OCA:
Oracle 10*g* Administration I
Study Guide

OCA: Oracle 10*g* Administration I Study Guide

Exam #1Z0-042

OBJECTIVES	CHAPTER
INSTALLING ORACLE DATABASE 10*G* SOFTWARE	
Identify system requirements.	1
Use Optimal Flexible Architecture.	1
Install software with Oracle Universal Installer.	1
Identify and configure commonly used environment variables.	1
CREATING AN ORACLE DATABASE	
Explain the Oracle database architecture.	1
Explain the instance architecture.	1
Use the management framework.	2
Use DBCA to Create a database.	2
Use DBCA to Configure a database.	2
Use DBCA to Drop a database.	2
Use DBCA to Manage templates.	2
DATABASE INTERFACES	
Use SQL*Plus and *i*SQL*Plus to access the Oracle Database 10*g*.	1
Use SQL*Plus and *i*SQL*Plus to describe the logical structure of tables.	1
Use SQL to query, manipulate, and define data using SELECT, UPDATE/INSERT/ DELETE and CREATE/ALTER/DROP statements.	1
Identify common database interfaces.	1
Describe a database transaction.	1
CONTROLLING THE DATABASE	
Start and stop *i*SQL*Plus.	2
Start and stop Enterprise Manager Database Control.	2
Start and stop the Oracle Listener.	4
Start up and shut down Oracle Database 10*g*.	2
Describe startup and shutdown options for the Oracle Database.	2
Handle Parameter files.	2
Locate and view the Database alert log.	2
STORAGE STRUCTURES	
Define the purpose of tablespaces and data files.	3
Create tablespaces.	3

SYBEX

Manage tablespaces (alter, drop, generate DDL, take offline, put on line, add data files, make read-only/read-write).	3
Obtain tablespace information from EM and the data dictionary.	3
Drop tablespaces.	3
Describe the default tablespaces.	3

ADMINISTERING USERS

Create and manage database user accounts.	6
Create and manage roles.	6
Grant and revoke privileges.	6
Control resource usage by users.	6

MANAGING SCHEMA OBJECTS

Create and modify tables.	3
Define constraints.	3
View the attributes of a table.	3
View the contents of a table.	3
Create indexes and views.	3
Name database objects.	3
Select appropriate data types.	3
Create and use sequences.	3

MANAGING DATA

Manipulate data through SQL using INSERT, UPDATE, and DELETE.	7
Use Data Pump to export data.	7
Use Data Pump to import data.	7
Load data with SQL Loader.	7
Create directory objects.	7

PL/SQL

Identify PL/SQL objects.	7
Describe triggers and triggering events.	7
Identify configuration options that affect PL/SQL performance.	7

ORACLE DATABASE SECURITY

Apply the principle of least privilege.	6
Manage default user accounts.	6
Implement standard password security features.	6

Exam objectives are subject to change at any time without prior notice and at Oracle's sole discretion. Please visit Oracle's Training and Certification website (http://www.oracle.com/education/certification/) for the most current exam objectives listing.

SYBEX

OCA:
Oracle 10g™ Administration I
Study Guide

Chip Dawes

Bob Bryla

Joseph C. Johnson

Matthew Weishan

San Francisco • London

Associate Publisher: Neil Edde
Acquisitions and Developmental Editor: Jeff Kellum
Production Editor: Mae Lum
Technical Editors: Christopher Guillaume, Robert Wahl
Copyeditor: Pat Coleman
Compositor: Craig Woods, Happenstance Type-O-Rama
Graphic Illustrator: Jeffrey Wilson, Happenstance Type-O-Rama
CD Coordinator: Dan Mummert
CD Technician: Kevin Ly
Proofreaders: James Brook, Sunah Cherwin, Amy Rasmussen, Nancy Riddiough
Indexer: Jack Lewis
Book Designers: Bill Gibson, Judy Fung
Cover Designer: Archer Design
Cover Photographer: Photodisc and Victor Arre

Library of Congress Card Number: 2004094992

ISBN: 0-7821-4367-9

SYBEX

To Our Valued Readers:

Thank you for looking to Sybex for your Oracle 10g exam prep needs. The OCA certification is designed to validate knowledge of basic database administration tasks and an understanding of the Oracle database architecture and how its components work and interact with one another. The OCA is also a prerequisite to becoming an OCP.

We at Sybex are proud of the reputation we've established for providing Oracle certification candidates with the practical knowledge and skills needed to succeed in the highly competitive IT marketplace. It has always been Sybex's mission to teach individuals how to utilize technologies in the real world, not to simply feed them answers to test questions. Just as Oracle is committed to establishing measurable standards for certifying database professionals, Sybex is committed to providing those professionals with the means of acquiring the skills and knowledge they need to meet those standards.

As always, your feedback is important to us. If you believe you've identified an error in the book, please send a detailed e-mail to support@sybex.com. And if you have general comments or suggestions, feel free to drop me a line directly at nedde@sybex.com. At Sybex, we're continually striving to meet the needs of individuals preparing for certification exams.

Good luck in pursuit of your Oracle certification!

Neil Edde
Associate Publisher—Certification
Sybex, Inc.

To my children Zachary and Charlie, you bring joy to my life.
—Chip Dawes

To my three wonderful daughters: Rachel, Laura, and Alyssa
—Matthew Weishan

To Brenda and Emily
—Joseph C. Johnson

To Mary Christine and the kids
—Bob Bryla

Acknowledgments

We would like to thank Oracle for producing the great database software that this book is about, as well as the Sybex team who did all the behind-the-scenes work on the book. We, the authors, get our names on the cover of the book, but the following people helped significantly in creating this Study Guide, and we want to thank and acknowledge their efforts: acquisitions and developmental editor Jeff Kellum; production editor Mae Lum; copyeditor Pat Coleman; technical editors Chris Guillaume and Bob Wahl; compositor Craig Woods of Happenstance Type-O-Rama; illustrator Jeffrey Wilson of Happenstance Type-O-Rama; proofreaders James Brook, Sunah Cherwin, Amy Rasmussen, and Nancy Riddiough; indexer Jack Lewis; and all the other unnamed individuals who had a hand in bringing this book to fruition.

I'd like to thank the good software engineers at Oracle for developing and continuing to improve a great software product. I've spent many good years learning about and teaching others to use Oracle databases, and I still have so much more to learn.

Lastly and most importantly, I'd like to thank my family for the unceasing support I get from them.

—Chip Dawes

I'd like to thank all the contributors to this book for their time and efforts. I'd also like to thank the entire Sybex team for their input and assistance in the production of this work. The third time has been a charm.

—Matthew Weishan

Many thanks to all those who helped me during the development of this book, in particular: Tony Gastel, Gerry Bustamente, Stephen Deutsch, Brook Swenson, Tami Van Dreese, Jamie Mudrick, Brenda, and Emily. Thanks too to my co-authors Chip, Bob, and Matt.

—Joseph C. Johnson

This book wouldn't be possible without the love and support from my family throughout the long nights and weekends when I still managed to find time to help the kids with their homework before bedtime. I loved every minute of it.

Thanks also to my professional colleagues, both past and present, who provided me with inspiration, support, and guidance and who pushed me a little further to take a risk now and then, starting with that math teacher in high school, whose name eludes me at the moment, who introduced me to computers on a DEC PDP-8 with a teletype and a paper tape reader.

—Bob Bryla

Contents at a Glance

Contents

Introduction

There is high demand for professionals in the information technology (IT) industry, and Oracle certifications are the hottest credentials in the database world. You have made the right decision to pursue your Oracle certification, because achieving it will give you a distinct advantage in this highly competitive market.

Most of you should already be familiar with Oracle and need no introduction to the Oracle database world. Here's some information for those who aren't. Oracle, founded in 1977, sold the first commercial relational database and is now the world's leading database company and second-largest independent software company, with revenues of more than $10 billion, serving more than 145 countries.

Oracle databases are the de facto standard for large Internet sites, and Oracle advertisers are boastful but honest when they proclaim, "The Internet Runs on Oracle." Almost all big Internet sites run Oracle databases. Oracle's penetration of the database market runs deep and is not limited to dot-com implementations. Enterprise resource planning (ERP) application suites, data warehouses, and custom applications at many companies rely on Oracle. The demand for DBA resources remains higher than others during weak economic times.

This book is intended to help you pass the Oracle Database 10*g*: Administration I exam, which will establish your credentials as an Oracle Database Administrator. The OCA certification is a prerequisite to obtaining the more comprehensive Oracle Certified Professional (OCP) certification and is the first step toward obtaining an Oracle Certified Master (OCM) certification. Using this book and a practice database, you can acquire the necessary skills to pass the 1Z0-042 Oracle Database 10*g*: Administration I exam.

Why Become Oracle Certified?

The number one reason to become an OCA or OCP is to gain more visibility and greater access to the industry's most challenging opportunities. Oracle certification is the best way to demonstrate your knowledge and skills in Oracle database systems.

Certification is proof of your knowledge and shows that you have the skills required to support Oracle core products. The Oracle certification program can help a company identify proven performers who have demonstrated their skills and who can support the company's investment in Oracle technology. It demonstrates that you have a solid understanding of your job role and the Oracle products used in that role.

OCPs are among the best paid in the IT industry. Salary surveys consistently show the OCP certification to yield higher salaries than other certifications, including Microsoft, Novell, and Cisco.

So whether you are beginning your career, changing your career, or looking to secure your position as a DBA, this book is for you!

Oracle Certifications

Oracle certifications follow a track that is oriented toward a job role. There are database administration, application developer, and web application server administrator tracks. Within each track, Oracle has a multitiered certification program.

Within the administration track, there are three tiers:

- The first tier is the Oracle 10*g* Certified Associate (OCA). To obtain OCA certification, you must pass the 1Z0-042 Oracle Database 10*g*: Administration I exam in a proctored setting.

- The second tier is the Oracle 10*g* Certified Professional (OCP), which builds on and requires OCA certification. To obtain OCP certification, you must attend an approved Oracle University hands-on class and pass the 1Z0-043 Oracle Database 10*g*: Administration II exam in a proctored setting.

- The third and highest tier is the Oracle 10*g* Certified Master (OCM), which builds on and requires OCP certification. To obtain OCM certification, you must attend advanced-level classes and take a two-day, hands-on practical exam.

The material in this book addresses only the Administration I exam. Other Sybex books—which can be found at www.sybex.com—can help students new to the DBA world prepare for the OCP exam Oracle Database 10*g*: Administration II exam (1Z0-043). You can also get information on the Oracle upgrade exam, the Oracle Database 10*g*: New Features for Administrators exam (1Z0-040).

 See the Oracle website at www.oracle.com/education/certification for the latest information on all of Oracle's certification paths along with Oracle's training resources.

Oracle DBA Certification

The role of the DBA has become a key to success in today's highly complex database systems. The best DBAs work behind the scenes, but are in the spotlight when critical issues arise. They plan, create, maintain, and ensure that the database is available for the business. They are always watching the database for performance issues and to prevent unscheduled downtime. The DBA's job requires broad understanding of the architecture of Oracle database and expertise in solving problems.

Because this book focuses on the DBA track, we will take a closer look at the tiers of the DBA track.

Oracle Database 10*g* Administrator Certified Associate

The Oracle 10*g* Administrator Certified Associate (OCA) certification is a streamlined, entry-level certification for the database administration track and is required to advance toward the more senior certification tiers. This certification requires you to pass one exam that demonstrates your knowledge of Oracle basics:

- 1Z0-042 Oracle Database 10*g*: Administration I

Oracle Database 10*g* Administrator Certified Professional

The OCP tier of the database administration track challenges you to demonstrate your enhanced experience and knowledge of Oracle technologies. The Oracle 10*g* Administrator Certified Professional (OCP) certification requires achievement of the OCA certification, attendance at one or more approved Oracle University classes, and successful completion of the following exam:

- 1Z0-043 Oracle Database 10*g*: Administration II

The approved courses for OCP candidates include the following:

- Oracle Database 10*g*: Administration I
- Oracle Database 10*g*: Administration II
- Oracle Database 10*g*: Introduction to SQL
- Oracle Database 10*g*: New Features for Administrators
- Oracle Database 10*g*: Program with PL/SQL

If you already have your OCP in 9*i* or earlier and have elected to take the upgrade path, you are not required to take the Oracle University class to obtain your OCP for Oracle 10*g*.

 Verify this list against the Oracle education website (www.oracle.com/education) as it can change without any notice.

Oracle Database 10*g* Certified Master

The Oracle Database 10*g* Administration Certified Master (OCM) is the highest level of certification that Oracle offers. To become a certified master, you must first obtain OCP certification, then complete advanced-level classes at an Oracle Education facility, and finally pass a hands-on, two-day exam at an Oracle Education facility. The classes and practicum exam are offered only at an Oracle Education facility and may require travel.

 More details on the required coursework will be available in late 2004.

Oracle 10*g* Upgrade Paths

Existing Oracle professionals can upgrade their certification in several ways:

- An Oracle9*i* OCP can upgrade to 10*g* certification by passing the 1Z0-040 Oracle Database 10*g*: New Features for Administrators exam.
- An Oracle8*i* OCP can upgrade directly to 10*g* by passing the 1Z0-045 Oracle Database 10*g*: New Features for Oracle8*i* OCP exam.
- Oracle7.3 and Oracle8 DBAs must first upgrade to an Oracle9*i* certification with the 1Z0-035 Oracle9*i* DBA: New Features for Oracle7.3 and Oracle8 OCP exam and then upgrade the 9*i* certification to 10*g* with the 1Z0-040 Oracle Database 10*g*: New Features for Administrators exam.

Oracle Database 10*g* Administrator Special Accreditations

New to the Oracle certification program are the Oracle Database 10*g* Administrator Special Accreditation programs. These accreditations formally recognize the specialized knowledge of OCPs in particular database administration areas such as high availability, security, and 10*g* Grid Control. OCPs who pass one of these special accreditation exams receive a certificate that formally recognizes their special competency.

Oracle Database 10*g* DBA Assessment

Oracle also provides an optional (and free) prerequisite to all the proctored exams, which is the Oracle Database 10*g* DBA Assessment online exam:

- 1Z0-041 Oracle Database 10*g*: DBA Assessment

This exam evaluates your proficiency with basic administration and management of an Oracle 10*g* database, and upon passing this online exam, you receive a certificate of completion from Oracle University. Although anybody can take this exam, it is designed for those new to Oracle and is an excellent measurement of how familiar you are with the new Oracle 10*g* database.

Oracle Exam Requirements

The Oracle Database 10*g*: Administration I exam covers several core subject areas. As with many typical multiple-choice exams, you can take advantage of several tips to maximize your score on the exam.

Skills Required for the Oracle Database 10*g*: Administration I Exam

To pass the Oracle 10*g* Administration I exam, you need to master the following subject areas in Oracle 10*g*:

Installing Oracle Database 10g Software

Identify system requirements.

Use Optimal Flexible Architecture (OFA).

Install software with Oracle Universal Installer.

Identify and configure commonly used environment variables.

Creating an Oracle Database

Explain the Oracle database architecture.

Explain the instance architecture.

Use the management framework.

Use DBCA (Database Configuration Assistant) to create a database.

Use DBCA to configure a database.

Use DBCA to drop (or delete) a database.

Use DBCA to manage templates.

Database Interfaces

Use SQL*Plus and *i*SQL*Plus to access an Oracle 10*g* database.

Use SQL*Plus and *i*SQL*Plus to describe the logical structure of tables.

Use SQL to query, manipulate, and define data using SELECT, UPDATE/INSERT/DELETE, and CREATE/ALTER/DROP statements.

Identify common database interfaces.

Describe a database transaction.

Controlling the Database

Start and stop *i*SQL*Plus.

Start and stop Enterprise Manager (EM) Database Control.

Start and stop the Oracle Listener.

Start up and shut down Oracle Database 10*g*.

Describe startup and shutdown options for Oracle Database 10*g*.

Handle parameter files.

Locate and view the Database alert log.

Storage Structures

Define the purpose of tablespaces and datafiles.

Create tablespaces.

Manage tablespaces (alter, drop, generate DDL, take offline, put on line, add data files, make read-only/read-write).

Obtain tablespace information from EM and the data dictionary views.

Drop tablespaces.

Describe the default tablespaces.

Administering Users

Create and manage database user accounts.

Create and manage roles.

Grant and revoke privileges.

Control resource usage by users.

Managing Schema Objects

Create and modify tables.

Define constraints.

View the attributes of a table.

View the contents of a table.

Create indexes and views.

Name database objects.

Select appropriate datatypes.

Create and use sequences.

Managing Data

Manipulate data through SQL using INSERT, UPDATE, and DELETE.

Use Data Pump to export data.

Use Data Pump to import data.

Load data with SQL*Loader.

Create directory objects.

PL/SQL

Identify PL/SQL (Procedural Language SQL) objects.

Describe triggers and triggering events.

Identify configuration options that affect PL/SQL performance.

Oracle Database Security

Apply the principle of least privilege.

Manage default user accounts.

Implement standard password security features.

Audit database activity.

Register for security updates.

Oracle Net Services

Use Database Control to create additional listeners.

Use Database Control to create Oracle Net service aliases.

Use Database Control to configure connect time failover.

Use Listener features.

Use the Oracle Net Manager to configure client and middle-tier connections.

Use `TNSPING` to test Oracle Net connectivity.

Describe Oracle Net Services.

Describe Oracle Net names resolution methods.

Oracle Shared Servers

Identify when to use Oracle Shared Servers.

Configure Oracle Shared Servers.

Monitor Shared Servers.

Describe the Shared Server architecture.

Performance Monitoring

Troubleshoot invalid and unusable objects.

Gather optimizer statistics.

View performance metrics.

React to performance issues.

Proactive Maintenance

Set warning and critical alert thresholds.

Collect and use baseline metrics.

Use tuning and diagnostic advisors.

Use the Automatic Database Diagnostic Monitor (ADDM).

Manage the Automatic Workload Repository.

Describe server-generated alerts.

Undo Management

Monitor and administer undo.

Configure undo retention.

Guarantee undo retention.

Use the Undo Advisor.

Describe the relationship between undo and transactions.

Size the undo tablespace.

Monitoring and Resolving Lock Conflicts

Detect and resolve lock conflicts.

Manage deadlocks.

Describe the relationship between transactions and locks.

Explain lock modes within Oracle Database 10*g*.

Backup and Recovery Concepts

Describe the basics of database backup, restore, and recovery.

Describe the types of failure that can occur in an Oracle 10*g* database.

Describe ways to tune instance recovery.

Identify the importance of checkpoints, redo log files, and archived log files.

Configure ARCHIVELOG mode.

Configure a database for recoverability.

Database Backups

Create consistent database backups.

Back up your database without shutting it down.

Create incremental backups.

Automate database backups.

Monitor the Flash Recovery area.

Describe the difference between image copies and backup sets.

Describe the different types of database backups.

Back up a control file to trace.

Manage backups.

Database Recovery

Recover from loss of a control file.

Recover from loss of a redo log file.

Recover from loss of a system-critical datafile.

Recover from loss of a non–system-critical datafile.

Tips for Taking the OCA Exam

Use the following tips to help you prepare for and pass the exam:

- The exam contains about 55–80 questions to be completed in 90 minutes. Answer the questions you know first so that you do not run out of time.

- At first glance, the answer choices to many questions look identical. Read the questions carefully. Do not jump to conclusions. Make sure that you clearly understand exactly what each question asks.

- Some questions are scenario-based. Some scenarios contain nonessential information and exhibits. You need to be able to identify what's important and what's not important.

- Do not leave any questions unanswered. There is no negative scoring. After selecting an answer, you can mark a difficult question or one that you're unsure of and come back to it later.

- When answering questions that you are not sure about, use a process of elimination to get rid of the obviously incorrect answers first. Doing this greatly improves your odds if you need to make an educated guess.

- If you're not sure of your answer, mark it for review, and then look for other questions that might help you eliminate any incorrect answers. At the end of the test, you can go back and review the questions that you marked for review.

 Be familiar with the exam objectives, which are included in the front of this book as a perforated tear-out card. You can also find them at www.oracle.com/education/certification/objectives/42.html. In addition, if you would like information on recommended classes and passing scores, visit www.oracle.com/education/certification/news/beta_042.html.

Where Do You Take the Certification Exam?

The Oracle Database 10g certification exams are available at any of the more than 900 Thomson Prometric Authorized Testing Centers around the world. For the location of a testing center near you, call 1-800-891-3926. Outside the United States and Canada, contact your local Thomson Prometric Registration Center.

To register for a proctored Oracle Certified Associate exam:

- Determine the number of the exam you want to take. For the OCA exam, it is 1Z0-042.

- Register with Thomson Prometric online at www.prometric.com or, in North America, by calling 1-800-891-EXAM (800-891-3926). At this point, you will be asked to pay in advance for the exam. At the time of this writing, the exams are $125 each and must be taken within one year of payment.

- When you schedule the exam, you'll get instructions regarding all appointment and cancellation procedures, the ID requirements, and information about the testing-center location.

You can schedule exams up to six weeks in advance or as soon as one working day before the day you want to take it. If something comes up and you need to cancel or reschedule your exam appointment, contact Thomson Prometric at least 24 hours or one business day in advance.

What Does This Book Cover?

This book covers everything you need to pass the Oracle Database10g Administration I exam. Each chapter begins with a list of exam objectives.

Chapter 1   Discusses some of the first activities you will need to perform. You will learn how to install the Oracle database software, about the architecture of both an Oracle database and instance, and how to use some common database interfaces as well as how to use SQL to define, manipulate, and access data in your database.

Chapter 2   Discusses creating and controlling the Oracle database environment. You will learn how to start and stop the database, EM Database Control, and iSQL*Plus.

Chapter 3   Discusses storage structures and schema objects. You will learn how to create and manage physical database structures such as tablespaces, datafiles, segments, extents, and blocks. You will also learn about logical database structures such as tables, indexes, views, and sequences.

Chapter 4   Discusses Oracle Net services. You will learn how to create and control database listeners, Net service names, and connect time failover.

Chapter 5   Discusses Oracle Shared Servers. You will learn about the Shared Server architecture, when to use Shared Servers, and how to configure and monitor Shared Servers.

Chapter 6   Discusses administering users and database security. You will learn how to create and manage user accounts, roles, privileges, password controls, and auditing.

Chapter 7   Discusses manipulating data and administering PL/SQL programs. You will learn how to work with data using SQL, Data Pump, SQL*Loader, and triggers and how to tune the database for PL/SQL performance.

Chapter 8   Discusses consistency and concurrency. You will learn how to configure and administer your undo tablespace. You will also learn about Oracle locking and how to detect and resolve locking conflicts.

Chapter 9   Discusses performance monitoring and proactive maintenance. You will learn how to administer invalid and unusable objects, gather optimizer statistics, work with performance metrics, set alert thresholds, and use the tuning and diagnostic advisors.

Chapter 10   Discusses backing up your Oracle 10g database. You will learn about Oracle backup concepts, how to create and manage consistent, online, and incremental backups. You will also learn how to monitor the Flash Recovery area.

Chapter 11   Discusses failures and how to recover your Oracle10g database from them. You will learn about the various kinds of failures that can occur with an Oracle10g database and how to recover from the loss of control files, redo logs, and datafiles.

Each chapter ends with a list of exam essentials, which gives you a highlight of the chapter, with an emphasis on the topics that you need to be extra familiar with for the exam. The chapter concludes with 20 review questions that are specifically designed to help you retain the knowledge presented. To really nail down your skills, read and answer each question carefully.

How to Use This Book

This book can provide a solid foundation for the serious effort of preparing for the Oracle 10*g* OCA exam. To best benefit from this book, use the following study method:

1. Take the Assessment Test immediately following this introduction. (The answers are at the end of the test.) Carefully read over the explanations for any questions you get wrong, and note which chapters the material comes from. This information should help you plan your study strategy.

2. Study each chapter carefully, making sure that you fully understand the information and the test objectives listed at the beginning of each chapter. Pay extra close attention to any chapter related to questions that you missed in the Assessment Test.

3. Complete all hands-on exercises in the chapter, referring to the chapter so that you understand the reason for each step you take. If you do not have an Oracle database available, be sure to study the examples carefully.

4. Answer the review questions related to that chapter. (The answers appear at the end of each chapter, after the "Review Questions" section.) Note the questions that confuse or trick you, and study those sections of the book again.

5. Take the two Bonus Exams that are included on the accompanying CD. This will give you a complete overview of what you can expect to see on the real test.

6. Remember to use the products on the CD included with this book. The electronic flashcards and the Sybex Test Engine exam preparation software have been specifically designed to help you study for and pass your exam.

To learn all the material covered in this book, you'll need to apply yourself regularly and with discipline. Try to set aside the same time period every day to study, and select a comfortable and quiet place to do so. If you work hard, you will be surprised at how quickly you learn this material. All the best!

What's on the CD?

We have worked hard to provide some really great tools to help you with your certification process. Load all the following tools on your workstation when you're studying for the test.

The Sybex Test Engine Preparation Software

This test-preparation software prepares you to pass the 1Z0-042 Oracle Database 10*g* Administration I exam. In this test, you will find all the questions from the book, plus two bonus exams that appear exclusively on the CD. You can take the Assessment Test, test yourself by chapter, or take the practice exams. The test engine will run on either a Microsoft Windows or a Linux platform.

Here is a sample screen from the Sybex Test Engine:

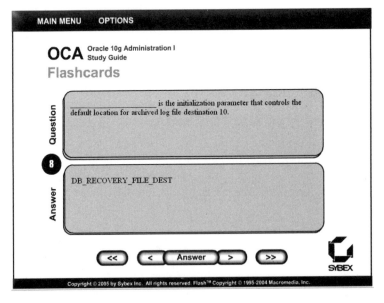

Electronic Flashcards for PC and Palm Devices

You can also test yourself with the flashcards included on the CD. The flashcards are designed to test your understanding of the fundamental concepts covered in the exam. Here is what the Sybex Flashcards interface looks like:

OCA: Oracle 10*g* Administration I Study Guide in PDF

Many people like the convenience of being able to carry their study guide on a CD, which is why we included the book in PDF format. This will be extremely helpful to readers who fly or commute on a bus or train and prefer an e-book, as well as to readers who find it more comfortable reading from their computer. We've also included a copy of Adobe Acrobat Reader on the CD.

About the Authors

Chip Dawes is an Oracle Certified Professional with more than 15 years' experience as a DBA. He lives, works, and plays in the Chicagoland area with his wife, Mary, children Zachary and Charlie, and dog Rex. Chip works for D&D Technologies, a Chicago-based consulting firm. To contact Chip, you can e-mail him at chipdawes@yahoo.com.

Matthew Weishan, OCP, is a senior specialist for EDS in Madison, Wisconsin. To contact Matt, you can e-mail him at mweishan@yahoo.com.

Joseph C. Johnson is an Oracle Certified Professional with more than 10 years of experience managing mission-critical Oracle databases. Joe is a Senior Database Administrator with Lands' End in Dodgeville, Wisconsin. You can e-mail him at josephcjohnson@yahoo.com.

Bob Bryla, OCP, currently works as a Data Analyst and Oracle DBA for Lands' End. To contact Bob, you can e-mail him at rjbryla@centurytel.net.

Assessment Test

1. Which of the following components is not part of an Oracle instance?

   A. System Global Area

   B. Server Process

   C. Database Writer

   D. System Monitor

2. Your organization has purchased an application that uses an Oracle database as the repository for application data. Your job is to install and configure the Oracle Database 10*g* software on the server. Which of the following should you do first?

   A. Create mount points and directories using the OFA model.

   B. Mount the Oracle CD and start the Oracle Universal Installer.

   C. Review the installation guides and release notes to familiarize yourself with the install process.

   D. Work with the Unix system administrator to configure kernel parameters.

3. All the following are examples of DML commands except which item?

   A. INSERT

   B. CREATE

   C. UPDATE

   D. DELETE

4. Assuming the ON DELETE CASCADE option was not used to define the constraint, what is the potential impact of a foreign key constraint on a DELETE statement?

   A. The foreign key constraint can prevent the delete if deleting the row violates the relationship defined in the foreign key.

   B. The foreign key constraint ensures that the user has the correct privileges on a table before the row is deleted.

   C. The foreign key is ignored if the delete removes only one row.

   D. Foreign key has no impact on DELETE statements.

5. You are a database administrator with databases in New York, Hong Kong, and London. You want to administer all your databases from a central console using Grid Control. Which of the following commands do you issue when using Grid Control?

   A. emctl start grid

   B. emctl start dbconsole

   C. emctl start agent

   D. isqlplusctl start

6. The lead DBA has requested that you set up a database that requires minimal disk management for a large data warehouse that is being implemented. He wants you to use a DBCA with and utilize one of the predefined templates. Which of the following combinations addresses this request?

A. Data Warehouse template with raw devices

B. Transactional template with file system disk management

C. Data Warehouse template with raw disk management

D. Data Warehouse template with the Automated Storage Management (ASM) disk option

7. You have created a database using DBCA and not saved the template definition. You now want to copy the database and all the data using the DBCA. Which of the following is the first step?

A. Create a new empty database using scripts, and import the data into the new database using the DBCA.

B. Use DBCA template management, and create a database template from an existing database with structure as well as data.

C. Choose the template of the previously created database created from the templates list and create the database.

D. Copy the datafiles from the existing database to a new location, and then use the DBCA to copy the database.

8. You are in the middle of an emergency drill at your organization. There is little time to notify database users, and you need to stop the Oracle database processes as quickly as possible. Which of the following would you perform?

A. SHUTDOWN ABORT

B. SHUTDOWN TRANSACTIONAL

C. SHUTDOWN

D. SHUTDOWN IMMEDIATE

E. None of the above

9. Where would you look to see if a tablespace is offline?

A. dba_tablespaces

B. v$tablespace

C. v$database

D. dba_datafile_status

10. Which of the following objects share the same namespace and therefore cannot have the same name?

A. Tables and sequences

B. Tables and indexes

C. Tables and tablespaces

D. Tables and constraints

11. Which of the following is not a valid column name?

    A. 1ST_ID

    B. CUST#

    C. ADDRESS1

    D. EXCEPTION

12. Oracle Advanced Security provides all the following except:

    A. Database profiles

    B. Data encryption

    C. Checksumming

    D. Biometrics option

13. You have just issued the command `lsnrctl stop LISTENER`. Which of the following statements are not true? (Choose all that apply.)

    A. New connections to the default listener will not succeed.

    B. Existing client connections will not be affected.

    C. Only new dedicated connections will fail

    D. Existing shared server connections will be dropped.

14. You issue the following command from the database server: `sqlplus scott/tiger` and receive the following error message: `ORA-01034: Oracle not available`. What is the state of the Oracle database:

    A. The database is open but in restricted mode.

    B. The instance is started but is in `MOUNT` mode.

    C. The database and the instance are not started.

    D. The instance is started in `NOMOUNT` mode.

15. You connect to the database using the command `sqlplus scott/tiger@abc.com:1522/orcl`. To which database are you connecting?

    A. `abc.com`

    B. `tiger`

    C. `orcl`

    D. `scott`

    E. None of the above

16. You are administering an Oracle database using Shared Server. The LARGE_POOL_SIZE is 50MB. You issue the command `ALTER SYSTEM SET LARGE_POOL_SIZE = 100M SCOPE=MEMORY`. You then shut down and restart the database. What will the LARGE_POOL_SIZE be?

    A. 50MB

    B. 100MB

    C. The default LARGE_POOL_SIZE

    D. The LARGE_POOL_SIZE as you have set it in the Oracle SPFILE that you are using

17. You have decided to implement connection pooling and set a timeout limit of 20 minutes for idle connections. You also want to support 500 concurrent connections with a maximum of 1500 sessions per dispatcher. Which of the following commands will accomplish this?

   A. `Dispatchers = "(PRO=TCP)(DIS=5)(POO=ON)(TICK=20)(CONN=500)(SESS=1500)"`

   B. `Dispatchers = "(PRO=TCP)(DIS=5)(POO=ON)(TICK=2)(CONN=500)(SESS=1500)"`

   C. `Dispatchers = "(PRO=TCP)(DIS=5)(POO=ON)(TICK=20)(CONN=1500)(SESS=500)"`

   D. `Dispatchers = "(PRO=TCP)(DIS=5)(POOLING=ON)(TICK=20)(CONN=500)(SESS=1500)"`

18. You issue the command `lsnrctl services`. What pieces of information can you see regarding shared server connections for each dispatcher listed? (Choose all that apply.)

   A. Established connections

   B. Refused connections

   C. Idle connections

   D. Current connections

   E. All the above

19. What status would you expect to see when querying **V$DISPATCHER** for a dispatcher that is not currently servicing any client requests?

   A. `IDLE`

   B. `WAIT`

   C. `SLEEP`

   D. `READY`

   E. None of the above

20. Which of the following statements sets the password for user simon to alakazaam?

   A. `alter user simon password alakazaam;`

   B. `update user simon set password=alakazaam;`

   C. `alter user simon identified by alakazaam;`

   D. `set password=alakazaam for simon;`

21. Which privilege allows the grantee to place the database in NOARCHIVELOG mode?

   A. `sysdba`

   B. `root`

   C. `dba`

   D. `operator`

22. Which of the following statements removes user brent together with all his schema objects from the database?

   A. `drop user brent;`

   B. `delete from dba_users where username='BRENT';`

   C. `alter system remove user brent cascade;`

   D. `drop user brent cascade;`

23. Which of the following parameters directs Data Pump export to capture the table definitions for, but not the contents of the tables owned by user sacagawea?

   A. `owner= sacagawea rows=no`

   B. `schemas= sacagawea content=metadata_only`

   C. `owner= sacagawea content=metadata_only`

   D. `tablespaces= sacagawea data=no`

24. Which of the following is not a valid Data Pump export mode?

   A. `JAVA`

   B. `SCHEMA`

   C. `TABLE`

   D. `TABLESPACE`

25. After updating a table, what must you execute to make the changes permanent?

   A. `COMMIT`

   B. `SAVEPOINT`

   C. Nothing. When the updates complete, the changes are permanent.

   D. `SAVE WORK`

26. When a table is updated, where is the before-image information (which can be used for undoing the changes) stored?

   A. Temporary segment

   B. Redo log buffer

   C. Undo buffer

   D. Undo segment

27. Which of the following will not implicitly begin a transaction?

   A. `INSERT`

   B. `UPDATE`

   C. `DELETE`

   D. `SELECT FOR UPDATE`

   E. None of the above; they all implicitly begin a transaction.

28. Select the invalid statements from the following regarding undo segment management. (Choose all that apply.)

   A. `ALTER SYSTEM SET UNDO_TABLESPACE = ROLLBACK;`

   B. `ALTER DATABASE SET UNDO_TABLESPACE = UNDOTBS;`

   C. `ALTER SYSTEM SET UNDO_MANAGEMENT = AUTO;`

   D. `ALTER SYSTEM SET UNDO_MANAGEMENT = MANUAL;`

29. The following table shows two concurrent transactions. Which statement about the result returned in Session 1 at 8:30 is true? Choose the best answer.

Session 1	Time	Session 2
`select sum(order_amt) from orders where order_date > trunc(sysdate);`	8:01	
	8:09	`insert into orders (cust_ num, order_date, order_amt) values (19581963, sysdate, 576.12);`
	8:10	`commit;`
`select` statement above reaches data block where insert from session 2 resides	8:15	
`select` statement completes and results returned to the user	8:30	

    A. The results include the changes committed by session 2 at 8:10.

    B. The results include the changes committed by session 2 at 8:10 if the two sessions were connected as the same user.

    C. The results of the query in session 1 do not include the changes committed by session 2 at 8:10.

    D. Session 1 instead returns a "Snapshot too old" error message at 8:30; no results are returned to the user, and the query must be resubmitted.

30. The Automatic Workload Repository (AWR) is primarily populated with performance statistics by which Oracle 10*g* background process?

    A. MMNL

    B. QMN1

    C. MMON

    D. MMAN

31. Which of the following advisors is used to determine if the database read-consistency mechanisms are properly configured?

    A. Undo Management Advisor

    B. SQL Access Advisor

    C. SQL Tuning Advisor

    D. Memory Advisor

32. You've decided to monitor your databases for CPU utilization based on baseline metrics. If you specify that you want a warning alert sent whenever CPU utilization is greater than 50 percent of the baseline and the high value for this metric is 300, when will the alert be sent?

   A. Whenever CPU utilization is 250 or less

   B. Whenever the CPU utilization is 450 or higher

   C. Whenever the CPU utilization is 300 or higher

   D. Whenever the CPU utilization is 225 or higher

33. Every evening you use SQL*Loader to perform direct-path loads of data into your company's data warehouse. Last night the load of the SALES table failed because the tablespace where the SALES table is stored ran out of space. As a result, the indexes on the SALES table are in an unusable state. Which of the following can you use to fix this problem?

   A. Drop and re-create the affected indexes.

   B. Use the ALTER INDEX … REBUILD command to rebuild the index.

   C. Use EM Database Control to rebuild the index.

   D. Any of the above will return the index to a usable state.

34. Which backup options are available for databases in NOARCHIVELOG mode? (Choose all that apply.)

   A. Online, incremental

   B. Offline, incremental

   C. Online, full, whole database

   D. Offline, full, whole database

35. According to Oracle, how many copies of the control file should you maintain?

   A. 1, since Oracle automatically multiplexes control files

   B. 2

   C. One copy on each Oracle-managed disk device

   D. 3

36. Identify the types of backups in the following list that RMAN performs. (Choose all that apply.)

   A. Backups to flat files

   B. Image copies

   C. Data Pump export dumps

   D. Backup sets

37. Archived log files can be written to as many as _____ locations. (Choose the best answer.)

   A. Ten, but they all have to be local, or they all have to be remote.

   B. Ten, with a maximum of five local destinations and five remote destinations

   C. Ten total

   D. Five total

   E. Twenty, a maximum of ten local destinations, and ten remote destinations

38. If a user inadvertently drops a table, this is considered what type of failure?

    A. Instance

    B. User error

    C. Statement

    D. User process

39. If the database instance fails, but will not shut down, you must use which command(s) before instance recovery can be performed? (Choose the best answer.)

    A. `STARTUP NOMOUNT`

    B. `STARTUP MOUNT`

    C. `SHUTDOWN IMMEDIATE; STARTUP FORCE`

    D. `SHUTDOWN ABORT; STARTUP`

40. Which of the following is not a valid database state?

    A. `OPEN`

    B. `SHUTDOWN`

    C. `STARTUP`

    D. `MOUNT`

    E. `NOMOUNT`

Answers to Assessment Test

1. **B.** The Server Process that is started on the server on behalf of each user connection is not considered part of the instance. An instance is defined as the System Global Area and all the Oracle background processes. For more information, see Chapter 1.

2. **C.** Review all relevant documentation before starting the Oracle installation. The documentation will help you determine whether your hardware and operating system meet the minimum specifications required for the installation. For more information, see Chapter 1.

3. **B.** The CREATE statement is an example of a DDL statement, not a DML statement. DROP and ALTER are also examples of DDL commands. For more information, see Chapter 1.

4. **A.** A foreign key constraint prevents the deletion of a record if other records in the same table or other tables still refer to that record. If the ON DELETE CASCADE option is used when the constraint is defined, deleting the primary key record also automatically deletes the associated foreign key records. For more information, see Chapter 1.

5. **C.** When you are using the Grid Control, start the agent on each managed target machine. The emctl start agent command initiates the agent process. For more information, see Chapter 2.

6. **D.** You use the Data Warehouse template with the ASM disk option to get the requested combination. For more information, see Chapter 2.

7. **B.** First, make a template definition of the existing database using the DBCA tool. You can then create the database from this definition. For more information, see Chapter 2.

8. **A.** Given the circumstances, the quickest way to shut down the Oracle processes is a SHUTDOWN ABORT. This is not the preferred shutdown method and requires instance recovery upon startup. For more information, see Chapter 2.

9. **A.** The dba_tablespaces and v$tablespace views contain information about tablespaces. The dba_tablespaces view includes the STATUS column, which indicates whether the tablespace is online or offline. For more information, see Chapter 3.

10. **A.** Tables share a namespace with views, sequences, private synonyms, procedures, functions, packages, materialized views, and user-defined types. Objects sharing a namespace cannot have the same name. For more information, see Chapter 3.

11. **A.** Column names cannot begin with a digit. They must begin with a letter and can contain letters, numbers, and the characters _, $, or # (underscore, dollar sign, or pound sign). Although a poor practice, PL/SQL keywords, such as EXCEPTION, can be used as a column name. For more information, see Chapter 3.

12. **A.** The Oracle Advanced Security feature provides additional database security options such as encryption, checksumming, and user authentication via options such as the biometrics. This feature is not necessary to use database profiles. For more information, see Chapter 4.

13. **C, D.** When you stop a listener, you affect only new client connections and not existing client connections, so C and D are false. For more information, see Chapter 4.

14. C.   Whenever you receive an ORA-01034, both the database and the instance are not started. For more information, see Chapter 4.

15. C.   The database is the parameter supplied after the port designation. Therefore, you connect to the orcl database. For more information, see Chapter 4.

16. D.   The LARGE_POOL_SIZE setting is determined by the setting in the Oracle SPFILE. Oracle always reads this file on startup if you are using it. The SCOPE=MEMORY parameter means that only the currently running instance is affected by the change. For more information, see Chapter 5.

17. B.   You would set the PRO, DIS, POO, TICK, CONN, and SESS attributes of the DISPATCHERS parameter accordingly. Remember that the TICK measurement is in 10-minute increments. For more information, see Chapter 5.

18. A, B, D.   You can see established, refused, and current connections for each dispatcher when you issue this command. You can also see the maximum number of connections allowed per dispatcher and the state of each dispatcher. For more information, see Chapter 5.

19. B.   The WAIT status indicates that the dispatcher is waiting to process a client request. For more information, see Chapter 5.

20. C.   You use the ALTER USER statement to change a password. The keywords IDENTIFIED BY tell the database to assign a new password to the user. For more information, see Chapter 6.

21. A.   The privilege SYSDBA is the most powerful system privilege; it allows the grantee to start up and shut down the database as well as enable ARCHIVELOG mode or NOARCHIVELOG mode. For more information, see Chapter 6.

22. D.   A DROP USER statement removes an account from the database. The keyword CASCADE tells the database to also drop all the schema objects owned by the user. For more information, see Chapter 6.

23. B.   The schemas parameter tells Data Pump export which object owners to include in the extract. The content parameter tells Data Pump what to export: DATA_ONLY, METADATA_ONLY, or ALL. The METADATA_ONLY value tells Data Pump to capture the object definitions but not the stored data values. For more information, see Chapter 7.

24. A.   Data Pump modes include FULL, SCHEMA, TABLE, and TABLESPACE, but not JAVA. For more information, see Chapter 7.

25. A.   After changing data with an INSERT, UPDATE, or DELETE statement, you must execute a COMMIT to make the changes permanent. A SAVEPOINT establishes an intermediate place holder in the data changes that you can optionally ROLLBACK to prior to a COMMIT. There is no SAVE statement in an Oracle 10g database. For more information, see Chapter 7.

26. D.   Before any DML operation is marked as complete, the undo information (the before image of data) is stored in the undo segments. This information is used to undo the changes and to provide a read-consistent view of the data. For more information, see Chapter 8.

27. E.   If a transaction is not currently in progress, any INSERT, UPDATE, MERGE, DELETE, SELECT FOR UPDATE, or LOCK statement implicitly begins a transaction. For more information, see Chapter 8.

28. B, C, D. Choice A is the only valid statement; an undo tablespace can have any name that follows the Oracle standard naming conventions for identifiers. Choice B is incorrect because undo tablespaces are not managed using ALTER DATABASE. Choices C and D are incorrect because the parameter UNDO_MANAGEMENT cannot be changed while the instance is running. For more information, see Chapter 8.

29. C. Read consistency ensures that the data visible to each session does not change when the statement is executing. For more information, see Chapter 8.

30. C. The Memory Monitor (MMON) process gathers performance statistics from the SGA (System Global Area) and stores them in the AWR. MMNL (Memory Monitor Light) also does some AWR-related statistics gathering, but not to the extent that MMON does. QMN1 is the process that monitors Oracle advanced queuing features. MMON is the process that dynamically manages the sizes of each SGA component when directed to make changes by the ADDM (Automatic Database Diagnostic Monitoring). For more information, see Chapter 9.

31. A. You can use the Undo Management Advisor to monitor and manage the undo segments to ensure maximum levels of read consistency and minimize occurrences of ORA-01555: Snapshot Too Old error messages. For more information, see Chapter 9.

32. B. The alert threshold will be defined as 300 * (1 + 50/100), or 450 percent. For more information, see Chapter 9.

33. D. Dropping or rebuilding an index changes the index from an unstable to a usable state. For more information, see Chapter 9.

34. D. If the database is in NOARCHIVELOG mode, only offline, full, whole database backups can be performed. As a result, any database failure loses committed transactions since the last backup. For more information, see Chapter 10.

35. D. Although you should have a minimum of two copies of the control file to guard against loss of one of them, Oracle strongly recommends three copies. For more information, see Chapter 10.

36. B, D. RMAN can make image copies of datafiles or place backups into backup sets. For more information, see Chapter 10.

37. C. Archived redo log files can be written to as many as ten different destinations, with any combination of local and remote locations. For more information, see Chapter 10.

38. B. Either dropping a table or inserting the wrong data into a table is considered a user error. For more information, see Chapter 11.

39. D. Instance recovery is performed automatically when ever the database instance is terminated without a NORMAL or IMMEDIATE shutdown. To force an abnormal termination of the instance, you must use SHUTDOWN ABORT and then you can use STARTUP to initiate automatic instance recovery. STARTUP NOMOUNT and STARTUP MOUNT will not start up an instance unless it is shut down first. STARTUP FORCE does not need a SHUTDOWN IMMEDIATE command first; it first performs a SHUTDOWN ABORT and then attempts a normal STARTUP. For more information, see Chapter 11.

40. C. STARTUP is not a valid state, but the command used to start the database. For more information, see Chapter 11.

Chapter

1

Oracle Database 10*g* Components and Architecture

ORACLE DATABASE 10*G*: ADMINISTRATION I EXAM OBJECTIVES COVERED IN THIS CHAPTER:

✓ **Installing Oracle Database 10*g* Software**

- Identify system requirements.
- Use Optimal Flexible Architecture.
- Install software with Oracle Universal Installer.
- Identify and configure commonly used environment variables.

✓ **Creating an Oracle Database**

- Explain the Oracle database architecture.
- Explain the instance architecture.

✓ **Database Interfaces**

- Use SQL*Plus and iSQL*Plus to access the Oracle Database 10*g*.
- Use SQL*Plus and iSQL*Plus to describe the logical structure of tables.
- Use SQL to query, manipulate, and define data using SELECT, UPDATE/INSERT/DELETE and CREATE/ALTER/DROP statements.
- Identify common database interfaces.
- Describe a database transaction.

Exam objectives are subject to change at any time without prior notice and at Oracle's sole discretion. Please visit Oracle's Training and Certification website (http://www.oracle.com/education/certification/) for the most current exam objectives listing.

With the release of Oracle Database 10g (Oracle 10g), Oracle Corporation has delivered a powerful and feature-rich database that can meet the performance, availability, recoverability, and security requirements of any mission-critical application. As the Oracle DBA, you are responsible for managing and maintaining the Oracle 10g database from initial installation, creation, and configuration to final deployment. Performing these tasks requires a solid understanding of Oracle's product offerings so that you can apply the proper tools and features to the application. You must also use relational database concepts to design, implement, and maintain the tables that store the application data. At the heart of these activities is the need for a thorough understanding of the Oracle architecture and the tools and techniques used to monitor and manage the components of this architecture.

This chapter introduces you to important concepts associated with the relational nature of Oracle 10g and its architecture. This chapter will also help you learn the specifics of how to install, configure, and manage an Oracle database. You need a solid understanding of these concepts before moving on to subsequent chapters.

The Oracle Product Family

Oracle Corporation is generally thought of as a database company—and for good reason. Oracle has been a leader in the development of reliable, scalable, and recoverable database technologies for more than 25 years. With the release of Oracle 10g, Oracle has further enhanced its reputation as an industry leader by producing a feature-rich, yet easy-to-manage database that can handle data from the busiest transactional systems to the largest data warehouses. However, Oracle Corporation also produces many other products that support a variety of data-related business activities. Currently, Oracle's product family consists of the following products and services:

- Oracle Database 10g
- Oracle Application Server 10g
- Oracle Developer Suite
- Oracle Applications 11i
- Oracle Collaboration Suite
- Oracle Services

Each of these products or services is described in detail in the following sections.

The following information regarding Oracle's products is included to provide a framework for understanding where Oracle 10*g* fits within the larger Oracle product line. This information is not part of the exam objectives.

Oracle 10*g*

Oracle 10g was released as version 10.1.0.2 in spring 2004. This release of Oracle's flagship database product introduces many new features, but the three primary thrusts are ease of management, enhanced scalability, and improved performance management.

The ease of management features include the automatic management of disk storage allocated to the database, proactive monitoring and self-tuning of the database's memory structures, preconfigured database alerts, and enhanced, web-based tools for monitoring and managing the entire Oracle architecture.

Scalability and performance improvements are largely based on Oracle's grid computing model. *Grid computing* is intended to allow businesses to move away from the idea of many individual servers, each of which is dedicated to a small number of applications. When configured in this manner, applications often either do not fully utilize the server's available hardware resources such as memory, CPU, and disk or fall short of these resources during peak usage. By comparison, databases running under Oracle's grid computing model can be spread across as few or as many servers as needed so as to make the most efficient use of each of the available hardware resources at all times. At the same time, Oracle 10g's automated performance monitoring and tuning mechanisms dynamically adjust the database's allocation of these resources to improve performance.

There are five editions of Oracle 10g:

- Enterprise
- Standard
- Standard Edition One
- Personal
- Lite

Table 1.1 compares these versions.

TABLE 1.1   Comparison of Oracle 10*g* Editions

Edition	Description
Enterprise Edition	Includes all available Oracle 10*g* features either bundled or as extra-cost options.
Standard Edition	Includes full clustering features and all Oracle 10*g* ease-of-management features for servers running as many as four processors.

TABLE 1.1   Comparison of Oracle 10g Editions *(continued)*

Edition	Description
Standard Edition One	Includes all Oracle 10g ease-of-management features for servers running as many as two processors.
Personal	Includes all available Oracle 10g features either bundled or as extra-cost options, but for an individual user database.
Lite	Includes all Oracle 10g features needed to build and deploy mobile database applications.

Most of the examples in this book are based on the Enterprise Edition.

Oracle Application Server 10*g*

Oracle's Application Server 10g is used to deploy web-based applications that, like the database, must be highly reliable and scalable to thousands of users. Like the database, Oracle Application Server 10g is also available in a number of versions, but all versions include full Java functionality and Oracle's HTTP server, with additional components such as portals, forms and reports servers, single sign-on capabilities, and wireless connectivity also available.

Oracle Developer Suite

Oracle's Developer Suite consists of several products that can be used to design, develop, and distribute web-based applications. These tools include the following:

- Oracle Designer for gathering business requirements and designing applications
- Oracle JDeveloper for creating Java-based applications
- Oracle Forms and Reports Developer for creating and deploying custom forms and reports
- Oracle Discoverer for developing and distributing ad hoc reporting capabilities against application data
- Oracle Warehouse Builder for designing and deploying data marts and warehouses.

Each of these tools is designed to integrate seamlessly with the Oracle database and application server products to provide a robust application development environment.

Oracle Applications 11*i*

Oracle's database, application server, and developer products make up the core infrastructure of the E-Business Suite of products collectively called Oracle Applications 11*i*. Oracle Applications 11*i* is composed of a number of modules that are used to manage the financial, personnel, manufacturing, order management, sales, service, and asset data of both businesses and public sector organizations.

Oracle Collaboration Suite

Oracle's Collaboration Suite offers a comprehensive system that integrates all of a business's communication technologies, from e-mail, voice mail, and faxes to wireless connectivity and web conferencing. Like Oracle Applications 11*i*, the Collaboration Suite also uses Oracle's database and application server technologies as the core technology infrastructure. This provides a scalable and reliable platform for true enterprise-wide collaboration.

Oracle Services

In addition to software development, Oracle also offers a variety of technical support and consulting services. Technical support is delivered primarily through Oracle's MetaLink website and is available to all customers with current maintenance agreements. In addition to this support, Oracle Services also offers consulting services to help customers select, install, and configure the Oracle technologies that best meet their needs.

You can access Oracle's MetaLink support site at `http://metalink.oracle.com`. This site provides a wealth of patches, documentation, notes, white papers, and user forums.

A valid Custom Support Identifier(CSI) is required to create a MetaLink account. A unique CSI number is usually issued for each Oracle product that is purchased.

Another service offered by Oracle is education. Oracle develops and delivers instructor-led and web-based training courses for all their products. These courses are taught at Oracle University sites and Oracle Approved Education Center locations throughout the world. Oracle Education is also responsible for coordinating all of Oracle's certification programs, including the Oracle Database 10*g* Oracle Certified Associate (OCA) and Oracle Certified Professional (OCP) certifications for which this book helps you prepare.

Relational Database Concepts

At the heart of all the Oracle products discussed in the previous section is the concept of using a database to store, manipulate, retrieve, and secure important business data. The manner in which these three tasks are performed has varied throughout the history of computing. Some early database technologies used flat files or hierarchical file structures to store application data. Others used networks of connections between sets of data to store and locate information.

Oracle 10g does not use any of these techniques for storing or accessing data. Instead, all releases of Oracle's database products have used a relational model to store application data in the database. This relational model on which Oracle is built is based on the ground-breaking work of Dr. Edgar Codd, which was first published in 1970 in his paper "A Relational Model of Data for Large Shared Data Banks."

 Oracle Corporation (then known as Relational Software, Inc.) released the first commercially available relational database in 1979.

IBM Corporation was an early adopter of Dr. Codd's model and also helped to develop the computer language that is used to access all relational databases today—*Structured Query Language (SQL)*. Using English-like commands, SQL users can easily interact with relational databases without having to write complex computer programs or needing to know where or how the data is physically stored on disk. Samples of SQL statements are used in examples throughout this book. In general, SQL commands are used to do the following:

- Display data stored in database tables using the SELECT command
- Add rows to tables using the INSERT command
- Remove rows from tables using the DELETE command
- Modify rows in tables using the UPDATE command
- Create, modify, or drop tables using the CREATE, ALTER, and DROP commands
- Grant or revoke user access to tables using the GRANT and REVOKE commands
- Control transactions using the COMMIT and ROLLBACK commands

Even though each of the previous commands is an SQL command, each type of SQL statement can be classified into one of four categories:

- *Queries* using the SELECT command.
- Statements using the CREATE, ALTER, or DROP command are classified as *Data Definition Language (DDL)* commands.
- Statements using the GRANT or REVOKE commands are classified as *Data Control Language (DCL)* commands.
- Statements using the INSERT, UPDATE, and DELETE commands are classified as *Data Manipulation Language (DML)* commands.

DML commands are used in transactions. A *transaction* begins with the first DML command that a user issues and ends when the user either makes their changes permanent by issuing a commit command or undoes their changes using the rollback command.

 Issuing a DDL or a DCL command also ends any prior transactions by causing an implicit commit command to occur. Abnormal terminations of a database connection to a network or a power failure can cause implicit rollbacks to occur.

Most SQL statements, whether they are queries, DMLs, DDLs, or DCLs, are directed at data stored in one or more Oracle tables. The next section examines important Oracle table concepts in detail.

Rows, Columns, Tables, and Databases

At the heart of the relational model is the concept of a table. A table is composed of columns and rows. The intersection of a column and a row is called a field. The collection of tables that store business data are stored within the Oracle 10g database. Figure 1.1 shows an example of a table, a column, a row, and a field for a table called DEPT that stores department data.

The DEPT table in Figure 1.1 is composed of three columns (DEPTNO, DNAME, and LOC) and contains four rows. Each row contains all the relevant data for a single department. The field at the intersection of the DNAME column and the first row contains the value "Accounting". When a table is created, each column is assigned a name and a datatype. Many datatypes are available in Oracle 10g, but most simply designate whether a column is intended to store characters, numbers, or dates. You can use the following DDL statement to create the DEPT table shown in Figure 1.1.

```
SQL> create table DEPT
  2  (DEPTNO   number(2),
  3   DNAME    varchar2(14),
  4   LOC      varchar2(13));

Table created.
```

FIGURE 1.1   An example of a table composed of columns, rows, and fields

DEPT (Department Table)

DEPTNO	DNAME	LOC
10	ACCOUNTING	NEW YORK	← Row
20	RESEARCH	DALLAS
30	SALES	CHICAGO
40	OPERATIONS	BOSTON

Column   Field

The DDL command creates a column called DEPTNO to store department numbers of as many as 2 digits, a column called DNAME to store department name data of as many as 14 characters, and a column called LOC to store department location data of as many as 13 characters. By specifying column datatypes in this manner, some basic data controls are automatically in place within the database. These controls prevent a user from storing incorrect data in a table. For example, attempting to insert a record that stores a word in a column that is set up to hold numeric values causes a SQL error. The following example shows an example of an INSERT statement that succeeds because all the data being inserted is of the correct datatype, and it shows another statement that fails because a character datatype was inserted into the numeric DEPTNO column:

```
SQL> insert into DEPT (DEPTNO, DNAME, LOC)
  2    values (50,'MANUFACTURING','MADISON');


1 row created.


SQL> insert into DEPT (DEPTNO, DNAME, LOC)
  2    values ('SIX','SHIPPING','MILWAUKEE');
values ('SIX','SHIPPING','MILWAUKEE')
        *
ERROR at line 2:
ORA-01722: invalid number
```

These are simplified examples. Oracle 10*g* can accommodate tables that have as many as 1,000 columns and billions of rows.

See Chapter 3, "Database Storage and Schema Objects," for more information about creating tables and other database objects.

In addition to tables such as DEPT that store important business data, Oracle databases also contain system tables that store data about the database itself. Examples of the type of information in these system tables include the names of all the tables in the database, the column names and datatypes of those tables, the number of rows those tables contain, and security information about which users are allowed to access those tables. This "data about the database" is referred to as *metadata*. As a DBA, you will frequently use this metadata when performing your tasks.

The metadata tables, however, have rather cryptic names such as OBJ$, FILE$, X$KSMSP, and X$KWQSI with unusual column names such as DATAOBJ#, CRSCNWRP, KSMCHCOM, and KWQSINCO. To make it easier to use SQL to examine the contents of metadata tables, Oracle builds views on the tables. A *view* is similar to a table in that it is made up of columns and rows. However, a view is only a logical structure that contains no data of its own. Instead, a view is like a window that can be used to look at the contents of another table or tables. Views greatly simplify access to the metadata because the names of the views and the columns in them are much more intuitive than the metadata tables on which they are based. An Oracle 10g database contains two types of metadata views:

- Data dictionary views
- Dynamic performance views

Examples of both data dictionary and dynamic performance views are described in the next section.

Data Dictionary Views

Depending on which features are installed and configured, an Oracle 10g database can contain more than 1,300 data dictionary views. Data dictionary views have names that begin with DBA_, ALL_, and USER_.

The difference between the DBA_, ALL_, and USER_ views can be illustrated using the DBA_ TABLES data dictionary view as an example. The DBA_TABLES view shows information on *all* the tables in the database. The corresponding ALL_TABLES view, despite its name, shows only the tables that a particular database user owns or has access to. For example, if you were logged in to the database as a user named SCOTT, the ALL_TABLES view would show all the tables owned by the user SCOTT and the tables to which SCOTT has been granted access by other users. The USER_TABLES view shows only those objects owned by a user. If the user SCOTT were to examine the USER_TABLES view, only those tables he owns would be displayed. Figure 1.2 shows a graphical representation of the relationship between the DBA_, ALL_, and USER_views.

FIGURE 1.2   A comparison of data dictionary views

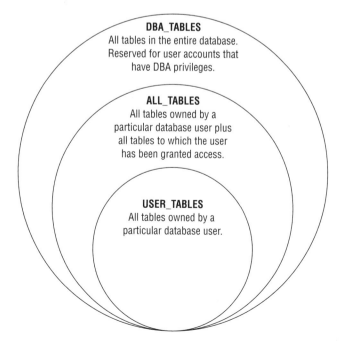

DBA_TABLES
All tables in the entire database.
Reserved for user accounts that
have DBA privileges.

ALL_TABLES
All tables owned by a
particular database user plus
all tables to which the user
has been granted access.

USER_TABLES
All tables owned by a
particular database user.

Because the DBA_ views provide the broadest metadata information, they are generally the data dictionary views used by DBAs. Table 1.2 provides more examples of DBA_ data dictionary views.

TABLE 1.2   Examples of Data Dictionary Views

Dictionary View	Description
DBA_TABLES	Shows the names and physical storage information about all the tables in the database.
DBA_USERS	Shows information about all the users in the database.
DBA_VIEWS	Shows information about all the views in the database.
DBA_TAB_COLUMNS	Shows all the names and datatypes of the table columns in the database.

A complete list of the Oracle 10*g* data dictionary views can be found in Chapters 2 and 3 of the *Oracle Database Reference 10*g *Release 1 (10.1) Part Number B10755-01* available at http://tahiti.oracle.com.

Dynamic Performance Views

Depending on which features are installed and configured, an Oracle 10*g* database can contain approximately 350 dynamic performance views. Most of these views have names that begin with V$. Table 1.3 describes a few of these dynamic performance views.

TABLE 1.3   Examples of Dynamic Performance Views

Dynamic Performance View	Description
V$DATABASE	Contains information about the database itself, such as the database name and when the database was created.
V$VERSION	Shows which software version the database is using.
V$OPTION	Displays which optional components are installed in the database.
V$SQL	Displays information about the SQL statements that database users have been issuing.

A complete list of the Oracle 10*g* data dictionary views can be found in Chapter 4 of the *Oracle Database Reference 10g Release 1 (10.1) Part Number B10755-01* available at http://tahiti.oracle.com.

Although the contents of the DBA_ and V$ metadata views are similar, there are some important differences between the two types. Table 1.4 compares these two types.

TABLE 1.4   A Comparison of Data Dictionary and Dynamic Performance Views

Dictionary Views	Dynamic Performance Views
The DBA_ views usually have plural names (for example, DBA_DATA_FILES).	The names of the V$ views are generally singular (for example, V$DATAFILE).
The DBA_ views are available only when the database is open and running.	Some V$ views are available even when the database is not fully open and running.
The data contained in the DBA_ views is generally uppercase.	The data contained in the V$ views is usually lowercase.
The data contained in the DBA_ views is static and is not cleared when the database is shut down.	The V$ views contain dynamic statistical data that is lost each time the database is shut down.

 As an alternative to querying data dictionary and dynamic performance views directly, you can use the web-based Oracle Enterprise Manager Database Control tools to graphically display metadata information.

Data dictionary views are useful for examining the relationships between tables and the rules defined for storing data in tables. These restrictions and relationships are examined in the next section.

Relationships and Constraints

Real-world Oracle databases are made up of hundreds or thousands of tables. To use these tables to more easily store and retrieve data, you can define rules about how the tables are related and how data should be stored in each table. These rules are referred to as constraints. A *constraint* allows the database designer to enforce business rules about the data stored in the database's tables and the relationships between tables. Table 1.5 describes the five types of constraints in an Oracle database.

TABLE 1.5   Types of Table Constraints

Constraint Type	Description
Not Null	A value must be supplied for this column, but values do not have to be unique.
Unique Key	Every value in this column must be unique, but null values are allowed.
Primary Key	Every value in the column must be unique and cannot be null.
Foreign Key	Every value in the column must match a value in another column in this table or some other table; otherwise, the value is null.
Check	The value entered in the table must match one of the specified values for this column.

A null value is the absence of any value; it is not the same as a space or a zero.

Constraint information is stored in the DBA_CONSTRAINTS and DBA_CONS_COLUMNS data dictionary views.

For example, suppose your database contains a table called EMP that holds employee information. Table 1.6 shows the structure of the EMP table.

TABLE 1.6   The Structure of an *EMP* Table

Column Name	Column Description	Column Datatype
EMPNO	Employee ID number	Number
ENAME	Employee name	Character
JOB	Job title	Character
MGR	Manager's employee ID	Number
HIREDATE	Date employee was hired	Date
SAL	Employee's monthly salary	Number

TABLE 1.6   The Structure of an *EMP* Table *(continued)*

Column Name	Column Description	Column Datatype
COMM	Employee's commission amount	Number
DEPTNO	Employee's department number	Number

If the business has a rule that every employee must have an employee ID and that no two employee IDs can be the same, placing a primary key constraint on the EMPNO column of the EMP table enforces this rule. Any records inserted without an employee number, or with the same employee number as an existing employee, are rejected. Therefore, the EMPNO column is referred to as the *primary key* of the EMP table because the EMPNO value uniquely identifies each record in the EMP table.

A business rule might require that each employee be assigned to a valid department. To enforce this rule, you can define a foreign key constraint between the EMP and DEPT tables so that the DEPTNO value entered for every employee in the EMP table must have a matching DEPTNO in the DEPT table. This relationship is shown graphically in Figure 1.3.

FIGURE 1.3   The relationship between the *EMP* and *DEPT* tables

EMP (Employee Table)

EMPNO	ENAME	JOB	MGR	HIREDATE	SAL	COMM	DEPTNO
7369	SMITH	CLERK	7902	17-DEC-80	800		20
7499	ALLEN	SALESMAN	7698	20-FEB-81	1600	300	30
7521	WARD	SALESMAN	7698	22-FEB-81	1250	500	30
7566	JONES	MANAGER	7839	02-APR-81	2975		20
7654	MARTIN	SALESMAN	7698	28-SEP-81	1250	1400	30
7698	BLAKE	MANAGER	7839	01-MAY-81	2850		30
7844	URNER	SALESMAN	7698	08-SEP-81	1500	0	30

Primary Key Column   Foreign Key Column

DEPT (Department Table)

DEPTNO	DNAME	LOC
10	ACCOUNTING	NEW YORK
20	RESEARCH	DALLAS
30	SALES	CHICAGO
40	OPERATIONS	BOSTON

Primary Key Column

In this example, the DEPTNO column of the EMP table is referred to as a *foreign key* because it has a relationship to the DEPTNO column in another (that is, foreign) table called DEPT. Designing database tables in this manner, so that the values in one table have a relationship to the values in another table, is referred to as *referential integrity (RI)*. Referential integrity is generally enforced through the use of primary key and foreign key table constraints.

 In addition to defining relationships between tables, you can also use foreign keys to define relationships between two columns within the same table. These types of constraints are referred to as *self-referencing foreign keys*.

Sample DDL commands to create the DEPT and EMP tables with the primary and foreign key constraints that we've described are shown here:

```
SQL> alter table DEPT
  2   add constraint DEPT_PK
  3   primary key (DEPTNO);
Table altered.

SQL> create table EMP
  2  (empno    number(4) constraint EMP_PK primary key,
  3  ename    varchar2(10),
  4  job      varchar2(9),
  5  mgr      number(4),
  6  hiredate date,
  7  sal      number(7,2),
  8  comm     number(7,2),
  9  deptno   number(2) constraint EMP_PK_DEPTNO references DEPT(deptno)
 10  );
```

Table created.

Notice that because the DEPT table did not have a primary key defined when we originally created it, the ALTER command is used to create one. Once the relationship between the two tables is defined, the database enforces the relationship for every DML statement performed on those tables. The following example shows an INSERT into the EMP table that fails because the DEPT table has no corresponding department record; it also shows how the same INSERT succeeds after the proper foreign key record is present in the DEPT table:

```
SQL> insert into EMP (empno, ename, deptno)
  2  values (84,'JOHNSON',99);
insert into EMP (empno, ename, deptno)
*
ERROR at line 1:
```

```
ORA-02291: integrity constraint (SCOTT.EMP_PK_DEPTNO) violated - parent key
    not found

SQL> insert into DEPT (deptno, dname, loc)
  2  values (99,'RESEARCH','FREEPORT');

1 row created.

SQL> insert into EMP (empno, ename, deptno)
  2  values (84,'JOHNSON',99);

1 row created.
```

Referential integrity not only enforces the relationship rules while rows are added to a table, but also enforces those rules when rows are being deleted or updated as well. For example, if a user attempts to delete a department from the DEPT table, that department must not have any employees assigned to it; if it does, the primary key/foreign key relationship will not allow the delete. If the employees in that department are deleted first, the DELETE statement on the DEPT table succeeds. The following example demonstrates this behavior when a DELETE statement is issued on tables with referential constraints:

```
SQL> delete from DEPT
  2  where deptno = 99;
delete from DEPT
*
ERROR at line 1:
ORA-02292: integrity constraint (SCOTT.EMP_PK_DEPTNO) violated - child
    record found


SQL> delete from EMP
  2  where deptno = 99;

1 row deleted.

SQL> delete from DEPT
  2  where deptno = 99;

1 row deleted.
```

The ORA-02292 error can be avoided if a foreign key constraint is defined with the ON DELETE CASCADE option. Defining a foreign key in this manner causes Oracle 10*g* to automatically delete child records when a parent record is deleted.

Constraints have a similar impact on UPDATE statements. If a department's number is updated, the database determines if there are employees in that department before allowing the update. If there are employees in that department, the UPDATE fails, because changing the department number will "orphan" these employees, leaving them without a valid department—which violates the business rule that the constraint was designed to enforce. The following example shows what happens when an UPDATE violates the RI rules in the database:

```
SQL> update DEPT
  2   set deptno = 1
  3   where deptno = 10;
update DEPT
       *
ERROR at line 1:
ORA-02292: integrity constraint (SCOTT.EMP_PK_DEPTNO) violated - child
       record found
```

Constraints also prevent a user from removing a table that has a defined relationship to another table. The following example shows how RI impacts an attempt to use the SQL DROP command on the DEPT table:

```
SQL> drop table DEPT;
drop table DEPT
             *
ERROR at line 1:
ORA-02449: unique/primary keys in table referenced by foreign keys
```

When two tables share a common column, such as when referential integrity constraints are defined on the columns between two tables, you can join those tables in a query and return rows from both tables simultaneously. The relationship between the two tables is defined in the WHERE clause of the query shown here.

```
SQL> select dname, ename
  2   from DEPT, EMP
  3   where DEPT.deptno = EMP.deptno;


DNAME          ENAME
-------------  ---------------
ACCOUNTING     CLARK
ACCOUNTING     KING
ACCOUNTING     MILLER
RESEARCH       SMITH
RESEARCH       ADAMS
RESEARCH       FORD
RESEARCH       SCOTT
RESEARCH       JONES
SALES          ALLEN
SALES          BLAKE
```

```
SALES       MARTIN
SALES       JAMES
SALES       TURNER
SALES       WARD
```

`14 rows selected.`

   This query joins the two tables on the common DEPTNO column. Because the DEPTNO column has the same name in both tables, each table's name is included in JOIN condition of the WHERE clause to explicitly tell Oracle how to perform the JOIN.

> In addition to the traditional Oracle JOIN syntax shown in the previous example, Oracle 10*g* is also fully compliant with the ANSI SQL: 1999 syntax that uses the JOIN, CROSS JOIN, or NATURAL JOIN keywords when joining tables.

> If you include two or more tables in the FROM clause, but forget to join the tables in the WHERE clause, the query produces a *Cartesian product*. Cartesian products simply join every row in the first table to every row in the second table without regard for the defined relationship between tables—usually producing a meaningless, I/O-intensive result.

Other Segment Types

The previous section described a variety of SQL commands that can be used against tables in the database. However, tables are just one type of segment in an Oracle 10*g* database. A *segment* is defined as any entity that consumes physical storage space within the database. Some of the more common segment types are described in Table 1.7.

TABLE 1.7   Oracle Segment Types

Segment Type	Description
Table	Stores data in column and row structure.
Index	Improves the access to table data.
Rollback	Special segment used to maintain read consistency during user transactions and perform transaction recovery. Rollback segments are described in Chapter 8, "Managing Consistency and Concurrency."
Partition	Divides a table into smaller, more manageable pieces for performance purposes.

Each Oracle segment is made up of contiguous chunks of storage space in the database called *extents*. Every segment must have at least one extent, but can have as many as 2 billion extents.

Each extent is itself made up of a collection of smaller chunks of space called Oracle *database blocks*. The minimum size of an extent is five database blocks. The default size of these database blocks is set at database creation, but Oracle 10g databases can use multiple block sizes within one database. The common database block sizes are 2KB, 4KB, 8KB, and 16KB.

Each database block is in turn composed of one or more *operating system blocks*. The size of an operating system block depends on the operating system, but most are 512 bytes to 2KB in size. Figure 1.4 summarizes the relationship between the segments, extents, database blocks, and operating system blocks.

Figure 1.4 illustrates how the DEPT table is made up of four extents. Each of these extents is made up of eight database blocks, and each database block is made up of four operating system blocks.

Once a segment such as a table is created, SQL is used to interact with it. The ways in which SQL accesses tables are described in the following section.

FIGURE 1.4   Segment space hierarchy

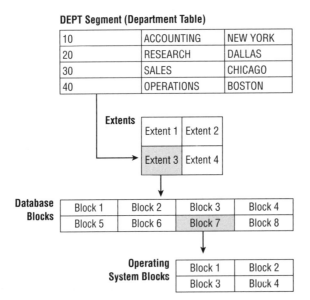

Interacting with Segments

The most common way to interact with an Oracle database is through the use of SQL. The SQL statements might be typed within an Oracle query tool, dynamically generated using a web-based development or management tool, or entered using a programming language such as C++ or COBOL. You can also use Oracle's own procedural language to extend the functionality of SQL within the database. Each of these methods of interacting with the database is explained in the following sections.

Structured Query Language

In their simplest form, SQL statements can be constructed using either of Oracle's command-line SQL tools: SQL*Plus or *i*SQL*Plus. Both SQL*Plus and *i*SQL*Plus allow you to type SQL commands and pass them directly to the database for processing. As described in the previous section, there are four types of SQL commands:

- Queries created using SELECT statements

- DML commands created using INSERT, UPDATE, and DELETE statements

- DDL commands created using CREATE, ALTER, or DROP commands

- DCL commands created using GRANT and REVOKE commands

 Whenever DML commands are performed on a table, the rows impacted by the change are locked by Oracle. Locking is described in detail in Chapter 8.

Short examples of each of these types of SQL statements will appear throughout the remainder of this chapter. However, most of the examples are of SELECT statements. SQL SELECT statements can be composed of many parts:

- The SELECT list, in which each of the columns you want to include in your output is specified. The SELECT clause is required in all queries. An * can be used in the SELECT clause if every column in a table is to be included in the query output.

- The FROM clause in which the name of the table or tables being queried is specified. The FROM clause is required in all queries.

- The WHERE clause in which the output of the query is further restricted by placing conditions on the rows that will be returned. The WHERE clause is optional. If it is not used, the query returns all rows from the table. When a query joins two or more tables, you can use the WHERE clause to define the JOIN condition.

- The GROUP BY clause, which allows you to group related rows of data to summarize their results.

- The HAVING clause, which, like the WHERE clause, is used to reduce the output of the query by limiting which rows are returned.

- The ORDER BY clause that sorts the query output in a specified order.

The following example shows an example of the parts of a SQL statement.

```
SQL> select dname, SUM(sal)
  2 from DEPT, EMP
  3 where DEPT.deptno=EMP.deptno
  4 group by dname
  5 having SUM(sal) > 10000
  6 order by SUM(sal);


DNAME          SUM(SAL)
-----------    --------

RESEARCH        10875
SALES           10100
```

The query examples used throughout this book use each of these clauses. The following sections show how you can use SQL*Plus and *i*SQL*Plus to issue SQL statements.

Using SQL*Plus to Access a Database

To access an Oracle database using SQL*Plus, you must have the following:

- The SQL*Plus client software on your local computer or accessible on the host server via a remote logon or Telnet session

- A valid database user name and password

- The Oracle Net connection string of the database to which you will connect

Figure 1.5 shows a user connecting with the Windows version of the SQL*Plus client to a database called PROD.

Once connected to the database via SQL*Plus, you can issue SQL statements from the SQL prompt. Figure 1.6 shows a query that returns all the columns and rows from the DEPT table.

Notice that the SELECT statement shown in Figure 1.6 ends with a semicolon (;). All SQL commands in SQL*Plus end with either a semicolon or a forward slash (/).

FIGURE 1.5   Accessing a database using SQL*Plus

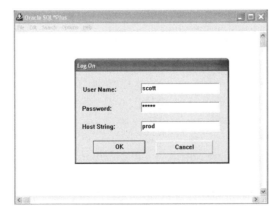

When a SQL statement ends with a forward slash (/), the forward slash should be alone on the last line of the statement.

The SQL examples in this book use mixed case to differentiate SQL reserved words from table and column names. However, SQL is not case sensitive, and you can type commands in upper, lower, or mixed case with the same results.

Another useful command that you can use in SQL*Plus is DESCRIBE. The DESCRIBE command is not a standard SQL command, but an Oracle-specific SQL*Plus command. It displays the logical structure of a table. Figure 1.7 shows the DESCRIBE command being used on the EMP table.

FIGURE 1.6   Querying the *DEPT* table

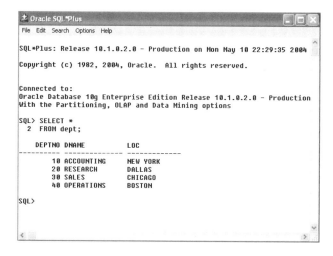

FIGURE 1.7   Describing the structure of the *EMP* table

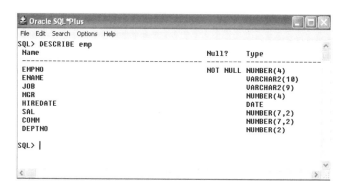

Using *i*SQL*Plus to Access a Database

To access an Oracle database using the browser-based *i*SQL*Plus tool, you must have the following:

- A web browser

- The URL address to the host server running the *i*SQL*Plus website

- A valid database user name and password

- The Oracle Net connection string of the database to which you will connect

Figure 1.8 shows a user connecting the *i*SQL*Plus client to a database called PROD.

The *i*SQL*Plus interface is composed of two windows. You enter SQL statements in the top window, click the Execute button, and the output from those statements is displayed in the bottom window. Just as in SQL*Plus, each *i*SQL*Plus statement can end with a semicolon or a forward slash (/). However, *i*SQL*Plus also allows you to execute SQL commands without specifying the semicolon or forward slash. Figure 1.9 shows a SELECT statement that displays two of the columns and all the rows from the EMP table.

Web-Based Management and Development Tools

In addition to *i*SQL*Plus, Oracle provides several other web-based tools for accessing and manipulating data in databases. Most of these tools do not require that the user construct their own SQL statements the way SQL*Plus or *i*SQL*Plus do. Instead, these tools either dynamically generate SQL code or use SQL code stored in the database to interact with the database. One example of this type of query tool is Oracle Discoverer. Discoverer is an end-user query tool that allows users to run predefined and ad hoc reports from their web browser simply by clicking the tables that they want to query. Oracle Forms and Reports also allows users to access databases using web-based forms and reports.

FIGURE 1.8   Accessing a database using *i*SQL*Plus

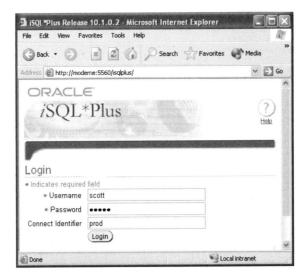

The *i*SQL*Plus listener process must be running on the host server before you can connect using your web browser. You can use the operating system command `isqlplusctl start` to start the *i*SQL*Plus listener on the host server.

Another tool, *Enterprise Manager (EM) Database Control*, is Oracle's web-based database administration tool. EM Database Control dynamically produces SQL commands that are sent to the database based on the navigational choices that are made within EM Database Control. A portion of the Administration page of EM Database Control is shown in Figure 1.10.

FIGURE 1.9 Querying the *EMP* table

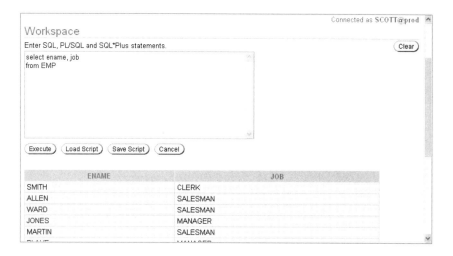

FIGURE 1.10 The EM Database Control main page

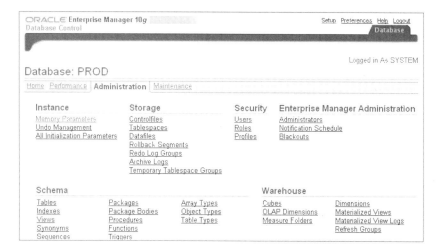

Most EM Database Control pages have a Show SQL button. Clicking this button displays the full text of any SQL statements that have been generated as a result of the user's actions within EM Database Control. In this manner, you can use the Show SQL button to review the SQL statements that EM sends to the database when the user clicks the OK button for the current operation.

The EM Database Control process must be running on the host server before you can connect using your web browser. You can use the operating system command emctl start dbconsole to start the EM process on the host server. The default URL for accessing EM Database Control is http://hostname:5500/em.

In addition to EM Database Control, you can install EM client software on your computer so that you can manage database tasks without using EM Database Control, if needed.

PL/SQL: Procedural Database Language

SQL is a powerful language for interacting with databases, but it does have some limitations. For example, SQL does not have very good mechanisms for condition testing, which would allow a SQL statement to execute if a given condition is true, but not execute if the condition is false. SQL also lacks looping capabilities, the ability to perform a specific SQL action for a specified number of times before stopping. Finally, SQL does not offer any exception-handling capabilities; all errors raised by SQL statements are returned directly to the user.

Oracle Procedural Language for SQL (PL/SQL) is the solution for all these limitations. PL/SQL is a powerful extension to SQL that not only adds condition testing, looping, and exception handling, but also allows developers to write application-specific functions, procedures, packages, and triggers. Table 1.8 describes each of these types of PL/SQL objects.

TABLE 1.8 Types of PL/SQL Objects

PL/SQL Object	Description
Anonymous Block	A block of PL/SQL code that is not stored in the database, but instead is embedded in a form, web page, or SQL script.
Procedure	A block of PL/SQL code that is stored in the database and performs a specific action.
Function	A block of PL/SQL code that is stored in the database and returns a value when called in a SQL statement.
Package	A collection of related procedures and/or functions that perform related functions.
Trigger	A block of PL/SQL code that runs whenever an INSERT, UPDATE, or DELETE activity occurs on a table. Can also be defined to run when certain database events occur.

Chapter 7, "Managing Data with SQL, PL/SQL, and Utilities," provides information on how to use PL/SQL.

Accessing the Database Using Java

Since its introduction in 1995, Java has emerged as a dominant development environment for web-based applications. The primary reason for Java's popularity is its operating system independence. Java programs can be developed on one operating system and then deployed on some other operating system without modification. This is made possible by running the Java programs in an operating system–specific engine called the *Java Virtual Machine (JVM)*. In this way, the only part of the Java architecture that is operating system–specific is the JVM—not the programs themselves.

By incorporating a JVM directly in the database, Oracle 10*g* can store and execute compiled Java code natively. This not only greatly improves the performance of Java-based applications, but also allows developers to incorporate Java code directly into PL/SQL procedures, functions, and packages.

Oracle also includes a Java-based driver, the JDBC (Java Database Connectivity) driver, for improved client-to-database Java connectivity.

Using Oracle Programming Interfaces

In addition to SQL, web-based tools, PL/SQL, and Java, Oracle also provides the ability to integrate SQL commands and database connectivity into traditional programming languages such as C, C++, and COBOL. This integration is achieved by using the Oracle precompilers and the Oracle Call Interface (OCI).

Oracle precompilers allow programmers to incorporate calls to the database directly into their program code. Precompilers are available for third-generation programming languages such as C and COBOL. The Oracle C++ Call Interface (OCCI) is used with C++ to provide full database interaction with that development environment. The OCCI provides substantial programmatic support for database security and password management, access to Oracle datatypes and object-relational features, management of distributed database transactions, and globalization features.

The Oracle Architecture

Each interface described in the previous section allows a user to interact with the database. Using these tools requires that user accounts be created in the database and connectivity to the database be in place across the network. Users must also have adequate storage capacity for the data that they insert, and they need recovery mechanisms for restoring the transactions that they are performing in the event of a hardware failure. As the DBA, you take care of each of these tasks, as well as others, which include the following:

- Selecting the server hardware on which the database software will run
- Installing and configuring the Oracle 10g software on the server hardware
- Creating the database itself
- Creating and managing the tables and other objects used to manage the application data
- Creating and managing database users
- Establishing reliable backup and recovery processes for the database
- Monitoring and tuning database performance

The remainder of this book is dedicated to helping you understand how to perform these and other important Oracle database administration tasks. But, first, to succeed as an Oracle DBA, you need to completely understand Oracle's underlying architecture and its mechanisms. Understanding the relationship between Oracle's memory structures, background processes, and I/O activities is critical before learning how to manage these areas.

The Oracle Server architecture can be described in three categories:

- User-related processes
- Logical memory structures that are collectively called an Oracle *instance*
- Physical file structures that are collectively called a *database*

Figure 1.11 shows all the parts of an Oracle instance and database.

The architecture in Figure 1.11 may at first seem complex. However, each of these architecture components is described in more detail in the following sections, beginning with the user-related processes.

 Taken together, the instance and the database are called an *Oracle Server*.

User Processes

At the user level, two processes allow a user to interact with the instance and, ultimately, with the database: the *User Process* and the *Server Process*.

Whenever a user runs an application, such as a human resources or order-taking application, Oracle starts a User Process to support the user's connection to the instance. Depending on the technical architecture of the application, the User Process exists either on the user's own PC or on the middle-tier application server. The User Process then initiates a connection to the instance. Oracle calls the process of initiating and maintaining communication between the User Process and the instance a *connection*. Once the connection is made, the user establishes a *session* in the instance.

After establishing a session, each user then starts a Server Process on the host server itself. It is this Server Process that is responsible for performing the tasks that actually allow the user to interact with the database.

FIGURE 1.11 The Oracle 10*g* architecture

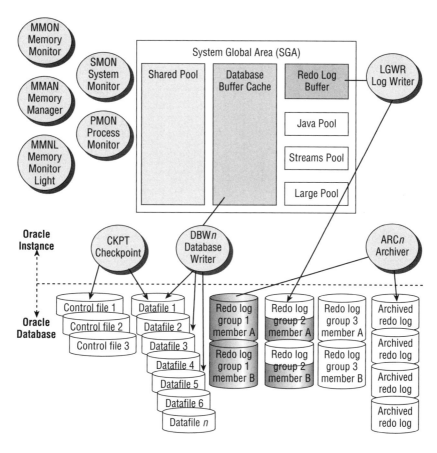

Examples of these interactions include sending SQL statements to the database, retrieving needed data from the database's physical files, and returning that data to the user.

Server Processes generally have a one-to-one relationship with User Processes—each User Process connects to one and only one Server Process. However, in some Oracle configurations, multiple User Processes can share Server Processes. See Chapter 5, "Oracle Shared Server," for details.

In addition to the User and Server processes that are associated with each user connection, an additional memory structure called the *Program Global Area (PGA)* is also created for each user. The PGA stores user-specific session information such as bind variables and session variables. Every Server Process on the server has a PGA memory area. Figure 1.12 shows the relationship between a User Process, Server Processes, PGA, and session.

FIGURE 1.12   The relationship between User and Server processes

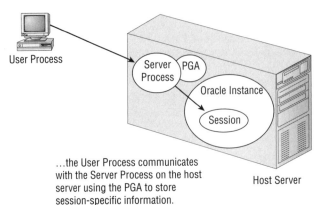

The Server Process communicates with the Oracle instance on behalf of the user. The Oracle instance is examined in the next section.

The Oracle Instance

An Oracle Server instance is made up of Oracle's main memory structure, called the *System Global Area (SGA)*, and several Oracle background processes. It is with the SGA that the Server Process communicates when the user accesses the data in the database. The components of the instance are described in the following sections.

The System Global Area

The SGA is made up of three required components and three optional components. Table 1.9 describes the required components, and Table 1.10 describes the optional components.

TABLE 1.9   Required SGA Components

SGA Component	Description
Shared Pool	Caches the most recently used SQL statements that have been issued by database users
Database Buffer Cache	Caches the data that has been most recently accessed by database users
Redo Log Buffer	Stores transaction information for recovery purposes

TABLE 1.10   Optional SGA Components

SGA Component	Description
Java Pool	Caches the most recently used Java objects and application code when Oracle's JVM option is used
Large Pool	Caches data for large operations such as Recovery Manager (RMAN) backup and restore activities and Shared Server components
Streams Pool	Caches the data associated with queued message requests when Oracle's Advanced Queuing option is used

Oracle uses a *least recently used (LRU) algorithm* to manage the contents of the Shared Pool and Database Buffer Cache. When a user's Server Process needs to put a SQL statement into the Shared Pool or copy a database block into the Buffer Cache, Oracle uses the space in memory that is occupied by the least recently accessed SQL statement or buffer to hold the requested SQL or block copy. Using this technique, Oracle keeps frequently accessed SQL statements and database buffers in memory longer, improving the overall performance of the server by minimizing parsing and physical disk I/O.

The sizes of these SGA components can be managed in two ways: manually and automatically. If you choose to manage these components manually, you must specify the size of each SGA component and then increase or decrease the size of each component according to the needs of the application. If these components are managed automatically, the instance itself will monitor the utilization of each SGA component and adjust their sizes accordingly, relative to a predefined maximum allowable aggregate SGA size.

Whether size is managed manually or automatically, Oracle accomplishes this dynamic allocation of space within the SGA by dividing the allocated SGA memory into chunks called *granules*. These granules of memory are dynamically allocated or deallocated from the Buffer Cache, Shared Pool, Large Pool, and Java Pool as needed according to the demands placed on these areas by the application users.

Depending on your server operating system and the size of the SGA, granules can be 4MB, 8MB, or 16MB in size.

Whether the instance operates in manual or automatic mode is determined by settings in a configuration file called the parameter initialization file. There are two types of parameter initialization files: *Parameter Files (PFILES)*, and *Server Parameter Files (SPFILES)*. You can use either type of file to configure instance and database options, including the size of the SGA and its components if manual SGA management is being used, or the overall memory allocated to the SGA if automatic SGA management is being used. However, there are some important differences between the two types of configuration files, as shown in Table 1.11.

TABLE 1.11   Comparison of PFILES and SPFILES

PFILE	SPFILE
Text file that can be edited using a text editor.	Binary file that cannot be edited directly.
When changes are made to the PFILE, the instance must be shut down and restarted before it takes effect.	Most changes to the SPFILE can be made dynamically, while the instance is open and running.
Is called init*instance name*.ora.	Is called spfile*instance name*.ora.
Can be created from an SPFILE using the create pfile from spfile command.	Can be created from a PFILE using the create spfile from pfile command.

The use of automatic SGA management features requires the use of the SPFILE for maximum benefit.

See the section "OFA Directory Paths" later in this chapter for details on the default locations of PFILES and SPFILES.

You can specify more than 250 documented configuration parameters in the PFILE or SPFILE. Oracle 10*g* divides these parameters into two categories: basic and advanced. Oracle recommends that you set only about 30 basic initialization parameters manually. Oracle also recommends that you do not modify the remaining 220 or so parameters unless directed to do so by Oracle Support or to meet the specific needs of your application. The basic initialization parameters are described in Table 1.12.

TABLE 1.12   Oracle 10*g* Basic Initialization Parameters

Parameter Name	Description
CLUSTER_DATABASE	Tells the instance whether it is part of a clustered environment.
COMPATIBLE	Specifies the release level and feature set that you want to be active in the instance.
CONTROL_FILES	Designates the physical location of the database control files.
DB_BLOCK_SIZE	Specifies the default database block size.

TABLE 1.12   Oracle 10*g* Basic Initialization Parameters *(continued)*

Parameter Name	Description
DB_CREATE_FILE_DEST	Specifies the directory location where database datafiles will be created if the Oracle Managed Files feature is used.
DB_CREATE_ONLINE_LOG_DEST_*n*	Specifies the location(s) where the database redo log files will be created if the Oracle Managed Files feature is used.
DB_DOMAIN	Specifies the logical location of the database on the network.
DB_NAME	Specifies the name of the database that is mounted by the instance.
DB_RECOVERY_FILE_DEST	Specifies the location where recovery files will be written if the Flash Recovery feature is used.
DB_RECOVERY_FILE_DEST_SIZE	Specifies the amount of disk space available for storing Flash Recovery files.
DB_UNIQUE_NAME	Specifies a globally unique name for the database within the enterprise.
INSTANCE_NUMBER	Identifies the instance in a Real Application Clusters (RAC) environment.
JOB_QUEUE_PROCESSES	Specifies the number of background processes to start for handling jobs submitted via Enterprise Manager or DBMS_JOBS.
LOG_ARCHIVE_DEST_*n*	Specifies as many as nine locations where archived redo log files are to be written.
LOG_ARCHIVE_DEST_STATE_*n*	Indicates how the specified locations should be used for log archiving.
NLS_LANGUAGE	Specifies the default language of the database.
NLS_TERRITORY	Specifies the default region or territory of the database.
OPEN_CURSORS	Sets the maximum number of cursors that an individual session can have open at one time.
PGA_AGGREGATE_TARGET	Establishes the overall amount of memory that all PGA processes are allowed to consume.
PROCESSES	Specifies the maximum number of operating system processes that can connect to the instance.

TABLE 1.12 Oracle 10*g* Basic Initialization Parameters *(continued)*

Parameter Name	Description
REMOTE_LISTENER	Specifies a network name that points to the address or list of addresses of remote Oracle Net listeners.
REMOTE_LOGIN_PASSWORDFILE	Determines whether the instance uses a password file and what type.
ROLLBACK_SEGMENTS	Specifies only if Automatic Undo Management is not being used.
SESSIONS	Determines the maximum number of sessions that can connect to the database.
SGA_TARGET	Establishes the maximum size of the SGA, within which space is automatically allocated to each SGA component when automatic memory management is used.
SHARED_SERVERS	Specifies the number of Shared Server processes to start when the instance is started. See Chapter 5 for details.
STAR_TRANSFORMATION_ENABLED	Determines whether the optimizer will consider star transformations when queries are executed. See Chapter 9, "Proactive Database Maintenance and Performance Monitoring," for details on the optimizer.
UNDO_MANAGEMENT	Establishes whether system undo is automatically or manually managed. See Chapter 8 for details on undo segments.
UNDO_TABLESPACE	Specifies which tablespace stores undo segments if the Automatic Undo Management option is used. See Chapter 8 for details on undo management.

As shown in Table 1.12, many initialization parameters are used to specify the size of the SGA and its components. Any parameters not specified in the PFILE or SPFILE take on their default values. The following is an example of the contents of a typical Unix Oracle 10*g* PFILE that contains both basic and advanced parameters:

```
db_block_size=8192
db_file_multiblock_read_count=16
open_cursors=300
db_name=PROD
background_dump_dest=/u01/app/oracle/admin/PROD/bdump
```

```
core_dump_dest=/u01/app/oracle/admin/PROD/cdump
user_dump_dest=/u01/app/oracle/admin/PROD/udump
control_files=(/u02/oradata/PROD/control01.ctl,
               /u03/oradata/PROD/control02.ctl,
               /u05/oradata/PROD/control03.ctl)
db_recovery_file_dest=/u01/app/oracle/flash_recovery_area/
db_recovery_file_dest_size=2147483648
job_queue_processes=10
compatible=10.1.0.2.0
sga_target=500M
max_sga_size=800M
processes=250
remote_login_passwordfile=EXCLUSIVE
pga_aggregate_target=25165824
sort_area_size=65536
undo_management=AUTO
undo_tablespace=UNDOTBS1
```

In this sample PFILE, the sizes of the Shared Pool, Database Buffer Cache, Large Pool, and Java Pool are not individually specified. Instead, Oracle 10g's automatic memory management features allow you to simply set one configuration parameter—SGA_TARGET—to establish the total amount of memory allocated to the SGA. Oracle then automatically allocates portions of this overall memory allocation to each of the SGA components at instance startup and also dynamically reallocates the space as needed to maximize performance while the database is in use. In addition to examining the PFILE/SPFILE, you can also use the V$SGA and V$SGA_DYNAMIC_COMPONENTS dynamic performance view to display the size of the SGA and some of its components, as shown here:

```
SQL> select *
  2  from V$SGA;
```

NAME	VALUE
Fixed Size	787988
Variable Size	145750508
Database Buffers	25165824
Redo Buffers	262144

The output from this query shows that the total size of the SGA is 171,966,464 bytes. This total size is composed of the variable space that is composed of the Shared Pool, the Large Pool, and the Java Pool (145,750,508 bytes), the Database Buffer Cache (25,165,824 bytes), the Redo Log Buffer (262,144 bytes), and some additional space (787,988 bytes) that stores information used by the instance's background processes. The V$SGA_DYNAMIC_COMPONENTS view displays additional detail about the allocation of space within the SGA, as shown in the following query:

```
SQL> select component,current_size
  2  from v$sga_dynamic_components;


COMPONENT                               CURRENT_SIZE
--------------------------------------- ------------
shared pool                                 83886080
large pool                                   8388608
java pool                                   50331648
streams pool                                       0
DEFAULT buffer cache                        25165824
KEEP buffer cache                                  0
RECYCLE buffer cache                               0
DEFAULT 2K buffer cache                            0
DEFAULT 4K buffer cache                            0
DEFAULT 8K buffer cache                            0
DEFAULT 16K buffer cache                           0
DEFAULT 32K buffer cache                           0
OSM Buffer Cache                                   0

13 rows selected.
```

The results of this query show that the Shared Pool is 83,886,080 bytes, the Large Pool is 8,388,608 bytes, the Java Pool is 50,331,648 bytes, and the Database Buffer Cache is 25,165,824 bytes.

You can also use EM Database Control to view the sizes of each of the SGA components, as shown in Figure 1.13.

FIGURE 1.13 EM Database Control showing SGA components

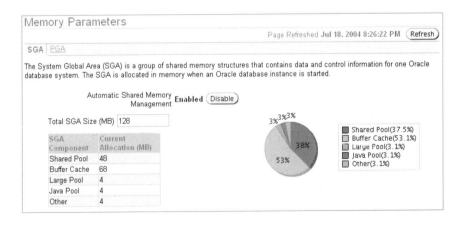

Real World Scenario

Handle With Care: Undocumented Configuration Parameters

You've just read a performance-tuning tip posted to the Oracle newsgroup at `comp.databases.oracle.server`. The person posting the tip suggests setting the undocumented PFILE parameter `_dyn_sel_est_num_blocks` to a value of 200 in order to boost your database's performance. Should you implement this suggestion?

More than 1000 undocumented configuration parameters are available in Oracle 10g. Undocumented configuration parameters are distinguished from their documented counterparts by the underscore that precedes their name, as with the parameter described in the newsgroup posting.

I do not recommend utilizing undocumented PFILE or SPFILE parameters on any of your systems because knowing the appropriate reasons to use these parameters, and the appropriate values to set these parameters to, is almost pure speculation because of their undocumented nature. Although some undocumented parameters are relatively harmless, using others incorrectly can cause unforeseen database problems. What does the `_dyn_sel_est_num_blocks` parameter do, and what value should you set it to? Only the engineers of the Oracle 10g kernel code know for sure.

One exception to this suggestion is when you are directed to use an undocumented configuration parameter by Oracle Support. Oracle Support occasionally uses these parameters to enhance the generation of debug information or to work around a bug in the kernel code.

Oracle Background Processes

There are many types of Oracle background processes. Each performs a specific job in helping to manage the instance. Five Oracle background processes are required, and several background processes are optional. The required background processes are found in all Oracle instances. Optional background processes may or may not be used depending on which optional Oracle features are being used in the database. Table 1.13 describes the required background processes, and Table 1.14 describes some of the optional background processes.

TABLE 1.13   Required Oracle Background Processes

Process Name	Operating System Process	Description
System Monitor	SMON	Performs instance recovery following an instance crash, coalesces free space in the database, and manages space used for sorting
Process Monitor	PMON	Cleans up failed user database connections

TABLE 1.13   Required Oracle Background Processes *(continued)*

Process Name	Operating System Process	Description
Database Writer	DBW*n**	Writes modified database blocks from the SGA's Database Buffer Cache to the datafiles on disk
Log Writer	LGWR	Writes transaction recovery information from the SGA's Redo Log Buffer to the online Redo Log files on disk
Checkpoint	CKPT	Updates the database files following a Checkpoint Event

*The *n* in any operating system process name signifies that more than one of these processes may be running. In these cases, the n is replaced with a numeric value. For example, if four database writer processes are running, their process names at the operating system level are DBW0, DBW1, DBW2, and DBW3.

TABLE 1.14   Optional Oracle Background Processes

Process Name	Operating System Process	Description
Archiver	ARC*n*	Copies the transaction recovery information written to disk by LGWR (log writer) to the online Redo Log files and to a secondary location in case it is needed for recovery. Nearly all production databases use this optional process. See Chapter 2, "Creating and Controlling a Database," for details on how to enable this process.
Recoverer	RECO	Recovers failed transactions that are distributed across multiple databases when using Oracle's distributed database feature.
Job Queue Monitor	CJQ*n*	Assigns jobs to the Job Queue processes when using Oracle's job scheduling feature.
Job Queue	J*nnn*	Executes database jobs that have been scheduled using Oracle's job scheduling feature.
Queue Monitor	QMN*n*	Monitors the messages in the message queue when Oracle's Advanced Queuing feature is used.
Parallel Query Slave	Q*nnn*	Used to carry out portions of a larger overall query when Oracle's Parallel Query feature is used.

TABLE 1.14   Optional Oracle Background Processes *(continued)*

Process Name	Operating System Process	Description
Dispatcher	D*nnn*	Assigns user's database requests to a queue where they are then serviced by Shared Server processes when Oracle's Shared Server feature is used. See Chapter 5 for details on using Shared Servers.
Shared Server	S*nnn*	Server Processes that are shared among several users when Oracle's Shared Server feature is used. See Chapter 5 for details on using Shared Servers.
Memory Manager	MMAN	Manages the size of each individual SGA component when Oracle's Automatic Shared Memory Management feature is used. See Chapter 9 for more information on using this feature.
Memory Monitor	MMON	Gathers and analyzes statistics used by the Automatic Workload Repository feature. See Chapter 9 for more information on using this feature.
Memory Monitor Light	MMNL	Gathers and analyzes statistics used by the Automatic Workload Repository feature. See Chapter 9 for more information on using this feature.
Recovery Writer	RVWR	Writes recovery information to disk when Oracle's Flashback Database Recovery feature is used. See Chapter 10, "Implementing Database Backups," and Chapter 11, "Implementing Database Recovery," for details on how to use the Flashback Database Recovery feature.
Change Tracking Writer	CTWR	Keeps track of which database blocks have changed when Oracle's incremental Recovery Manager feature is used. See Chapters 10 and 11 for details on using Recovery Manager to perform backups.

On Unix systems, you can view these background processes from the operating system using the ps command, as shown here:

```
$ ps -ef |grep PROD
oracle   3969   1  0 10:02 ?     00:00:05 ora_pmon_PROD
oracle   3971   1  0 10:02 ?     00:00:00 ora_mman_PROD
```

```
oracle    3973    1  0 10:02 ?         00:00:07  ora_dbw0_PROD
oracle    3975    1  0 10:02 ?         00:00:07  ora_lgwr_PROD
oracle    3977    1  0 10:02 ?         00:00:10  ora_ckpt_PROD
oracle    3979    1  0 10:02 ?         00:00:20  ora_smon_PROD
oracle    3981    1  0 10:02 ?         00:00:00  ora_reco_PROD
oracle    3983    1  0 10:02 ?         00:00:09  ora_cjq0_PROD
oracle    3985    1  0 10:02 ?         00:00:00  ora_d000_PROD
oracle    3987    1  0 10:02 ?         00:00:00  ora_s000_PROD
oracle    4052    1  0 10:02 ?         00:00:00  ora_qmnc_PROD
oracle    4054    1  0 10:02 ?         00:00:29  ora_mmon_PROD
oracle    4057    1  0 10:02 ?         00:00:08  ora_mmnl_PROD
oracle    4059    1  0 10:02 ?         00:01:04  ora_j000_PROD
oracle    27544   1  0 20:29 ?         00:00:00  ora_q000_PROD
```

This output shows that 15 background processes are running on the Unix server for the PROD database.

User Server processes are not considered part of the instance.

In Windows environments, a Windows service called OracleService*Instance-Name* is also associated with each instance. This service must be started in order to start up the instance in Windows environments.

The Oracle Database

An instance is a temporary memory structure, but the Oracle database is made up of a set of physical files that reside on the host server's disk drives. These files are called *control files*, *datafiles*, and *redo logs*. Additional physical files that are associated with the Oracle database, but are not technically part of the database, are the *password file*, the PFILE and SPFILE described previously, and any *archived redo log files*. Table 1.15 summarizes the role that each of these files plays in the database architecture.

Creating and managing these files is discussed in detail in Chapter 2.

The three files that make up a database—the control file, datafile, and redo logs—are described in the following sections.

TABLE 1.15   Oracle Physical Files

File Type	Information Contained in File(s)
Control	Locations of other physical files, database name, database block size, database character set, and recovery information. These files are required to open the database.
Datafile	All application data and internal metadata.
Redo log	Record of all changes made to the database; used for recovery.
Parameter (PFILE or SPFILE)	Configuration parameters for the SGA, optional Oracle features, and background processes.
Archived log	Copy of the contents of previous online redo logs, used for recovery.
Password	Optional file used to store names of users who have been granted the SYSDBA and SYSOPER privileges. See Chapter 6 for details on SYSDBA and SYSOPER privileges.
Oracle Net	Entries that configure the database listener and client-to-database connectivity. See Chapter 4 for details.

Control Files

Control files are critical components of the database because they store important information that is not available anywhere else. This information includes the following:

- The name of the database
- The names, locations, and sizes of the datafiles and redo log files
- Information used to recover the database in the case of a disk failure or user error

The control files are created when the database is created in the locations specified in the control_files parameter in the parameter file. Because loss of the control files negatively impacts the ability to recover the database, most production databases multiplex their control files to multiple locations. Oracle uses the CKPT background process to automatically update each of these files as needed, keeping the contents of all copies of the control synchronized. You can use the dynamic performance view V$CONTROLFILE to display the names and locations of all the database's control files. A sample query of V$CONTROLFILE on a Unix system is shown here:

```
SQL> select name from v$controlfile;

NAME
-----------------------------------
/u02/oradata/PROD/control01.ctl
```

/u03/oradata/PROD/control02.ctl
/u05/oradata/PROD/control03.ctl

   This query shows that the database has three control files, called control01.ctl, control02.ctl, and control03.ctl, which are stored in the directories /u02/oradata/ PROD/, /u03/oradata/PROD/, and /u05/oradata/PROD/ respectively. You can also monitor control files using EM Database Control, as shown in Figure 1.14.

> Control files are usually the smallest files in the database, generally between 1MB and 5MB in size. However, they can be larger depending on the PFILE/ SPFILE setting for CONTROLFILE_RECORD_KEEP_TIME when the Recovery Manager feature is used.

   One thing that the control files keep track of in the database are the names, locations, and sizes of the database datafiles. Datafiles, and their relationship to another database structure called a tablespace, are examined in the next section.

Datafiles

Datafiles are the physical files that actually store the data that has been inserted into each table in the database. The size of the datafiles is directly related to the amount of table data that they store. Datafiles are the physical structure behind another database storage area called a *tablespace*. A tablespace is a logical storage area within the database. Tablespaces group logically related segments. For example, all the tables for the Accounts Receivable application might be stored together in a tablespace called AR_TAB, and the indexes on these tables might be stored in a tablespace called AR_IDX.

FIGURE 1.14   EM Database Control showing control files

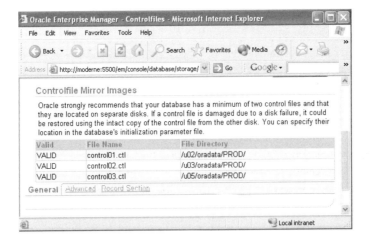

By default, every Oracle 10*g* database must have at least three tablespaces. These tablespaces are described in Table 1.16.

TABLE 1.16   Required Tablespaces in Oracle 10*g*

Tablespace Name	Description
SYSTEM	Stores the data dictionary tables and PL/SQL code.
SYSAUX	Stores segments used for database options such as the Automatic Workload Repository, Online Analytical Processing (OLAP), and Spatial.
TEMP	Used for performing large sort operations. TEMP is required when the SYSTEM tablespace is created as a locally managed tablespace; otherwise, it is optional. See Chapter 3 for details.

In addition to these three required tablespaces, most databases have tablespaces for storing other database segments similar to those shown in Table 1.17.

TABLE 1.17   Common Tablespaces in Oracle 10*g* Databases

Tablespace Name	Description
TOOLS	Used to store segments for nonapplication management tools.
USERS	Used as the default tablespace for database users.
UNDOTBS1	Used to store transaction information for read consistency and recovery purposes. See Chapter 8 for details.

Beyond the six common tablespaces listed in Tables 1.16 and 1.17, production databases often have many more tablespaces for storing application segments. Either you or the application vendor determines the total number and names of these tablespaces. You can use the DBA_ TABLESPACES data dictionary view to display a list of all the tablespaces in the database. This is a sample query on DBA_TABLESPACES:

```
SQL> select tablespace_name
  2  from dba_tablespaces
  3  order by tablespace_name;


TABLESPACE_NAME
------------------------------
APPL_IDX
```

```
APPL_TAB
EXAMPLE
SYSAUX
SYSTEM
TEMP
UNDOTBS1
```

```
7 rows selected.
```

This output shows that this database consists of seven tablespaces: SYSTEM, UNDOTBS1, SYSAUX, TEMP, EXAMPLE, APPL_TAB, and APPL_IDX. You can also monitor tablespaces using EM Database Control, as shown in Figure 1.15.

 The current release of Oracle's Application 11*i* uses more than 375 tablespaces to store application data and indexes.

For each of the tablespaces shown in Figure 1.15, there must be at least one datafile. Some tablespaces may be composed of several datafiles for management or performance reasons. The data dictionary view DBA_DATA_FILES shows the datafiles associated with each tablespace in the database. The following SQL statement shows a sample query on the DBA_DATA_FILES data dictionary view.

```
SQL> select tablespace_name, file_name
  2  from dba_data_files
  3  order by tablespace_name;
```

TABLESPACE_NAME	FILE_NAME
APPL_IDX	/u01/oradata/PROD/appl_idx01.dbf
APPL_IDX	/u03/oradata/PROD/appl_idx02.dbf
APPL_TAB	/u01/oradata/PROD/appl_tab01.dbf
APPL_TAB	/u03/oradata/PROD/appl_tab02.dbf
EXAMPLE	/u02/oradata/PROD/example01.dbf
SYSAUX	/u04/oradata/PROD/sysaux01.dbf
SYSTEM	/u05/oradata/PROD/system01.dbf
UNDOTBS1	/u02/oradata/PROD/undotbs101.dbf

This output shows that the datafiles for the six tablespaces in this database are stored in the /u01/oradata/PROD through /u05/oradata/PROD directories. The APPL_DATA and APPL_INDX tablespaces are each made up of two datafiles; the rest of the tablespaces are each made up of only one datafile. You can also monitor datafiles using EM Database Control, as shown in Figure 1.16.

 Temporary tablespaces are not displayed in DBA_TABLESPACES. They are listed in DBA_TEMP_FILES.

FIGURE 1.15   EM Database Control showing tablespaces

Results

Create

Edit View Delete Actions Add Datafile ⌄ Go

Select	Name	Type	Extent Management	Segment Management	Status	Size (MB)	Used (MB)	Used (%)	
⊙	APPL_IDX	PERMANENT	LOCAL	MANUAL	ONLINE	100.000	.063		0.06
○	APPL_TAB	PERMANENT	LOCAL	MANUAL	ONLINE	100.000	.063		0.06
○	EXAMPLE	PERMANENT	LOCAL	AUTO	ONLINE	500.000	117.813		23.56
○	SYSAUX	PERMANENT	LOCAL	AUTO	ONLINE	450.000	344.875		76.64
○	SYSTEM	PERMANENT	DICTIONARY	MANUAL	ONLINE	250.000	200.813		80.33
○	TEMP	TEMPORARY	LOCAL	MANUAL	ONLINE	500.000	37.000		7.40
○	UNDOTBS1	UNDO	LOCAL	MANUAL	ONLINE	800.000	19.938		2.49

FIGURE 1.16   EM Database Control showing datafiles

Results

Create

Edit View Actions Create Like ⌄ Go

Select	File Name	Tablespace	Status	Size (MB)	Used (MB)	Used (%)	
⊙	/u20/oradata/PROD/appl_idx01.dbf	APPL_IDX	ONLINE	100.000	.063		0.06
○	/u20/oradata/PROD/appl_idx02.dbf	APPL_IDX	ONLINE	100.000	.063		0.06
○	/u20/oradata/PROD/appl_tab01.dbf	APPL_TAB	ONLINE	100.000	.063		0.06
○	/u20/oradata/PROD/appl_tab02.dbf	APPL_TAB	ONLINE	100.000	.063		0.06
○	/u20/oradata/PROD/example01.dbf	EXAMPLE	ONLINE	500.000	117.813		23.56
○	/u20/oradata/PROD/sysaux01.dbf	SYSAUX	ONLINE	450.000	344.875		76.64
○	/u20/oradata/PROD/system01.dbf	SYSTEM	SYSTEM	250.000	200.813		80.33
○	/u20/oradata/PROD/temp01.dbf	TEMP	ONLINE	500.000	37.000		7.40
○	/u20/oradata/PROD/undotbs101.dbf	UNDOTBS1	ONLINE	800.000	19.938		2.49

Chapter 3 discusses the creation and management of tablespaces in further detail.

Datafiles are usually the largest files in the database, ranging from megabytes to gigabytes or terabytes in size.

When a user performs a SQL operation on a table, the user's Server Process copies the affected data from the datafiles into the Database Buffer Cache in the SGA. If the user has performed a committed transaction that modifies that data, the Database Writer process (DBWn) ultimately writes the modified data back to the datafiles.

When Does Database Writer Write?

The DBWn background process writes to the datafiles whenever one of the following events occurs:

- A user's Server Process has searched too long for a free buffer when reading a buffer into the Buffer Cache.

- The number of modified and committed, but unwritten, buffers in the Database Buffer Cache is too large.

- At a database Checkpoint event. See Chapters 10 and 11 for information on checkpoints.

- The instance is shut down using any method other than a shutdown abort.

- A tablespace is placed into backup mode.

- A tablespace is taken offline to make it unavailable or changed to READ ONLY.

- A segment is dropped.

Redo Log Files

Whenever a user performs a transaction in the database, the information needed to reproduce this transaction in the event of a database failure is automatically recorded in the Redo Log Buffer. The contents of the Redo Log Buffer are ultimately written to the redo logs by the LGWR background process.

Because of the important role that redo logs play in Oracle's recovery mechanism, they are usually multiplexed, or copied. This means that each redo log contains one or more copies of itself in case one of the copies becomes corrupt or is lost due to a hardware failure. Collectively, these sets of redo logs are referred to as *redo log groups*. Each multiplexed file within the group is called a *redo log group member*. Oracle automatically writes to all members of the redo log group to keep the files in sync. Each redo log group must be composed of one or more members. Each database must have a minimum of two redo log groups because redo logs are used in a circular fashion, as shown in Figure 1.17.

Figure 1.17 shows a database that has three redo log groups: group 1, group 2, and group 3. Each group is composed of two members. The first member of each group is stored in the directory /u02/oradata/PROD. The second, multiplexed member is stored in the directory /u04/oradata/PROD. You can use the V$LOGFILE dynamic performance view to view the names of the redo log groups and the names and locations of their members, as shown next. The following SQL statement shows a sample query on a Unix system of the DBA_DATA_FILES data dictionary view.

```
SQL> select group#, member
  2  from v$logfile
  3  order by group#;

   GROUP# MEMBER
---------- ------------------------------
        1 /u02/oradata/PROD/redo01a.rdo
```

```
1 /u04/oradata/PROD/redo01b.rdo
2 /u02/oradata/PROD/redo02a.rdo
2 /u04/oradata/PROD/redo02b.rdo
3 /u02/oradata/PROD/redo03a.rdo
3 /u04/oradata/PROD/redo03b.rdo

6 rows selected.
```

When Does Log Writer Write?

The LGWR background process writes to the current redo log group whenever one of the following database events occurs:

- Every three seconds.

- A user commits a transaction.

- The Redo Log Buffer is one-third full.

- The Redo Log Buffer contains 1MB worth of redo information.

- Before the DBW*n process* whenever a database checkpoint occurs. See Chapter 10 for more information on checkpoints.

FIGURE 1.17   How redo logs are used in the database

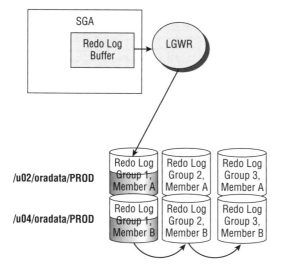

This output shows that the database has a total of three redo log groups and that each group has two members. Each of the members is located in a separate directory and disk volume on the server's disk drives so that the loss of a single disk drive will not cause the loss of the recovery information stored in the redo logs. You can also monitor redo logs using EM Database Control, as shown in Figure 1.18.

When a user performs a DML activity on the database, the recovery information for this transaction is written to the redo log buffer by the user's Server Process. LGWR eventually writes this recovery information to the active redo log group until that log group is filled. Once the current log fills with transaction information, LGWR switches to the next redo log until that log group fills with transaction information, and so on, until all available redo logs are used. When the last redo log is used, LGWR wraps around and starts using the first redo log again. As shown in the following query, you can use the V$LOG dynamic performance view to display which redo log group is currently active and being written to by LGWR:

```
SQL> select group#, members, status
  2  from v$log
  3  order by group#;

    GROUP#    MEMBERS STATUS
---------- ---------- ----------------
         1          2 CURRENT
         2          2 INACTIVE
         3          2 INACTIVE
```

This output shows that redo log group number 1 is currently active and being written to by LGWR. Once redo log group 1 is full, LGWR switches to redo log group 2.

FIGURE 1.18 EM Database Control showing redo logs

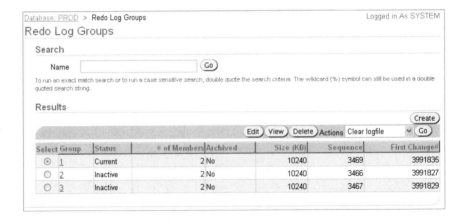

When LGWR wraps around from the last redo log group back to the first redo log group, any recovery information previously stored in the first redo log group is overwritten and therefore no longer available for recovery purposes. However, if the database is operating in *archive log mode*, the contents of these previously used logs are copied to a secondary location before the log is reused by LGWR. If this archiving feature is enabled, it is the job of the ARC*n* background process described in the previous section to copy the contents of the redo log to the archive location. These copies of old redo log entries are called archive logs. This process is shown graphically in Figure 1.19.

In Figure 1.19, the first redo log group has been filled, and LGWR has moved to on to redo log group 2. As soon as LGWR switches from redo log group 1 to redo log group 2, the ARC*n* process starts copying the contents of redo log group 1 to the archive log file location. Once the first redo log group is safely archived, LGWR is free to wrap around and reuse the first redo log group once redo log group 3 is filled.

Nearly all production databases run in archive log mode because they need to be able to redo all transactions since the last backup in the event of a hardware failure or user error that damages the database.

If LGWR needs to write to the redo log group that ARC*n* is trying to copy but cannot because the destination is full, the database hangs until space is cleared on the drive.

The next section talks about how to install and configure the Oracle software on your server so that you can then create a database. Creating a database is described in detail in Chapter 2.

FIGURE 1.19 How *ARCn* copies redo log entries to disk

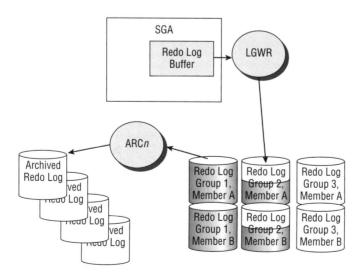

Installing Oracle 10*g*

One of your duties as an Oracle DBA is to install and configure the Oracle 10*g* software on the server so that a database can be created to store application data. This section discusses each of the steps that you must perform in order to successfully install Oracle 10*g*.

The examples in this section are for a Unix server, but most of the concepts apply equally to Windows platforms. Significant differences between Unix and Windows are noted.

Review the Documentation

Before beginning an installation of Oracle 10*g*, you need to review several documents so that you completely understand the installation requirements. These documents include the following:

- The installation guide for your operating system
    - *Oracle Database Installation Guide 10g* Release 1 (10.1) for Unix Systems: AIX-Based Systems, HP-UX, HP Tru64 Unix, Linux, and Solaris Operating System (SPARC), Part No. B10811-02
    - *Oracle Database Installation Guide 10g* Release 1 (10.1.0.2.0) for Windows, Part No. B10130-01
- The general release notes for the version of Oracle that you are installing
- The operating system–specific release notes for the version of Oracle that you are installing
- Any "quick start" installation guides

Before you begin, review each of these documents so that you are thoroughly familiar with the install process and any known associated issues.

All these documents are available on Oracle's Technology Network website located at http://otn.oracle.com/index.html and on Oracle's MetaLink website at http://metalink.oracle.com. Unlike MetaLink accounts, OTN user accounts are free.

Review the System Requirements

The next task is to review your server hardware specifications to see if they meet or exceed the specifications in the install documentation. Minimally, this means that you must confirm that your server meets the installation requirements in these four areas:

- The operating system is of the proper release level
- The server has adequate memory to perform the install and run an instance
- The server has adequate CPU resources to perform the install and run an instance
- The server has adequate disk storage space to perform the install and run a database

The recommended minimum hardware requirements for an Oracle 10*g* installation are shown in Table 1.18.

TABLE 1.18   Recommended Minimum Hardware Requirements for Oracle 10*g*

Hardware Component	Recommended Requirement
Memory	512MB.
Swap space	1GB or two times the amount of RAM.
Temp space	400MB of free space in the /tmp directory on Unix systems.
Free disk space	1.5GB of disk space is required for the base Oracle 10*g* installation. 1GB of disk space is needed to create a database using the Database Configuration Assistant.

The Oracle Universal Installer, which is described in the subsequent section, "Using the Oracle Universal Installer," will perform a quick system check prior to starting an installation to see if your system meets the specific requirements for your operating system. If your system does not meet the minimum requirements, the installer returns an error and aborts.

On Unix systems, you must examine one critical system requirement before installation: Unix kernel parameters. Unix kernel parameters are used to configure the Unix operating system settings for operating system–level operations that impact Oracle-related activities such as the following:

- The maximum size allowed for a sharable memory segment on the server, which can impact the SGA size
- The maximum number of files that can be open on the server at one time, which impacts the total number of users and files in the database
- The number of processes that can run concurrently on the server, which impacts the number of users and the ability to use some optional features

The systems administrator usually makes Unix kernel changes, which may require a server reboot in order to take effect. The install guide and/or release notes provides details on the appropriate kernel setting for your operating system. In addition to kernel settings, the system administrator may have to configure the server's disk storage system and backup hardware before installing the Oracle software.

Plan Your Install

Once you review the documentation and system requirements, you are ready to begin planning your installation. This is the last step before actually running the Oracle Universal Installer.

One way to simplify installation planning is to adopt the *Optimal Flexible Architecture (OFA)* model that Oracle recommends as a best-practice methodology for managing Oracle installations in Unix environments (and to a lesser extent, Windows environments). Cary Millsap designed the OFA model to produce database installations that are easier to manage, upgrade, and back up while at the same time minimizing problems associated with database growth. The OFA model addresses four areas:

- Naming conventions for Unix file systems and mount points
- Naming conventions for directory paths
- Naming conventions for database files
- Standardized locations for Oracle-related files

 You can download Cary Millsap's original 1995 OFA white paper at www.hotsos.com/downloads/visitor/00000019.pdf.

In addition to using the OFA model, planning your install also means answering the following questions:

- Which operating system user will own the installed Oracle software?
- On which disk drive and directory will the Oracle software be installed?
- What directory structure will be used to store the Oracle software, its related configuration files, and the database itself?
- How should the database files be laid out so that the maximum performance benefits will be realized?
- How should the database files be laid out so that the maximum recoverability benefits will be realized?

Creating the Oracle User Account

On Unix systems, every file is owned by an operating system user account. Therefore, before you can install the Oracle software, you must create a Unix user account that will own the Oracle binaries. The user name for this account can be anything, but common Oracle user names include oracle, ora10g, and ora101. Each Unix user is also in one or more operating system groups. Create a new operating system group for the Oracle Unix user. This group is usually called dba, and you will be prompted for it later during the installation.

Naming Volumes and Mount Points

Unless Oracle's automatic storage management feature or raw devices are used, almost all files on a Unix server are stored on logical storage areas called volumes, which are attached, or mounted, to directories, or mount points, by the Unix system administrator. The OFA model suggests that these mount points be given a name that consists of a combination of a character and numeric values. Examples of common OFA mount points for Unix systems include the following:

- /u01
- /mnt01

- /du01

- /d01

Notice that the naming convention for these mount points is generic. The mount point's name has no relationship to what type of file it will ultimately hold. The OFA model recommends this generic naming convention because it provides the greatest flexibility for future management of the server's file systems.

 The concept of mount points does not apply directly to Windows environments. Windows environments assign a standard Windows drive letter (for example, C:, D:) to each volume.

Creating OFA Directory Paths

The OFA model prescribes that the directory structures under the mount points use a consistent and meaningful naming convention. In addition to this naming convention, the OFA model also assigns standard operating system environment variable names to some of these directory paths as "nicknames" to aid in navigation and ensure portability of the directory structures in the event that they need to be moved to new file systems.

Tables 1.19 and 1.20 show the two operating system environment variables used in the OFA model, along with the directories with which the variables are associated, for both Unix and Windows systems.

TABLE 1.19   Comparison of Unix Directory Paths and Variables

Environment Variable	Directory Path	Description
$ORACLE_BASE	/u01/app/oracle	Top-level directory for Oracle software on the host server
$ORACLE_HOME	/u01/app/oracle/product/10.1.0	Directory into which the Oracle 10g software will be installed

TABLE 1.20   Comparison of Windows Directory Paths and Variables

Environment Variable	Directory Path	Description
%ORACLE_BASE%	D:\ORACLE	Top-level directory for Oracle software on the host server
%ORACLE_HOME%	D:\ORACLE\ORA101	Directory into which the Oracle 10g software will be installed

These environment variables are used extensively when installing, patching, upgrading, and managing Oracle systems. Table 1.21 shows several examples of how these variables define the locations of other Oracle directories.

TABLE 1.21   Common Uses of *ORACLE_BA*SE and *ORACLE_HOME*

Directory	Description
$ORACLE_HOME/dbs	Default location for PFILES and SPFILES on Unix systems
%ORACLE_HOME%\database	Default location for PFILES and SPFILES on Windows systems
$ORACLE_BASE/admin/PROD/pfile	Location of the PFILE for a database called PROD on Unix systems
%ORACLE_BASE%\admin\PROD\pfile	Location of the PFILE for a database called PROD on Windows systems
$ORACLE_HOME/network/admin	Default location for Oracle Net configuration files on Unix systems
%ORACLE_HOME%\network\admin	Default location for Oracle Net configuration files on Windows systems
$ORACLE_HOME/rdbms/admin	Location of many Oracle database configuration scripts on Unix systems
%ORACLE_HOME%\rdbms\admin	Location of many database configuration scripts on Windows systems

For Unix systems, Table 1.21 says $ORACLE_HOME/dbs is the default location for the PFILE and SPFILE, but then says that PFILES should be stored in $ORACLE_BASE/admin/PROD/pfile. Windows systems are similar. This implies that the same file needs to be in two locations at the same time. You can accomplish this using two tricks. Which you use depends on your operating system.

On Unix systems, you can create the PFILE in the $ORACLE_BASE/admin/PROD/pfile directory and then create a symbolic link in $ORACLE_HOME/dbs that points to the file in $ORACLE_BASE/admin/PROD/pfile using this syntax:

```
ln -s $ORACLE_BASE/admin/PROD/pfile/initPROD.ora
   $ORACLE_HOME/dbs/initPROD.ora
```

On Windows systems, you can create the PFILE in the %ORACLE_BASE%\admin\PROD\pfile directory and then put another PFILE in %ORACLE_HOME%\database that contains a single entry that points to the other PFILE in %ORACLE_BASE%\admin\PROD\pfile like this:

ifile=D:\oracle\admin\PROD\pfile\initPROD.ora

Using these techniques allows you to put the initialization parameter files in their default locations under $ORACLE_HOME, but also in their desired location under $ORACLE_BASE.

Other Administrative Directories

According to the OFA model, for a database called PROD, the initialization parameter file should be located in $ORACLE_BASE/admin/PROD/pfile. However, the OFA model also recommends that several other directories be built under this location for other management purposes. These directories are located under $ORACLE_BASE/admin/PROD:

adhoc   This directory is designed to store ad hoc SQL scripts for the PROD database.

arch   If the database is in archive log mode, this directory is specified as the location where the archived redo logs are to be written by LGWR. The PFILE/SPFILE parameter called LOG_ARCHIVE_DEST specifies the location of the arch directory.

adump   If database auditing is turned on, this directory is specified as the location where the audit trail information is to be written. The PFILE/SPFILE parameter AUDIT_FILE_DEST specifies the location of the adump directory.

bdump   This directory is the location of the database Alert log file and any trace files generated by background processes. The PFILE/SPFILE parameter BACKGROUND_DUMP_DEST specifies the location of the bdump directory.

cdump   This directory is the location where core dump files will be written by operating system processes that crash. The PFILE/SPFILE parameter CORE_DUMP_DEST specifies the location of the cdump directory.

create   This directory stores the SQL scripts that were used to initially create the database. These scripts may have been manually created or created using the Oracle Database Configuration Assistant described in Chapter 2.

exp   This directory stores files that have been created using the Oracle export utility.

logbook   This directory stores files that document the activities you performed on the database.

pfile   This directory stores the parameter initialization file, or PFILE, for the database.

udump   This directory is the location where any trace files generated by user processes will be written. The PFILE/SPFILE parameter USER_DUMP_DEST specifies the location of the udump directory.

Why should the "real" copy of the PFILES be stored under $ORACLE_BASE instead of $ORACLE_HOME? Because it is a good idea to keep only version-specific files under $ORACLE_HOME. That way, when you eventually uninstall the software from an old $ORACLE_HOME, you won't lose your carefully tailored initialization files.

In addition to $ORACLE_BASE and $ORACLE_HOME, a few other non-OFA-related operating system environment variables on Unix and Windows systems are important to be aware of. These are described in Table 1.22.

TABLE 1.22   Common Non-OFA Environment Variables

Operating System Variable	Description
$ORACLE_SID	Defines which instance a Unix user session should be connecting to on the server.
%ORACLE_SID%	Defines which instance a Windows user session should connect to on the server.
$TNS_ADMIN	Specifies where the Oracle Net configuration files are stored on Unix systems—if they are to be stored outside their default location of $ORACLE_HOME\network\admin.
%TNS_ADMIN%	Specifies where the Oracle Net configuration files are stored on Windows systems—if they are to be stored outside their default location of %ORACLE_HOME%/network/admin.
$TWO_TASK	Establishes a default Oracle Net connection string that will be used on Unix systems if none is specified by the user.
%LOCAL%	Establishes a default Oracle Net connection string that will be used on Windows systems if none is specified by the user.
$LD_LIBRARY_PATH	Specifies the locations of the Oracle shared object libraries. This variable usually points to $ORACLE_HOME/lib or $ORACLE_HOME/lib32 on Unix systems.
$PATH	Tells the operating system in which directories to look for executable files on Unix systems.
%PATH%	Tells the operating system in which directories to look for executable files on Windows systems.

The directories described in the "Other Administrative Directories" sidebar are merely guidelines. On large production databases, you will likely not want to store the database archived redo logs and export files under $ORACLE_HOME/admin/PROD because of their size, number, and need to be actively managed.

You'll need many of the environment settings discussed in this section in order to install Oracle 10g. You will see examples of their use later in this chapter, in the section "Responding to OUI Prompts."

Creating OFA Directories Structures

The OFA directory structure and its associated operating system environment variables are primarily used to manage the Oracle 10g software binaries and the supporting files for an instance such as the PFILE and SPFILES. However, the OFA model also prescribes a directory naming convention and structure for the physical database files. In general, the OFA model recommends that the physical database file be located in a directory structure like the one shown here for a database called PROD with five mount points:

- /u01/oradata/PROD
- /u02/oradata/PROD
- /u03/oradata/PROD
- /u04/oradata/PROD
- /u05/oradata/PROD

Notice that the directory naming convention incorporates the database name in the path. This makes it easier to have multiple files from multiple databases on the same mount points, on the same server. In addition to these directory paths, the names of the physical database files themselves also have an OFA naming convention, which is discussed in the following sections.

Control Files

Control files use names such as control$n$.ctl, in which n is the number of the copy of the multiplexed control file, for example, control01.ctl, control02.ctl, and so on.

The query shown earlier on V$CONTROLFILE demonstrates an OFA-compliant naming convention for control files.

Datafiles

Datafiles use names such as filename$n$.dbf, in which n is the number of the datafile of a tablespace that is composed of multiple datafiles. The datafile names should also describe the tablespace to which they belong. For example, if a tablespace called TOOLS comprises four datafiles, those datafiles might be called tools01.dbf, tools02.dbf, tools03.dbf, and tools04.dbf.

Databases that use the Oracle Managed Files (OMF) feature will use system-generated filenames. See Chapter 3 for details.

The query shown earlier on DBA_DATA_FILES demonstrates an OFA-compliant naming convention for datafiles.

Redo Log Files

Redo logs use names such as redo*gm*.log, in which *g* is the group number of the redo log and *m* is the member number. For example, if a database has three redo log groups, and each redo log group is multiplexed with two members, the first redo log group's files might be called redo1a.log and redo1b.log.

The query shown earlier on V$LOGFILE demonstrates an OFA-compliant naming convention for redo logs.

Many of these environment variables and OFA file locations are used by the Oracle Universal Installer during the installation process. An example of using the Oracle Universal Installer to install Oracle 10g is shown in the next section.

Using the Oracle Universal Installer

You use the *Oracle Universal Installer (OUI)* to install and configure the Oracle 10g software. The OUI is a Java-based application that provides the same installation look and feel no matter which operating system the install is being run on. The OUI process consists of six primary operations:

- Mounting the CD and starting the OUI
- Performing preinstallation checks
- Responding to server-specific prompts for file locations, names, and so on
- Selecting the products that you want to install
- Copying the files from the install media to $ORACLE_HOME
- Compiling the Oracle binaries
- Performing post-install operations using Configuration Assistants

Mounting the CD and Starting the OUI

To begin the install process, insert the Oracle 10g CD in the server. On some Unix systems, you may have to use the appropriate operating system command to mount the CD in your server before it is accessible.

Once the CD is mounted, take a moment to set the environment variables $ORACLE_BASE, $ORACLE_HOME, $PATH, and $LD_LIBRARY_PATH. OUI installations on Unix systems must also set the X Windows *DISPLAY* environment variable as shown here before continuing; otherwise, the OUI will not display correctly:

```
$ ORACLE_BASE=/u01/app/oracle; export ORACLE_BASE
$ ORACLE_HOME=$ORACLE_BASE/product/10.1.0; export ORACLE_HOME
$ PATH=$ORACLE_HOME/bin:$PATH; export PATH
$ LD_LIBRARY_PATH=$ORACLE_HOME/lib; export LD_LIBRARY_PATH
$ DISPLAY=192.168.1.100:0.0; export DISPLAY
```

After mounting the CD, you may want to copy its contents to a staging directory so that you can install from there instead of from the CD.

Performing Preinstallation Checks

Once these operating system variables are set, start the OUI using the `runInstaller.sh` command shown here:

```
$ /cdrom/runInstaller
Starting Oracle Universal Installer...

Checking installer requirements...

Checking operating system version: must be redhat-2.1, UnitedLinux-1.0
     or redhat-3
                              Passed


All installer requirements met.

Preparing to launch Oracle Univeral Installer from
     /tmp/OraInstall2004-07-16_01-53-28PM. Please wait...
```

Notice that the output shows that the OUI checked the server's operating system version, available RAM, kernel settings, and so on that we described earlier in this chapter.

If needed, you can turn off the system verification that occurs prior to the installation by using the `-ignoreSysPrereqs` option of the `runInstaller` command.

Once the preinstallation tests are completed and passed, the OUI displays the initial OUI screen shown in Figure 1.20.

Click the Next button on the OUI screen to proceed with the installation.

Responding to OUI Prompts

The next OUI screen prompts you for two pieces of information:

- The location for the inventory files that the OUI uses to keep track of which Oracle products are installed on the server
- The name of the operating system group of which the user doing the install is a member

  You can see both items in Figure 1.21.

FIGURE 1.20   The initial OUI installation screen

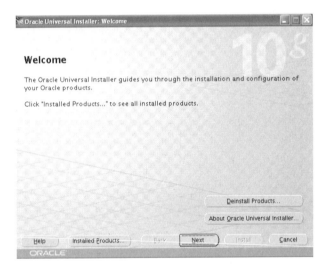

FIGURE 1.21   The OUI Specify Inventory Directory and Credentials screen

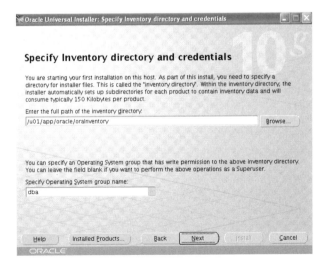

The value suggested for the oraInventory location, /u01/app/oracle/oraInventory, was selected based on the $ORACLE_BASE environment variable. The value suggested for the operating system group, dba, is the Oracle default value. Because both settings are correct for our environment, click the Next button to continue the installation. When you click the Next button on a Unix system, the OUI displays the screen shown in Figure 1.22.

This screen asks you to open a second session on the Unix server as the superuser root so that the script orainstRoot.sh can be executed. The following example shows this orainstRoot.sh script being executed from another session:

```
$ su -
Password:
# cd /u01/app/oracle/oraInventory
./orainstRoot.sh
Creating the Oracle inventory pointer file (/etc/oraInst.loc)
Changing groupname of /u01/app/oracle/oraInventory to dba.
#
```

Running the script creates some directory structures that are used to support the Oracle installation and sets the proper file permissions on those directories as well as other files. Once the orainstRoot.sh script executes, click the Continue button to open the Specify File Locations screen, which is shown in Figure 1.23.

On this screen, you specify the location of the source CD and the destination location of the Oracle software (for example, $ORACLE_HOME). Additionally, you can assign a nickname to this $ORACLE_HOME (OraDb10g_home1, in this example). The value of /u01/app/oracle/product/ 10.0.1 is filled in automatically by the installer based on the $ORACLE_HOME environment variable setting that you established before starting the OUI. Click the Next button to open the Select Installation Type screen, as shown in Figure 1.24, and continue with the installation.

FIGURE 1.22   The OUI *orainstRoot.sh* screen

FIGURE 1.23 The Specify File Locations screen

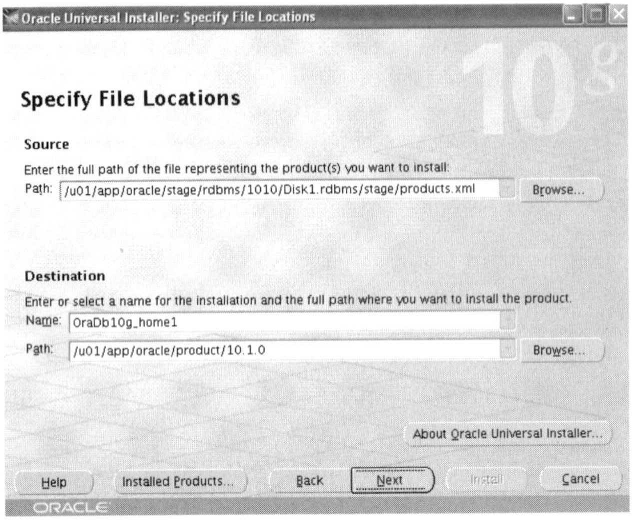

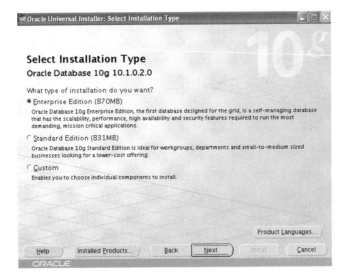

FIGURE 1.24 The Select Installation Type screen

Selecting Products to Install

This screen prompts you to select the type of installation to perform. In this example, we selected the Enterprise Edition option.

Click the Next button to open the next screen, which is shown in Figure 1.25.

The OUI goes thorough a second round of installation checks that confirm that the server's operating system version and configuration are appropriate for the Enterprise Edition install of Oracle 10g. If all the verification checks complete successfully, click the Next button to open the Select Database Configuration screen, as shown in Figure 1.26.

FIGURE 1.25   The OUI verifies system version and configuration.

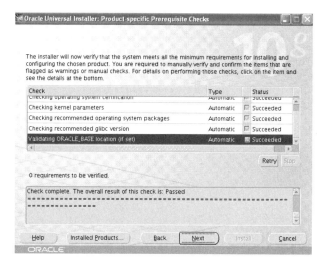

FIGURE 1.26   The Select Database Configuration screen

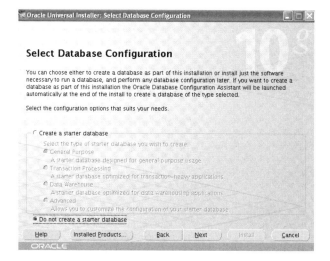

This screen asks if you want to create a database following the installation process. Because creating a database is covered in Chapter 2, we'll skip this step for now. Click the Do Not Create A Starter Database option, and then click Next to open the Summary screen, as shown in Figure 1.27.

This screen summarizes all the options that you selected and all the components that will be installed. If you need to make changes, click the Back button to go back and modify your previous selections. If you are satisfied with your selections, click the Next button to start copying the Oracle binaries from the CD to the $ORACLE_HOME directory.

Copying and Compiling Files

As shown in Figure 1.28, a bar is displayed to indicate the progress of the copy process.

FIGURE 1.27   The Summary screen

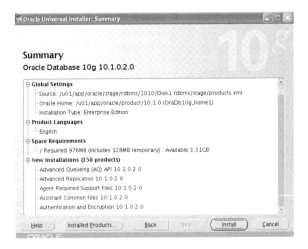

FIGURE 1.28   To track the copy progress, keep an eye on the bar.

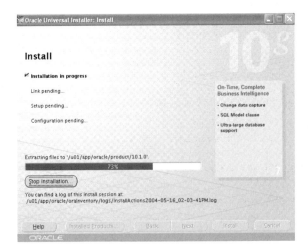

If these operating system checks do not succeed, you must correct the areas failing the checks before continuing.

Once the file copy portion of the installation is complete, the OUI begins linking the binaries to create the executable files needed to make the Oracle 10g software run on the server. Figure 1.29 shows the linking progress bar.

FIGURE 1.29   You can track the linking process by watching the bar.

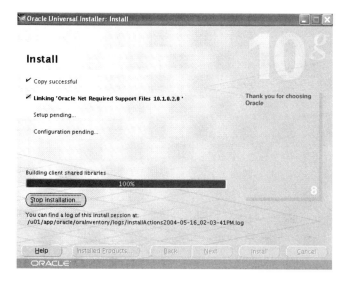

On Unix systems, following the linking process, you are prompted to execute a second configuration script as the superuser root from the Unix command line, as shown in Figure 1.30.

FIGURE 1.30   Running the script as root

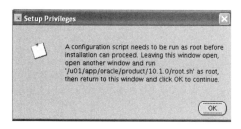

Like the first root script, the root.sh script should be executed from a second session as shown here:

$ su -
Password:

```
# cd /u01/app/oracle/product/10.1.0
./root.sh
Running the Oracle10 root.sh script...
The following environment variables are set as:
  ORACLE_OWNER= oracle
  ORACLE_HOME= /u01/app/oracle/product/10.1.0

Enter the full pathname of the local bin directory: [/usr/local/bin]:

Creating /etc/oratab file...
Adding entry to /etc/oratab file...
Entries will be added to the /etc/oratab file as needed by
Database Configuration Assistant when a database is created
Finished running generic part of root.sh script.
Now product-specific root actions will be performed.
Successfuly accumulated necessary OCR keys.
Creating OCR keys for the user 'root', privgrp 'root'..
Operation successful.
Oracle Cluster Registry for cluster has been initialized

Adding to inittab
Checking the status of Oracle init process...
Expecting the CRS daemons to be up within 600 seconds.
CSS is active on these nodes.
        moderne
CSS is active on all nodes.
Oracle CSS service is installed and running under init(1M)
#
```

Executing the root.sh script copies some files to a location outside $ORACLE_HOME and sets the permissions on several files inside and outside $ORACLE_HOME. Once the root.sh script executes successfully, click OK to continue the installation.

If you have multiple installations to perform, you can speed up the process and minimize errors by building an OUI response file. This text file contains all the necessary responses to the OUI prompts so that an unattended, silent install is possible.

The OUI on Windows systems also offers a Basic Installation mode in which only a few installation questions are asked before the copying of files begins. If you select the Advanced Installation mode, the prompts will closely follow those shown for Unix in this section.

Performing Post-Install Tasks

Once the `root.sh` script has completed, the OUI will perform some brief post-installation configuration activities before displaying the End Of Installation screen shown in Figure 1.31.

FIGURE 1.31   The End Of Installation Screen

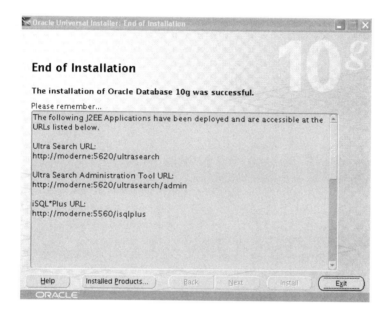

Click the Exit button and then the OK button on the pop-up screen to exit the OUI and return to the Unix prompt.

Once the OUI is complete, you should have a completely installed and configured `$ORACLE_HOME`. We'll use this software to create your first database in Chapter 2.

Summary

Oracle offers a broad product mix that includes not only their popular database software, but also application servers, development tools, and enterprise-level applications and services. At the heart of Oracle's product mix is the relational database model that uses tables to store application data and constraints to enforce relationships between tables and implement business rules. Examples of these constraints include Primary and Foreign Key, Not Null and Unique, and Check.

You use SQL to retrieve, add, modify, and delete data in Oracle tables. SQL statements are broadly categorized as query, DML, DDL, or DCL commands. SELECT statements are composed of the SELECT and FROM clauses and, optionally, WHERE, HAVING, and ORDER BY clauses. INSERT, UPDATE, and DELETE commands are examples of SQL DML commands. You can enter these commands directly through tools such as SQL*Plus or *i*SQL*Plus or through applications such as Enterprise Manager and compiled C++, COBOL, or Java programs. CREATE, ALTER, and DROP are examples of SQL DDL commands, and GRANT and REVOKE are examples of SQL DCL commands. Oracle also provides a procedural extension to SQL called PL/SQL.

Oracle uses a number of data dictionary views and dynamic performance views to provide information about the database and its contents. These contents include segments of many types, including tables, indexes, and partitions. A segment is composed of extents, which are composed of database blocks, which are composed of operating system blocks.

Extents are stored within tablespaces. A database must have at least three tablespaces, SYSTEM, SYSAUX, and TEMP, but may have many more depending on the application that it supports. Each tablespace is associated with a physical file or files on disk called a datafile. The datafiles store the data that has been inserted into application tables. Other files that make up the Oracle database include control files and redo log files.

The datafiles are accessed by the user's Server Process whenever a SQL command is issued against the database. The user's Server Process parses each SQL statement and places it into the Shared Pool component of the SGA before copying the database blocks that contain the desired data into the Database Buffer Cache component of the SGA. If the user performs a DML statement, the recovery information needed to reproduce this statement is placed in the Redo Log Buffer component of the SGA where it is ultimately written to disk by the LGWR background process. Other processes that are part of the Oracle instance include Database Writer, System Monitor, Process Monitor, and Checkpoint. The parameter initialization file (PFILE or SPFILE) is used to configure the instance.

The OFA model is useful for establishing a manageable directory structure for a new Oracle server. The OFA model recommends mount point, directory, and file-naming conventions. Once the OFA structure is established, you can use the OUI to install the Oracle 10g software into the location you've selected.

Exam Essentials

Describe the Oracle tools and what they are used for.   Know which tools are available for connecting to and interacting with an Oracle database. Understand how these tools differ from one another.

Understand relational database concepts.   Understand important relational database concepts such as primary and foreign keys and how these are used to enforce business rules within the database.

Identify how SQL is used to interact with the database.   Be able to describe how SQL and *i*SQL*Plus, GUI management tools, Java, PL/SQL, and Oracle's programming interfaces can be used to connect to an Oracle database; describe the structure of the tables; and use SELECT, INSERT, UPDATE, and DELETE statements to perform transactions.

Understand the Oracle architecture components.   Be able to describe the logical and physical components of the Oracle architecture and the components that make up each. Know the relationship between segments, extents, database blocks, and operating system blocks.

Explain Oracle 10g system requirements.   Know what the requirements are for available server disk space and memory prior to performing an Oracle 10g installation.

Describe the Optimal Flexible Architecture.   Be able to explain the concepts associated with the OFA model and how to implement an OFA-compliant installation and database directory structure.

Identify common environment variables.   Know which environment variables are generally required for a successful Oracle 10g installation and what each variable is used for.

Describe steps for installation and configuration.   Know how to set up the Oracle installation environment so that the OUI can be used to install and configure the Oracle 10g software.

Review Questions

1. Which of the following SQL commands is an example of a DML command?

    A. SELECT

    B. CREATE

    C. INSERT

    D. GRANT

2. You have just started a database transaction by inserting a row into a table. Which of the following actions will end this transaction?

    A. Inserting another row

    B. Issuing a COMMIT command

    C. Issuing an END TRANSACTION command

    D. Deleting the row you just inserted

3. You are designing an application that will enforce business rules through table design. One of the tables in the application contains information about parts that are used to manufacture your product. When creating the PARTS table, what could you do to make certain that each part receives a part number and that each part number will be unique?

    A. Place a Unique constraint on the part number column of the PARTS table.

    B. Place a Not Null constraint on the part number column of the PARTS table.

    C. Place a Primary Key constraint on the part number column of the PARTS table.

    D. Place a Foreign Key constraint on the part number field of the PARTS table.

4. Which of the following is not an advantage of SQL over traditional programming languages?

    A. SQL statements use English-like commands.

    B. A user can choose from several interfaces when interacting with SQL.

    C. SQL has sophisticated condition testing and looping capabilities.

    D. Users do not have to know how or where their data is physically stored in order to access it.

5. How much free disk space is required to install Oracle Database 10*g*?

    A. 1.5MB

    B. 15GB

    C. 1.5KB

    D. 1.5GB

6. You've just been hired as a DBA for a large company. During the interview process, you were shown the job description for the position. Which of the following tasks might have been included on this job description?

   A. Install and configure Oracle 10g software.

   B. Implement database installations according to OFA guidelines.

   C. Use OFA-compliant naming conventions for database files and directories.

   D. Any of the above may have been included on the DBA job description.

7. Which of the following is not one of the differences between SQL*Plus and iSQL*Plus?

   A. iSQL*Plus is accessed via a web browser, but SQL*Plus must be run from a client or on the server.

   B. iSQL*Plus output is displayed in a separate window from the commands, but SQL*Plus displays everything in one window.

   C. iSQL*Plus can use SQL and PL/SQL to access the database, as can SQL*Plus.

   D. iSQL*Plus can only be used to access databases on Windows servers, but SQL*Plus can be used to access databases on Unix or Windows servers.

8. Which of the following is an example of an environment variable that might be defined on a Unix system prior to starting the OUI?

   A. ORACLE_DIR

   B. $ORACLE_HOME

   C. $ORA_HOME

   D. $ORACLE_HM

9. The DBA_TABLES data dictionary view contains a column called OWNER that shows the user name of the account who owns each table. What SQL clause would you add to a query on DBA_TABLES to view only those tables owned by a user called APPS?

   A. WHERE

   B. GROUP BY

   C. HAVING

   D. ALTER

10. You have just logged on to the database as the user APPS and need to know which tables you own or have been granted access to. Which of the following data dictionary views would you query to see a listing of these tables?

   A. DBA_TABLES

   B. USER_TABLES

   C. ALL_TABLES

   D. MY_TABLES

11. You want to configure the instance so that the sizes of the Shared Pool, Buffer Cache, Large Pool, and Java Pool are automatically managed by Oracle. Which initialization parameter do you need to set to allow this to happen?

   A. SGA_TARGET

   B. SHARED_POOL_SIZE

   C. LARGE_POOL_SIZE

   D. DB_CACHE_SIZE

12. Which of the following is not considered part of an Oracle database?

   A. Datafiles

   B. Redo logs

   C. PFILE and SPFILE

   D. Control files

13. Which of the following statements is not always true?

   A. Every database has at least three tablespaces.

   B. Every database has at least three datafiles.

   C. Every database has at least three multiplexed redo logs.

   D. At least three types of segments can exist in a database.

14. The LRU algorithm is used to manage what part of the Oracle architecture?

   A. Users who log on to the database infrequently and may be candidates for being dropped.

   B. The datafile that stores the least amount of information and will need the least frequent backup.

   C. The tables that users rarely access so that they can be moved to a less active tablespace.

   D. The Shared Pool and Database Buffer Cache portions of the SGA.

15. Two structures make up an Oracle server: an instance and a database. Which of the following best describes the difference between an Oracle instance and a database?

   A. An instance is made up of memory structures and processes, whereas a database is composed of physical files.

   B. An instance is only used during database creation; after that, the database is all that is needed.

   C. An instance is started whenever the demands on the database are high, but the database is used all the time.

   D. An instance is configured using a PFILE, whereas a database is configured using an SPFILE.

16. Which of the following is the proper order of Oracle's storage hierarchy, from smallest to largest?

   A. Operating system block, database block, segment, extent

   B. Operating system block, database block, extent, segment

   C. Segment, extent, database block, operating system block

   D. Segment, database block, extent, operating system block

17. You've been asked to install Oracle 10*g* on a new Unix server. You're likely to ask the Unix system administrator to do all but which of the following for you in order to get the new server ready for Oracle?

   A. Modify the server's kernel parameters.

   B. Create a new Unix user to own the Oracle software.

   C. Create the mount points and directory structure using the OFA model.

   D. Determine which directory will be used for $ORACLE_HOME.

18. Oracle's OFA model specifies a naming convention for all but which of the following?

   A. User names

   B. Mount points

   C. Directory paths

   D. Database filenames

19. The Oracle Universal Installer is started by executing which program?

   A. `emctl`

   B. `runInstaller`

   C. `ouistart`

   D. `isqlplusctl`

20. On Unix systems, the script `root.sh` must be executed during the installation process. What is the purpose of this script?

   A. It creates the root user in the database.

   B. It creates the root directory for the server.

   C. It grants root superuser privileges to the Oracle Unix account.

   D. It copies files and sets permissions on files outside $ORACLE_HOME.

Answers to Review Questions

1. **C.** Examples of DML, or data manipulation commands, include INSERT, UPDATE, and DELETE. DDL, or data definition language commands, include CREATE, ALTER, or DROP. DCL, or data control language commands, include GRANT and REVOKE.

2. **B.** Transactions are ended when the transaction is either committed using the COMMIT command, or rolled back using the ROLLBACK command.

3. **C.** Tables with a Primary Key constraint on them require that any rows inserted into the table have a value that is unique and not null for the primary key column.

4. **C.** SQL does not provide any condition testing or looping capabilities. Oracle provides PL/SQL to allow for these types of programming constructs.

5. **D.** Oracle 10g requires 1.5GB of free disk space for installation. An additional 1GB is required if a sample database is created using the OUI.

6. **D.** The tasks that a DBA performs encompass all these areas plus managing database storage, security, and availability.

7. **D.** iSQL*Plus can be used to access databases on both Unix and Windows servers, as can SQL*Plus.

8. **B.** The $ORACLE_HOME environment variable would point to the location where the Oracle binaries should be installed.

9. **A.** The SQL WHERE clause qualifies the results of the query and limits the rows that are returned to those that match the condition specified in the WHERE clause.

10. **C.** The ALL_TABLES view displays information about the tables that the user owns or has been granted access to. The DBA_TABLES view displays information about all tables in the database. The USER_TABLES view shows only information about the user's own tables. There is no view called MY_TABLES.

11. **A.** Setting SGA_TARGET to a nonzero value in the PFILE or SPFILE allows the automated memory management feature to dynamically assign space to these four areas of the SGA.

12. **C.** Although PFILEs and SPFILEs are physical files used to configure the Oracle instance, they are not considered part of the database.

13. **C.** Every database must have at least two redo log files, which may or may not be multiplexed.

14. **D.** The LRU mechanism ensures that each user's Server Process can find free space in the Shared Pool and Database Buffer Cache whenever they need it, but also keeps frequently used objects cached in those memory areas.

15. **A.** The instance consists of the SGA and all the Oracle background processes. The database is composed of the control files, datafiles, and redo logs.

16. B. Multiple operating system blocks make up database blocks, contiguous chunks of which make up extents, which comprise segments.

17. D. While the Unix system administrator is responsible for creating volume groups and mount points, the DBA generally decides where the Oracle binaries will be installed—the location designated by the $ORACLE_HOME environment variable.

18. A. The OFA model does not include any reference to naming conventions for things inside the database, such as users, tables, or tablespaces.

19. B. The runInstaller executable performs a preinstall check of the operating system and hardware resources before starting the OUI graphical tool.

20. D. The root.sh script copies configuration files to directories outside $ORACLE_HOME and sets the permissions on those files accordingly.

Chapter

2

Creating and Controlling a Database

ORACLE DATABASE 10*G*: ADMINISTRATION I EXAM OBJECTIVES COVERED IN THIS CHAPTER:

✓ **Creating an Oracle Database**

- Use the management framework.
- Use DBCA to Create a database.
- Use DBCA to Configure a database.
- Use DBCA to Drop a database.
- Use DBCA to Manage templates.

✓ **Controlling the Database**

- Start and stop *i*SQL*Plus.
- Start and stop Enterprise Manager Database Control.
- Start up and shut down Oracle Database 10*g*.
- Describe startup and shutdown options for the Oracle Database.
- Handle Parameter files.
- Locate and view the Database alert log.

Exam objectives are subject to change at any time without prior notice and at Oracle's sole discretion. Please visit Oracle's Training and Certification website (http://www.oracle.com/education/certification/) for the most current exam objectives listing.

As a DBA, you are responsible for creating and managing Oracle databases and services within your organization. Oracle provides a comprehensive and cohesive set of tools to help the DBA perform these tasks. It is important for you to understand these tools and how to use them properly.

This chapter discusses the Oracle Enterprise Management Framework and explains how you can use this framework to administer the entire Oracle environment. It also describes how to use the Oracle Database Configuration Assistant to create and remove Oracle databases and how you can use templates to create databases.

In addition, we'll explore how to start and stop the Oracle Enterprise Manager control interface and the iSQL*Plus interface. You will use these tools extensively to manage the Oracle environment.

We'll describe the various database startup and shutdown options and explain the circumstances under which you use these options. We will explain what parameter files are, the different types of parameter files, and how you can manage parameter files. Finally, we will discuss how to locate, manage, and view the database alert log, and explain the contents of the alert log.

The Oracle Enterprise Management Framework

While computer systems have been growing larger and more complex, IT organizations have been performing an increasing number of tasks with the same or fewer resources. This is especially true of the DBA. Traditionally, you have spent most of your time creating databases and objects, managing space, and monitoring performance. Today, you need to take care of these tasks in less time and more effectively in order to meet other IT needs and challenges.

Businesses are becoming increasingly dependent on systems that must be available around the clock. You must constantly monitor these mission-critical operations, and you need to know when the system is not functioning correctly or is not available for use. You need to be able to answer questions quickly about the performance and availability of the components that constitute an Oracle enterprise. The Oracle management framework is designed to meet these needs and challenges.

The Oracle Enterprise Management Framework provides a comprehensive set of integrated tools that you can use to perform your traditional tasks more easily and efficiently as well as effectively monitor the components in the enterprise. You can customize this framework and use it to manage your applications via a web-based interface. Having this type of tool is vital if you manage larger and more complex databases, especially if they are spread over disparate geographic regions.

You can extend the management framework using the software developer's kit (SDK). The extensions give you flexibility in monitoring organizational components. For example, you can quickly define new target types to allow users to collect monitoring information from managed targets specific to their enterprise environment. Figure 2.1 provides an overview of management framework components.

All communication between the targets of the Oracle Enterprise Management Framework is orchestrated by Oracle Management Agents. Management Agents are responsible for identifying and collecting data about the entities of interest within the Management Framework. For example, agents can monitor an Oracle database and send out an alert if the database is not available. Normally, one Oracle Management Agent is on each of the host systems that you are interested in monitoring via the Oracle Enterprise Management Framework. The agents store the data collected about the managed targets in the Management Repository.

The Oracle Enterprise Management Framework is divided into these functional areas:

Managed Targets   You administer *managed targets* using the Enterprise Manager. Examples of managed targets include databases, application servers, web servers, applications, and Oracle agents such as the Oracle Net listener and Connection Manager. You can add and remove managed targets as the needs of the enterprise change. Many managed targets are preconfigured to function and communicate with the Oracle Enterprise Management Framework.

Management Service   The Oracle Management Service is a Java-based web component that is the actual interface you use to monitor and control managed targets within the Management Framework.

FIGURE 2.1   Oracle Enterprise Management Framework components

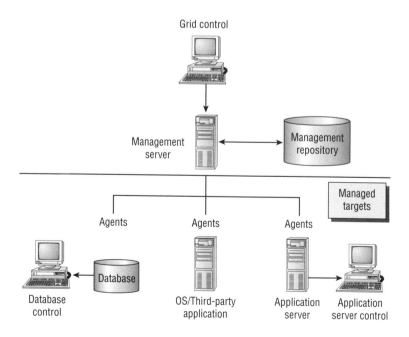

Oracle Management Repository   Configuration and monitoring information collected about the managed targets is stored in an Oracle Management Repository. The repository comprises two tablespaces in an Oracle database that contain information about administrators, targets, and applications that are managed within Enterprise Manager.

The Management Agents communicate with the Management Service to place data into the repository. The Management Repository is organized for easy retrieval and display within the Oracle Management Service.

Oracle Enterprise Manager 10g Grid Control   Enterprises that must manage many databases, application servers, web servers, and other components can use the Enterprise Manager *Grid Control*. The EM Grid Control is a web-based user interface that communicates with and centrally manages all the components within the Oracle enterprise.

You can use the EM Grid Control to monitor and administer the entire computing environment from a centralized location, including hosts, databases, listeners, application servers, HTTP servers, and web applications.

Oracle Enterprise Manager 10g Database Control   The EM Database Control is a web-based component of the Enterprise Management Framework for managing Oracle Database 10g Release 1 (10.1). The Enterprise Manager 10g Database Control allows you to monitor and administer a single Oracle database instance or a single Real Application Cluster (RAC) environment.

Application Server Control   The *Application Server Control* is a web-based component of Enterprise Manager that monitors the Oracle Application Server 10g (9.0.4). The Application Server Control allows you to monitor and administer a single Oracle Application Server instance, a collection of Oracle Application Server instances, or Oracle Application Server Clusters.

Now that you have an understanding of the components that comprise the Oracle Enterprise Management Framework, let's discuss how to control and access the various components within the framework.

In the following sections, we will explore how to stop and start the Oracle Management Agent. We will also explain how to start and use the *i*SQL*Plus tool.

Starting and Stopping the Oracle Management Agent

As we discussed in the previous section, if you elect to use the Oracle Enterprise Management Framework, there are two methods of administering your databases within the enterprise. You can centrally administer all of your databases using the Oracle Enterprise Manager 10g Grid Control or you can manage each database individually using the Oracle Enterprise Manager 10g Database Control. In either case, you need to understand how to stop and start the necessary agents to use these tools.

If you are centrally managing all your Oracle databases via Oracle Enterprise Manager Grid Control Framework, you need to start an agent process on each managed target server that you want available to the framework.

An Oracle management agent is a background process that runs on each managed target server. The agent collects information about the managed target and then communicates with the central management service, which maintains the information about the managed target.

You use the *EMCTL* command-line utility to start and stop the Oracle management agent. To start the agent, use the `emctl start agent` command. Here is an example:

```
/u01/app/oracle/product/10.0.1/bin> emctl start agent
Oracle Enterprise Manager 10g Database Control Release 10.1.0.2.0
Copyright © 2002, 2004 Oracle Corporation, All rights reserved
Start agent. . . . .started.
```

Once the agent starts, you can manage the target using the Oracle Enterprise Manager Grid Control.

To stop the agent, use the `emctl stop agent` command. Here is an example of using the command:

```
/u01/app/oracle/product/10.0.1/bin> emctl stop agent
Oracle Enterprise Manager 10g Database Control Release 10.1.0.2.0
Copyright © 2002, 2004 Oracle Corporation, All rights reserved
This will stop the Oracle Enterprise Manager 10g Database Control process.
    Contuinue [y/n] :y
Enter Management Password :
Stopping Oracle Enterprise Manager 10g Database Control . . . . Stopped
Agent is not running.
```

If you are going to manage your databases as separate entities and not within the centralized Grid Control framework, you can use the Enterprise Manager Database Control web tool. To start the Database Control Agent, which is similar to the Grid Control process, issue the `emctl start dbconsole` command. In a Unix environment, the emctl program can be found in your ORACLE_HOME/bin directory. In the following examples, /u01/app/oracle/product/10.0.1/bin refers to the ORACLE_HOME directory where the emctl program is located.

Here is an example of issuing the `emctl start dbconsole` command:

```
/u01/app/oracle/product/10.0.1/bin> emctl start dbconsole
TZ set to US/Central
Oracle Enterprise Manager 10.0.1.0.0
Copyright © 2002, 2004 Oracle Corporation, All rights reserved
http://10.19.200.50:5500/em/cosole/aboutApplication
http://10.19.200.50:/emd/console/aboutApplication
Starting DB Console. . . . . . . . . started.
```

To stop the Database Control agent, use the `emctl stop dbconsole` as follows:

```
/u01/app/oracle/product/10.0.1/bin> emctl stop dbconsole
TZ set to US/Central
```

```
Oracle Enterprise Manager 10.0.1.0.0
Copyright © 2002, 2004 Oracle Corporation, All rights reserved
http://10.19.200.50:5500/em/cosole/aboutApplication
http://10.19.200.50:/emd/console/aboutApplication
Enter Management password:
Stopping dbconsole. . . . . . Stopped.
```

You can also view the status of the agent by issuing the emctl status dbconsole command:

```
/u01/app/oracle/product/10.0.1/bin> emctl status dbconsole
E:\>emctl status dbconsole
Oracle Enterprise Manager 10g Database Control Release 10.1.0.2.0
Copyright (c) 1996, 2004 Oracle Corporation.  All rights reserved.
http://Ldn6f751-mw.corp.goxroads.net:5500/em/console/aboutApplication
Oracle Enterprise Manager 10g is not running.
-----------------------------------------------------------------
Logs are generated in directory E:\oracle\product\10.1.0\Db_1\Ldn6f751-
    mw.corp.goxroads.net_ORCL/sysman/log
```

In this example, the agent is not running. You can view information about the status of the agent in the log files that are created. In this example, you see the location of the logs listed. You can access and view the logs with any text editor.

Accessing a Database Using the Database Control

After you start the Database Control agent, you can access the web-based tool. To do so, open your web browser and enter the URL as shown below. Note that port 5500 is the default port.

```
http://hostname:portnumber/em
```

If your database is open, you will see the Database Control Login screen, as shown in Figure 2.2.

To log in, enter a user ID and a password. When your database is first created, the initial login user ID will most likely be SYS, SYSTEM, or SYSMAN. Once you are connected to the database via Database Control, you can perform a variety of administrative tasks from the console.

Using iSql*Plus

Oracle provides a web-based version of the SQL*Plus tool called iSQL*Plus. iSQL*Plus has a server-side listener process that must be started in order for clients to connect to a database through the browser interface. To start the listener process on a Windows server, run the following command:

```
%ORACLE_HOME%\bin\isqlplusctl start
```

FIGURE 2.2   The Database Control Login screen

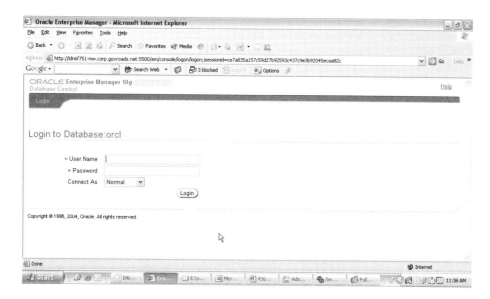

Here are the results:

```
D:\oracle\product\10.1.0\Db_1\BIN> isqlplusctl start
iSQL*Plus 10.1.0.2.0
Copyright (c) 2004 Oracle.  All rights reserved.
Starting iSQL*Plus ...
iSQL*Plus started.
```

To start the *i*SQL*Plus listener process on a Unix server, run the following command:

```
$ORACLE_HOME/bin/isqlplusctl start
```

If you are working in a Windows environment, you can also start the server-side listener process by starting the *i*SQL*Plus Application Server service.

*i*SQL*Plus uses the default port number 5560 for the server-side listener process.

To stop the *i*SQL*Plus listener process on a Unix server, run the following command:

```
$ORACLE_HOME/bin/> isqlplusctl stop
iSQL*Plus 10.1.0.2.0
Copyright (c) 2004 Oracle.  All rights reserved.
Stopping iSQL*Plus ...
iSQL*Plus stopped.
$ORACLE_HOME/bin/>
```

Obtaining a List of Ports Used by the Oracle Components

To view a summary of which ports are in use by the various Oracle components, you can view the portlist.ini file. This file is normally located in the $ORACLE_HOME/install directory on Unix or %ORACLE_HOME/install directory on Windows. Here is an example of what you might see in the portlist.ini file:

```
Ultra Search HTTP port number =5620
Enterprise Manager Agent Port =
iSQL*Plus HTTP port number =5560
Enterprise Manager Console HTTP Port (orcl) = 5500
Enterprise Manager Agent Port (orcl) = 1830
```

After you start the process, you can access *i*SQL*Plus by entering the following URL in your web browser. Note that the default port number is 5560.

```
http://machine_name.domain_name:port/iSQLplus
```

You will be presented with a login screen like the one in Figure 2.3.

FIGURE 2.3   The *i*SQL*Plus Login screen

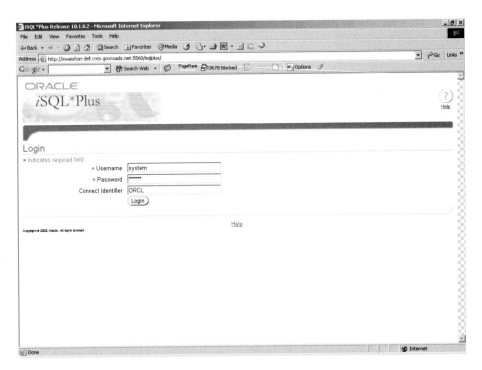

When you are logged in to the *i*SQL*Plus tool, you can run commands and load and save scripts much the same as you can using SQL*Plus. Enter one or more commands in the Workspace box and click the Execute button. If you enter multiple commands in this box, Oracle runs each command in order. Any output is displayed in a results panel at the bottom of the screen when the query is complete.

To view a summary of your last 10 commands, click the History tab. You can change the number of queries stored in history by clicking the Preferences icon and modifying History Size.

You can also describe table structures within *i*SQL*Plus. Run the DESCRIBE command to display a description of a database object. For example, if you describe a table, you will see a summary of the table columns, datatypes, and column sizes in the results window. Figure 2.4 shows an example of describing a table.

> **NOTE**   It is possible to set up *i*SQL*Plus to allow connections to the database with SYSOPER or SYSDBA privileges. To allow this type of connection, the user must be authenticated by the *i*SQL*Plus application server. You must perform a number of steps to set up the authentication. For a complete summary of these steps, refer to "Database Storage and Schema" in the section "Enabling *i*SQL*Plus DBA Access" in *SQL*Plus Users Guide and Reference Release 10.1* (Part Number B12170-01).

Now that you have an understanding of the Oracle Enterprise Management Framework and some of the tools provided within the framework, we will explore how to create a database using the Database Configuration Assistant.

FIGURE 2.4   The *i*SQL*Plus query results screen

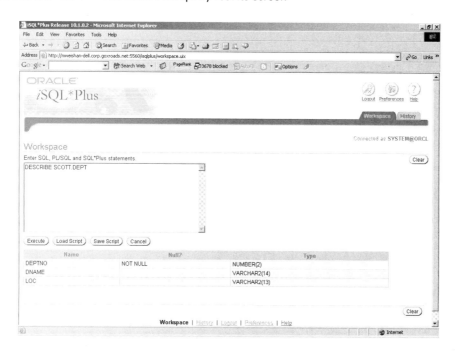

Using the Oracle Database Configuration Assistant

The Oracle *Database Configuration Assistant (DBCA)* is a Java-based tool used to create Oracle databases. If you've been a DBA for a few years, you probably remember the days of writing and maintaining scripts to create databases. Although it is still possible to manually create a database, the DBCA provides a flexible and robust environment in which you can not only create databases but also generate templates containing the definitions of the databases created. This provides you the ease of using a GUI-based interface with the flexibility of Oracle-generated XML-based templates that you can use to maintain a library of database definitions.

You can also use the DBCA to add options to an existing database or to remove a database. We recommend using the DBCA facility to create your databases, even if you are a die-hard command-line DBA.

You can use the DBCA to create a database when the Oracle software is installed, or you can invoke the DBCA later to manually create a database. In the following sections, we will show you the steps necessary to create an Oracle database using the DBCA tool.

Creating an Oracle Database Using the DBCA

You can invoke the DBCA from a command line in the Unix environment or as an application choice in a Windows 2000 environment. If you are using the Windows 2000 environment, choose Start ➢ Programs ➢ Oracle *Oracle Home* ➢ Configuration And Migration Tools ➢ Database Configuration Assistant.

If you are in a Unix environment or would prefer to work from the command line in Windows, type **dbca** from the $ORACLE_HOME/bin location.

After you open the DBCA, you should see the Welcome screen, as shown in Figure 2.5.

Click Next to open the Operations screen, as shown in Figure 2.6. You can create a database, configure database options, delete a database, or manage templates.

Table 2.1 lists and describes the DBCA database management options.

TABLE 2.1   The DBCA Database Management Options

Option	Description
Create A Database	Allows for the step-by-step creation of a database. The database can be created based on an existing template or customized for the specific needs of the organization.
Configure Database Options	Performs the necessary changes to move from a dedicated server to a Shared Server. You can also add database options that have not been previously configured for use with your database.
Delete A Database	Completely removes a database and all associated files.

TABLE 2.1   The DBCA Database Management Options *(continued)*

Option	Description
Manage Templates	Manages database templates. The *database templates* are definitions of your database configuration saved in an XML file format on your local hard disk. You can choose from several pre-defined templates, or you can create customized templates.

FIGURE 2.5   The DBCA Welcome screen

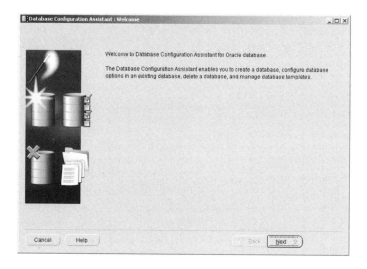

FIGURE 2.6   The DBCA Operations screen

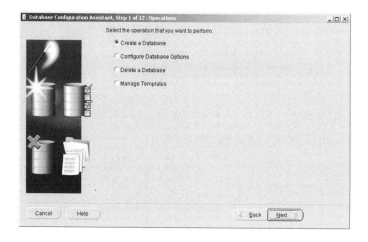

Click Next to open the Database Templates screen.

In the next two sections, we'll explore the various kinds of database templates and how to assign your database a name.

Database Templates

The DBCA comes with several preconfigured database templates. These XML-based documents contain the information necessary to create the Oracle database. You can choose one of these predefined templates, or you can build a custom database definition. The predefined database templates are Data Warehouse, General Purpose, and Transaction Processing (see Figure 2.7). These templates were designed to create databases that are optimized for a particular type of workload.

To display the configuration definitions for these preconfigured databases, click Show Details. Table 2.2 displays information about what is contained in template definition. Each section of the page gives further information about the template. For example, under the Common Options section, you will see a list of each of the database options that gets installed for the template definition you have chosen.

After you have chosen the appropriate template to use, click Next. You will then be presented with the Database Identification Screen.

TABLE 2.2 Template Definition Details

Section	Description
Common Options	Displays which options will be installed
Initialization Parameters	Displays the common initialization parameters and their settings
Character Sets	Character sets to be used
Control Files	Control filenames and locations
Tablespaces	Tablespace names and types
Datafiles	Datafile names for each tablespace and their size
Redo Log Groups	Group number and size

Database Identification

The Database Identification screen (see Figure 2.8) allows you to enter the global database name and Oracle system identification name, commonly referred to as the Oracle SID.

The global database name is the fully qualified name of the database in the enterprise. It is composed of a database name and a database domain and takes the format *database_name* .*database_domain*, for example, `marketing.us.aceinc.com`.

In this example, the first part of the global database name, `marketing`, is the name of your database. The second part of the global database name—in this example, `us.aceinc.com`—is the domain. Normally, the database domain is the same as the network domain within the enterprise. A global database name must be unique within a given network domain.

FIGURE 2.7   The DBCA Database Templates screen

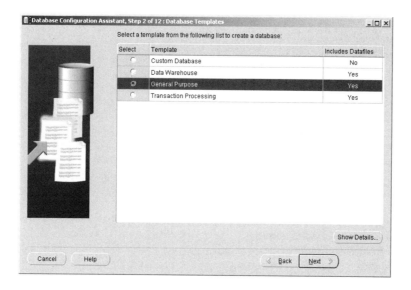

FIGURE 2.8   The DBCA Database Identification screen

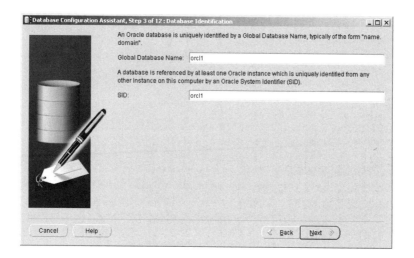

The Oracle system identification (SID) name is the name of the instance associated with the database. The Oracle SID was of greater significance in earlier releases of Oracle, but is still required when creating a database in Oracle 10*g*. The Oracle SID can be a maximum of eight characters and must be unique on the server. For example, you cannot have two Oracle SIDs called PROD on a single server.

Management Options

After you choose the database name, you can configure Enterprise Manager to monitor and manage your database using the DBCA Management Options screen (see Figure 2.9).

You can choose from two options: You can centrally manage all your databases from a single management console if the Management Agent is installed on the database server, or you can manage each database individually.

If the Oracle Management Agent is installed, the DBCA detects its presence and lists the name of the agent service. You can select this name if you want this existing agent to manage this database. Your new database becomes one of the managed targets for the existing agent.

If you don't have an agent installed or are not doing centralized database management, you can still use Enterprise Manager to monitor and maintain the database. Choose Use Database Control For Database Management if you want to install EM installed and configure it locally.

FIGURE 2.9   The DBCA Management Options screen

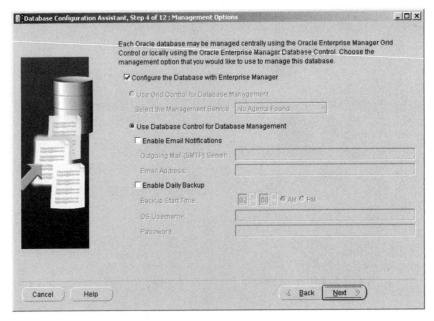

From the Management Options screen, you can also configure e-mail notifications from Enterprise Manager. E-mail notifications are generated when certain database thresholds are reached, for example, the maximum number of database sessions. After installing Enterprise Manager, you can configure notification of these database thresholds. To get these e-mail notifications, you'll need the name of your SMTP mail server and the e-mail address to which you want e-mail notifications sent.

Finally, using the Management Options screen, you can configure backups of your database. If you select Enable Daily Backup, Enterprise Manager backs up your database based on the start time you enter. The database is backed up to a designated area on your system that is specified later in the configuration process. You have to supply an operating system username and password that Enterprise Manager will log in as to perform the backup. This user should have the proper write authorization to the area of the disk where you want the backup stored.

Database Credentials

You use the Database Credentials screen (see Figure 2.10) to configure passwords for the various user accounts that are set up automatically when the database is configured. You can select the same password for all the critical accounts, or you can elect to have a different password for each of the preconfigured accounts. How you elect to set your passwords may depend on the policies of your particular organization. Typically, the same critical passwords are set for these accounts, and the accounts that you won't need to access are selectively locked.

FIGURE 2.10   The DBCA Database Credentials screen

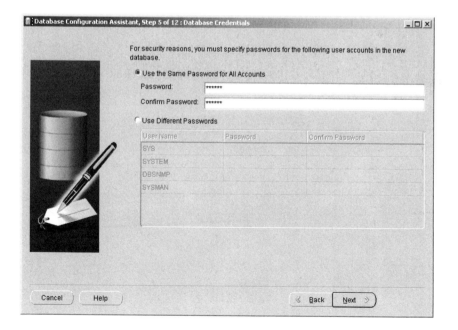

Four accounts are preconfigured when you set up your database:

SYS   The SYS user owns all the internal Oracle tables that constitute the data dictionary. Normally, you should not perform any actions as the SYS user and should ensure that this account is locked down. Also, don't manually modify the underlying objects owned by the SYS user.

SYSTEM   SYSTEM is an additional support user that contains additional administrative tables and views. This account should also be locked down to prevent unauthorized use of it.

DBSNMP   DBSNMP is a login used by the Enterprise Manager facility to monitor and gather performance statistics about the database.

SYSMAN   SYSMAN is the equivalent of the SYS user for the Enterprise Manager facility. This Enterprise Manager administrator can create and modify other Enterprise Manager administrator accounts, as well as administer the database instance itself.

Once you have completed the Database Credentials page, click Next. You will now be presented the Storage Options screen.

Storage Options

The Storage Options screen (see Figure 2.11) is used to define how you want to configure the disk storage areas used by the database. You have three choices:

- File System
- Automatic Storage Management (ASM)
- Raw Devices

Let's take a look at these options in more detail.

FIGURE 2.11   The DBCA Storage Options screen

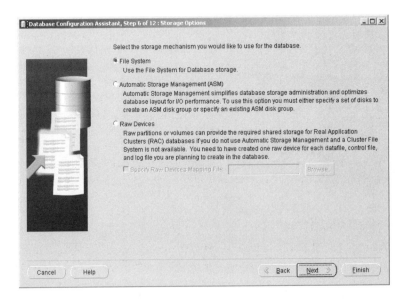

File System Storage

File system storage is the most common type of storage configuration for pre–Oracle 10g databases. This type of storage definition relies on the underlying operating system to maintain and manage the actual files that you as the DBA define. When you choose this option, the DBCA suggests a set of datafile names and directory locations for those files. You can modify this information at a later step in the database creation process.

The DBCA uses the Optimal Flexible Architecture (OFA) directory design for laying out the suggested file locations. The OFA is an Oracle-recommended method for designing a flexible directory structure and naming convention for your Oracle database files.

ASM Storage

Automated Storage Management (ASM) is a new type of storage mechanism available in Oracle 10g. ASM is designed to relieve the burden of disk and storage management and relies on Oracle to maintain your database storage. Instead of your managing many individual database files, ASM allows you to define disk groups for file management.

Using disk groups, you can define one or more groups of disks as a logical unit that Oracle views as a single unit of storage. This concept is similar in nature to the way that some operating systems, including various flavors of Unix, define volume groups.

Oracle manages the storage definitions of the database within a second database used exclusively by ASM to keep track of the disk group allocations. When you create a database and select the ASM option in the Storage Options screen, a series of screens guides you through the process of defining the secondary ASM database instance.

For more information on the new ASM feature, see Chapter 12 in the *Oracle Database Administrator's Guide 10g Release 1* (Part Number B10739-01). This book is part of the standard Oracle documentation CD collection that accompanies your Oracle software. You can also find this documentation on the Oracle Technet website at http://technet.oracle.com. The website is free but you have to create a user ID and password to view the documentation.

Raw Devices

You can also select a raw device as your storage definition. *Raw devices* are disks that are not managed by the underlying operating system. Instead of the underlying operating system controlling disk reading and writing activities, Oracle performs the actions directly to the underlying hardware without handing the responsibilities off to the operating system.

Typically, the systems administrator predefines the raw disk partitions that will constitute the specific raw devices. Then, you as the DBA map the raw devices to specific datafiles and redo log files.

Database File Locations

After you define the type of storage that you want to use for your database, you define where you want to put the files that will constitute the database (see Figure 2.12). Depending on the type of storage option you choose, you may have more or fewer location options available. For example, if you are using raw devices, you or your systems administrator created raw device definitions before creating the database. You use these raw devices as the locations for you database files.

 For more information on how to configure raw devices, consult *Oracle Real Application Clusters Installation and Configuration Guide 10*g *Release 1 (10,1.0.2.0)* (Part Number B20766-04). This book is part of the standard Oracle documentation CD collection that accompanies your Oracle software. You can also find this documentation on the Oracle Technet website at http://technet .oracle.com. The website is free but you have to create a user ID and password to view the documentation.

You are presented with three options on the Database File Locations screen:

- Use Database File Locations From Template
- Use Common Location For All Database Files
- Use Oracle-Managed Files

Let's take a look at these options.

Use Database File Locations from Template

If you chose one of the predefined database templates or a previously defined database template to use for this database, Oracle uses the previously defined locations from the template as the basis for the database file locations. You still have the opportunity later in the database definition process to review and modify the filenames and locations even if you choose this option.

FIGURE 2.12 The DBCA Database File Locations screen

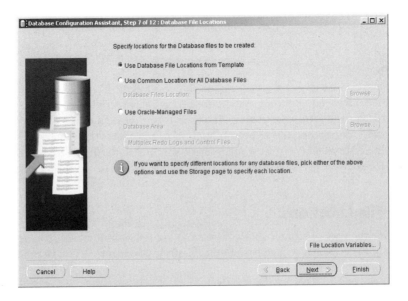

Use Common Location for all Database Files

If you choose this option, you can specify a new directory for all your database files. Again, even if you choose this option, you can change the filenames and locations later in the database definition process.

Use Oracle-Managed Files

If you chose Automated Storage Management (ASM) on the Storage Options screen, you choose Use Oracle-Managed Files and select the appropriate directory path to the area of the disk that will be used to store the database. This area of disk will be fully managed by a secondary ASM Oracle database. If you choose this option, you will not be able to review or make changes later in the database definition process.

Once you have chosen the appropriate storage option for your database, click Next. The next screen you are presented with is the Recovery Configuration screen.

Recovery Configuration

You use the Recovery Configuration screen, as shown in Figure 2.13, to set up your database backup and recovery strategy. Oracle provides robust mechanisms for full point of failure recovery. As a DBA, it is critical to understand the backup and recovery requirements of your application so that you can choose the appropriate backup strategy.

You can configure several options on this screen, the Flash Recovery options—new in Oracle 10*g*—and your archive log options. Let's take a look at each of these options.

FIGURE 2.13 The DBCA Recovery Configuration screen

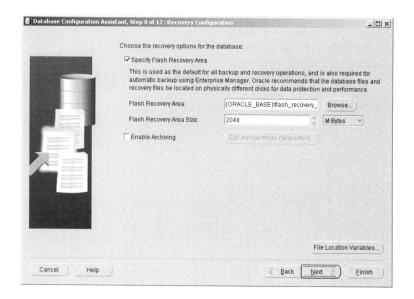

Flash Recovery

Oracle Flash Recovery is a new option available in Oracle 10*g*. It is the foundation of the new Automated Disk-Based recovery feature. Flash Recovery is designed to simplify your life in terms of Oracle backups by providing a centralized location to maintain and manage all the files related to database backups.

The Flash Recovery area is an area of the disk dedicated to the storage and management of files needed for recovering an Oracle database. This area is completely separate from the other components of the Oracle database such as the datafiles, redo logs, and control files.

Oracle uses the Flash Recovery Area to store and manage the archive logs. Enterprise Manager can store its backups in the Flash Recovery area and uses it when restoring files during media recovery. The Oracle Recovery Manager (RMAN) uses the Flash Recovery area and ensures that the database is recoverable based on the files being stored in the Flash Recovery area. All files necessary to recover the database following a media failure are part of the Flash Recovery area.

 We will explore the Flash Recovery feature in more detail in Chapter 10, "Implementing Database Backups."

You can specify the directory location and the size of the disk area that you want to dedicate to the Flash Recovery area. The default location of the directory is ORACLE_BASE\flash_recovery_area. For example, if your ORACLE_BASE location in a Unix environment is /u01/app/oracle/oradata/ORCL, your Flash Recovery area is a directory called /u01/app/oracle/oradata/ORCL/flash_recovery_area.

You can click File Location Variables on the Recovery Configuration screen to display a summary of the Oracle file location parameters, including the current setting of the ORACLE_BASE parameter (see Figure 2.14).

FIGURE 2.14   The DBCA File Location Variables screen

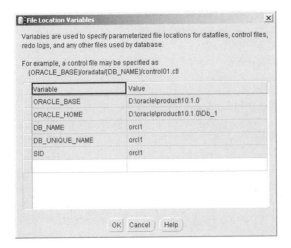

The size of the Flash Recovery area defaults to 2048MB and can be set larger or smaller by changing the Flash Recovery Size setting.

Enabling Archive Logging

From the Recovery Configuration screen, you also have the ability to enable the Oracle archive logging feature. Archive logging is the mechanism Oracle uses to enable you to perform point-of-failure recovery of a database. To enable Archive Logging, mark the Enable Archiving check box. Once you do so, the button Edit Archive Mode Parameters will be enabled. If you click this button, you are presented with a screen that enables you to set the various parameters that are used to configure archive logging (see Figure 2.15).

We will explore archive logging in more detail in Chapter 10.

After completing the Recovery Configuration screen, click Next. You will then be presented with the Database Content screen.

Database Content

If you chose to create a custom database in the Database Templates screen, you will be presented with the Database Content screen as shown in Figure 2.16.

FIGURE 2.15   The DBCA Edit Archive Mode Parameters screen

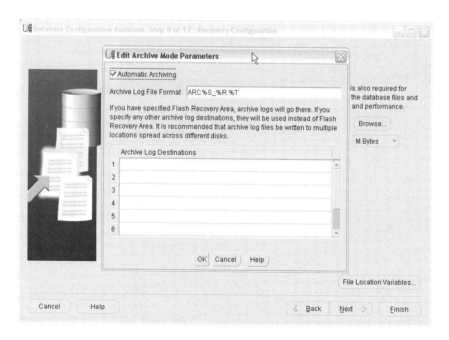

FIGURE 2.16 The DBCA Database Content screen

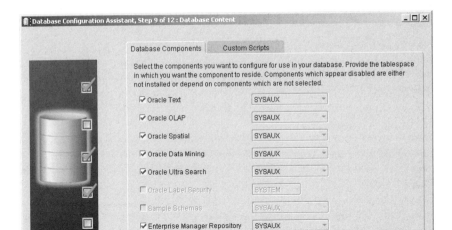

You use the options on this screen to specify which Oracle database components you want to install. Table 2.3 lists and describes the components that can be included and configured automatically by the DBCA.

TABLE 2.3 Oracle Optional Components

Component	Description
Oracle Text	Provides support for multimedia content such as audio and video.
Oracle OLAP	Provides facilities for creating and deploying online analytical processing applications
Oracle Spatial	Provides the components and infrastructure for Oracle to manage and maintain geographic and spatial information such as map coordinates.
Oracle Data Mining	Adds a set of analytical tools and extended algorithms to the database to facilitate data mining.
Oracle Ultra Search	Provides capabilities to perform extended text and searches within the Oracle database.

TABLE 2.3   Oracle Optional Components *(continued)*

Component	Description
Oracle Label Security	Manages and controls access to sensitive information within the database.
Sample Schemas	Provides working examples of how to configure and use certain extended features of the Oracle database.
Enterprise Manager Repository	Specifies the location of the schema used to manage the content of the OEM repository. If you chose to do local management of your database, this schema is required.

Click the Standard Database Components button to display any additional standard features that Oracle will automatically configure for you and recommend as part of a standard database installation (see Figure 2.17). These features are the Oracle JVM, Oracle Intermedia, and Oracle XML DB.

Sample Schemas and Custom Scripts

The DBCA also lets you install examples of actual working databases. Oracle provides a set of example schemas and applications that use these schemas. You can install these sample schemas now or later by running a series of SQL scripts.

These sample schemas include the following:

- Human Resources
- Order Entry
- Product Media
- Sales History
- Queued Shipping

To select these schemas, click the Sample Schemas tab in the DBCA Database Content screen, mark the Sample Schemas check box, and click Next (see Figure 2.18).

FIGURE 2.17   The DBCA Standard Database Components box

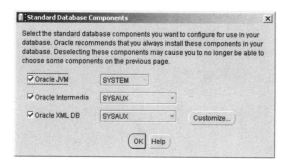

FIGURE 2.18   DBCA Database Content Sample Schemas Tab

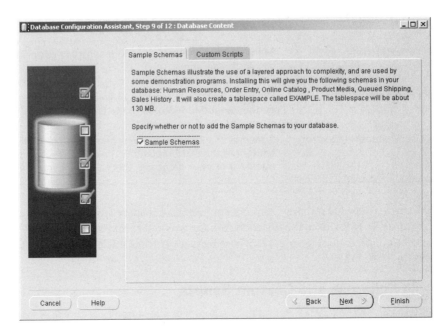

These schemas are designed to provide you with working examples of how to use and implement a variety of features within Oracle. For example, the Product Media schema shows how to use the Oracle Intermedia option, which is used to manage binary large objects (BLOBs) such as images and sound clips.

If you choose to create the sample schemas, Oracle creates a tablespace called EXAMPLES and stores all the necessary tables within that tablespace. Be aware that this adds about 130MB to your database definition.

You can also run custom scripts as part of the database creation process. Click the Custom Scripts tab in the Database Content screen to enter the names and locations of the custom scripts that you want to run at database creation (see Figure 2.19).

For example, you might want the DBCA to automatically create the schema and define the tables that you will use for this database. You can create a script that performs all the necessary work and have the DBCA run the script as part of the database creation process. The custom scripts are run using the command-line utility SQL*Plus, so you will have to define a user ID and password within the body of the script. For example, your script might contain the line:

```
connect some_userid/some_password
```

This line directs Oracle to connect to the current Oracle database, which is determined by your ORACLE_SID environment variable using the supplied user ID and password.

After completing the Database Content screen, click Next. You will then be presented with the Initialization Parameters screen.

FIGURE 2.19   The DBCA Database Content Custom Scripts tab

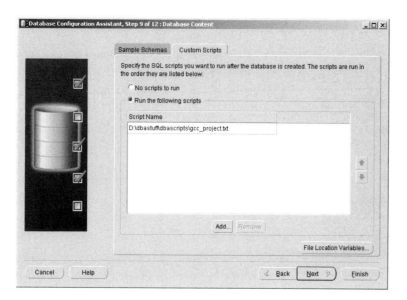

Initialization Parameters

You use the Initialization Parameters screen to define the various initialization parameter settings used to configure size and setup characteristics of the Oracle instance. The following four tabs are categorized according to the parameters used to manage the Oracle instance:

- Memory
- Sizing
- Character Sets
- Connection Mode

Let's take a look at each of these tabs and what settings you can manage under each tab.

The Memory Tab

You use the options on the Memory tab to control the size of the database parameters that configure the overall memory footprint of the Oracle instance (see Figure 2.20). There are two general approaches to managing the memory database parameters: Oracle can set and manage most of the parameters for you, or you can customize each of the initialization parameters for your specific database.

If you choose the Typical setting, Oracle allocates memory to the various components within the Oracle System Global Area (SGA) and Process Global Area (PGA). This memory allocation is automatic and is a percentage of the overall physical memory available on the server. The default is 40 percent of total memory available, but you can change this setting. If you choose this setting, click the Show Memory Distribution button to see how Oracle will allocate the memory between the SGA and the PGA.

FIGURE 2.20 The Memory tab in the Initialization Parameters screen

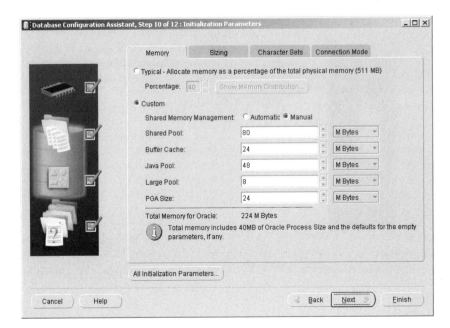

If you choose the Custom option, you have full control over how much each of the specific areas of the SGA will take. The main areas that you will configure are the Shared Pool, Buffer Cache, Java Pool, Large Pool, and PGA size. Each of the settings maps to a specific Oracle parameter.

The Sizing Tab

You use the options on the Sizing tab (see Figure 2.21) to configure the block size of your database and the number of processes that can connect to this database. The Block Size setting corresponds to the smallest unit of storage within the Oracle database. All storage of database objects (tables, indexes, and so on) are governed by the block size. The block size defaults to 8KB, but you can modify it. Once the database is created, you cannot modify this setting.

The maximum and minimum size of an Oracle block depends on the operating system. Generally, 8KB is sufficient for most transaction-oriented applications, and larger block sizes such as 16KB and higher are used in data warehouse–type applications.

The Processes setting specifies the maximum number of simultaneous operating system processes that can be connected to this Oracle database. You must include at least six processes for each of the Oracle background processes. You can increase this number on this screen.

 This parameter does have a bearing on the overall size of your Oracle instance. The larger you make this number, the more room Oracle must reserve in the SGA to track the processes.

FIGURE 2.21   The Sizing tab in the Initialization Parameters screen

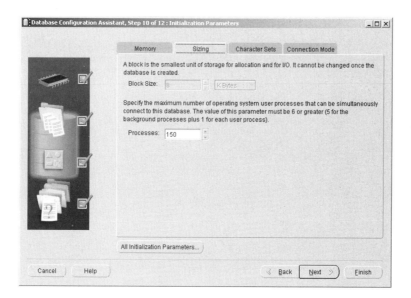

The Character Sets Tab

You use the options on the Character Sets tab to configure the character sets you will use within your database (see Figure 2.22). You will determine the database character set, the national character set, the default language, and the default date format.

Specifying a database character set defines the type of encoding scheme that Oracle uses to determine how characters are displayed and stored within your Oracle environment. The character set you choose determines the languages that can be represented in your environment. It also controls other nuances such as how your database interacts with your operating system and how much storage is required for your data. The default character set is based on the language setting of the operating system.

Specifying a national character set defines how your database represents unicode characters in a database that does not use a Unicode-enabled character set.

You use the Default Language setting to manage certain aspects of how your database represents information pertaining to different locales. For example, this setting determines how your database displays time and monetary values.

You use the Default Date setting to specify how Oracle displays dates by default. For example, the AMERICA setting shows dates in the DD-MON-YYYY format by default.

The Connection Mode Tab

You use the options on the Connection Mode tab to specify the type of connections to use for this database (see Figure 2.23). You can choose dedicated or shared server mode. The default connection mode is dedicated server.

FIGURE 2.22 The Character Sets tab in the Initialization Parameters screen

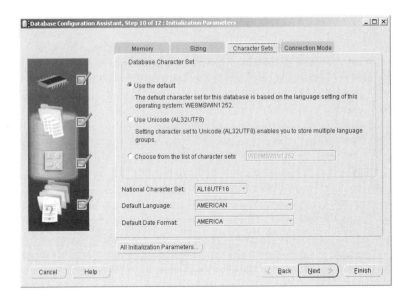

FIGURE 2.23 The Connection Mode tab on the Initialization Parameters screen

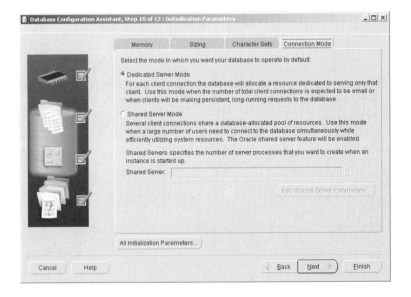

 Connection types are covered in more detail in Chapter 4, "Oracle Net Services."

After completing the Initialization Parameters screen, click Next. You will then be presented with the Database Storage screen.

Database Storage

The Database Storage screen provides you with the opportunity to review and change the locations of the actual objects that compose the Oracle database, namely, the datafiles, control files, and redo logs (see Figure 2.24).

This screen displays a tree structure in the left pane. You can click the various elements within the tree to expand and display the details of each component. Selecting an element displays details about the element in the pane on the right. For example, clicking Controlfile displays a summary of the control filenames and locations in the right pane. You can make manual changes to the names and locations of the control files in the right pane.

If you are creating a custom database definition that does not use a template, you can add new objects to a particular group. For example, clicking the Redo Logs folder and then clicking Create lets you add redo log groups to your database definition. If you selected a database template that included datafile definitions, you cannot add or remove datafiles, tablespaces, or rollback segments, but you can modify the location of the datafiles, control files, and redo log groups. As with many of the other screens in the DBCA, you can click the File Location Variables button to display the settings for the various Oracle file location parameters, such as the ORACLE_BASE and ORACLE_HOME settings.

After completing the Database Storage screen, click Next to create your database.

FIGURE 2.24   The DBCA Database Storage screen

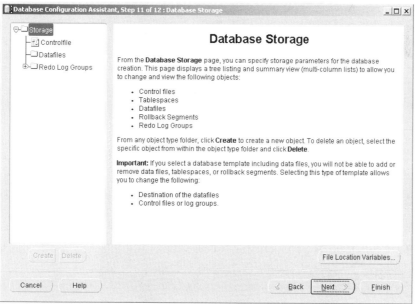

Creation Options

The Creation Options screen (see Figure 2.25) provides you with two options:

Create Database   Use this option to have the DBCA immediately create your database.

Save as a Database Template   You actually have two choices with this option. You can elect to save your database definition to a template and create the database at a later time or you can have the DBCA create the template and immediately create your database.

If you elect to create your database immediately, the DBCA uses the information you have provided in the previous screens to create all the necessary components of your database, populate the database with sample schemas if they were chosen, start your database, and allow you to configure the network components of your database such as the Oracle Net listener.

We will discuss the listener component in more detail in Chapter 4.

If you elect to save your database to a template definition, this definition is added to the list of database definitions that you can select on subsequent executions of the DBCA.

You can also let the DBCA create a set of scripts that you can run manually to create the database.

FIGURE 2.25   The DBCA Creation Options screen

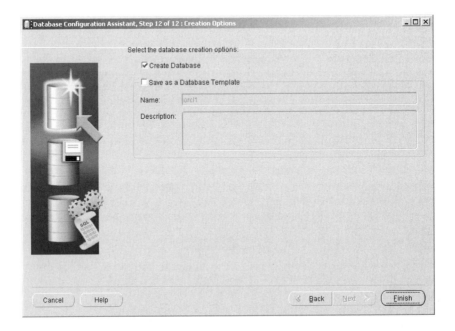

This option is available only if you chose to create a new database template and did not choose an existing template.

You can choose a location to store your scripts and then you can run the scripts manually to generate your database. If you choose a manual creation process, you will also have to manually configure several items, including the Oracle Internet Directory Service if you elect to use centralized naming and your listener. Also, depending on your operating system, you will have to configure or modify the ORATAB file on Unix or create a service in the Windows environment.

If you elect to have the DBCA create the database immediately, click Finish. You will see the Confirmation screen that summarizes the database configuration options that you chose for this database (see Figure 2.26). You can scroll down the window to examine the following:

- Options to install into the database
- The initialization parameter settings
- Character set settings
- Datafilenames and locations
- Redo log filenames and locations
- Control filenames and locations

You can save this summary screen as an HTML file for later reference.

FIGURE 2.26   The DBCA Confirmation screen

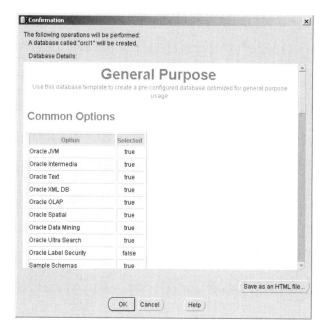

Once you start the database creation process, Oracle creates the database as you have specified. It starts the instance, creates all the necessary database components, and configures all the database options that you specified. Depending on how large a database you create and how many options you are installing, the process can take anywhere from several minutes to an hour or more.

When the creation process is complete, connect to the database with one of the tools such as SQL*Plus, *i*SQL*Plus, or Enterprise Manager to ensure that all the database options and components were installed properly.

Configuring an Oracle Database Using DBCA

The DBCA lets you change various aspects of an existing database. To change the database configuration, select Configure Database Options in the DBCA Operations screen (shown earlier in this chapter in Figure 2.6). If the database is not started, the DBCA starts it for you automatically. You must connect to the database as a user that has DBA authority.

Once you have selected and started the database, you can add options that may not have been previously included in the database. You can also change the server type.

Deleting an Oracle Database Using DBCA

You can also delete a database using the DBCA. In the Operations screen (shown earlier in this chapter in Figure 2.6), choose Delete A Database and click Next to open the Database screen, as shown in Figure 2.27. The DBCA lists all the databases available for deletion.

If you click Finish, the DBCA removes all files on the disk associated with this database you have chosen. If you are using Windows, the DBCA also removes the service associated with the database.

FIGURE 2.27 The DBCA Database screen

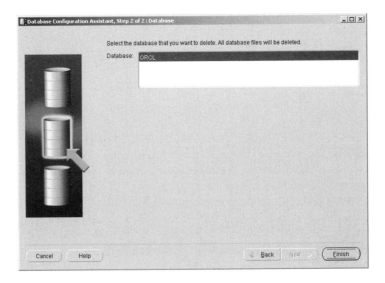

Deleting an Oracle Database Manually

Some DBAs prefer to use a command-line interface to perform their tasks. You can delete a database using the command-line tool SQL*Plus.

To do so, first connect to SQL*Plus as an administrator that has the ability to start up the database, that is, an administrator with either SYSOPER or SYSDBA privileges.

For example:

```
/u01/app/oracle>sqlplus sys/oracle as sysdba
```

Once you are connected, you need to put the database in MOUNT mode. Issue the following command if the database is not running:

```
Startup mount;
```

Next, issue the following command:

```
Drop database;
```

This command deletes all the files associated with the database. If you are using raw disk devices, the special files created for these devices are not deleted. Also, you may have to remove any archived logs from the database archive area using the appropriate operating system command.

Managing Database Templates Using DBCA

As we explained earlier in this chapter, the DBCA can store and use XML-based templates to create your Oracle database. As the DBA, you can manage these database definition templates. Saving a definition of your database in a template format makes it easier to perform various tasks. For example, you can copy a preexisting template to modify new database definitions. The template definition is normally stored in the $ORACLE_HOME/assistants/dbca/templates directory on Unix and in the %ORACLE_HOME%\assistants\dbca\templates directory on Windows systems.

The DBCA can use two types of templates: seed and nonseed. Seed templates are template definitions that contain database definition information and the actual datafiles and redo log files. The advantage of a seed template is that the DBCA makes a copy of the datafiles and redo logs included in the definition file. These prebuilt datafiles include all schema information, which makes for a faster database creation process. The seed templates carry a .dbc extension. The associated predefined redo logs and datafiles are stored as files having a .djf extension. When you use a seed template, you can change the database name, the datafile locations, the number of control files and redo log groups, and the initialization parameters.

Nonseed templates contain custom-defined database definitions. Unlike seed templates, they do not come with preconfigured datafiles and redo logs. Nonseed templates carry a .dbt extension.

Now we'll explore the various options we have to manage templates.

Creating Template Definitions Using the DBCA

You can use the DBCA interface to create new database templates. When you connect to the DBCA, select Manage Templates in the Operations screen (see Figure 2.6, shown earlier in this chapter) and click Next to open the Template Management screen (Figure 2.28).

You have three choices for creating templates. Table 2.4 summarizes your options.

TABLE 2.4   Template Creation Options

Selection	Description
From An Existing Template	Creates a new template definition from a preexisting template. This allows you to modify a variety of template settings, including parameters and datafile storage characteristics.
From An Existing Database (Structure Only)	Creates a new template based on the structural characteristics of an existing database. The datafiles are created from scratch and will not include data from the original database. Choose this option when you want a database that is structurally like another database but does not contain any data. The database that you are copying from can reside anywhere in your network.
From An Existing Database (Structure As Well As Data)	Creates a new template based on the structural characteristics of an existing database. The datafiles and all corresponding user data are included in the new database. Choose this option when you want an exact copy of an existing database. The database you are copying must reside on the same physical server as the new database you are creating.

FIGURE 2.28   The DBCA Template Management Screen

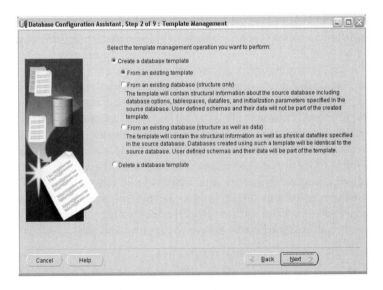

Depending on the option selected, you are presented with a set of forms to save your template definition. If you elected to create a template from an existing database, you will have to connect to the database so that the DBCA can obtain information about the database. You must connect to the database as a user that has DBA credentials to perform this task.

If you are copying a definition from an existing template, you can configure the template by following a series of screens that are similar to those used to create a database. These screens allow you to configure the various aspects of the template, including initialization parameters and datafile and redo log locations.

Deleting Template Definitions Using the DBCA

You can also delete an existing template definition. In the Operations screen (see Figure 2.6, shown earlier in this chapter), click Manage Templates. You will be presented with the Template Management screen (see Figure 2.28, shown earlier in this chapter). Select the option Delete A Database Template. You can then choose the template to delete. When you remove the template, the DBCA removes the XML file from the system.

Managing Parameter Initialization Files

Oracle uses parameter initialization files to store information about initialization parameters used when an Oracle instance starts. Oracle reads the parameter file to obtain information about how the Oracle instance should be sized and configured upon startup.

As you learned in Chapter 1, the parameter file can be either a plain text file, commonly referred to as a *PFILE*, or it can be a binary parameter file, commonly referred to as an SPFILE. The default location that Oracle searches to find the PFILE and SPFILE parameter files is $ORACLE_HOME/dbs on Unix systems and %ORACLE_HOME%/database on Windows systems.

Oracle uses a search hierarchy when a startup command is issued without specifying either a PFILE or an SPFILE. Oracle first looks for a parameter file called spfile$ORACLE_SID.ora. If it doesn't find that, it searches for spfile.ora. Finally it searches for a traditional text PFILE with the default name of init$ORACLE_SID.ora.

If the parameter files do not exist in the default location or you want to use a different parameter file to start your database, you can specify a parameter file to use when you issue a startup command to start the Oracle database.

In some instances, you may need to change the initialization parameters. For example, you might need to increase the number of sessions allowed to connect to the database because you are adding users. Whatever the case, you need to know how to make these changes.

You can make changes manually, or you can use the EM Database Control tool to modify the parameters. To use the EM Database Control tool to modify existing database parameters, navigate to the Administration menu. In the Instance section, you can modify your initialization parameters. If you choose All Initialization Parameters, you will see a list of all the parameters that can be modified (see Figure 2.29).

FIGURE 2.29 The EM Database Control Initialization Parameters screen

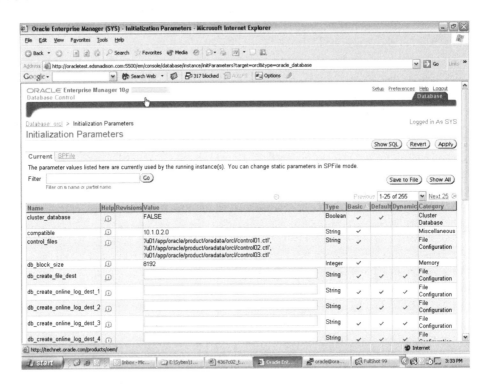

 Parameter initialization files were described in Chapter 1, "Installing Oracle 10g."

 You will see examples of how this is done later in this chapter.

The Initialization Parameters screen has two tabs: Current and SPFile. The Current tab displays all the currently active settings for initialization parameters for the database instance. If a parameter is marked Dynamic, you can modify it, and this modification immediately affects the parameter that affects the currently running instance without stopping the database. The changes you make from the Current tab are not permanent, so the next time the database is stopped and restarted, the settings revert to their original values.

If you are using a server parameter file, or SPFILE, you will see the SPFile tab. This screen also lets you change existing database parameters. The difference between changing parameters in this screen and changing parameters in the Current tab is that changes to the SPFILE are persistent across database startups and shutdowns because the changes are saved to the SPFILE definition. You can also apply your changes to the SPFILE only or to the SPFILE and the currently running instance.

Starting Up and Shutting Down an Oracle Database

As a DBA, you are responsible for startup and shutdown of the Oracle instance. Oracle gives authorized administrators the ability to perform this task using a variety of interfaces. It is important to understand the options that are available to you to start up and shut down the Oracle instance and when the various options can or should be used.

To start up or shut down an Oracle instance, you need to be connected to the database with the appropriate privileges. Two special connection accounts authorizations are available for startup and shutdown: *SYSDBA* or *SYSOPER*. The SYSDBA authorization is an all-empowering authorization that allows you to perform any database task. The SYSOPER authorization is a less powerful authorization that allows startup and shutdown abilities but restricts other administrative tasks, such as access to nonadministrative schema objects. These authorizations are managed either through a passwords file or via operating-system control.

When a database is initially installed, only the SYS schema can connect to the database with the SYSDBA authorization. You can grant this authorization and the SYSOPER authorization to give others the ability to perform these tasks without connecting as the SYS user.

Now we will discuss how to perform a database startup.

Oracle 10*g* Database Startup

As described in Chapter 1, the Oracle instance is composed of a set of logical memory structures and background processes that users interact with to communicate with the Oracle database. When Oracle is started, these memory structures and background processes are initialized and started so that users can communicate with the Oracle database.

Whenever an Oracle database is started, it goes through a series of steps to ensure database consistency. When it starts up, a database passes through three modes: NOMOUNT, MOUNT, and OPEN. We will review each of these startup modes and a few other special startup options and discuss when you need to use these options. We'll then discuss how to use the available interfaces to start up an Oracle instance.

STARTUP NOMOUNT

STARTUP NOMOUNT starts the instance without mounting the database. When a database is started in this mode, the parameter file is read and the background processes and memory structures are initiated, but they are not attached or communicating with the disk structures of the database. When the instance is in this state, the database is not available for use.

If a database is started in NOMOUNT mode, you can perform certain tasks. One of the most common is to run a script that creates the underlying database.

At times, a database may not be able to go to the next mode (called MOUNT mode) and remains in NOMOUNT mode. For example, this can occur if Oracle has a problem accessing the control file structures, which contain important information to continue with the startup process. If these structures are damaged or not available, the database startup process cannot continue until the problem is resolved.

STARTUP MOUNT

The STARTUP MOUNT option performs all the work of the STARTUP NOMOUNT option but also attaches and interacts with the database structures. At this point, Oracle obtains information from the control files that it uses to locate and attach to the main database structures.

Certain administrative tasks can be performed while the database is in this mode, for example, recovery. You can also physically change file locations or place the database in archive log mode.

STARTUP OPEN

The STARTUP OPEN option is the default startup mode if no mode is specified on the STARTUP command line. STARTUP OPEN performs all the steps of the STARTUP NOMOUNT and STARTUP MOUNT options. This option makes the database available to all users.

Although you typically use the STARTUP NOMOUNT, STARTUP MOUNT, and STARTUP OPEN options, a few other startup options are available that you can use in certain situations: STARTUP FORCE and STARTUP RESTRICT. These are discussed next.

STARTUP FORCE

You can use the STARTUP FORCE startup option if you are experiencing difficulty starting the database in a normal fashion. For example, if a database server lost power and the database stopped abruptly, it can leave the database in a state in which a STARTUP FORCE startup is necessary. This type of startup should not normally be required but can be used if a normal startup does not work. What is also different about STARTUP FORCE is that it can issued no matter what mode the database is in. STARTUP FORCE does a shutdown abort and then restarts the database.

STARTUP RESTRICT

The STARTUP RESTRICT option starts up the database and places it in OPEN mode, but gives access only to users who have the RESTRICTED SESSION privilege. You might want to open a database using the RESTRICTED option when you want to perform maintenance on the database while it is open but ensure that users cannot connect and perform work on the database. You might also want to open the database using the RESTRICTED option to perform database exports or imports and guarantee that no users are accessing the system during these activities. After you are done with your work, you can disable the restricted session, ALTER SYSTEM DISABLE RESTRICTED SESSION, so everyone can connect to the database.

Starting Up Oracle Using EM Database Control

Now that you understand the various startup options, let's look at how to use the EM Database Control to start up the Oracle instance.

When you invoke the Enterprise Manager console, you are notified that the database instance is down (see Figure 2.30).

Click the Startup button located on the Database Control screen to open the Startup/Shutdown: Specify Host And Target Database Credentials screen (see Figure 2.31). On this screen, you need to supply an operating system username and password and an Oracle user ID and password that has either the SYSDBA or SYSOPER account authentication. After you enter the appropriate user ID and password information, click OK to open the Startup/Shutdown: Confirmation screen, as shown in Figure 2.32.

FIGURE 2.30   The EM Database Control database status screen

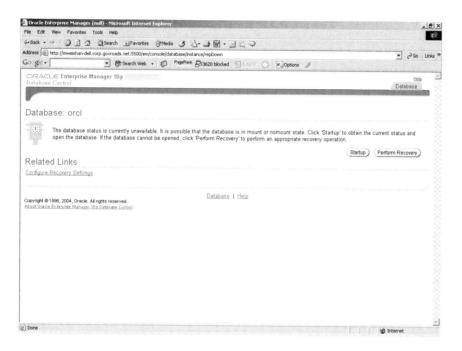

FIGURE 2.31   Startup/Shutdown: Specify Host And Target Database Credentials screen

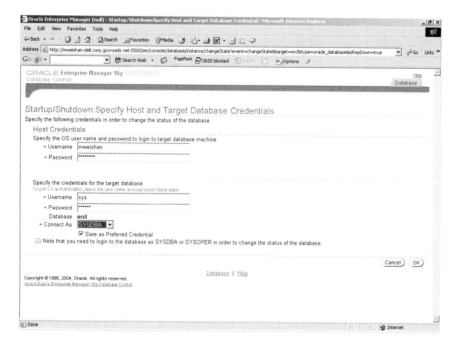

From here, you can click Yes to continue, No to cancel, or Advanced Options to select advanced startup options.

If you click Advanced Options, you can select the type of startup you want (see Figure 2.33). You can choose your startup mode (NOMOUNT, MOUNT, or OPEN), you can choose the parameter file to use, and you can choose to force database startup or to start the database in RESTRICTED mode. Click OK to return the previous screen. By default, Oracle starts with the OPEN option and uses the default initialization file.

 You can also click Show SQL to see the actual startup command that will be executed.

After you choose the type of startup, click Yes. The startup process may take some time to complete depending on system speed and whether Oracle has to perform any recovery operations during the startup process. You will be presented with a screen indicating that the database is being started (see Figure 2.34). If Oracle does not encounter any problems with the startup process, you will be notified that the database is now open and available.

Starting Oracle Using SQL*Plus

You can also use the command-line facility SQL*Plus to start the Oracle database. You will need to connect to SQL*Plus as a user with SYSOPER or SYSDBA privileges. Here is a syntax diagram of the startup options available:

STARTUP [NOMOUNT|MOUNT|OPEN] [PFILE/SPFILE=] [RESTRICT]

FIGURE 2.32 Startup/Shutdown: Confirmation screen

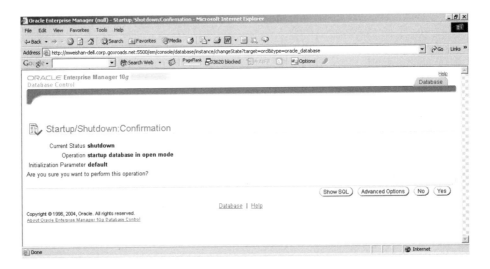

FIGURE 2.33   Startup/Shutdown: Advanced Startup Options screen

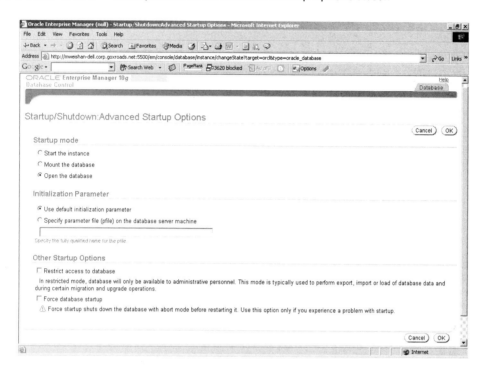

FIGURE 2.34   Startup/Shutdown: Activity Information screen

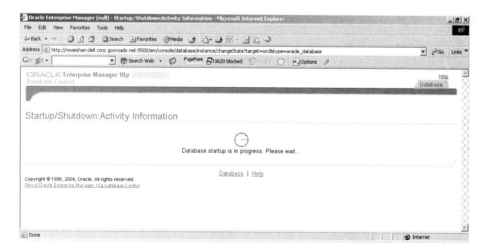

Table 2.5 shows some examples of startup commands that you can use from within SQL*Plus.

TABLE 2.5 SQL*Plus Startup Command Examples

Command	Description
STARTUP NOMOUNT pfile=/u01/oracle/init.ora	Start up Oracle in NOMOUNT mode using a non-default parameter file
STARTUP MOUNT	Start up Oracle in MOUNT mode using a default SPFILE or PFILE
STARTUP OPEN	Start up Oracle in OPEN mode using a default SPFILE or PFILE
STARTUP RESTRICT	Start up Oracle in OPEN mode and allow only users with restricted session privileges to connect to the database
STARTUP FORCE	Force database startup using the default PFILE or SPFILE
STARTUP OPEN PFILE=/u01/sp01.ora	Start up Oracle in OPEN mode using a nondefault parameter file

Here is an example of how you can use the STARTUP FORCE command with a nondefault parameter file to start up an Oracle database using SQL*Plus:

```
D:\oracle\ora10g>sqlplus "/ as sysdba"
SQL*Plus: Release 10.1.0.2.0 - Production on Mon Jul 19 15:59:22 2004
Copyright (c) 1982, 2004, Oracle.  All rights reserved.
Connected to an idle instance.
SQL> startup force pfile=d:\oracle\ora10g\initORCL1.ora
ORACLE instance started.
Total System Global Area  171966464 bytes
Fixed Size                   787988 bytes
Variable Size             145750508 bytes
Database Buffers           25165824 bytes
Redo Buffers                 262144 bytes
Database mounted.
Database opened.
SQL>
```

If you are running Oracle on Windows, you can also start the database when you start the associated Oracle service. Starting the Oracle service automatically starts the Oracle database.

Shutting Down an Oracle 10*g* Database

In some instances, you will need to shut down a database, for example, to perform regularly scheduled cold backups of the database or to perform database upgrades. Whatever the case, you need to understand the shutdown options. Just as with database startup, several options are available, as well as a variety of interfaces that you can use.

SHUTDOWN NORMAL

A normal shutdown is the default type of shutdown that Oracle performs if no shutdown options are provided. You need to be aware of the following when doing a normal shutdown:

- No new Oracle connections are allowed from the time the SHUTDOWN NORMAL command is issued.

- The database will wait until all users are disconnected to proceed with the shutdown process.

   Because Oracle waits until all users are disconnected before shutting down, you can find yourself waiting indefinitely for a client who may be connected but is no longer doing any work or may have left for the day. This can require extra work, identifying which connections are still active and either notifying the users to disconnect or forcing the client disconnections by killing their session. This type of shutdown is also known as a "clean" shutdown because when you start Oracle again, no recovery is necessary.

SHUTDOWN TRANSACTIONAL

A transactional shutdown of the database is a bit more aggressive than a normal shutdown. The characteristics of the transactional shutdown are as follows:

- No new Oracle connections are allowed from the time the SHUTDOWN TRANSACTIONAL command is issued.

- No new transactions are allowed to start from the time the SHUTDOWN TRANSACTIONAL command is issued.

- Once all active transactions on the database have completed, all client connections are disconnected.

   A transactional shutdown does allow client processes to complete prior to the disconnection. This can prevent a client from losing work and can be valuable especially if the database has long-running transactions that need to be completed prior to shutdown. This type of shutdown is also a clean shutdown and does not require any recovery on a subsequent startup.

SHUTDOWN IMMEDIATE

The immediate shutdown method is the next most aggressive option. An immediate shutdown is characterized as follows:

- No new Oracle connections are allowed from the time the SHUTDOWN IMMEDIATE command is issued.

- Any uncommitted transactions are rolled back. Thus, a user in the middle of a transaction will lose all the uncommitted work.

- Oracle does not wait for clients to disconnect. Any unfinished transactions are rolled back, and their database connections are terminated.

This type of shutdown works well if you want to perform unattended or scripted shutdowns of the database and you need to ensure that the database will shut down without getting hung up during the process by clients who are connected. Even though Oracle is forcing transactions to roll back and disconnecting users, an immediate shutdown is still considered a clean shutdown. No recovery activity takes place when Oracle is subsequently restarted.

SHUTDOWN ABORT

A shutdown abort is the most aggressive type of shutdown and has the following characteristics:

- No new Oracle connections are allowed from the time the SHUTDOWN ABORT command is issued.

- Any SQL statements currently in progress are terminated, regardless of their state.

- Uncommitted work is not rolled back.

- Oracle disconnects all client connections immediately upon the issuance of the SHUTDOWN ABORT command.

Do not use SHUTDOWN ABORT regularly. Use it only if the other options for database shutdown fail or if you are experiencing some type of database problem that is preventing Oracle from performing a clean shutdown. This type of shutdown is not a clean shutdown and requires recovery when the database is subsequently started.

Shutting Down Oracle Using EM Database Control

You can use the EM Database Control to shut down the Oracle database. To do so, invoke the EM Database Control from your web browser. Click the Shutdown button in the General section (see Figure 2.35).

After you click Shutdown, you are presented with the Startup/Shutdown: Specify Host and Target Database Credentials screen (see Figure 2.36). You must supply an OS user ID and password to log into the target database machine. If you are not using Operating System Authentication, you must also enter an Oracle user ID and password that has SYS-DBA authority.

After you authenticate, the Startup/Shutdown: Confirmation screen is displayed (see Figure 2.37). The default shutdown selected when you are using the EM Database Control is SHUTDOWN IMMEDIATE. Oracle also displays the current status of the database on this form.

FIGURE 2.35   The EM Database Control Home screen

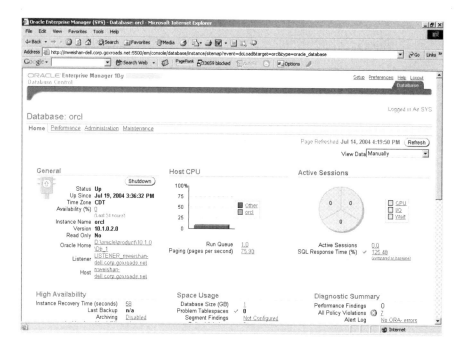

FIGURE 2.36   Startup/Shutdown: Specify Host and Target Database Credentials screen

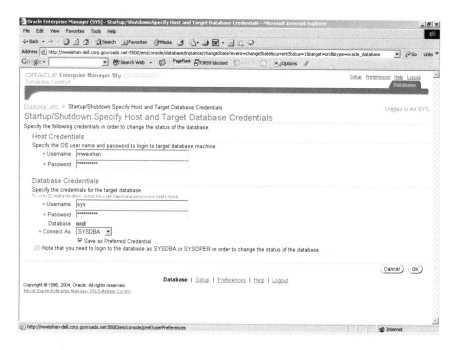

To perform a nondefault type of shutdown, click the Advanced Options button. In the Startup/Shutdown: Advanced Shutdown Options screen (see Figure 2.38), you can select the type of shutdown.

After you select the type of shutdown, click OK, and then click Yes in the Confirmation screen to open a screen informing you that the database shutdown is in progress (see Figure 2.39). Once the process has completed, click the Refresh button, and you will see that the database is now shut down (see Figure 2.40). In this EM Database Control database status screen, you can start the database.

FIGURE 2.37 The Startup/Shutdown: Confirmation screen

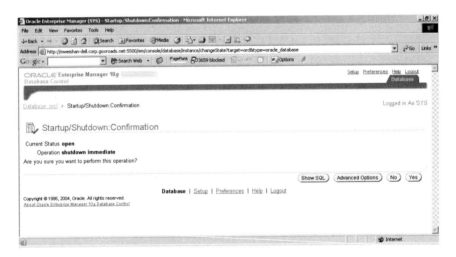

FIGURE 2.38 The Startup/Shutdown: Advanced Shutdown Options screen

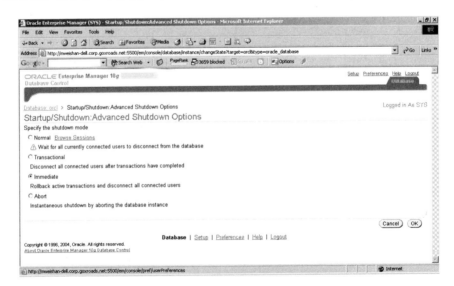

FIGURE 2.39   The Startup/Shutdown: Activity Information screen

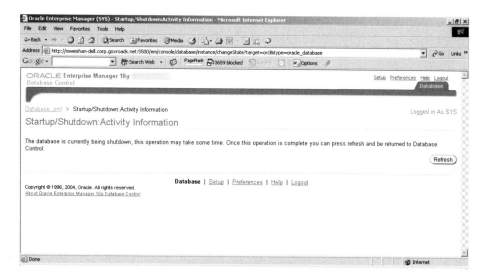

FIGURE 2.40   The EM Database Control database status screen

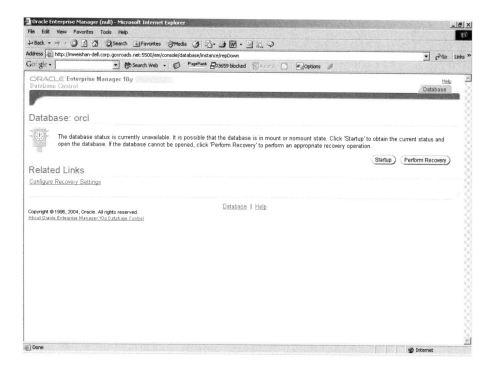

Shutting Down Oracle Using SQL*Plus

You can also use the command-line facility SQL*Plus to shut down the Oracle database. You will need to connect to SQL*Plus as a user with SYSOPER or SYSDBA privileges. Here is a syntax diagram of the shutdown options available to you:

```
SHUTDOWN [NORMAL|IMMEDIATE|RESTRICT|ABORT]
```

Here is an example of how to use the SHUTDOWN IMMEDIATE command to shut down an Oracle database using SQL*Plus:

```
SQL*Plus: Release 10.1.0.2.0 - Production on Mon Jul 19 15:30:25 2004
Copyright (c) 1982, 2004, Oracle.  All rights reserved.
Connected to:
Oracle Database 10g Enterprise Edition Release 10.1.0.2.0 - Production
With the Partitioning, OLAP and Data Mining options
SQL> shutdown immediate
Database closed.
Database dismounted.
ORACLE instance shut down.
SQL>
```

If you are running in a Windows environment and shut down the database using either the Database Control or SQL*Plus tools, the Oracle Service will continue to run. Even though the Oracle Windows service is running, the database is not available until a subsequent startup command is issued.

Monitoring the Database Alert Log

The Database alert log, sometimes referred to as the alert file, contains information about certain activities and errors that occur within your database. The alert log contains a chronological summary of these events. The alert log contains a wealth of information that you can use to diagnose system problems and review histories of activities that have occurred on the system. Some of the events and actions recorded in the alert log include the following:

- Startup and shutdown information, including a record of every time a database is started or shut down

- Certain types of administrative actions, such as ALTER SYSTEM or ALTER DATABASE commands

- Certain types of database errors, such as internal Oracle errors (ORA-600 errors) or space errors (ORA-1642, for example)

- The values of initialization parameters that have had values different from their default values

Here is an excerpt from an Oracle 10*g* alert log:

```
Starting ORACLE instance (normal)
SYS auditing is disabled
Starting up ORACLE RDBMS Version: 10.1.0.2.0.
System parameters with non-default values:
  processes              = 150
  shared_pool_size       = 83886080
  large_pool_size        = 8388608
  java_pool_size         = 50331648
  control_files          =
D:\ORACLE\PRODUCT\10.1.0\ORADATA\ORCL\CONTROL01.CTL,
    D:\ORACLE\PRODUCT\10.1.0\ORADATA\ORCL\CONTROL02.CTL,
    D:\ORACLE\PRODUCT\10.1.0\ORADATA\ORCL\CONTROL03.CTL
  db_block_size          = 8192
  db_cache_size          = 25165824
  compatible             = 10.1.0.2.0
  db_file_multiblock_read_count= 16
  db_recovery_file_dest  = D:\oracle\product\10.1.0\flash_recovery_area
  db_recovery_file_dest_size= 2147483648
  undo_management        = AUTO
  undo_tablespace        = UNDOTBS1
  remote_login_passwordfile= EXCLUSIVE
  db_domain              =
  dispatchers            = (PROTOCOL=TCP) (SERVICE=orclXDB)
  job_queue_processes    = 10
  background_dump_dest   = D:\ORACLE\PRODUCT\10.1.0\ADMIN\ORCL\BDUMP
  user_dump_dest         = D:\ORACLE\PRODUCT\10.1.0\ADMIN\ORCL\UDUMP
  core_dump_dest         = D:\ORACLE\PRODUCT\10.1.0\ADMIN\ORCL\CDUMP
  sort_area_size         = 65536
  db_name                = orcl
  open_cursors           = 300
  pga_aggregate_target   = 25165824
Thu Jul 22 15:25:55 2004
starting up 1 dispatcher(s) for network address
  '(ADDRESS=(PARTIAL=YES)(PROTOCOL=TCP))'...
starting up 1 shared server(s) ...
LGWR started with pid=5, OS id=2140
SMON started with pid=7, OS id=2136
RECO started with pid=8, OS id=2184
PMON started with pid=2, OS id=2132
```

```
CKPT started with pid=6, OS id=2180
MMAN started with pid=3, OS id=2116
CJQ0 started with pid=9, OS id=2192
DBW0 started with pid=4, OS id=2128
Thu Jul 22 15:26:01 2004
alter database mount exclusive
Thu Jul 22 15:26:17 2004
Controlfile identified with block size 16384
Thu Jul 22 15:26:21 2004
Setting recovery target incarnation to 2
Thu Jul 22 15:26:22 2004
Successful mount of redo thread 1, with mount id 1059986201
Thu Jul 22 15:26:22 2004
Database mounted in Exclusive Mode.
Completed: alter database mount exclusive
Thu Jul 22 15:26:22 2004
alter database open
Thu Jul 22 15:26:23 2004
Beginning crash recovery of 1 threads
Thu Jul 22 15:26:24 2004
Started first pass scan
Thu Jul 22 15:26:25 2004
Completed first pass scan
 1579 redo blocks read, 169 data blocks need recovery
Thu Jul 22 15:26:25 2004
Started redo application at
 Thread 1: logseq 19, block 3084, scn 0.0
Recovery of Online Redo Log: Thread 1 Group 3 Seq 19 Reading mem 0
  Mem# 0 errs 0: D:\ORACLE\PRODUCT\10.1.0\ORADATA\ORCL\REDO03.LOG
Thu Jul 22 15:26:28 2004
Completed redo application
Thu Jul 22 15:26:28 2004
Completed crash recovery at
 Thread 1: logseq 19, block 4663, scn 0.490142
 169 data blocks read, 169 data blocks written, 1579 redo blocks read
Thu Jul 22 15:26:31 2004
Thread 1 advanced to log sequence 20
Maximum redo generation record size = 120832 bytes
Maximum redo generation change vector size = 116476 bytes
Private_strands 7 at log switch
Thread 1 opened at log sequence 20
```

```
Current log# 1 seq# 20 mem# 0:
    D:\ORACLE\PRODUCT\10.1.0\ORADATA\ORCL\RED001.LOG
Successful open of redo thread 1
Thu Jul 22 15:26:31 2004
Starting background process MMON
MMON started with pid=15, OS id=2248
Thu Jul 22 15:27:11 2004
Starting background process MMNL
MMNL started with pid=16, OS id=2296
Thu Jul 22 15:27:17 2004
Completed: alter database open
```

This excerpt shows a successful startup of a database. Notice the section that lists the non-default initialization parameters. Also notice that Oracle performed an automatic recovery of the database. This indicates that the database was not shut down cleanly prior to this startup. You can also see that Oracle is starting dispatcher processes, which indicates that we are running Oracle Shared Server.

The parameter that governs the location of the alert log is called *BACKGROUND_DUMP_DEST*. This parameter is set to a path that designates where Oracle should place the log. Here is an example of this setting on a Unix system in the initialization parameter file:

```
BACKGROUND_DUMP_DEST = /u01/app/oracle/admin/PROD/bdump
```

The alert log is continuously appended to, so it is a good idea to periodically purge it. Many DBAs do so daily or weekly, saving a copy of the current alert log to a backup and clearing the current alert log. It is a good idea to save the log contents. You can use it to review when initialization parameters changed and to review database errors or problems recorded in the log.

Summary

Oracle provides a comprehensive framework for you to monitor and manage your Oracle infrastructure. The Oracle Enterprise Management Framework provides a comprehensive set of integrated tools that allow you to perform your traditional tasks more easily and efficiently as well as effectively monitor the various components in the enterprise. This framework, which you can customize, allows for centralized management of your applications using a web-based interface.

The Oracle Enterprise Management Framework is divided into these functional areas:

- Managed targets
- Management Services
- Oracle Management Repository
- Oracle Enterprise Manager 10g Grid Control
- Oracle Enterprise Manager 10g Database Control
- Application Server Control

Managed targets can be administered using the Enterprise Manager. Examples of managed targets include databases, application servers, web servers, applications, and Oracle agents such as the Oracle Net listener and Oracle Connection Manager Listener.

The Oracle Management Service is a Java-based web component that is the actual interface you use to monitor and control managed targets within the Management Framework.

Configuration and monitoring information collected about managed targets is stored in an Oracle Management Repository. The repository is composed of two tablespaces in an Oracle database that contain information about administrators, targets, and applications that are managed within Enterprise Manager.

The Oracle Enterprise Manager 10g Grid Control is a web-based user interface that communicates with and centrally manages all the components within the Oracle Enterprise. The Grid Control agent needs to be started when using this facility.

The Oracle Enterprise Manager 10g Database Control allows you to monitor and administer a single Oracle database instance or a single Real Application Cluster (RAC) environment. The Database Control agent needs to be started when using this facility.

The Application Server Control is a web-based component of Enterprise Manager used to monitor the Oracle Application Server 10g (9.0.4).

You can access and monitor the database using the Database Control facility. You can also interact with the database using the web-based iSQL*Plus facility. The iSQL*Plus server provides many of the same features found in the SQL*Plus command line and Windows utility but is accessed from within a web browser interface. To use the iSQL*Plus interface, you need to start the iSQL*Plus server.

You can use the Database Configuration Assistant (DBCA) to create databases. You can choose from preexisting database definitions stored as XML templates or create a database definition from scratch. All aspects of the database, including database name, file location, sizing, and initialization parameter settings, are defined within the DBCA. You can create a database after completing the database definition, or you can save the definition as a template or series of scripts to be run at a later time. You can also use the DBCA to remove databases or add options to existing databases.

You can manage and create new template definitions using the DBCA interface. This is advantageous because it serves as a way to centrally manage all your database definitions. You can also create new databases from existing databases using the DBCA. This simplifies the cloning of databases.

Oracle uses parameter initialization files to store information about initialization parameters used when an Oracle instance starts. Oracle reads the parameter file to obtain information about how the Oracle instance should be sized and configured upon startup. The parameter file can be either a plain text file, commonly referred to as a PFILE, or a binary file that is referred to as a SPFILE. You can use the Database Control facility to change existing database parameters.

The database needs to be started in order for work to be done against it. You can start up the database in one of several modes: MOUNT, NOMOUNT, and OPEN. You can also start up the database with the RESTRICT option to restrict general access to the database. You can also start up a database using the FORCE option if other startup methods fail. You can start the database using a variety of interfaces, including the Database Control utility, SQL*Plus, and iSQL*Plus.

You can shut down the database using one of several options: NORMAL, TRANSACTIONAL, IMMEDIATE, and ABORT. NORMAL, TRANSACTIONAL, and IMMEDIATE are considered clean shutdowns because no recovery is necessary upon a subsequent startup. You can shut down the database using a variety of interfaces, including the Database Control utility, SQL*Plus, and *i*SQL*Plus.

The alert log contains information about certain activities and errors that occur within your database. The Alert log contains a chronological summary of these events. The alert log contains a wealth of information that you can use to diagnose system problems and review histories of activities that occurred on the system.

Exam Essentials

Define the Oracle Enterprise Management Framework.   Describe what the Oracle Enterprise Management Framework is and the components of the framework. Understand how the components of the Management Framework communicate using agents.

Know how to start and stop Grid Control.   Understand the commands necessary to start and stop the Grid Control. Be able to describe the circumstances in which the Grid Control is utilized in the Oracle enterprise.

Know how to start and stop the EM Database Control.   Know the command necessary to start and stop the EM Database Control. Be able to describe the difference between the Database Control and the Grid Control and under what circumstances the Database Control is used in the Oracle enterprise.

Know how to start and stop the *i*SQL*Plus agent.   You should understand how to stop and start the *i*SQL*Plus agent. The agent must be started in order to use the *i*SQL*Plus tool to interact with the database.

Understand how to login and interact with the database using *i*SQL*Plus.   You need to understand how to connect to the database using the *i*SQL*Plus tool and how to enter and run commands using the tool.

Be able to create a database using the DBCA.   Describe the steps involved in creating a database using the Oracle Database Configuration Assistant (DBCA). Understand how the DBCA uses templates to store information about databases and how templates are used by the DBCA to create databases. Be familiar with the various options available to you when creating an Oracle database using the DBCA.

Know how to delete a database using the DBCA.   Understand how to use the DBCA tool to delete a database.

Know how to manage DBCA templates.   Understand how to use the DBCA to manage templates and the various options available when creating new database templates. Understand what each option is and when it should be used.

Describe the database startup modes.   Understand the various modes of database startup. Understand what each database startup option is and when you might use the option.

Recognize how to start up an Oracle database.   Understand how to use the database tools to start up an Oracle database.

Describe the shutdown database modes.   Understand the various modes of database shutdown. Understand what each database shutdown option is and when you might use the option.

Be able to shut down an Oracle database.   Understand how to use the database tools to shut down an Oracle database.

Know how to manage the Oracle parameter file.   Be able to identify the Oracle parameter file and the different types of parameter files. Also understand how you can change the parameter files.

View and understand the contents of the Oracle alert log.   Be able to identify the Oracle alert log and the kinds of information Oracle writes to the alert log. Be able to identify the database initialization parameter that provides the location of the alert log.

Review Questions

1. You need to start up the *i*SQL*Plus server. Which of the following commands do you use?

   A. `isqlplus startup`

   B. `isqlplusctl startup`

   C. `isqlplusctl start`

   D. `sqlplus start`

2. You need to find the directory where the Oracle alert log is being written. Which initialization parameter contains this information?

   A. `ALERT_LOG_DEST`

   B. `BACKGROUND_DUMP_DEST`

   C. `LOG_DESTINATION`

   D. `INIT_LOG_DUMP_DEST`

3. An Oracle application server is an example of what component in the Oracle Enterprise Management Framework?

   A. Managed targets

   B. Application Entity

   C. Destination

   D. Background Object

   E. None of the above

4. You need to start up the Enterprise Manager Grid Control facility. Which command should you use?

   A. `agctl start agent`

   B. `emctl startup agent`

   C. `agctl enable agent`

   D. `emctl startup framework`

   E. `emctl start agent`

5. All the following are functional areas within the Oracle Enterprise Management Framework except which?

   A. Repository Agent

   B. Management Services

   C. Database Control

   D. Oracle Management Repository

   E. Managed targets

6. You want to view the EMP table structure from within the *i*SQL*Plus interface. Which command produces the desired output?

   A. DEFINE EMP

   B. SHOW EMP

   C. DESCRIBE EMP

   D. DISPLAY EMP

7. All the following are database management options within the Database Configuration Assistant except which?

   A. Change Database Initialization Parameters

   B. Create A Database

   C. Manage Templates

   D. Delete A Database

8. Which of the following is another term for the fully qualified name of a database?

   A. ORACLE SID

   B. Global Database Name

   C. Global identifier

   D. Oracle global name

   E. ORACLE ID

9. Which of the following Oracle accounts is not automatically configured by the DBCA?

   A. SYS

   B. SYSTEM

   C. SYSMAN

   D. DBSNMP

   E. All the above accounts are configured automatically by DBCA.

10. You have worked with your systems administrator to set up predefined disk partitions dedicated to and controlled by Oracle for meeting your database storage requirements. What is another name for this type of storage?

   A. File system storage

   B. Oracle managed storage

   C. Raw devices

   D. Defined storage

   E. None of the above

11. Which new Oracle 10*g* feature provides a centralized location to maintain and manage all the files related to database backups?

- **A.** Archive logging
- **B.** Automated Storage Management
- **C.** Flash Recovery
- **D.** Data Guard

12. Which of the following best describes seed templates?

- **A.** DBCA template definitions that contain database definition information and the actual datafiles and redo log files
- **B.** DBCA template definitions that contain database definition information only
- **C.** DBCA template definitions that contain database definition information and the actual datafiles
- **D.** DBCA template definitions that contain database definition information redo log file and control file definitions
- **E.** None of the above

13. You find a file on disk that has a .DJF extension. What type of information would you expect to be stored in the file?

- **A.** The associated predefined redo logs and datafiles for nonseed templates
- **B.** The associated predefined redo logs and datafiles for seed templates
- **C.** The associated predefined redo logs and control files for seed templates
- **D.** The associated predefined redo logs and control files for nonseed templates

14. Which of the following is not a valid Create A Database Template option in the DBCA?

- **A.** From An Existing Template
- **B.** From An Existing Database And Don't Copy The Data
- **C.** From An Existing Database And Copy The Structure And Data
- **D.** From An Existing Template And Copy The Structure And Data

15. Which of the following startup options does not perform a database recovery?

- **A.** STARTUP
- **B.** STARTUP FORCE RESTRICT
- **C.** STARTUP NOMOUNT
- **D.** STARTUP OPEN
- **E.** STARTUP RESTRICT

16. Which of the following shutdown statements does not perform a clean shutdown?

A. SHUTDOWN ABORT

B. SHUTDOWN TRANSACTIONAL

C. SHUTDOWN

D. SHUTDOWN IMMEDIATE

E. All the above are considered clean shutdowns.

17. You would like to export the system and limit access to only the DBA staff during the export process. Which of the following startup options should you use?

A. STARTUP NOMOUNT RESTRICT

B. STARTUP RESTRICT

C. STARTUP MOUNT RESTRICT

D. STARTUP MOUNT FORCE RESTRICT

18. You want to start up the database using a binary initialization file. What is another name for this file?

A. CONFIGFILE

B. PFILE

C. SPFILE

D. init_pfile.ora

19. Under normal circumstances, which of the following actions or events is not found in the Oracle alert log?

A. Database startup and shutdown information

B. Nondefault initialization parameters

C. ORA-00600 errors

D. New columns added to a user table

20. On your Unix database server, you have installed and configured a database using the DBCA. You need to find out what ports are being used for the various Oracle tools. Where would you find this information?

A. $ORACLE_HOME/bin/portlist.ini

B. $ORACLE_HOME/rdbms/admin/portlist.ini

C. $ORACLE_HOME/install/portlist.ini

D. $ORACLE_HOME/bin/portlist.ini

Answers to Review Questions

1. C. To use the *i*SQL*Plus tool, you need to start the *i*SQL*Plus server. Connect to the location where the server is going to be started, get to a command prompt, and type **isqlplusctl start**. In a Windows environment, you can start the associated service to perform the same task.

2. B. BACKGROUND_DUMP_DEST is the initialization parameter that determines where the Oracle alert log is written. This is a directory path designation.

3. A. In the Oracle Enterprise Management Framework, managed targets can be administered using the Enterprise Manager. Application servers are one example of a managed target. Other examples include databases, web servers, applications, and Oracle agents.

4. E. To use the Grid Control facility, you must start the associated agent process. This process can be started from a command-line prompt using the `emctl start agent` command. In a Windows environment, you can start the agent by starting the appropriate service.

5. A. Management Services, Database Control, Oracle Management Repository, and managed targets are functional areas of the Oracle Enterprise Management Framework.

6. C. You can use the DESCRIBE command within SQL*Plus and *i*SQL*Plus to display the structure of a table or a view. This information includes the column name, column width, datatype, and whether the column allows null values.

7. A. The Database Configuration Assistant lets you create databases, manage templates, add database options, and delete databases. Although you can change initialization parameters when you are defining a database, this is not one of the management options available.

8. B . The Global Database Name is another term for the fully qualified name of a database. The global database name is composed of the database name and database domain.

9. E. The DBCA creates the SYS, SYSTEM, SYSMAN, and DBSNMP accounts by default. You can lock the accounts and set the initial password.

10. C. Raw devices are disk partitions set up as special devices and managed by Oracle. The underlying operating system does not control the reading or writing of information to these special areas of disk.

11. C. The Flash Recovery feature is designed to ease configuration and administration of all aspects of Oracle backup and recovery. It predefines a location of disk to centrally store files that Oracle will use in case database recovery is needed.

12. A. Seed templates are template definitions that contain database definition information and the actual datafiles and redo log files. Nonseed templates contain the database definition but don't contain the actual datafiles and redo log files.

13. B. Files that have a .DJF extension contain the predefined redo logs and datafiles for seed templates.

14. D. From the Template Management screen of the DBCA, you can create a new template from an existing template, create a new template from an existing database and copy the structure only, and create a new template from an existing database, copying the structure and the data. You cannot create a new template from an existing template and copy structure and data.

15. C. Recovery of a database occurs when the database moves from the MOUNT mode to the OPEN mode. All these options attempt to start up and open the database except for option C, which only puts the database in NOMOUNT mode.

16. A. Any time you perform a SHUTDOWN ABORT, Oracle does not perform a clean shutdown. All other types of shutdowns are considered clean shutdowns because Oracle will not have to perform recovery on a subsequent database startup.

17. B. The STARTUP RESTRICT choice opens the database and allows only users with RESTRICTED database access to connect and use it.

18. C. The SPFILE is another term for a server-side binary file that Oracle reads when a database startup is performed. This binary file contains all the nondefault initialization parameters used at startup.

19. D. The Oracle alert log contains a chronological history of administrative events and actions and certain types of database errors that occur within the database. Adding a column to a user table is not an administrative action and is not recorded in the alert log.

20. C. The $ORACLE_HOME/install/portlist.ini file contains information about what ports are being used by the various Oracle tools.

Chapter

3

Database Storage and Schema Objects

ORACLE DATABASE 10*G*: ADMINISTRATION I EXAM OBJECTIVES COVERED IN THIS CHAPTER:

✓ **Storage Structures**

  ▪ Define the purpose of tablespaces and data files.

  ▪ Create tablespaces.

  ▪ Manage tablespaces (alter, drop, generate DDL, take offline, put on line, add data files, make read-only/read-write).

  ▪ Obtain tablespace information from EM and the data dictionary.

  ▪ Drop tablespaces.

  ▪ Describe the default tablespaces.

✓ **Managing Schema Objects**

  ▪ Create and modify tables.

  ▪ Define constraints.

  ▪ View the attributes of a table.

  ▪ View the contents of a table.

  ▪ Create indexes and views.

  ▪ Name database objects.

  ▪ Select appropriate data types.

  ▪ Create and use sequences.

Exam objectives are subject to change at any time without prior notice and at Oracle's sole discretion. Please visit Oracle's Training and Certification website (http://www.oracle.com/education/certification/) for the most current exam objectives listing.

The Oracle Database 10g (Oracle 10g) database stores schema objects—such as tables—logically in tablespaces while physically placing them in data files. An Oracle database consists of two or more tablespaces, and each *tablespace* sits on one or more datafiles. When you create a *table*, you can tell the database which tablespace to put the table's data into.

In this chapter, you will learn how to create and manage tablespaces and about the schema objects that reside in them.

Identifying Segments, Extents, and Data Blocks

Starting with the highest level of Oracle disk-space management are tablespaces. Drilling down, you find *segments* that can reside in only one tablespace. Each segment is constructed from one or more *extents*. Each of these extents can reside in only one datafile. Thus, for a segment to straddle multiple datafiles, it must be constructed from multiple extents, which are located in separate datafiles. An extent is composed of a contiguous set of *data blocks*, which is at the lowest level of space management. A data block is a fixed number of bytes of disk space.

Figure 3.1 shows the relationship among segments, extents, and data blocks.

The data block size is a tablespace attribute. The SYSTEM and SYSAUX tablespaces have the database's standard data block size, defined at creation time by the initialization parameter db_block_size. Other tablespaces can have different data block sizes, defined at tablespace creation time. A database can have as many as five data block sizes. The database always allocates and uses disk space in units of data blocks. The data block size is typically 8KB to 32KB and must be a multiple of the physical block size of the storage device. Larger data block sizes are more common in data warehousing environments where the larger block size can yield shallower Btree indexes and thus better performance.

Managing Tablespaces

Tablespaces physically group schema objects for administration convenience. They bridge physical structures, such as datafiles or extents, and logical structures, such as tables and indexes. Tablespaces can store zero or more segments. Segments are schema objects that require storage outside the data dictionary. Tables and indexes are examples of segments. *Constraints* and *sequences* are examples of schema objects that do not store data outside the data dictionary and are therefore not segments.

FIGURE 3.1   Segment, extents, and data blocks

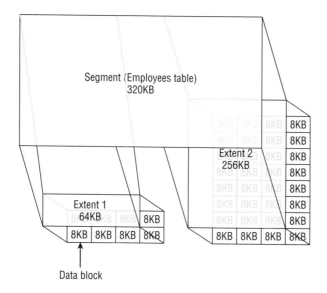

You can place the tables and indexes associated with an application into a set of tablespaces in order to manage that data more easily. You can take a tablespace offline and recover it (potentially to a different point in time), separate from the rest of the database. You can also move it to another database and configure it as read-only so that you do not have to make additional backups of static data.

Another common use for tablespaces is performance related. You can physically separate tables from indexes onto separate disk drives without using a logical volume manager. By placing tables into a tablespace that sits on datafiles residing on one set of disk drives and placing the indexes for those tables into another tablespace that sits on datafiles residing on different disk drives, you can separate table and *index* segments, thereby reducing any disk contention that might otherwise occur on heavily accessed tables. The following example creates two tablespaces—one for tables and one for indexes:

```
CREATE TABLESPACE HR_DATA DATAFILE 'D:\oracle\oradata\ora10\HR_DATA01.DBF'
    SIZE 2G;

CREATE TABLESPACE HR_INDX DATAFILE 'F:\oracle\oradata\ora10\HR_INDX01.DBF'
    SIZE 2G;
```

In the following sections, you will learn how to create and manage tablespaces in your database.

Identifying Default Tablespaces

The SYSTEM tablespace is used for the data dictionary and should not be used to store schema objects other than those that the database places there. The SYSAUX tablespace is new to Oracle10*g* and stores schema objects associated with Oracle-provided features, such as the spatial data option, XMLDB (eXtensible Markup Language DataBase), or Intermedia.

The SYSTEM and SYSAUX tablespaces are always created when the database is created. (SYSAUX is created when you upgrade an older database to Oracle 10g.) One or more temporary tablespaces are usually created in a database as well as an undo tablespace and several application tablespaces. Because SYSTEM and SYSAUX are the only tablespaces always created with the database, they are the default tablespaces. You should not, however, continue to use them as the default tablespace for your users or applications. In the following sections, you will learn how to create additional tablespaces and enable their use as better defaults.

Creating and Maintaining Tablespaces

You create tablespaces using either the CREATE DATABASE or the CREATE TABLESPACE statement. You must make several choices when creating a tablespace: whether to make the tablespace bigfile or smallfile, whether to manage extents locally or with the dictionary, and whether to manage segment space automatically or manually. Additionally, there are specialized tablespaces for temporary segments and undo segments.

Creating Bigfile and Smallfile Tablespaces

New to Oracle10g is the bigfile tablespace. *Bigfile tablespaces* are built on a single datafile (or temp file), which can be as many as 2^{32} data blocks in size. So, a bigfile tablespace that uses 8KB data blocks can be as much as 32TB in size.

Bigfile tablespaces are intended for very large databases. When a very large database has thousands of read/write datafiles, operations that must update the datafile headers, such as checkpoints, can take a relatively long time. If you reduce the number of datafiles, these operations can complete faster.

To create a bigfile tablespace, use the keyword BIGFILE in the CREATE statement, like this:

```
CREATE BIGFILE TABLESPACE hist2004apr
DATAFILE '/ORADATA/PROD/HIST2004APR.DBF' SIZE 25G;
```

Smallfile tablespace is the new name for the old Oracle tablespace datafile option. With a smallfile tablespace, you can have multiple datafiles for a tablespace. Each datafile can be as many as 2^{22} data blocks in size. So datafiles in a smallfile tablespace that uses 8KB data blocks are limited to 32GB. The smallfile tablespace can have as many as 1,022 datafiles, limiting the 8KB data block tablespace to slightly less than 32TB—about the same as a bigfile tablespace. The SYSTEM and SYSAUX tablespaces are always created as smallfile tablespaces.

To create a smallfile tablespace, either omit the keyword BIGFILE or explicitly use the keyword SMALLFILE, like this:

```
CREATE TABLESPACE hist2004apr
DATAFILE '/ORADATA/PROD/HIST2004APR.DBF' SIZE 25G;
```

If you are not using a logical volume manager that supports dynamic volume resizing as well striping and/or mirroring, do not use bigfile tablespaces.

Working with Oracle Managed File Tablespaces

Oracle Managed Files (OMF) can ease the administration of files used by an Oracle10*g* database. Using OMF, you specify operations in terms of tablespaces and not operating system files. You don't explicitly name datafiles or temp files; the database does this for you.

To enable OMF, set the initialization parameter DB_CREATE_FILE_DEST to the directory where you want the database to create and manage your data and temp files, like this:

```
ALTER SYSTEM SET
  db_create_file_dest = 'D:\oracle\oradata\ora10\OMF'
  SCOPE=BOTH;
```

When creating a tablespace using OMF, you simply omit the filename:

```
CREATE TABLESPACE hr_data;
```

Oracle creates a tablespace using a unique datafile name, such as O1_MF_HR_DATA_ 0DC3Z9WL_.DBF. This datafile will have auto extend enabled and be 100MB unless you specify a different size. By default, the tablespace is a smallfile tablespace, but you can specify a bigfile tablespace by including the keyword BIGFILE, like this:

```
CREATE BIGFILE TABLESPACE hr_data;
```

If you work in an environment in which many databases are managed under both Windows and Unix, you can use OMF to eliminate operating system–specific filenames from your administrative scripts.

Choosing Extent Management

You can use tablespaces with either local *extent management* or the older technique of dictionary extent management. With dictionary extent management, the database tracks free and used extents in the data dictionary, changing the FET$ and UET$ tables with recursive SQL. With local extent management, the database tracks extents through the use of bitmaps, eliminating the recursive SQL. Local extent management is the default if not specified and is generally the preferred technique.

With locally managed tablespaces, you have two options for how extents are allocated: UNIFORM or AUTOALLOCATE. The UNIFORM option tells the database to allocate and deallocate extents in the tablespace with the same unvarying size that you can specify or let extents default to 1MB. UNIFORM is the default for temporary tablespaces and cannot be specified for undo tablespaces. To create consistent 100MB extents, use the clause EXTENT MANAGEMENT LOCAL UNIFORM SIZE 100M in the CREATE TABLESPACE statement. Here is an example:

```
CREATE TABLESPACE hist2004apr
DATAFILE '/ORADATA/PROD/HIST2004APR.DBF' SIZE 25G
EXTENT MANAGEMENT LOCAL UNIFORM SIZE 100M;
```

AUTOALLOCATE, on the other hand, tells the database to vary the size of extents for each segment. For example, on Windows and Linux with 8KB data blocks, each segment starts out with

64KB extents for the first 16 extents, and then extents increase in size to 1MB for the next 63 extents. The size then increases to 8MB for the next 120 extents, then 64MB, and so on as the segment grows. This algorithm allows small segments to remain small and large segments to grow without gaining too many extents. AUTOALLOCATE is best used for a general-purpose mixture of small and large tables. Here is an example of creating a tablespace using AUTOALLOCATE:

```
CREATE TABLESPACE hist2004apr
DATAFILE '/ORADATA/PROD/HIST2004APR.DBF' SIZE 25G
EXTENT MANAGEMENT LOCAL AUTOALLOCATE;
```

You can convert a tablespace from dictionary extent management to local extent management and back with the Oracle-supplied PL/SQL package DBMS_SPACE_ADMIN. The SYSTEM tablespace and any temporary tablespaces, however, cannot be converted from local to the older style dictionary management.

Choosing Segment Space Management

For tablespaces that have local extent management, you can use either manual or automatic *segment space management*. Manual segment space management exists for backward compatibility and uses free block lists to identify the data blocks available for inserts together with the parameters PCT_FREE and PCT_USED, which control when a block is made available for inserts.

After each INSERT or UPDATE, the database compares the remaining free space in that data block with the segment's PCT_FREE setting. If the data block has less than PCT_FREE free space (meaning that it is almost full), it is taken off the free block list and is no longer available for inserts. The remaining free space is reserved for update operations that may increase the size of rows in that data block. After each UPDATE or DELETE, the database compares the used space in that data block with that segment's PCT_USED setting. If the data block has less than PCT_USED used space, the data block is deemed empty enough for inserts and is placed on the free block list.

To specify manual segment space management, use the SEGMENT SPACE MANAGEMENT MANUAL clause of the CREATE TABLESPACE statement, or simply omit the SEGMENT SPACE MANAGEMENT clause. Although Oracle strongly recommends AUTOMATIC segment space management for permanent, locally managed tablespaces, the default behavior of Oracle 10*g* is MANUAL. Here is a statement that creates a tablespace with manual segment space management:

```
CREATE TABLESPACE hist2004apr
DATAFILE '/ORADATA/PROD/HIST2004APR.DBF' SIZE 25G
EXTENT MANAGEMENT LOCAL AUTOALLOCATE
SEGMENT SPACE MANAGEMENT MANUAL;
```

When automatic segment space management is specified, bitmaps are used instead of free lists to identify which data blocks are available for inserts. The parameters PCT_FREE and PCT_USED are ignored for segments in tablespaces with automatic segment space management. Automatic segment space management is available only on tablespaces configured for local extent management; it is not available for temporary or system tablespaces. Automatic segment space management performs better and reduces your maintenance tasks, making it the preferred technique.

To specify automatic segment space management, use the SEGMENT SPACE MANAGEMENT AUTO clause of the CREATE TABLESPACE statement, like this:

```
CREATE TABLESPACE hist2004apr
DATAFILE '/ORADATA/PROD/HIST2004APR.DBF' SIZE 25G
EXTENT MANAGEMENT LOCAL AUTOALLOCATE
SEGMENT SPACE MANAGEMENT AUTO;
```

 Although the name segment space management sounds similar to extent management, it is quite different and can be more accurately regarded as free space management. Moreover, because the default behavior of the database differs from Oracle's recommended implementation, be sure that you understand these options.

Creating Temporary Tablespaces

A temporary tablespace is used for temporary segments, which are created, managed, and dropped by the database as needed. These temporary segments are most commonly generated during sorting operations such as ORDER BY, GROUP BY, and CREATE INDEX. They are also generated during other operations such as hash joins or inserts into temporary tables.

You create a temporary tablespace at database creation time with the DEFAULT TEMPORARY TABLESPACE clause of the CREATE DATABASE statement or after the database is created with the CREATE TEMPORARY TABLESPACE statement, like this:

```
CREATE TEMPORARY TABLESPACE temp
TEMPFILE 'C:\ORACLE\ORADATA\ORA10\TEMP01.DBF' SIZE 2G
;
```

Notice that the keyword TEMPFILE is used instead of DATAFILE. Temp files are only available with temporary tablespaces, never need to be backed up, and do not log data changes in the redo logs.

 Although it is always a good practice to create a separate temporary tablespace, it is required when the SYSTEM tablespace is locally managed.

Temporary tablespaces are created using temp files instead of datafiles. Temp files are allocated slightly differently than datafiles. Although datafiles are completely allocated and initialized at creation time, temp files are not always guaranteed to allocate the disk space specified. This means that on some Unix systems a temp file will not actually allocate disk space until a sorting operation requires it. Although this delayed allocation approach allows rapid file creation, it can cause problems down the road if you have not reserved the space that may be needed at runtime.

Workaround for Deferred Temp File Disk Space Allocations

A workaround for allocating temp file space at runtime is to preallocate it, just like you do with a datafile. In fact, you first allocate it as a datafile and then drop the tablespace, leaving the file. Finally, you create your temp tablespace reusing the old datafile as a temp file.

```
-- first create it as a permanent tablespace
-- to force the disk space to be allocated
CREATE TABLESPACE temp
DATAFILE '/ORADATA/PROD/TEMP01.DBF' SIZE 2G;


-- dropping the tablespace does not remove
-- the file from the file system
DROP TABLESPACE temp;


-- the keyword REUSE is needed to use the existing
-- file created in the previous steps
CREATE TEMPORARY TABLESPACE temp
TEMPFILE '/ORADATA/PROD/TEMP01.DBF' SIZE 2G REUSE
```

Creating Undo Tablespaces

An undo tablespace stores undo segments, which are used by the database for several purposes, including the following:

- Rolling back a transaction explicitly with a ROLLBACK statement
- Rolling back a transaction implicitly (for example, through recovery of a failed transaction)
- Reconstructing a read-consistent image of data
- Recovering from logical corruptions

To create an undo tablespace at database creation time, set the initialization parameter UNDO_MANAGEMENT=AUTO and include an UNDO TABLESPACE clause in your CREATE DATABASE statement, like this:

```
CREATE DATABASE TEST
  CONTROLFILE REUSE
  LOGFILE
     GROUP 1 'C:\ORADATA\TEST\REDO01.LOG'  SIZE 10M,
     GROUP 2 'C:\ORADATA\TEST\REDO02.LOG'  SIZE 10M,
     GROUP 3 'C:\ORADATA\TEST\REDO03.LOG'  SIZE 10M
  DATAFILE  'C:\ORADATA\TEST\SYSTEM01.DBF' SIZE 500M
     AUTOEXTEND ON NEXT 50M MAXSIZE UNLIMITED
```

```
   EXTENT MANAGEMENT LOCAL
SYSAUX DATAFILE 'C:\ORADATA\TEST\SYSAUX01.DBF' SIZE 250M
   AUTOEXTEND ON NEXT 50M MAXSIZE UNLIMITED
   EXTENT MANAGEMENT LOCAL
DEFAULT TEMPORARY TABLESPACE temp
   TEMPFILE 'C:\ORADATA\TEST\TEMP01.DBF' SIZE 100M
   AUTOEXTEND ON NEXT 100M MAXSIZE 8000M
UNDO TABLESPACE undo
   DATAFILE 'C:\ORADATA\TEST\undo01.DBF' SIZE 500M
   AUTOEXTEND ON NEXT 100M MAXSIZE UNLIMITED
   EXTENT MANAGEMENT LOCAL
CHARACTER SET WE8MSWIN1252
NATIONAL CHARACTER SET AL16UTF16
USER SYS    IDENTIFIED BY SOUPERSEEKRET
USER SYSTEM IDENTIFIED BY MYSEEKRET
;
```

You can create an undo tablespace after database creation with the CREATE UNDO TABLESPACE statement, like this:

```
CREATE UNDO TABLESPACE undo
DATAFILE '/ORADATA/PROD/UNDO01.DBF' SIZE 2G;
```

 Although it is always a good practice to create a separate undo tablespace, it is required when the system tablespace is locally managed.

Removing a Tablespace

To remove a tablespace from the database, use the DROP TABLESPACE statement. The optional clause INCLUDING CONTENTS recursively removes any segments (tables, indexes, and so on) in the tablespace, like this:

```
DROP TABLESPACE dba_sandbox INCLUDING CONTENTS;
```

Dropping a tablespace does not automatically remove the datafiles from the file system. Use the additional clause INCLUDING CONTENTS AND DATAFILES to remove the underlying datafiles as well as the stored objects, like this:

```
DROP TABLESPACE hr_data INCLUDING CONTENTS AND DATAFILES;
```

Modifying Tablespaces

Use an ALTER TABLESPACE statement to modify the attributes of a tablespace. Some of the actions that you can perform on tablespaces include renaming the tablespace, adding a datafile to a smallfile tablespace, taking a tablespace offline or online, making a tablespace read-only or read/write, or changing the user-managed backup state. To rename a tablespace, use an ALTER TABLESPACE statement with a RENAME clause, like this:

```
ALTER TABLESPACE fin RENAME TO payables;
```

The following sections detail additional modifications that you may perform on your tablespaces.

Adding a Datafile to a Tablespace

Smallfile tablespaces can have multiple datafiles and can thus be spread over multiple file systems without engaging a logical volume manager. To add a datafile to a smallfile tablespace, use an ADD DATAFILE clause with the ALTER TABLESPACE statement. For example, the following statement adds a 2GB datafile on in the /u02 file system to the receivables tablespace:

```
ALTER TABLESPACE receivables ADD DATAFILE
  '/u02/oradata/ORA10/receivables01.dbf'
  SIZE 2G;
```

Taking a Tablespace Offline or Online

You need to take a tablespace offline to perform some maintenance operations, such as recovering the tablespace or moving the datafiles to a new location. Use the OFFLINE clause with an ALTER TABLESPACE statement to take a tablespace offline. For example, to take the receivables tablespace offline to move a datafile from the H drive to the G drive, follow these steps.

1. Take the receivables tablespace offline:

    ```
    ALTER TABLESPACE receivables OFFLINE;
    ```

2. Use an operating system program to physically move the file, such as Copy in Microsoft Windows or cp in Unix.

3. Tell the database about the new location:

    ```
    ALTER TABLESPACE receivables RENAME DATAFILE
        'H:\ORACLE\ORADATA\ORA10\RECEIVABLES02.DBF'
      TO 'G:\ORACLE\ORADATA\ORA10\RECEIVABLES02.DBF' ;
    ```

4. Bring the tablespace back online:

    ```
    ALTER TABLESPACE receivables ONLINE;
    ```

Making a Tablespace Read-Only

If a tablespace contains static data, it can be marked read-only. Tablespaces that contain historic or reference data are typical candidates for read-only. When a tablespace is read-only, it does not have to be backed up with the nightly or weekly database backups. One backup after being marked read-only is all that is needed for future recoveries. Tables in a read-only tablespace can only be selected from; their rows cannot be inserted, updated, or deleted.

Use a READ ONLY clause with an ALTER TABLESPACE statement to mark a tablespace read-only. For example, to mark the SALES2003 tablespace read-only, execute the following:

```
ALTER TABLESPACE sales2003 READ ONLY;
```

If you need to make changes to a table in a read-only tablespace, make it read writable again with the key words READ WRITE, like this:

```
ALTER TABLESPACE sales2003 READ WRITE;
```

Putting a Tablespace in Backup Mode

If you perform non-RMAN (non–Recovery Manager) online backups, sometimes called user-managed backups, you need to put a tablespace in backup mode before you begin to copy the datafiles using an operating system program. While the tablespace is in backup mode, the database continues to write data to the datafiles (checkpoints occur), but the occurrence of these checkpoints is not recorded in the header blocks of the datafiles. This omission tells the database that recovery may be needed if the database instance gets terminated abruptly.

While a tablespace is in backup mode, some additional information is written to the redo logs to assist with recovery, if needed.

  See Chapter 10, "Implementing Database Backups" for more information on backups, and see Chapter 11, "Implementing Database Recovery," for more information on recovery.

Some companies perform backups by splitting a third mirror, mounting these mirrored file systems onto another server, and then copying them to tape. To safely split the mirror, alter all your tablespaces into backup mode, make the split, and then alter all the tablespaces out of backup mode. Put them into backup mode like this:

```
ALTER TABLESPACE system BEGIN BACKUP;
```

Use the keywords END BACKUP to take a tablespace out of backup mode, like this:

```
ALTER TABLESPACE system END BACKUP;
```

If you forget to take a tablespace out of backup mode, the next time you bounce your database, it will see that the checkpoint number in the control file is later than the one in the datafile headers and report that media recovery is required.

Obtaining Tablespace Information

You can get information on tablespaces using the Enterprise Manager (EM) Database Control from several data dictionary views, such as the following:

- DBA_TABLESPACES
- DBA_DATA_FILES

- DBA_TEMP_FILES
- V$TABLESPACE

The DBA_TABLESPACES *view* has one row for each tablespace in the database and includes the following information:

- The tablespace block size
- The tablespace status: online, offline, or read-only
- The contents of the tablespace: undo, temporary, or permanent
- Whether it uses dictionary or locally managed extents
- Whether the segment space management is automatic or manual
- Whether it is a bigfile or smallfile tablespace

To get a listing of all the tablespaces in the database, their status, contents, extent management policy, and segment management policy, run the following query:

```
SELECT tablespace_name, status,contents
      ,extent_management extents
      ,segment_space_management free_space
FROM dba_tablespaces
```

TABLESPACE_NAME	STATUS	CONTENTS	EXTENTS	FREE_SPACE
SYSTEM	ONLINE	PERMANENT	LOCAL	MANUAL
UNDOTBS1	ONLINE	UNDO	LOCAL	MANUAL
SYSAUX	ONLINE	PERMANENT	LOCAL	AUTO
TEMP	ONLINE	TEMPORARY	LOCAL	MANUAL
USERS	ONLINE	PERMANENT	LOCAL	AUTO
EXAMPLE	ONLINE	PERMANENT	LOCAL	AUTO
DATA	ONLINE	PERMANENT	LOCAL	AUTO
INDX	ONLINE	PERMANENT	LOCAL	AUTO

The V$TABLESPACE view also has one row per tablespace, but it includes some information other than DBA_TABLESPACES, such as whether the tablespace participates in database flashback operations:

```
SELECT name, bigfile, flashback_on
FROM v$tablespace;
```

NAME	BIGFILE	FLASHBACK_ON
SYSTEM	NO	YES
UNDOTBS1	NO	YES
SYSAUX	NO	YES
USERS	NO	YES

```
TEMP       NO      YES
EXAMPLE    NO      YES
DATA       NO      YES
INDX       NO      YES
```

 See Chapter 10 for more information on flashback operations.

The DBA_DATA_FILES and DBA_TEMP_FILES views contain information on datafiles and temp files, respectively. This information includes the tablespace name, filename, file size, and autoextend settings.

```
SELECT tablespace_name, file_name, bytes/1024 kbytes
FROM dba_data_files
UNION ALL
SELECT tablespace_name, file_name, bytes/1024 kbytes
FROM dba_temp_files;
```

```
TABLESPACE FILE_NAME                                    KBYTES
---------- -------------------------------------------- -------
USERS      C:\ORACLE\ORADATA\ORA10\USERS01.DBF          102400
SYSAUX     C:\ORACLE\ORADATA\ORA10\SYSAUX01.DBF         256000
UNDOTBS1   C:\ORACLE\ORADATA\ORA10\UNDOTBS01.DBF         51200
SYSTEM     C:\ORACLE\ORADATA\ORA10\SYSTEM01.DBF         460800
EXAMPLE    C:\ORACLE\ORADATA\ORA10\EXAMPLE01.DBF        153600
INDX       C:\ORACLE\ORADATA\ORA10\INDX01.DBF           102400
TEMP       C:\ORACLE\ORADATA\ORA10\TEMP01.DBF            51200
```

In addition to the data dictionary, tablespace information can be obtained from several sources. Some of these sources are the DDL and the Enterprise Manager.

Generating DDL for a Tablespace

Another way to quickly identify the attributes of a tablespace is to ask the database to generate DDL to re-create the tablespace. The CREATE TABLESPACE statement that results contains the attributes for the tablespace. Use the PL/SQL package DBMS_METADATA to generate DDL for your database objects. For example, to generate the DDL for the USERS tablespace, execute this:

```
SELECT DBMS_METADATA.GET_DDL('TABLESPACE','USERS')
FROM dual;
```

The output from this statement is a CREATE TABLESPACE statement that contains all the attributes for the USERS tablespace:

```
CREATE TABLESPACE "USERS" DATAFILE
```

```
'C:\ORACLE\ORADATA\ORA10\USERS01.DBF' SIZE 5242880
AUTOEXTEND ON NEXT 1310720 MAXSIZE 32767M
LOGGING ONLINE PERMANENT BLOCKSIZE 8192
EXTENT MANAGEMENT LOCAL AUTOALLOCATE SEGMENT SPACE
MANAGEMENT AUTO;
```

Obtaining Tablespace Information with the Enterprise Manager

Instead of querying the data dictionary views with a command-line tool such as SQL*Plus or
*i*SQL*Plus, you can use the interactive GUI tool EM Database Control to monitor and manage
database structures, including tablespaces. The EM Database Control is an alternative to a command-line interface.

To use the Database Control, follow these steps:

1. Point your browser to the Enterprise Manager URL for your database.

2. Log in to the database, and navigate to the Administration tab of the main screen, which
   is shown in Figure 3.2.

FIGURE 3.2 The Enterprise Manager Administration tab

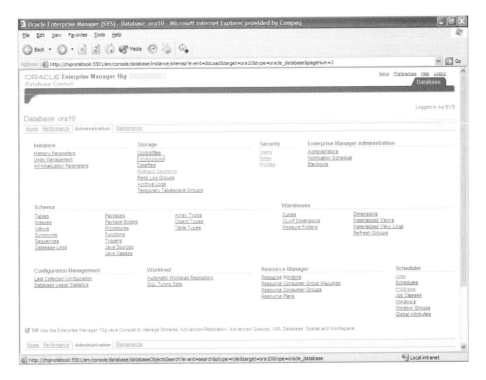

3. Click the Tablespaces link under the heading Storage to display a list of tablespaces like that shown in Figure 3.3.

4. Click the radio button next to the tablespace that you want to work with, and then click the Edit button. You can navigate to the tablespace General, Storage, and Thresholds edit screens, as shown in Figure 3.4.

You use the screens and options in EM Database Control to manipulate and change your tablespaces with many of the same options that the command-line interface supports. For example, to increase the size of the datafile in the USER3_DATA tablespace, click the edit button next to the datafile. The EM Database Control displays the tablespace edit screen, as shown in Figure 3.5.

Edit the File Size field, increasing it to 300 MB. The change will be applied when you click Continue.

FIGURE 3.3 The Enterprise Manager Tablespaces screen

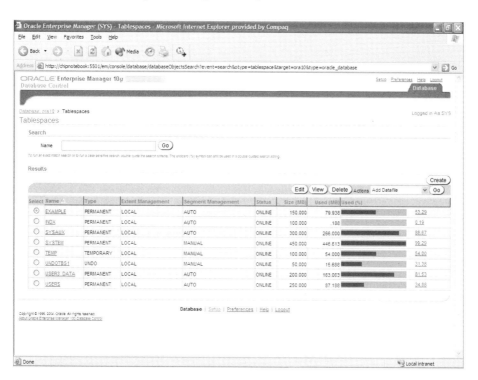

FIGURE 3.4   The Enterprise Manager tablespace editor

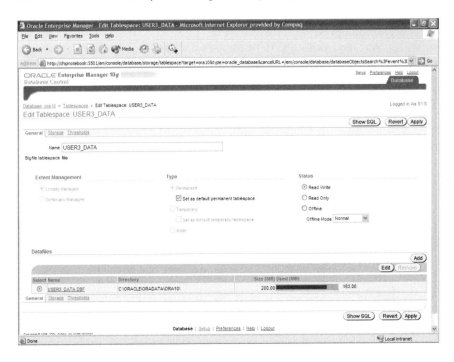

FIGURE 3.5   Editing the datafile size

Managing Datafiles

If you are not using OMF, you will need to manage datafiles yourself. The database will create or reuse one or more datafiles in the sizes and locations that you specify whenever you create a tablespace. A datafile belongs to only one tablespace and only one database at a time. Temp files are a special variety of datafile that are used in temporary tablespaces. When the database creates or reuses a datafile, the operating system file is allocated and initialized—filled with a regular pattern of mostly binary zeros. This initialization will not occur with temp files.

Operations that you may need to perform on datafiles include the following:

- Resizing them

- Taking them offline or online

- Moving (renaming) them

- Recovering them

A useful technique for managing disk space used by datafiles is to enable AUTOEXTEND, which tells the database to automatically enlarge a datafile when the tablespace runs out of free space. The AUTOEXTEND attributes apply to individual datafiles and not to the tablespace.

To resize a datafile manually, use the ALTER DATABASE DATAFILE statement, like this:

```
ALTER DATABASE DATAFILE
   'C:\ORACLE\ORADATA\ORA10\DATA01.DBF' RESIZE 2000M;
```

To configure a datafile to automatically enlarge as needed by adding 100MB at a time up to a maximum of 8,000MB, execute the following:

```
ALTER DATABASE DATAFILE
   'C:\ORACLE\ORADATA\ORA10\DATA01.DBF'
AUTOEXTEND ON NEXT 100M MAXSIZE 8000M;
```

Even if you do not plan to manage disk space using AUTOEXTEND, consider enabling it on your datafiles to avoid out-of-space failures in your applications.

To relocate a datafile, take it offline, move it using an operating system command, rename it, recover it (sync the file header with the rest of the database), and then bring it back online. Here is an example:

1. Take it offline:

```
ALTER DATABASE DATAFILE
   'C:\ORACLE\DATA02.DBF' OFFLINE;
```

2. Copy it:

```
HOST COPY C:\ORACLE\DATA02.DBF
   C:\ORACLE\ORADATA\ORA10\DATA02.DBF
```

3. Change the filename in the control files:

```
ALTER DATABASE RENAME FILE
   'C:\ORACLE\DATA02.DBF' TO
   'C:\ORACLE\ORADATA\ORA10\DATA02.DBF';
```

4. Sync the file header with the database:

```
RECOVER DATAFILE 'C:\ORACLE\ORADATA\ORA10\DATA02.DBF';
```

5. Bring it back online so it can be used.

```
ALTER DATABASE DATAFILE
   'C:\ORACLE\ORADATA\ORA10\DATA02.DBF' ONLINE;
```

Working with Schema Objects

A *schema* is collection of database objects owned by a specific database user. In an Oracle10g database, the schema has the same name as the database user, so the two terms are synonymous.

Schema objects include the segments (tables, indexes, and so on) you have seen in tablespaces as well as nonsegment database objects owned by a user. These nonsegment objects include constraints, views, synonyms, procedures, and packages. Database objects that are not owned by one user and thus are not schema objects include roles, tablespaces, and directories.

In this section, you will learn about the built-in datatypes that Oracle provides for use in your tables, how to create and manage tables, how to implement business rules as constraints on your tables, and how to improve the performance of your tables with indexes. Finally, we will briefly cover other schema objects that you can use in your applications.

Specifying Datatypes

Oracle10g has several built-in datatypes that you can use in your tables. These datatypes fall into six major categories:

- Character
- Numeric
- Datetime
- LOB (Large Object)
- ROWID
- Binary

Oracle 10g supports additional datatypes, but we will focus on these six major categories.

Character Datatypes

Character datatypes store alphanumeric data in the database character set or the Unicode character set. The database character set is specified when the database is created and indicates which languages can be represented in the database. The US7ASCII character set supports the English language as well as any other language that uses a subset of the English alphabet. The WE8ISO8859P1 character set supports several European languages, including English, French, German, and Spanish. The Unicode character set AL16UTF16 is intended to concurrently support every known language, although there are a few not yet included, such as Egyptian hieroglyphs and cuneiform.

The database character datatypes are as follows:

CHAR(`size [byte|char]`), NCHAR(`size`)   Fixed width types that always store the column-width amount of data, right padding with spaces as needed. The size specification is in bytes if you do not include the keyword `char`. The NCHAR variation uses the Unicode character set, and the size is always given in characters.

VARCHAR(`size [byte|char]`), VARCHAR2(`size [byte|char]`), NVARCHAR2(`size`)   Variable width types. Unlike their CHAR counterparts, the VARCHAR types store only the amount of data that is actually used. The size specification is in bytes if you do not include the keyword `char`. The NVARCHAR2 variation uses the Unicode character set and is always given in characters. VARCHAR and VARCHAR2 are synonymous in Oracle10g, but Oracle reserves the right to change comparison semantics of VARCHAR in future releases; so the VARCHAR2 type is preferred.

LONG   A legacy datatype that exists for backward compatibility. It stores variable-length alphanumeric data up to 2GB in size. There are many restrictions on the usage of the columns of type LONG: there is a limit of one column of type LONG per table, tables containing a LONG cannot be partitioned, LONG datatypes cannot be used in subqueries, and few functions will work with LONG data. The CLOB datatype is the preferred datatype for character data larger than VARCHAR2.

Here is an example of the character datatypes in use:

```
CREATE TABLE number_samples
(name          VARCHAR2(48)
,country_code  CHAR(2)
,address       NVARCHAR2(100)
,city          NVARCHAR2(64)
);
```

Numeric Datatypes

Numeric datatypes can store positive and negative fixed and floating-point numbers, zero, infinity, and the special value Not A Number.

The database numeric datatypes are as follows:

NUMBER[(`precision[, scale]`)]   Stores zero, positive numbers, and negative numbers. `precision` is the total number of digits and defaults to 38—the maximum. `Scale` is the number of digits to the right of the decimal point and defaults to 0. A negative scale tells the database to round off data to the left of the decimal point. *scale* has a valid range of −84 to 127. Table 3.1 shows how *precision* and *scale* affect the way number types are stored.

TABLE 3.1 Precision, Scale, and Rounding

Specification	Actual Value	Stored Value
NUMBER(11,4)	12345.6789	12345.6789
NUMBER(11,2)	12345.6789	12345.68
NUMBER(11,-2)	12345.6789	12300
NUMBER(5,2)	12345.6789	Error – Precision is too small
NUMBER(5,2)	123456	Error – Precision is too small

BINARY_FLOAT, BINARY_DOUBLE   Store single-precision and double-precision floating-point data or one of the special floating-point values listed in Table 3.2.

TABLE 3.2 Floating-Point Constants

Constant	Description
BINARY_FLOAT_NAN	Not a number
BINARY_FLOAT_INFINITY	Infinite
BINARY_FLOAT_MAX_NORMAL	3.40282347e+38
BINARY_FLOAT_MIN_NORMAL	1.17549435e-038
BINARY_FLOAT_MAX_SUBNORMAL	1.17549421e-038
BINARY_FLOAT_MIN_SUBNORMAL	1.40129846e-045
BINARY_DOUBLE_NAN	Not a number
BINARY_DOUBLE_INFINITY	Infinite
BINARY_DOUBLE_MAX_NORMAL	1.7976931348623157E+308
BINARY_DOUBLE_MIN_NORMAL	2.2250738585072014E-308

TABLE 3.2   Floating-Point Constants *(continued)*

Constant	Description
BINARY_DOUBLE_MAX_SUBNORMAL	2.2250738585072009E-308
BINARY_DOUBLE_MIN_SUBNORMAL	4.9406564584124654E-324

Here is an example of the number datatypes in use:

```
CREATE TABLE number_samples
(id       NUMBER
,cost     NUMBER(11,2)
,mass     BINARY_FLOAT
,velocity BINARY_DOUBLE
);
```

Datetime Datatypes

Oracle10*g* has several datetime datatypes that can store dates, time, and time periods:

DATE   Stores a date and time with a one-second granularity. The date portion can be from January 1, 4712 BCE to December 31, 9999. The time portion of a DATE datatype defaults to midnight, or 00:00:00 hours, minutes, and seconds.

TIMESTAMP[(*precision*)]   Stores a date and time with subsecond granularity. The date portion can be from January 1, 4712 BCE to December 31, 9999. *precision* is the number of digits of subsecond granularity. *precision* defaults to 6 and can range from 0 to 9.

TIMESTAMP[(*precision*)] WITH TIMEZONE   Extends the TIMESTAMP datatype by also storing a time zone offset. This time zone offset defines the difference (in hours and minutes) from the local time zone and UTC (Coordinated Universal Time, also known as Greenwich mean time or GMT). Like TIMESTAMP, *precision* defaults to 6 and can range from 0 to 9. Two TIMESTAMP WITH TIMEZONE values are considered equal if they represent the same chronological time. For example, 10:00AM EST is equal to 9:00AM CST or 15:00 UTC.

TIMESTAMP[(*precision*)] WITH LOCAL TIMEZONE   Extends the TIMESTAMP datatype by also storing a time zone offset. The TIMESTAMP WITH LOCAL TIMEZONE datatype does not store the time zone offset with the column data. Instead, the timestamp value is converted from the local time to the database time zone. Likewise, when data is retrieved, it is converted from the database time zone to the local time zone. Like TIMESTAMP, *precision* defaults to 6 and can range from 0 to 9.

INTERVAL YEAR[(*precision*)] TO MONTH   Stores a period of time in years and months. *precision* is the maximum number of digits needed for the year portion of this period, with a default of 2 and a range of 0 to 9. Use the INTERVAL YEAR TO MONTH datatype to store the difference between two datetime values if yearly or monthly granularity is needed.

INTERVAL DAY[(*d_precision*)] TO SECOND[(*s_precision*)]   Stores a period of time in days, hours, minutes, and seconds. *d_precision* is the maximum number of digits needed for the day portion of this period, with a default of 2 and a range of 0 to 9. *s_precision* is the number of digits to the right of the decimal point needed for the fractional seconds portion of this period, with a default of 6 and a range of 0 to 9. Use the INTERVAL DAY TO SECOND datatype to store the difference between two datetime values if granularity down to a fractional second is needed.

Here is an example of the datetime datatypes in use:

```
CREATE TABLE datetime_samples
(dt        DATE
,ts        TIMESTAMP(3)
,ts2       TIMESTAMP
,tstz      TIMESTAMP(3) WITH TIME ZONE
,tsltz     TIMESTAMP WITH LOCAL TIME ZONE
,long_duration  INTERVAL YEAR(4) TO MONTH
,short_duration INTERVAL DAY(3) TO SECOND(2)
);
```

LOB Datatypes

As the name implies, LOB datatypes store large objects, up to $2^{32} - 1$, or 4,294,967,295 data blocks. With an 8KB data block size, this comes out to about 32TB per field. LOBs are designed for text, image video, audio, and spatial data. When you create a table with LOB columns, you can specify a different tablespace and different attributes for the LOB data than for the rest of the table. The LOB locator, a kind of pointer, is stored inline with the row and is used to access the LOB data.

The database LOB datatypes are as follows:

CLOB   Stores variable-length character data.

NCLOB   Stores variable-length character data using the Unicode character set.

BLOB   Stores binary variable-length data inside the database. BLOB data does not undergo character set conversion when passed between databases or between client and server processes.

BFILE   Stores binary variable-length data outside the database. BFILEs are limited to a maximum of 4GB of data and even less in some operating systems.

Here is an example of the LOB datatypes in use:

```
CREATE TABLE lob_examples
( id NUMBER
, name VARCHAR2(32)
, description VARCHAR2(4000)
```

```
, definition CLOB
, mp3 BLOB
)TABLESPACE USERS
LOB (definition) STORE AS
    (TABLESPACE user3_data);
```

ROWID Datatypes

ROWIDs are either physical or logical addresses that uniquely identify each row in an Oracle10*g* table. The database ROWID datatypes are as follows:

ROWID   Stores the base64-encoded physical address of any row in a heap-organized table in the database. ROWIDs incorporate the Object ID (OID), relative file number, block number, and row slot within the block. They are used internally in indexes and via the ROWID pseudocolumn in SQL. You can use ROWID datatype columns in your tables to store "row pointers" to rows in other tables.

UROWID (**Universal ROWID**)   Stores the base64-encoded string representing the logical address of a row in an index-organized table.

Here is an example of the ROWID datatypes in use:

```
CREATE TABLE rowid_samples
(tab_rowid        ROWID
,iot_rowid        UROWID
);
```

Binary Datatypes

Oracle10*g* binary datatypes can be used to store unstructured data. Unlike regular character data, binary data does not undergo character set conversion when passed from database to database via a database link or export/import utility or when passed between database client and server processes.

The database binary datatypes are as follows:

RAW(*size*)   Stores unstructured data up to 2000 bytes in size.

LONG RAW   Stores unstructured data up to 2GB in size. Like the LONG datatype, it exists to support backward compatibility, and there are several restrictions on LONG RAW columns—Oracle discourages their use. Consider using the BLOB datatype instead.

Here is an example of the binary datatypes in use:

```
CREATE TABLE binary_samples
(init_string    RAW(2000)
,logo_image     LONG RAW
);
```

Creating Tables

As you know from Chapter 1, "Installing Oracle 10g," tables are the primary data storage containers in an Oracle database. Data in a table is organized into rows and columns. Each column is named, has a specific datatype and size, such as CHAR(16), VARCHAR2(50), TIMESTAMP(6), or NUMBER. A row is a single occurrence of this set of columns. You can think of columns as fields, and you can think of rows as records.

When you create a table, you must give it a name as well as specify the column names and datatypes. You can optionally specify many additional attributes, such as column default values, extent sizes, which tablespace to use, and so on. Table and column names have the following requirements:

- Must be from 1 to 30 bytes in length.

- Must begin with a letter.

- Can include letters, numbers, the underscore symbol (_), the pound symbol (#), and the dollar symbol ($). (However, Oracle discourages the use of pound and dollar symbols in names.)

- Cannot be a reserved word such as NUMBER or INDEX.

If the name is enclosed in double quotation marks (" "), the only requirement is that the name be from 1 to 30 bytes long and not contain an embedded double quotation mark. Each column name must be unique within a table, and the table name must be unique within the namespace for tables, views, sequences, private synonyms, procedures, functions, packages, materialized views, and user-defined types. The namespace is simply the domain of allowable names for the set of schema objects that it serves.

In addition to the namespace shared by tables and views, the database has separate namespaces for each of the following:

- Indexes

- Constraints

- Clusters

- Database triggers

- Private database links

- Dimensions

- Roles

- Public synonyms

- Public database links

- Tablespaces

- Profiles

- Parameter files (PFILEs)

For example, if you have a view named BOOKS, you cannot name a table BOOKS (tables and views share a namespace), although you can create an index named BOOKS (indexes and tables have separate namespaces) and a constraint named BOOKS (constraints and tables have separate namespaces).

In the following sections, you will see how to create and manage tables.

Creating a Table

To create a table, use the CREATE TABLE statement. At a minimum, you need to list the column names and datatypes for the table. Here is an example:

```
CREATE TABLE change_log
(log_id      NUMBER
,who         VARCHAR2(64)
,when        TIMESTAMP
,what        VARCHAR2(200)
);
```

Commas delimit or separate the column definitions, which start with the column name: log_id, who, when, and what are the columns in this example. You can add some attributes to your table definition such as the tablespace in which you want your table stored:

```
CREATE TABLE change_log
(log_id      NUMBER
,who         VARCHAR2(64)
,when        TIMESTAMP
,what        VARCHAR2(200)
) TABLESPACE users;
```

After you create the table, you can display the structure of a table with the SQL*Plus DESCRIBE command:

```
SQL> describe change_log
 Name                      Null?    Type
 ----------------------- -------- ----------------
 LOG_ID                             NUMBER
 WHO                                VARCHAR2(64)
 WHEN                               TIMESTAMP(6)
 WHAT                               VARCHAR2(200)
```

Creating a Table Using a Query

When you can create a table based on a query, you do not need to specify the column attributes; they are inherited from the existing schema object. Queries used in a CREATE TABLE AS SELECT statement can be on a single table, a view, or can join multiple tables.

This table creation syntax is frequently identified with the abbreviation CTAS (Create Table As Select):

```
CREATE TABLE january2004_log
NOLOGGING COMPRESS
TABLESPACE archives
```

```
AS SELECT * FROM change_log
WHERE when BETWEEN TO_DATE('01-JAN-2004','DD-Mon-YYYY')
 AND TO_DATE('31-JAN-2004','DD-Mon-YYYY');

SQL> describe january2004_log
 Name                          Null?    Type
 ----------------------------- -------- ----------------
 LOG_ID                                 NUMBER
 WHO                                    VARCHAR2(64)
 WHEN                                   TIMESTAMP(6)
 WHAT                                   VARCHAR2(200)
```

The option NOLOGGING tells the database not to log the contents of the table to the redo log and not to log subsequent direct-path insert operations to the redo log. The COMPRESS option tells the database to add the data to the table using data compression, thus requiring less disk space. The TABLESPACE option tells the database where to store the table.

Creating a Temporary Table

You can create a temporary table whose contents are transitory and only visible to the session that inserted data into it. The definition of the table persists, but the data in a temporary table lasts only for either the duration of the transaction (ON COMMIT DELETE ROWS) or for the duration of the session (ON COMMIT PRESERVE ROWS). Here is an example:

```
CREATE GLOBAL TEMPORARY TABLE my_session
(category       VARCHAR2(16)
,running_count NUMBER
) ON COMMIT DELETE ROWS;
```

Programs can manipulate data in temporary tables or join them to permanent tables in the same manner as any other table.

Setting Default Values

You can set default values for the columns in your table. When subsequent INSERT statements do not explicitly populate these columns, the database assigns the default value to the column.

Having a default value does not ensure that the column will always have a value. An INSERT or an UPDATE statement can always explicitly set a column to NULL unless there is a NOT NULL constraint on the column.

See the section "Creating Constraints" later in this chapter for more information on creating or using constraints.

Default values can be any SQL expression that does not reference a PL/SQL function, other columns, or the pseudocolumns ROWNUM, NEXTVAL, CURRVAL, LEVEL, or PRIOR. To implement more complex rules in PL/SQL for assigning default values, you can use a BEFORE INSERT trigger.

See Chapter 7, "Managing Data with SQL, PL/SQL, and Utilities," for more information on creating triggers.

Default values are defined as part of a column specification. This definition can be made at table creation time, like this:

```
CREATE TABLE change_log
(log_id      NUMBER
,who         VARCHAR2(64) DEFAULT USER
,when        TIMESTAMP    DEFAULT SYSTIMESTAMP
,what        VARCHAR2(200)
) TABLESPACE users;
```

To define a default value after a table has been created, use the ALTER TABLE statement to modify the column specification, like this:

```
ALTER TABLE change_log MODIFY
who          VARCHAR2(64) DEFAULT USER;
```

Adding Comments to a Table or a Column

You can add descriptive comments to your tables and columns in order to better describe the content or usage of these database objects. Comments can be a maximum of 4,000 bytes in length and can have embedded white space and punctuation.

Use the COMMENT ON statement to assign a comment to either a table or a column, like this:

```
COMMENT ON TABLE change_log IS
  'This table is where you record changes
 to the configuration of the DEMO system';

COMMENT ON COLUMN change_log.log_id IS
'System generated key for change log table
 Populated with the change_seq sequence.';
```

The comment must be enclosed in single quotes, but can span physical lines. To display the comments on a table, query the DBA_TAB_COMMENTS, ALL_TAB_COMMENTS, or USER_TAB_COMMENTS data dictionary views:

```
SELECT owner, table_name, comments
FROM all_tab_comments
```

```
WHERE table_name = 'CHANGE_LOG';
```

```
OWNER   TABLE_NAME   COMMENTS
------  -----------  ----------------------------------------
CHIP    CHANGE_LOG   This table is where you record changes
                     to the configuration of the DEMO system
```

To display the comments on a column, query the DBA_COL_COMMENTS, ALL_COL_COMMENTS, or USER_COL_COMMENTS data dictionary views:

```
SELECT table_name, column_name, comments
FROM user_col_comments
WHERE table_name = 'CHANGE_LOG'
AND    column_name = 'LOG_ID';
```

```
TABLE_NAME COLUMN COMMENTS
---------- ------ ----------------------------------------
CHANGE_LOG LOG_ID System generated key for change log table
                  Populated with the change_seq sequence.
```

Renaming a Table

You can use the RENAME statement to change the name of a table, view, sequence, or private synonym—objects that share a namespace with tables. The syntax is RENAME *old_name* TO *new_name*. When you rename a table, the database invalidates all objects that depend on (refer to) the table, such as views, procedures, or synonyms. The database automatically alters associated indexes, grants, and constraints to reference the new name.

To change the name of the change_log table to demo_change_log, execute this:

```
RENAME change_log TO demo_change_log;
```

Another way to rename a table is with the RENAME TO clause of the ALTER TABLE statement. For example:

```
ALTER TABLE change_log RENAME TO demo_change_log;
```

Neither syntax is preferred; both semantics are fully supported.

Adding and Dropping Columns in a Table

One task that you will need to perform while managing tables is adding new columns to an existing table. Use the ALTER TABLE statement to add columns. When adding a single column, use the syntax ALTER TABLE *table_name* ADD *column_spec*.

When you add multiple columns to a table, enclose a comma-delimited list of column specifications with parentheses. The column specification includes the column name, the column's datatype, and any default value that the column will have.

For example, to add a column named HOW to the change_log table, execute the following SQL:

```
ALTER TABLE change_log ADD how VARCHAR2(45);
```

To add the two columns—HOW and WHY—to the change_log table, use the syntax with parentheses, like this:

```
ALTER TABLE change_log ADD
(how      VARCHAR2(45)
,why      VARCHAR2(60)
);
```

To remove a column from a table, use the ALTER TABLE DROP COLUMN statement, as in this example:

```
ALTER TABLE change_log DROP COLUMN how;
```

To drop multiple columns, you don't use the keyword COLUMN, and instead enclose the comma-delimited list of columns in parentheses:

```
ALTER TABLE change_log DROP (how,why);
```

Modifying Columns

You may need to occasionally make changes to the columns of a table—increase or decrease the size of a column, rename a column, or assign a default value to a column. You use the ALTER TABLE MODIFY statement to make these column-level changes. As with the ADD and DROP options, you have two syntactical options: one for modifying a single column and one for modifying multiple columns.

To make changes to a single column, you specify the column name together with the new characteristics. For example, to change the column WHAT from VARCHAR2(200) to VARCHAR2(250), you execute:

```
ALTER TABLE change_log MODIFY what VARCHAR2(250);
```

To change multiple columns, enclose a comma-delimited list of modified column specs in parentheses, like this:

```
ALTER TABLE change_log MODIFY
(what      VARCHAR2(250)
,who       VARCHAR2(50)  DEFAULT user
);
```

Viewing the Attributes of a Table

You can use several data dictionary views to display the attributes of a table. The first place to start is usually with the DESCRIBE command from SQL*Plus or *i*SQL*Plus:

```
SQL> describe employees
 Name                    Null?     Type
 ----------------------- --------- ----------------
 EMPLOYEE_ID             NOT NULL  NUMBER
 HIRE_DATE               NOT NULL  DATE
 FIRST_NAME                        VARCHAR2(42)
 LAST_NAME                         VARCHAR2(42)
 PAYROLL_ID                        VARCHAR2(10)
 DEPT_NBR                          NUMBER
 MANAGER                           NUMBER
```

The DESCRIBE command displays the column names, datatypes, and nullity of each column. To see the table physical attributes, query the ALL_TABLES or USER_TABLES dictionary view, like this:

```
SELECT * FROM user_tables
WHERE table_name = 'EMPLOYEES';
```

To see what constraints are declared on a table, use the ALL_CONSTRAINTS and ALL_CONS_COLUMNS views, like this:

```
SELECT constraint_name,constraint_type ,r_constraint_name
FROM user_constraints
WHERE table_name = 'EMPLOYEES';
```

CONSTRAINT_NAME	CONS TYPE	R_CONSTRAINT_NAME
NN_EMP_ID	C	
SYS_C005286	C	
EMPLOYEES_PK	P	
UNIQ_PAYROLL_ID	U	
EMP_DEPT_FK	R	DEPARTMENT_PK
MGR_EMP_FK	R	EMPLOYEES_PK
HIRE_DATE_CHECK	C	

The CONSTRAINT_TYPE column indicates the kind of constraint:

- C is for Check
- P is for Primary Key

- R is for Referential (or Foreign Key)
- U is for Unique

   NOT NULL constraints are stored both as a column attribute and as a check constraint.
   The SEARCH_CONDITION column of the USER_CONSTRAINTS view is only applicable for
CHECK constraints:

```
SELECT search_condition
FROM user_constraints
WHERE constraint_name = 'SYS_C005286';


SEARCH_CONDITION
-------------------------------------------------
"HIRE_DATE" IS NOT NULL
```

   The columns participating in a FOREIGN KEY constraint can be found in the ALL_CONS_
COLUMNS view, like this:

```
SELECT column_name, position
FROM all_cons_columns
WHERE constraint_name = 'EMP_DEPT_FK';


COLUMN_NAME                     POSITION
------------------------------ ----------
DEPT_NBR                               1
```

Viewing the Contents of a Table

To view the contents of a table, simply select the columns of interest from the table. You can
use the column list reported in the DESCRIBE command to limit your column selection or you
can specify * for the column list to view all columns in the table. Use a WHERE clause to filter the
rows, like this:

```
SELECT * FROM employees;


SELECT employee_id, first_name, last_name, hire_date
FROM employees
WHERE hire_date > SYSDATE - 90
;
```

Working With Constraints

Constraints enforce business rules in the database. In other words, they limit the acceptable data
values for a table. Constraints are optional schema objects that depend on tables. Although you
can have a table without any constraints, you cannot create a constraint without a table.

Oracle lets you create several types of constraints on your tables to enforce your business rules, including the following:

- NOT NULL
- UNIQUE
- PRIMARY KEY
- REFERENTIAL
- CHECK

You can create constraints together with the table in the CREATE TABLE statement. After you create a table, you add or remove a constraint from a table with an ALTER TABLE statement. You specify the constraint information with either the in-line syntax as a column attribute or the out-of-line syntax as part of the table definition. Constraints do not require a name; if you do not name the constraint, Oracle generates one for you. However, the generated names are simply numbers prefixed with SYS_C and may not be very meaningful.

The following sections describe each of the constraint types in detail.

Working with *NOT NULL* Constraints

By default, all columns in a table allow NULL as a valid value. A NULL represents unknown or nonexistent information. Some business rules can be enforced with a NOT NULL constraint. For example, an employee may not be considered a valid employee if their hire date is not known. You enforce this business rule by placing a NOT NULL constraint on the hire_date column of the employees table. Any INSERT or UPDATE statements fail if the protected column does not have a value.

NOT NULL constraints must be declared together with the column definition using in-line syntax. Here is an example using the NOT NULL constraint:

```
CREATE TABLE employees
(employee_id   NUMBER  CONSTRAINT nn_emp_id  NOT NULL
,hire_date     DATE                          NOT NULL
,first_name    VARCHAR2(42)
,last_name     VARCHAR2(42)
);
```

Working with *UNIQUE* Constraints

A UNIQUE constraint ensures that each occurrence of the columns protected by this constraint is different from all other occurrences in the table. UNIQUE constraints cannot be created on columns of type CLOB, NCLOB, BLOB, LONG, LONG RAW, or TIMESTAMP WITH TIMEZONE.

Here is how you create an employees table that has a UNIQUE constraint on the payroll_id column using the out-of-line syntax:

```
CREATE TABLE employees
(employee_id   NUMBER       NOT NULL
```

```
,hire_date      DATE        NOT NULL
,first_name     VARCHAR2(42)
,last_name      VARCHAR2(42)
,payroll_id     VARCHAR2(10)
,CONSTRAINT uniq_payroll_id UNIQUE (payroll_id)
);
```

Using the in-line syntax, the statement looks like this:

```
CREATE TABLE employees
(employee_id    NUMBER      NOT NULL
,hire_date      DATE        NOT NULL
,first_name     VARCHAR2(42)
,last_name      VARCHAR2(42)
,payroll_id     VARCHAR2(10)
   CONSTRAINT uniq_payroll_id UNIQUE
);
```

No two rows in this table can have the same value in payroll_id. NULL values do not count as a distinct value, so this employees table can have multiple rows with a NULL payroll_id. To ensure that payroll_id is always present, you need a NOT NULL constraint.

The database uses an index to help enforce this constraint. The index is usually a unique index, and if you create the UNIQUE constraint together with the table, the database automatically creates a unique index on the columns protected by the UNIQUE constraint, and the name of the index defaults to the name of the constraint. To assign attributes to this index, take advantage of the USING INDEX clause, like this:

```
CREATE TABLE employees
(employee_id    NUMBER      NOT NULL
,hire_date      DATE        NOT NULL
,first_name     VARCHAR2(42)
,last_name      VARCHAR2(42)
,payroll_id     VARCHAR2(10)
,CONSTRAINT uniq_payroll_id UNIQUE (payroll_id)
  USING INDEX TABLESPACE indx
);
```

You can add a UNIQUE constraint after the table is built by using an ALTER TABLE statement, like this:

```
ALTER TABLE employees ADD
CONSTRAINT uniq_payroll_id UNIQUE (payroll_id)
  USING INDEX TABLESPACE indx
;
```

When adding a UNIQUE constraint to an existing table, Oracle raises an exception, and the statement fails if there are any duplicate keys (that is, violations of the constraint). To assist you in identifying any duplicates, you can specify an EXCEPTIONS INTO clause. First, create an exceptions table with the utlexcpt.sql (using ROWID) or utlexpt1.sql (using UROWID) script located in the *oracle_home*/rdbms/admin directory. These scripts create a table named EXCEPTIONS that contains columns for the ROWID, owner, table_name, and constraint that is in violation. You can use this information to fix any data that violates the constraint and then try the ALTER statement again to create the constraint.

Here is an example:

```
ALTER TABLE employees ADD
  CONSTRAINT uniq_payroll_id UNIQUE (payroll_id)
  USING INDEX TABLESPACE indx
  EXCEPTIONS INTO exceptions;
```

Working with *PRIMARY KEY* Constraints

Primary keys are defined in a relational model as being the unique identifier for any tupple in an entity. PRIMARY KEY constraints enforce the validity of a primary key, so a table can have only one PRIMARY KEY constraint. A PRIMARY KEY constraint implicitly includes both NOT NULL constraints on each column in the key as well as a UNIQUE constraint, enforced with an index, on all columns in the key. You can create a PRIMARY KEY constraint at the same time that you create a table.

Here is an example of creating a PRIMARY KEY constraint together with a table, using out-of-line syntax:

```
CREATE TABLE employees
(employee_id    NUMBER       NOT NULL
,hire_date      DATE         NOT NULL
,first_name     VARCHAR2(42)
,last_name      VARCHAR2(42)
,payroll_id     VARCHAR2(10)
,CONSTRAINT employees_pk PRIMARY KEY (employee_id)
  USING INDEX TABLESPACE indx
);
```

As with UNIQUE constraints, PRIMARY KEY constraints cannot be created on columns of type CLOB, NCLOB, BLOB, LONG, LONG RAW, or TIMESTAMP WITH TIMEZONE.

Working with *FOREIGN KEY* Constraints

FOREIGN KEY constraints are also known as referential integrity constraints because they enforce referential integrity. FOREIGN KEY constraints enforce referential integrity by ensuring that data values referenced in one table are defined in another table. FOREIGN KEY constraints tie these two tables together in a parent/child or referenced/dependent relationship.

When you declare a FOREIGN KEY constraint, you identify the columns in one table whose values must also appear in the primary key or unique key of another table. The table with the primary or unique key is known as the parent or referenced table, and the table with the FOREIGN KEY constraint is known as the child or dependent table.

As with UNIQUE and PRIMARY KEY constraints, FOREIGN KEY constraints cannot be created on columns of type CLOB, NCLOB, BLOB, LONG, LONG RAW, or TIMESTAMP WITH TIMEZONE.

Here is an example of creating a parent table (DEPARTMENTS) and child table (EMPLOYEES) with a PRIMARY KEY constraint on the parent and a FOREIGN KEY constraint on the child table, using out-of-line syntax:

```
CREATE TABLE departments
(dept_nbr       NUMBER    NOT NULL
   CONSTRAINT department_pk PRIMARY KEY
,dept_name      VARCHAR2(32)
,manager_id     NUMBER
);


CREATE TABLE employees
(employee_id    NUMBER       NOT NULL
,hire_date      DATE         NOT NULL
,first_name     VARCHAR2(42)
,last_name      VARCHAR2(42)
,payroll_id     VARCHAR2(10)
,dept_nbr       NUMBER
,CONSTRAINT uniq_payroll_id UNIQUE (payroll_id)
   USING INDEX TABLESPACE indx
,CONSTRAINT employees_pk PRIMARY KEY (employee_id)
   USING INDEX TABLESPACE indx
,CONSTRAINT emp_dept_fk FOREIGN KEY (dept_nbr)
   REFERENCES departments(dept_nbr)
);
```

In this example, each employee belongs to a department, so we put a DEPT_NBR column in the EMPLOYEES table, which will hold each employee's department number. The DEPARTMENTS table defines all the valid department numbers to ensure that DEPT_NBR values appearing in the EMPLOYEES table are defined in the DEPARTMENTS table—in essence that an employee belongs to a valid department. You implement this relationship or rule with a FOREIGN KEY constraint. By default, FOREIGN KEYs allow NULLs.

By default, the database raises an exception and does not allow you to delete rows from a parent table if those rows are referenced in the child table. If this behavior isn't what you want, you can tell the database to automatically maintain referential integrity in a couple of ways: by deleting the child rows and specifying ON DELETE CASCADE or by setting the columns in the child table to NULL with the ON DELETE SET NULL clause, like this:

```
ALTER TABLE employees
   ADD CONSTRAINT emp_dept_fk FOREIGN KEY (dept_nbr)
     REFERENCES departments(dept_nbr) ON DELETE CASCADE;
```

```
ALTER TABLE departments ADD CONSTRAINT
   dept_mgr_fk FOREIGN KEY (manager_id) REFERENCES
     employees(employee_id) ON DELETE SET NULL;
```

The first statement tells the database that deleting a department should cause a cascading deletion of that department's employees. The second statement tells the database that deleting an employee who is a department manager should cause that department's MANAGER_ID column to revert to NULL.

A Self-Referencing Foreign Key

The parent and child tables do not always have to be separate tables; they can be separate columns of the same table. This configuration is known as a self-referencing foreign key. An example of a self-referencing foreign key can be added to the EMPLOYEES table used in the previous section. The business rule that will be enforced requires that each employee report to a manager and also that the manager be a valid employee. To add this rule to the EMPLOYEES table, add the MANAGER column together with a FOREIGN KEY constraint on which it references the EMPLOYEES table, like this:

```
ALTER TABLE employees ADD
   (manager    NUMBER
   ,CONSTRAINT mgr_emp_fk FOREIGN KEY (manager)
     REFERENCES employees(employee_id)
     ON DELETE SET NULL
   );
```

Deferred Constraint Checking

It's possible that your programs might temporarily violate a FOREIGN KEY constraint without really violating the underlying business rule if a program adds data to both tables participating in a FOREIGN KEY constraint within the scope of a single transaction.

For example, if you hire a new employee and create a new department for that person to manage, you need to add a row to both the EMPLOYEES table (which references the new department) as well as the DEPARTMENTS table (which references the new employee). Although this temporary violation will not go against the intent of the business rule, you will need to create the constraints with some additional options, like this:

```
ALTER TABLE employees
   ADD CONSTRAINT emp_dept_fk FOREIGN KEY (dept_nbr)
```

```
    REFERENCES departments(dept_nbr) ON DELETE CASCADE
    DEFERRABLE;

ALTER TABLE departments ADD CONSTRAINT
  dept_mgr_fk FOREIGN KEY (manager_id) REFERENCES
    employees(employee_id) ON DELETE SET NULL
    DEFERRABLE INITIALLY DEFERRED;
```

By default, the database checks that a FOREIGN KEY constraint is satisfied at the end of each statement. You define this behavior with the keywords INITIALLY IMMEDIATE. Also by default, the database will not allow programs to defer constraint checking to the end of the transaction. You define this behavior with the keywords NOT DEFERRABLE.

When you create a constraint, you can tell the database to allow either immediate or deferred constraint checking by specifying the keyword DEFERRABLE. If you normally want a DEFERRABLE constraint to be deferred, create it with the INITIALLY DEFERRED option. Only DEFERRABLE constraints can be set to INITIALLY DEFERRED. Once you create a constraint, you cannot change its deferability (for example, from NOT DEFERRABLE to DEFERABLE); instead, you must drop and re-create the constraint with the new specification.

Working with *CHECK* Constraints

CHECK constraints verify that a column or set of column values meet a specific condition that must evaluate to a Boolean. If the condition evaluates to FALSE, the database raises an exception, and the INSERT or UPDATE statement fails. The condition cannot include subqueries, references to other tables, or calls to functions that are not deterministic. A function is deterministic if it always returns the same result when passed the same input parameters. Examples of deterministic functions include SQRT, TO_DATE, and SUBSTR. The functions SYSDATE, USER, and DBTIMEZONE are not deterministic. The condition must be a Boolean SQL expression enclosed in parentheses.

Add a CHECK constraint to ensure that every employee's hire date is later than the company's founding date, like this:

```
ALTER TABLE employees ADD CONSTRAINT
  validate_hire_date CHECK
  (hire_date > TO_DATE('15-Apr-1999','DD-Mon-YYYY'));
```

Modifying Constraints

Once created, constraints can be dropped, disabled (temporarily not enforced), enabled (enforced again), or renamed. You make these changes to constraints using an ALTER TABLE statement. Take care in disabling UNIQUE or PRIMARY KEY constraints because disabling these constraints results in the supporting index being dropped (unless you also specify KEEP INDEX.

To drop a constraint, use an ALTER TABLE statement with the constraint name, like this:

```
ALTER TABLE employees DROP CONSTRAINT validate_hire_date;
```

Because there can be only one PRIMARY KEY constraint on a table, you can drop it by simply specifying DROP PRIMARY KEY without actually using the constraint's name. If FOREIGN KEY constraints reference your PRIMARY KEY or UNIQUE constraint, you need to drop these dependent constraints before or in conjunction (using the CASCADE keyword) with the PRIMARY KEY constraint:

```
ALTER TABLE employees DROP PRIMARY KEY CASCADE;
```

To rename a constraint, give the old and new names:

```
ALTER TABLE employees
  RENAME CONSTRAINT validate_hire_date TO hire_date_check;
```

When bulk loading data into a table, it is often more efficient to disable FOREIGN KEY and CHECK constraints, load the data, and then re-enable these constraints, like this:

```
ALTER TABLE employees DISABLE CONSTRAINT mgr_emp_fk;
-- bulk load the table
ALTER TABLE employees ENABLE  CONSTRAINT mgr_emp_fk;
```

Disabling either a PRIMARY KEY or a UNIQUE constraint may drop the supporting index and therefore may not be desirable for a load process that uses that index.

Working with Indexes

Indexes are optional data structures built on tables. Indexes can improve data retrieval performance by providing a direct access method instead of the default full table scan retrieval method. You can build Btree or bitmap indexes on one or more columns in a table. An *index key* is defined as one data value stored in the index. A Btree index sorts the keys into a binary tree and stores these keys together with the table's ROWIDs. In a bitmap index, a bitmap is created for each key. There is a bit in each bitmap for every ROWID in the table, forming the equivalent of a two-dimensional matrix. The bits are set if the corresponding row in the bitmap exists.

Btree indexes are the default index type, can be unique or non-unique, and are appropriate for medium- to high-*cardinality* columns—those having many distinct values. Btree indexes support row-level locking and so are appropriate for multiuser, transactional applications. The indexes supporting a PRIMARY KEY or UNIQUE constraints are Btree indexes.

Bitmap indexes, on the other hand, are best for multiple combinations of low- to medium-cardinality columns (you cannot create a unique bitmap index), and they do not support row-level locking. Bitmap indexes are best in environments in which changes to data are limited and controlled, such as many data warehousing applications. Because bitmap indexes cannot efficiently make changes to the indexed data, they are often dropped prior to data loading and then re-created after a data load.

In the following section, we will show you how to create, drop, and manage indexes.

Creating and Dropping Indexes

To create an index, you first need a table. In the CREATE INDEX statement, you tell the database the name of the new index, which table to create the index on, and which columns to include. If multiple columns will be included, use a comma-delimited list.

To create a Btree index on the DEPT_NBR column of the EMPLOYEES table used in the preceding sections, use a CREATE INDEX statement, like this:

```
CREATE INDEX emp_dept_nbr ON employees (dept_nbr)
   TABLESPACE indx;
```

A unique index requires the additional keyword UNIQUE, like this:

```
CREATE UNIQUE INDEX dname_uix ON departments (dept_name);
```

If you frequently access employees by seniority, you can create a multicolumn index on both department number and hire date, like this:

```
CREATE INDEX emp_seniority ON
   employees (dept_nbr, hire_date)
   TABLESPACE indx;
```

To create three single-column bitmap indexes on the STATE, REGION, and METRO_AREA columns of the GEOGRAPHY table, execute the following:

```
CREATE BITMAP INDEX state_bix  ON geography (state);
CREATE BITMAP INDEX region_bix ON geography (region);
CREATE BITMAP INDEX metro_bix  ON geography (metro_area);
```

To drop an index, use a DROP INDEX statement, like these:

```
DROP INDEX emp_seniority;
DROP INDEX state_bix;
```

Managing Indexes

You can perform several maintenance actions on an index, including rebuilding an index, moving it to a new tablespace, coalescing it, or renaming the index. All these actions are performed with different clauses of an ALTER INDEX statement.

To rebuild an index, which will shrink its size and possibly reduce the Btree depth (making it more efficient), use a REBUILD clause, like this.

```
ALTER INDEX emp_seniority REBUILD;
```

To move an index from one tablespace to another, you specify a new tablespace in conjunction with REBUILD:

```
ALTER INDEX uniq_payroll_id REBUILD TABLESPACE hr_indx;
```

Coalescing an index is like a quick-and-dirty rebuild. Instead of re-creating the Btree, a coalesce combines entries in nearby leaf blocks with the intent of freeing space from some of the leaf blocks. The space and resources required for a coalesce is much less than the full rebuild. But when you coalesce an index, you cannot move the index or reduce the depth of the Btree. Here is an example of coalescing an index:

```
ALTER INDEX uniq_payroll_id COALESCE;
```

Renaming an index is beneficial if you have a poorly named index. It also comes in handy if you need to take care of some high-availability maintenance actions that include staging the new version of an index using a temporary name and then in a short deployment window renaming the old and new indexes. Here is an example of renaming an index:

```
ALTER INDEX sys_c001428 RENAME TO employee_pk;
```

Working with Views

Views are virtual tables consisting of a stored query. A view is created with a query that incorporates one or more base tables. Although views are often used for selecting data, some views can also be updated, deleted, or inserted into. You can use views to restrict access to a subset of a table, or you can make an awkward join appear as a simple table, reducing a query's complexity.

The data dictionary is a good example of a collection of complex joins appearing as more simple tables. The ALL_CONSTRAINTS view, for example, is a complex nine-table join that also includes two subqueries. Trying to navigate the base tables used in the dictionary views is a bit daunting, but the dictionary views are much more usable because they hide a great deal of the underlying complexity.

Likewise, some data is deemed too sensitive for most access, such as the passwords associated with a database link. The data is stored in the underlying base table link$, but not revealed in the dictionary views DBA_DB_LINKS or ALL_DB_LINKS. Because access to the base table is restrictive, but the dictionary views are widely accessed, the database can hide the sensitive data in the base tables.

To create a view named empv that is based on a combination of data in both the EMPLOYEES and DEPARTMENTS tables, you can execute the following:

```
CREATE OR REPLACE VIEW empv
(employee_name
,department
,manager
,hire_date
) AS SELECT
 E.first_name||' '||E.last_name
,D.dept_name
,M.first_name||' '||M.last_name
,E.hire_date
```

```
FROM employees    E
    ,departments D
    ,employees    M
WHERE E.dept_nbr = D.dept_nbr
 AND  D.manager_id = M.employee_id
;
```

The OR REPLACE keywords tell the database to replace the view definition if it already exists. If the OR REPLACE keyword is not included, the statement fails if the view already exists. The column list in the parentheses is the list of column names as they appear in the view and correspond positionally with the column expressions in the query—the first expression the query maps to the first column name for the view, the second expression in the query, to the second column name, and so on. You can choose not to include salary or commission in the view definition and only grant privileges on the view, thus restricting access to sensitive data.

To remove a view from the database, use a DROP VIEW statement, like this:

```
DROP VIEW empv;
```

Working with Sequences

Sequences are schema objects that generate unique integers. They are frequently used to generate primary key values.

The CREATE SEQUENCE statement creates new sequences. You must, at a minimum, give the sequence a name. You can also assign the following attributes to the sequence in the CREATE statement:

START WITH   Defines the initial value for the sequence.

INCREMENT BY   Defines how the subsequent sequence numbers will be generated. The default is 1, and valid values are nonzero integers of less than 29 digits. A negative INCREMENT BY results in a descending sequence that generates progressively lower numbers. A positive INCREMENT BY results in an ascending sequence that generates progressively higher numbers.

MAXVALUE   Defines the highest value that the sequence can generate. The default is the special keyword NOMAXVALUE, which evaluates to 10^{27} for an ascending sequence and to -1 for a descending sequence.

MINVALUE   Defines the lowest value that the sequence can generate. The default for MINVALUE is the special keyword NOMINVALUE, which evaluates to -10^{26} for an ascending sequence and to -1 for a descending sequence.

CACHE   Defines how many values will be preallocated and held in memory. The default is 20, and the valid values range from 2 to the number returned from the formula:

```
(CEIL (MAXVALUE - MINVALUE)) / ABS(INCREMENT BY)
```

To create a sequence called `employees_seq` that generates unique integers, starting with 100500 and incrementing by 1, use the following statement:

```
CREATE SEQUENCE employees_seq START WITH 100500 NOMAXVALUE NOMINVALUE;
```

To request the next integer from the sequence, reference the pseudocolumn `NEXTVAL` in a SQL statement, like this:

```
SELECT employees_seq.nextval FROM dual;
```

These values can be used in `INSERT` statements or in `UPDATE` statements, like this:

```
INSERT INTO employees (employee_id, hire_date)
  SELECT employees_seq.NEXTVAL, hired_date
  FROM merged_employees;
```

You can use the `ALTER SEQUENCE` statement to modify the `INCREMENT BY`, `MAXVALUE`, `MINVALUE`, `CYCLE`, and `CACHE` attributes, but not the `START WITH` attribute, like this:

```
ALTER SEQUENCE employees_seq INCREMENT BY -1;
```

If you need to reset the next value that a sequence will generate, drop it, re-create it, and then re-grant any privileges on it. To drop a sequence, use the `DROP SEQUENCE` statement, like this:

```
DROP SEQUENCE employee_seq;
```

Summary

In this chapter, you learned about the purpose of tablespaces and datafiles. You found out how to create and manage tablespaces as well as how Oracle stores some schema objects as segments in extents and data blocks.

You learned how to create and modify tables, indexes, constraints, views, and sequences. We covered deferred constraint checking and how to configure foreign key constraints to support either deferrable or not deferrable implementations.

Exam Essentials

Know the relationship of datafiles to tablespaces.   Tablespaces are built on one or more datafiles—bigfile tablespaces on a single datafile and smallfile tablespaces on one or more datafiles.

Understand the statements needed to create, modify, and drop tablespaces.   Use a CREATE TABLESPACE, ALTER TABLESPACE, or DROP TABLESPACE statement to create, modify, and drop a tablespace.

Know how to take tablespaces offline and what consequences the offline immediate option poses. Use an ALTER TABLESPACE statement to take a tablespace offline or bring it online. If you use the offline immediate option, you must perform media recovery when you bring it back online.

Know how to use the EM Database Control to view tablespace information. The EM Database Control can be used to view tablespace information as well as perform various administrative tasks. A working knowledge of this tool is required.

Know the difference between segment space management and extent management. Extent management deals with segment-level space allocations, and segment space management deals with data block–level space allocations.

Know what initialization parameter controls Oracle Managed Files (OMF) placement. The DB_CREATE_FILE_DEST parameter tells the database where to place Oracle Managed Files.

Know what constitutes a valid name for a database object. Database object names can be a maximum of 30 bytes, must begin with a letter, and can be composed of letters, numbers, and the special characters underscore, dollar sign, or pound sign. If the database name is enclosed in double quotes, it can be mixed case and contain other punctuation marks.

Know what a namespace is and how it determines which objects can have the same name. Database object names must be unique within a namespace. One namespace is shared by tables, views, sequences, private synonyms, procedures, functions, packages, materialized views, and user-defined types. There are separate namespaces for each of the following: indexes, constraints, clusters, database triggers, private database links, and dimensions.

Know the different types of constraints and which have dependencies with others. There are CHECK, NOT NULL, UNIQUE, PRIMARY KEY, and FOREIGN KEY constraints. A PRIMARY KEY constraint implicitly includes NOT NULL and UNIQUE constraints. A FOREIGN KEY constraint must refer to a PRIMARY KEY or UNIQUE constraint.

Know the types of indexes and when they are appropriate. There are Btree and bitmap indexes. Btree indexes are medium- to high-cardinality columns in applications in which data can change frequently. Bitmap indexes are best for low- to medium-cardinality columns in applications that control data changes, usually in batches.

Review Questions

1. Which of the following statements about tablespaces is true?

   A. A tablespace is the physical implementation of logical structure called a namespace.

   B. A tablespace can hold the objects of only one schema.

   C. A bigfile tablespace can have only one datafile.

   D. The SYSAUX tablespace is an optional tablespace only created if you install certain database options.

2. Automatic segment space management on the tablespace causes which of the following table attributes in that tablespace to be ignored?

   A. The whole storage clause

   B. NEXT and PCTINCREASE

   C. BUFFERPOOL and FREEPOOL

   D. PCTFREE and PCTUSED

3. Which objects share the same namespace and therefore cannot have the same name?

   A. Tables and indexes

   B. Tables and procedures

   C. Tables and constraints

   D. Tables and triggers

4. Which is not a type of segment that is stored in a tablespace?

   A. Undo

   B. Redo

   C. Permanent

   D. Temporary

5. With which parameters do you specify unlimited datafile growth?

   A. MAXSIZE UNLIMITED

   B. UNLIMITED GROWTH

   C. MAXEXTENTS UNLIMITED

   D. Datafile size cannot change.

6. Which of the following is not a character datatype that can be used in a table column definition?

   A. char

   B. varchar

   C. nvarchar2

   D. string

7. With which numeric datatype can you represent infinity?

   A. double

   B. float

   C. binary_float

   D. Infinity cannot be represented in the database.

8. A table name can never include the special meta-character dollar sign ($).

   A. True

   B. False

   C. Only if the table name is enclosed in double quotes

   D. Only if the table name is enclosed in single quotes

9. Which of the following column specifications results in a column that will store time values down to the microsecond decimals of precision?

   A. timestamp(3)

   B. time(3)

   C. datetime(3)

   D. date(3)

10. Which type of index can specify as a unique index?

   A. Bitmap

   B. Heap organized

   C. Btree

   D. XOR

11. Which operation can you not do to a table that is created with the following SQL statement?

```
CREATE TABLE properties
("Location"  NUMBER primary key
,value       NUMBER(15)
,lot         varchar2(12)
,constraint positive_value check
   (value > 0)
);
```

   A. Rename the primary key to properties.

   B. Insert a null into the value column.

   C. Add a column named owner.

   D. Rename the index supporting primary key to properties.

   E. None of the above.

12. Which of the statements is true regarding the table created with the following SQL statement?

```
CREATE TABLE autos
(vin          VARCHAR2(64) primary key
,style        VARCHAR2(15) default 'TUDOR'
,year         char(4)
,make         varchar2(12)
,model        varchar2(30)
);
```

    A. MAKE is a reserved word; the CREATE TABLE will fail.

    B. The column style will always have a value.

    C. There is no index on this table.

    D. The column style can have a NULL value.

13. Which constraint-checking model is the default?

    A. Initially immediate and deferrable

    B. Initially immediate and not deferrable

    C. Initially deferred and not immediately

    D. Initially deferrable and not immediate

14. Which statement on views is true?

    A. A view can only be on one base table, although that base table can be joined to itself.

    B. A view cannot be created with the same name and columns as the base table.

    C. Inserts into a view are not allowed.

    D. Privileges on a view can be different from those on the base table.

15. What can tablespaces be used for?

    A. To organize tables and indexes into manageable groupings

    B. To make sure that data stored in the tablespace does not change

    C. To move data from one database to another

    D. All of the above

16. Which allocation unit is the smallest?

    A. Datafile

    B. Extent

    C. Data block

    D. Segment

17. Which is a valid tablespace extent management specification?

    A. Automatic

    B. Local

    C. Manual

    D. Temporary

18. Which of the following is not a valid Oracle10*g* datatype?

    A. `timestamp with local timezone`

    B. `binary`

    C. `blob`

    D. `urowid`

19. How do you specify that a temporary table will be emptied at the end of a user's session?

    A. Create the temporary table with the `ON COMMIT PRESERVE ROWS` option.

    B. Create the temporary table with the `ON DISCONNECT PRESERVE ROWS` option.

    C. Create the temporary table with the `ON DISCONNECT PURGE ROWS` option.

    D. Create the temporary table with the `ON COMMIT DELETE ROWS` option.

20. How can you change the comment assigned to the columns in a table?

    A. Use the `ALTER TABLE MODIFY COLUMN` statement.

    B. Use the `COMMENT ON TABLE` statement.

    C. Use the `RENAME` statement.

    D. Use the `COMMENT ON COLUMN` statement.

Answers to Review Questions

1. C. Bigfile tablespaces are new to Oracle10g and can have only a single datafile. The traditional or smallfile tablespace can have many datafiles.

2. D. Segment space management refers to free space management, with automatic segment space management using bitmaps instead of FREELISTS, PCTFREE, and PCTUSED.

3. B. Indexes, constraints, and triggers all have separate namespaces. Tables share a namespace with views, sequences, private synonyms, procedures, functions, packages, materialized views, and user-defined types. Objects within the same schema sharing a namespace must have unique names.

4. B. Redo information is not stored in a segment; it is stored in the redo logs. Undo segments are stored in the undo tablespace, temporary segments are in the temporary tablespace, and permanent segments go into all the other tablespaces.

5. A. The autoextend MAXSIZE parameter tells Oracle how large a data or temp file can grow to. UNLIMITED specifies no bounds to the automatic growth.

6. D. The character datatypes include char, nchar, varchar, varchar2, nvarchar2, and long but do not include string.

7. C. With Oracle 6 through Oracle 9i, infinity could not be represented in the database. With Oracle10g, however, binary_float and binary_double can represent infinity, not a number (NAN), as well as several other special values.

8. B. Objects in an Oracle10g database can always include letters, numbers, and the characters $, _, and # (dollar sign, underscore, and pound sign). Names can include any other character only if they are enclosed in double quotes. The character dollar sign is not a special meta-character in an Oracle10g database.

9. A. There is no time or datetime datatype in Oracle10g. The date datatype cannot store subsecond granularity. The timestamp datatype stores subsecond granularity, defaulting to six digits of precision.

10. C. Heap organized is a table that is not index organized; it is not an index type. XOR is bitwise function and not an index type. Bitmap is an index type, but cannot be used for a unique index. Btree indexes make fine unique indexes.

11. E. You can rename both a constraint and an index to the same name as a table—they are in separate namespaces. Columns can be added, and owner is a valid column name. If the check constraint condition evaluates to FALSE, the data value will not be allowed; if the condition evaluates to either TRUE or NULL, the value is allowed.

12. D. A default clause ensures that the column does not contain a NULL after an insert, but not after an update. MAKE is not a reserved word, and an index will be created on the primary key.

13. B. Constraints can be created as deferrable and initially deferred, but deferred constraint checking is not the default.

14. D. Views can be created on one or more base table. Views share the same namespace as tables and therefore cannot have the same name; columns, however, can be named the same as the base table. SELECT, INSERT, UPDATE, and DELETE are all valid operations on a view. One of the uses for a view is to hide portions of the base table, by granting different privileges to the view than the base table.

15. D. The primary use for a tablespace is to organize tables and indexes into manageable units. Some of the manageable operations that you can do to a tablespace include making it read-only or moving it from one database to another.

16. C. An extent is composed of two or more data blocks; a segment is composed of one or more extents, and a datafile houses all these.

17. B. A tablespace can have either dictionary extent management or local extent management.

18. B. Although binary_float and binary_double are valid datatypes, binary is not.

19. A. The options for temporary tables are either ON COMMIT DELETE ROWS, with causes the table to flush at the end of each transaction, or ON COMMIT PRESERVE ROWS, which causes the table to flush at the end of each session.

20. D. You assign or change comments on a column with the COMMENT ON COLUMN statement. The COMMENT ON TABLE statement is used to add or change the comment assigned to a table.

Chapter

4

Oracle Net Services

ORACLE DATABASE 10G: ADMINISTRATION I EXAM OBJECTIVES COVERED IN THIS CHAPTER:

✓ **Controlling the Database**

 ▪ Start and stop the Oracle Listener.

✓ **Oracle Net Services**

 ▪ Use Database Control to Create additional listeners.

 ▪ Use Database Control to Create Oracle Net service aliases.

 ▪ Use Database Control to Configure connect time failover.

 ▪ Use Listener features.

 ▪ Use the Oracle Net Manager to configure client and middle-tier connections.

 ▪ Use TNSPING to test Oracle Net connectivity.

 ▪ Describe Oracle Net Services.

 ▪ Describe Oracle Net names resolution methods.

Exam objectives are subject to change at any time without prior notice and at Oracle's sole discretion. Please visit Oracle's Training and Certification website (http://www.oracle.com/education/certification/) for the most current exam objectives listing.

Networks have evolved from simple terminal-based systems to complex multitiered systems. Today's networks can comprise many computers on multiple operating systems using a wide variety of protocols and communicating across wide geographic areas. We need look no further than the explosion of the Internet to see how networking has matured and what a profound impact networks have on the way we work and communicate.

Although networks have become increasingly complex, they also have become easier to use and manage. For instance, we all take advantage of the Internet without knowing or caring about the components that make this communication possible because the complexity of this huge network is completely hidden from us.

The experienced Oracle database administrator has seen this maturation process in the Oracle network architecture as well. From the first version of SQL*Net to the latest releases of Oracle Net, Oracle has evolved its network strategy and infrastructure to meet the demands of the rapidly changing landscape of network communications.

This chapter highlights the areas that you need to consider when implementing an Oracle network strategy and the responsibilities that you have when managing an Oracle Database 10g (Oracle 10g) network. We'll also discuss the most common network configurations. The chapter introduces the features of Oracle Net—the connectivity management software that is the backbone of the Oracle network architecture. We'll explain how to configure the main client and server-side components of Oracle Net, and we'll discuss the tools that you have at your disposal to perform these tasks.

Network Design Considerations

Many factors are involved in making network design decisions. First and foremost, you need to understand the design of the Oracle network architecture itself. Oracle Net is flexible and configurable and has the scalability to accommodate a range of network sizes. You can choose from a variety of network configurations that are designed to meet the needs of both small and large organizations. The sections that follow summarize the areas that you need to consider.

Network Complexity Issues

The complexity of the network plays an important role in many of your network design decisions. To determine network complexity, you need to answer the following questions:

- How many clients will the network need to support?

- What type of work will the clients be doing?

- Where are the clients? In complex networks, clients can be geographically dispersed over a wide area.

- What types of clients are going to be supported? Will they be PC-based or terminal-based? Will these be thin clients that do little processing or fat clients that do most of the application processing?

- What is the projected growth of the network?

- Where will the processing take place? Will any middle-tier servers be involved, such as an application server or a transaction server?

- What types of network protocols will be used to communicate between the clients and servers?

- Will Oracle servers have to communicate with other Oracle servers in the enterprise?

- Will the network involve multiple operating systems?

- Do the applications that will be used require any special networking? This is especially important to consider when you are dealing with third-party applications.

Answering these questions will provide you with guidance in determining the size and amount of the network hardware and software required to monitor and manage the network. You will also start to gain insights into the staffing levels and time requirements needed to support the network.

Network Security Issues

Network security has become even more critical as companies expose their systems to larger and larger numbers of users through Internet and intranet connections. To determine the security of a network, you need to answer the following questions:

- Does the organization have any special requirements for secure network connections? What kinds of information will be sent across the Oracle network?

- Can you ensure secure connections across a network without risk of information tampering? This may involve sending the data in a format that makes it tamper-proof and also ensures that the data cannot be captured and read by parties other than the client and the intended Oracle server.

- Is there a need to centralize the authorizations that an individual has to each of the Oracle servers? In large organizations that have many Oracle services, this can be a management and administration issue.

Once you gain an understanding of what the network security requirements are, you should know the following:

- The network hardware and software requirements

- The modifications to applications to meet these security requirements

- The policy and procedure changes within the organization to meet the requirements

- The staffing levels to monitor and manage security

Interfacing Existing Systems with New Systems

Many organizations are faced with the challenge of interfacing legacy systems to new systems. Often these legacy systems contain mission-critical information, and must be able to communicate to new applications as the business evolves. If existing computer systems must communicate with Oracle server networks, you need to answer the following questions:

- Does the application that needs to perform the communication require a seamless, real-time interface?

- Does the existing system use a non-Oracle database such as IBM DB2 or Microsoft SQL Server?

- Will information be transferred periodically from the existing system to the Oracle server? If so, what is the frequency and which transport mechanisms should be used? Will the Oracle server need to send information back to the existing system?

- Do applications need to gather data from multiple sources, including Oracle and non-Oracle databases, simultaneously?

- What are the applications involved that require this interface?

- Will these network requirements necessitate design changes to existing systems?

Answering these questions will give you a better understanding of what systems need to be able to communicate with Oracle Net and to what degree these systems need to be integrated.

Network Responsibilities for the DBA

As a database administrator, you have many design issues to consider when implementing a network of Oracle servers in the enterprise. Here are some of your key responsibilities:

- Understand the network configuration options available and know which options should be used based on the requirements of the organization.

- Understand the underlying network architecture of the organization in order to make informed design decisions.

- Work closely with the network engineers to ensure consistent and reliable connections to the Oracle servers.

- Understand the tools available for configuring and managing the network.

- Troubleshoot connection problems on the client, middle tier, and server.

- Ensure secure connections and use the available network configurations, when necessary, to attain higher degrees of security for sensitive data transmissions.

- Stay abreast of trends in the industry and changes to the Oracle architecture that might have an impact on network design decisions.

Network Configurations

You can select from three basic types of network configurations when designing an Oracle infrastructure:

- Single tier
- Two tier
- *n*-tier

Single tier is the simplest type. It has been around for years and is characterized by the use of terminals for serial connections to the Oracle server. The two-tier configuration is also referred to as the client/server architecture, and more recently the *n*-tier architecture has been introduced. Let's take a look at each of these configuration alternatives.

Single-Tier Architecture

Single-tier architecture was the standard for many years before the birth of the PC. Applications using single-tier architecture are sometimes referred to as green-screen applications because most of the terminals that used them, such as the IBM 3270, had green screens. Single-tier architecture is commonly associated with mainframe-type applications.

This architecture is still in use today for many mission-critical applications, such as order processing and fulfillment and inventory control, because it is the simplest architecture to configure and administer. Because the terminals are directly connected to the host computer, the complexities of network protocols and multiple operating systems don't exist.

When a single-tier architecture is used, users interact with the database using terminals, which are nongraphical, character-based devices. Figure 4.1 shows an example of the single-tier architecture. In this type of architecture, client terminals are directly connected to larger server systems such as mainframes. All the intelligence exists on the mainframe, and all processing takes place there. Simple serial connections also exist on the mainframe. Although no complex network architecture is necessary, a single-tier architecture is somewhat limiting in terms of scalability and flexibility. Because all the processing must take place on the server, the server can become the bottleneck to increasing performance.

FIGURE 4.1 Single-tier architecture

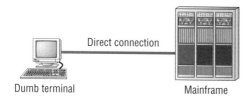

Direct connection

Dumb terminal   Mainframe

Two-Tier Architecture

Two-tier architecture gained popularity with the introduction of the PC and is commonly referred to as client/server computing. In a two-tier environment, clients connect to servers over a network using a network protocol, which is the agreed-upon method for the client to communicate with the server. TCP/IP (Transmission Control Protocol/Internet Protocol) is a popular network protocol and has become the de facto standard of network computing. Whether you choose TCP/IP or some other network protocol, both the client and the server must be able to understand it. Figure 4.2 shows an example of a two-tier architecture.

This architecture has definite benefits over single-tier architecture. First, client/server computing introduces the graphical user interface (GUI). This interface is easier to understand and learn, and it offers more flexibility than the traditional character-based interfaces of the single-tier architecture. Also, two-tier architecture allows the client computer to share the application process load. To a certain degree, this reduces the processing requirements of the server.

The two-tier architecture does have some faults, even though at one time, this configuration was thought to be the panacea of all networking architectures. Unfortunately, the main problem—that being scalability—persists. Notice that the term *client/server* contains a slash (/). The slash represents the invisible component of the two-tier architecture and the one that is often overlooked: the network! The limitation of client/server computing is one of scalability.

When prototyping projects, many developers fail to consider the network component and soon find out that what worked well in a small environment does not scale effectively to larger, more complex systems. The two-tier architecture model was subject to a great deal of redundancy because application software was required on every desktop. As a result, many companies end up with bloated PCs and large servers that still do not perform adequately. What is needed is a more scalable model for network communications. That is what *n*-tier architecture provides.

N-Tier Architecture

N-tier architecture is the next logical step after two-tier architecture. Instead of dividing application processing work between a client and a server, you divide the work among three or more machines. The n-tier architecture introduces *middleware* components, such as application servers or web servers, situated between the client and the database server, which can be used for a variety of tasks, including the following:

- Moving data between machines that work with different network protocols

- Serving as firewalls that can control client access to the servers

- Offloading processing of the business logic from the clients and servers to the middle tier

- Executing transactions and monitoring activity between clients and servers to balance the load among multiple servers

- Acting as a gateway to bridge existing systems to new systems

The Internet is an example of the ultimate *n*-tier architecture, with the user's browser providing a consistent presentation interface. This common interface means less training of staff and also increases the potential reuse of client-side application components.

FIGURE 4.2   Two-tier architecture

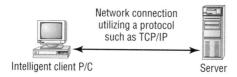

N-tier architecture is rapidly becoming the architecture of choice for enterprise networks. This model is scalable and divides the tasks of presentation, business logic and routing, and database processing among many machines, which means that this model accommodates large applications. Many factors are driving *n*-tier computing, such as the Internet and Oracle grid computing, which uses a large number of back-end processors to scale database services and connectivity.

By reducing the processing load on the database servers, those servers can do more work with the same number of resources. Also, the transaction servers can balance the flow of network transactions intelligently, and application servers can reduce the processing and memory requirements of the client (see Figure 4.3).

An Overview of Oracle Net Features

Oracle Net is the glue that bonds the Oracle network together. It is responsible for handling client-to-server and server-to-server communications, and it can be configured on the client, the middle-tier application, web servers, and the Oracle server.

Oracle Net manages the flow of information in the Oracle network infrastructure. First, it establishes the initial connection to the Oracle server, and then it acts as the messenger, passing requests from the client back to the server or passing them between two Oracle servers. Oracle Net handles all negotiations between the client and server during the client connection.

In addition to functioning as an information manager, Oracle Net supports the use of middleware products such as Oracle Application Server and Oracle Connection Manager. These products allow *n*-tier architectures to be used in the enterprise, which increases the flexibility and performance of application designs.

FIGURE 4.3   Connection requests in *n*-tier architecture

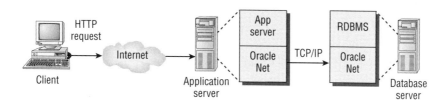

To provide a further understanding of the features of Oracle Net, the following sections discuss in detail the five categories of networking solutions that Oracle Net addresses:

- Connectivity
- Manageability
- Scalability
- Security
- Accessibility

Connectivity

There are many ways in which a client can interact with an Oracle database. A client may be running a PC-based application or a dumb terminal application, or perhaps the client is connecting to the database via the Internet. Let's take a look at how Oracle supports connectivity to the database through these and other interfaces.

Multi-Protocol Support

Oracle Net supports a wide range of industry-standard protocols such as TCP/IP and named pipes. This support is handled transparently and allows Oracle Net to connect to a wide range of computers and a wide range of operating environments.

Multiple Operating Systems

Oracle Net can run on many operating system platforms, from Windows XP, to all variants of Unix, to large mainframe-based operating systems. This range allows users to bridge existing systems to other Unix or PC-based systems, which increases the data access flexibility of the organization without making wholesale changes to the existing systems.

Java and JDBC

Applications written in Java can take advantage of the Java Database Connectivity (JDBC) drivers provided with Oracle to connect to an Oracle server. The two basic types of JDBC drivers are JDBC Oracle Call Interface (OCI) and JDBC thin.

The JDBC Oracle Call Interface driver is a client-side installed driver that is used if the Java application is resident on a client computer. This driver is also called a type II driver because the driver software is installed on the computer that is using the application. It uses OCI to interact with the Oracle Net infrastructure. Figure 4.4 shows how a client and server communicate when using a JDBC OCI connection.

In this example, the Java application installed on the client uses the JDBC OCI driver and Oracle database server. When an application makes a database request, it uses the JDBC OCI driver to translate the JDBC calls and send them to Oracle Net. Oracle Net is used on both the client and server to broker all communications between the two endpoints.

The JDBC thin driver is written entirely in Java and, as such, is platform independent. It does not have to be installed on a client computer (hence, the term *thin driver*). The driver interfaces directly with a layer of the Oracle Net infrastructure called the Two-Task Common Layer.

FIGURE 4.4   Oracle JDBC OCI connection

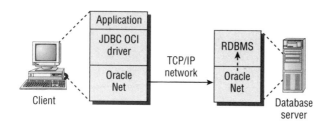

Manageability

Oracle Net provides a variety of features that allow you to manage the components of an Oracle network. Let's review the key manageability features of Oracle Net.

Web Applications

Oracle Net supports a variety of connectivity solutions from a web browser interface. Connections can be made through a middle-tier web or application server or directly from a web browser to an Oracle service.

When a middle-tier solution is used, the web browser uses HTTP to contact a database service and request information. Typically, an application or web server receives this request and hands it off to Oracle Net, which manages the connection between the web server and the database server. Once the database server receives the connection request, the request is processed and passed back to the web server. The web server then sends the response back to the client's web browser. This type of request fulfillment requires that the middle-tier application server be loaded with the Oracle Net software, but the client does not require any additional software.

Oracle also supports web connectivity directly from a web client. For example, a Java applet running within a web browser can use a JDBC driver to connect directly to an Oracle server without the need for an application or web server.

Location Transparency

Oracle Net provides the infrastructure to manage the database location. This is important especially in large organizations that support many databases and clients. Each database in the organization is represented as one or more services. Database services are defined by one or more service names. The actual definition of the service names is managed within Oracle Net. The definition holds information about the type and location of the service on the network. This layer of abstraction provides location transparency to the client and centralizes the management of connection information within Oracle Net, which simplifies the job of managing the network.

Directory Naming

Directory Naming allows service names to be resolved through a centralized naming repository. The central repository takes the form of a Lightweight Directory Access Protocol (LDAP)–compliant server. LDAP is a protocol and language that defines a standard method for storing, identifying, and retrieving services. It provides a simplified way to manage directories of information, whether this information is about users in an organization or Oracle services connected to a network. The LDAP server allows for a standard form of managing and resolving names in an Oracle environment. The quality of these services excels because LDAP provides a single, industry-standard interface to a directory service such as Oracle Internet Directory (OID). By using OID, you ensure security and reliability of the directory information because information is stored in the Oracle database.

As of Oracle 10*g*, Directory Naming is the preferred method of centralized naming within an Oracle environment, replacing the Oracle Names Server, which is no longer supported for centralized naming.

Scalability

Many enterprise systems are growing rapidly, supporting larger and larger databases and user communities. Your network capabilities need to be able support this growth. Oracle Net provides features that allow you to expand your network reach and maximize your system resources to meet these demands.

Oracle Shared Server

Oracle Shared Server is an optional configuration of the Oracle server that allows support for a large number of concurrent connections without increasing physical resource requirements. This is accomplished by sharing resources among groups of users.

Directory Services: Oracle Internet Directory

The OID is an LDAP 3–compliant directory service that provides the repository and infrastructure needed to enable a centralized naming solution using Directory Naming. OID is compatible with older releases of Oracle such as Oracle8*i* and Oracle9*i*. In Oracle 10*g*, the OID runs as an application. The OID service can run on a remote server, and it can communicate with the Oracle server using Oracle Net. The OID is a scalable architecture, and it provides mechanisms for replicating service information among other Oracle servers.

OID also provides security in a number of ways. First, it can be integrated into a Secure Sockets Layer (SSL) environment to ensure user authentication. Also, an administrator can maintain policies that grant or deny access to services. These policies are defined for entities within the OID tree structure.

Oracle Shared Server is discussed in detail in Chapter 5, "Oracle Shared Server."

Connection Manager

Oracle Connection Manager is a middleware solution that provides three additional scalability features:

Multiplexing   Connection Manager can group many client connections and send them as a single multiplexed network connection to the Oracle server. This reduces the total number of network connections that the server has to manage.

Network access   You can configure Connection Manager with rules that restrict access by IP address. You can set up this rules-based configuration to accept or reject client connection requests. Also, connections can be restricted by point of origin, destination server, or Oracle server.

Cross-protocol connectivity   This feature allows clients and servers that use different network protocols to communicate. Connection Manager acts as a translator, providing two-way protocol conversion.

Oracle Connection Manager is controlled by a set of background processes that manage the communications between clients and servers. Figure 4.5 provides an overview of the Connection Manager architecture.

FIGURE 4.5   Connection Manager architecture

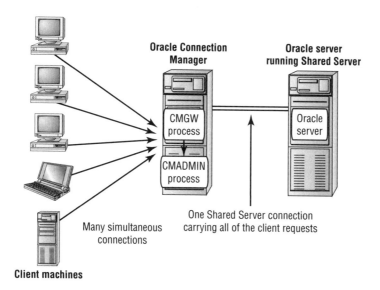

Security

The threat of data tampering and database security is an issue of major concern in many organizations, as network systems continue to grow in number and complexity and as users gain increasing access to systems. Sensitive business transactions are being conducted with greater frequency and, in many cases, are not protected from unauthorized tampering or message interception. Oracle Net is capable of providing organizations with a secure network environment to conduct business transactions.

Advanced Security

Oracle Advanced Security, formerly known as the Advanced Security Option and the Advanced Networking Option, not only provides the tools necessary to ensure secure transmissions of sensitive information, but it also provides mechanisms to confidently identify and authenticate users in the Oracle enterprise.

When configured on the client and the Oracle server, Oracle Advanced Security supports secured data transactions by encrypting and optionally checksumming the transmission of information that is sent in a transaction. Oracle supports encryption and checksumming by taking advantage of industry-standard algorithms, such as RSA RC4, Standard DES and Triple DES, and MD5 checksumming. These security features ensure that data transmitted from the client has not been altered during transmission to the Oracle server.

Oracle Advanced Security also gives you the ability to authenticate users connecting to the Oracle servers. In fact, a number of authentication features ensure that users really are who they claim to be. These are offered in the form of token cards, which use a physical card and a user-identifying PIN number to gain access to the system; the biometrics option, which uses fingerprint technology to authenticate user connection requests; public key; and certificate-based authentication.

Another feature of Oracle Advanced Security is the ability to have a single sign-on mechanism for clients. Single sign-on is accomplished with a centralized security server that allows the user to connect to any of the Oracle services in the enterprise using a single user ID and password. Oracle leverages the industry-standard features of Kerberos to enable these capabilities. This greatly simplifies the privilege matrix that administrators must manage when they are dealing with large numbers of users and systems.

Kerberos is an authentication mechanism based on the sharing of secrets between two systems.

Firewall Support

Firewalls are an important security mechanism in corporate networks. Firewalls are generally a combination of hardware and software used to control network traffic and prevent intruders from compromising corporate network security. Firewalls fall into two broad categories:

IP-Filtering Firewalls *IP-filtering firewalls* monitor the network packet traffic on IP networks and filter out packets that either originated or did not originate from specific groups of machines.

The information contained in the IP packet header is interrogated to obtain this information. Vendors of this type of firewall include Network Associates and Axent Communications.

Proxy-Based Firewalls   *Proxy-based firewalls* prevent information from outside the firewall from flowing directly into the corporate network. The firewall acts as a gatekeeper, inspecting packets and sending only the appropriate information through to the corporate network. This prevents any direct communication between clients outside the firewall and applications inside the firewall. Check Point Software Technologies and Cisco are examples of vendors that market proxy-based firewalls.

Oracle works closely with the vendors of both types of firewalls to ensure support of database traffic through these types of mechanism. Oracle supplies the Oracle Net Application Proxy Kit to the firewall vendors. This product can be incorporated into the firewall architecture to allow database packets to pass through the firewall and still maintain a high degree of security.

Accessibility

In many organizations, workers need to be able to communicate across a variety of systems and databases. They spend a lot of time bringing together data from different systems. The accessibility features of Oracle Net have capabilities that allow you to communicate with non-database data sources. This ability opens up new opportunities to provide customers with accurate and timely information.

Real World Scenario

Know Thy Firewall

It is important to understand your network infrastructure, the network routes that you are using to obtain database connections, and the type of firewall products that you are using. In more than one situation, I've seen firewalls cause connectivity issues between a client and an Oracle server.

For instance, a small patch was applied to a firewall when I was working as a DBA for one of my former employers. In this case, employees started experiencing intermittent disconnects from the Oracle database. After many days of investigation and network tracing, we pinned down the exact problem. We then contacted the firewall vendor, who sent us a new patch to apply that corrected the problem.

In another instance, I was working as a DBA for a large corporate client. The development staff started experiencing a similar connection problem. It turned out that the networking routes for the development staff had been modified to connect through a new firewall, with connections timing out after 20 minutes. This timeout was too short for this department. Increasing the timeout parameter solved the problem.

These are examples of the types of network changes that you need to be aware of to avoid unnecessary downtime and to avoid wasting staff time and resources.

Heterogeneous Services

Heterogeneous Services provide the ability to communicate with non-Oracle databases and services. These services allow organizations to leverage and interact with their existing data stores without having to necessarily move the data to an Oracle server.

The suite of Heterogeneous Services comprises the *Oracle Transparent Gateway* and *Generic Connectivity*. These products allow Oracle to communicate with non-Oracle data sources in a seamless configuration. Heterogeneous Services also integrate existing systems with the Oracle environment, which allows you to leverage your investment in those systems. These services also allow for two-way communication and replication from Oracle data sources to non-Oracle data sources.

Transparent Gateway seamlessly extends the reach of Oracle to non-Oracle data stores, which allows you to treat non-Oracle data sources as if they were part of the Oracle environment. In fact, the user is not even aware that the data being accessed is coming from a non-Oracle source. This can significantly reduce the time and investment necessary to transition from existing systems to the Oracle environment. Transparent Gateway fully supports SQL and the Oracle transaction control features, and it currently supports access to more than 30 non-Oracle data sources.

Generic Connectivity provides a set of agents, which contain basic connectivity capabilities. It also provides a foundation so that you can custom-build connectivity solutions using standard OLE Database, Microsoft's interface to data access. OLE DB requires an ODBC driver to interface to the agents. You can also use ODBC as a stand-alone connection solution. For example, with the proper Oracle ODBC driver, you can access an Oracle database from programs such as Microsoft Excel. (You can obtain these drivers from Oracle or third-party vendors.) Because these drivers are generic in nature, they do not provide as robust an interface to external services as does the Transparent Gateway.

External Procedures

In some development efforts, interfacing with procedures that reside outside the database may be necessary. These procedures are typically written in a third-generation language, such as C. Oracle Net provides the ability to invoke such external procedures from Oracle PL/SQL callouts. When a call is made, a process is started that acts as an interface between Oracle and the external procedure. This callout process defaults to the name *extproc*. The listener is then responsible for supplying information, such as a library or procedure name and any parameters, to the called procedure. These programs are then loaded and executed under the control of the extproc process.

Configuring Oracle Net on the Server

Now that you understand the basic features that Oracle Net provides, you need to understand how to configure the major components of Oracle Net. You must configure Oracle Net on the server in order for client connections to be established. This section will focus on how to configure the network elements of the Oracle server. It will also describe the types of connection methods that Oracle Net supports. We will then discuss how to manage Oracle Net on the server and troubleshoot connections from the server if clients experience connection problems.

Understanding the Oracle Listener

The Oracle *listener* is the main server-side Oracle networking component that allows connections to be established between client computers and an Oracle database. You can think of the listener as a big ear that listens for connection requests to Oracle services.

The type of Oracle service being requested is part of the connection descriptor information supplied by the process requesting a connection, and the service name resolves to an Oracle database. The listener can listen for any number of databases configured on the server, and it is able to listen for requests being transported on a variety of protocols. A client connection can be initiated from the same machine that the listener resides on, or it may come from some remote location.

The listener is controlled by a centralized file called *listener.ora*. Though only one listener.ora file is configured per machine, there may be numerous listeners on a server, and this file contains all the configuration information for every listener configured on the server. If multiple listeners are configured on a single server, they are usually set up for failover purposes or to balance connection requests and minimize the burden of connections on a single listener.

Multiple listeners may also be used when you configure Oracle Real Application Clusters. In a Real Application Clusters environment, these listeners typically span multiple server nodes, and all the corresponding nodes connect to a single database. Later in this chapter, in the section "Additional Configurations When Using Multiple Listeners," we'll discuss other reasons to configure multiple listeners.

 The content and structure of the listener.ora file is discussed later in this chapter, in the section "Managing Oracle Listeners."

Every listener is a named process that runs on either a middle-tier server or the database server. The default name of the Oracle listener is LISTENER, and it is typically created when you install Oracle. If you configure multiple listeners, each has a unique name. The following is an example of the contents of the listener.ora file:

```
# listener.ora Network Configuration File:
    D:\oracle\ora10g\NETWORK\ADMIN\listener.ora
# Generated by Oracle configuration tools.

SID_LIST_LISTENER =
  (SID_LIST =
    (SID_DESC =
      (SID_NAME = PLSExtProc)
      (ORACLE_HOME = D:\oracle\ora10g)
      (PROGRAM = extproc)
    )
    (SID_DESC =
      (GLOBAL_DBNAME = ORCL.COM)
```

```
      (ORACLE_HOME = d:\oracle\ora10g)
      (SID_NAME = ORCL)
    )
  )


LISTENER =
  (DESCRIPTION_LIST =
    (DESCRIPTION =
      (ADDRESS = (PROTOCOL = TCP)(HOST = mjworn.corp.testenv.net)(PORT = 1521))
    )
    (DESCRIPTION =
      (ADDRESS = (PROTOCOL = IPC)(KEY = EXTPROC))
    )
  )
```

Now that you have a basic understanding of the Oracle Listener, let's explore the main function of the Listener, responding to client connection requests.

How Do Listeners Respond to Connection Requests?

A listener can respond to a client request for a connection in several ways. The response depends on several factors, such as how the server-side network components are configured and what type of connection the client is requesting. The listener then responds to the connection request in one of two ways.

The listener can spawn a new process and pass control of the client session to the process. In a *dedicated server* environment, every client connection is serviced by its own server-side process. Server-side processes are not shared among clients. Two types of dedicated connection methods are possible: direct and redirect. Each method results in a separate process that handles client processing, but the mechanics of the actual connection initiation process are different. For remote clients to use dedicated connections, the listener process must be running on the same physical server as the database or databases for which it is listening.

The listener can also pass control of a connection request to a dispatcher. This type of connection takes place in an Oracle Shared Server environment. There are also two types of connection methods when using Oracle Shared Server: direct and redirect.

Let's take a look at each of these connection method types.

 We'll discuss Oracle Shared Server in detail in Chapter 5.

Dedicated Connections: Direct Handoff Method

Direct handoff connections are possible when the client and database exist on the same server. For example, a direct handoff method is used when the client connection request originates from the same machine on which the listener and database are running.

Another name for direct handoff connections is bequeath connections.

The following steps, which show the connection process for the bequeath connections, are illustrated in Figure 4.6:

1. The client contacts the Oracle listener after resolving the service name.
2. The listener starts a dedicated process, and the client connection inherits the dedicated server process network connect endpoint from the listener.
3. The client now has an established connection to the dedicated server process.

Dedicated Connections: Redirect Method

Redirect connections occur in a dedicated server environment when the client exists on a machine that is separate from the listener and database server. The listener must inform the client of the address of the spawned process in order for the process to contact the newly created dedicated server process.

The following steps, which show the connection process for redirect connections in a dedicated server environment, are illustrated in Figure 4.7:

1. The client contacts the Oracle listener after resolving the service name.
2. The listener starts a dedicated process.
3. The listener sends an acknowledgment back to the client with the address of the dedicated server connect endpoint on the database server to which the client will connect.
4. The client establishes a connection to the dedicated server connect endpoint.

FIGURE 4.6 Dedicated connection: direct handoff method

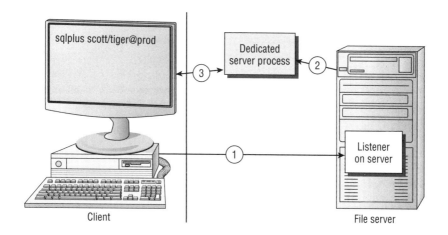

FIGURE 4.7 Dedicated connections: redirect method

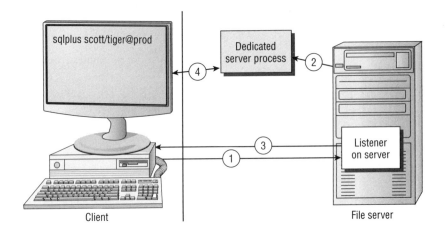

Oracle Shared Server: Direct Handoff Method

When you are using Oracle Shared Server, the client connection can also be established using a direct handoff method. This would be the case, for example, when the client request originates from the same machine as the listener and the database are running. Figure 4.8 outlines the connection steps when using Oracle Shared Server and the direct handoff method:

1. The client contacts the Oracle listener after resolving the service name.
2. The Oracle Listener passes the connection request to the least loaded dispatcher.
3. The client now has an established connection to the dispatcher process.

FIGURE 4.8 Oracle Shared Server: direct handoff method

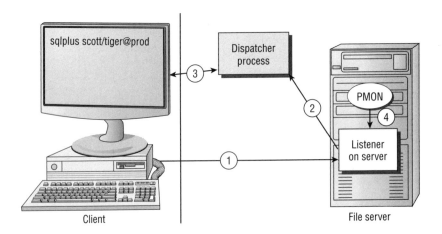

Oracle Shared Server: Redirect Method

The listener can also redirect the user to a server process or a dispatcher process when using Oracle Shared Server. This type of connection can occur when the operating system does not directly support direct handoff connections or the listener is not on the same physical machine as the Oracle server.

The following steps are illustrated in Figure 4.9:

1. The client contacts the Oracle server after resolving the service name.

2. The listener sends information back to the client, redirecting the client to the dispatcher port. The original network connection between the listener and the client is disconnected.

3. The client then sends a connect signal to the server or dispatcher process to establish a network connection.

4. The dispatcher or server process sends an acknowledgment back to the client.

5. PMON (process monitor) sends information to the listener about the number of connections being serviced by the dispatchers. The listener uses this information to maintain consistent loads between the dispatchers.

Managing Oracle Listeners

You can configure the server-side listener files in a number of ways. As part of the initial Oracle installation process, the installer prompts you to create a default listener. If you choose this method, the installer uses the set of screens that are a part of the Oracle Net Configuration Assistant to do the initial listener configuration. Figure 4.10 shows an example of the opening screen for this assistant.

FIGURE 4.9   Oracle Shared Server: redirect connection method

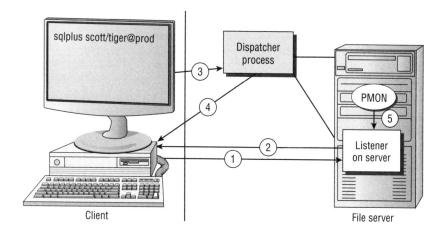

FIGURE 4.10 Oracle Net Configuration Assistant opening screen

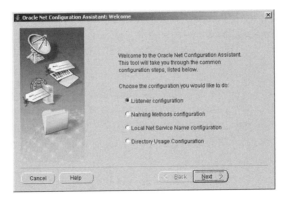

If you want to set up more than just basic configurations of Oracle network files, you will have to use the Oracle Net Manager, the web-based tool Oracle Enterprise Manager (EM), or the command-line facility `lsnrctl`. In the next few sections, you will learn how to use these tools to configure the server-side network files.

Managing Listeners with Oracle Net Manager

Oracle Net Manager is a tool you can use to create and manage most client- and server-side configuration files. The Oracle Net Manager has evolved from the Oracle7 tool, Network Manager, to the latest Oracle 10g version. Throughout this evolution, Oracle has continued to enhance the functionality and usability of the tool.

If you are using a Windows environment, you can start the Oracle Net Manager by choosing Start ≻ Programs ≻ *Your Oracle 10g Programs choice* ≻ Configuration and Migration Tools ≻ Oracle Net Manager. In a Unix environment, you can start it by running `./netmgr` from your `$ORACLE_HOME/bin` directory.

Figure 4.11 shows an example of the Oracle Net Manager opening screen.

Configuring Listener Services Using the Oracle Net Manager

Oracle Net Manager provides an easy-to-use graphical interface for configuring most of the network files that you will be using. By using Oracle Net Manager, you can ensure that the files are created in a consistent format, which will reduce the potential for connection problems.

When you first start the Oracle Net Manager, the opening screen displays a tree structure with a top level called Oracle Net Configuration. If you click the plus (+) sign next to this icon, you will see the Local folder. The choices under the Local folder relate to different network configuration files. Here are the network file choices and what each configures:

Icon	File Configured
Profile	`sqlnet.ora`
Service Naming	`Tnsnames.ora`
Listeners	`Listener.ora`

FIGURE 4.11   The opening screen for Oracle Net Manager

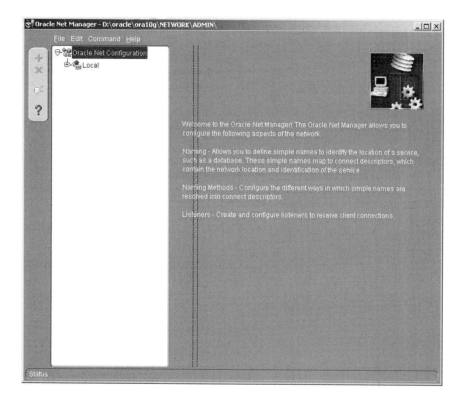

Creating the Listener

Earlier, we said that, by default, Oracle creates a listener called LISTENER when it is initially installed. The default settings that Oracle uses for the `listener.ora` file are shown here:

Section of the File	Setting
Listener Name	LISTENER
Port	1521
Protocols	TCP/IP and IPC
Host Name	Default Host Name
SID Name	Default Instance

You can use Oracle Net Manager to create a non-default listener or change the definition of existing listeners. The Oracle Net Manager has a wizard interface for creating most of the basic network elements, such as the `listener.ora` and `tnsnames.ora` files.

Follow these steps to create the listener:

1. Click the plus (+) sign next to the Local icon.

2. Click the Listeners folder.

3. Click the plus sign icon or choose Edit ➢ Create to open the Choose Listener Name dialog box.

4. The Oracle Net Manager defaults to LISTENER or to LISTENER1 if the default listener is already created. Click OK if this is correct, or enter a new name and then click OK to open the Listening Locations screen, as shown in Figure 4.12.

5. To configure the listening locations, click the Listening Locations drop-down list and make your selection. Then click the Add Address button at the bottom of the screen to open a new window.

FIGURE 4.12 The Listening Locations screen

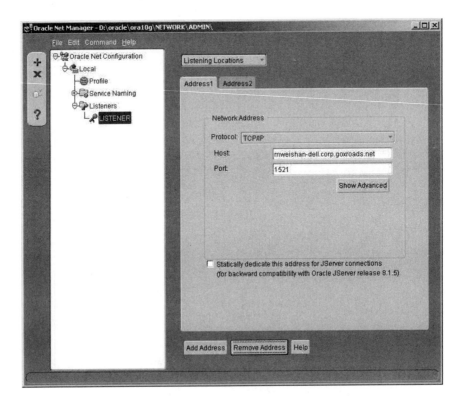

The prompts on this screen depend on your protocol. By default, TCP/IP information is displayed. If you are using TCP/IP, the Host and Port fields are filled in for you. The *host* is the name of the machine in which the listener is running, and the *port* is the listening location for TCP/IP connections. The default value for the port is 1521.

6. To save your information, choose File ➢ Save Network Configuration, and then look in the directory where the files was saved.

You can add additional listeners by following these steps. Listeners must have unique names and listen on separate ports, so assign the listener a new name and a new port (1522, for example). You also must assign service names to the listener. We'll see how to add service information in the next section.

You always know where the files are stored by looking at the top banner of the Oracle Net Manager screen.

The Oracle Net Manager actually creates three files in this process: `listener.ora`, `tnsnames.ora`, and `sqlnet.ora`. The `tnsnames.ora` file does not contain any information. The `sqlnet.ora` file may contain a few entries at this point, but you can ignore them for the time being. The `listener.ora` file contains information as shown in the following code.

```
# listener.ora Network Configuration File:
    D:\oracle\ora10g\network\admin\listener.ora
# Generated by Oracle configuration tools.

LISTENER =
  (DESCRIPTION_LIST =
    (DESCRIPTION =
      (ADDRESS_LIST =
        (ADDRESS = (PROTOCOL = TCP)(HOST = mjworn.corp.testenv.net)
    (PORT = 1521))
      )
      (ADDRESS_LIST =
        (ADDRESS = (PROTOCOL = IPC)(KEY = EXTPROC))
      )
    )
  )
```

We'll discuss the structure and content of the `listener.ora` file later in this chapter.

Adding Service Name Information to the Listener

After you create the listener with the name, protocol, and listening location information, you can define the network services to which the listener is responsible for connecting. This is called *static service registration*, because Oracle is not automatically registering the service with the listener. In releases of Oracle prior to Oracle 8*i*, static service registration was the only method to associate services with a listener.

A listener can listen to an unlimited number of network service names. Follow these steps to add the service name information:

1. To select the listener to configure, click the Listeners icon and highlight the name of the listener that you want to configure.

2. From the drop-down list at the top right of the screen, select Database Services.

3. Click the Add Database button at the bottom of the screen. This opens the window that allows you to add the database (see Figure 4.13).

4. Enter values in the Global Database Name, Oracle Home Directory, and SID fields. The entries for SID and Global Database Name are the same if you are using a flat naming convention.

5. Choose File ➢ Save to save your configuration.

FIGURE 4.13 The Database Services screen

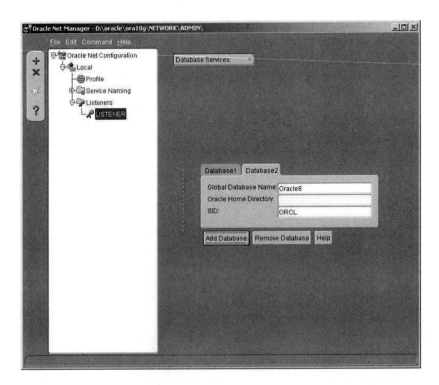

Here is an example of the completed listener.ora file:

```
# listener.ora Network Configuration File:
    D:\oracle\ora10g\NETWORK\ADMIN\listener.ora
# Generated by Oracle configuration tools.

SID_LIST_LISTENER =
  (SID_LIST =
    (SID_DESC =
      (SID_NAME = PLSExtProc)
      (ORACLE_HOME = D:\oracle\ora10g)
      (PROGRAM = extproc)
    )
    (SID_DESC =
      (GLOBAL_DBNAME = ORCL.COM)
      (ORACLE_HOME = d:\oracle\ora10g)
      (SID_NAME = ORCL)
    )
  )


LISTENER =
  (DESCRIPTION_LIST =
    (DESCRIPTION =
      (ADDRESS = (PROTOCOL = TCP)(HOST = mjworn.corp.testenv.net)(PORT = 1521))
    )
    (DESCRIPTION =
      (ADDRESS = (PROTOCOL = IPC)(KEY = EXTPROC))
    )
  )
```

Table 4.1 lists and describes each of the listener.ora parameters for the Listening Location section of the listener.ora file.

TABLE 4.1   Parameters for the Listening Location Section of *listener.ora*

Parameter	Description
LISTENER	Indicates the starting point of a listener definition. This is actually the name of the listener being defined. The default name is LISTENER.
DESCRIPTION	Describes each of the listening locations.

TABLE 4.1   Parameters for the Listening Location Section of *listener.ora* (continued)

Parameter	Description
ADDRESS_LIST	Contains address information about the locations where the listener is listening.
PROTOCOL	Designates the protocol for this listening location.
HOST	Holds the name of the machine on which the listener resides.
PORT	Contains the address on which the listener is listening.
SID_LIST_LISTENER	Defines the list of Oracle services for which the listener is configured.
SID_DESC	Describes each Oracle SID.
GLOBAL_DBNAME	Identifies the global database name. This entry should match the SERVICE_NAMES entry in the init.ora file for the Oracle service.
ORACLE_HOME	Shows the location of the Oracle executables on the server.
SID_NAME	Contains the name of the Oracle SID for the Oracle instance.

Optional *listener.ora* Parameters

You can set optional parameters that add functionality to the listener. To do so, select a parameter from the General Parameters drop-down list at the top right of the screen. Table 4.2 describes these parameters and where they can be found in the Oracle Net Manager.

Understanding Service Registration

Static service registration occurs when entries are added to the listener.ora file manually by using one of the Oracle tools. It is static because you are adding this information manually. Static service registration is necessary if you will be connecting to pre-Oracle8 *i* instances using Oracle Enterprise Manager or if you will be connecting to external services.

Another way to manage listeners that does not require manual updating of service information in the listener.ora file is called *dynamic service registration*. Dynamic service registration allows an Oracle instance to automatically register itself with an Oracle listener. The benefit of this feature is that it does not require you to perform any updates of server-side network files when new Oracle instances are created. Dynamic service registration will be covered in more detail later in this chapter, in the section "Dynamically Registering Services."

TABLE 4.2   Optional *listener.ora* Parameter Definitions

Oracle Net Manager Prompt	*listener.ora* Parameter	Description
Startup Wait Time	STARTUP_WAIT_TIME	Defines how long a listener will wait before it responds to a STATUS command in the lsnrctl command-line utility.
(Unavailable from Net Manager)	INBOUND_CONNECT_TIMEOUT	Defines how long a listener will wait for a valid response from a client once a session is initiated. The default is 10 seconds.
Save Configuration On Shutdown	SAVE_CONFIG_ON_STOP	Specifies whether modifications made during an lsnrctl session should be saved when exiting.
Log File	LOG_FILE. Will not be in listener.ora file if default setting is used. By default, listener logging is enabled with the log created in the default location.	Specifies where a listener will write log information. This is ON by default and defaults to %ORACLE_HOME%\network\log\listener.log.
Trace Level	TRACE_LEVEL. Not present if tracing is disabled. Default is OFF.	Sets the level of detail if listener connections are being traced. Valid values include Off, User, Support, and Admin.
Trace File	TRACE_FILE	Specifies the location of listener trace information. Defaults to $ORACLE_HOME\network\trace\listener.trc.
Require A Password For Listener Operations	PASSWORDS	Specifies password required to perform administrative tasks in the lsnrctl command-line utility.

As you will see, you cannot add some parameters directly from the Oracle Net Manager and must do so manually. These optional parameters also have the listener name appended to them so that you can identify the listener definition to which they belong. For example, if the parameter STARTUP_WAIT_TIME is set for the default listener, the parameter created is STARTUP_WAIT_TIME_LISTENER.

Managing Listeners with Oracle Enterprise Manager

Oracle Enterprise Manager (EM) is a web-based tool that allows you to manage many aspects of an Oracle 10*g* server. Being able to perform administrative functions via a web interface lets you administer the database from any location where a web browser is available.

You can also manage Oracle Net using EM. Once EM is installed and configured, you can invoke it via a URL from a web browser. Here is an example of a URL used to invoke the tool:

`http://mweishan-dell.corp.goxroads.net:5500/em`

You are presented with a login screen, as shown in Figure 4.14. If you want to perform administrative functions such as administering the listener, log in as a user that has the SYSDBA privilege.

Once you are connected to the database, you are presented with the main database console. Oracle provides a wealth of information about your database configuration and performance-related information within the EM framework. Figure 4.15 shows an example of the main EM console screen.

Notice under the General section a list of listeners that are available to manage. Click a listener to display a screen (see Figure 4.16) that gives you details about that listener, including when the listener was started, the net address and port information for the listener, and listening location information.

You can also add and edit listeners using the Database Control interface. Let's take a look at how to do so using the Oracle Enterprise Manager Database Control console.

FIGURE 4.14 The Oracle Enterprise Manager Login screen

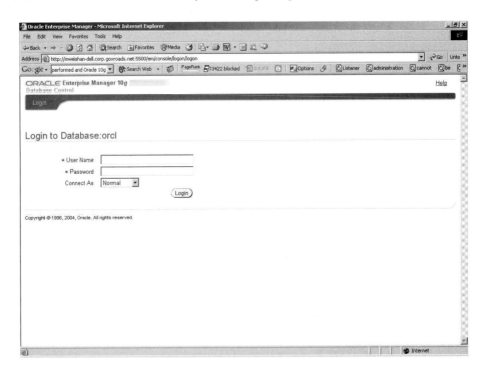

FIGURE 4.15   The Oracle Enterprise Manager main console

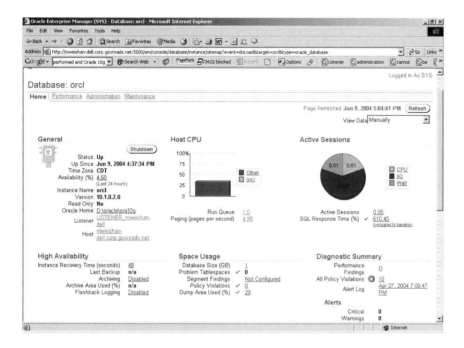

FIGURE 4.16   The Oracle Enterprise Manager Listener console

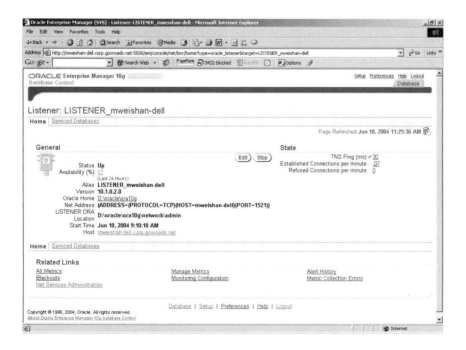

Adding a Listener using Enterprise Manager Database Control

To add a new listener using the Database Control, select the Net Services Administration option listed under the Related Links section to open the Net Services Administration screen, as shown in Figure 4.17.

From the Administer drop-down list, select Listeners and click Go to open a login screen. Connect to the server with a valid operating system user ID and password to open the listener control screen, as shown in Figure 4.18.

In this example, a listener is already configured and named LISTENER. To create an additional listener, click the Create button to open the Create Listener screen, as shown in Figure 4.19.

FIGURE 4.17 The Oracle Enterprise Manager Net Services Administration screen

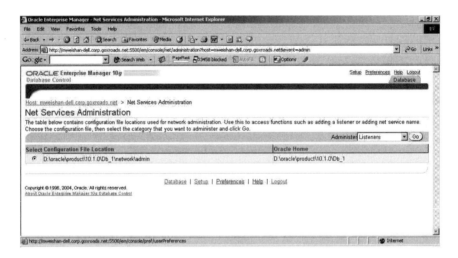

FIGURE 4.18 The Oracle Enterprise Manager listener control screen

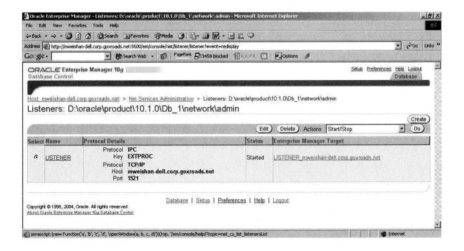

Oracle will choose a new name for you and place that in the Listener Name field. In Figure 4.19, LISTENER0 is the new listener to be created.

You can fully configure the new listener using this interface. At a minimum, the listener needs listening address information. Click the Add button to open the Add Address screen, as shown in Figure 4.20.

FIGURE 4.19   The Oracle Enterprise Manager Create Listener screen

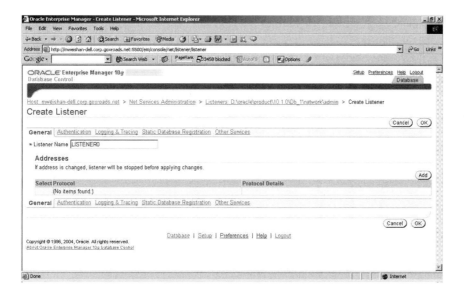

FIGURE 4.20   The Oracle Enterprise Manager Add Address screen

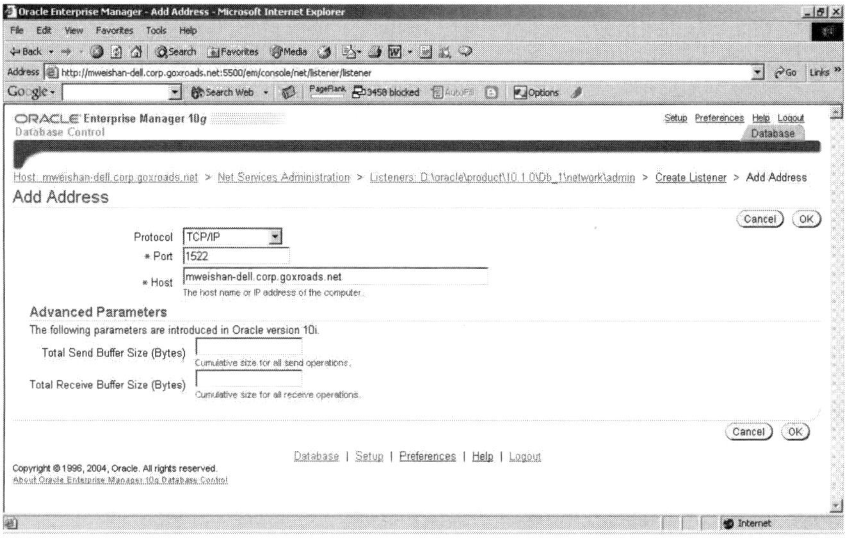

You can choose a protocol, such as TCP/IP, for which the listener will be listening. You also need to designate a listening port and host where the listener will be listening for connections. The other parameters, send and receive buffer size, are optional, advanced parameters. Click OK to save your information. You will then see the new listener listed on the Listeners screen, and you can control the listener from here (see Figure 4.21). To start the new listener, select Start/Stop from the Actions drop-down list and click Go.

Editing Existing Listeners Using Database Control

From the Oracle Enterprise Manager Listener console (shown earlier in this chapter in Figure 4.16), you can also make changes to an existing listener. Choose Edit to modify the `listener.ora` parameters, and save this information to the existing `listener.ora` file. To perform these functions, you must be logged in to the machine on which the listener file is located. From the login screen, enter the appropriate user ID and password for the machine and choose Login.

Once you are connected to the machine, you can administer all aspects of the listener. Figure 4.22 shows a snapshot of the main Enterprise Manager Oracle Net listener administration screen.

You use the tabs across the top of the listener administration screen to configure various aspects of the listener. You can manage logging and tracing, add listener services, and enter service name information to statically register new services with the listener. You can also manage the listening location and port information. If you choose to edit the port or listening location of the listener, click the Edit button to open the Edit Address screen, as shown in Figure 4.23. You can change the host name and port. Once you make a change, the listener is stopped and restarted with the new configuration information.

FIGURE 4.21   The Oracle Enterprise Manager listener control screen, with the new listener listed

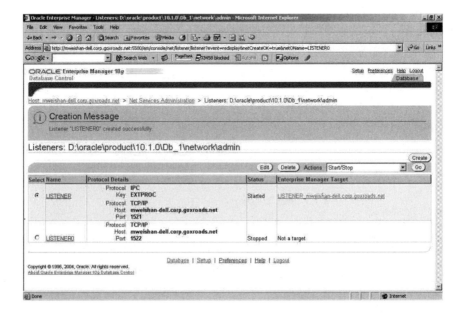

FIGURE 4.22 The Oracle Enterprise Manager listener administration screen

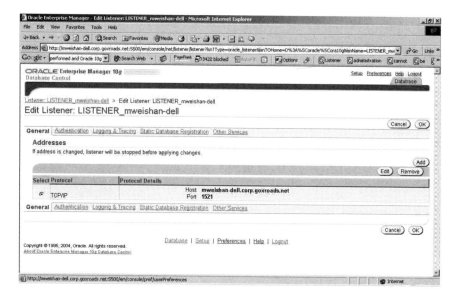

FIGURE 4.23 The Oracle Enterprise Manager Edit Address screen

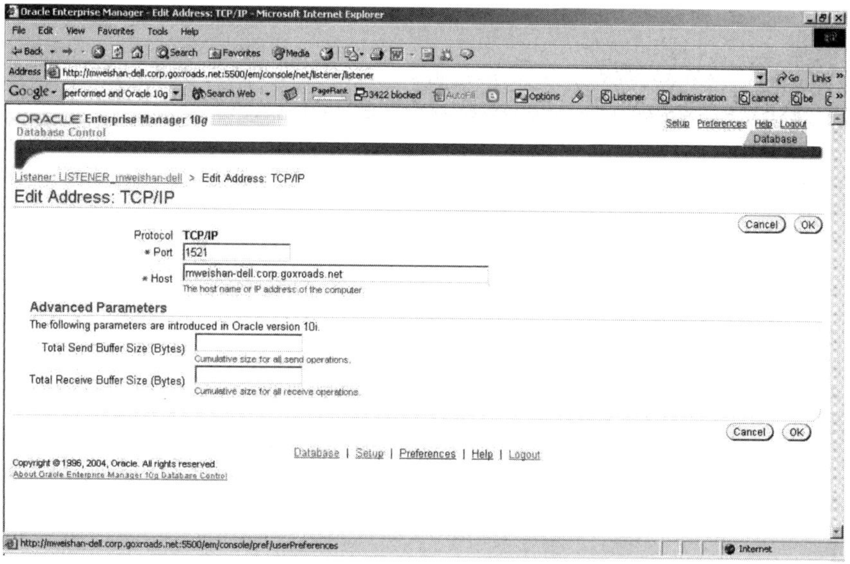

Managing Listeners with lsnrctl

You can also use a command-line interface, lsnrctl, to administer the listener. This tool gives you full configuration and administration capabilities. If you have been using Oracle, this tool should be familiar. This command-line interface has been around since the early releases of the Oracle product. Other Oracle network components, such as Connection Manager, also have command-line tools that are used to administer their associated processes.

 On Windows, the listener runs as a service. Services are programs that run in the background on Windows. You can start the listener from the Windows Services panel. Then select the name of the listener service from the list of services. If the name of your listener is Listener, for example, look for an entry such as OracleOra10gListener. Select the listener name and choose Start.

To invoke the command-line utility, type **lsnrctl** at the command line. The following code shows a resulting login screen:

```
D:\oracle\ora10g\BIN>lsnrctl

LSNRCTL for 32-bit Windows: Version 10.1.0.2.0 - Production on
    10-JUN-2004 09:57
:59

Copyright (c) 1991, 2004, Oracle. All rights reserved.

Welcome to LSNRCTL, type "help" for information.

LSNRCTL>
```

You can perform a variety of functions from within the lsnrctl utility. Let's take a look at the most common functions you'll perform on the listener using this utility.

Starting the Listener

The listener has commands to perform various functions. You can type **help** at the LSNRCTL> prompt to display a list of these commands. To start the default listener named LISTENER, type **start** at the prompt. To start a different listener, type **start** and then that listener name. For example, typing **start listener1** starts the LISTENER1 listener.

The following code shows the results of starting the default listener:

```
D:\oracle\ora10g\BIN>lsnrctl start

LSNRCTL for 32-bit Windows: Version 10.1.0.2.0 - Production on
    10-JUN-2004 09:58
:45
```

Copyright (c) 1991, 2004, Oracle. All rights reserved.

Starting tnslsnr: please wait...

TNSLSNR for 32-bit Windows: Version 10.1.0.2.0 - Production
System parameter file is D:\oracle\ora10g\network\admin\listener.ora
Log messages written to D:\oracle\ora10g\network\log\listener.log
Listening on: (DESCRIPTION=(ADDRESS=(PROTOCOL=tcp)(HOST=mweishan-
    dell.corp.goxroads.net)(PORT=1522)))

Connecting to (DESCRIPTION=(ADDRESS=(PROTOCOL=TCP)(HOST=mweishan-
    dell.corp.goxroads.net)(PORT=1522)))
STATUS of the LISTENER

Alias   LISTENER
Version   TNSLSNR for 32-bit Windows:
     Version 10.1.0.2.0 - Production
Start Date   10-JUN-2004 09:58:47
Uptime   0 days 0 hr. 0 min. 2 sec
Trace Level   off
Security   ON: Local OS Authentication
SNMP   OFF
Listener Parameter File D:\oracle\ora10g\network\admin\listener.ora
Listener Log File   D:\oracle\ora10g\network\log\listener.log
Listening Endpoints Summary...
  (DESCRIPTION=(ADDRESS=(PROTOCOL=tcp)(HOST=mweishan-
  dell.corp.goxroads.net)(POR
T=1522)))
Services Summary...
Service "PLSExtProc" has 1 instance(s).
  Instance "PLSExtProc", status UNKNOWN, has 1 handler(s) for this service...
Service "orcl.com" has 1 instance(s).
  Instance "ORCL", status UNKNOWN, has 1 handler(s) for this service...
The command completed successfully

This listing shows a summary of information, including the services that the listener is listening for, the log locations, and whether tracing is enabled for the listener.

Reloading the Listener

If the listener is running and modifications are made to the listener.ora file manually, with Oracle Net Manager, or with Enterprise Manager, you must reload the listener to refresh the listener with the most current information. The reload command rereads the listener.ora file for the new definitions. As you can see, it is not necessary to stop and start the listener to reload it. Although stopping and restarting the listener can also accomplish a reload, using the reload command is better because the listener is not actually stopped, which makes this process more efficient. The following code shows an example of the reload command:

 Reloading the listener has no effect on clients connected to the Oracle server.

```
D:\oracle\ora10g\BIN>lsnrctl reload

LSNRCTL for 32-bit Windows: Version 10.1.0.2.0 - Production on
    10-JUN-2004 10:00:02

Copyright (c) 1991, 2004, Oracle.  All rights reserved.

Connecting to (DESCRIPTION=(ADDRESS=(PROTOCOL=TCP)(HOST=mweishan-
    dell.corp.goxro
ads.net)(PORT=1522)))
The command completed successfully
```

In the code example above, Oracle has reread the listener.ora file and applied any changes that we made to the file against the currently running listener process. We can see the address, protocol, and port designation of the default listener. Notice that this listener is listening on a non-default port of 1522.

Showing the Status of the Listener

You can display the status of the listener by using the status command. The status command shows whether the listener is active, the locations of the logs and trace files, how long the listener has been running, and the services for the listener. This is a quick way to verify that the listener is up and running with no problems.

The following code shows the result of the lsnrctl status command:

```
D:\oracle\ora10g\BIN>lsnrctl status

LSNRCTL for 32-bit Windows: Version 10.1.0.2.0 - Production on
    10-JUN-2004 10:00:36

Copyright (c) 1991, 2004, Oracle.  All rights reserved.
```

```
Connecting to (DESCRIPTION=(ADDRESS=(PROTOCOL=TCP)(HOST=mweishan-
   dell.corp.goxroads.net)(PORT=1522)))
STATUS of the LISTENER
------------------------
Alias                    LISTENER
Version                  TNSLSNR for 32-bit Windows: Version
                         10.1.0.2.0 - Production
Start Date               10-JUN-2004 09:58:47
Uptime                   0 days 0 hr. 1 min. 50 sec
Trace Level              off
Security                 ON: Local OS Authentication
SNMP                     OFF
Listener Parameter File  D:\oracle\ora10g\network\admin\listener.ora
Listener Log File        D:\oracle\ora10g\network\log\listener.log
Listening Endpoints Summary...
   (DESCRIPTION=(ADDRESS=(PROTOCOL=tcp)(HOST=mweishan-
    dell.corp.goxroads.net)(PORT=1522)))
Services Summary...
Service "PLSExtProc" has 1 instance(s).
  Instance "PLSExtProc", status UNKNOWN, has 1 handler(s) for this service...
Service "orcl.com" has 1 instance(s).
  Instance "ORCL", status UNKNOWN, has 1 handler(s) for this service...
The command completed successfully
```

This code example depicts a listener that has recently been started. We also see what the log file and parameter file locations are for the listener. This is a good facility to use to get a quick listing of vital information for the listener.

Listing the Services for the Listener

The lsnrctl services command displays information about the services, such as whether the services have any dedicated prespawned server processes or dispatched processes associated with them and how many connections have been accepted and rejected per service. Use this method to check if a listener is listening for a particular service.

The following code shows an example of running the services command:

```
D:\oracle\ora10g\BIN>lsnrctl services

LSNRCTL for 32-bit Windows: Version 10.1.0.2.0 - Production on
     10-JUN-2004 10:01:48
Copyright (c) 1991, 2004, Oracle.  All rights reserved.


Connecting to (DESCRIPTION=(ADDRESS=(PROTOCOL=TCP)(HOST=mweishan-dell.corp
   ➥.goxroads.net)(PORT=1522)))
```

```
Services Summary...
Service "PLSExtProc" has 1 instance(s).
  Instance "PLSExtProc", status UNKNOWN, has 1 handler(s) for this service...
    Handler(s):
      "DEDICATED" established:0 refused:0
        LOCAL SERVER
Service "orcl.com" has 1 instance(s).
  Instance "ORCL", status UNKNOWN, has 1 handler(s) for this service...
    Handler(s):
      "DEDICATED" established:0 refused:0
        LOCAL SERVER
The command completed successfully
```

In this example, you can see that the listener is listening for connections to the service ORCL. The line "DEDICATED" established:0 refused:0 shows us how many connections to this service have been accepted or rejected by the listener. One reason why a listener may reject servicing a request is if the database were not available.

Other Commands in *lsnrctl*

You can run other commands in lsnrctl. Table 4.3 summarizes these other commands. Type the command at the lsnrctl prompt to execute it.

TABLE 4.3 A Summary of the *lsnrctl* Commands

Command	Definition
change_password	Allows a user to change the password needed to stop the listener.
exit	Exits the lsnrctl utility.
quit	Performs the same function as exit.
reload	Rereads the listener.ora file without stopping the listener. Refreshes the listener if the file changes.
save_config	Copies the listener.ora file called listener.bak when changes are made to the listener.ora file from lsnrctl.
services	Lists a summary of services and details information on the number of connections established and the number of connections refused for each protocol service handler.
start listener	Starts the named listener.

TABLE 4.3   A Summary of the *lsnrctl* Commands *(continued)*

Command	Definition
status listener	Shows the status of the named listener.
stop listener	Stops the named listener.
trace	Turns on tracing for the listener.
version	Displays the version of the Oracle Net software and protocol adapters.

Using the *set* Commands in *lsnrctl*

The lsnrctl utility also has commands called set commands. To issue these commands, type **set commandname** at the LSNRCTL> prompt. You use the set commands to modify the listener.ora file. For example, you can use this command to set up logging and tracing. You can set most of these parameters using the Oracle Net Manager.

To display the current setting of a parameter, use the show command, which displays the current settings of the parameters set using the set command. Table 4.4 summarizes the lsnrctl set commands. Type **set** or **show** to display a listing of all the commands.

TABLE 4.4   A Summary of the *lsnrctl set* Commands

Command	Description
current_listener	Sets the listener to modify or shows the name of the current listener.
displaymode	Sets display for the lsnrctl utility to RAW, COMPACT, NORMAL, or VERBOSE.
inbound_connect_ timeout	Specifies the time in seconds for a client to complete a connection request to the listener after the network connection is established. An ORA-12525 error will be generated if the listener fails to receive the request in the allotted time.
log_status	Shows whether logging is on or off for the listener.
log_file	Shows the name of listener log file.
log_directory	Shows the log directory location.
rawmode	Shows more detail on STATUS and SERVICES when set to ON. Values: ON or OFF.
startup_waittime	Sets the length of time that a listener will wait to respond to a status command in the lsnrctl command-line utility.

TABLE 4.4   A Summary of the *lsnrctl set* Commands *(continued)*

Command	Description
save_config_on_stop	Saves changes to the listener.ora file when exiting lsnrctl.
trc_level	Sets the trace level to OFF, USER, ADMIN, SUPPORT.
trc_file	Sets the name of the listener trace file.
trc_directory	Sets the name of the listener trace directory.

Stopping the Listener

To stop the listener, you must issue the *lsnrctl stop* command. This command stops the default listener. To stop a non-default listener, include the name of the listener. For example, to stop LISTENER1, type **lsnrctl stop listener1**. If you are in the lsnrctl> facility, you will stop the current listener defined by the current_listener setting. To see what the current listener is set to, use the show command. The default value is LISTENER.

Stopping the listener does not affect clients connected to the database. It only means that no new connections can use this listener until the listener is restarted.

The following code shows what the stop command looks like:

```
D:\oracle\ora10g\BIN>lsnrctl stop

LSNRCTL for 32-bit Windows: Version 10.1.0.2.0 - Production on 10-JUN-
    2004 10:05:51

Copyright (c) 1991, 2004, Oracle.  All rights reserved.

Connecting to (DESCRIPTION=(ADDRESS=(PROTOCOL=TCP)(HOST=mweishan-
    dell.corp.goxroads.net)(PORT=1522)))
The command completed successfully
```

Dynamically Registering Services

Oracle 10*g* databases can automatically register their presence with an existing listener. The instance registers with the listener defined on the local machine. Dynamic service registration allows you to take advantage of other features, such as load balancing and automatic failover. The PMON process is responsible for registering this information with the listener.

When dynamic service registration is used, you will not see the service listed in the listener.ora file. To see the service listed, run the lsnrctl services command. Be aware that if the listener is started after the Oracle instance, there may be a time lag before the instance actually registers information with the listener.

For an instance to automatically register with a listener, the listener must be configured as a default listener, or you must specify the `init.ora` parameter LOCAL_LISTENER. The LOCAL_ LISTENER parameter defines the location of the listener with which you want the Oracle server to register. A default listener definition is shown here:

```
Listener Name = LISTENER
Port = 1521
Protocol = TCP/IP
```

And here is an example of the LOCAL_LISTENER parameter being used to register the Oracle server with a non-default listener:

```
local_listener="(ADDRESS_LIST = (Address =
(Protocol = TCP) (Host=weishan) (Port=1522)))
```

In the previous example, the Oracle server registers with the listener listening on port 1522 using TCP/IP. This is a non-default port location, so you must use the LOCAL_LISTENER parameter in order for the registration to take place.

You must configure two other `init.ora` parameters to allow an instance to register information with the listener. Two parameters are used to allow automatic registration: INSTANCE_ NAME and SERVICE_NAMES.

The INSTANCE_NAME parameter is set to the name of the Oracle instance that you want to register with the listener. The SERVICE_NAMES parameter is a combination of the instance name and the domain name. The domain name is set to the value of the DB_DOMAIN initialization parameter. For example, if your DB_DOMAIN is set to GR.COM and your Oracle instance is DBA, set the parameters as follows:

```
Instance_name = DBA
Service_names = DBA.GR.COM
```

If you are not using domain names, set the INSTANCE_NAME and SERVICE_NAMES parameters to the same values.

Additional Configurations When Using Multiple Listeners

If you have a more complex network environment with a large number of simultaneous connection requests or if you are using an advanced database design such as Oracle Real Application Clusters, you can configure multiple listeners to better manage connection loads. You also gain functionality when multiple listeners service your database connection requests. These features include Connect-Time Failover, Transparent Application Failover, Client Load Balancing, and Connection Load Balancing.

Connect-Time Failover

The Connect-Time Failover feature allows clients to connect to another listener if the initial connection to the first listener fails. Multiple listener locations are specified in the clients `tnsnames.ora` file. If a connection attempt to the first listener fails, a connection request to the next listener in the list is attempted. This feature increases the availability of the Oracle service should a listener location be unavailable.

Here is an example of what a tnsnames.ora file looks like with connect-time failover enabled:

```
ORCL =
  (DESCRIPTION=
    (ADDRESS_LIST=
      (ADDRESS=(PROTOCOL=TCP)(HOST=DBPROD)(PORT=1521))
      (ADDRESS=(PROTOCOL=TCP)(HOST=DBFAIL)(PORT=1521))
    )
    (CONNECT_DATA=(SERVICE_NAME=PROD)(SERVER=DEDICATED)
    )
  )
```

> We will discuss the tnsnames.ora file in detail later in this chapter in the section "Configuring Oracle Net for the Client."

Notice the additional entry under the ADDRESS_LIST section. Two listeners are specified. If a connection is unsuccessful when attempting to connect to the DBPROD host on port 1521, a connection attempt is made to the DBFAIL host on port 1521. The time that the connection waits before attempting to failover is operating system dependent.

Transparent Application Failover

The Transparent Application Failover (TAF) feature is a runtime failover for high-availability environments, such as Oracle Real Application Clusters. TAF fails over and reestablishes application-to-service connections. It enables client applications to automatically reconnect to the database if the connection fails and, optionally, resume a SELECT statement that was in progress. The reconnection happens automatically from the OCI library.

The following code shows an example of the tnsnames.ora file setup for using Transparent Application Failover:

```
ORCL =
  (DESCRIPTION=
    (FAILOVER=ON)
    (ADDRESS_LIST=
      (ADDRESS=(PROTOCOL=TCP)(HOST=DBPROD)(PORT=1521))
      (ADDRESS=(PROTOCOL=TCP)(HOST=DBFAIL)(PORT=1521))
    )
    (CONNECT_DATA=(SERVICE_NAME=PROD)(SERVER=DEDICATED)
      (FAILOVER_MODE=(TYPE=select)(METHOD=basic))
    )
  )
```

In this example, notice additional entries in the `tnsnames.ora` file that enable the Transparent Application Failover. There are two hosts, DBPROD and DBFAIL. If DBPROD becomes unavailable, the connections will failover to the DBFAIL host and connect to the associated service. The database service of PROD must be the same on both the DBPROD and DBFAIL servers for this example to work properly.

Client Load Balancing

Client Load Balancing is a feature that allows clients to randomly select from a list of listeners. Oracle Net moves through the list of listeners and balances the load of connection requests across the available listeners. Here is an example of the `tnsnames.ora` entry that allows for load balancing:

```
ORCL =
  (DESCRIPTION=
    (LOAD_BALANCE=ON)
    (ADDRESS_LIST=
      (ADDRESS=(PROTOCOL=TCP)(HOST=MWEISHAN-DELL)(PORT=1522))
      (ADDRESS=(PROTOCOL=TCP)(HOST=MWEISHAN-DELL)(PORT=1521))
    )
    (CONNECT_DATA=
(SERVICE_NAME=ORCL)
    )
    )
```

Notice the additional parameter of LOAD_BALANCE. This enables load balancing between the two listener locations specified.

Connection Load Balancing

Connection Load Balancing is a feature that enables better distribution of connection among a group of dispatchers in an Oracle Shared Server environment. The next chapter explains this concept in more detail.

Troubleshooting Server-Side Connection Problems

Even if it seems that you have configured Oracle server-side components correctly, network errors can still occur that will require troubleshooting. You can experience a connection problem for a variety of reasons:

- The client, middle-tier, or Oracle server is not configured properly.
- The client cannot resolve the net service name.
- The underlying network protocol is not active on the server; for example, the TCP/IP process on the server is not running.
- The user enters an incorrect net service name, user ID, or password.

You can diagnose and correct these types of errors. In the next section, "Server-Side Computer and Database Checks," you will see how to diagnose and correct connection problems originating from the Oracle server. In the next chapter, we discuss troubleshooting problems with client-side network configuration.

When a client has a connection problem that is up to you to fix, it is helpful to first gather information about the situation. Make sure you record the following information:

- The Oracle error that the client received.

- The location of the client. Is the client connecting from a remote location, or is the client connected directly to the server?

- The name of the Oracle server to which the client is attempting to connect.

- Check to see if other clients are having connection problems. If so, are these clients in the same general location?

- Ask the user what is failing. Is it the application being used or the connection?

We will now look at the particular network areas to check and the methods used to further diagnose connection problems from the Oracle server. We will also look at the Oracle error codes that will help identify and correct the problems.

Server-Side Computer and Database Checks

You can perform several server-side checks if a connection problem occurs. Before running such checks, be sure that the machine is running, that the Oracle server is available, and that the listener is active. In the following sections, we'll summarize the checks to perform on the server.

Check the Server Machine

Make sure that the server machine is active and available for connections. On some systems, it is possible to start a system in a restricted mode that allows only supervisors or administrators to log in to the computer. Make sure that the computer is open and available to all users.

On a TCP/IP network, you can use the *ping* utility to test for connectivity to the server. Here is an example of using ping to test a network connection to a machine called `matt`:

```
C:\users\default>ping matt

Pinging cupira03.cmg.com [10.69.30.113] with 32 bytes of data:

Reply from 10.69.30.113: bytes=32 time=10ms TTL=248
Reply from 10.69.30.113: bytes=32 time=10ms TTL=248
Reply from 10.69.30.113: bytes=32 time<10ms TTL=248
Reply from 10.69.30.113: bytes=32 time=10ms TTL=248
```

The reply indicates that the machine can be seen on the network.

Check the Database

Make sure that the database is running. Connect to the Oracle server and log in to the database using a tool such as SQL*Plus. First attempt a local connection, which does not use the Oracle listener.

To connect to the Oracle server using a local connection, set your ORACLE_SID environmental variable to the name of the Oracle instance that you want to connect to. Then, attempt to connect to SQL*Plus.

The following example is a connection sequence on Windows that fails because the database is not running. For example, if the database that you are attempting to connect to is named MJW, you can use the following code example in a Windows environment for your test:

```
D:\oracle\ora10g\BIN>sqlplus system/manager

SQL*Plus: Release 10.1.0.2.0 - Production on Thu Jun 10 10:08:16 2004

Copyright (c) 1982, 2004, Oracle.  All rights reserved.

ERROR:
ORA-01034: ORACLE not available
ORA-27101: shared memory realm does not exist
```

An ORA-01034 error indicates that the Oracle instance is not running. You need to start the Oracle instance. The ORA-27101 error indicates that no instance is currently available to connect to for the specified ORACLE_SID.

Verify That the Database Is Open to All Users

You can open a database in restricted mode. This means that only users with restricted mode access can use the system. This is not a networking problem, but it will lead to clients being unable to connect to the Oracle server. Here is an example of a connection that fails because the user does not have the restricted session privilege.

```
D:\>sqlplus scott/tiger@ORCL

SQL*Plus: Release 10.1.0.2.0 - Production on Thu Jun 10 10:09:19 2004

Copyright (c) 1982, 2004, Oracle.  All rights reserved.

ERROR:
ORA-01035: ORACLE only available to users with RESTRICTED SESSION privilege
```

As we can see, the user Scott is attempting to connect to the ORCL service. The error message tells us that user Scott does not have the restricted session privilege and cannot log in until the DBA either grants this privilege to Scott or takes the database out of restricted session mode.

Check User Privileges

Make sure that the user attempting to establish the connection has been granted the CREATE SESSION privilege to the database. This privilege is needed for a user to connect to the Oracle server. If the client does not have this privilege, you must grant it to the user. To do so, follow this example:

```
D:\oracle\ora10g\BIN>sqlplus matt/matt
SQL*Plus: Release 10.1.0.2.0 - Production on Thu Jun 10 10:09:19 2004
Copyright (c) 1982, 2004, Oracle.  All rights reserved.
ERROR:
ORA-01045: user MATT lacks CREATE SESSION privilege; logon denied
```

Here is an example of how you can grant the CREATE SESSION privilege to a user:

```
SQL> grant create session to matt;
Grant succeeded
SQL>
```

In this example, the DBA has granted the CREATE SESSION privilege to user Matt. Matt now has the ability to make a connection to the database.

Server-Side Network Checks

After you validate that the server where the database is located is up and available and you verify that the user has proper privileges, begin checking for any underlying network problems on the server. In the following sections, we will detail some of the common areas of the server to check when you are experiencing connection problems.

Check Listener

Make sure that the listener is running on the Oracle server. Make sure that you check the services for all the listeners on the Oracle server; you can use the lsnrctl status command to do this. The following command shows the status of the default listener named LISTENER:

```
D:\oracle\ora10g\BIN>lsnrctl status

LSNRCTL for 32-bit Windows: Version 10.1.0.2.0 - Production on 10-JUN-
    2004 10:00:36

Copyright (c) 1991, 2004, Oracle.  All rights reserved.
Connecting to (DESCRIPTION=(ADDRESS=(PROTOCOL=TCP)(HOST=mweishan-
    dell.corp.goxroads.net)(PORT=1522)))
STATUS of the LISTENER
------------------------
Alias                    LISTENER
Version                  TNSLSNR for 32-bit Windows: Version
                         10.1.0.2.0 - Production
```

```
Start Date                10-JUN-2004 09:58:47
Uptime                    0 days 0 hr. 1 min. 50 sec
Trace Level               off
Security                  ON: Local OS Authentication
SNMP                      OFF
Listener Parameter File   D:\oracle\ora10g\network\admin\listener.ora
Listener Log File         D:\oracle\ora10g\network\log\listener.log
Listening Endpoints Summary...
  (DESCRIPTION=(ADDRESS=(PROTOCOL=tcp)(HOST=mweishan-
   dell.corp.goxroads.net)(PORT=1522)))
Services Summary...
Service "PLSExtProc" has 1 instance(s).
  Instance "PLSExtProc", status UNKNOWN, has 1 handler(s) for this service...
Service "orcl.com" has 1 instance(s).
  Instance "ORCL", status UNKNOWN, has 1 handler(s) for this service...
The command completed successful
```

Also check the services for which the listener is listening. You must see the service to which the client is attempting to connect. If the service is not listed, the client may be entering the wrong service, or the listener may not be configured to listen for this service.

Check *GLOBAL_DBNAME*

If the client is using the hostnaming method, make sure that the GLOBAL_DBNAME parameter is set to the name of the host machine. You can find this parameter in the service definition of the listener.ora file. Verify the setting by reviewing the listener.ora configuration. In the following sample code, we can see that the GLOBAL_DBNAME parameter has been set to mweishan-dell.

```
SID_LIST_LISTENER =
  (SID_LIST =
    (SID_DESC =
      (GLOBAL_DBNAME = mweishan-dell) – machine listener is on
      (ORACLE_HOME = d:\oracle\ora10g)
      (SID_NAME = orcl)
```

Check Listener Protocols

Check the protocols for which the listener is configured. This is displayed by the lsnrctl services command. You can see an example of this command in the section, "Listing the Services for the Listener," earlier in this chapter. Make sure that the protocol of the service matches the protocol the client is using when requesting a connection. If the client is requesting to connect with a protocol that the listener is not listening for, the user will receive an ORA-12541 "No Listener" error message.

Check Server Protocols

Make sure that the underlying network protocol on the server is active. For systems that run TCP/IP, you can attempt to use the ping command to ping the server. This will verify that the TCP/IP daemon process is active on the server. You can also check this by verifying the services on Windows or using the ps command on Unix. An example of the ping command can be found earlier in this chapter in the section "Check Server Machine."

Check Server Protocol Adapters

Make sure that the appropriate protocol adapters are installed on the server. On most platforms, you can invoke the Oracle Universal Installer program and check the list of installed protocols. On Unix platforms, you can use the adapter utility to ensure that the appropriate adapters are linked to Oracle. The following example shows how to run this utility, which is located in the $ORACLE_HOME/bin directory.

The following adapters summarize all of the protocol adapters that have been installed as part of this Oracle installation. You can see that we have installed four types of adapters.

```
[root@localhost] ./adapters oracle

Net protocol adapters linked with oracle are:

    BEQ
    IPC
    TCP/IP
    RAW


Net Naming Adapters linked with oracle are:

    Oracle TNS Naming Adapter
    Oracle Naming Adapter
Advanced Networking Option/Network Security products
 linked with oracle are:

    Oracle Security server Authentication Adapter
```

If the required protocol adapter is not listed, you have to install the adapter. You can do so by using the Oracle Installer, installing the Oracle Net Server software, and choosing the appropriate adapters during the installation process.

Check for Connection Timeouts

If the client is receiving an ORA-12535 or an ORA-12547 error message, the client is timing out before a valid connection is established. This can occur if you have a slow network connection. You can attempt to solve this problem by increasing the time that the listener will wait for a valid response from the client; simply set the `INBOUND_CONNECT_TIMEOUT` parameter to a higher number. This is the number of seconds that the listener waits for a valid response from the client when establishing a connection.

Oracle Net Logging and Tracing on the Server

If a network problem persists, you can use logging and tracing to help resolve it. Oracle generates information into log files and trace files that can assist you in tracking down network connection problems. You can use logging to find out general information about the success or failure of certain components of the Oracle network. You can use tracing to get in-depth information about specific network connections.

By default, Oracle produces logs for clients and the Oracle listener. You cannot disable client logging.

Logging records significant events, such as starting and stopping the listener, along with certain kinds of network errors. Errors are generated in the log in the form of an error stack. The listener log records information such as the version number, connection attempts, and the protocols for which it is listening. You can enable logging at the client, middle-tier, and server locations.

Use Tracing Sparingly

Use tracing only as a last resort if you are having connectivity problems between the client and server. Complete all the server-side checks described earlier before you resort to tracing. The tracing process generates a significant amount of overhead, and, depending on the trace level set, it can create some rather large files. This activity will impede system I/O performance because of all the information that is written to the logs, and if left unchecked, it could fill your disk or file system.

I was once involved with a large project that was using JDBC to connect to the Oracle server. We were having difficulty with connections being periodically dropped between the JDBC client and the Oracle server. We enabled tracing to try to find the problem. We did eventually correct the problem (it was with how our DNS names server was configured), but the tracing was left on inadvertently. When the system eventually went into production, the trace files grew so large that they filled the disk where tracing was being collected. To prevent this from happening, periodically ensure that the trace parameters are not turned on, and if they are, turn them off.

Tracing, which you can also enable at the client, middle-tier, or server location, records all events that occur on a network, even when an error does not occur. The trace file provides a great deal of information that logs do not, such as the number of network round-trips made during network connection or the number of packets sent and received during a network connection. Tracing enables you to collect a thorough listing of the actual sequence of the statements as a network connection is being processed. This gives you a much more detailed picture of what is occurring with connections that the listener is processing.

Use the Oracle Net Manager to enable most logging and tracing parameters. Many of the logging and tracing parameters are found in the `sqlnet.ora` file. Let's take a look at how to enable logging and tracing for the various components in an Oracle network.

Server Logging

By default, the listener is configured to enable the generation of a log file. The log file records information about listener startup and shutdown, successful and unsuccessful connection attempts, and certain types of network errors. By default, the listener log location is $ORACLE_HOME/network/log on Unix and %ORACLE_HOME%\network\log on Windows. The default name of the file is `listener.log`.

Information in the `listener.log` file is a fixed-length, delimited format with each field separated by an asterisk. If you want to further analyze the information in the log, you can load the data into an Oracle table using a tool such as SQL*Loader. Notice in the following sample listing that the file contains information about connection attempts, the name of the program executing the request, and the name of the client attempting to connect. The last field contains a zero if a request was successfully completed.

```
TNSLSNR for 32-bit Windows: Version 10.1.0.2.0 - Production on 27-APR-
    2004 16:05:13

Copyright (c) 1991, 2004, Oracle.  All rights reserved.

Log messages written to D:\oracle\ora10g\network\log\listener.log
Trace information written to
    D:\oracle\ora10g\network\trace\listener.trc
Trace level is currently 0

Started with pid=2260
Listening on: (DESCRIPTION=(ADDRESS=(PROTOCOL=tcp)(HOST=mweishan-
    dell.corp.goxroads.net)(PORT=1521)))

TIMESTAMP * CONNECT DATA [* PROTOCOL INFO] * EVENT [* SID] * RETURN CODE
27-APR-2004 16:05:17 *
    (CONNECT_DATA=(CID=(PROGRAM=)(HOST=)(USER=mweishan))(COMMAND=status)
    (ARGUMENTS=64)(SERVICE=LISTENER)(VERSION=168821248)) * status * 0
```

```
27-APR-2004 16:05:18 *
  (CONNECT_DATA=(CID=(PROGRAM=)(HOST=__jdbc__)(USER=))(SERVICE_NAME=or
  cl)) * (ADDRESS=(PROTOCOL=tcp)(HOST=206.122.131.90)(PORT=2021)) *
  establish * orcl * 12514
TNS-12514: TNS:listener does not currently know of service requested in
  connect descriptor
```

Server Tracing

As mentioned earlier, tracing gathers information about the flow of traffic across a network connection. Data is transmitted back and forth in the form of packets. A packet contains sender information, receiver information, and data. Even a single network request can generate a large number of packets.

In the trace file, each line file starts with the name of the procedure executed in one of the Oracle Net layers and is followed by a set of hexadecimal numbers. The hexadecimal numbers are the actual data transmitted. If you are not encrypting the data, sometimes you will see the actual data after the hexadecimal numbers.

Each of the Oracle Net procedures is responsible for a different action. The code type of each packet depends on the action being taken. All the packet types start with NSP. Here is a summary of the common packet types:

Packet Keyword	Packet Type
NSPTAC	Accept
NSPTRF	Refuse
NSPTRS	Resend
NSPDA	Data
NSPCNL	Control
NSPTMK	Marker

If you are doing server-to-server communications and have a sqlnet.ora file on the server, you can enter information in the Server Information section located on the Tracing tab from the Profile screen in Oracle Net Manager tracing. This provides tracing information for server-to-server communications.

Several numeric codes are also used to help diagnose and troubleshoot problems with Oracle Net connections. These codes can be found in the trace files. Here is an example of a line from the trace file that contains a code value:

```
nspsend: plen=12, type=4
```

Here is a summary of the numeric codes that you could encounter in a trace file:

Code	Packet Type
1	Connect
2	Accept
3	Acknowledge
4	Refuse
5	Redirect
6	Data
7	Null, empty data
9	Abort
11	Resend
12	Marker
13	Attention
14	Control information

Enabling Server Tracing

You can enable server tracing from the same Oracle Net Manager screens shown earlier. Simply click the Tracing Enabled radio button. The default filename and location is $ORACLE_HOME/ network/trace/listener.trc in Unix and %ORACLE_HOME%\network\trace\listener.trc on Windows. You can set the trace level to OFF, USER, ADMIN, or SUPPORT. The USER level detects specific user errors. The ADMIN level contains all the user-level information along with installation-specific errors. SUPPORT is the highest level and can produce information that might be beneficial to Oracle Support personnel. This level also can produce large trace files. The following listing shows an example of a listener trace file:

```
nsglhfre: entry
nsglhrem: entry
nsglhrem: entry
nsglhfre: Deallocating cxd 0x4364d0.
nsglhfre: exit
nsglma: Reporting the following error stack:
TNS-01150: The address of the specified listener name is incorrect
 TNS-01153: Failed to process string:
   (DESCRIPTION=(ADDRESS=(PROTOCOL=TC)(HOST=mprntw507953)
   (PORT=1521)))
nsrefuse: entry
nsdo: entry
```

```
nsdo: cid=0, opcode=67, *bl=437, *what=10, uflgs=0x0, cflgs=0x3
nsdo: rank=64, nsctxrnk=0
nsdo: nsctx: state=2, flg=0x4204, mvd=0
nsdo: gtn=152, gtc=152, ptn=10, ptc=2019
nscon: entry
nscon: sending NSPTRF packet
nspsend: entry
nspsend: plen=12, type=4
ntpwr: entry
ntpwr: exit
```

You can tell which section of the Oracle Net the trace file is in by looking at the first two characters of the program names in the trace file. In the previous example, nscon refers to the network session (NS) sublayer of Oracle Net. A message is being sent back to the client in the form of an NSPTRF packet. This is a *refuse packet*, which means that the requested action is being denied.

You see the Oracle error number embedded in the error message. In the previous example, a TNS-01153 error was generated. This error indicates that the listener failed to start. It also shows the line of information on which the listener is failing. This error could be the result of a problem with another process listening on the same location, or it could be a syntax problem in the listener.ora file. Basically, this error message states that a syntax error has occurred because the protocol was specified as TC and not TCP. In addition to this error, there are some more recent ones. The most recent errors are at the bottom of the file.

The following example shows a section of the listener.ora file with the logging and tracing parameters enabled:

```
# D:\ORACLE\ora10g\NETWORK\ADMIN\LISTENER.ORA Configuration
# File:D:\Oracle\ora10g\NETWORK\ADMIN\listener.ora
# Generated by Oracle Oracle Net Manager

TRACE_LEVEL_LISTENER = ADMIN
TRACE_FILE_LISTENER = LISTENER.trc
TRACE_DIRECTORY_LISTENER = D:\Oracle\ora10g\network\trace
LOG_DIRECTORY_LISTENER = D:\Oracle\ora10g\network\log
LOG_FILE_LISTENER = LISTENER.log
```

Table 4.5 summarizes the meaning of each of these parameters.

TABLE 4.5   *listener.ora* Log and Trace Parameters

Parameter	Definition
TRACE_LEVEL_LISTENER	Turns tracing on and off. The levels are OFF, USER, ADMIN, and SUPPORT. SUPPORT generates the greatest amount of data.
TRACE_FILE_LISTENER	The name of the trace file.

TABLE 4.5   *listener.ora* Log and Trace Parameters *(continued)*

Parameter	Definition
TRACE_DIRECTORY_LISTENER	The directory where trace files are written.
LOG_DIRECTORY_LISTENER	The directory where log files are written.
LOG_FILE_LISTENER	The name of the listener log file.

Configuring Oracle Net for the Client

Once the Oracle server is properly configured, you can focus on configuring the clients to allow for connectivity to the Oracle server. It is important to understand how to configure Oracle clients. Without proper knowledge of how to configure the client, you are limited in your connection choices to the server. As a DBA, you must understand the network needs of the organization, the type of connectivity that is required, and client/server connections versus *n*-tier connectivity, for example, in order to make the appropriate choices about client-side configuration. This section should help clarify the client-side connectivity options available to you and show you how to troubleshoot client connection problems

Client-Side Names Resolution Options

When a client needs to connect to an Oracle server, the client must supply three pieces of information: their user ID, password, and net service name. The net service name provides the necessary information, in the form of a connect descriptor, to locate an Oracle service in a network.

This connect descriptor describes the path to the Oracle server and its service name, which is an alias for an Oracle database. The location where this information is kept depends on the names resolution method you choose. The five methods of net service name resolution are Oracle Internet Directory, External Naming, hostnaming, Oracle Easy Connect, and local-naming. Normally, you choose just one of these methods, but you can use any combination.

Oracle Internet Directory is advantageous when you are dealing with complex networks that have many Oracle servers. When you choose this method, you can configure and manage Net Service Names and connect descriptor information in a central location.

External Naming uses a non-Oracle facility to manage and resolve Oracle service names. For example, if an organization is using an external names resolution method such as Network Information Service (NIS), the database service information could be stored in this external location and used by clients to resolve service names.

You should only be casually familiar with these two naming resolution options. For a more detailed description of how to configure External Naming and how to configure and use this method, please consult the *Oracle Database Net Services Administrator's Guide 10g Release 1* (10.1) Part Number B10775-01.

In the following sections, we will take a closer look at the hostnaming, Oracle Easy Connect, and localnaming methods.

The Hostnaming Method

In small networks with few Oracle servers to manage, you can take advantage of the *hostnaming method*. Hostnaming is advantageous when you want to reduce the amount of configuration work necessary. Hostnaming saves you from configuring on the clients, although it does have limitations. There are four prerequisites to using hostnaming:

- You must use TCP/IP as your network protocol.

- You must not use any advanced networking features, such as Oracle Connection Manager.

- You must have an external naming service, such as DNS, or a HOSTS file available to the client.

- The listener must be set up with the GLOBAL_DBNAME parameter equal to the name of the machine.

Now let's discuss how to configure this naming method.

Configuring the Hostnaming Method

By default, Oracle attempts to use the hostnaming method from the client only after it attempts connections using localnaming. To override this default search path for resolving names, set the NAMES.DIRECTORY_PATH parameter in the sqlnet.ora file on the client so that it searches for hostnaming only. You can configure this parameter using the Oracle Net Manager (see Figure 4.24).

FIGURE 4.24   Oracle Net Manager *sqlnet.ora* Naming screen

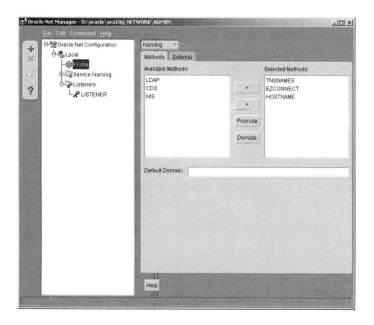

To configure the parameter using Oracle Net Manager, choose Profile from the Local tab and select Naming from the drop-down list at the top of the screen to open a list of naming methods. The Selected Methods list displays the naming methods being used and the order in which they are used to resolve service names. The Available Methods list displays the methods not included in the Selected Methods list.

To change the list of available methods, highlight a method name and click the arrow key (>) to include it in the Selected Methods list. To remove a name, select it and click the other arrow key (<). You can also change the order of the list. Select a name from the Selected Methods list and click the Demote button to move the name down the list or click the Promote button to move the name up the list. Make sure that HOSTNAME shows up in the Selected Methods column.

Once you save the configuration, Oracle updates the `sqlnet.ora` file with the changes you made.

The following is an example of the `sqlnet.ora` file.

```
# SQLNET.ORA Network Configuration File:
    D:\oracle\ora10g\network\admin\sqlnet.ora
# Generated by Oracle configuration tools.


NAMES.DEFAULT_DOMAIN = mjw.com
NAMES.DIRECTORY_PATH= (TNSNAMES,EZCONNECT,HOSTNAME)
```

> The hostnaming and the Oracle Easy Connect Naming methods do not require any client-side configuration files. We'll discuss these connection methods later in this section.

You can check TCP/IP connectivity from the client using the TCP/IP utility ping. Ping attempts to contact the server by sending a small request packet. The server responds in kind with an acknowledgment.

The following code shows an example of how ping works and the speed of the round-trip from client to server and back:

```
C:\>ping mil02ora

Pinging mil02ora [10.1.5.210] with 32 bytes of data:

Reply from 10.1.5.210: bytes=32 time<10ms TTL=128
Reply from 10.1.5.210: bytes=32 time<10ms TTL=128
Reply from 10.1.5.210: bytes=32 time<10ms TTL=128
Reply from 10.1.5.210: bytes=32 time<10ms TTL=128
```

The server must be configured with a listener running TCP/IP, and the listener must be listening on the default port of 1521. If the instance has not been dynamically registered with the listener, you must configure the listener with the GLOBAL_DBNAME parameter. The following code shows what the `listener.ora` file looks like when it is configured with this parameter.

In this example, the hostname is mweishan-dell, the name of the physical machine on which the listener process is running.

```
# listener.ora Network Configuration File:
  D:\oracle\ora10g\network\admin\listener.ora
# Generated by Oracle configuration tools.
LISTENER =
  (DESCRIPTION =
    (ADDRESS = (PROTOCOL = TCP)(HOST = mweishan-dell)
    (PORT = 1521))
    (PROTOCOL_STACK =
      (PRESENTATION = TTC)
      (SESSION = NS)
    )
  )

SID_LIST_LISTENER =
  (SID_LIST =
    (SID_DESC =
      (GLOBAL_DBNAME = mweishan-dell) - machine listener is on
      (ORACLE_HOME = d:\oracle\ora10g)
      (SID_NAME = orcl)
    )
  )
```

Figure 4.25 shows the Oracle Net Manager Database Services screen. Each database that the listener will be serving is created as a separate entry. Provide the global database name, Oracle Home directory, and Oracle SID information. This completes the configuration work for the database portion of listener configuration.

The Connection Process When Using Hostnaming

When you use hostnaming, the client must supply a user ID and password along with the name of the machine to which they want to connect. For example, if the user matt with the password casey wants to connect to a database residing on machine mweishan-dell, he enters **Sqlplus matt/casey@mweishan-dell**.

The hostname is resolved either by a HOSTS file or by an external naming environment, such as DNS. External naming methods, such as DNS, are preferred over a HOSTS file because they facilitate centralized management of hostnames. The following code contains an example of a HOSTS file from a Windows environment. The default location for the HOSTS file on a Unix system is in the /etc directory. On Windows, the default location is c:\winnt\system32\drivers\etc. Once the hostname is resolved, the connection is made to the machine.

```
# Copyright (c) 1993-1999 Microsoft Corp.
#
```

```
# This is a sample HOSTS file used by Microsoft
# TCP/IP for Windows NT.
#
# This file contains the mappings of IP addresses
# to hostnames. Each
# entry should be kept on an individual line.
# The IP address should
# be placed in the first column followed
# by the corresponding hostname.
# The IP address and the hostname should be separated
# by at least one
# space.
#
# Additionally, comments (such as these) may be
# inserted on individual
# lines or following the machine name denoted
# by a '#' symbol.
#
# For example:
#
#   102.54.94.97    rhino.acme.com    # source server
#    38.25.63.10    x.acme.com        # x client host

127.0.0.1       localhost
10.2.0.91       mweishan-dell # Oracle Database Server
```

🌐 Real World Scenario

A Word about the *HOSTS* file

If you have a small TCP/IP network and a names resolution method such as DNS is not used or available, you can use the HOSTS file to resolve network service names. Even in larger networks that use DNS or other names resolution methods, the HOSTS file can be a handy tool when troubleshooting connections. For example, if a client is having a connection problem, try configuring a local HOSTS file on the client that points to the IP address of the server to which you want to connect. When a HOSTS file is configured and the hostname is contained within the file, the client can use it for hostname resolution. If you are successful in pinging or connecting to the server using the local HOSTS, chances are the problem lies somewhere in the routing information within one of the network devices on your network. It could be a bad route statement or a mislabeled hostname within the routing table of the network device. I've used this technique more than once to help network administrators detect and solve connection problems.

FIGURE 4.25   The Oracle Net Manager *listener.ora* setup for hostnaming

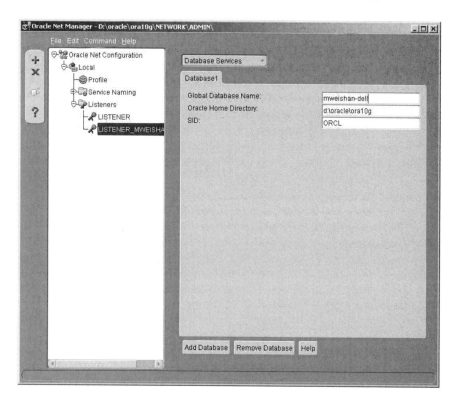

The listener receives the request and looks for a matching GLOBAL_DBNAME. If it is found, the connection is established as a dedicated, or dispatched, connection depending on the configuration of the Oracle server.

Figure 4.26 illustrates the following hostnaming connection process:

1. The client contacts the DNS server or local HOSTS file.

2. The client contacts the Oracle server.

3. The server spawns a dedicated process and redirects the connection to the newly spawned process or redirects the connection to a dispatched process when you are using the Oracle Shared Server.

4. The server passes connection information back to the client.

5. The client is now in direct contact with the server process or dispatcher.

Configuring Multiple Services on the Same Host Using Hostnaming

If you have multiple Oracle servers on the same machine, it is possible to continue using the hostnaming method. To do so, you must have separate hostname address entries in your HOSTS file or in your external naming service for each of the separate Oracle services. For example, if you have two Oracle services, one called DBA and one called PROD, on a machine with an IP address of 10.2.0.91, you can configure your HOSTS name with the following entry:

```
10.2.0.91      DBA  # Alias for MACH1 server for DBA  DBA
10.2.0.91      PROD # Alias for MACH1 server for PROD  PROD
```

Notice that each of these names resolve to the same IP address. You also need to configure your listener with two entries, one for DBA and one for PROD, both with the GLOBAL_DBNAME parameter set to DBA and PROD, respectively. (If you are using the hierarchical naming model with domain names, include the domain name on the GLOBAL_DBNAME parameter.)

The Oracle Easy Connect Naming Method

The *Oracle Easy Connect Naming method* is a new connection resolution technique introduced in Oracle 10g. This method is similar to the hostnaming method described in the previous section but adds parameters that allow for a port and service name specification. By default, the Oracle Easy Connect names resolution method is configured when Oracle Net is installed.

FIGURE 4.26 Hostnaming connection summary

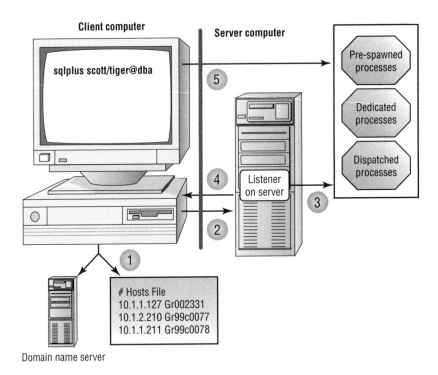

Like the hostnaming method, the Oracle Easy Connect Naming method eliminates the need for any connection information to be configured on the client. This makes for less setup and administrative work. It enhances the hostnaming method by allowing for a port and service specification. Remember from the previous section that the hostnaming method requires a listener to be listening on the default port of 1521. Allowing a port specification addresses one of the limitations of the hostnaming method. Using the Oracle Easy Connect Naming method requires that certain conditions be met:

- Oracle Net Services 10g must be installed on the client.

- Oracle Net TCP/IP services must be enabled and supported on both the client and the server.

- No advanced connection descriptor features are allowed such as connection pooling or external procedure calls.

The following describes the connect descriptor components when you are using the Oracle Easy Connect Naming method:

Syntax Component	Description
//	Optional: Used when you are connecting via a URL.
Host	Required: The host or IP address to connect to.
Port	Optional: The port to connect to. The default is 1521.
Service Name	The service name for the database. The default is the hostname of the computer on which the database resides. If the database name is different from the hostname, enter the service name.

Here are a few examples of how to connect to a database using the Easy Connect method:

```
CONNECT scott/tiger@mweishan-dell:1522/orcl.com
CONNECT scott/tiger@//mweishan-dell/orcl
```

The first example shows how a user connects to a database service orcl.com that is running on the mweishan-dell server and has an Oracle listener listening for TCP/IP connections on port 1522. The second example shows how you can use the Easy Connect method with the default port via JDBC or a URL-type connection. This type of connection requires a double slash (//) between the password and server descriptor.

As stated previously, this method is configured automatically when you install Oracle Net. If you want the Oracle Easy Connect Naming method to be the first method chosen by a client when a connection request is made, you can modify the NAMES.DIRECTORY_PATH parameter in the sqlnet.ora file. The following discussion shows how to do this.

You can use the Oracle Net Manager tool to configure the Easy Connect method as the default names resolution method. Start the Oracle Net Manager tool, then follow these steps:

1. Choose Local ➢ Profile pane in the Navigator pane.

2. Select Naming from the panel on the right.

3. Select the Methods tab.

4. Select EZCONNECT in the Selected Methods list. You can click the promote arrows to move EZCONNECT to the top of the Selected Methods list.

5. Choose File ➢ Save Network Configuration to save your changes.

When you check your `sqlnet.ora` file, you should see the following entry:

```
NAMES.DIRECTORY_PATH=(EZCONNECT,TNSNAMES)
```

The Localnaming Method

The *localnaming method* is probably the most widely used and well-known method for resolving net service names. Most users know this method as the `tnsnames.ora` method because it uses the `tnsnames.ora` file.

To use the localnaming method, you must configure the *tnsnames.ora* file, which can be in any location as long as the client can get to it. The default location for the `tnsnames.ora` file and the `sqlnet.ora` file is `%ORACLE_HOME%\network\admin` on Windows and `$ORACLE_HOME/network/admin` on Unix systems. If you want to change the location of this file, set the environmental variable `TNS_ADMIN`. In Unix-based systems, you can export `TNS_ADMIN` to the user's shell environment or in the user's profile. In Windows, this setting is in the Registry. The Windows Registry key that stores the `TNS_ADMIN` depends on your particular setup. Generally, it is somewhere under `Hkey_local_machine/software/oracle`, but it may be at a lower level depending on your configuration.

Most installations probably keep the files in these default locations on the client and server. Some users create shared disks and place the `tnsnames.ora` and `sqlnet.ora` files in this shared location to take a centralized approach to managing these files. If server-to-server communication is necessary, these files need to be on the server. The default location on the server is the same as the default location on the client.

Now that you have an understanding of the localnaming method, we will discuss how to configure this method using Oracle Net Manager.

Configuring the Localnaming Method Using Oracle Net Manager

To configure the localnaming method, you use Oracle Net Manager. To start this configuration, open the Net Manager and select Service Naming on the Local tab. Click the plus sign on the left side of the screen, or choose Edit ➢ Create (see Figure 4.27).

The Oracle Net Manager starts the Net Service Name wizard, which guides you through the process of creating the Net Service Names definition.

Choosing a Net Service Name

When you configure a client to use the localnaming method, you must first choose a *net service name*. This is the name that users enter when they are referring to the location to which they want to connect. The name you supply here should not include the domain portion if you are using the hierarchical naming mode. Figure 4.28 shows an example of choosing the net service name. Click the Next button to continue.

FIGURE 4.27 The Oracle Net Manager title screen with the Service Naming option chosen

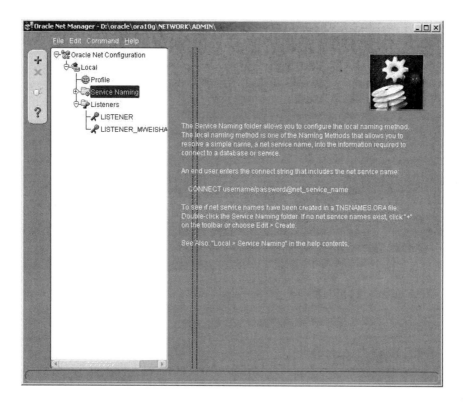

FIGURE 4.28 Choosing a net service name

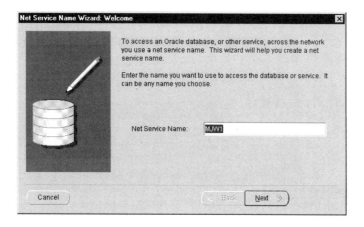

Choosing a Network Protocol

The next step is to enter the type of protocol that the client should use when they connect to the server for this net service name. By default, TCP/IP is chosen (see Figure 4.29). The list of protocols depends on your platform. Click the Next button to continue.

Choosing the Hostname and the Port

This step depends on the protocol you chose in the previous step. If you chose TCP/IP, you are prompted for the hostname and the port number. The hostname is the name of the machine on which the listener process is running. The port number is the listening location for the listener. The default port is 1521 (see Figure 4.30).

FIGURE 4.29 Choosing a network protocol

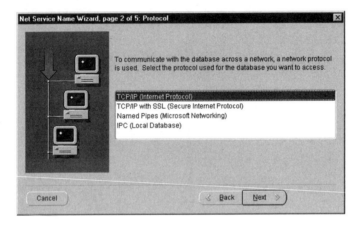

FIGURE 4.30 Choosing a hostname and a port

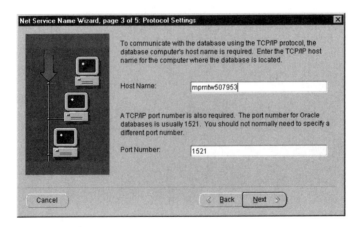

Choosing the Service Name

The next step is to define the service name. For Oracle 10g, the service name does not have to be the same as the ORACLE_SID because a database can have multiple service names. In Oracle 10g, the service name is normally the same as the global database name. This is the service name that is supplied to the listener, so the listener has to be listening for this service. You can also choose whether this service is for Oracle8i or later databases or Oracle8 and previous databases. You can also select the connection type from one of these choices:

- Database Default
- Shared Server
- Dedicated Server

Figure 4.31 shows an example of the Oracle Net Manager service name screen.

Testing the Net Service Name Connection

The last step is to test the net service name and verify that all the connection information entered is correct. Click the Test button to test the network connection. Figure 4.32 displays an example of the Oracle Net Manager test network connection screen.

By default, the test connection tries to connect to the database with a username of scott and the password tiger. If your connection fails, check to see if you have a scott/tiger user. You can change which login to test with by clicking the Change Login button in the test connection screen. You can also create the user scott by running a script called scott.sql located in the $ORACLE_HOME/rdbms/admin directory on Unix or %ORACLE_HOME%\rdbms\admin on Windows.

FIGURE 4.31   Choosing the service name

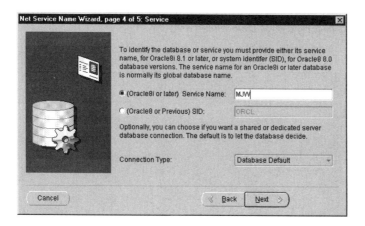

FIGURE 4.32 The Oracle Net Manager test network connection screen

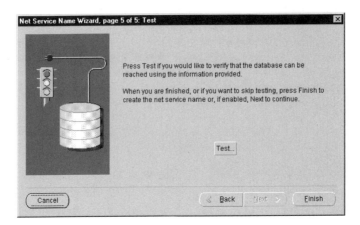

If everything is correct, you should see a result similar to Figure 4.33.

After you complete all this, save your changes by choosing File ➢ Save Network Configuration. This creates and saves the tnsnames.ora file.

Contents and Structure of the *tnsnames.ora* File

Here is an example of the tnsnames.ora file:

```
# tnsnames.ora Network Configuration File:
   D:\oracle\ora10g\NETWORK\ADMIN\tnsnames.ora
# Generated by Oracle configuration tools.

ORCL =
  (DESCRIPTION =
    (ADDRESS_LIST =
      (ADDRESS = (PROTOCOL = TCP)(HOST = mweishan-dell)(PORT = 1521))
    )
    (CONNECT_DATA =
      (SERVICE_NAME = ORCL)
    )
  )
```

FIGURE 4.33   The Oracle Net Manager *tnsnames.ora* wizard test result screen

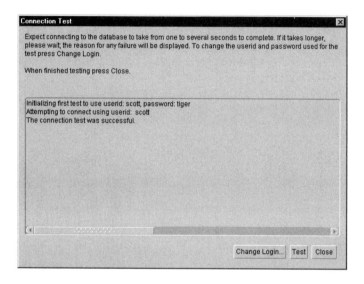

Table 4.6 summarizes the parameters in the tnsnames.ora file.

TABLE 4.6   The *tnsnames.ora* Parameters

Parameter	Description
DESCRIPTION	Starts the connect descriptor section of the file.
ADDRESS_LIST	Starts a list of all connect descriptor address information.
ADDRESS	Specifies the connect descriptor for the net service name.
PROTOCOL	Specifies the protocol used, such as TCP/IP.
HOST	Specifies the name of the machine on which the listener is running. An IP address can also be specified in TCP/IP.
PORT	Specifies the listening location of the listener specific to TCP/IP.
CONNECT_DATA	Starts the services section for this net service name.
SERVICE_NAME	Replaces the SID parameter from older releases of Oracle. Defines which service to connect to, which can be the same as the ORACLE_SID or the global database name. Databases can now be referred to by more than a single service name.

Configuring Localnaming Using Enterprise Manager

You can also use Oracle Enterprise Manager to configure localnaming. You do so from the Net Services Administration screen as described in the "Adding a Listener Using Enterprise Manager Database Control" section earlier in this chapter. You will see the screen shown in Figure 4.17. Choose Local Naming from the Administer drop-down list and click Go to open the Local Naming screen, as shown in Figure 4.34.

FIGURE 4.34   Using Enterprise Manager to configure localnaming

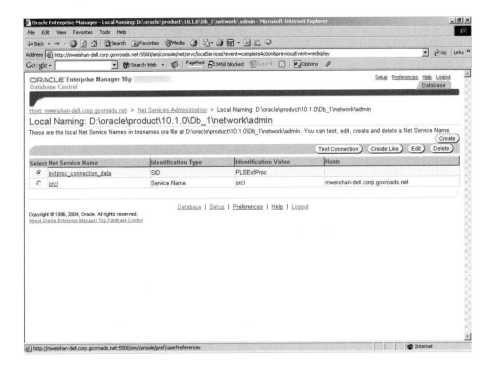

Click the Create button to open the Create Net Service Name page. Here you can enter the Unique Service Name that you want users to use to connect to this Oracle Service. This can also be the Oracle SID. You can select the type of connection to use for this service: dedicated server, shared server, or the database default. The address information also needs to be specified. This includes the protocol, port, and host used by the service being connected to. Click the Add button under addresses to open the Add Address screen to fill in the appropriate information (see Figure 4.35).

On the Create New Service Name page, there is a section to configure failover and load balancing options. The earlier section in this chapter, "Additional Configurations When Using Multiple Listeners" discusses the concepts of failover and load balancing. Five choices are listed under the Connect Time Failover and Load Balancing section. Table 4.7 summarizes these prompts. If you have multiple listeners listening for this service or are using Oracle Connection Manager, you can select from this list. The default is to use the first address only; this is the case where a single listener is being used.

FIGURE 4.35   The Add Address screen

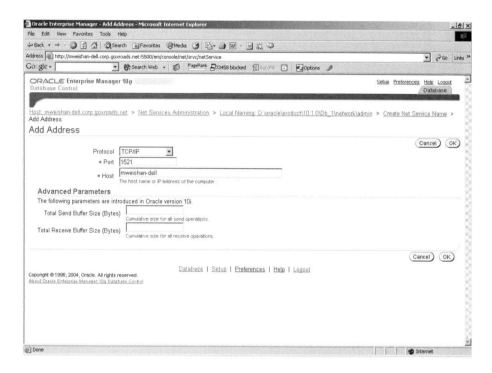

TABLE 4.7   Advanced Features Summary

Option	Advanced Feature
Try each address, in order, until one succeeds.	Failover
Try each address, randomly, until one succeeds.	Failover Load Balancing
Try one address, selected at random.	Load Balancing
Use each address in order until you reach the destination.	Source Routing
Use only the first address.	None

Source Routing is used with Oracle Connection Manager. Oracle passes control from the first address listed to the next address and so on until the ultimate destination is reached. Every address listed is used in the case of source routing.

Troubleshooting Client-Side Connection Problems

Connection problems can also occur from the Oracle client. A number of areas affect the ability of a client to connect successfully to the server. The client must be able to contact both the computer on which the Oracle server is located and the listener listening for connections to the Oracle server. The client must also be able to resolve the net service name. Let's take a look at the checks to perform on the client to verify connectivity to the Oracle server and to detect and troubleshoot client-side connection problems. Use the following list to systematically check various aspects of the client connection process:

- Verify that the client can contact the server.

- Determine the network route that the client is taking to the server.

- Verify localnaming configuration files.

- Check for multiple-client network configuration files.

- Check network file locations.

- Check the NAMES.DIRECTORY_PATH parameter.

- Check the NAMES.DEFAULT_DOMAIN parameter.

- Check the client protocol adapters installed.

- Check for any common client-side error codes.

Checking Client/Server Contact

Make sure that the client can see the host computer. If you are using TCP/IP, you can attempt to ping the host computer. Simply type **ping** and the name of the host. If the host is not found, try using the IP address of the host computer instead of the hostname. If this works, the problem may be that your HOSTS file is not correct or your DNS server does not recognize the host computer name. For example, you can ping a computer with the hostname of mweishan-dell as follows:

```
D:\oracle\ora10g\NETWORK\ADMIN>ping mweishan-dell

Pinging mweishan-dell.corp.goprod.net [211.209.111.50] with 32 bytes of
   data:

Reply from 211.209.111.50: bytes=32 time<10ms TTL=128
Reply from 211.209.111.50: bytes=32 time<10ms TTL=128
Reply from 211.209.111.50: bytes=32 time<10ms TTL=128
```

Determining the Network Route that the Client Is Using to Get to the Server

If you are using a TCP/IP network, you can see a summary of the network path or "hops" made from a client to some network destination using the tracert (on Windows) or traceroute (on Unix) utility. This utility is helpful because it displays the route taken by a TCP/IP connection from one location to another. It can help to diagnose situations in which some users are experiencing network problems or slowness while others are not having the problem. It is also helpful if new hardware such as routers have been added to the network and you want to see if the new hardware is being used to route the IP traffic from your client to the server. You and your network team can use this information to ensure that appropriate network routes are being used to connect to databases.

Here is an example of using the traceroute utility:

```
Cupx001:/home/oracle>traceroute 10.15.9.11
traceroute to 10.15.9.11 (10.19.5.11), 30 hops max, 20 byte packets
    1 211.118.131.20 (211.118.131.20)          1 ms    3 ms    0 ms
    2 trx001.mweishan.com (10.15.9.11)         1 ms    1 ms    1 ms
```

This example shows a traceroute being performed from a server called Cupx001. The user is attempting to see which network route is being taken to connect to the TCP/IP destination 10.15.9.11. You can see that an initial network hop is made to 211.118.131.20. This is possibly a router in the network. The connection was established in about 1 millisecond, as you can see in the first numeric column.

From there, the TCP/IP packet was sent to our destination of 10.15.9.11. This also was done in about 1 millisecond. Long network delays or many hops could indicate where and why network problems are occurring.

In the following example, we can see an example of using the tracert utility on a Windows platform.

```
E:\>tracert 10.20.0.39
Tracing route to rep02.cgnsmadison.com [10.20.0.39]
over a maximum of 30 hops:
    1    <1 ms    <1 ms    <1 ms   211.139.222.26
    2    <1 ms    <1 ms    <1 ms   rep02.cgnsmadisono.com [10.20.0.39]
Trace complete.
E:\>
```

Checking Client/Listener Contact

Next, check to see if the client can contact the listener. You can use a utility called *tnsping* to verify this. The tnsping Oracle utility attempts to contact an Oracle listener. It works similarly to ping in that you can enter a net service name and the number of times to contact the listener. This utility verifies that the client can contact the listener. However, it does not verify that the client can actually connect to the Oracle server. You can also specify a number of attempts. In the following example, two attempts are made to contact the ORCL database:

```
D:\oracle\ora10g\NETWORK\ADMIN>tnsping orcl 2

TNS Ping Utility for 32-bit Windows: Version 10.1.0.2.0 - Production on
    10-JUN-2004 10:18:05
```

```
Copyright (c) 1997, 2003, Oracle.  All rights reserved.

Used parameter files:
D:\oracle\ora10g\network\admin\sqlnet.ora

Used TNSNAMES adapter to resolve the alias
Attempting to contact (DESCRIPTION = (ADDRESS_LIST = (ADDRESS =
   (PROTOCOL = TCP)
(HOST = mweishan-dell)(PORT = 1521))) (CONNECT_DATA = (SERVICE_NAME =
   ORCL)))
OK (20 msec)
OK (10 msec)
```

The tnsping utility shows how long the round-trip took to contact the listener. This information can also assist you in uncovering the connection problem, as discussed in the following sidebar.

 Real World Scenario

The Mysterious Timeout Problem

I have used tnsping to help troubleshoot some interesting connection problems. One such problem involved a client who was experiencing intermittent connection timeouts. Sometimes the client could connect, but other times the client received a timeout error message. The client also reported that logging in to the Oracle server always took an inordinate amount of time.

This problematic client machine happened to be sitting adjacent to another client machine that had no connection or timeout problems whatsoever. I ran some connection tests with tnsping and discovered that the client having problems took, on average, 3000 milliseconds to connect to the listener while the other client took only 30 milliseconds. Both clients were using the same network routes to connect to the server.

After further investigation, I discovered that the machines were using different implementations of TCP/IP, which was the cause of the intermittent timeout problems. With the help of the tnsping utility, I was able to narrow down the problem to a difference in the client machine configurations.

Verifying Localnaming Configuration Files

If the client is using the localnaming method for net service name resolution, check the entries in the tnsnames.ora file. Make sure that the entries are syntactically correct and that there is an entry for the net service name. Also make sure that the protocol is correct.

Looking for Multiple Client Network Configuration Files

Make sure that all copies of these files are identical. Normally there should be only one copy of the client-side networking files such as `tnsnames.ora` and `sqlnet.ora`. In some situations, such as when you are using other Oracle tools (such as Oracle Developer), these products are installed on a client in a separate `ORACLE_HOME` directory and have their own copies of the network files. This can make it necessary for a client to have more than one copy of the networking files.

Checking Network File Locations

One of the most common problems encountered is clients moving network files and not setting the `TNS_ADMIN` environmental variable to the new file location. Oracle expects the `tnsnames.ora` and `sqlnet.ora` files to be in the default location. If it cannot locate the files and you have not set `TNS_ADMIN`, you receive an ORA-12154 error message. You also receive this error if the supplied net service name is invalid. The following codes shows an example of this error message:

```
D:\oracle\ora10g\NETWORK\ADMIN>sqlplus scott/tiger@ora

SQL*Plus: Release 10.1.0.2.0 - Production on Thu Jun 10 10:21:22 2004

Copyright (c) 1982, 2004, Oracle.  All rights reserved.

ERROR:
ORA-12154: TNS:could not resolve the connect identifier specified
```

If you decide to move network files, be sure to set the `TNS_ADMIN` environmental variable to the location of the files. Oracle first searches the default location for the files and then searches the `TNS_ADMIN` location for the files.

Checking *NAMES.DIRECTORY_PATH*

Make sure that the client has the proper names resolution setting. The *NAMES.DIRECTORY_ PATH* parameter in the `sqlnet.ora` file controls the order in which the client resolves net service names. If the parameter is not set, the default is localnaming, OID, and then hostnaming.

If this parameter is set incorrectly, the client may never check the appropriate names resolution type. For example, if you are using localnaming and the parameter is set to `HOSTNAMES`, the `tnsnames.ora` file will never be used to resolve the net service name. You will receive an ORA-12154 "Cannot Resolve Connect Identifier Specified" error message.

Checking *NAMES.DEFAULT_DOMAIN*

NAMES.DEFAULT_DOMAIN is another common error. It was more common in older releases of Oracle because the parameter defaulted to the value WORLD. Check the client sqlnet.ora file to see if the parameter is set. If the parameter has a value and you are using unqualified net service names, the parameter value is appended to the end of the net service name. An unqualified service name is a service name that does not contain domain information.

For example, if you entered **Sqlplus matt/casey@PROD**, and the NAMES.DEFAULT_DOMAIN is set to WORLD, Oracle appends .WORLD to the net service name; as a result, Oracle passes the command as sqlplus matt/casey@PROD.WORLD. You will receive an ORA-12154 "Cannot Resolve Connect Identifier Specified" error message if the service name should not include the .WORLD domain extension. You use this parameter only if you are using a hierarchical naming convention.

Checking Client Protocol Adapters

Verify that the appropriate protocol adapters are installed on the client. You can invoke the Universal Installer and check the client setup. Look for the listing of client protocol adapters installed.

Checking for Client-Side Error Codes

You should next check for client-side error codes. Here is a summary of some of the common client-side Oracle error messages that you might encounter. They are discussed in detail in the following sections.

```
ORA-12154 "TNS: could not resolve connect identifier specified"
ORA-12198 "TNS: could not find path to destination"
ORA-12203 "TNS: Unable to connect to destination"
ORA-12533 "TNS: illegal address parameters"
ORA-12541 "TNS: No listener"
```

ORA-12154   Indicates that the client cannot find the service listed in the tnsnames.ora file. Some of the causes of this are described previously, such as the file is not in the proper directory or the TNS_ADMIN variable is not specified or specified incorrectly.

ORA-12198 and ORA-12203   Indicate that the client found an entry for the service in the tnsnames.ora file but the service specified was not found. Check to make sure that the service specified in the tnsnames.ora file actually points to a valid database service.

ORA-12533   Indicates that you have configured the ADDRESS section of the tnsnames.ora file incorrectly. Check to make sure the syntax is correct or re-create the definition using the Oracle Net Manager tool.

ORA-12541   Indicates that the client contacted a server that does not have a listener running on the specified port. Make sure that the listener is started on the server and that the listening port specifications on the client and the server match.

Summary

You need to understand several key components in order to succeed when networking in an Oracle environment. The main responsibilities of the DBA include determining the applications and type of connections that will be supported, the number of users and the locations from which they will be accessing the network, and the security issues involved in protecting sensitive information, such as single sign-on and data encryption.

In addition, you need to choose from the three basic types of network configurations when setting up an Oracle network: single-tier architecture, two-tier architecture, and *n*-tier architecture. Because systems have evolved from the simpler single-tier architecture to the more complex *n*-tier architecture, which can include connections through middle-tier servers and the Internet, you will most likely choose between the two architectures that Oracle Net is an integral part of: two-tier or *n*-tier.

Oracle Net manages the flow of information from client computers to Oracle servers and forms the foundation of all networked computing in the Oracle environment. Oracle Net provides services that can be divided into five main categories: connectivity, directory services, scalability, security, and accessibility. Connectivity solutions include support for multiple protocols, multiple operating systems, and Java and Internet. Directory services provide an infrastructure to resolve Oracle service names through a centralized naming repository. Scalability solutions include Connection Manager and Oracle Shared Server. Security options include Oracle Advanced Security, which provides an additional layer of security options and robust support for many varieties of firewalls. Accessibility support includes Heterogeneous Services and support for calling external procedures. Oracle Net also provides connectivity to Java stored procedures and URL connections.

The listener is the main server-side component in the Oracle Net environment. Listener configuration information is stored in the `listener.ora` file, and you manage the listener using the lsnrctl command-line utility. You configure the listener by using the Oracle Net Manager. The Oracle Net Manager provides a graphical interface for creating most of the Oracle Net files that you will use for Oracle, including the `listener.ora` file. If multiple listeners are configured, each one has a separate entry in the `listener.ora` file.

Oracle10g provides a feature called dynamic service registration. This feature allows an Oracle instance to automatically register itself with a listener. The listener must be configured with TCP/IP and listen on port 1521, or you must specify the parameter `LOCAL_LISTENER` in the `init.ora` file. You must set the parameters `INSTANCE_NAME` and `SERVICE_NAMES` in the `init.ora` file for the Oracle instance to enable dynamic service registration.

You can configure logging and tracing on the Oracle server using Oracle Net Manager, Oracle Enterprise Manager, or the lsnrctl utility. Logging records significant events, such as starting and stopping the listener, along with certain kinds of network errors. Errors are generated in the log in the form of an error stack. Tracing records all events that occur even when an error does not happen. The trace file provides a great deal of information that logs do not. Tracing uses much more space than logging and can also have an impact on system performance. Enable tracing only if other methods of troubleshooting fail to resolve the problem.

Configuring the Oracle server components correctly is the first step to successfully implementing Oracle in a network environment. If you do not have the Oracle server network components configured correctly, you will be unable to provide connection support to clients in the Oracle environment. Configure and test the server network components before configuring the Oracle clients.

Depending on your network environment, the client configuration setups can vary from no work to configuring a number of files on the client. The names resolution methods available for clients include hostnaming, Oracle Easy Connect, localnaming, Oracle Internet Directory, and External Naming. Hostnaming, which can only be used if you are using TCP/IP, is mainly used for simple Oracle networks. Oracle Easy Connect is an extension of hostnaming and allows for the inclusion of additional information such as the hostname and port specification. Localnaming is the most popular of the names resolution methods, and it uses the `tnsnames.ora` file, which is typically located on each client, to resolve net service names. The client looks up the net service name in the `tnsnames.ora` file and uses the resulting connect descriptor information to connect to the Oracle server. The hostnaming and localnaming methods are configured using the Oracle Net Manager or Oracle Enterprise Manager. Oracle Internet Directory is a Lightweight Directory Access Protocol (LDAP)–compliant server that provides for centralized management of Oracle database connection identifier information. External Naming uses a non-Oracle facility, such as DNS, to manage and resolve Oracle service names.

It is important to know how to troubleshoot connection problems. You should know the general format and content of the `tnsnames.ora` and `sqlnet.ora` files to be able to identify syntax errors. You should know where these files reside on the client. You should understand how the various names resolution methods work. You should become familiar with the tools that can be used, such as the TCP/IP-supplied ping utility and the Oracle-supplied tnsping utility to assist you when troubleshooting these problems. Finally, you should familiarize yourself with the most common Oracle error messages that can occur as a result of connection problems.

This chapter provides the foundation of knowledge that you will need when you are designing, configuring, and managing the Oracle network infrastructure. The decisions you make about the network design have ramifications in terms of the scalability, security, and flexibility of your Oracle environment. When you understand the underlying network architecture, network options available to you, and how to configure and manage the Oracle Net infrastructure, you will be able to provide consistent and reliable connections to Oracle services for your clients.

Exam Essentials

Know the database administrator's responsibilities and how they relate to network administration.   Be able to list the responsibilities of the database administrator with respect to network administration. Can you define the basic network configuration choices and summarize the strengths and weaknesses of these options?

Understand what Oracle Net is and the functionality it provides.   Be able to list the five categories of functionality that Oracle Net provides and explain the functionality that falls into each category. Also understand what functionality the Oracle Shared Server and Oracle Connection Manager options provide. In addition, be able to define Oracle Advanced Security and know when to use it.

Be familiar with Oracle's Internet connection options. Have a basic understanding of the connection options that Oracle provides from the Internet. This includes connections made via an application server and connections made directly to the Oracle server from a web browser.

Be able to define the main responsibilities of the Oracle listener. To fully understand the function of the Oracle listener, you should understand how the listener responds to client connection requests. In addition, know the difference between bequeath connections and redirect connections, and know under what circumstances the listener will use each. Also, be able to outline the steps involved in using each of these connection types.

Be able to define the listener.ora file and the ways in which the file is created. To understand the purpose of this file, know its default contents and how to change the file using the various Oracle tools. In addition, be able to define the sections of the file and know the definitions of the optional parameters it contains. Also understand the structure of the listener.ora file when one or more listeners are configured.

Understand how to use the lsnrctl command-line utility. To start up and shut down the listener, know how to use the lsnrctl command-line utility. Be able to explain the command-line options for the lsnrctl utility, such as services, status, and reload. When using this utility, also know the options available to you, and be able to define the various set commands.

Understand the concepts of static and dynamic service registration. Be able to define the difference between static service registration and dynamic service registration and know the advantages of using dynamic service registration over static service registration. Also, be aware of the situations in which you have to use static service registration. Lastly, be familiar with the init.ora parameters that you will need to set in order to enable dynamic service registration.

Be able to diagnose and correct network connectivity problems. Know the types of server-side errors that can occur and how to diagnose and correct these problems. Be able to define the difference between logging and tracing and know how to use the types of packet information that you may find in a trace file.

Define the Oracle client-side names resolution options. Be able to define the Oracle client-side names resolution options. Know in which situations to use localnaming, Oracle Easy Connect Naming, hostnaming, and OID.

Define the prerequisites for using the hostnaming method. Know how to configure this method using the Oracle Net Manager, and understand the connection process when you use this method. You also need to be able to define the parameter that you may have to add to the listener.ora file. In addition, understand the HOSTS file.

Use the Oracle tools to configure the client. Be able to use various Oracle tools to configure the sqlnet.ora file on the client. Understand the meaning of the NAMES.DEFAULT_DOMAIN and NAMES.DIRECTORY_PATH parameters within the sqlnet.ora file.

Define the localnaming method. In addition to knowing the meaning of the localnaming method and what it does, understand how to use the Oracle Net Manager to configure this names resolution method. Understand the primary file used in the localnaming method, the tnsnames.ora file.

Define the contents and structure of the tnsnames.ora file. Be able to describe the tnsnames.ora file and the various sections of the file and to explain how the file is used. Understand the contents of the tnsnames.ora file so that you can identify syntax problems with the structure of entries in the file. Be familiar with the common locations of this file and how to set the TNS_ADMIN parameter to override the default location of this and the other client-side network files.

Define and correct client-side errors. Understand the types of client-side connection errors that can occur. Be able to define these errors and understand the situations in which a client might encounter them.

Review Questions

1. All of the following are examples of networking architectures except:

   A. Client/server

   B. N-tier

   C. Single-tier

   D. Two-tier

   E. All the above are examples of network architectures.

2. You manage one non-Oracle database and several Oracle databases. An application needs to access the non-Oracle database as if it were part of the Oracle databases. What tool allows you to do this? (Choose the best answer.)

   A. Oracle Advanced Security

   B. Oracle Connection Manager

   C. Heterogeneous Services

   D. Oracle Net

   E. None of the above

3. Which of the following is true about Oracle Net?

   A. It is not an option included in the Oracle Enterprise installation.

   B. It works only on TCP/IP platforms.

   C. It has the ability to communicate with non-Oracle data sources.

   D. It is never installed directly on a client workstation.

4. You want to centrally administer all the Oracle network services in a large Oracle 10*g* installation that runs many network services. Which of the following facilities would best provide this functionality at minimal cost?

   A. Advanced Security

   B. Heterogeneous Services

   C. Oracle Shared Server

   D. Oracle Internet Directory

5. Which of the following files must be present on the Oracle server to start a non-default Oracle listener?

   A. `listener.ora`

   B. `lsnrctl.ora`

   C. `sqlnet.ora`

   D. `tnsnames.ora`

6. Which of the following is the correct way to start the default listener?

    A. lsnrctl startup listener

    B. lsnrctl start

    C. listener start

    D. listener start listener

7. Which of the following parameters sets the number of seconds a server process waits to get a valid client request?

    A. connect_waittime_*listener_name*

    B. connect_wait_*listener_name*

    C. timeout_*listener_name*

    D. inbound_connect_timeout_*listener_name*

8. When dynamic service registration is used, you will not see the service listed in which of the following files where it would normally be located?

    A. sqlnet.ora

    B. tnsnames.ora

    C. listener.ora

    D. None of the above

9. You have just made changes to the listener.ora file for the listener called listener1 using Oracle Net Manager. Which of the following commands or combinations of commands would you use to put the changes into effect with the least amount of client disruption?

    A. lsnrctl stop listener1 followed by lsnrctl start listener1

    B. lsrnctl restart listener1

    C. lsnrctl reload listener1

    D. lsnrctl reload

10. What is the default name of the process that makes external calls via Oracle Net?

    A. lsnrctl

    B. external

    C. extproc

    D. procext

11. What are the ways in which a client can resolve a net service name? (Choose all that apply.)

    A. Localnaming

    B. Hostnaming

    C. Easy Connect Naming

    D. Oracle Global Naming

    E. All the above

12. Connection Manager provides which of the following?

   A. Multiplexing

   B. Cross-protocol connectivity

   C. Network access control

   D. All the above

13. Which is a requirement for using hostnaming?

   A. You must use `tnsnames.ora` on the client.

   B. You must be using TCP/IP.

   C. You must have an OID present.

   D. You must have a `sqlnet.ora` file present on the client.

   E. None of the above.

14. To which of the choices below does the following statement apply? "Prevents direct communication between a client outside the corporate network and applications inside the corporate network."

   A. Proxy-based firewalls

   B. Filter-based firewalls

   C. Both types of firewalls

   D. Neither type of firewall

15. Which of the following statements about `tnsnames.ora` is false?

   A. It is used to resolve an Oracle service name.

   B. It can exist on the client.

   C. It is used for localnaming.

   D. It does not support the TCP/IP protocol

16. You manage a large network of servers with many Oracle10*g* instances configured on each server. The company would like to centralize the Oracle services into a common location for ease of maintenance. Which of the following would be the best choice for centralized naming services?

   A. Oracle Easy Connect Naming

   B. Localnaming

   C. Oracle Names Server

   D. Oracle Internet Directory

17. A client receives the following error message:

```
"ORA-12154 TNS:could not resolve the connect identifier
    specified"
```

Which of the following could be possible causes of the error? (Choose all that apply.)

A. The listener is not running on the Oracle server.

B. The user entered an invalid net service name.

C. The user supplied the correct net service name, but the net service name is misspelled in the tnsnames.ora file.

D. The listener is not configured to listen for this service.

18. What portion of the tnsnames.ora file specifies the name or IP address of the server where the listener process is listening?

A. CONNECT_DATA

B. PORT

C. SERVICE_NAME

D. HOST

19. Which of the following is the utility that you can use to test the network connections across TCP/IP?

A. trcasst

B. lsnrctl

C. namesctl

D. ping

E. None of the above

20. A client wants to connect to the database dbprod.com located on the dbprod.com server to a non-default port using Oracle Easy Connect. Which of the following connect strings is the best choice for the client use?

A. CONNECT scott/tiger@dbprod.com:1522

B. CONNECT scott/tiger@1521:dbprod.com/dbprod.com

C. CONNECT scott/tiger@dbprod.com/1522:dbprod.com

D. CONNECT scott/tiger@dbprod.com:1521/dbprod.com

E. CONNECT scott/tiger@dbprod.com:1522/dbprod.com

Answers to Review Questions

1. E. All these are examples of network connectivity configurations. Networking can be as simple as a dumb terminal connected directly to a server via a serial connection. It can also be as complex as an *n*-tier architecture that involves clients, middleware, the Internet, and database servers.

2. C. Heterogeneous Services is the correct answer because these services provide cross-platform connectivity to non-Oracle databases. Oracle Advanced Security would not solve this application problem because it addresses security and not accessibility to non-Oracle databases. Oracle Net would be part of the solution, but another Oracle Network component is necessary. Connection Manager would also not be able to accommodate this requirement on its own.

3. C. When you are using the Heterogeneous Services capabilities of Oracle Net, you do have the ability to communicate with non-Oracle data sources.

4. D. The best solution to the problem is the Oracle Internet Directory because it facilitates centralized naming. Advanced Security, Heterogeneous Services, and Oracle Shared Server would not provide a solution to this business need because none of these address the issue of centrally managing network services.

5. A. The listener is the process that manages incoming connection requests. The `listener.ora` file is used to configure the listener and must be configured to start a non-default listener. The `sqlnet.ora` file is an optional client- and server-side file. The `tnsnames.ora` file is used for doing local naming resolution. There is no such file as `lsnrctl.ora`.

6. B. Because the default listener name is LISTENER, simply enter `lsnrctl start`. The name LISTENER is assumed to be the listener to start in this case.

7. D. When a user makes a connection request, the listener passes control to some server process or dispatcher. Once the user is attached to this process, all negotiations and interaction with the database pass through this process. If the user supplies an invalid user ID or password, the process waits for a period of time for a valid response. If the user does not contact the server process with a valid response in the allotted time, the server process terminates, and the user must contact the listener so that the listener can again spawn a process or redirect the client to an existing dispatcher. This period of time that the process waits is specified by the `connect_timeout_listener_name` parameter. This parameter is specified in seconds.

8. C. When services are dynamically registered with the listener, their information is not present in the `listener.ora` file.

9. C. Although you can use choice A to stop and start the listener, doing so temporarily disrupts clients attempting to connect to the database. Choice D is fine if you are starting and stopping the default listener called LISTENER, but we are using a non-default listener. Choice B is not valid because RESTART is not a valid command-line argument for lsnrctl. Therefore, the best method is C, to use the `lsnrctl reload listener1` command to load the new set of values in for the listener without disrupting connection service to the databases that the listener is servicing.

10. C. The default name of the external procedure process is `extproc`. lsnrctl is a utility used to manage the listener service. `External` and `procext` are not valid responses.

11. A, B, C. Oracle uses service names in networks in much the same way it uses synonyms in the database. Service names provide location transparency and hide the complexity of connect string information. You can configure Oracle Net to connect in several ways, including host-naming, localnaming, OID, and Oracle Easy Connect Naming. Oracle Global Naming is not a valid Oracle option.

12. D. Connection Manager is a middleware solution that provides for multiplexing of connections, cross-protocol connectivity, and network access control. All the answers describe Connection Manager.

13. B. Hostnaming is typically used in small installations that have few Oracle databases. This is an attractive option when you want to minimize client-side configuration. TCP/IP is a requirement when you use hostnaming.

14. A. Proxy-based firewalls prevent any direct contact between a client outside the corporate firewall and applications inside a corporate firewall. Filter-based firewalls inspect the packet headers but pass the packet on without modification to the destination application. Proxy-based firewalls act more as a relay between external clients and internal applications.

15. D. A `tnsnames.ora` file is configured when you want to use localnaming, and it typically exists on the client workstation. It is also used to resolve a service name. The `tnsnames.ora` file used in localnaming does indeed support the TCP/IP protocol.

16. D. OID is Oracle's preferred centralized naming service. Oracle Names Server is no longer supported in Oracle 10*g*.

17. B, C. Supplying a net service name that is not contained in the `tnsnames.ora` file can cause this error. Problems with the `tnsnames.ora` file can cause this error too. Listener problems would not cause this error.

18. D. The `HOST` portion specifies the name of the server to contact. `CONNECT_DATA` specifies the database service to connect to. The `PORT` portion specifies the location where the listener is listening on the `HOST`. `SERVICE_NAME` is the name of the actual database service.

19. D. Protocols come with tools that allow you to test network connectivity. One such utility for TCP/IP is ping. The user supplies either an IP address or a hostname to the ping utility. It then searches the network for this address. If it finds one, it displays information on data that is sent and received and how quickly it found this address. The other choices are Oracle-supplied utilities.

20. A. The correct syntax to use with the Oracle Easy Connect Naming method when you are connecting to a non-URL location is as follows: *connect username/password@host:port/ service_name*. If the service name and the host are identical, you do not have to include the service name. If the port is any port other than the default port of 1521, it must be specified. Because we want to connect to a non-default port where the database name and the hostname are the same, the best answer is A.

Chapter

5

Oracle Shared Server

ORACLE DATABASE 10G: ADMINISTRATION I EXAM OBJECTIVES COVERED IN THIS CHAPTER:

✓ **Oracle Shared Servers**

- Identify when to use Oracle Shared Servers.
- Configure Oracle Shared Servers.
- Monitor Shared Servers.
- Describe the shared server architecture.

Exam objectives are subject to change at any time without prior notice and at Oracle's sole discretion. Please visit Oracle's Training and Certification website (http://www.oracle.com/education/certification/) for the most current exam objectives listing.

As the number of users connecting to Oracle databases in the enterprise grows, the system requirements of the servers increase—particularly the memory and process requirements. When a system starts to encounter these capacity issues, you need to know which alternatives are available within the Oracle environment that can address the problem. One configuration alternative that may help to overcome this capacity problem is Oracle Shared Server.

It is important to understand the Oracle Shared Server architecture and how and when to use it appropriately. When used properly, this feature can help alleviate problems with servers that are being taxed in terms of the number of processes running on the server. When the Shared Server is configured properly, it can help stave off system upgrades that may have seemed imminent, thus saving the organization time and money.

This chapter discusses the Oracle Shared Server and its benefits. You will learn about the client connection process and how Oracle Shared Server processes user requests. You will also learn how to configure Oracle Shared Server and how to manage Oracle Shared Server using various Oracle dynamic performance views. Finally, you will learn where to find information to help you tune the Oracle Shared Server.

An Overview of Oracle Shared Server

Oracle Shared Server is an optional configuration of Oracle Server that allows the server to support a larger number of concurrent connections without increasing physical resource requirements. It does so by sharing resources among groups of users.

Shared Server is suitable for "high think" applications. High think applications are composed of small transactions with natural pauses in the transaction patterns, which makes them good candidates for Oracle Shared Server connections. Many web-based applications fit this model. These types of applications are typically form-based and involve submissions of small amounts of information to the database with small result sets returned to the client.

When determining whether an application is a good candidate for using Shared Server, review the application and consider the amount of network traffic generated by a typical client interaction with the database server. Look at the size of the data sets returned to the client. Generally speaking, given the speed of most current networks, if a typical client interaction for the application involves 16KB or less data, it is a good candidate for using Oracle Shared Server. If an application client returns large results sets, such as an ad hoc reporting application for a data warehouse, it is probably not a good candidate for Oracle Shared Server. You will understand why when we discuss how Oracle Shared Server connections are managed later in this section.

Data set size is one factor that impacts the performance of Oracle Shared Server. Other factors are the speed of the network, the speed of the database server, and the number of client processes that the application must support concurrently.

Oracle manages dedicated server and Shared Server connections differently. As a DBA, you need to be able to identify these differences. This knowledge will help you to better understand the advantages and disadvantages of Oracle Shared Server and when it might be advantageous to use Oracle Shared Server in your environment.

Dedicated Server versus Shared Server

If you have ever gone to an upscale restaurant, you may have had your own personal waitperson. That waitperson is there to greet you and escort you to your seat. They take your order for food and drinks and even help prepare your order. No matter how many other patrons enter the restaurant, your waitperson is responsible for serving only your requests. Therefore, your service is consistent—if the person is a good waitperson.

A dedicated server environment works in much the same way. Every client connection is associated with a dedicated server process, sometimes called a *shadow process,* on the machine, where the Oracle server exists. No matter how many other connections are made to the server, the same dedicated server is always responsible for processing only your requests. You use the services of that server process until you disconnect from the Oracle Server.

Most restaurants operate more like shared servers. When you walk in, you are assigned a waitperson, but they may be responsible for serving many other tables. This is good for the restaurant because they can serve more customers without increasing the staff. It may be fine for you as well, if the restaurant is not too busy and the waitperson is not responsible for too many tables. Also, if most of the orders are small, the staff can keep up with the requests, and the service will be as good as if you had your own waitperson.

In the diner, things work slightly different; the waitperson takes your order and places it on a turnstile. If the diner has multiple cooks, the order is picked up from the turnstile and prepared by one of the available cooks. When the cook completes the preparation of the dinner, it is placed in a location where the waitperson can pick it up and bring it to your table.

This is how an Oracle Shared Server environment works. In an Oracle Shared Server environment, *dispatcher* processes are responsible for servicing client requests. These processes are capable of handling requests from many clients. This is different from the dedicated server environment, where a single client process is handled by a single server process. Like the waitperson in the diner, a dispatcher can be responsible for taking the orders of many clients.

When you request something from the server, it is the dispatcher's responsibility to take your request and place it in a location called a *request queue*. The request queue functions like the turnstile in the diner analogy. All dispatcher processes place their client requests in one request queue, which is a structure contained in the System Global Area (SGA).

Shared Server processes, like cooks in a diner, are responsible for fulfilling the client requests. The Oracle Shared Server process executes the request and places the result into an area of the SGA called a *response queue*. Every dispatcher has its own response queue. The dispatcher picks up the completed request from the response queue and returns the results to the client. Figure 5.1 illustrates the following processing steps for a Shared Server request:

1. The client passes a request to the dispatcher serving it.

2. The dispatcher places the request on a request queue in the SGA.

3. One of the Shared Server processes executes the request.

4. The Shared Server places the completed request on the dispatchers' response queue of the SGA.

5. The dispatcher picks up the completed request from the response queue.

6. The completed request is passed back to the client.

Requests placed in the request queue are processed on a first-in, first-out basis (FIFO). Currently, there is no way to prioritize requests within the queue.

FIGURE 5.1   Request processing in Shared Server

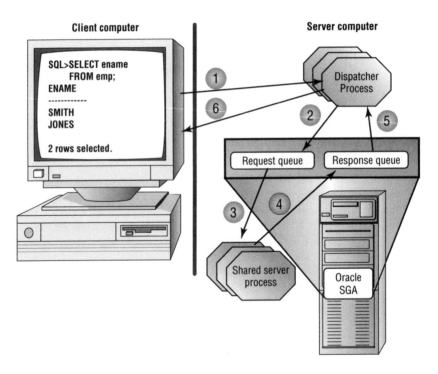

Advantages and Disadvantages of Shared Server

Oracle Shared Server is used when server resources, such as memory and active processes, become constrained. People tend to throw more hardware at problems such as these; this will likely remedy the problem, but it may be an unnecessary expense.

If your system is experiencing these problems, Oracle Shared Server allows you to support the same or greater number of connections without requiring additional hardware. As a result, Oracle Shared Server tends to decrease the overall memory and process requirements on the server. Because clients are sharing processes, the total number of processes is reduced. This translates into resource savings on the server.

Shared Server also allows for connection pooling. Connection pooling enables the database server to disconnect an idle Oracle Shared Server connection to service an incoming request. The idle connection is still active and is reenabled once the client makes the next request. The connection pooling feature of Oracle Shared Server allows it to handle a larger number of requests without having to start additional dispatcher processes. You configure connection pooling by adding attributes to one of the Oracle Shared Server parameters.

See the section "Configuring Connection Pooling with the Dispatchers Parameter" later in this chapter to see how connection pooling is configured.

Shared Server is also required to take advantage of certain network options, such as connection multiplexing and client access control, which are features of Oracle Connection Manager. Oracle Connection Manager is a facility provided by Oracle that controls access to database services and multiplex connections in an Oracle environment. The access control component of Oracle Connection Manager allows you to configure rules that allow or disallow fulfillment of a connection request. The multiplexing component acts as a concentrator feature. It funnels multiple client sessions through a shared network connection from the Oracle Connection Manager server to the database server.

You can find out more about Oracle Connection Manager in the *Oracle Database Net Services Administrators Guide 10g Release 1 (10.1)*, Part Number B10755-01.

Oracle Shared Server also has some disadvantages. Applications that generate a significant amount of network traffic or result in large result sets are not good candidates for Shared Server connections. Think of the earlier diner analogy. Your service is fine until two parties of 12 people show up. All of a sudden, the waitperson is overwhelmed with work from these two other tables, and your service begins to suffer. The same thing would happen in a shared server environment. If requests for large quantities of information start going to the dispatchers, the dispatchers can become overwhelmed, and you can see performance suffer for the other clients connected to the dispatcher. This, in turn, increases your response times. Dedicated processes better serve these types of applications.

Some functions are not allowed when you are using an Oracle Shared Server connection. You cannot start up, shut down, or perform certain kinds of recovery of an Oracle server when you are connected via a shared server.

Also, you should not perform certain administrative tasks using Oracle Shared Server connections, including bulk loads of data, index and table rebuilds, and table analysis. These types of tasks deal with manipulating large data sets and should use dedicated connections.

Oracle Shared Server is a scalability enhancement option, not a performance enhancement option. If you are looking for a performance increase, Shared Server is not what you should be configuring. Use Shared Server only if you are experiencing the system constraint problems discussed earlier in this chapter. In general, you will have equal or better performance in a dedicated server environment.

Oracle Shared Server Infrastructure

As described in the previous section, you manage client connections quite differently when using Oracle Shared Server as opposed to using a dedicated server. To accommodate the change, several modifications take place inside the internal memory structures of the Oracle Server. The way in which the database and listener interact is also affected when using Oracle Shared Server. It is important to understand these changes when configuring and managing the Oracle Shared Server.

Certain changes are necessary to the memory structures within Oracle to provide the Shared Server capability. Let's see what changes within the Oracle infrastructure are necessary to provide this support.

PGA and SGA Changes When Using Oracle Shared Server

When Oracle Shared Server is configured, Oracle adds two new types of structures to the SGA: request queues and response queues. These structures do not exist in a dedicated server environment. There is one request queue for all dispatchers, but each dispatcher has its own response queue. Therefore, if you have four dispatchers, you will have one request queue and four response queues. The request queue is located in the SGA where the dispatcher places client requests. A Shared Server process executes each request and places the completed request in the dispatchers' response queue.

In a dedicated server environment, each server has a memory segment called a *Program Global Area (PGA)*. The PGA is an area of memory where information about each client session is maintained. This information includes bind variables, cursor information, and the client's sort area. In an Oracle Shared Server environment, this information is moved from the PGA to an area of the SGA called the *User Global Area (UGA)*. You can configure a special area of the SGA called the *Large Pool* to accommodate the bulk of the UGA.

You will see how to configure the Large Pool in the section "Configuring the Large Pool" later in this chapter.

Figure 5.2 shows how the SGA and PGA structures differ between a dedicated server and an Oracle Shared Server environment.

Each connection being serviced by a dispatcher is bound to a shared memory segment and forms a *virtual circuit*. The dispatcher uses the shared memory segment to manage communications between the client and the Oracle database. The Oracle Shared Server processes use the virtual circuits to send and receive information to the appropriate dispatcher process.

FIGURE 5.2   An SGA dedicated server versus Oracle Shared Server

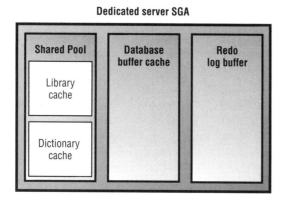

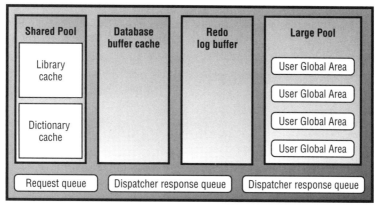

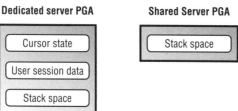

The Role of the Listener in an Oracle Shared Server Environment

The listener plays an important role in the Oracle Shared Server environment. The listener supplies the client with the address of the dispatcher to connect to when a user requests connections to an Oracle Shared Server. The listener maintains a list of dispatchers available from the Oracle Shared Server. The Oracle background process PMON (process monitor) notifies the listener as to which dispatcher is responsible for servicing each virtual circuit. The listener is then aware of the number of connections that the dispatcher is managing. This information allows the listener to take advantage of dispatcher load balancing.

Load balancing allows the listener to make intelligent decisions about which dispatcher to redirect client connections to so that no one dispatcher becomes overburdened. When the listener receives a connection request, it looks at the current connection load for each dispatcher and redirects the client connection request to the least-loaded dispatcher. The listener determines the least-loaded dispatcher for all nodes, if Real Application Clusters (RAC) are being used, followed by the least-loaded instance for the node, and finally by the least-loaded dispatcher for the instance. By doing so, the listener ensures that connections are evenly distributed across dispatchers.

The listener can either redirect the client connection to an available dispatcher or directly hand off the request to the dispatcher. The latter is performed whenever possible and is done typically when the listener and database service exist on the same node. When the listener and database service exist on different nodes, the redirection method is used.

When a client connection terminates, the listener is updated to reflect the change in the number of connections that the dispatcher is handling.

Figure 5.3 illustrates the following steps in the Oracle Shared Server connection process after the database has been started and the dispatcher processes have been started:

1. The client contacts the Oracle database server after resolving the service name.

2. The listener validates the Oracle Service Name supplied by the client and hands off or redirects the client connection to the least-busy dispatcher.

3. The listener sends information back to the client so the client can redirect the connection to the appropriate dispatcher process.

4. The dispatcher process manages the client server request.

5. PMON registers connection information with the listener.

Configuring the Oracle Shared Server

You can configure Oracle Shared Server in a number of ways. You can configure it at the time the database is created, you can use the Enterprise Manager (EM) to configure it after the database has been created, or you can manually configure it by editing initialization parameters. We'll discuss the parameters necessary to configure Oracle Shared Server. We'll also give examples of how to configure Shared Server at database creation or after the database is created using EM.

FIGURE 5.3   The Shared Server connection process

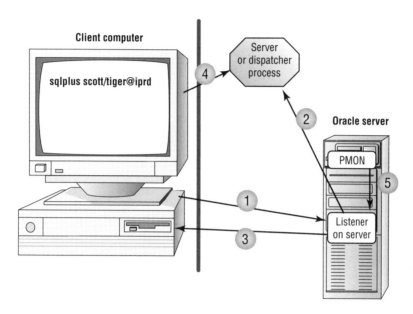

    With the release of Oracle Database 10*g* (Oracle 10*g*), configuring the Oracle Shared Server option has been simplified. You do not have to specify the DISPATCHERS parameter in order to enable shared servers in a default network environment. A default network environment is one in which a listener is configured with TCP/IP listening on the default port (1521). In this scenario, Oracle automatically starts a dispatcher, listening for TCP/IP connections on the default port. If a non-default setting or additional options are required, you must configure the DISPATCHERS parameter manually.

Defining the Shared Server Parameters

You configure Oracle Shared Server by adding or modifying parameter values in the Oracle initialization file. These parameters identify the number and type of dispatchers, the number of shared servers, and the name of the database that you want to associate with the Shared Server.

One advantage of Oracle 10*g* is that all the parameters necessary to manage Oracle Shared Server can be changed dynamically. This fulfills one of your primary goals of ensuring the highest degree of database availability possible. Let's take a look at the parameters used to manage Oracle Shared Server.

Using the *DISPATCHERS* Parameter

The DISPATCHERS parameter defines the number of dispatchers that should start when the instance is started. This parameter specifies the number of dispatchers and the type of protocol to which the dispatchers can respond. If you configured your database using the Database Configuration Assistant, this parameter may already be configured.

You can add dispatchers dynamically using the ALTER SYSTEM command. You can also configure the parameter using the EM, which will be discussed later in this chapter in the section "Configuring Shared Server using Enterprise Manager."

The DISPATCHERS parameter has a number of optional attributes. Table 5.1 lists and describes several of these. You need to specify only ADDRESS, DESCRIPTION, or PROTOCOL for a DISPATCHERS definition. All the attributes for this parameter can be abbreviated.

TABLE 5.1   Summary of *DISPATCHER* Attributes

Attribute	Abbreviations	Description
ADDRESS	ADD or ADDR	Specifies the network protocol address of the end point on which the dispatchers listen.
CONNECTIONS	CON or CONN	The maximum number of network connections per dispatcher. The default value varies by operating system.
DESCRIPTION	DES or DESC	The network description of the end point where the dispatcher is listening, including the protocol being listened for.
DISPATCHERS	DIS or DISP	The number of dispatchers to start when the instance is started. The default is 1.
LISTENER	LIS or LIST	The address of the listener to which PMON sends connection information. This attribute needs to be set only when the listener is nonlocal, uses a port other than 1521, the default port and the LOCAL_LISTENER parameter have not been specified, or the listener is resident on a different network node.
PROTOCOL	PRO or PROT	The network protocol for the dispatcher to listen for. This is the only required attribute.
SESSIONS	SES or SESS	The maximum number of network sessions allowable for this dispatcher. This will vary by operating system but predominantly defaults to 16K.
SERVICE	SER or SERV	The Oracle Net Service Name that the dispatcher registers with the listener. If it is not supplied, the dispatcher registers with the services listed in the SERVICE_NAMES initialization parameter.
POOL	POO	Provides connection pooling capabilities to provide the ability to handle a larger number of connections.

For a complete summary of the optional DISPATCHER attributes, please consult *Oracle Database Reference 10g Release 1 (10.1)*, Part Number B10755-01.

The two main attributes are DISPATCHERS and PROTOCOL. For example, if you want to configure three TCP/IP dispatchers and two IPC dispatchers, you set the parameter as follows:

```
DISPATCHERS = "(PRO=TCP)(DIS=3)(PRO=IPC)(DIS=2)"
```

You must consider several factors (discussed in the following section) when determining the appropriate setting for the DISPATCHERS parameter.

Determining the Number of Dispatchers to Start

The number of dispatchers that you start depends on your particular configuration. Your operating system may place a limit on the number of connections that one dispatcher can handle. Consult your operating system documentation to obtain this information.

When determining the number of dispatchers to start, consider the type of work that the database sessions will be performing and the number of concurrent connections that your database will be supporting. The more data intensive the operations and the larger the number of concurrent connections, the fewer sessions each dispatcher should handle. Generally speaking, a starting point is to allow 50 concurrent sessions for each dispatcher.

You can use the following formula to determine the number of dispatchers to configure initially:

```
Number of Dispatchers = CEIL  (maximum number of concurrent sessions /
  connections per dispatcher)
```

For example, if you have 500 concurrent TCP/IP connections, and you want each dispatcher to manage 50 concurrent connections, you need 10 dispatchers. You set your DISPATCHERS parameter as follows:

```
DISPATCHERS = "(PRO=TCP)(DIS=10)"
```

You can determine the number of concurrent connections by querying the V$SESSION view. This view shows you the number of clients currently connected to the Oracle server. Here is an example of the query:

```
SQL> select sid,serial#,username,server,program from v$session
  2* where username is not null
      SID   SERIAL# USERNAME   SERVER    PROGRAM
--------- --------- ---------- --------- ---------------
        7        13    SCOTT   DEDICATED SQLPLUS.EXE
        8        12    SCOTT   DEDICATED SQLPLUS.EXE
        9         4   SYSTEM   DEDICATED SQLPLUS.EXE
```

In this example, three users are connected to the server. You can ignore any sessions that do not have a user name because these would be the Oracle background processes such as PMON and SMON. If you take a sampling of this view over a typical work period, you get an idea of the average number of concurrent connections for your system. You can then use this number as a guide when you establish the starting number of dispatchers.

You can also query the V$LICENSE view and check the SESSION_CURRENT and SESSION_HIGHWATER columns to see the current number of sessions and the maximum number of concurrent sessions since the instance was started.

Managing the Number of Dispatchers

You can start additional dispatchers or remove dispatchers dynamically using the ALTER SYSTEM command. You can start any number of dispatchers up to the MAX_DISPATCHERS setting, which is discussed next. Here is an example of adding three TCP/IP dispatchers to a system configured with two TCP/IP dispatchers:

```
ALTER SYSTEM SET DISPATCHERS="(PRO=TCP)(DIS=5)";
```

Notice that you set the number to the total number of dispatchers that you want, not to the number of dispatchers that you want to add.

You use additional attributes to the DISPATCHERS parameter to configure connection pooling.

Configuring Connection Pooling with the *DISPATCHERS* Parameter

Connection pooling gives Oracle Shared Server the ability to handle a larger volume of connections by automatically disconnecting idle connections and using the idle connection to service an incoming client request. If the idle connection becomes active again, the connection to the dispatchers is automatically reestablished. This provides added scalability to Oracle Shared Server. If you manage applications that have a large number of possible client connections but also have a large number of idle connections, you might want to consider configuring this Oracle Shared Server option. Web applications are good candidates for connection pooling because they are typically composed of a large client base with small numbers of concurrent connections.

You enable connection pooling by adding attributes to the DISPATCHERS parameter. The POOL attribute specifies that a dispatcher is allowed to perform connection pooling. Set this attribute to the value ON to enable connection pooling for a dispatcher. You also need to specify the TICK attribute, which sets the number of 10-minute increments of inactivity for a connection to be considered idle.

Here is an example that turns on connection pooling:

```
DISPATCHERS="(PROTOCOL=tcp)(DISPATCHERS=1)(POOL=on)(TICK=1)
  (CONNECTIONS=500)(SESSIONS=1000)"
```

In this example, we want to turn on connection pooling. An idle connection is considered any connection with 10 minutes of inactivity. We want the TCP/IP dispatcher to handle a maximum of 500 concurrent connections and a maximum of 1,000 sessions per dispatcher.

Using the *MAX_DISPATCHERS* Parameter

You set the MAX_DISPATCHERS parameter to the maximum number of dispatchers that you anticipate needing for the Oracle Shared Server. In Oracle 10g, this parameter can now be set dynamically using the ALTER SYSTEM command. The maximum number of processes that a dispatcher can run concurrently is operating-system dependent. Use the following formula to set this parameter:

```
MAX_DISPATCHERS = (maximum number of concurrent sessions/connections
    per dispatcher)
```

Here is an example of the parameter and adjusting the parameter using the ALTER SYSTEM command:

```
MAX_DISPATCHERS = 5
ALTER SYSTEM SET MAX_DISPATCHERS=10;
```

In the ALTER SYSTEM example, the MAX_DISPATCHERS parameter is being set to 10. This will be the maximum number of dispatchers that Oracle Shared Server can start simultaneously.

Using the *SHARED_SERVERS* Parameter

The SHARED_SERVERS parameter specifies the minimum number of Shared Servers to start and retain when the Oracle instance is started. A setting of 0 or no setting means that Shared Servers will not be used. If dispatchers have been configured, the default value of SHARED_SERVERS is 1. This parameter can be changed dynamically, so even if shared servers are not configured when the instance starts, they can be configured without bringing the Oracle instance down and restarting it.

The number of servers necessary depends on the type of activities that your users are performing. Oracle monitors the response queue loads, starts additional shared servers as needed, and removes these shared servers when the servers are no longer needed. Generally, for the types of high think applications that will be using shared server connections, 25 concurrent connections per shared server should be adequate. If the users are going to require larger result sets or are doing more intensive processing, you'll want to reduce this ratio.

Here is an example of setting the SHARED_SERVERS parameter:

```
SHARED_SERVERS = 3
```

You can start additional Oracle Shared Servers or reduce the number of Oracle Shared Servers dynamically using the ALTER SYSTEM command. You can start any number of Oracle Shared Servers up to the MAX_SERVERS setting. Here is an example of adding three additional Oracle Shared Servers to a system initially configured with two Shared Servers:

```
ALTER SYSTEM SET SHARED_SERVERS = 5;
```

Notice that you set the number to the total number of Oracle Shared Servers that you want, not to the number of Oracle Shared Servers that you want to add.

Using the *SHARED_SERVER_SESSIONS* Parameter

The SHARED_SERVER_SESSIONS parameter specifies the total number of Oracle Shared Server sessions that are allowed for the Oracle instance. If the number of Oracle Shared Server client connections reaches this limit, any clients that attempt to connect via an Oracle Shared Server connection will receive the following error message:

```
ERROR:
ORA-00018 maximum number of sessions exceeded
```

Once the number of Oracle Shared Server connections falls below this number, additional shared server connections can be established. Using this parameter limits the total number of shared server sessions. Dedicated server connections are still allowed if this limit is reached. This parameter can be set in the Oracle initialization file and can be modified dynamically using the ALTER SYSTEM command. Here is an example of how you specify the initialization parameter:

```
SHARED_SERVER_SESSIONS = 2
```

Here is an example of how to dynamically modify the parameter using the ALTER SYSTEM command:

```
ALTER SYSTEM SET SHARED_SERVER_SESSIONS = 5;
```

Using the *MAX_SHARED_SERVERS* Parameter

The MAX_SHARED_SERVERS parameter sets the maximum number of Oracle Shared Servers that can be running concurrently. This number can be modified dynamically using the ALTER SYSTEM command. Generally, you should set this parameter to accommodate your heaviest work times. If no value is specified for MAX_SHARED_SERVERS, the number of Oracle Shared Servers that can be started is unlimited, which is also the default setting.

The V$SHARED_SERVER_MONITOR view can assist in determining the maximum number of Oracle Shared Servers that have been started since the Oracle instance was started.

We will discuss the Dynamic Performance View later in this chapter, in the section "Using Dynamic Performance Views for Shared Server."

Here is an example of the parameter and the ALTER SYSTEM command that will change the value MAX_SHARED_SERVER value to 20:

```
MAX_SHARED_SERVERS = 5
ALTER SYSTEM SET MAX_SHARED_SERVERS = 20;
```

Using the *CIRCUITS* Parameter

The CIRCUITS parameter manages the total number of virtual circuits allowed for all incoming and outgoing network sessions. There is no default value for this parameter, and it does influence the total size of the SGA at system startup. Generally, you do not manually configure this parameter unless there is a need to specifically limit the number of virtual circuits.

Here is an example of the parameter:

```
CIRCUITS = 200
```

Now that you understand the parameters that are needed to use the Oracle Shared Server, you need to know how to configure these parameters. You can also use the ALTER SYSTEM command to change the parameter as follows:

```
ALTER SYSTEM SET CIRCUITS = 300;
```

Configuring Shared Server at Database Creation

The Oracle Shared Server option can be configured when a database is created using the Database Configuration Assistant. The Database Configuration Assistant (DBCA) devotes several screens to configuring this option. We will look at these in the following sections.

Selecting the Connection Mode

During the process of creating a database using the DBCA, you are presented with the option of selecting a connection mode. You can either select dedicated server or Oracle Shared Server. Figure 5.4 shows the database if you elect to configure it as a shared server. You can provide the number of shared servers to start at instance startup.

FIGURE 5.4   Configuring Shared Server with the DBCA

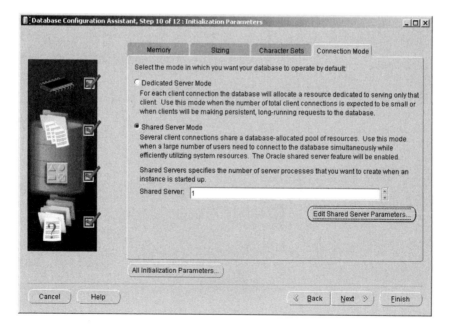

Editing Shared Server Parameters

You can also modify other aspects of the Oracle Shared Server configuration during database creation. Click the Edit Shared Server Parameters button on the Connection Mode tab to change the maximum number of Oracle Shared Servers and dispatchers, the number of dispatchers to start up, and other shared server options.

In the General tab, you can override the default values and choose a value for the maximum number of shared servers and dispatchers (see Figure 5.5).

The Dispatcher tab (see Figure 5.6) allows you to configure other attributes of the Oracle Shared Server DISPATCHERS parameter. The attributes include the maximum number of sessions and connections (the SESSIONS and CONNECTIONS attributes), the service name that the database should register with the listener (the SERVICE attribute), and the name of the listener to register with if it is not the default listener (the LISTENER attribute).

The Advanced Dispatcher Configuration screen allows you to set up advanced attributes of the DISPATCHERS parameter (see Figure 5.7). To open this screen, click the Advanced Options button in the Dispatcher tab. The advanced features of Oracle Shared Server are multiplexing and connection pooling and can be configured in this screen.

 See the section "Configuring Connection Pooling with the DISPATCHERS Parameter" (earlier in this chapter) for a discussion on connection pooling. Multiplexing requires that the Oracle Connection Manager option be configured, which is briefly described earlier in this chapter in the section "Advantages and Disadvantages of Oracle Shared Server." A more detailed discussion of Oracle Connection Manager can be found in *Oracle Database Net Services Administrators Guide 10*g *Release 1 (10.1)*, Part Number B10755-01.

FIGURE 5.5   The General tab in the DBCA

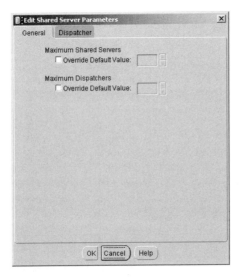

FIGURE 5.6   The Dispatcher tab in the DBCA

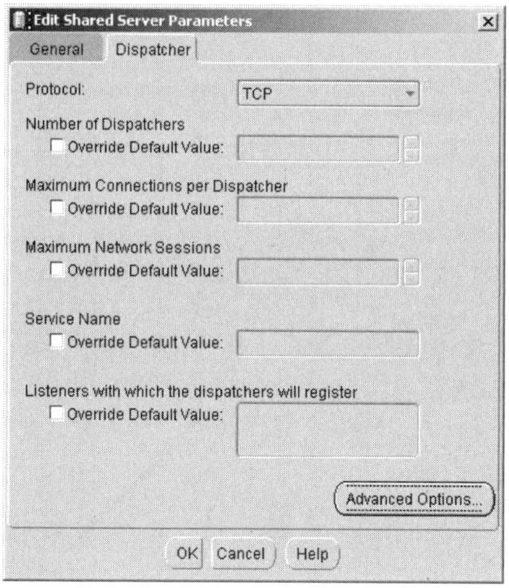

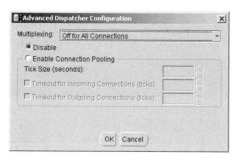

FIGURE 5.7   Configuring *DISPATCHER* in the Advanced Dispatcher Configuration screen

Configuring Shared Server Using Enterprise Manager

You can also configure the Oracle Shared Server using Enterprise Manager. Once you connect to Enterprise Manager via your web browser, click the Administration tab to display a form that allows you to manage all aspects of your Oracle environment. To modify the initialization parameters for Oracle Shared Server, click the All Initialization Parameters link in the Instance section. Figure 5.8 shows the Initialization Parameters screen.

FIGURE 5.8 The Enterprise Manager Initialization Parameters screen

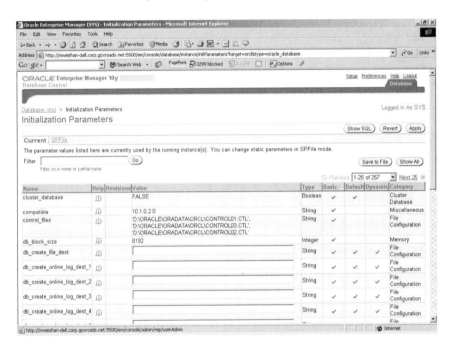

Initially, this form lists only the parameters that are being used for the instance. If you've already configured the Oracle Shared Server, you will see the parameters described in the previous section listed with their current values. If you are configuring the Oracle Shared Server for the first time, you will not see these parameters. Click the Show All button to display all the available initialization parameters. You can then scroll down to the initialization parameter that you want to modify and type appropriate values for the parameter.

You can also select only those parameters that you want to modify. Type the partial or full name of the parameter that you want to change in the Filter field and click Go to display only the specific parameters or parameters that match the name entered. Enter the new value for the parameter in the Value field next to each parameter.

It is a good idea to validate the change you are making. To do so, click the Show SQL button to display the actual ALTER SYSTEM command that runs to make the change. Figure 5.9 shows an example of an ALTER SYSTEM command that modifies the DISPATCHERS parameter, setting the number of TCP/IP dispatchers to two.

After you make all your changes, you can choose how you want to save them. If you click the Apply button, your changes take effect immediately. The currently running instance is affected by these changes. This is the choice if you want the changes to be effective right away. If you want to save the changes but not have the changes affect the currently running instance, click the Save To File button. This saves all your currently active initialization parameter values along with your newly modified parameter values to a file. This is the best choice if you are using an Oracle initialization parameter file. You can save a copy of the modifications to a file in the location of your choice and then cut and paste the new values into your initialization file. These changes will then be in force the next time your instance starts. If the Oracle Shared Server parameters were configured dynamically using the ALTER SYSTEM command or at database creation, it isn't necessary to stop and start the server.

FIGURE 5.9   The Enterprise Manager SQL screen

Using the *SCOPE* Attribute with *ALTER SYSTEM*

When you use the ALTER SYSTEM command to modify the initialization parameters, an additional attribute called SCOPE determines when the change takes effect. The possible settings for the SCOPE attribute are MEMORY, SPFILE, or BOTH. The default setting of the attribute depends on how the database was started.

If your database was started using a server-side spfile, the default action is to modify both the currently running instance and change the SPFILE setting (using the BOTH attribute). The changes are preserved for the next time the database is started using the SPFILE. If the database was started using a parameter file, sometimes called a PFILE, the change affects only the currently running instance (using the MEMORY attribute). If you want to make the changes permanent, you will have to modify the init.ora file resident on the database server. Here is an example of syntax to modify only the currently running instance using the ALTER SYSTEM command:

```
ALTER SYSTEM SET SHARED_SERVERS = 10 SCOPE=MEMORY;
```

Managing Shared Server

After you configure the Oracle Shared Server parameters, you need to understand how to view information about Oracle Shared Server. Oracle provides a set of dynamic performance views that you can use to gather information about the Oracle Shared Server configuration and the performance of the Oracle Shared Server. You can also gather information about Oracle Shared Server connections by using the lsnrctl utility.

In the following sections, we will explain how to display information about Oracle Shared Server connections using the listener utility and discuss the various dynamic performance views used to manage Shared Server.

Displaying Information about Shared Server Connections Using the Listener Utility

You can use the *lsnrctl* command-line listener utility to display information about the dispatcher processes. Remember from the previous section that the Oracle background process PMON registers dispatcher information with the listener. The listener keeps track of the current connection load for all the dispatchers.

Use the lsnrctl services query to view information about dispatchers. The following example shows a listener listening for two TCP/IP dispatchers:

```
D:\>lsnrctl services

LSNRCTL for 32-bit Windows: Version 10.1.0.2.0 - Production on 21-APR-2004
    20:50:35

Copyright (c) 1991, 2004, Oracle.  All rights reserved.

Connecting to (DESCRIPTION=(ADDRESS=(PROTOCOL=TCP)(HOST=MJW01)
(PORT=1521)))
Services Summary...
Service "PLSExtProc" has 1 instance(s).
  Instance "PLSExtProc", status UNKNOWN, has 1 handler(s) for this service...
    Handler(s):
      "DEDICATED" established:0 refused:0
        LOCAL SERVER
  Instance "MJW", status READY, has 3 handler(s) for this service...
    Handler(s):
      "DEDICATED" established:0 refused:0 state:ready
        LOCAL SERVER
```

```
     "D001" established:11 refused:1 current:1 max:1002 state:ready
        DISPATCHER <machine: MJW01, pid: 504>
        (ADDRESS=(PROTOCOL=tcp)(HOST=MJW01)
        (PORT=4152))
     "D000" established:15 refused:3 current:2 max:1002 state:ready
        DISPATCHER <machine: MJW01, pid: 3846>
        (ADDRESS=(PROTOCOL=tcp)(HOST=MJW01)
        (PORT=3845))
The command completed successfully
```

Notice that the listing displays how many connections each dispatcher is managing, the listening location of the dispatcher, and the process ID of the dispatcher. This example has three active connections, two belong to dispatcher D000 and one belongs to dispatcher D001. The display also shows how many total client connections were established and how many were refused by each dispatcher since the time it was started. This summary information can be helpful when looking at how well the connections are balanced across all the dispatchers. It also can be helpful to see how many connections were refused. A connection can be refused if a user supplies an invalid user ID or password or reaches the MAX_SHARED_SERVER limit.

Using Dynamic Performance Views for Shared Server

Oracle provides dynamic performance views, also known as the V$ views that provide the DBA with a wealth of system statistics and performance information, including information about Oracle Shared Server. These views provide information about the number of dispatchers and shared servers configured, the activity among the shared servers and dispatchers, the activity in the request and response queue, as well as the clients that are connected with shared server connections. We will look at the dynamic performance views in the following sections.

 For a complete listing of all the column definitions for the V$ views, consult the *Oracle Database Reference 10g Release 1 (10.1)*, Part Number B10755-01.

Using the *V$DISPATCHER* Dictionary View

The V$DISPATCHER view contains information about the dispatchers, including dispatcher activity, the number of connections the dispatchers are currently handling, and the total number of connections each dispatcher has handled since instance startup.

Here is sample output from the V$DISPATCHER view:

```
SQL> select name,status,messages,idle,busy,bytes,breaks from
  2 v$dispatcher
```

```
NAME STATUS   MESSAGES   IDLE BUSY  BYTES BREAKS
---- ------   ---------  ------- ---- ------ ------
D000 WAIT          168  389645  108  12435      0
D001 WAIT           94  389668   48   6940      0
```

This example lists two dispatchers: D000 and D001. The WAIT status indicates that the dispatchers are both idle and waiting for a client request to process. The IDLE and BUSY columns display information on how many hundredths of a second each dispatcher has either been waiting to process a client request or actually processing a client request. The MESSAGES column displays the number of messages that a dispatcher has processed since instance startup and the BYTES column is the total size of all messages processed by the dispatcher. Finally, the BREAKS column displays the total number of breaks that the dispatcher has handled since instance startup. A break is an interrupt passed from a client that allows a transaction to be stopped prior to completion. For example, pressing Ctrl+C in some applications will cause a break request to be generated and passed to the dispatcher process. SQL*Plus is an example of an application that will cause a break request to be sent by pressing this keyboard combination.

Using the *V$DISPATCHER_CONFIG* Dictionary View

The V$DISPATCHER_CONFIG view is a new Oracle 10g view that contains configuration information about the dispatchers. This view summarizes the dispatcher configuration and gives information such as the protocol, the listener or listening address of the dispatcher, maximum settings for connection and sessions, and service names information.

The following sample shows a system configured with three dispatchers listening for TCP/IP connections to the orcl service. (The maximum connections and sessions are set at the system at 1,002.)

```
SQL> select conf_indx,dispatchers,connections,sessions "SESS",service
2  from v$dispatcher_config
3  where network like '%TCP%'


CONF_INDX DISPATCHERS CONNECTIONS   SESS SERVICE
--------- ----------- ----------- ------ -------
        0           3        1002   1002 orcl
```

Using the *V$DISPATCHER_RATE* Dictionary View

The V$DISPATCHER_RATE view shows statistics for the dispatchers, such as the average number of bytes processed, the maximum number of inbound and outbound connections, and the average rate of bytes processed per client connection. The columns in the table that begin with CUR show current statistics. Columns that begin with AVG or MAX show historical statistics taken at some time interval. The time interval is typically measured in hundredths of a second. The scale measurement periods used for each of the column types is contained in the columns that begin with SCALE. This information can be useful when you are taking load measurements for the dispatchers.

Here is a sample of the output from this view.

```
SQL>select name,cur_event_rate,cur_msg_rate,
    cur_svr_byte_rate
 from v$dispatcher_rate
```

NAME	CUR_EVENT_RATE	CUR_MSG_RATE	CUR_SVR_BYTE_RATE
D000	5300	4	0	0
D001	5205	3	0	1

This code example shows two dispatchers, D000 and D001, running on the database. The CUR_EVENT_RATE column is a measure of how quickly dispatchers are responding to client requests. From this example, we can determine that client requests are being responded to at a rate of 5,300 per minute for D000 and 5,205 per minute for D001. This is not the actual number of events handled, but the measure of the rate of requests per minute that the dispatcher is handling. The CUR_MSG_RATE is a measure of how quickly the dispatcher has been sending a client request to the Shared Servers. We can see in this example that on average D000 has been passing four requests per second to the Shared Servers for processing and that D001 has been passing three requests per minute to the Shared Servers for processing. Notice the scale for the CUR_EVENT_RATE is events per minute and that the scale for CUR_MSG_RATE is messages per second. These measures give some indication as to how quickly the Shared Servers and dispatchers are responding to client requests. The other columns provide information on the maximum and average rates at which the dispatcher is servicing client requests.

Using the *V$QUEUE* Dictionary View

The V$QUEUE view contains information about the request and response queues, such as how long requests are waiting in the queues. This information is valuable when you are trying to determine if more shared servers are needed.

The following example shows the COMMON request queue and two response queues:

```
SQL> select * from v$queue;
```

PADDR	TYPE	QUEUED	WAIT	TOTALQ
00	COMMON	0	0	152
03C6C244	DISPATCHER	0	0	91
03C6C534	DISPATCHER	0	0	71

The PADDR column lists the address of the process that owns the queue. This example shows that no items are waiting in the queue because the QUEUED column is zero. We also have not experienced any queue waits because all WAIT values are zero. We would want to make sure that the WAIT column stays close to zero so no processes are waiting in the queues. The TOTALQ column represents the total number of messages that have ever been in the queue.

Using the *V$CIRCUIT* Dictionary View

The V$CIRCUIT dictionary view displays information about Oracle Shared Server virtual circuits, such as the volume of information that has passed between the client and the dispatcher and the current status of the client connection. The SADDR column displays the session address for the connected session. This can be joined to the V$SESSION view to display information about the user to whom this connection belongs.

Here is a sample output from this view:

```
SQL> select circuit,dispatcher,server,waiter WTR,
  2 status,queue,bytes from v$circuit;


CIRCUIT   DISPATCH SERVER   WTR STATUS QUEUE  BYTES SADDR
--------  -------- -------- --- ------ ------ ----- ------
03E2A624  03C6C244 00        00 NORMAL NONE   47330 03C7AB68
03E2A724  03C6C534 03C6BC64  00 NORMAL SERVER 43572 03C79BE8
```

You can see from this example that two active connections are being managed by the dispatchers. The value of SERVER in the QUEUE column displayed for the second circuit tells us that the circuit is currently active and processing a user request.

Using the *V$SHARED_SERVER* Dictionary View

The V$SHARED_SERVER view contains information about the shared server processes. It displays information about the number of requests and the amount of information processed by the shared servers. It also indicates the status of the shared server (that is, whether it is active or idle).

Here is a sample output from this view:

```
SQL> select name,status,messages,bytes,idle,busy,
  2 requests from v$shared_server;


NAME STATUS MESSAGES  BYTES  IDLE   BUSY REQUESTS
---- ------ -------- ------ ------ ---- --------
S000 EXEC        372  86939  98472  300      175
S001 EXEC         26   9851  98703   38       13
```

The sample depicts two shared servers: S000 and S001. The status of EXEC signifies that the shared servers are currently executing SQL statements. You can see that S000 has had more activity than S001. This would typically be the case in a lightly loaded system. S000 is the first shared server in our sequence and will be the first shared server used when a client request comes in if it is available. If the S000 shared server is not available, S001 is used.

Using the *V$SHARED_SERVER_MONITOR* Dictionary View

The V$SHARED_SERVER_MONITOR view contains information that can assist in tuning the Oracle Shared Server, including the maximum number of concurrent connections attained since instance startup and the total number of servers started since instance startup.

The following query shows an example of output from the V$SHARED_SERVER_MONITOR view:

```
SQL> select maximum_connections "MAX CONN",maximum_sessions "MAX SESS",
    servers_started "STARTED" from v$shared_server_monitor;


MAX CONN MAX SESS  STARTED
-------- --------- --------
115      120       10
```

This example shows that we have reached a maximum of 115 concurrent connections since the instance was started. It also shows that the highest number of concurrent sessions since instance startup is 120. It is important to compare the MAX SESS value returned by the query to the value of the initialization parameter SHARED_SERVER_SESSIONS. If the maximum sessions value reaches the SHARED_SERVER_SESSIONS value, users will be unable to connect via Shared Server until the number of sessions falls below this value. If this occurs, Oracle records an ORA-00018 error in the alert log, indicating that you have exceeded the maximum number of sessions. If you see that the maximum sessions value is being approached, you might want to consider increasing the SHARE_SERVER_SESSIONS value. You need to monitor this value to avoid unnecessary disruptions in client connections.

Using the *V$SESSION* Dictionary View

The V$SESSION view contains a wealth of information about the client session, such as the client session address, user name, session status, and the operating system user name. The SERVER column indicates whether this client is using a dedicated session or a dispatcher. The following listing shows an example of the V$SESSION view displaying the server information. (This listing ignores any rows that do not have a user name to avoid listing information about the background processes.)

```
SQL> select username,program,server from v$session
    where username is not null;


USERNAME         PROGRAM          SERVER
---------------  ---------------  ---------
SYSTEM           SQLPLUS.EXE      NONE
SCOTT            SQLPLUS.EXE      SHARED
```

Notice that user Scott has a server value of SHARED. This means that Scott is connected to a dispatcher. The SYSTEM user is connected using a local connection because the server value is NONE. If a user connects using a dedicated connection, the server value is DEDICATED.

The V$MTS view has been depreciated and is replaced by the V$SHARED_SERVER_ MONITOR view. V$MTS was the name for this view in Oracle8*i*.

Requesting a Dedicated Connection in a Shared Server Environment

You can configure Oracle Shared Server connections and dedicated server connections to connect to a single Oracle server. This is advantageous if you have a mix of database activity. Some types of activities are well suited to Oracle Shared Server connections, and other types of activities are better suited to dedicated connections.

By default, if Oracle Shared Server is configured, a client is connected to a dispatcher unless the client explicitly requests a dedicated connection. As part of the connection descriptor, the client has to send information requesting a dedicated connection. Clients can request dedicated connections if the names resolution method is localnaming. You cannot use this option when using the hostnaming names resolution method. If localnaming is being used, you can make the necessary changes to the tnsnames.ora file to allow dedicated connections. You can make these changes manually, or you can use Oracle Net Manager.

Configuring Dedicated Connections Manually

If you are using localnaming, you can add a parameter to the service name entry in the tnsnames.ora file. The parameter (SERVER=DEDICATED) is added to the DBA net service name. (The SERVER parameter can be abbreviated as SRVR.) Here is an example of the entry in the tnsnames.ora file:

```
# tnsnames.ora Network Configuration File:
# C:\oracle\product\10.1.0\db_1\network\admin\tnsnames.ora

ORCL =
  (DESCRIPTION =
    (ADDRESS = (PROTOCOL = TCP)(HOST = MJW01)(PORT = 1521))
    (CONNECT_DATA =
      (SERVICE_NAME = orcl)
      (SRVR = DEDICATED)  # Request a dedicated connection for DBA
    )
  )
```

Configuring Dedicated Connections Using Oracle Net Manager

You can use Oracle Net Manager to modify the connection type for a service. In Windows, Oracle Net Manager is a tool; in Unix, you open Oracle Net Manager by executing netasst.

After you start Oracle Net Manager, follow these steps:

1. Under Service Naming in the left pane, select the service name that you want to modify.

2. Click the Connection Type drop-down list in the Service Identification section and choose Dedicated Server.

Figure 5.10 shows an example what your Net Manager screen should look like if you configured the Dedicated Server selection properly.

FIGURE 5.10 You can configure a dedicated connection using Oracle Net Manager.

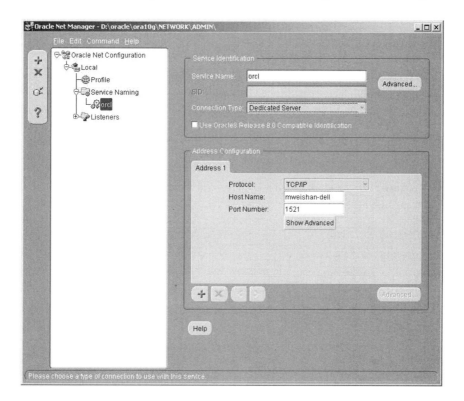

Tuning the Shared Server Option

Before tuning the Oracle Shared Server, examine the performance of the dispatchers and the shared server processes. You want to make sure that you have enough dispatchers so that clients are not waiting for dispatchers to respond to their requests, and you want enough shared server processes so that requests are not waiting to be processed. You also want to configure the Large Pool SGA memory area. The Large Pool stores the UGA, which contains much of the information that is stored in the PGA in a dedicated server configuration.

The Large Pool is designed to allow the database to request large amounts of memory from a separate area of the SGA. Before the database had a Large Pool design, memory allocations for Shared Server came from the Shared Pool. This caused Shared Server to compete with other processes updating information in the Shared Pool. The Large Pool alleviates the memory burden on the Shared Pool and enhances performance of the Shared Pool.

You need to understand how to set the Large Pool to the appropriate size and to monitor the performance of the dispatchers and shared servers in the Oracle Shared Server environment. The following section discusses how to appropriately size the Large Pool and how to determine if the correct number of dispatchers and shared servers have been configured.

Configuring the Large Pool

You can configure the Large Pool by setting the parameter LARGE_POOL_SIZE in the init.ora file. You can set this parameter to a minimum of 300KB and a maximum of at least 2GB; the maximum setting is operating-system dependent. When you use a default value, Oracle adds 250KB per session for each shared server if you specified the DISPATCHERS parameter. If you do not configure a Large Pool, Oracle places the UGA in the Shared Pool. Because of this, configure a Large Pool when using Oracle Shared Server so that you don't affect the performance of the Shared Pool.

Here is an example of setting the LARGE_POOL_SIZE parameter in the init.ora file:

```
LARGE_POOL_SIZE = 50M
```

As with many of the Oracle 10g parameters, you can also modify the LARGE_POOL_SIZE parameter dynamically using the ALTER SYSTEM command. For example:

```
ALTER SYSTEM SET LARGE_POOL_SIZE = 100M
```

This example sets the large pool size to 100 megabytes.

You can see how much space the Large Pool is using by querying the V$SGASTAT view. The free memory row shows the amount available in the Large Pool, and the session heap row shows the amount of space used in the Large Pool. Here is a listing that shows an example of the query:

```
SQL> select * from v$sgastat where pool = 'large pool';
```

POOL	NAME	BYTES
large pool	free memory	251640
large pool	session heap	48360

 If a LARGE_POOL_SIZE is not given, the size of the Large Pool is determined by a number of initialization parameters, including the DISPATCHERS parameter.

Sizing the Large Pool

The Large Pool should be large enough to hold information for all your shared server connections. Generally, each connection needs between 1 and 3 megabytes of memory, but this depends on that client's type of activity. Clients that do a great deal of sorting or open many cursors will use more memory.

You can gauge how much memory shared server connections are using by querying the V$SESSTAT view. This view contains information about memory utilization per user. The following query shows how to measure the maximum amount of memory for all shared server sessions since the instance was started. You can use this as a guide to determine how much memory you should allocate for the Large Pool. This example shows that the maximum amount of memory used for all shared server sessions is about 240KB:

```
select sum(value) "Max MTS Memory Allocated"from v$sesstat ss, v$statname st
where name = 'session uga memory max'and ss.statistic# =st.statistic#;


Max MTS Memory Allocated
-----------------------
                244416
```

You can determine a good starting point for the Large Pool by taking into account the number of shared server connections that you want to manage and multiply that by the maximum UGA memory for a session. In this example, a single Oracle Shared Server connection happens to be using 240KB of Large Pool space. If you want to support 200 concurrent connections in this environment, configure LARGE_POOL_SIZE to about 50MB (240KB multiplied by 200 concurrent connections). This would be a good starting point for the Large Pool.

If the Large Pool has not been sized correctly, clients can encounter connection errors. The error message looks similar to this:

```
ORA-04031: unable to allocate 490 bytes of shared memory
      ("large pool","MWEIS","session heap","define var info")
```

This error message indicates that the LARGE_POOL_SIZE needs to be increased. In Oracle 10*g*, you can modify the LARGE_POOL_SIZE dynamically using the ALTER SYSTEM command. Here is an example of how to modify the LARGE_POOL_SIZE using the ALTER SYSTEM command:

```
ALTER SYSTEM SET LARGE_POOL_SIZE = 51200000 SCOPE=MEMORY
```

You can limit the amount of space that a session can allocate in the SGA by using a session profile. Session profiles allow you to control and manage thresholds for a variety of characteristics of a database session. The PRIVATE_SGA setting in a profile sets the per session memory threshold. A discussion of profiles is beyond the scope of this book. For a complete description of profiles, please consult *Oracle Database SQL Reference 10*g *Release (10.1)*, Part Number B10759-01.

Determining Whether You Have Enough Dispatchers

You can monitor the dispatcher processes by querying the V$DISPATCHER view, which contains information about how busy the dispatcher processes are. Query this view to determine whether it will be advantageous to start more dispatchers.

The following sample query runs against the **V$DISPATCHER** view to show what percentage of the time dispatchers are busy:

```
Select name, (busy / (busy + idle))*100
"Dispatcher % busy Rate"
From V$DISPATCHER

Protocol        Dispatcher % Busy Rate
-----------     --------------------------
D000             .00070079
D001             .0059
```

These dispatchers show little busy time. If dispatchers are busy more than 50 percent of the time, consider starting more dispatchers. You can do so dynamically using the ALTER SYSTEM command. The following example would set the number of TCP/IP dispatchers to 4.

```
ALTER SYSTEM SET DISPATCHERS="(PRO=TCP)(DIS=4)";
```

Add one or two more dispatchers and monitor the busy rates of the dispatchers to see if they fall below 50 percent.

Measuring How Long Users Are Waiting for Dispatchers

To measure how long users are waiting for the dispatchers to execute their request, look at the combined V$QUEUE and V$DISPATCHER views. The following listing shows an example:

```
SELECT decode(sum(totalq),0,'No Responses',
              Sum(wait)/sum(totalq)) "Average Wait time"
FROM V$QUEUE q, V$DISPATCHER d
WHERE q.type = 'DISPATCHER'
AND q.paddr = d.paddr;

Average Wait Time
-----------------
  .0413
```

In this example, the average wait time for dispatchers is a little more than 0.04 second. Monitor this measure over time. If the number increases consistently, consider adding more dispatchers. You can do so dynamically using the ALTER SYSTEM command.

 See the section "Using the DISPATCHERS Parameter" (earlier in this chapter) for the proper syntax for modifying this parameter.

Determining Whether You Have Enough Shared Servers

You can monitor shared servers by using the V$SHARED_SERVER and V$QUEUE dictionary views. The shared servers are responsible for executing client requests and placing the requests in the appropriate dispatcher response queue.

   The measurement you are most interested in is how long client requests are waiting in the request queue. The longer the request remains in the queue, the longer the client will wait for a response. The following statement tells you how long requests are waiting in the queue:

```
Select decode(totalq,0,'No Requests') "Wait Time",
Wait/totalq || ' hundredths of seconds'
"Average Wait time per request"
from V$QUEUE
where type = 'COMMON'


Wait Time Average Wait time per request
-------- ----------------------------------
.023132   hundredths of a second
```

Real World Scenario

Choosing the Appropriate Connection Method Makes a Difference

As a DBA, you've configured the Oracle Shared Server and are monitoring the dispatchers and shared server performance daily. The Shared Server environment has been running smoothly for months, but your monitoring starts to indicate that the wait times have increased significantly over the past week. You are also starting to receive complaints from the user community regarding system response time.

You start to investigate if there have been any significant changes to the hardware, the network, or the database application. You confer with the systems administration and network group and find that no changes have taken place. Then your discussion with the applications group reveals that a new ad hoc reporting utility has been installed and a small number of administrators are starting to use the tool. These users are connecting via Oracle Shared Server and are requesting large data sets via the ad hoc reporting tool.

You suggest to the applications team that the administrators connect to the database using dedicated connections to alleviate the load on the Shared Servers. After modifying the appropriate network files, you again monitor the shared server wait times and discover that the waits have fallen back in line with what you were seeing prior to the deployment of the ad hoc reporting tool.

The average wait time in the request queue is a little more than 0.02 second. Monitor this measure over time. If the number increases consistently, consider adding more shared servers. You can do so dynamically using the ALTER SYSTEM command.

The following example shows how you would query V$SHARED_SERVER:

```
SQL> select name,status,requests,messages,bytes,breaks from v$shared_server;
NAME STATUS                 REQUESTS   MESSAGES       BYTES      BUSY
---- ------------------- ---------- ---------- ---------- ----------
S000 WAIT(COMMON)             300        212    1024963    210433
```

In this example, one shared server is configured. We can see how many requests and messages the server has handled in the REQUESTS and MESSAGES columns and the total size of the messages in the BYTES column. We can also see many milliseconds of time this shared server has been actively processing requests since the last instance startup: it has been busy for roughly 2,100 seconds since instance startup.

See the section "Using the SHARED_SERVERS Parameter" (earlier in this chapter) for the proper syntax for modifying this parameter.

Summary

The Shared Server is a configuration of the Oracle Server that allows you to support a greater number of connections without the need for additional resources. It is important to understand the shared server option because it can stave off potentially unnecessary hardware upgrades when you face the problem of the number of processes that your server can manage.

In this configuration, user connections share processes called dispatchers. Dispatchers replace the dedicated server processes in a dedicated server environment. The Oracle Server is also configured with shared server processes that can process the requests of many clients.

The Oracle Server is configured with a single request queue in which dispatchers place the client requests that the shared servers process. The shared server processes put the completed requests in the appropriate dispatcher's response queue. The dispatcher then sends the completed request back to the client. These request and response queues are structures added to the SGA.

You add a number of parameters to the init.ora file to configure Shared Server. You can add dispatchers and shared servers dynamically after the Oracle Server is started. You can add more shared servers and dispatchers up to the maximum value specified.

You can monitor Shared Server using several V$ views. The information contained in these views pertains to dispatchers, shared server processes, and the clients that are connected to the dispatcher processes.

You can use the V$ views to tune the Shared Server. It is most important to measure how long clients are waiting for dispatchers to process their requests and how long it is taking before a shared server processes the client requests. These factors may lead to increasing the number of shared server and dispatcher processes. You also want to monitor the usage of the Large Pool.

Exam Essentials

Define Oracle Shared Server.   Be able to list the advantages of Shared Server versus a dedicated server and when it is appropriate to consider both options.

Understand the architecture of the Oracle Shared Server.   Be able to summarize the steps that a client takes to initiate a connection with a shared server and the processes behind those steps. Understand what happens during client request processing, and outline the steps.

Understand the changes that are made in the SGA and the PGA.   Make sure you understand that in a Shared Server environment, many PGA structures are moved in the Large Pool inside the SGA. This means that the SGA will become larger and that the Large Pool will need to be configured in the init.ora file.

Know how to configure the Oracle Shared Server.   Be able to define each of the parameters involved in the configuration of Oracle Shared Server. Know what parameters can be dynamically modified and what parameters require the Oracle instance to be restarted to take effect.

Know how to configure clients running in Shared Server mode.   Be able to configure clients that need a dedicated connection to Oracle if it is running in Shared Server mode.

Know which views to use to monitor the Shared Server performance.   Be able to use the available V$ views to monitor and tune the Shared Server and know how to adjust settings when necessary.

Review Questions

1. All the following are reasons to configure the server using Shared Server *except*:

   A. Overall memory utilization is reduced.

   B. The system is predominantly used for decision support with large result sets returned.

   C. The system is predominantly used for small transactions with many users.

   D. The number of idle connections on the server is reduced.

2. Which of the following is true about Shared Server?

   A. Dedicated connections cannot be made when Shared Server is configured.

   B. It is recommended that index rebuilds be performed when connected via Shared Server.

   C. The database can be started when connected via Shared Server.

   D. The database cannot be stopped when connected via Shared Server.

3. The administrator wants to allow a user to connect via a dedicated connection into a database configured in Shared Server mode. Which of the following lines accomplishes this?

   A. (SERVER=DEDICATED)

   B. (CONNECT=DEDICATED)

   C. (INSTANCE=DEDICATED)

   D. (MULTITRHEADED=FALSE)

   E. None of the above

4. In which of the following files would you find the Shared Server configuration parameters?

   A. listener.ora

   B. mts.ora

   C. init.ora

   D. tnsnames.ora

   E. sqlnet.ora

5. Which of the following is a component of Shared Server?

   A. Shared user processes

   B. Checkpoint processes

   C. Dispatcher processes

   D. Dedicated server processes

6. You want to put the database in Shared Server mode. Which of the following files will you modify?

   A. tnsnames.ora

   B. cman.ora

   C. names.ora

   D. init.ora

7. What choice in the Oracle Net Manager allows for the configuration of Shared Server?

   A. Local

   B. Service Naming

   C. Listeners

   D. Profile

   E. None of the above

8. You want two TCP/IP dispatchers and one IPC dispatcher to start when the instance is started. Which of the following lines will accomplish this?

   A. `dispatchers=(protocol=tcp)(dispatchers=2)(protocol=IPC)`
      `(dispatchers=1)dispatchers=(protocol=tcp)(dispatchers=2)`
      `(protocol=IPC)(dispatchers=1)`

   B. `dispatchers="(protocol=tcp)(dispatchers=2)(protocol=IPC)(dispatchers=1)"`

   C. `dispatchers_start=(protocol=tcp)(dispatchers=2)(protocol=IPC)`
      `(dispatchers=1)`

   D. `dispatchers_start=(pro=tcp)(dis=2)(pro=IPC)(dis=1)`

9. What is the name of the piece of shared memory that client connections are bound to during communications via Shared Server?

   A. Program Global Area

   B. System Global Area

   C. Virtual Circuit

   D. Database Buffer Cache

   E. None of the above

10. What is the first step that the dispatcher performs after it receives a request from the user?

   A. Pass the request to a shared server.

   B. Place the request in a request queue in the PGA.

   C. Place the request in a request queue in the SGA.

   D. Process the request.

11. Dispatchers have all the following characteristics *except*:

   A. Dispatchers can be shared by many connections.

   B. More dispatchers can be added dynamically with the `ALTER SYSTEM` command.

   C. A dispatcher can listen for multiple protocols.

   D. Each dispatcher has its own response queue.

12. When configured in Shared Server mode, which of the following is contained in the PGA?

    A. Cursor state

    B. Sort information

    C. User session data

    D. Stack space

    E. None of the above

13. Which of the following is false about shared servers?

    A. Shared servers can process requests from many users.

    B. Shared servers receive their requests directly from dispatchers.

    C. Shared servers place completed requests on a dispatcher response queue.

    D. The SHARED_SERVERS parameter configures the number of shared servers to start at instance startup.

14. Which of the following is *not* a step in the processing of a Shared Server request?

    A. Shared servers pass information back to the client process.

    B. Dispatchers place information in a request queue.

    C. Users pass requests to a dispatcher.

    D. The dispatcher picks up completed requests from its response queue.

    E. None of the above.

15. When you are configuring Shared Server, which initialization parameter would you likely need to modify?

    A. DB_CACHE_SIZE

    B. DB_BLOCK_BUFFERS

    C. LARGE_POOL_SIZE

    D. BUFFER_SIZE

    E. None of the above

16. Which of the following is *false* about request queues?

    A. They reside in the SGA.

    B. They are shared by all the dispatchers.

    C. Each dispatcher has its own request queue.

    D. The shared server processes remove requests from the request queue.

17. You want to gather information about users connected via Shared Server connections. Which of the following is the view that contains this information?

A. V$USERS

B. V$QUEUE

C. V$SESS_STATS

D. V$CIRCUIT

E. None of the above

18. What is the process that notifies the listener after a database connection is established?

A. SMON

B. DBWR

C. PMON

D. LGWR

19. You want to gather performance and tuning-related information for the shared server processes. You should start by querying which of the following views?

A. V$USERS

B. V$CIRCUIT

C. V$SHARED_SERVER_MONITOR

D. V$SESS_STATS

20. Which command can you execute to get details about the number of sessions connected via Shared Server?

A. lsnrctl sessions

B. lsnrctl conn

C. lsnrctl status

D. lsnrctl services

E. None of the above

Answers to Review Questions

1. B. Shared Server is a scalability option of Oracle. It provides a way to increase the number of supported user processes while reducing the overall memory usage. This configuration is well suited to high-volume, small-transaction-oriented systems with many users connected. Because users share processes, the number of overall idle processes is also reduced. It is not well suited for large data retrieval type applications such as decision support.

2. D. Users can request dedicated connections in a Shared Server configuration. Index rebuilds and data-intensive activities should be performed using dedicated server. The database cannot be started when connecting via Shared Server. So the correct answer is D.

3. A. A user must explicitly request a dedicated connection when a server is configured in Shared Server mode. Otherwise, the user gets a Shared Server connection. The correct parameter is (SERVER=DEDICATED).

4. C. The Shared Server configuration parameters exist in the init.ora file on the Oracle Server machine.

5. C. In Shared Server, users connect to a pool of shared resources called dispatchers. A client connects to the listener, and the listener redirects the request to a dispatcher. The dispatchers handle all the user requests for the session. Many users can share dispatchers.

6. D. Because the database has to be configured in Shared Server mode, you must change the init.ora file. The other choices are also configuration files, but none of them are used to configure Shared Server.

7. E. This is one of the tricky questions again! You can use Oracle Net Manager to configure many options and files, including tnsnames.ora and sqlnet.ora. But because Shared Server is a characteristic of the database server and not of the network, you cannot use Oracle Net Manager to configure it.

8. B. The DISPATCHERS parameter of the init.ora file is used to configure dispatchers, so the correct answer is option B. All the other choices are invalid parameters.

9. C. The System Global Area is the shared memory segment that Oracle obtains on instance startup. The Program Global Area is an area of memory used primarily during dedicated connections. The Database Buffer Cache is actually a component of the Program Global Area. Virtual Circuits are the shared memory areas to which clients bind.

10. C. Once a dispatcher receives a request from the user process, it places the request on the request queue. Remember that in a Shared Server environment, a request can be handled by a shared server process. This is made possible by placing the request and user information in the SGA.

11. C. Many users can connect to dispatchers, and dispatchers can be added dynamically. Also, each dispatcher does have its own response queue. The only one of these options that is false is option C because dispatchers can listen for only one protocol. You can configure multiple dispatchers so that each is responsible for different protocols.

12. D. A small PGA is maintained even though most of the user-specific information is moved to the SGA (specifically called the UGA in the Shared Pool or the Large Pool). The only information left in the reduced PGA is stack space.

13. B. Shared Servers can process requests from many users. The completed requests are placed into the dispatchers' response queues. The servers are configured with the SERVERS parameter. However, shared servers do not receive requests directly from dispatchers. The requests are taken from the request queue.

14. A. Study the steps of what happens during a request via Shared Server. Dispatchers receive requests from users and place the requests on request queues. Only dispatchers interact with client processes. Shared servers merely execute the requests and place the results back on the dispatcher's response queue.

15. C. Shared Server requires a shift of memory away from individual session processes to the SGA. More information has to be kept in the SGA (in the UGA) within the Shared Pool. A Large Pool is configured and is responsible for most of the SGA space allocation. Option C is the correct answer. The cache size and block buffers settings do not affect Shared Server.

16. C. Request queues reside in the SGA, and there is one request queue per instance. This is where shared server processes pick up requests that are made by users. Dispatchers have their own response queues, but they *share* a single request queue.

17. D. You can use several V$ views to manage the Shared Server. V$QUEUE gives information regarding the request and response queues. V$USERS and V$SESS_STATS are not valid views. V$CIRCUIT gives information about the users who are connected via Shared Server connections, and it provides the necessary information.

18. C. The PMON process notifies the listener after a client connection is established. This is so that the listener can keep track of the number of connections being serviced by each dispatcher.

19. C. You can query the V$SHARED_SERVER_MONITOR view to display information about the maximum number of connections and sessions, the number of servers started and terminated, and the server high-water mark. These numbers can help determine whether you should start more shared servers.

20. D. Dispatchers register with listeners so that when a listener redirects a connection to a dispatcher, the listener knows how many active connections the dispatcher is serving. The lsnrctl status command summarizes the number of connections established, connections currently active, and other valuable information regarding Shared Server. The lsnrctl services command summarizes only dispatchers and does not display any details about connections.

Chapter 6

User Administration and Security

ORACLE DATABASE 10*G*: ADMINISTRATION I EXAM OBJECTIVES COVERED IN THIS CHAPTER:

✓ **Administering Users**

- Create and manage database user accounts.
- Create and manage roles.
- Grant and revoke privileges.
- Control resource usage by users.

✓ **Oracle Database Security**

- Apply the principle of least privilege.
- Manage default user accounts.
- Implement standard password security features.
- Audit database activity.
- Register for security updates.

Exam objectives are subject to change at any time without prior notice and at Oracle's sole discretion. Please visit Oracle's Training and Certification website (http://www.oracle.com/education/certification/) for the most current exam objectives listing.

DBAs must maintain the security, integrity, performance, and availability of their databases. In this chapter, you will learn about managing database security: how to manage user accounts, implement password expiration and complexity rules, and configure security policies using object, system, and role privileges. To further enhance your ability to monitor and manage database access, you will learn how to use auditing mechanisms to fine-tune your security policy, identify attempts to access areas of your database that the user is not authorized to visit, and identify intrusion attempts.

Creating and Managing User Accounts

One of the most basic administrative requirements for a database is to identify the users. Each user who connects to your database should have an account. Shared accounts are difficult to troubleshoot and audit , and having them are a poor security practice.

You create a new database account with the CREATE USER statement. When you create a new account, at a minimum, you must assign a unique username and authentication method. You can optionally assign additional attributes to the user account with the CREATE USER statement. To change or assign new attributes to an existing user account, use the ALTER USER statement.

The terms *user account*, *account*, *user*, and *schema* are all interchangeable and refer to a database user account that owns schema objects.

In the following sections, you will learn how to create a new account, how to assign and change the authentication mechanism, and how to define how this account will allocate and use certain database resources.

Configuring Authentication

When you connect to an Oracle database instance, your user account must be authenticated. Authentication involves validating the identity of the user and confirming that they have the authority to use the database. Oracle offers three authentication methods for your user accounts: password authentication (the most common), external authentication, and global authentication.

We will look at each of these authentication methods in the following sections.

Password Authenticated Users

When a user with password authentication attempts to connect to the database, the database verifies that the username is a valid database account and that the password supplied matches that user's password as stored in the database.

Password authenticated user accounts are the most common and are sometimes referred to as database authenticated accounts. With a password authenticated account, the database stores the encrypted password in the data dictionary. For example, to create a password authenticated user named `rajesh` with a password of `welcome`, you execute the following:

```
CREATE USER rajesh IDENTIFIED BY welcome;
```

The keywords `IDENTIFIED BY` *password* (in this case, *password* is `welcome`) tell the database that this user account is a password authenticated account.

Externally Authenticated Users

When an externally identified user attempts to connect to the database, the database verifies that the username is a valid database account and trusts that the operating system has performed authentication.

Externally authenticated user accounts do not store or validate a password in the database. These accounts are sometimes referred to as OPS$ (pronounced *ahps dollar*) accounts, because when Oracle introduced them in Oracle 6, the account had to be prefixed with the keyword OPS$.

With all releases of the database since then, including Oracle 10g, you can configure this `OS_AUTHENT_PREFIX` in the initialization or SPFILE file. For example, to create an externally authenticated user named `oracle`, using the default `OS_AUTHENT_PREFIX`, you execute the following:

```
CREATE USER ops$oracle IDENTIFIED EXTERNALLY;
```

The keywords `IDENTIFIED EXTERNALLY` tell the database that this user account is an externally authenticated account.

Externally authenticated accounts are frequently used for administrative scripts so that a password does not have to be embedded in a human-readable script.

Globally Authenticated Users

When a globally identified user attempts to connect to the database, the database verifies that the username is valid and passes the connection information to the advanced security option for authentication. The advanced security option supports several mechanisms for authentication, including biometrics, X.509 certificates, Kerberos, and RADIUS.

Globally authenticated user accounts do not store or validate a password in the database as a password authenticated account does. These accounts rely on authentication provide by a service supported through the advanced security option.

The syntax for creating a globally authenticated account depends on the service called, but all use the keywords IDENTIFIED GLOBALLY, which tell the database to engage the advanced security option for authentication. Here is an example:

```
CREATE USER spy_master IDENTIFIED GLOBALLY AS 'CN=spy_master, OU=tier2,
    O=security, C=US';
```

Assigning a Default Tablespace

Every user is assigned a default tablespace. The default tablespace for a user is that tablespace where schema objects are stored when no TABLESPACE clause is given in statements that create tables or indexes. If you execute a CREATE TABLE statement and do not explicitly specify a tablespace, the database uses your default tablespace.

If you do not explicitly assign a default tablespace to a user at the time you create the user, the database assigns the database's default tablespace to the new user account. Use the keywords DEFAULT TABLESPACE *tablespace_name* to assign a default tablespace to either a new user via a CREATE USER statement or an existing user, like this:

```
CREATE USER rajesh IDENTIFIED BY welcome
DEFAULT TABLESPACE users;
```

Or via an ALTER USER statement:

```
ALTER USER rajesh
DEFAULT TABLESPACE users;
```

To change the database default tablespace (the value that users inherit if no default tablespace is provided), use the ALTER DATABASE statement, like this:

```
ALTER DATABASE DEFAULT TABLESPACE users;
```

Assigning a Temporary Tablespace

Every user is assigned a temporary tablespace in which the database stores temporary segments. Temporary segments are created during large sorting operations, such as ORDER BY, GROUP BY, SELECT DISTINCT, MERGE JOIN, or CREATE INDEX.

Temporary segments are also used when a temporary table is used. The database creates and drops temporary segments transparently to the user. Because of the transitory nature of temporary segments, you must use a dedicated tablespace of type TEMPORARY for your user's temporary tablespace setting.

For more information on temporary tablespaces, see Chapter 3, "Database Storage and Schema Objects."

If you do not explicitly assign a temporary tablespace at user creation time, the database assigns the database default temporary tablespace to the new user account. Use the keywords TEMPORARY TABLESPACE *tablespace_name* to assign a temporary tablespace either to a new user via the CREATE USER statement:

```
CREATE USER rajesh IDENTIFIED BY welcome
DEFAULT TABLESPACE users
TEMPORARY TABLESPACE temp;
```

Or to an existing user via an ALTER USER statement:

```
ALTER USER rajesh
TEMPORARY TABLESPACE temp;
```

To change the database default temporary tablespace, use the ALTER DATABASE statement, like this:

```
ALTER DATABASE DEFAULT TEMPORARY TABLESPACE temp;
```

To avoid having to set the default and temporary tablespace for each user account that you create, change the database defaults with the ALTER DATABASE statement.

Assigning a Profile to a User

In addition to default and temporary tablespaces, every user is assigned a profile. A profile serves two purposes: first, it can limit the resource usage of some resources, and second, it can enforce password-management rules.

The default profile is appropriately named default. To explicitly assign a profile to a user, include the keywords PROFILE *profile_name* in the CREATE USER or ALTER USER statement. For example, to assign the profile named resource_profile to the new user jiang as well as to the existing user hamish, execute the following SQL:

```
CREATE USER jiang IDENTIFIED BY "kneehow.ma"
DEFAULT TABLESPACE users
TEMPORARY TABLESPACE temp
PROFILE resource_profile;

ALTER USER hamish
PROFILE resource_profile;
```

Removing a User from the Database

You use the DROP USER statement to remove a user from the database. You can optionally include the keyword CASCADE to tell the database to recursively drop all objects owned by that user.

To drop both user `rajesh` and all objects he owns, execute the following:

```
DROP USER rajesh CASCADE;
```

Dropping a user implicitly drops any object (but not role or system) privileges in which the user was the grantor. The data dictionary records both grantee and grantor for object privileges, but only the grantee is recorded for role and system privileges.

Granting and Revoking Privileges

Privileges allow a user to access database objects or execute stored programs that are owned by another user. Privileges also enable a user to perform system-level operations, such as connecting to the database, creating a table, or altering the database.

Privileges are assigned to a user, to the special user PUBLIC, or to a role with the GRANT statement and can be rescinded with the REVOKE statement.

An Oracle 10*g* database has three types of privileges:

Object privileges   Permissions on schema objects such as tables, views, sequences, procedures, and packages. To use a schema object owned by another user, you need privileges on that object.

System privileges   Permissions on database-level operations, such as connecting to the database, creating users, altering the database, or consuming unlimited amounts of tablespace.

Role privileges   Object and system privileges that a user has by way of a role. Roles are tools for administering groups of privileges.

We will look at each of these privileges and how to grant them in the following sections.

Granting Object Privileges

Object privileges bestow upon the grantee the permission to use a schema object owned by another user in a particular way. There are several types of object privileges. Some privileges apply only to certain schema objects. For example, the INDEX privilege applies only to tables, and the SELECT privilege applies to tables, views, and sequences.

The following object privileges can be granted individually, grouped in a list, or with the keyword ALL to implicitly grant all available object privileges for a particular schema object.

WARNING   Be careful when using ALL. It may implicitly grant powerful privileges.

Table object privileges   Oracle 10g provides several object privileges for tables. These privileges give the table owner considerable flexibility in controlling how schema objects are used and by whom. The following privileges are commonly granted, and you should know them well.

SELECT   The most commonly used privilege for tables. With this privilege, the table owner permits the grantee to query the specified table with a SELECT statement.

INSERT   Permits the grantee to create new rows in the specified table with an INSERT statement.

UPDATE   Permits the grantee to modify existing rows in the specified table with an UPDATE statement.

DELETE   Permits the grantee to remove rows from the specified table with a DELETE statement.

The following are powerful administrative privileges on tables; grant them cautiously.

ALTER   Permits the grantee to execute an ALTER TABLE statement on the specified table. This privilege can be used to add, modify, or rename columns in the table, to move the table to another tablespace, or even to rename the specified table.

DEBUG   Permits the grantee to access, via a debugger, the PL/SQL code in any triggers on the specified table.

INDEX   Permits the grantee to create new indexes on the table. These new indexes will be owned by a different user than the table, which is an unusual practice. In most cases, the indexes on a table are owned by the same user who owns the table itself.

REFERENCES   Permits the grantee to create foreign key constraints that reference the specified table.

View object privileges   Oracle 10g offers a smaller set of object privileges for views than it does for tables.

SELECT   The most commonly used privilege for views. With this privilege, the view owner permits the grantee to query the view.

INSERT   Permits the grantee to execute an INSERT statement on the specified view to create new rows.

UPDATE   Permits the grantee to modify existing rows in the specified view with an UPDATE statement.

DELETE   Permits the grantee to execute a DELETE statement on the specified view to remove rows.

DEBUG   Permits the grantee to access, via a debugger, the PL/SQL code in the body of any trigger on this view.

REFERENCES   Permits the grantee create foreign key constraints on the specified view.

Sequence object privileges   Oracle 10*g* provides only two object privileges for sequences.

SELECT   Permits the grantee to access the current and next values (CURRVAL and NEXTVAL) of the specified sequence.

ALTER   Permits the grantee to change the attributes of the specified sequence with an ALTER statement.

Stored functions, procedures, packages, and Java object privileges   Oracle 10*g* provides only two object privileges for stored PL/SQL programs.

DEBUG   Permits the grantee to access, via a debugger, all the public and private variables and types declared in the specified program. If the specified object is a package, both the specification and the body are accessible to the grantee. The grantee can also use a debugger to place breakpoints in the specified program.

EXECUTE   Permits the grantee to execute the specified program. If the specified object is a package, any program, variable, type, cursor, or record declared in the package specification is accessible to the grantee.

You use the GRANT statement to confer object privileges on either a user or a role. The optional keywords WITH GRANT OPTION additionally allow the grantee to confer these privileges on other users and roles. For example, to give SELECT, INSERT, UPDATE, and DELETE privileges on the table CUSTOMERS to the role SALES_MANAGER, execute the following statement while connected as the owner of table CUSTOMERS:

```
GRANT SELECT,INSERT,UPDATE,DELETE ON customers TO sales_manager;
```

If you grant privileges to the special user PUBLIC, you make them available to all current and future database users. For example, to give all database users the SELECT privilege on table CUSTOMERS, execute the following while connected as the owner of the table:

```
GRANT SELECT ON customers TO public;
```

When you extend a privilege to another user or role, you can also extend the ability for that grantee to turn around and grant the privilege to others. To extend this extra option, include the keywords WITH GRANT OPTION in the GRANT statement. For example, to give the SELECT privilege on table SALES.CUSTOMERS to the user SALES_ADMIN together with the permission for SALES_ADMIN to grant the SELECT privilege to others, execute the following:

```
GRANT SELECT ON sales.customers TO sales_admin WITH GRANT OPTION;
```

You can only include the WITH GRANT OPTION keywords when the grantee is a user or the special account PUBLIC. You cannot use WITH GRANT OPTION when the grantee is a role.

If you grant an object privilege using the WITH GRANT OPTION keywords and later revoke that privilege, the revoke cascades, and the privileges created by the grantee are also revoked. For example, Mary grants SELECT privileges on her table clients to Zachary with the WITH GRANT OPTION keywords. Zachary then creates a view based on the table mary.clients and grants the SELECT privilege on it to Rex. If Mary revokes the SELECT privilege from Zachary, the revoke cascades and removes the privilege from Rex. See Figure 6.1 for an illustration of this example.

FIGURE 6.1   The revoking of object privilege cascades

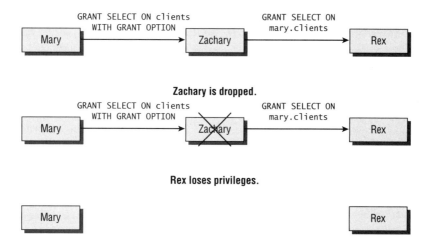

With object privileges, the database records both the grantor and the grantee. Therefore, a grantee can obtain a privilege from more than one grantor. When this multiple grant of the same privilege occurs, revoking one of these grants does not remove the privilege. To remove the privilege, all grants must be revoked. (See Figure 6.2 for an illustration.)

FIGURE 6.2   The revoking of object privilege with multiple grant paths

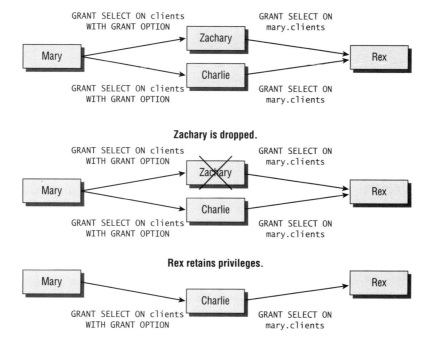

Extending our previous example: Mary has granted SELECT on her table clients to Zachary using WITH GRANT OPTION. Zachary has then granted SELECT on mary.clients to Rex. Mary has also granted SELECT on her table clients to Charlie, who has in turn granted to Rex. Rex now has the SELECT privilege from more than one grantee. If Zachary leaves and his account is dropped, the privilege from Charlie remains and Rex can still select from mary.clients.

Granting System Privileges

In general, system privileges permit the grantee to execute Data Definition Language (DDL) statements—such as CREATE, ALTER, and DROP—or Data Manipulation Language (DML) statements system wide. Oracle 10g has more than 170 system privileges, all of which are listed in the data dictionary view SYSTEM_PRIVILEGE_MAP.

 You will not be required to know all these privileges for the certification exam (thank goodness!), as many are for features that fall outside the scope of the exam.

You should be familiar with the following groups.

Database   Oracle 10g gives you four database-oriented system privileges.

ALTER DATABASE   Permits the grantee to execute the ALTER DATABASE statement.

ALTER SYSTEM   Permits the grantee to execute the ALTER SYSTEM statement.

AUDIT SYSTEM   Permits the grantee to execute AUDIT and NOAUDIT statements to perform statement auditing.

AUDIT ANY   Permits the grantee to execute AUDIT and NOAUDIT statements to perform object auditing on objects in any schema.

Debugging   Oracle 10g gives you two debugging-oriented system privileges.

DEBUG CONNECT SESSION   Permits the grantee to connect the current session to a debugger.

DEBUG ANY PROCEDURE   Permits the grantee to debug all PL/SQL and Java code in the database. This system privilege is equivalent to granting the object privilege DEBUG for every applicable object in the database.

Indexes   Oracle 10g gives you three system privileges related to indexes.

CREATE ANY INDEX   Permits the grantee to create an index in any schema.

ALTER ANY INDEX   Permits the grantee to alter indexes in any schema.

DROP ANY INDEX   Permits the grantee to drop indexes from any schema.

Job Scheduler   Oracle 10g gives you several system privileges related to the job scheduler.

CREATE JOB   Permits the grantee to create jobs, programs, or schedules in their own schema.

CREATE ANY JOB   Permits the grantee to create jobs, programs, or schedules in any schema.

The CREATE ANY JOB privilege gives the grantee the ability to execute programs using any other user's credentials. Grant it cautiously.

EXECUTE ANY PROGRAM   Permits the grantee to use any program in a job in their own schema.

EXECUTE ANY CLASS   Permits the grantee to specify any job class for jobs in their own schema.

MANAGE SCHEDULER   Permits the grantee to create, alter, or delete any job class, window, or window group.

Procedures   Oracle 10*g* gives you several system privileges related to stored procedures.

CREATE PROCEDURE   Permits the grantee to create procedures in their own schema.

CREATE ANY PROCEDURE   Permits the grantee to create procedures in any schema.

ALTER ANY PROCEDURE   Permits the grantee to recompile any procedure in the database.

DROP ANY PROCEDURE   Permits the grantee to remove procedures from any schema.

EXECUTE ANY PROCEDURE   Permits the grantee to run any procedure in any schema.

Profiles   Oracle 10*g* gives you three system privileges related to user profiles.

CREATE PROFILE   Permits the grantee to create profiles. To cause a profile to be used requires an ALTER USER statement (which requires the ALTER USER privilege).

ALTER PROFILE   Permits the grantee to modify existing profiles.

DROP PROFILE   Permits the grantee to drop profiles from the database.

Roles   Oracle 10*g* gives you several system privileges related to roles. Because roles deal with security, some of these privileges are very powerful.

CREATE ROLE   Permits the grantee to create new roles.

ALTER ANY ROLE   Permits the grantee to change the password for any role in the database.

DROP ANY ROLE   Permits the grantee to remove any role from the database.

GRANT ANY ROLE   Permits the grantee to grant any role to any user or revoke any role from any user or role.

The GRANT ANY ROLE privilege permits grantees to assign or rescind powerful administrative roles, such as SCHEDULER_ADMIN and IMP_FULL_DATABASE to or from any user, including themselves or other DBAs. Grant it cautiously.

Sequences   Oracle 10*g* gives you several system privileges to manage sequences.

CREATE SEQUENCE   Permits the grantee to create new sequences in their own schema.

CREATE ANY SEQUENCE   Permits the grantee to create new sequences in any schema.

ALTER ANY SEQUENCE   Permits the grantee to change the characteristics of any sequence in the database.

DROP ANY SEQUENCE   Permits the grantee to remove any sequence from any schema in the database.

SELECT ANY SEQUENCE   Permits the grantee to select from any sequence.

Sessions   Oracle 10*g* gives you four session-oriented system privileges.

CREATE SESSION   Permits the grantee to connect to the database. This privilege is required for user accounts, but may be undesirable for application owner accounts.

ALTER SESSION   Permits the grantee to execute ALTER SESSION statements.

ALTER RESOURCE COST   Permits the grantee to change the way that Oracle calculates resource cost for resource restrictions in a profile.

For more information on managing resource consumption with profiles, see the section "Assigning Resource Limits with a Profile," later in this chapter.

RESTRICTED SESSION   Permits the grantee to connect when the database has been opened in RESTRICTED SESSION mode, typically for administrative purposes. User accounts should not normally be granted this privilege.

Synonyms   Oracle 10*g* gives you several system privileges related to synonyms.

CREATE SYNONYM   Permits the grantee to create new synonyms in their own schema.

CREATE ANY SYNONYM   Permits the grantee to create new synonyms in any schema.

CREATE PUBLIC SYNONYM   Permits the grantee to create new public synonyms, which are accessible to all users in the database.

DROP ANY SYNONYM   Permits the grantee to remove any synonyms in any schema.

DROP PUBLIC SYNONYM   Permits the grantee to remove any public synonym from the database.

Tables   Oracle 10*g* gives you several system privileges for managing tables.

CREATE TABLE   Permits the grantee to create new tables in their own schema.

CREATE ANY TABLE   Permits the grantee to create new tables in any schema.

ALTER ANY TABLE   Permits the grantee to alter existing tables in any schema.

DROP ANY TABLE   Permits the grantee to drop tables from any schema.

COMMENT ANY TABLE   Permits the grantee to assign table or column comments to any table or view in any schema.

SELECT ANY TABLE   Permits the grantee to query any tables in any schema.

INSERT ANY TABLE   Permits the grantee to insert new rows into any table in any schema.

UPDATE ANY TABLE   Permits the grantee to modify rows in any table in any schema.

DELETE ANY TABLE   Permits the grantee to delete rows from tables in any schema.

LOCK ANY TABLE   Permits the grantee to execute a LOCK TABLE statement to explicitly lock a table in any schema.

 See Chapter 8, "Managing Consistency and Concurrency," for more information on locking tables.

FLASHBACK ANY TABLE   Permits the grantee to execute a SQL flashback query, using the AS OF syntax, on any table or view in any schema.

 See Chapter 10, "Implementing Database Backups," for more information on using flashback queries.

Tablespaces   Oracle 10*g* gives you four system privileges to control tablespace management.

CREATE TABLESPACE   Permits the grantee to create new tablespaces.

ALTER TABLESPACE   Permits the grantee to alter existing tablespaces with the ALTER TABLESPACE statement.

DROP TABLESPACE   Permits the grantee to delete tablespaces from the database.

MANAGE TABLESPACE   Permits the grantee to alter a tablespace ONLINE, OFFLINE, BEGIN BACKUP or END BACKUP.

 See Chapter 3 for more information on altering a tablespace.

UNLIMITED TABLESPACE   Permits the grantee to consume unlimited disk quota in any tablespace. This system privilege is equivalent to granting unlimited quota in each tablespace to the specified grantee.

Triggers   Oracle 10*g* gives you several system privileges to control trigger management.

CREATE TRIGGER   Permits the grantee to create new triggers on tables in their own schema.

CREATE ANY TRIGGER   Permits the grantee to create new triggers on tables in any schema.

ALTER ANY TRIGGER   Permits the grantee to enable, disable, or compile existing triggers on tables in any schema.

DROP ANY TRIGGER   Permits the grantee to remove triggers from tables in any schema.

ADMINISTER DATABASE TRIGGER   Permits the grantee to create new ON DATABASE triggers. The grantee must also have the CREATE TRIGGER or CREATE ANY TRIGGER privilege before they can create an ON DATABASE trigger.

Users   Oracle 10g gives you several system privileges to control who can manage user accounts.

CREATE USER   Permits the grantee to create new database users.

ALTER USER   Permits the grantee to change the authentication method or password and assign quotas, temporary tablespace, default tablespace, or profile for any user in the database. All users can change their own password without this privilege.

The ALTER USER privilege allows the grantee to change the authentication method or password for any user (and also change it back). This makes it possible for the grantee to masquerade as another user. Grant this privilege cautiously.

DROP USER   Permits the grantee to remove users together with any objects they own from a database.

Views   Oracle 10g gives you several system privileges to manage views. Note that some of these privileges include the word TABLE and not VIEW. These privileges apply to either tables or views.

CREATE VIEW   Permits the grantee to create new views in their own schema.

CREATE ANY VIEW   Permits the grantee to create new views in any schema.

DROP ANY VIEW   Permits the grantee to remove views from any schema.

COMMENT ANY TABLE   Permits the grantee to assign table or column comments to any table or view in any schema.

FLASHBACK ANY TABLE   Permits the grantee to execute a SQL flashback query, using the AS OF syntax, on any table or view in any schema.

See Chapter 10 for more information on using flashback queries.

Others   Oracle 10g gives you several system privileges for managing your database that don't fit into the other categories. These privileges include powerful administrative capabilities and should not be granted lightly.

ANALYZE ANY   Permits the grantee to execute an ANALYZE statement on tables, indexes, or clusters in any schema.

GRANT ANY OBJECT PRIVILEGE   Permits the grantee to assign object privileges on any object in any schema.

GRANT ANY PRIVILEGE   Permits the grantee to assign any system privilege to other users or roles.

GRANT ANY ROLE   Permits the grantee to assign any role to other users or roles.

SELECT ANY DICTIONARY   Permits the grantee to select from the SYS-owned data dictionary tables, such as TAB$ or SYSAUTH$.

SYSDBA   The most powerful system privilege, it permits the grantee to create, alter, start-up, or shut down databases, enable ARCHIVELOG and NOARCHIVELOG mode, recover a database, and create an SPFILE, in addition to having all system privileges the database has to offer, including RESTRICTED SESSION.

SYSOPER   Only slightly less powerful than SYSDBA, this privilege permits the grantee to start up, shut down, alter, mount, back up, and recover a database. The grantee can create or alter an SPFILE and enter restricted session mode.

As with object privileges, you use the GRANT statement to confer system privileges on either a user or a role. Unlike object privileges, the optional keywords WITH ADMIN OPTION are required to additionally allow the grantee to confer these privileges on other users and roles. For example, to give the CREATE USER, ALTER USER, and DROP USER privileges to the role APPL_DBA, you execute the following statement:

```
GRANT create user, alter user, drop user TO appl_dba;
```

 NOTE   System and role privileges require the wording WITH ADMIN OPTION; object privileges require the wording WITH GRANT OPTION. Because the function is so similar, but the syntax is different, be sure you know when to use ADMIN and when to use GRANT—a question involving this subtle difference may appear on the exam.

As with object privileges, you can grant system privileges to the special user PUBLIC. Granting privileges to PUBLIC allows anyone with a database account to exercise this privilege. In general, because system privileges are more powerful than object privileges, take care when granting a system privilege to PUBLIC. For example, to give all current and future database users the FLASHBACK ANY TABLE privilege, execute the following:

```
GRANT flashback any table TO public;
```

To give the INDEX ANY TABLE privilege to the role APPL_DBA together with the permission to allow anyone with the role APPL_DBA to grant this privilege to others, execute the following:

```
GRANT index any table TO appl_dba WITH ADMIN OPTION;
```

If you grant a system privilege `WITH ADMIN OPTION` and later revoke that privilege, the privileges created by the grantee will not be revoked. Unlike object privileges, revocation of system privileges does not cascade. Think of it this way: `WITH GRANT OPTION` includes the keyword `GRANT` and so implies that a revoke cascades, but `WITH ADMIN OPTION` does not mention `GRANT`, so a revoke has no effect. Here's an example. Mary grants `SELECT ANY TABLE` privilege to new DBA Zachary with `ADMIN OPTION`. Zachary then grants this privilege to Rex. Later, Zachary gets promoted and leaves the department, so Mary revokes the `SELECT ANY TABLE` privilege from Zachary. Rex's privilege remains unaffected. You can see this in Figure 6.3.

This behavior differs from object privileges, because the database does not record both grantor and grantee for system privileges—only the grantee is recorded.

Role Privileges

Role privileges confer on the grantee a group of system, object, and other role privileges. Users who have been granted a role inherit the privileges that have been granted to that role. Roles can be password protected, so users may have a role granted to them, yet not be able to use that role in all database sessions. We will look more closely at roles and role privileges—including how to grant them—in the following section.

Creating and Managing Roles

A *role* is a tool for administering privileges. Privileges (discussed in the preceding section "Granting and Revoking Privileges") can be granted to a role, and then that role can be granted to other roles and users. Users can thus inherit privileges via roles. Roles serve no other purpose than to administer privileges.

FIGURE 6.3   The revoking of system or role privileges

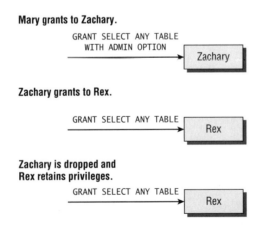

Mary grants to Zachary.

GRANT SELECT ANY TABLE
WITH ADMIN OPTION
→ Zachary

Zachary grants to Rex.

GRANT SELECT ANY TABLE
→ Rex

**Zachary is dropped and
Rex retains privileges.**

GRANT SELECT ANY TABLE
→ Rex

The database only records the privilege granted, not who granted it.

To create a role, use the CREATE ROLE statement. You can optionally include an INDENTIFIED BY clause that requires users to authenticate themselves before enabling the role. Roles requiring authentication are typically used inside an application, where a user's activities are controlled by the application. To create the role APPL_DBA, execute the following:

```
CREATE ROLE appl_dba IDENTIFIED BY seekwrit;
```

To enable a role, execute a SET ROLE statement, like this:

```
SET ROLE appl_dba IDENTIFIED BY seekwrit;
```

Granting Role Privileges

As with object and system privileges, you use the GRANT statement to confer role privileges on either a user or another role. Also, like system privileges, the optional keywords WITH ADMIN OPTION allow the grantee to confer these privileges on other users and roles. For example, to give the OEM_MONITOR role to user charlie, execute the following:

```
GRANT oem_monitor TO charlie;
```

As with the other privileges, you can grant role privileges to the special user PUBLIC. Granting privileges to PUBLIC allows anyone with a database account to exercise this privilege. For example, to give all current and future database users use of the plustrace role, execute the following:

```
GRANT plustrace TO public;
```

To give the INDEX ANY TABLE privilege to the role APPL_DBA together with the permission to allow anyone with the role APPL_DBA to grant this privilege to others, execute the following:

```
GRANT index any table TO appl_dba WITH ADMIN OPTION;
```

When it comes to granting a role WITH ADMIN OPTION, roles behave like system privileges, and subsequent revocations do not cascade.

Enabling Roles

Roles can be enabled—or disabled for that matter—selectively in each database session. If you have two concurrent sessions, the roles in effect for each session can be different. Use the SET ROLE *role_list* statement to enable one or more roles. *role_list* is a comma-delimited list of roles to enable. This list can include the keyword ALL, which enables all the roles granted to the user. You can optionally append a list of roles to exclude from the ALL list by specifying ALL EXCEPT *exclusion_list*.

If a role has a password associated with it, the keywords IDENTIFIED BY *password* must immediately follow the role name in the *role_list*.

For example, to enable the password-protected role HR_ADMIN, together with the unprotected role EMPLOYEE, execute the following:

```
SET ROLE hr_admin IDENTIFIED BY "my!seekrit", employee;
```

To enable all roles except HR_ADMIN, run this:

```
SET ROLE ALL EXCEPT hr_admin;
```

You can enable as many roles as have been granted to you, up to the MAX_ENABLED_ROLES initialization parameter.

Identifying Enabled Roles

The roles that are enabled in your session are listed in the data dictionary view SESSION_ROLES. To identify these enabled roles for your session, run the following:

```
SELECT role FROM session_roles;
```

These roles include the roles that have been granted to you, the roles that have been granted to the special user PUBLIC, and the roles that you have inherited by way of other roles. To identify the roles granted to either user or the special user PUBLIC, run the following:

```
SELECT granted_role FROM user_role_privs
WHERE username IN (USER, 'PUBLIC');
```

The role DBA includes the role SCHEDULER_ADMIN, which in turn has system privileges (such as CREATE ANY JOB). A user who has been granted the DBA role inherits the SCHEDULER_ADMIN role indirectly. To identify the roles that are both enabled in your session and granted directly to you or PUBLIC but not those roles that you inherited, run this:

```
SELECT role FROM session_roles
INTERSECT
SELECT granted_role FROM user_role_privs
WHERE username IN (USER, 'PUBLIC');
```

In your sessions, you can disable only these directly granted and public roles.

Disabling Roles

Roles can be disabled in a database session either en masse or by exception. Use the SET ROLE NONE statement to disable all roles. Use the SET ROLE ALL EXCEPT *role_list* statement to enable all roles except those in the comma-delimited *role_list*.

There is no way to selectively disable a single role. Also, you cannot disable roles that you inherit by way of another role without disabling the parent role. For example, you cannot disable the SCHEDULER_ADMIN role without disabling the DBA role.

Setting Default Roles

Roles that are enabled by default when you log on are called default roles. You do not need to specify a password for default roles and do not have to execute a SET ROLE statement to enable a default role. Change the default roles for a user account with an ALTER USER DEFAULT ROLE *role_list* statement. The *role_list* can include the keywords ALL, NONE, and EXCEPT, in the same manner as with a SET ROLE statement.

Including a password-protected role in the *role_list* defeats the purpose of password protecting the role as it is automatically enabled without the password. When you create a role, you are implicitly granted that role with the admin option, and it is configured as a default role for your account.

For example, to create the role EMPLOYEE, grant it to user scott, and configure all of scott's roles except PLUSTRACE as default roles, run the following:

```
CREATE ROLE employee;
GRANT employee TO scott;
ALTER USER scott DEFAULT ROLE ALL EXCEPT plustrace;
```

Because the creator of a role automatically has that role assigned as a default role, administrative users (such as SYS or SYSTEM) who create many roles may need to alter their default role list. If you attempt to log on with more default roles than allowed by the MAX_ENABLED_ROLES initialization parameter, you will raise an exception and your logon will fail.

Real World Scenario

Password-Protected Role

Lucinda works in HR and needs to be able to modify an employee's salary after they have a review and their raise is approved. The HR application ensures that the raise is approved and falls within corporate guidelines. Although Lucinda needs to be able to change employee salaries, she should be allowed to do so only from within the HR application, because it ensures that business rules are followed.

You wisely choose to use a password-protected role to satisfy these requirements. Update on the salary table is granted to the password-protected role salary_admin. Lucinda is then granted the salary_admin role, but she is not told the password for it. The HR application has the password encoded within it, so when Lucinda runs the HR application, unbeknownst to her, a SET ROLE salary_admin IDENTIFY BY *password* statement is executed, enabling the role and allowing her to change the salary.

If Lucinda tries to execute an UPDATE statement on the salary table from *i*SQLPlus, she will get an insufficient privileges error.

Controlling Resource Usage by Users

An Oracle 10*g* database lets you limit some resources that your user accounts consume. Disk-space limits are governed by tablespace quotas, and CPU, memory, and hybrid limits are implemented with profiles. In the following sections, you will learn how to manage resource consumption in your database with roles and quotas.

Assigning Tablespace Quotas

Before a user can create objects in a tablespace, they must have a space usage quota for that tablespace. Tablespace quotas limit the amount of disk space that a user can consume. The default quota is none, which is why you need to assign a quota before you can create objects in a tablespace. You can assign a space usage quota at the same time you create a user, with the CREATE USER statement:

```
CREATE USER chip IDENTIFIED BY "Seek!r3t"
QUOTA 100M ON USERS;
```

Or after the user has been created with the ALTER USER statement:

```
ALTER USER bart
QUOTA UNLIMTED ON USERS;
```

The special keyword UNLIMITED tells the database that the user should not have a preset limit on the amount of space that their objects can consume.

Assigning Resource Limits with a Profile

CPU and session-oriented resource limits are managed through the use of a profile. Profiles let you set limits for several resources, including CPU time, memory, and the number of logical reads performed during a user session or database call. A database call is either a parse, an execute, or a fetch. Usually, the database implicitly performs these calls for you. You can explicitly make these database calls from Java, PL/SQL, or OCI (Oracle Call Interface) programs.

A logical read is a measure of the amount of work that the database performs while executing SQL statements. Statements that generate more logical reads require the database to perform more work than statements generating fewer logical reads. Technically, a logical read is counted for each row accessed via ROWID (index access) and for each data block accessed via multiblock read (full table scan or index fast full scan).

To enable resource limit restrictions with profiles, first enable them in the database by setting the initialization parameter resource_limit to true, like this:

```
ALTER SYSTEM SET resource_limit = TRUE SCOPE = BOTH;
```

To assign resource limits to a profile, use the CREATE PROFILE or ALTER PROFILE statement with one or more of the kernel resource parameters. These statements support the following clauses to limit resources:

CONNECT_TIME   Limits any session established by a user having this profile to the specified number of minutes. Connection time is sometimes called "wall clock time" to differentiate it from CPU time. When a session exceeds the specified number of minutes, the database rolls back any uncommitted changes and terminates the session. The next call to the database raises an exception. You can use the special value UNLIMITED to tell the database that there is no limit to a session's duration. Set this parameter in a CREATE PROFILE or ALTER PROFILE statement like this:

```
CREATE PROFILE agent LIMIT CONNECT_TIME 10;


ALTER PROFILE data_analyst LIMIT CONNECT_TIME UNLIMITED;
```

CPU_PER_CALL   Limits the amount of CPU time that can be consumed by any single database call in any session established by a user with this profile. The specified value is in hundredths of a second and applies to a parse, an execute, or a fetch call. These calls are implicitly performed by the database for any SQL statement executed in SQL*Plus and can be explicitly called from OCI, Java, or PL/SQL programs. When this limit is breached, the statement fails and is automatically rolled back, and an exception is raised. The user can then commit or roll back any uncommitted changes in the transaction. Set this parameter in a CREATE PROFILE or ALTER PROFILE statement like this:

```
CREATE PROFILE agent LIMIT CPU_PER_CALL 3000;


ALTER PROFILE data_analyst LIMIT CPU_PER_CALL UNLIMITED;
```

CPU_PER_SESSION   Limits the amount of CPU time that can be consumed in any session established by a user with this profile. The specified value is in hundredths of a second. When this limit is breached, the current statement fails, the transaction is automatically rolled back, and an exception is raised. The user can then commit or roll back any uncommitted changes in the transaction before logging off. Set this parameter in a CREATE PROFILE or ALTER PROFILE statement like this:

```
CREATE PROFILE agent LIMIT CPU_PER_CALL 30000;
ALTER PROFILE data_analyst LIMIT CPU_PER_CALL UNLIMITED;
```

IDLE_TIME   Limits the duration of time between database calls to the specified number of minutes. If a user having this profile exceeds this setting, the next statement fails, and the user is allowed to either commit or roll back any uncommitted changes before logging off. Long-running statements are not affected by this setting. Set IDLE_TIME in a CREATE PROFILE or ALTER PROFILE statement like this:

```
CREATE PROFILE agent LIMIT IDLE_TIME 10;


ALTER PROFILE daemon LIMIT IDLE_TIME UNLIMITED;
```

LOGICAL_READS_PER_CALL   Caps the amount of work that any individual database call performs to the specified number of logical reads. The database call is either a parse, an execute, or a fetch. If the limit is exceeded, the database rolls back the statement, returns an error to the calling program, and allows the user to either commit or roll back any uncommitted changes.

Logical reads are computed as the sum of consistent gets plus current mode gets. Set this parameter in a CREATE PROFILE or ALTER PROFILE statement like this:

```
CREATE PROFILE agent LIMIT LOGICAL_READS_PER_CALL 2500;

ALTER PROFILE data_analyst LIMIT LOGICAL_READS_PER_CALL 1000000;
```

LOGICAL_READS_PER_SESSION   Limits the amount of database work that a user's session can consume to the specified number of logical reads. When the limit is exceeded, the current statement fails and an exception is raised, and the user must either commit or roll back the transaction and end the session. Logical reads are computed as the sum of consistent gets plus current mode gets. Set this parameter in a CREATE PROFILE or ALTER PROFILE statement like this:

```
CREATE PROFILE agent LIMIT LOGICAL_READS_PER_SESSION 250000;

ALTER PROFILE data_analyst
   LIMIT LOGICAL_READS_PER_SESSION 35000000;
```

PRIVATE_SGA   Limits the amount of SGA (System Global Area) memory in bytes that a user connecting with shared servers (via multithreaded server [MTS]) can allocate to the persistent area in the PGA (Program Global Area). This area contains bind information among other items. Set this parameter in a CREATE PROFILE or ALTER PROFILE statement like this:

```
CREATE PROFILE agent LIMIT PRIVATE_SGA 2500;

ALTER PROFILE data_analyst LIMIT PRIVATE_SGA UNLIMITED;
```

SESSIONS_PER_USER   Restricts a user with this profile to the specified number of database sessions. This setting can be useful to discourage DBAs from all connecting to a shared administrative account to do their work when corporate policy indicates that they should be connecting to their individual accounts. Set this parameter in a CREATE PROFILE or ALTER PROFILE statement like this:

```
CREATE PROFILE admin_profile LIMIT SESSIONS_PER_USER 2;

ALTER PROFILE data_analyst LIMIT SESSIONS_PER_USER 6;
```

COMPOSITE_LIMIT   Limits the number of service units that can be consumed during a user session. Service units are calculated as the weighted sum of CPU_PER_SESSION, LOGICAL_READS_PER_SESSION, CONNECT_TIME, and PRIVATE_SGA values. The weightings are established with the ALTER RESOURCE COST statement and can be viewed from the RESOURCE_COST data dictionary view. This COMPOSITE_LIMIT allows you to cap the resource consumption of user groups in more complex ways than a single resource limit. Set this parameter in a CREATE PROFILE or ALTER PROFILE statement like this:

```
CREATE PROFILE admi_profile LIMIT COMPOSITE_LIMIT UNLIMITED;
```

```
ALTER PROFILE data_analyst LIMIT COMPOSITE_LIMIT 100000;
```

To enforce the resource limits established with profiles, you must enable them by setting the initialization parameter RESOURCE_LIMIT to TRUE. The default setting is FALSE. Set this parameter with the ALTER SYSTEM statement, like this:

```
ALTER SYSTEM SET resource_limit = TRUE SCOPE=BOTH;
```

You can also use profiles to manage passwords.

For information on managing passwords, see the section "Implementing Standard Password Security Features," later in this chapter.

Applying the Principle of Least Privilege

The principle of least privilege states that each user should only be given the minimal privileges needed to perform their job. This principle is a central tenet to the initially closed philosophy whereby all access is initially closed or unavailable and access is opened on a need-to-know basis. Highly secure environments typically operate under an initially closed philosophy. The contrasting philosophy is an initially open philosophy, whereby all access is by default open to all users and only sensitive areas are closed. Academic or learning environments typically operate under an initially open philosophy.

Many IT organizations want the most secure policies for production systems, which calls for the initially closed approach to security. To support the need for administrators and programmers to quickly learn new technology, these shops frequently create "sandbox" systems that follow the initially open philosophy. These sandbox systems afford their limited users the learning benefit of the initially open approach, while not storing or giving gateway access to any sensitive information elsewhere in the enterprise.

To implement the principle of least privilege on your production or development systems, you should take several actions, or best practices, while setting up or locking down the database.

Protect the data dictionary.   Ensure that users with the SELECT ANY TABLE privilege cannot access the tables that underlie the data dictionary by setting O7_DICTIONARY_ACCESSIBILITY = FALSE. This is the default setting.

Revoke unnecessary privileges from *PUBLIC*.   By default, several packages and roles are granted to the special user PUBLIC. Review these privileges and revoke the EXECUTE privilege from PUBLIC if these packages are not necessary. Some of these packages include the following:

UTL_TCP   Permits the grantee to establish a network connection to any waiting TCP/IP network service. Once a connection is established, arbitrary information can be sent and received directly from the database to and from the other TCP services on your network. If your organization is concerned about information exchange over TCP/IP, revoke the EXECUTE privilege on this package from PUBLIC. Grant privileges on this package only to those users who need it.

UTL_SMTP   Permits the grantee to send arbitrary e-mail. If your organization is concerned about information exchange via e-mail, revoke the EXECUTE privilege on this package from PUBLIC. Grant privileges on this package only to those users who need it.

UTL_HTTP   Permits the grantee to send and receive arbitrary data via the HTTP protocol. If your organization is concerned about information exchange via HTTP, revoke the EXECUTE privilege on this package from PUBLIC. Grant privileges on this package only to those users who need it.

UTL_FILE   Permits the grantee to read and write text data to and from arbitrary operating system files that are in the designated directories. UTL_FILE does not manage concurrency, so multiple user sessions can step on each other, overwriting changes via UTL_FILE. Consider revoking the EXECUTE privilege on this package from PUBLIC.

DBMS_OBFUSCATION_TOOLKIT and *DBMS_CRYPTO*   Permit the grantee to employ encryption technologies. In a managed environment using encryption, the keys are stored and managed. If encryption keys are lost, the encrypted data is undecipherable. Consider revoking the EXECUTE privilege on these packages from PUBLIC.

You can revoke the EXECUTE privileges like this:

```
REVOKE EXECUTE ON utl_tcp FROM PUBLIC;
REVOKE EXECUTE ON utl_smtp FROM PUBLIC;
REVOKE EXECUTE ON utl_http FROM PUBLIC;
REVOKE EXECUTE ON utl_file FROM PUBLIC;
REVOKE EXECUTE ON dbms_obfuscation_toolkit
    FROM PUBLIC;
REVOKE EXECUTE ON dbms_crypto FROM PUBLIC;
```

You can query the data dictionary to see what other packages may need to be locked down by revoking the EXECUTE privilege from PUBLIC. Here is a query to list the packages, owned by user SYS, that have EXECUTE privilege granted to PUBLIC:

```
SELECT table_name
FROM dba_tab_privs p
    ,dba_objects  o
WHERE p.owner=o.owner
```

```
AND    p.table_name = o.object_name
AND    p.owner = 'SYS'
AND    p.privilege = 'EXECUTE'
AND    p.grantee = 'PUBLIC'
AND    o.object_type='PACKAGE';
```

Limit the users who have administrative privileges.   Grant administrative privileges to user accounts cautiously. Some powerful administrative privileges and roles to exercise caution with include the following:

SYSDBA   Gives the grantee the highest level of privileges with the Oracle database software. A clever user with the SYSDBA role can circumvent most database security measures. There is usually no good reason to grant this role to any account except SYS, and the SYS password should be both cautiously guarded and changed regularly. Also guard operating system accounts carefully. If you are logged on to the database server using a privileged operating system account, you might be able to connect to the database with SYSDBA authority and no password by entering **connect / as sysdba** in SQL*Plus.

DBA   Permits the grantee to assign privileges and manipulate data throughout the database. A clever user with the DBA role can circumvent most database security measures. Grant this role only to those users who need it.

The *ANY* system privileges   SELECT ANY TABLE, GRANT ANY ROLE, DELETE ANY TABLE, and so on permit the grantee to assign privileges and manipulate data throughout the database. A malicious user with the one of these roles can wreak havoc in your database. Grant these privileges only to those users who need them.

Do not enable *REMOTE_OS_AUTHENT*.   The default setting for the initialization parameter REMOTE_OS_AUTHENT is FALSE. There is rarely a reason to enable this feature. When set to TRUE, this parameter tells the database to trust any client to authenticate externally authenticated accounts. For example, if you have an externally identified account named ORACLE that has DBA privileges for use in administrative scripts running on the database server (a common practice), setting this parameter to TRUE will allow someone with a notebook or desktop PC with a locally created ORACLE account to connect to your database with DBA credentials and no password.

Managing Default User Accounts

The SYS and SYSTEM user accounts are always created with an Oracle 10*g* database. Additionally, the SYSMAN and DBSNMP accounts are created together with a database via the Database Configuration Assistant (DBCA).

Other special accounts may be created to support installed products, such as RMAN (Recovery Manager) or XMLDB. When created via the DBCA, these special accounts are locked and expired, leaving only SYS, SYSTEM, SYSMAN, and DBSNMP open. The SYS and SYSTEM accounts are the data dictionary owner and an administrative account, respectively. SYSMAN and DBSNMP are used by Enterprise Manager.

If your database is created via any means other than DBCA, ensure that the accounts are locked and expired, and that the default passwords are changed. You expire and lock an account using the ALTER USER statement like this:

```
ALTER USER mdsys PASSWORD EXPIRE ACCOUNT LOCK;
```

Depending on the functionality installed in your Oracle 10g database, you may need to lock and expire several default user accounts. Your database-created user accounts may include the following:

csmig	odm	sysman
ctxsys	odm_mtr	system
dbsnmp	olapsys	tracesvr
demo	ordplugins	websys
dip	ordsys	wkproxy
dmsys	outln	wksys
exfsys	perfstat	wk_test
lbacsys	rman	wmsys
mddata	scott	xdb
mdsys	si_informtn_schema	xdm
oas_public	sys	

Implementing Standard Password Security Features

For users who are configured for database authentication, password security rules are enforced with profiles and password-complexity rules with verification functions. Profiles have a set of standard rules that define how long a password can remain valid, the elapsed time, the number of password changes before a password can be reused, the number of failed login attempts that will lock the account, and how long the account will remain locked.

If you want a parameter to inherit the setting from the DEFAULT profile, set the parameter's value to the keyword DEFAULT. Explicitly assign password rules to a profile using the CREATE PROFILE or ALTER PROFILE statement. These profile assignment statements support the following clauses to configure the standard password rules:

FAILED_LOGIN_ATTEMPTS* and *PASSWORD_LOCK_TIME   The FAILED_LOGIN_ ATTEMPTS parameter specifies how many times in a row the user can fail password authentication.

If this limit is breached, the account is locked for PASSWORD_LOCK_TIME days. If the PASSWORD_LOCK_TIME parameter is set to UNLIMITED and a user exceeds FAILED_LOGIN_ATTEMPTS, the account must be manually unlocked. You can set these parameters in a CREATE PROFILE or ALTER PROFILE statement like this:

```
-- lock account for 10 minutes if 3 consecutive logins fail
CREATE PROFILE agent LIMIT
   FAILED_LOGIN_ATTEMPTS 3
   PASSWORD_LOCK_TIME 10/1440;

-- remove failed login restrictions
ALTER PROFILE student LIMIT FAILED_LOGIN_ATTEMPTS UNLIMITED;

-- manually unlock an account
ALTER USER scott ACCOUNT UNLOCK;
```

PASSWORD_LIFE_TIME and *PASSWORD_GRACE_TIME*   The PASSWORD_LIFE_TIME parameter specifies the maximum number of days that a password can remain in force, and the PASSWORD_GRACE_TIME is the number of days after the first successful login following password expiration, during which the user will be reminded to change their password, but allowed to log in. After the PASSWORD_GRACE_TIME limit is reached, the user must change their password. If you set PASSWORD_LIFE_TIME to a value and set PASSWORD_GRACE_TIME to UNLIMITED, users will be reminded to change their password every time they log in, but never forced to actually do so. You can set these two parameters in a CREATE PROFILE or ALTER PROFILE statement like this:

```
-- limit the password lifetime to 90 days
-- during the last 14 days the user will be reminded
-- to change the password
CREATE PROFILE agent LIMIT
   PASSWORD_LIFE_TIME 90 - 14
   PASSWORD_GRACE_TIME 14;

-- set no limit to password lifetime
ALTER PROFILE student LIMIT
   PASSWORD_LIFE_TIME UNLIMITED
   PASSWORD_GRACE_TIME DEFAULT;
```

PASSWORD_REUSE_TIME and *PASSWORD_REUSE_MAX*   The PASSWORD_REUSE_TIME parameter specifies the minimum number of days that must transpire before a password can be reused. PASSWORD_REUSE_MAX specifies the minimum number of password changes that must occur before a password can be reused. If you specify a value for one of these two parameters and UNLIMITED for the other, passwords can never be reused. If you set both PASSWORD_REUSE_TIME and PASSWORD_REUSE_MAX to UNLIMITED, these parameters are essentially disabled. You can set these password parameters in a CREATE PROFILE or ALTER PROFILE statement like this:

```
-- require at least 4 password changes and 1 year
-- before a password may be reused.
CREATE PROFILE agent LIMIT
   PASSWORD_REUSE_TIME 365
   PASSWORD_REUSE_MAX 4;

-- remove password reuse constraints
ALTER PROFILE student LIMIT
   PASSWORD_REUSE_TIME UNLIMITED
   PASSWORD_REUSE_MAX UNLIMITED;
```

> Several password attributes are durations expressed in days. These durations are normally set with integer values, such as 30, 90, or 365 days. But decimal values are supported as well. You can set the password timeout to 5 minutes (5/1,440 days) or 5 seconds (5/86,400 days). Using a fractional number of days is a great way to try out combinations of values and observe the results of setting these password rules.

PASSWORD_VERIFY_FUNCTION　The PASSWORD_VERIFY_FUNCTION parameter lets you codify additional rules that will be verified when a password is changed. These rules usually verify password complexity such as minimal password length or check that a password does not appear in a dictionary. The PASSWORD_VERIFY_FUNCTION must be created under the user SYS and must have three pass parameters of type VARCHAR2. These pass parameters must contain the username in the first parameter, the new password in the second, and the old password in the third. You can set this parameter in a CREATE PROFILE or ALTER PROFILE statement like this:

```
-- use a custom password function
CREATE PROFILE agent LIMIT PASSWORD_VERIFY_FUNCTION my_function;

-- disable use of a custom function
ALTER PROFILE student LIMIT PASSWORD_VERIFY_FUNCTION DEFAULT;
```

Auditing Database Activity

Auditing involves monitoring and recording specific database activity. An Oracle 10*g* database supports four levels of auditing and affords you two locations for recording these activities.

Real World Scenario

Implementing a Corporate Password Security Policy

Many companies have security policies requiring that several password complexity rules be followed. For your Oracle 10*g* database, these rules can be incorporated into a password verify function. Here is an example of three password-complexity requirements and how they are satisfied through a password verify function named MY_PASSWORD_VERIFY.

The first rule specifies that the password must be at least six characters in length. The second rule disallows passwords containing some form of either the username or the word *password*. The third rule requires the password to contain at least one alphabetic character, at least one digit, and at least one punctuation character. If the new password fails any of these tests, the function raises an exception, and the password change fails.

After creating this function as user SYS, assign it to a profile, like this:

```
ALTER PROFILE student LIMIT password_verify_function my_password_verify;
```

Any user having the student profile will have to abide by the password rules enforced by the my_password_verify function:

```
CREATE OR REPLACE FUNCTION my_password_verify
    (username VARCHAR2
    ,password VARCHAR2
    ,old_password VARCHAR2
    ) RETURN BOOLEAN
IS

BEGIN
    -- Check for the minimum length of the password
    IF LENGTH(password) < 6 THEN
        raise_application_error(-20001
            ,'Password must be at least 6 characters long');
    END IF;

    -- Check that the password does not contain any
    -- upper/lowercase version of either the user name
    -- or the keyword PASSWORD
    IF (   regexp_like(password,username,'i')
        OR regexp_like(password,'password','i')) THEN
        raise_application_error(-20002
            ,'Password cannot contain username or PASSWORD');
```

```
      END IF;

   -- Check that the password contains at least one letter,
   -- one digit and one punctuation character
   IF NOT(    regexp_like(password,'[[:digit:]]')
         AND regexp_like(password,'[[:alpha:]]')
         AND regexp_like(password,'[[:punct:]]')
       ) THEN
      raise_application_error(-20003
         ,'Password must contain at least one digit '||
          'and one letter and one punctuation character');
   END IF;

   -- password is okey dokey
   RETURN(TRUE);
END;
/
```

Audit records can be stored in the database or in operating system files for greater security. You tell the database where to record audit trail records by setting the initialization parameter audit_trail. The default is NONE. AUDIT_TRAIL=DB tells the database to record audit records in the database. AUDIT_TRAIL=DB_EXTENDED tells the database to record audit records in the database together with bind variables (SQLBIND) and the SQL statement triggering the audit entry (SQLTEXT). AUDIT_TRAIL=OS tells the database to record audit records in operating system files. You cannot change this parameter in memory, only in your PFILE or SPFILE. For example, the following statement will change the location of audit records in the SPFILE:

```
ALTER SYSTEM SET audit_trail=DB SCOPE=SPFILE;
```

After changing the audit_trail parameter, you will need to bounce (shut down and start up) your database instance for the change to take effect.

When recorded in the database, most audit entries are recorded in the SYS.AUD$ table. On Unix systems, operating system audit records are written into files in the directory specified by the initialization parameter audit_file_dest (which defaults to $ORACLE_HOME/rdbms/audit). On Microsoft Windows systems, these audit records are written to the Event Viewer log file.

The four levels of auditing—statement, privilege, object, and fine-grained access—are described in detail in the following sections.

Managing Statement Auditing

Statement auditing involves monitoring and recording the execution of specific types of SQL statements. In the following sections, you will learn how to enable and disable statement auditing as well as identify what statement auditing options are enabled.

Enabling Statement Auditing

You enable auditing of specific SQL statements with an AUDIT statement. For example, to audit the SQL statements CREATE TABLE, DROP TABLE, or TRUNCATE TABLE, use the TABLE audit option like this:

```
AUDIT table;
```

To record audit entries for specific users only, include a BY *USER* clause in the AUDIT statement. For example, to audit CREATE, DROP, or TRUNCATE TABLE statements for user juanita only, execute the following:

```
AUDIT table BY juanita;
```

Frequently, you want to record only attempts that fail—perhaps to look for users who are probing the system to see what they can get away with. To further limit auditing to only these unsuccessful executions, use a WHENEVER clause like this:

```
AUDIT table BY juanita WHENEVER NOT SUCCESSFUL;
```

You can alternately specify WHENEVER SUCCESSFUL to record only successful statements. If you do not include a WHENEVER clause, both successful and unsuccessful statements trigger audit records.

You can further configure non-DDL statements to record one audit entry for the triggering session or one entry for each auditable action during the session. Specify BY ACCESS or BY SESSION in the AUDIT statement, like this:

```
AUDIT INSERT TABLE BY juanita BY ACCESS;
```

There are many auditing options other than TABLE or INSERT TABLE. Table 6.1 shows all of the statement auditing options.

TABLE 6.1   Statement Audit Options

Statement Auditing Option	Triggering SQL Statements
ALTER SEQUENCE	ALTER SEQUENCE
ALTER TABLE	ALTER TABLE
COMMENT TABLE	COMMENT ON TABLE COMMENT ON COLUMN
DATABASE LINK	CREATE DATABASE LINK DROP DATABASE LINK
DELETE TABLE	DELETE
EXECUTE PROCEDURE	Execution of any procedure, function or access to any cursor or variable in a package

TABLE 6.1 Statement Audit Options *(continued)*

Statement Auditing Option	Triggering SQL Statements
GRANT PROCEDURE	GRANT on a function, package, or procedure
GRANT SEQUENCE	GRANT on a sequence
GRANT TABLE	GRANT on a table or view
INDEX	CREATEINDEX
INSERT TABLE	INSERT into table or view
LOCK TABLE	LOCK
NOT EXISTS	all SQL statements
PROCEDURE	CREATE FUNCTION DROP FUNCTION CREATE PACKAGE CREATE PACKAGE BODY DROP PACKAGE CREATE PROCEDURE DROP PROCEDURE
PROFILE	CREATE PROFILE ALTER PROFILE DROP PROFILE
ROLE	CREATE ROLE ALTER ROLE DROP ROLE SET ROLE
SELECT SEQUENCE	SELECT on a sequence
SELECT TABLE	SELECT from table or view
SEQUENCE	CREATE SEQUENCE DROP SEQUENCE
SESSION	LOGON
SYNONYM	CREATE SYNONYM DROP SYNONYM
SYSTEM AUDIT	AUDIT NOAUDIT

TABLE 6.1   Statement Audit Options *(continued)*

Statement Auditing Option	Triggering SQL Statements
SYSTEM GRANT	GRANT REVOKE
TABLE	CREATE TABLE DROP TABLE TRUNCATE TABLE
TABLESPACE	CREATE TABLESPACE ALTER TABLESPACE DROP TABLESPACE
TRIGGER	CREATE TRIGGER ALTER TRIGGER (to enable or disable) ALTER TABLE (to enable all or disable all)
UPDATE TABLE	UPDATE on a table or view
USER	CREATE USER ALTER USER DROP USER
VIEW	CREATE VIEW DROP VIEW

Identifying Enabled Statement Auditing Options

You can identify the statement auditing options that have been enabled in your database by querying the DBA_STMT_AUDIT_OPTS data dictionary view. For example, the following example shows that SESSION auditing is enabled for all users, NOT EXISTS auditing is enabled for all users, and TABLE auditing WHENEVER NOT SUCCESSFUL is enabled for user juanita:

```
SELECT audit_option, failure, success, user_name
FROM dba_stmt_audit_opts
ORDER BY audit_option, user_name;

AUDIT_OPTION         FAILURE     SUCCESS     USER_NAME
-------------------- ----------- ----------- -------------
CREATE SESSION       BY ACCESS   BY ACCESS
NOT EXISTS           BY ACCESS   BY ACCESS
TABLE                BY ACCESS   NOT SET     JUANITA
```

Disabling Statement Auditing

To disable auditing of a specific SQL statement, use a NOAUDIT statement, which allows the same BY and WHENEVER options as the AUDIT statement. If you enable auditing for a specific user, specify that user in the NOAUDIT statement as well. However, it is not necessary to include the WHENEVER NOT SUCCESSFUL clause in the NOAUDIT statement.

For example, to disable the three audit options in the previous section, execute the following three statements:

```
NOAUDIT session;
NOAUDIT not exists;
NOAUDIT table BY juanita;
```

Examining the Audit Trail

Statement, privilege, and object audit records are written to the SYS.AUD$ table and made available via the data dictionary views DBA_AUDIT_TRAIL and USER_AUDIT_TRAIL. These data dictionary views may not contain values for every record because this view is used for three different types of audit records. For example, you can view the user, time, and type of statement audited for user juanita by executing the following:

```
SELECT username, timestamp, action_name
FROM dba_audit_trail
WHERE username = 'JUANITA';
```

USERNAME	TIMESTAMP	ACTION_NAME
JUANITA	15-Jun-2004 18:43:52	LOGON
JUANITA	15-Jun-2004 18:44:19	LOGOFF
JUANITA	15-Jun-2004 18:46:01	LOGON
JUANITA	15-Jun-2004 18:46:40	CREATE TABLE

If you enable AUDIT SESSION, the database creates one audit record when a user logs on and updates that record when the user logs off successfully. These session audit records contain some valuable information that can help you narrow the focus of your tuning efforts. Among the information recorded in the audit records are the username, logon time, logoff time, and the number of physical reads and logical reads performed during the session. By looking for sessions with high counts of logical or physical reads, you can identify high-resource-consuming jobs and narrow the focus of your tuning efforts.

Managing Privilege Auditing

Privilege auditing involves monitoring and recording the execution of SQL statements that require a specific system privilege, such as SELECT ANY TABLE or GRANT ANY PRIVILEGE. You can audit any system privilege. In the following section, you will learn how to enable and disable privilege auditing as well as identify which privilege auditing options are enabled in your database.

Enabling Privilege Auditing

You enable privilege auditing with an AUDIT statement, specifying the system privilege that you want to monitor. For example, to audit statements that require the system privilege CREATE ANY TABLE, execute the following:

```
AUDIT create any table;
```

To record audit entries for specific users only, include a BY *USER clause* in the AUDIT statement. For example, to audit SQL statements made by user juanita that require the CREATE ANY TABLE privilege, execute the following:

```
AUDIT create any table BY juanita;
```

Just as you do with statement auditing, you can further configure non-DDL privileges to record one audit entry for the triggering session or one for each auditable action during the session by specifying BY ACCESS or BY SESSION in the AUDIT statement, like this:

```
AUDIT DELETE ANY TABLE BY juanita BY ACCESS;
```

Identifying Enabled Privilege Auditing Options

You can report on the privilege auditing that has been enabled in your database by querying the DBA_PRIV_AUDIT_OPTS data dictionary view. For example, the following report shows that ALTER PROFILE auditing is enabled for all users and that ALTER USER and DELETE ANY TABLE auditing is enabled for user juanita:

```
SELECT privilege, user_name
FROM dba_priv_audit_opts
ORDER BY privilege, user_name

PRIVILEGE            USER_NAME
-------------------- ----------------
ALTER PROFILE
DELETE ANY TABLE     JUANITA
ALTER USER           JUANITA
```

Disabling Privilege Auditing

To disable auditing of a system privilege, use a NOAUDIT statement. The NOAUDIT statement allows the same BY options as the AUDIT statement. If you enable auditing for a specific user, you need to specify that user in the NOAUDIT statement. For example, to disable the three audit options in the previous section, execute the following three statements:

```
NOAUDIT alter profile;
NOAUDIT delete any table BY juanita;
NOAUDIT alter user BY juanita;
```

Managing Object Auditing

Object auditing involves monitoring and recording the execution of SQL statements that require a specific object privilege, such as SELECT, INSERT, UPDATE, DELETE, or EXECUTE. Unlike either statement or system privilege auditing, schema object auditing cannot be restricted to specific users—it is enabled for all users or no users. In the following sections, you will learn how to enable and disable object auditing options as well as identify which object auditing options are enabled.

Enabling Object Auditing

You enable object auditing with an AUDIT statement, specifying both the object and object privilege that you want to monitor. For example, to audit SELECT statements on the HR.EMPLOYEE_SALARY table, execute the following:

```
AUDIT select ON hr.employee_salary;
```

You can further configure these audit records to record one audit entry for the triggering session or one for each auditable action during the session by specifying BY ACCESS or BY SESSION in the AUDIT statement. This access/session configuration can be defined differently for successful or unsuccessful executions. For example, to make one audit entry per auditable action for successful SELECT statements on the HR.EMPLOYEE_SALARY table, execute the following:

```
-- one audit entry for each trigging statement
AUDIT select ON hr.employee_salary
   BY ACCESS WHENEVER SUCCESSFUL;

-- one audit entry for the session experiencing one or more
-- triggering statements
AUDIT select ON hr.employee_salary
   BY SESSION WHENEVER NOT SUCCESSFUL;
```

Identifying Enabled Object Auditing Options

The object auditing options that are enabled in the database are recorded in the DBA_OBJ_
AUDIT_OPTS data dictionary view. Unlike the statement and privilege _AUDIT_OPTS views, the
DBA_OBJ_AUDIT_OPTS always has one row for each auditable object in the database. There are
columns for each object privilege that auditing can be enabled on, and in each of these columns,
a code is reported that shows the auditing options. For example, the following report on the
HR.EMPLOYEES table shows that no auditing is enabled for the INSERT object privilege and that
the SELECT object privilege has auditing enabled with one audit entry for each access when the
access is successful and one audit entry for each session when the access is not successful:

```
SELECT owner, object_name, object_type, ins, sel
FROM dba_obj_audit_opts
WHERE owner='HR'
AND   object_name='EMPLOYEE_SALARY';


OWNER         OBJECT_NAME                OBJECT_TY INS SEL
-----------   -------------------------  --------- --- ---
HR            EMPLOYEE_SALARY            TABLE     -/- A/S
```

The coding for the object privilege columns contains one of three possible values: a dash (-) to
indicate no auditing is enabled), an A to indicate BY ACCESS, or an S to indicate BY SESSION. The
first code (preceding the slash) denotes the action for successful statements, and the second code
(after the slash) denotes the action for unsuccessful statements.

Disabling Object Auditing

To disable object auditing, use a NOAUDIT statement, which allows the same WHENEVER options
as the AUDIT statement. For example, to disable auditing of unsuccessful SELECT statements
against the HR.EMPLOYEES table, execute the following:

```
NOAUDIT select ON hr.employee_salary  WHENEVER NOT SUCCESSFUL;
```

Purging the Audit Trail

Database audit records for statement, privilege, and object auditing are stored in the table
SYS.AUD$. Depending on how extensive your auditing and retention policies are, you will need
to periodically delete old audit records from this table. The database does not provide an interface to assist in deleting rows from the audit table, so you will need to do so yourself. To purge
audit records older than 90 days, execute the following as user SYS:

```
DELETE FROM sys.aud$ WHERE timestamp# < SYSDATE -90;
```

You might want to copy the audit records into a different table for historical retention or export them to an operating system file before removing them. It is a good practice to audit changes to the AUD$ table so that you can identify when changes were made.

> The audit table does not have a self-managing purge job and will grow without bounds. To keep your SYSTEM tablespace from getting too large, you should regularly delete old entries from the sys.aud$ table.

Managing Fine-Grained Auditing

Fine-grained auditing (FGA) lets you monitor and record data access based on the content of the data. With FGA, you define an audit policy on a table and optionally a column. When the specified condition evaluates to TRUE, an audit record is created, and an optional event-handler program is called. You use the PL/SQL package DBMS_FGA to configure and manage FGA.

In the following sections, you will learn how to create, drop, enable, and disable fine-grained auditing policies.

Creating an FGA Policy

To create a new FGA policy, use the packaged procedure DBMS_FGA.ADD_POLICY. This procedure has the following parameters:

object_schema   This is the owner of the object to be audited. The default is NULL, which tells the database to use the current user.

object_name   This is the name of the object to be monitored.

policy_name   This is a unique name for the new policy.

audit_condition   This is a SQL expression that evaluates to a Boolean. When this condition evaluates to either TRUE or NULL (the default), an audit record can be created. This condition cannot directly use the SYSDATE, UID, USER, or USERENV functions, it cannot use subqueries or sequences, nor can it reference the pseudocolumns LEVEL, PRIOR, or ROWNUM.

audit_column   This is a comma-delimited list of columns that the database will look to access. If a column in audit_column is referenced in the SQL statement and the audit_condition is not FALSE, an audit record is created. Columns appearing in audit_column do not have to also appear in the audit_condition expression. The default value is NULL, which tells the database that any column being referenced should trigger the audit record.

handler_schema   This is the owner of the event-handler procedure. The default is NULL, which tells the database to use the current schema.

handler_module   This is the name of the event-handler procedure. The default NULL tells the database to not use an event handler. If the event handler is a packaged procedure, the handler_module must reference both the package name and program, using dot notation, like this:

```
UTL_MAIL.SEND_ATTACH_RAW
```

enable   This is a Boolean that tells the database if this policy should be in effect. The default is TRUE.

statement_types   This tells the database which types of statements to monitor. Valid values are a comma-delimited list of SELECT, INSERT, UPDATE, and DELETE. The default is SELECT.

audit_trail   This parameter tells the database whether to record the SQL statement and bind variables for the triggering SQL in the audit trail. The default value DBMS_FGA.DB_EXTENDED indicates that the SQL statement and bind variables should be recorded in the audit trail. Set this parameter to DBMS_FGA.DB to save space by not recording the SQL statement or bind variables in the audit trail.

audit_column_ops   This parameter has only two valid values: DBMS_FGA.ALL_COLUMNS and DBMS_FGA.ANY_COLUMNS. When set to DBMS_FGA.ALL_COLUMNS, this parameter tells the database that all columns appearing in the audit_column parameter must be referenced in order to trigger an audit record. The default is DBMS_FGA.ANY_COLUMNS, which tells the database that if any column appearing in the audit_column also appears in the SQL statement, an audit record should be created.

To create a new disabled audit policy named COMPENSATION_AUD that looks for SELECT statements that access the HR.EMPLOYEES table and references either SALARY or COMMISSION_PCT, execute the following:

```
DBMS_FGA.ADD_POLICY(object_schema=>'HR'
   ,object_name=>'EMPLOYEES'
   ,policy_name=>'COMPENSATION_AUD'
   ,audit_column=>'SALARY, COMMISSION_PCT'
   ,enable=>FALSE
   ,statement_types=>'SELECT');
```

Enabling an FGA Policy

Use the procedure DBMS_FGA.ENABLE_POLICY to enable an FGA policy. This procedure will not raise an exception if the policy is already enabled. For example, you can enable the COMPENSATION_AUD policy added in the previous section like this:

```
DBMS_FGA.ENABLE_POLICY(object_schema=>'HR'
   ,object_name=>'EMPLOYEES'
   ,policy_name=>'COMPENSATION_AUD');
```

If you use direct path inserts, be careful with FGA auditing. If an FGA policy is enabled on a table participating in a direct path insert, the auditing overrides the hint, disabling the direct path access and causing conventional inserts. As with all hints, the database does not directly tell you that your hint is being ignored.

Disabling an FGA Policy

To turn off a fine-grained access policy, use the DBMS_FGA.DISABLE_POLICY procedure. Here is an example:

```
DBMS_FGA.DISABLE_POLICY(object_schema=>'HR'
   ,object_name=>'EMPLOYEES'
   ,policy_name=>'COMPENSATION_AUD');
```

Dropping an FGA Policy

To remove an FGA audit policy, use the DBMS_FGA.DROP_POLICY procedure. For example, to drop the COMPENSATION_AUD policy used in this section, run this:

```
DBMS_FGA.DROP_POLICY(object_schema=>'HR'
   ,object_name=>'EMPLOYEES'
   ,policy_name=>'COMPENSATION_AUD');
```

Identifying FGA Policies in the Database

Query the DBA_AUDIT_POLICIES data dictionary view to report on the FGA policies defined in your database. For example, the following report shows that the policy named COMPENSATION_AUD on the column SALARY in the table HR.EMPLOYEES is defined, but not enabled:

```
SELECT policy_name ,object_schema||'.'||
     object_name object_name
     ,policy_column
     ,enabled ,audit_trail
FROM dba_audit_policies;


POLICY_NAME      OBJECT_NAME   POLICY ENABLED AUDIT_TRAIL
---------------- ------------- ------ ------- -----------
COMPENSATION_AUD HR.EMPLOYEES  SALARY NO      DB_EXTENDED
```

Audit records from this policy, when enabled, capture the standard auditing information as well as the text of the SQL statement that triggered the auditing (DB_EXTENDED).

Reporting on the FGA Audit Trail Entries

The DBA_FGA_AUDIT_TRAIL data dictionary view is used in reporting on the FGA audit entries that have been recorded in the database. The following example shows audit trail entries for the COMPENSATION_AUD policy, listing the database username and the timestamp of the audit record and computer from which the database connection was made.

```
SELECT db_user, timestamp, userhost
FROM dba_fga_audit_trail
```

```
WHERE policy_name='COMPENSATION_AUD'

DB_USER      TIMESTAMP            USERHOST
-----------  -------------------- --------------------
CHIPD        10-Jun-2004 09:48:14 XYZcorp\CHIPNOTEBOOK
JUANITA      19-Jun-2004 14:50:47 XYZcorp\HR_PC2
```

Summary

Oracle 10*g* gives you a well-stocked toolkit for managing your users and securing your database. You create and manage user accounts with the CREATE, ALTER, and DROP USER statements. You can assign tablespace resources to be used for sorting that are different than those for tables or indexes. You can limit the disk, CPU, and memory resources that your users consume by employing tablespace quotas and kernel resource limits in user profiles.

To protect your data from unwanted access or manipulation, you can employee object and system privileges. You can create and use roles to make managing these database privileges easier. You can enable object, statement, privilege and fine-grained auditing to help you monitor and record sensitive database activity.

Your Oracle 10*g* database has several powerful features (user accounts and packages) that will need to be locked down in your production systems, and in this chapter you learned which user accounts need to be locked, as well as which standard packages should be locked down to better protect your company's data.

Exam Essentials

Be familiar with the authentication methods. Database accounts can be authenticated by the database (identified by password), by the operating system (identified externally), or by an enterprise security service (identified globally).

Know how to assign default and temporary tablespaces to users. Assign default and temporary tablespaces with either a CREATE USER or an ALTER USER statement.

Be able to identify and grant object, system, and role privileges. Know the difference between these types of privileges and when to use each type.

Know the differences between the *WITH ADMIN OPTION* and the *WITH GRANT OPTION* keywords. The ADMIN option applies to role or system privileges, but the GRANT option applies to object privileges

Know how to enable roles. Know when a role needs to be enabled and how to enable it.

Be able to secure your database. Make sure you know how to lock down you database. Know which packages should be secured and how to secure them.

Know how to implement password security. An Oracle 10*g* database affords you several standard password security settings. Know what is available in a profile and what needs to be implemented in a password-verify function.

Know how to enable, disable and identify enabled auditing options. Be able to describe the types of auditing, how to enable them, and how to report on the audit trail.

Review Questions

1. Which of the following statements creates an Oracle account, but lets the operating system authenticate logons?

   A. `create user ops$admin identified by os;`

   B. `create user ops$admin identified externally;`

   C. `create user ops$admin nopassword;`

   D. `create user ops$admin authenticated by os;`

2. Which of the following types of statements can use a temporary tablespace?

   A. An index creation

   B. SQL statements with a GROUP BY clause

   C. A hash join operation

   D. All of the above

3. Which of the following statements gives user desmond the ability to alter table gl.accounts?

   A. `grant alter on gl.accounts to desmond;`

   B. `grant alter to desmond on gl.accounts;`

   C. `grant alter table to desmond;`

   D. `allow desmond to alter table gl.accounts;`

4. Which of the following statements gives user desmond the ability to alter table gl.accounts as well as give this ability to other accounts?

   A. `grant alter any table with grant option to desmond;`

   B. `grant alter on gl.accounts to desmond with admin option;`

   C. `grant alter any table to desmond with grant option;`

   D. `grant alter any table to desmond with admin option;`

5. The following SQL statement will allow user regina to perform which operations on sequence oe.orders_seq?

   `GRANT ALL ON oe.orders_seq TO regina;`

   A. Select the next value from oe.orders_seq.

   B. Alter sequence oe.orders_seq to change the next value.

   C. Change the number of sequence numbers that will be cached in memory.

   D. Both A and C.

   E. All of the above.

6. User system granted SELECT on sh.products to user ian using WITH GRANT OPTION. Ian then granted SELECT on sh.products to user stuart. Ian has left the company, and his account is dropped. What happens to Stuart's privileges on sh.products?

   A. Stuart loses his SELECT privilege on sh.products.

   B. Stuart retains his SELECT privilege on sh.products.

   C. Stuart loses his SELECT privilege if Ian was dropped with the CASCADE REVOKE option.

   D. Stuart retains his SELECT privilege if Ian was dropped with the NOCASCADE REVOKE option.

7. User system granted SELECT ANY TABLE to user ian using WITH ADMIN OPTION. Ian then granted SELECT ANY TABLE to user stuart. Ian has left the company, and his account is dropped. What happens to Stuart's privileges?

   A. Stuart loses his privileges.

   B. Stuart retains his privileges.

   C. Stuart loses his privileges if Ian was dropped with the CASCADE REVOKE option.

   D. Stuart retains his privileges if Ian was dropped with the NOCASCADE REVOKE option.

8. Which of the following system privileges can allow the grantee to masquerade as another user and therefore should be granted judiciously?

   A. CREATE ANY JOB

   B. ALTER USER

   C. CREATE ANY PROCEDURE

   D. All of the above

9. Which of the following statements enables the role user_admin in the current session?

   A. alter session enable role user_admin;

   B. alter session set role user_admin;

   C. alter role user_admin enable;

   D. set role user_admin;

10. Which of the following SQL statements allows user augustin to use the privileges associated with the password-protected role info_czar, which has been granted to him?

    A. set role all;

    B. alter user augustin default role all;

    C. alter session enable role info_czar;

    D. alter session enable info_czar identified by brozo

11. By default, how much tablespace can any account use for a new table?

    A. None

    B. Up to the current free space in the tablespace

    C. Unlimited space, including autoextends

    D. Up to the default quota established at tablespace creation time

12. Which of the following SQL statements results in a disconnection after a session is idle for 30 minutes?

    A. `alter session set idle_timeout=30;`

    B. `alter session set idle_timeout=1800;`

    C. `alter profile limit idle_time 30;`

    D. `alter profile set idle_timout 30;`

13. Which of the following prevents a user from reusing a password when they change their password?

    A. Setting the initialization parameter NO_PASSWORD_REUSE to TRUE

    B. Altering that user's profile to UNLIMITED for PASSWORD_REUSE_TIME and 1 for PASSWORD_REUSE_MAX

    C. Altering that user's profile to UNLIMITED for both PASSWORD_REUSE_TIME and PASSWORD_REUSE_MAX

    D. Using a password verify function to record the new password and compare the new passwords to those recorded previously

14. How can you prevent someone from using an all-numeric password?

    A. Set the initialization parameter PASSWORD_COMPLEXITY to ALPHANUM.

    B. Alter that user's profile setting PASSWORD_COMPLEXITY to ALPHNANUM.

    C. Alter the user's profile to use a password verify function that performs REGEX comparisons to validate the password.

    D. There is no mechanism that lets you prevent an all-numeric password.

15. Which of the following is not an object privilege on a table?

    A. SELECT

    B. DEBUG

    C. REFERENCES

    D. READ

16. Which of the following statements about user administration and security is the *most* true? Select the best answer.

    A. Password-protected roles require a password before they can become enabled.

    B. You can disable any role that you find in your `session_roles` view.

    C. If you execute `alter profile student limit idle_time 10;` and then execute `alter user scott profile student;`, then user `scott` will be disconnected from future sessions after 10 minutes of idle time.

    D. You can limit a table to a maximum size on disk.

17. Which of the following SQL statements limit attempts to guess passwords by locking an account after three failed logon attempts?

    A. `alter profile default limit failed_login_attempts 3;`

    B. `alter system set max_logon_failures = 3 scope=both;`

    C. `alter user set failed_login_attempts = 3;`

    D. `alter system set failed_login_attempts = 3 scope=both;`

18. Where can the database write `audit_trail` records?

    A. In a database table

    B. In a file outside the database

    C. Both in the database and in an operating system file

    D. Either in the database or in an operating system file

19. Which of the following activities can be audited?

    A. Unsuccessful deletions from the `audit_trail` table

    B. Unsuccessful selects from the `employee_salary` table

    C. All GRANT and REVOKE statements on procedures executed by user system

    D. All of the above

20. How do you manage fine-grained auditing?

    A. With the AUDIT and NOAUDIT statements

    B. With the DBMS_FGA package

    C. With the GRANT and REVOKE statements

    D. With the CREATE, ALTER, and DROP statements

Answers to Review Questions

1. B. Authentication by the operating system is called external authentication, and the Oracle account name must match the operating system account name prefixed with the OS_AUTHENT_ PREFIX string.

2. D. Any operation that requires a large sort or other creation of temporary segments will create, alter, and drop those temporary segments in the TEMPORARY tablespace.

3. A. Altering a table in another user's schema requires either the object privilege ALTER on that object or the system privilege ALTER ANY TABLE. Option A has the correct syntax for granting the object privilege on ALTER gl.accounts to user desmond. Although option C would allow user desmond to alter his own tables, he would need the ALTER ANY TABLE privilege to alter another user's table.

4. D. Either the ALTER ANY TABLE system privilege or the ALTER object privilege is required. To confer the ability to further grant the privilege requires the keywords WITH ADMIN OPTION for system or role privileges or the keywords WITH GRANT OPTION for object privileges. Only option D has both the correct syntax and the correct keywords.

5. D. The ALL option for a sequence includes the SELECT and ALTER privileges. The SELECT privilege lets Regina select the next value from the sequence. The ALTER privilege lets Regina change the cache but not the next value.

6. A. When object privileges are granted through an intermediary, they are implicitly dropped when the intermediary is dropped. There are no CASCADE REVOKE or NOCASCADE REVOKE options.

7. B. When system privileges are granted through an intermediary, they are not affected when the intermediary is dropped. There are no CASCADE REVOKE or NOCASCADE REVOKE options.

8. D. The CREATE ANY JOB and CREATE ANY PROCEDURE system privileges allow the grantee to create and run programs with the privileges of another user. The ALTER USER PRIVILEGE allows the grantee to change a user's password, connect as that user, and then change the password back. These are all powerful system privileges and should be restricted to as few administrative users as practical.

9. D. The SET ROLE statement enables or disables roles in the current session.

10. B. To enable a password-protected role, you need to either execute a SET ROLE statement specifying the password or alter the user to make the role a default role. Default roles do not require a set role statement or a password to become enabled.

11. A. By default, user accounts have no quota in any tablespace. Before a user can create a table or an index, you need to either give the user a quota in one or more specific tablespaces, or grant the UNLIMITED TABLESPACE system privilege to give unlimited quota (including autoextends) in all tablespaces.

12. C. Profiles limit the amount of idle time, CPU time, logical reads, or other resource-oriented session limits. Option C uses the correct syntax to limit idle time for a session to 30 minutes.

13. B. Although option D could also work, it involves storing the passwords in a table in the database, which could be a security concern. It also takes a lot more effort to configure and maintain. The better technique is to use the standard database profile features PASSWORD_RESUSE_TIME and PASSWORD_REUSE_MAX. Setting one of these profile parameters to UNLIMITED and the other to a specific value prevents passwords from being reused. If both of these profile parameters are set to UNLIMITED, these parameters are essentially disabled. There is no initialization parameter called NO_PASSWORD_REUSE.

14. C. There are no standard password complexity settings in either the initialization parameters or profiles. A password verify function can validate new passwords against any rules that you can code in PL/SQL, including regular expression comparisons.

15. D. The object privileges on a table include SELECT, INSERT, UPDATE, DELETE, ALTER, INDEX, REFERENCES, and DEBUG, but not READ. READ is a valid object privilege, but only on a directory—a database object that is outside the scope of the OCA exam.

16. D. This question is tricky. All the options look correct and in fact are mostly true. But option D is the most correct option. Password-protected roles that are included in a user's default role list are enabled by default and do not need a password. Your session_roles view contains both roles granted directly to you and those you inherit through another role. You cannot disable roles that you inherit by way of another role without disabling the role granted directly to you. For example, you cannot disable SCHEDULER_ADMIN without disabling DBA. Limiting a profile to 10 minutes of idle time will cause future sessions to timeout after 10 idle minutes, but only if the initialization parameter RESOURCE_LIMIT is set to TRUE (the default is FALSE). Because each schema owner can be assigned tablespace quotas, you can effectively limit all of a user's segments to a maximum size, thus setting an upper limit on the size of any single table.

17. A. You limit the number of failed logon attempts with a profile.

18. D. The destination of audit_trail records is controlled by the initialization parameter audit_trail. Setting this parameter to DB or DB_EXTENDED causes the audit trail to be written to a database table. Setting the parameter to OS causes the audit trail to be written to an operating system file.

19. D. Audit unsuccessful deletions from the audit table with the following SQL:

AUDIT DELETE ON sys.aud$ WHENEVER NOT SUCCESSFUL;

Audit unsuccessful selects from all tables with the following:

AUDIT NOT EXISTS;

Audit all grant and revoke statements on procedures executed by user SYSTEM with the following:

AUDIT grant procedure BY system;

20. B. Fine-grained auditing is managed using the DBMS_FGA package. The AUDIT and NOAUDT statements are used to manage statement, privilege, or object auditing. The GRANT and REVOKE statements are used to manage system, object, and role privileges. The CREATE, ALTER, and DROP statements are used to manage several types of database objects and settings.

Chapter

7

Managing Data With SQL, PL/SQL, and Utilities

ORACLE DATABASE 10*G*: ADMINISTRATION I EXAM OBJECTIVES COVERED IN THIS CHAPTER:

✓ **Managing Data**

- Manipulate data through SQL using INSERT, UPDATE, and DELETE.
- Use Data Pump to export data.
- Use Data Pump to import data.
- Load Data with SQL Loader.
- Create directory objects.

✓ **PL/SQL**

- Identify PL/SQL objects.
- Describe triggers and triggering events.
- Identify configuration options that affect PL/SQL performance.

Exam objectives are subject to change at any time without prior notice and at Oracle's sole discretion. Please visit Oracle's Training and Certification website (http://www.oracle.com/education/certification/) for the most current exam objectives listing.

Oracle supports manipulating data via several interfaces, but the most common are SQL and PL/SQL. Understanding how to use and manage PL/SQL programs is an important skill for any DBA. Some database functionality is delivered only as PL/SQL programs, such as fine-grained auditing, and some functionality is available in both a command-line version or as PL/SQL programs, such as Data Pump export and Data Pump import. As you gain experience, you will increasingly rely on using PL/SQL to manage your databases. So you need to have a solid grasp of SQL and PL/SQL fundamentals to be a successful Oracle10g DBA.

In this chapter, you will learn how to create, change, and remove information from an Oracle database using SQL and PL/SQL.

Manipulating Data through SQL

The Structured Query Language, SQL for short, includes Data Definition Language (DDL) statements, Data Control Language (DCL) statements, and Data Manipulation Language (DML) statements. You learned how to create, alter, and delete objects using DDL statements in Chapter 3, "Database Storage and Schema Objects." Chapter 6, "User Administration and Security," showed you how to use the DCL statements GRANT and REVOKE to give and take privileges on database objects. In this section, you will learn how to use the DML statements INSERT, UPDATE, and DELETE to add, modify, and remove data from your tables.

After using DML statements to add rows to a table, update rows in a table, or delete rows from a table, you must make these changes permanent by executing a COMMIT command. Alternatively, you can undo the DML changes with a ROLLBACK command. Until you commit the changes, other database sessions will not be able to see your changes.

Using *INSERT* Statements

You use the INSERT statement to add rows to one or more tables. You can create these rows with specific data values or copy them from existing tables using a subquery.

Inserting into a Single Table

When using SQL, the only way to add rows to an Oracle10g table is with an INSERT statement and the most common variety of INSERT statement is the single table insert. Figure 7.1 shows a diagram of the syntax for the single-table INSERT statement.

FIGURE 7.1   The syntax for a single-table *INSERT* statement

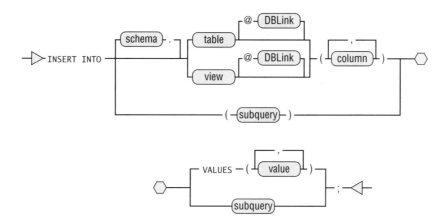

The column list is optional, with the default being a list of all columns in the table in COLUMN_ ID order. See the data dictionary views USER_TAB_COLUMNS, ALL_TAB_COLUMNS, or DBA_TAB_ COLUMNS for the COLUMN_ID. While inserting into a table is more common, you can also insert into a view, as long as the view does not contain one of the following:

- A DISTINCT operator

- A set operator (UNION, MINUS, and so on)

- An aggregate function (SUM, COUNT, AVG, and so on)

- A GROUP BY, ORDER BY, or CONNECT BY clause

- A subquery in the SELECT list

Here are some examples of using the INSERT statement to insert rows into a single table. The following inserts one row, channel 3, in the channels table:

```
INSERT INTO channels (channel_id ,channel_desc
  ,channel_class ,channel_class_id
  ,channel_total ,channel_total_id) VALUES
  (3 ,'Direct Sales' ,'Direct'
  ,12 ,'Channel total' ,1);
```

The following inserts one row, channel 5, in the channels table:

```
INSERT INTO channels VALUES
  (5 ,'Catalog' ,'Indirect' ,13 ,'Channel total' ,1);
```

The following copies zero or more rows from the territories table in the home_office database into the regions table:

```
INSERT INTO regions (region_id ,region_name)
  SELECT region_seq.NEXTVAL , terr_name
```

```
FROM territories@home_office
WHERE class = 'R';
```

The number and datatypes of values in the VALUES list must match the number and datatypes in the column list. The database will perform implicit datatype conversion if necessary to convert the values into the datatype of the target.

Inserting into Multiple Tables

Most INSERT statements are the single-table variety, but Oracle also supports a multiple-table INSERT statement. You most frequently use multitable inserts in data warehouse Extract, Transform, and Load (ETL) routines.

With a multitable insert, you can make a single pass through the source data and load the data into more than one table. By reducing the number of passes through the source data, you can reduce the overall work and thus achieve faster throughput. Figure 7.2 shows a diagram of the multitable INSERT statement syntax.

If a WHEN condition evaluates to TRUE, the corresponding INTO clause is executed. If no WHEN condition evaluates to TRUE, the ELSE clause is executed. The keyword ALL tells the database to check each WHEN condition. On the other hand, the keyword FIRST tells the database to stop checking WHEN conditions after finding the first TRUE condition.

In the following example, an insurance company has policies for both property and casualty in the policy table, but in their data mart, they break out these policy types into separate fact tables. During the monthly load, new policies are added to both the property_premium_fact and casualty_premium_fact tables. You can use a multitable INSERT to add these rows more efficiently than two separate INSERT statements. The multitable INSERT would look like this:

```
INSERT FIRST
WHEN policy_type = 'P' THEN
   INTO property_premium_fact(policy_id
       ,policy_nbr ,premium_amt)
   VALUES (property_premium_seq.nextval
         ,policy_number ,gross_premium)
WHEN p.policy_type = 'C' THEN
   INTO casualty_premium_fact(policy_id
       ,policy_nbr ,premium_amt)
   VALUES (property_premium_seq.nextval
         ,policy_number ,gross_premium)
SELECT policy_nbr ,gross_premium ,policy_type
FROM policies
WHERE policy_date >=
      TRUNC(SYSDATE,'MM') - TO_YMINTERVAL('00-01');
```

By using this multitable INSERT statement instead of two separate statements, the code makes a single pass through the policy table instead of two and thus loads the data more efficiently.

FIGURE 7.2 The syntax for the multitable *INSERT* statement

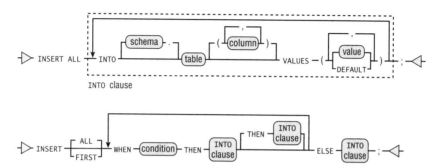

Using *UPDATE* Statements

You use an UPDATE statement to change existing rows in a table. Figure 7.3 shows a diagram of the syntax for the UPDATE statement.

The column list can be either a single column or a comma-delimited list of columns. A single list of columns lets you assign single values—either literals or from a subquery. The following updates customer XYZ's phone and fax numbers, and sets their quantity based on their orders:

```
UPDATE order_rollup r
SET phone = '3125551212'
   ,fax   = '7735551212'
   ,qty   = (SELECT SUM(d.qty)
             FROM order_details d
             WHERE d.customer_id = r.customer_id)
WHERE r.customer_id = 'XYZ';
```

Like the CREATE TABLE and ALTER TABLE statements you saw in Chapter 6, when you use a comma-delimited list of columns, you must enclose them in parentheses. The comma-delimited list lets you assign multiple values from a subquery. The following updates both the quantity and price for customer XYZ for the order they placed on October 1, 2004:

```
UPDATE order_rollup
SET (qty, price) = (SELECT SUM(qty), SUM(price)
                    FROM order_details
                    WHERE customer_id = 'XYZ')
WHERE customer_id = 'XYZ'
 AND   order_period = TO_DATE('01-Oct-2004');
```

FIGURE 7.3 The syntax for the *UPDATE* statement

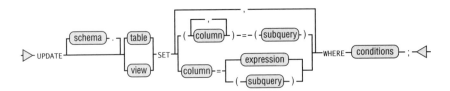

Assigning multiple values from a single subquery can save you from having to perform multiple subqueries, thus improving the efficiency of your SQL.

Using *DELETE* Statements

You use the DELETE statement to remove rows from a table. A diagram of the syntax for the DELETE statement is shown in Figure 7.4.

Here are some examples of a DELETE statement. The following removes orders from certain states:

```
DELETE FROM orders
WHERE state IN ('TX','NY','IL')
 AND  order_date < TRUNC(SYSDATE) - 90
```

The following removes customer GOMEZ:

```
DELETE FROM customers
WHERE customer_id = 'GOMEZ';
```

The following removes duplicate line_detail_ids. Note that the keyword FROM is not needed.

```
DELETE line_details
WHERE rowid NOT IN (SELECT MAX(rowid)
                    FROM line_detail
                    GROUP BY line_detail_id)
```

```
--Remove all rows from the table order_staging
DELETE FROM order_staging;
```

The WHERE clause is optional, and when it is not present, all rows from the table are removed. If you need to remove all rows from a table, consider using the TRUNCATE statement. TRUNCATE is a DDL statement and, unlike the DELETE statement, does not support a ROLLBACK. Using TRUNCATE, unlike using DELETE, does not generate undo and executes much faster for a large table. If you want to empty a table of all rows, use a TRUNCATE statement instead of a DELETE. The TRUNCATE executes faster and may generate significantly less undo.

FIGURE 7.4   The syntax for the *DELETE* statement

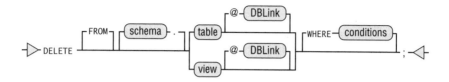

Identifying PL/SQL Objects

PL/SQL is Oracle's Procedural Language extension to SQL. This Oracle proprietary language was derived from Ada and has evolved to include a robust feature set, including sequential and conditional controls, looping constructs, exception handing, records, and collections, as well as object-oriented features such as methods, overloading, upcasting, and type inheritance.

Full knowledge of the PL/SQL language is well beyond the scope of the OCA/OCP exams, and more developers than DBAs create PL/SQL programs. But a significant number of database features are delivered as PL/SQL programs, and knowledge of how to identify and work with these programs is crucial to your effectiveness. In this section, you will learn what kinds of PL/SQL programs are available, when each is appropriate, and what configuration options are applicable to working with PL/SQL programs.

The exam covers five types of named PL/SQL programs, which are usually stored in the database: *functions*, *procedures*, packages, *package bodies*, and *triggers*. Each of these program types is covered in the following sections. The name and source code for each stored PL/SQL program is available from the data dictionary views DBA_SOURCE and DBA_TRIGGERS, although some packages are supplied "wrapped," which means that the source code is a binary form. You can wrap your programs as well with the wrap utility.

See the *PL/SQL Users Guide and Reference* for details on using wrap.

Working with Functions

Functions are PL/SQL programs that execute zero or more statements and return a value through a RETURN statement. Functions can also receive or return zero or more values through their parameters. Oracle provides several built-in functions such as the commonly used SYSDATE, COUNT, and SUBSTR functions. There are over 200 SQL functions that come with your Oracle10g database and hundreds of PL/SQL functions. See the Oracle Database SQL Reference 10g manual (part B10759-01) for a complete list of these SQL functions and the PL/SQL Packages and Types Reference 10g manual (part B10802-01) for the functions available with the built-in PL/SQL packages. Because functions have a return value, a datatype is associated with them. Functions can be invoked anywhere an expression of the same datatype is allowed. Here are some examples:

- As a default value

```
DECLARE
   today  DATE DEFAULT SYSDATE;
```

- In an assignment

```
today := SYSDATE;
```

- In a Boolean expression

```
IF TO_CHAR(SYSDATE,'Day') = 'Monday'
```

- In a SQL expression

```
SELECT COUNT(*)
FROM employees
WHERE hire_date > SYSDATE-30;
```

- In the parameter list of another procedure or function

```
SELECT TRUNC(SYSDATE)
```

Create a function with the CREATE FUNCTION statement, like this:

```
CREATE OR REPLACE FUNCTION is_weekend(
  check_date IN DATE DEFAULT SYSDATE)
  RETURN VARCHAR2 AS
BEGIN
   CASE TO_CHAR(check_date,'DY')
   WHEN 'SAT' THEN
      RETURN 'YES';
   WHEN 'SUN' THEN
      RETURN 'YES';
   ELSE
      RETURN 'NO';
   END CASE;
END;
```

Functions, like all named PL/SQL, have the OR REPLACE keywords available in the CREATE statement. When present, OR REPLACE tells the database to not raise an exception if the object already exists. This behavior differs from a DROP and CREATE, in that privileges are not lost during a REPLACE operation and any objects that reference this object will *not* become invalid.

Working with Procedures

Procedures are PL/SQL programs that execute one or more statements. Procedures can receive and return values only through their parameter lists. Unlike functions, only a few built-in procedures, such as RAISE_APPLICATION_ERROR are built into the PL/SQL language.

You create a procedure with the CREATE PROCEDURE statement, like this:

```
CREATE OR REPLACE PROCEDURE archive_orders
   (cust_id    IN NUMBER
   ,retention IN NUMBER) IS
BEGIN
   DELETE orders
   WHERE customer = cust_id
   AND    order_date < SYSDATE - retention;

   INSERT INTO maint_log
      (action, action_date, who) VALUES
      ('archive orders '||retention||' for '||cust_id
      ,SYSDATE ,USER);
END;
```

The keyword IS, in the third line, is synonymous with the keyword AS, seen in the third line of the last example function in the previous section. Both are syntactically valid for all named SQL.

You invoke a procedure as a stand-alone statement within a PL/SQL program by using the CALL or EXEC commands. Here is an example:

```
EXEC DBMS_OUTPUT.PUT_LINE('Hello world!');
Hello world!

PL/SQL procedure successfully completed.

CALL  DBMS_OUTPUT.PUT_LINE('Hello world!');
Hello world!

Call completed.
```

Working with Packages

A package is a container for functions, procedures, and data structures, such as records, cursors, variables and constants. A package has a publicly visible portion, called the specification (or *spec* for short) and a private portion called the package body. The package spec describes the programs and data structures that can be accessed from other programs. The package body contains the implementation of the procedures and functions. The package spec is identified in the data dictionary as the type PACKAGE, and the package body is identified as the type PACKAGE BODY.

To create a package spec, use the CREATE PACKAGE statement. In the following, the package spec table_util contains one function and one procedure:

```
CREATE OR REPLACE PACKAGE table_util IS
  FUNCTION version RETURN VARCHAR2;
  PROCEDURE truncate (table_name IN VARCHAR2);
END table_util;
```

Privileges on a package are granted at the package-spec level. The EXECUTE privilege on a package allows the grantee to execute any program or use any data structure declared in the *package specification*. You cannot grant the EXECUTE privilege on only some of the programs declared in the spec.

A package body depends on a package spec having the same name. The package body can only be created after the spec. The package body implements the programs that were declared in the package spec and can optionally contain private programs and data accessible only from within the package body.

To create a package body, use the CREATE PACKAGE BODY statement:

```
CREATE OR REPLACE PACKAGE BODY table_util IS
```

Here is an example of a private variable that can be referenced only in the package body:

```
version_string VARCHAR2(8) := '1.0.0';
```

Here is the code for the version function:

```
FUNCTION version RETURN VARCHAR2 IS
  BEGIN
    RETURN version_string;
  END;
```

Here is the code for the truncate procedure:

```
PROCEDURE truncate (table_name IN VARCHAR2) IS
  BEGIN
    IF  UPPER(table_name) = 'ORDER_STAGE'
    OR UPPER(table_name) = 'SALES_ROLLUP'
    THEN
       EXECUTE IMMEDIATE 'truncate table ' ||
          UPPER(table_name);
    ELSE
       RAISE_APPLICATION_ERROR(-20010
```

```
                   ,'Invalid table for truncate: '|| table_name);
      END IF;
   END;
END table_util;
```

The package name following the END statement is optional, but encouraged, as it improves readability.

Working with Triggering Events and Managing Triggers

Triggers are PL/SQL programs that are invoked in response to an event in the database. Three sets of events can be hooked, allowing you to integrate your business logic with the database in an event-driven manner. Triggers can be created on DML events, DDL events, and database events. These three trigger event classes provide developers and you, the DBA, with a robust toolkit with which to design, build, and troubleshoot systems.

We will look at each of these events in more detail in the following sections. We will also discuss how to enable and disable triggers.

DML Event Triggers

DML triggers are invoked, or "fired," when the specified DML events occur. If the keywords FOR EACH ROW are included in the trigger definition, the trigger fires once for each row that is changed. If these keywords are missing, the trigger fires once for each statement that causes the specified change. If the DML event list includes the UPDATE event, the trigger can be further restricted to fire only when updates of specific columns occur.

The following example creates a trigger that fires before any insert and before an update to the hire_date column of the employee table:

```
CREATE OR REPLACE TRIGGER employee_trg
 BEFORE INSERT OR UPDATE OF hire_date
 ON employees FOR EACH ROW
BEGIN
   log_update(USER,SYSTIMESTAMP);
   IF INSERTING THEN -- if fired due to insert
     :NEW.create_user :=  USER;
     :NEW.create_ts   :=  SYSTIMESTAMP;
   ELSEIF UPDATING THEN -- if fired due to update
     IF :OLD.hire_date <> :NEW.hire_date THEN
        RAISE_APPLICATION_ERROR(-20013,
          'update of hire_date not allowed');
     END IF;
   END IF;
END;
```

This trigger will fire once for each row affected, because the keywords FOR EACH ROW are included. When the triggering event is an INSERT, two columns are forced to the specific values returned by USER and SYSTIMESTAMP. DML triggers cannot be created on SYS-owned objects. Table 7.1 shows the DML triggering events.

TABLE 7.1   DML Trigger Events

Event	When It Fires
INSERT	When a row is added to a table or a view.
UPDATE	When an UPDATE statement changes a row in a table or view. Update triggers can also specify an OF clause to limit the scope of changes that fire this type of trigger.
DELETE	When a row is removed from a table or a view.

Multiple triggers on a table fire in the following order:

- Before statement triggers
- Before row triggers
- After row triggers
- After statement triggers

DDL Event Triggers

DDL triggers fire either for DDL changes to a specific schema or to all schemas in the database. The keywords ON DATABASE specify that the trigger will fire for the specified event on any schema in the database.

The following is an example of a trigger that fires for a DDL event in only one schema:

```
CREATE OR REPLACE TRIGGER NoGrantToPublic
BEFORE GRANT ON engineering.SCHEMA
DECLARE
    grantee_list     dbms_standard.ora_name_list_t;
    counter          BINARY_INTEGER;
BEGIN
    -- get the list of grantees
    counter := GRANTEE(grantee_list);
    FOR loop_counter IN
      grantee_list.FIRST..grantee_list.LAST
    LOOP
        -- if PUBLIC is on the grantee list, stop the action
```

```
    IF REGEXP_LIKE(grantee_list(loop_counter)
          ,'public','i') THEN
        RAISE_APPLICATION_ERROR(-20113
            ,'No grant to PUBLIC allowed for '
            ||DICTIONARY_OBJ_OWNER||'.'
            ||DICTIONARY_OBJ_NAME);
    END IF;
  END LOOP;
END;
```

In the preceding example, the DDL event is a GRANT statement issued by user engineering. The code examines the grantee list, and if it finds the special user/role PUBLIC, an exception is raised, causing the grant to fail. Table 7.2 shows the DDL triggering events.

TABLE 7.2   DDL Trigger Events

Event	When It Fires
ALTER	When an ALTER statement changes a database object.
ANALYZE	When the database gathers or deletes statistics or validates the structure of an object.
ASSOCIATE STATISTICS	When the database associates a statistic with a database object with an ASSOCIATE STATISTICS statement.
AUDIT	When the database records an audit action (except FGA).
COMMENT	When a comment on a table or column is modified.
CREATE	When the database object is created.
DDL	In conjunction with any of the following: ALTER, ANALYZE, ASSOCIATE STATISTICS, AUDIT, COMMENT, CREATE, DISASSOCIATE STATISTICS, DROP GRANT, NOAUDIT, RENAME, REVOKE, or TRUNCATE.
DISASSOCIATE STATISTICS	When a database disassociates a statistic type from a database object with a DISASSOCIATE STATISTICS statement.
DROP	When a DROP statement removes an object from the database.
GRANT	When a GRANT statement assigns a privilege.
NOAUDIT	When a NOAUDIT statement changes database auditing.

TABLE 7.2 DDL Trigger Events *(continued)*

Event	When It Fires
RENAME	When a RENAME statement changes an object name.
REVOKE	When a REVOKE statement rescinds a privilege.
TRUNCATE	When a TRUNCATE statement purges a table.

Database Event Triggers

Database event triggers fire when the specified database-level event occurs. Most of these triggers are available only before or after the database event, but not both.

The following example creates an after-server error trigger that sends an e-mail notification when an ORA-01555 error occurs:

```
CREATE OR REPLACE TRIGGER Email_on_1555_Err
AFTER SERVERERROR ON DATABASE
DECLARE
    mail_conn          UTL_SMTP.connection;
    smtp_relay         VARCHAR2(32) := 'mailserver';
    recipient_address  VARCHAR2(64) := 'DBA@hotmail.com';
    sender_address     VARCHAR2(64) := 'oracle@sybex.com';
    mail_port          NUMBER := 25;
    msg                VARCHAR2(200);
BEGIN
    IF USER = 'SYSTEM' THEN
        -- Ignore this error
        NULL;
    ELSIF IS_SERVERERROR (1555) THEN
        -- compose the message
        msg := 'Subject: ORA-1555 error';
        msg := msg||'Snapshot too old err at '||systimestamp;
        -- send email notice
        mail_conn := UTL_SMTP.open_connection(smtp_relay
            ,mail_port);
        UTL_SMTP.HELO(mail_conn, smtp_relay);
        UTL_SMTP.MAIL(mail_conn, sender_address);
        UTL_SMTP.RCPT(mail_conn, recipient_address);
        UTL_SMTP.DATA(mail_conn, msg);
        UTL_SMTP.QUIT(mail_conn);
    END IF;
END;
```

WARNING   Be careful when using database triggers. Fully test them in development before deploying them to production.

Table 7.3 shows the database triggering events.

TABLE 7.3   Database Trigger Events

Event	When It Fires
LOGON	When a database session is established—only AFTER trigger is allowed
LOGOFF	When a database session ends normally—only BEFORE trigger is allowed
STARTUP	When the database is opened—only AFTER trigger is allowed
SHUTDOWN	When the database is closed—only BEFORE trigger is allowed
SERVERERROR	When a database exception is raised—only AFTER trigger is allowed
SUSPEND	When a server error causes a transaction to be suspended

Enabling and Disabling Triggers

The database automatically enables a trigger when you create it. After creating a trigger, you can disable it (temporarily prevent it from firing) or re-enable it. You can disable and enable triggers by name with an ALTER TRIGGER statement. Here are two examples:

```
ALTER TRIGGER after_ora60 DISABLE;

ALTER TRIGGER load_packages ENABLE;
```

Alternatively, you can enable and disable multiple DML triggers with an ALTER TABLE statement, like this:

```
ALTER TABLE employees DISABLE ALL TRIGGERS;
ALTER TABLE employees ENABLE ALL TRIGGERS;
```

You can query the STATUS column of the DBA_TRIGGERS or USER_TRIGGERS view to find out whether a trigger is enabled or disabled.

Using and Administering PL/SQL Programs

Oracle10*g* comes bundled with hundreds of built-in packages that give you significant capabilities for administering your database. Many features in the database are implemented through one or more of these built-in packages. To use the job scheduler, collect and manage optimizer statistics, implement fine-grained auditing, send e-mail from the database, and use Data Pump or Log Miner, you must engage the built-in packages. As you gain experience, you will use these built-in packages more extensively.

To view the names and parameter lists for stored programs (except triggers), use the SQL*Plus DESCRIBE command like this:

```
describe dbms_monitor
-- some output is deleted for brevity


PROCEDURE SESSION_TRACE_DISABLE
Argument Name      Type                 In/Out Default?
---------------    -------------------  ------ --------
SESSION_ID         BINARY_INTEGER       IN     DEFAULT
SERIAL_NUM         BINARY_INTEGER       IN     DEFAULT


PROCEDURE SESSION_TRACE_ENABLE
Argument Name      Type                 In/Out Default?
---------------    -------------------  ------ --------
SESSION_ID         BINARY_INTEGER       IN     DEFAULT
SERIAL_NUM         BINARY_INTEGER       IN     DEFAULT
WAITS              BOOLEAN              IN     DEFAULT
BINDS              BOOLEAN              IN     DEFAULT
```

You can see in this output from DESCRIBE that the packaged procedure DBMS_MONITOR contains several procedures, including SESSION_TRACE_DISABLE and SESSION_TRACE_ENABLE. Furthermore, you can see the names, datatypes, and in/out mode for each parameter (SESSION_ID, SERIAL_NUM, and so on).

An extensive list of Oracle built-in PL/SQL packages is available in the manual *PL/SQL Packages and Types Reference*, a weighty 3,700-page tome. Fortunately, you don't have to know all these programs to sit for the certification exam!

A PL/SQL program is invalidated whenever a dependent object is changed through the ALTER command. The database automatically recompiles the package body the next time it is called, but you can choose to compile invalid PL/SQL programs yourself and thus eliminate a costly recompile during regular system processing. To explicitly compile a named SQL program, use the ALTER ... COMPILE statement, like this:

```
ALTER PROCEDURE archive_orders COMPILE;
ALTER FUNCTION is_weekend COMPILE;
ALTER PACKAGE table_util COMPILE BODY;
```

Other objects, such as views or types, are similarly compiled.

Configuring PL/SQL for Better Performance

There are several great features that PL/SQL gives a developer to fine-tune their code and prepare it for promotion to production. But like many development-oriented features, they may not be appropriate for production or may need to be disabled to support legacy code. The database initialization parameters that affect PL/SQL performance include:

- PLSQL_WARNING
- PLSQL_DEBUG
- PLSQL_OPTIMIZE_MODE
- PLSQL_CODE_TYPE

> For advanced tuning of PL/SQL programs, see the white paper "PL/SQL Just Got Faster" by Bryn Llewellyn and Charles Wetherell. It is located on the Oracle Technet website. At the time of publication, the URL was www.oracle.com/technology/tech/pl_sql/htdocs/New_In_10gR1.htm.

PL/SQL compiler warnings are new to Oracle10*g*. These optional compile-time warnings can help developers create better programs by identifying potential problems that might result in runtime errors or poor performance. In general, disable compile-time warnings in production. To ensure these warnings are disabled, execute the following:

```
ALTER SYSTEM SET plsql_warnings='DISABLE:ALL' SCOPE=BOTH;
```

The PLSQL_DEBUG parameter forces all subsequent PL/SQL compilations to be interpreted and include additional debugging information. Again, although this feature can be beneficial in development, disable it in production. To ensure that it is disabled, execute the following:

```
ALTER SYSTEM SET plsql_debug=FALSE SCOPE=BOTH;
```

Oracle10*g* introduced an optimizing compiler that significantly improves PL/SQL performance of computing-intensive programs. Unless testing has shown this optimization to be detrimental to your programs, enable it fully in both production and development. To fully enable this feature, execute this:

```
ALTER SYSTEM SET plsql_optimize_mode=2 SCOPE=BOTH;
```

The parameter PLSQL_CODE_TYPE specifies whether to compile the PL/SQL code into the default-interpreted byte code or native machine code. The native machine code provides faster runtime performance at a cost of longer compilation times and slightly greater administrative overhead. To enable native compilation, you need the C compiler supplied by your platform vendor. Set PLSQL_NATIVE_LIBRARY_DIR and make sure the directory exists. Finally, set your PLSQL_CODE_TYPE to 'NATIVE' and CREATE OR REPLACE your programs.

Creating Directory Objects

Directory objects are named directory locations on the database server. Directories are used with several database features, including BFILEs, external tables, utl_file, and Data Pump. Of these, only Data Pump is germane to the certification exam.

Under Unix, you create directories with the CREATE DIRECTORY statement, like this:

```
CREATE DIRECTORY dump_dir AS '/oracle/data_pump/dumps';
CREATE DIRECTORY log_dir  AS '/oracle/data_pump/logs';
```

Under Windows, you create directories like this:

```
CREATE DIRECTORY dpump_dir  AS 'G:\datadumps';
```

Directories are not schema objects, like tables or synonyms, as they are not owned by a schema. Instead, directories are like profiles or roles in that they are owned by the database. To control access to a directory, you need to grant the READ or WRITE object privilege on that directory, like this:

```
GRANT read,write ON DIRECTORY dump_dir TO PUBLIC;
```

To create directories, you must have the CREATE ANY DIRECTORY system privilege. By default, only users SYSTEM and SYS have this privilege. Be careful in granting this system privilege to users, because the database employs the operating system credentials of the database instance owner.

Data Pump Overview

The Data Pump facility is new to Oracle10*g*. It is a high-speed mechanism for transferring data or metadata from one database to another or to and from operating system files. Data Pump employs direct-path unloading and direct-path loading technologies. Unlike the older export and import programs (exp and imp), which operated on the client side of a database session, the Data Pump facility runs on the server. Thus, you must use a database directory to specify dump file and log file locations.

You can use Data Pump to copy data from one schema to another between two databases or within a single database. You can also use it to extract a logical copy of the entire database, a list of schemas, a list of tables, or a list of tablespaces to portable operating system files. Data Pump can be used to transfer or extract the metadata (DDL statements) for a database, schema, or table.

Data Pump is called from the command-line programs expdp and impdp or through the *DBMS_DATAPUMP* PL/SQL package.

Using Data Pump to Export Data

You initiate a Data Pump export by running the **expdp** program or by running a PL/SQL program that calls DBMS_DATAPUMP procedures. The EM Database Control also provides a graphical user interface for running Data Pump exports.

In this section, you will learn how to export data using both the command-line program **expdp** and the DBMS_DATAPUMP procedures. You will also be introduced to some of the EM Database Control screens for exporting data with Data Pump.

    The EXP_FULL_DATABASE role is required to export data from a schema different than yours.

Executing Data Pump Exports from the Command Line

The Data Pump export program can operate in several modes, including database, schema, table, and tablespace. In a database mode export, the entire database is exported to operating system files, including user accounts, public synonyms, roles, and profiles. In a schema mode export, all data and metadata for a list of schemas is exported. At the most granular level is the table mode export, which includes the data and metadata for a list of tables. A tablespace mode export extracts both data and metadata for all objects in a tablespace list as well as any object dependent on those in the specified tablespace list. Therefore, if a table resides in your specified tablespace list, all its indexes are included whether or not they also reside in the specified tablespace list. In each of these modes, you can further specify that only data or only metadata be exported. The default is to export both data and metadata.

With some objects, such as indexes, only the metadata is exported; the actual internal structures contain physical addresses and are always rebuilt on import.

The files created by a Data Pump export are called dump files, and one or more of these files can be created during a single Data Pump export job. Multiple files are created if your Data Pump job has a parallel degree greater than one or if a single dump file exceeds the **filesize** parameter. All the export dump files from a single Data Pump export job are called a dump file set.

In the following sections, we will discuss how to execute the different modes of Data Pump exports.

Running Database Mode Exports

A full database export requires the database user to have the EXP_FULL_DATABASE role. For example, to perform a full database export to files in the chap7a and chap7b directories, execute the following:

```
expdp system/secret full=Y dumpfile=chap7a:fulla%U.dmp, chap7b:fullb%U.dmp
    filesize 2G parallel=2 logfile=chap7:full.log
```

These parameters tell the Data Pump program to connect to the database as user SYSTEM with a password of SECRET. The **full=y** parameter tells Data Pump to perform a database mode export. Data Pump writes a series of dump files alternating between the chap7a and chap7b directories. (These are database directory objects.) The %U in the filename tells Data Pump to insert a sequential number (00, 01, 02, 03, and so on, up to 99) into each filename. Each file is filled to 2GB in size. Data Pump spawns up to two slave processes to parallelize the load. Finally, the log file is placed in the chap7 directory (also a database directory object) and has the filename full.log.

Running Schema Mode Exports

To perform a schema mode export, omit the full=y parameter and instead include a schemas=*schema_list* parameter. The schema list is a comma-delimited list of schemas. Alternatively, to export your own schema, omit both the full= and the schema= parameters. Data Pump defaults to a schema mode export of your schema. To export another user's schema, you must have the EXP_FULL_DATABASE role.

For example, to Data Pump export the HR schema, run this:

```
expdp hr/hr dumpfile=chap7:hr.dmp logfile=chap7:hr.out
```

The dumpfile and logfile parameters work the same in all export modes—the database directory object is followed by a colon and then the filename. If your operating system is case sensitive, these names will be case sensitive as well.

Running Table Mode Exports

To perform a table mode export, include a tables=*table_list* parameter and omit any full or schema parameters. The *table_list* is a comma-delimited list of tables to export. These tables may be qualified with the owner using dot notation, such as HR.EMPLOYEES.

For example, to export the metadata only for the HR-owned jobs and job_history tables, run this:

```
expdp hr/hr dumpfile=chap7:job_tabs.dmp nologfile=y
    content=metadata_only tables=jobs,job_history
```

While the log is always displayed, the parameter nologfile=y tells Data Pump not to write a log file to disk. The content=metadata_only parameter tells Data Pump to export only the metadata, not the data in the tables. To specify data only (no metadata), replace the metadata_only value with data_only.

Running Tablespace Mode Exports

A tablespace mode export requires that the database user have the EXP_FULL_DATABASE role. To export in tablespace mode, use the tablespaces=*tablespace_list* parameter to specify the tablespaces to be exported. The tablespace list is a comma-delimited list of tablespaces.

For example, to export all the objects, including their dependent objects, from the tablespace USERS, run this:

```
expdp system/password dumpfile=chap7:users_ts.dmp
    logfile=chap7:users_ts.out tablespaces=users
```

You can ask **expdp** for a full list of the supported parameters by specifying the parameter **help=y**. If your command line starts getting long, place some or all of the parameters in a file, and then direct **expdp** to read the file for additional parameters. Use **parfile=***directory:filename* to tell **expdp** where to find the additional parameters. The *directory* parameter is a database directory object, and *filename* is the name of the parameter file.

TABLE 7.4   Data Pump Export Parameters

Parameter	Description
full=y	Specifies a database mode export.
schemas=schema_list	Specifies a schema mode export where *schema_list* is a comma-delimited list of schemas to export.
tables=table_list	Specifies a table mode export where *table_list* is a comma-delimited list of tables to export.
tablesspaces=tablespace_list	Specifies a tablespace mode export where *tablespace_list* is a comma-delimited list of tablespaces to export.
content=content_option	Specifies whether data, metadata, or both are exported. Valid values are: DATA_ONLY (data only), METADATA_ONLY (metadata only), or the default ALL (both).
network_link=db_link	Specifies that a remote database accessed via the database link *db_link* should be used as the export source.
dumpfile=dir:file	Specifies the dump file location and name. *dir* is a database directory object. *file* is the filename. If the filename includes a %U substitution variable, the database will substitute a two-digit file sequence number starting with 00.
filesize=size_limit	Specifies the maximum size of each dump file. Can be specified in bytes, kilobytes, megabytes, or gigabytes. The default is bytes.
logfile=dir:file	Specifies the log file location and name. *dir* is a database directory object and *file* is the filename.
directory=dir	Specifies the file location to use for both the dump file and log file. *dir* is a database directory object.
nologfile=y	Specifies that no log file should be written.
job_name=identifier	Specifies a name for the import job. This name is visible from data dictionary views. The default is system generated.

TABLE 7.4 Data Pump Export Parameters *(continued)*

Parameter	Description
parallel=*degree*	Specifies the maximum number of active threads/processes operating on behalf of the import. The default is 1.
parfile= *dir:file*	Specifies the file location and name of the parameter file that Data Pump import should use. *dir* is a database directory object. *file* is the filename.

Executing Data Pump Exports Using *DBMS_DATAPUMP*

The DBMS_DATAPUMP PL/SQL package provides a programmatic interface to Data Pump. This mechanism is ideal for scheduling export jobs from the database scheduler. Setting up a Data Pump export using the DBMS_DATAPUMP PL/SQL package is a little more verbose than the stand-alone program, but provides greater functionality and control.

The most important options are covered in this chapter, but see the section "DBMS_DATAPUMP" in the *PL/SQL Packages and Types Reference* manual for full details on all the options.

The basic flow of a PL/SQL-initiated Data Pump session is the following:

- Obtain a handle to a Data Pump session.
- Define the dump and log files.
- Define any filtering conditions, such as a list of schemas or tables to include or exclude.
- Launch the Data Pump session.
- Disconnect from the session.

The following example exports a schema mode of the user HR:

```
DECLARE
   h1   NUMBER;  -- handle for the Data Pump session
BEGIN
   -- Obtain a handle to an export Data Pump session
   h1 := dbms_datapump.open (
            operation => 'EXPORT'    -- export not import
           ,job_mode => 'SCHEMA');  -- schema mode
--         ,job_mode => 'FULL');    -- database mode
--         ,job_mode => 'TABLE');   -- table mode
```

```
--            ,job_mode => 'TABLESPACE'); -- tablespace mode

    -- define the log file
    dbms_datapump.add_file(
        handle => h1          -- from the OPEN call
        ,filename => 'hr.out' -- file name
        ,directory => 'CHAP7' -- database directory object
        ,filetype =>dbms_datapump.ku$_file_type_log_file);

    -- define the dump file
    dbms_datapump.add_file(
        handle => h1          -- from the OPEN call
        ,filename => 'hr.dmp' -- file name
        ,directory => 'CHAP7' -- database directory object
        ,filetype => dbms_datapump.ku$_file_type_dump_file);

    -- define the schemas to export
    dbms_datapump.metadata_filter(
        handle => h1                -- from the OPEN call
        ,name => 'SCHEMA_EXPR'     -- schema name filter
--      ,name => 'INCLUDE_NAME_EXPR' -- table name filter
--      ,name => 'EXCLUDE_NAME_EXPR' -- table name filter
--      ,name => 'TABLESPACE_EXPR' -- tablespace name filter
        ,value => 'IN(''HR'')'); -- name list

    -- invoke Data Pump
    dbms_datapump.start_job(
        handle => h1);       -- from the OPEN call

    -- run the job in the background
    dbms_datapump.detach(handle => h1);
END;
```

The code in this PL/SQL example exports a schema. If you want to run an export in a different mode, change the comments on the JOB_MODE parameter in the OPEN procedure. Use 'FULL' for a database mode export, 'TABLE' for a table mode export, or 'TABLESPACE' for a tablespace mode export. A full database export does not require the METADATA_FILTER procedure call. When you execute this PL/SQL block, the job scheduler initiates the Data Pump job. You can monitor it through the data dictionary views DBA_DATAPUMP_JOBS or USER_ DATAPUMP_JOBS or by examining the log file.

Executing Data Pump Exports with Enterprise Manager Database Control

You can use the Enterprise Manager (EM) Database Control as a menu-driven interface to Data Pump export jobs. This program steps you through several options and then shows you the PL/SQL code that it will execute. Therefore, you can also use the EM Database Control to learn more about using the PL/SQL interface.

Open Database Control by pointing your browser to the appropriate URL, and then follow these steps:

1. On the Maintenance tab of the EM Database Control main menu, click the Export To Files link, as shown in Figure 7.5.

FIGURE 7.5   The EM Database Control main menu

2. Select an export type, as shown in Figure 7.6, and click Continue.

FIGURE 7.6   Selecting an export type

3. After stepping through several menu-driven pages, you can review the export job settings as well as the PL/SQL code that will initiate the job, as shown in Figure 7.7.

When you submit the job, it is scheduled to run from the job scheduler, so you won't see the results immediately.

FIGURE 7.7   The Data Pump Export: Review screen

Using Data Pump to Import Data

Import is the counterpart to export. Export extracts data and metadata from your database, and import loads this extracted data into the same database or into a different database, optionally transforming metadata along the way. These transformations let you, for example, copy tables from one schema to another or remap a tablespace from one database to another.

Data Pump imports, like exports, can be initiated from a standalone program, from a PL/SQL program using DBMS_DATAPUMP, or from the EM Database Control. In this section, you will learn how to use these Data Pump interfaces to import data or metadata into your database.

Executing Data Pump Imports from the Command Line

The Data Pump import program, impdp, has several modes of operation, including full, schema, table, and tablespace. In the full mode, the entire content of an export file set is loaded. In a schema mode import, all content for a list of schemas in the specified file set is loaded. The specified file set for a schema mode import can be from either a database or a schema mode export. With a table mode import, only the specified table and dependent objects are loaded from the export file set. With a tablespace mode import, all objects in the export file set that were in the specified tablespace list are loaded.

With all these modes, the source can be a live database instead of a set of export files. Table 7.5 shows the supported mapping of export mode to import mode.

TABLE 7.5 Export to Import Modes

Source Export Mode	Import Mode
Database Schema Table Tablespace Live database	Full
Database Schema Live database	Schema
Database Schema Table Tablespace Live database	Table
Database Schema Table Tablespace Live database	Tablespace

The IMP_FULL_DATABASE role is required if the source is a live database or the export session required the EXP_FULL_DATABASE role. Several parameters control the behavior of the Data Pump import program. These parameters are listed in Table 7.6.

TABLE 7.6 Data Pump Import Parameters

Import Parameter	Description
Full=y	Specifies a full mode import.
Schemas=*schema_list*	Specifies a schema mode import. *schema_list* is a comma-delimited list of schemas to import.
Tables=*table_list*	Specifies a table mode import. *table_list* is a comma-delimited list of tables to import.

TABLE 7.6   Data Pump Import Parameters *(continued)*

Import Parameter	Description
tablesspaces=*tablespace_list*	Specifies a tablespace mode import. *tablespace_list* is a comma-delimited list of tablespaces to import.
content=*content_option*	Specifies whether data, metadata, or both are imported. Valid values are: DATA_ONLY (data only), METADATA_ONLY (metadata only), and the default ALL (both).
network_link=*db_link*	Specifies the live database accessed via the database link. *db_link* should be used as the import source.
dumpfile=*dir:file*	Specifies the dump file location and name. *dir* is a database directory object. *file* is the filename.
logfile=*dir:file*	Specifies the log file location and name. *dir* is a database directory object. *file* is the filename.
directory=*dir*	Specifies the file location to use for both the dump file and log file. *dir* is a database directory object.
nologfile=y	Specifies that no log file should be written.
sqlfile=*dir:file*	Specifies the file location and name to write the metadata/DDL statements to. *dir* is a database directory object. *file* is the filename.
job_name=*identifier*	Specifies a name for the import job. This name is visible from data dictionary views. The default is system generated.
parallel=*degree*	Specifies the maximum number of active threads/processes operating on behalf of the import. The default is 1.
parfile=*dir:file*	Specifies the file location and name of the parameter file that Data Pump Import should use. *dir* is a database directory object. *file* is the filename.
reuse_datafiles=*option*	Specifies whether datafiles should be overwritten in CREATE TABLESPACE statements. Valid values for *option* are: Y, which means overwrite existing files, and N, which means do not overwrite existing files.
remap_datafile=*source:target*	Specifies how to change the source and target datafile names that appear in CREATE TABLESPACE, CREATE LIBRARY and CREATE DIRECTORY statements. *source* is the datafile name from the export or live database. *target* is the datafile name to use in the import.

TABLE 7.6 Data Pump Import Parameters *(continued)*

Import Parameter	Description
remap_schema=*source*:*target*	Specifies the source and target schema names when importing into a different schema than the export was taken from. Multiple remap_schema entries can be used. *source* is the schema from the export or live database. *target* is the schema to import into.
remap_tablespace=*source*:*target*	Specifies the source and target tablespace names when they change between the source export files / live database and database. Multiple remap_tablespace entries can be used. *source* is the tablespace name from the export or live database. *target* is the tablespace name that the source objects should be placed in.
include=*object_list*	Specifies a comma-delimited list of object types to include in the import. See the examples following this table for more information.
exclude=*object_list*	Specifies a comma-delimited list of object types to exclude from the import. See the examples following this table for more information.

You must include one parameter to specify the mode, either full, schemas, tables, or tablespaces. You can include several other parameters on the command line or place them in a file and use the parfile= parameter to instruct impdp where to find them. Here are some examples of imports:

- Read the dump file FULL.DMP and extract all DDL, placing it in the file FULL.SQL. Do not write a log file.

  ```
  impdp system/password full=y dumpfile=chap7:FULL.DMP
      nologfile=y sqlfile=chap7:FULL.SQL
  ```

- Read the data accessed via database link PROD and import schema HR into schema HR_TEST, importing only metadata, writing the log file to the database directory chap7, and naming this log file HR_TEST.imp.

  ```
  impdp system/password network_link=prod schemas="HR"
      remap_schema="HR:HR_TEST" content=metadata_only
      logfile=chap7:HR_TEST.imp
  ```

- Read the dump file HR.DMP and write to the SQL file HR_proc_give.sql all the DDL to create any procedures with a name LIKE 'GIVE%'. Do not write a log file.

  ```
  impdp system/password full=y dumpfile=chap7:HR.DMP
      nologfile=y sqlfile=chap7:HR_proc_give.SQL
      include=PROCEDURE:"LIKE 'GIVE%'"
  ```

- Read the data accessed via database link PROD and import only the data from HR.DEPARTMENTS into schema HR_TEST.DEPARTMENTS. Write a log file to file DEPT_DATA.log.

```
impdp system/password network_link=prod schemas="HR"
   remap_schema="HR:HR_TEST" content=data_only
   include=TABLE:"= 'DEPARTMENTS'"
   logfile=chap7:HR_TEST.imp
```

The combinations of parameters that you can use in copying data and metadata allow you, the DBA, flexibility in administering your databases.

Executing Data Pump Imports Using *DBMS_DATAPUMP*

The DBMS_DATAPUMP PL/SQL package supports import operations as well as export operations. As with the export functionality, this PL/SQL technique is more verbose and easily integrated into database-scheduled jobs. All the functionality available in the standalone program impdp is also available with the PL/SQL package. This section shows you the important options and coding syntax that you will need for the exam.

NOTE   To obtain full documentation, see the *PL/SQL Packages and Types Reference* manual.

The following example shows how to use the PL/SQL package to read the data accessed via database link PROD and import schema HR into schema HR_TEST, importing only metadata, writing the log file to the database directory chap7, and naming this log file HR_TEST.imp:

```
DECLARE
  h1    NUMBER;   -- handle for the Data Pump session
BEGIN
  -- Obtain a handle to an import Data Pump session
  h1 := dbms_datapump.open (
          operation => 'IMPORT'   -- import not export
          ,job_mode => 'SCHEMA'    -- schema mode
          ,remote_link=>'PROD');     -- db_link name

  -- define the schemas to import
  dbms_datapump.metadata_filter(
     handle => h1             -- from the OPEN call
     ,name => 'SCHEMA_EXPR'    -- schema name filter
     ,value => 'IN(''HR'')'); -- name list

  -- define the schema remapping
  dbms_datapump.metadata_remap(
     handle => h1             -- from the OPEN call
     ,name => 'REMAP_SCHEMA'   -- change schema referencess
```

```
--    ,name => 'REMAP_TABLESPACE' -- change tablespace refs
--    ,name => 'REMAP_DATAFILE'   -- change datafiel refs
      ,old_value => 'HR'          -- source value
      ,value => 'HR_TEST');       -- target value

   -- Do not import data (only metadata)
   dbms_datapump.data_filter(
      handle => h1            -- from the OPEN call
      ,name => 'INCLUDE_ROWS' -- data filter name
      ,value => 0);           -- do not include data

   -- define the log file
   dbms_datapump.add_file(
      handle => h1            -- from the OPEN call
      ,filename => 'HR_TEST.imp' -- file name
      ,directory => 'CHAP7' -- database directory object
      ,filetype =>dbms_datapump.ku$_file_type_log_file);

   -- invoke Data Pump
   dbms_datapump.start_job(
      handle => h1);          -- from the OPEN call

   -- run the job in the background
   dbms_datapump.detach(handle => h1);
END;
```

The Data Pump import via PL/SQL gives you the most options to execute Data Pump imports, but as you can see in the previous example, it is also the most programmatic and requires you to be very familiar with the constructs used by Data Pump. To help familiarize yourself with these constructs, you can use the GUI interface provided by the EM Database Control, which is discussed in the next section.

Executing Data Pump Imports with EM Database Control

One of the simplest ways to get experience with Data Pump is to use EM Database Control to step through setting up an import job. The EM program helps you define the necessary parameters for a Data Pump session, shows you the PL/SQL program that will be executed, and gives you the option of initiating the import job immediately or running it later at a specific time.

To execute a Data Pump import job from the EM Database Control, follow these steps:

1. On the EM Database Control main menu, click the Maintenance tab, and then either click Import From Files to import from a previously created export dump file set or click Import From Database to import from a live database.

2. Enter the dumpfile name and location if you are importing from an export file set (displayed as Import From Files), or enter the db_link name if you are importing from a live database. You will also need to select which mode of import you want to run: full, schema, or table. The full option is displayed as Entire Files in the EM Database Control.

3. The EM Database Control prompts you to specify any remapping—schema, tablespace, or datafile. See Figure 7.8 for the remapping options. Remapping a schema allows you to change the schema owner between the source and target databases; for example, you can copy all of the objects owned by user HR in the source to user HR_TEST in the target. Likewise, you can remap a tablespace or datafile, so that all objects in the source tablespace/datafile remap to a different target tablespace/datafile.

FIGURE 7.8   Defining the import remapping options

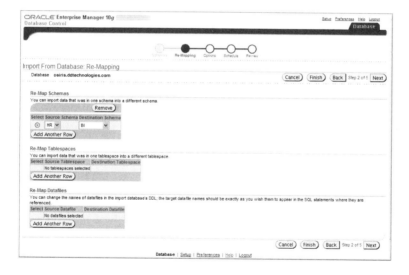

4. The EM Database Control now prompts you to specify any additional options. To see the full range, click the Show Advanced Options link. You can choose the content (data, metadata, or both) as well as any filtering conditions you choose to specify. Figure 7.9 shows the import options.

FIGURE 7.9 Defining the import remapping options

5. Name the job and schedule its start time—immediately or at a future time. The PL/SQL program and your selected options will be presented for review before you initiate the job.

Monitoring the Progress of a Data Pump Job

You can monitor the progress of all Data Pump jobs in the database by querying the DBA_DATAPUMP_JOBS data dictionary view. The following example shows how to query this dictionary view:

```
SELECT owner_name owner, job_name ,operation
     ,job_mode,state
FROM dba_datapump_jobs;


OWNER   JOB_NAME           OPERATION  JOB_MODE STATE
------  ----------------   ---------- -------- -----------
SYSTEM  full_meta          EXPORT     FULL     EXECUTING
SYSTEM  ESTIMATE000026     EXPORT     SCHEMA   NOT RUNNING
```

Once the Data Pump job completes, it will be deleted from this view.

Loading Data with SQL*Loader

*SQL*Loader* is a program that reads data files in many possible formats, parses the data (breaks it into meaningful pieces), and loads the data into database tables. Like Data Pump, myriad options and a hefty book could be devoted to its use. The Oracle Database Utilities manual (part B10825-01) devotes 275 pages of reference material to SQL*Loader alone. This section will not be so comprehensive or attempt to cram all possible uses of SQL*Loader into a few short pages. Instead we will cover the basics and teach you what we feel is necessary for the exam.

SQL*Loader uses the following file types:

Log   A mandatory file. If you do not specify a log file, SQL*Loader will try to create one in the current directory with the name of your control file and a .log filename extension. If SQL*Loader cannot create the log file, execution is aborted. The log file contains a summary of the SQL*Loader session, including any errors that were generated.

Control   A mandatory file. This file tells SQL*Loader where the other files are, how to parse and load the data, and which tables to load the data into and can contain the data as well.

Data   Data files are optional and, if included, hold the data that SQL*Loader reads and loads into the database. The data can be located in the control file, so these files are optional.

Bad   Hold the "bad" data records—those that did not pass validation by either SQL*Loader or the database. Bad files are created only if one or more records fail validation. Just as with the log file, if you do not specify a bad file, the database will create one with the name of your control file and a .bad filename extension.

Discard   Hold data records that did not get loaded because they did not satisfy the record selection criteria in the control file. Discard files are created only if data records were discarded because they did not satisfy the selection criteria.

SQL*Loader provides a robust toolkit to build data-loading programs for your Oracle10g database. It can operate either on the database server or on a client machine.

The following section will show you how to employ SQL*Loader to load data into your database tables.

Specifying SQL*Loader Command-Line Parameters

To invoke the SQL*Loader program, use the command sqlldr followed by one or more command-line parameters. These parameters can be identified positionally on the command line or with a *keyword=value* pair. You can mix positional and keyword notation provided that all the keyword notation parameters appear after all the positional parameters.

For example, to invoke SQL*Loader, telling it to use the connect string system/password and use the control file regions.ctl, you can execute any of the following command lines:

```
sqlldr system/password regions.ctl
sqlldr control=regions.ctl userid=system/password
sqlldr system/password control=regions.ctl
```

The command-line parameters include those in Table 7.7, which are shown in positional notation order (through bindsize), and can be seen by executing the sqlldr command with no parameters.

TABLE 7.7   SQL*Loader Command-Line Parameters

Parameter	Description
userid	The database connect string, for example, scott/tiger@prod).
control	The name of the control file.
log	The name of the log file. The default is the control filename with a .log extension.
bad	The name of the bad file. The default is the datafile name, but with a .bad extension.
data	The name of the datafile. The default is the control filename with a .dat extension.
discard	The name of the discard file. The default is the datafile name, but with a .dsc extension.
discardmax	The maximum number of discards to allow before failing. The default is all.
skip	The number of records to skip before starting to load. The default is none.
load	The number of records to load. The default is all.
errors	The number of errors to allow before failing. The default is 50.
rows	The number of rows in a conventional path bind array or between direct path data saves. The default is 64 rows in conventional path mode and all rows in direct path mode.
bindsize	The size of the conventional path bind array in bytes. The default is 256KB.
direct	If TRUE, use direct path. The default is FALSE, indicating conventional path.
parfile	The name of a file containing additional command-line parameters. There is no default.

Many of the command-line parameters can also appear in the control file. When they appear as both command-line parameters and in the control file, the command-line options take precedence.

Specifying Control File Options

The control file contains commands to tell SQL*Loader where to find the data, how to parse it, how to load it, what to do when errors occur, and what to do with records that fail validation.

A control file has two or three main sections. The first contains session-wide-oriented information, such as log filename, bind size, and whether direct or conventional path loading will be used. The second section contains one or more INTO TABLE blocks. These blocks specify the target tables and columns. The third section, if present, is the actual data. Comments can appear anywhere in the control files (except in the data lines) and should be used liberally. The control file language can be somewhat cryptic, so generous use of comments is encouraged. Comments in a control file start with a double dash and end with a new line. The control file must begin with the line LOAD DATA or CONTINUE LOAD DATA and also have an INTO TABLE clause, together with directions on how to parse the data and load it into which columns.

The best way to learn how to construct a control file is to look at examples and then use variations of them to build your control file. This section gives you several examples, but is certainly not a comprehensive sampling. Again, the intent is to present you with enough information to get you going.

For a comprehensive reference, see the Oracle manual *Oracle Database Utilities 10g*.

The first example is rather simple and straightforward. The control file contains both control file commands and the data. The command line is:

```
sqlldr hr/hr control=regions.ctl
```

The control file `regions.ctl` contains the following:

```
LOAD DATA
-- Control file begins with LOAD DATA
INFILE *
-- The * tells SQL*Loader the data is inline
INTO TABLE regions TRUNCATE
-- truncate the target table before loading
FIELDS TERMINATED BY ',' OPTIONALLY ENCLOSED BY '"'
-- how to parse the data
 (region_id, region_name)
-- positional mapping of data file fields to table columns
-- lines following BEGINDATA are loaded
-- no comments are allowed after BEGINDATA
BEGINDATA
1,"Europe"
2,"Americas"
3,"Asia"
4,"Middle East and Africa"
```

The LOAD DATA command tells SQL*Loader that you are beginning a new data load. If you are continuing a data load that was interrupted, specify CONTINUE LOAD DATA. The command

INFILE * tells SQL*Loader that the data will appear in the control file. The table REGIONS is loaded. The keyword TRUNCATE tells SQL*Loader to truncate the table before loading it. Instead of TRUNCATE, you can specify INSERT (the default), which requires the table to be empty at the start of the load. APPEND tells SQL*Loader to add the data to any existing data in the table. REPLACE tells SQL*Loader to issue a DELETE to empty out the table before loading. DELETE differs from a TRUNCATE in that delete DML triggers fire, and DELETE can be rolled back.

The lines in the control file that follow BEGINDATA contain the data to parse and load. The parsing specification tells SQL*Loader that the data fields are comma-delimited and that text data can be enclosed by double quotation marks. These double quotation marks should not be loaded as part of the data. The list of columns enclosed in parentheses are the table columns that will be loaded with the data fields.

In the second example, the same data is loaded into the same table, but it is located in a stand-alone file called regions.dat and is in the following pipe-delimited, fixed format:

```
1|Europe                 |
2|Americas                |
3|Asia                    |
4|Middle East and Africa |
```

The command line is:

```
sqlldr hr/hr control=regions.ctl
```

The content of the control file is:

```
LOAD DATA
INFILE '/apps/seed_data/regions.dat'
BADFILE '/apps/seed_data/regions.bad'
DISCARDFILE '/apps/seed_data/regions.dsc'
OPTIONS (DIRECT=TRUE)
-- data file spec
INTO TABLE regions APPEND
-- add this data to the existing target table
(region_id   POSITION(1)    INTEGER EXTERNAL
,region_name POSITION(3:25) NULLIF region_name = BLANKS
) -- how to parse the data
```

The control file tells SQL*Loader where to find the data file (INFILE) as well as the bad and discard files (BADFILE and DISCARDFILE). The OPTIONS line specifies direct path loading. With fixed-format data, the column specification identifies the starting and ending positions. A numeric datatype can be identified as INTEGER EXTERNAL. The directive NULLIF region_name = BLANKS tells SQL*Loader to set the region_name column to NULL if the data field contains only white space.

You shouldn't have to know the minutiae of how to tell SQL*Loader precisely how to parse data—the options are far too arcane to expect you to recite them off the top of your head for an exam—but knowing the SQL*Loader capabilities of reading fixed format and variable format data is essential. More important to your job is knowing about direct path loads and unusable indexes, which are discussed in the next section.

Using Direct Path Loading

Direct path loading is a SQL*Loader option that allows you, under certain conditions, to use the direct path interface to load data into a table. The direct path interface can be significantly faster than conventional path loading. With conventional loading, SQL*Loader loads data into a bind array and passes it to the database engine to process with an INSERT statement. Full undo and redo mechanisms operate on conventional path loads.

With direct path loading, SQL*Loader reads data, passing it to the database via the direct path API. The API formats it directly into Oracle data blocks in memory and then flushes these blocks, en masse, directly to the datafiles using multiblock I/O, bypassing the buffer cache, as well as the redo and undo mechanisms. Direct path loads always write to a table above the high-water mark; thus, always increase the number of data blocks that a table is actually using.

The important thing to remember about direct path load is that it is fast, but has restrictions, including the following:

- Indexes are rebuilt at the end of a direct path load. If unique constraint violations are found, the unique index is left in an unusable state. To correct the index, you must find and remove the constraint violations and then rebuild the index.

Unusable indexes are a possible result of direct path loading. Make sure you know what causes an unusable index and how to fix it.

- Direct path load cannot occur if there are active transactions against the table being loaded.
- Triggers do not fire during direct path loads.
- Direct path loading into clustered tables is not supported.
- During direct path loads, foreign key constraints are disabled at the beginning of the load and then reenabled after the load.

Summary

In this chapter, you learned how to use SQL to create, change, and remove data from an Oracle database. You also learned how to identify, execute, and tune PL/SQL programs, including triggers, to manage an Oracle10g database. Finally, you learned how to use the utilities Data Pump import, Data Pump export, and SQL*Loader to bulk load, unload, and copy data or metadata between your databases.

Exam Essentials

Know how to create database directory objects.   Directory objects are required for use in the Data Pump Export and and Data Pump Import programs.

Know the syntax for how to insert data with either a list of values or a subquery.   A list of values requires the keyword VALUES, while a subquery does not.

Know the difference between DELETE TABLE and TRUNCATE TABLE.   DELETE TABLE generates undo and must be committed for the changes to be made permanent. TRUNCATE TABLE does not generate undo and issues an implicit commit.

Know that PL/SQL functions have a RETURN clause.   Functions have a datatype and a RETURN clause. The other PL/SQL programs do not.

Know how to enable and disable triggers.   Use the ALTER TRIGGER statement to enable or disable any individual trigger and the ALTER TABLE ENABLE ALL TRIGGERS or ALTER TABLE DISABLE ALL TRIGGERS statement to enable or disable triggers en masse.

Be aware of the default settings for the PL/SQL initialization parameters.   By default, native compilation, PL/SQL warnings, and debug are all disabled, while optimization is set to maximum.

Know that directory objects are not owned by individual schema.   Directory objects are not schema objects. Instead, they are owned by the database like roles or profiles.

Be aware of the Data Pump export and import modes.   Data Pump export has database, schema, table, and tablespace modes, and Data Pump import has full, schema, table, and tablespace modes. Although these modes sound similar, they differ between the two tools.

Be familiar with the Data Pump options that let you transfer both data and metadata from one schema to another.   The content= parameter controls whether data, metadata, or both are copied. The remap_schema parameter allows you to transfer data from one schema to another.

Be aware of the limitations of SQL*Loader direct path mode, including unusable indexes.   SQL*Loader direct path mode has several limitations, the most prominent being that it locks the table in exclusive mode for the duration of the load. Unique indexes are marked unusable if unique violations are found after a direct path load. These unique violations must be resolved before the index can be rebuilt.

Review Questions

1. Which of the following conditions prevents you from being able to insert into a view?

   A. A TO_NUMBER function on one of the base table columns

   B. A CONNECT BY clause in the view definition

   C. A column of type RAW

   D. All of the above

2. Changes made with an UPDATE statement are made permanent in the database after what occurs?

   A. DBWR flushes the changes to disk.

   B. You issue a SAVEPOINT statement.

   C. You issue a COMMIT statement.

   D. A checkpoint occurs.

3. Which of the following is not a PL/SQL program?

   A. Library

   B. Trigger

   C. Function

   D. Procedure

4. Why would you execute a CREATE OR REPLACE PROCEDURE statement instead of a DROP PROCEDURE and a CREATE PROCEDURE?

   A. It is less typing.

   B. There is no difference between the two.

   C. CREATE OR REPLACE PROCEDURE does not invalidate dependent objects.

   D. DROP PROCEDURE and CREATE PROCEDURE require regranting of privileges.

5. Which of the following is not a trigger event?

   A. UPDATE

   B. SELECT

   C. NOAUDIT

   D. SERVERERROR

6. Which of the following statements can be used to enable triggers?

   A. ALTER SYSTEM

   B. ALTER TABLE

   C. ALTER USER

   D. ALTER PACKAGE

7. Which of the following is true?

   A. Directories are like roles or profiles; they are not owned by any individual user.

   B. Directories are like synonyms or database links; they can be public or private.

   C. Directories are like triggers and packages; they are owned by a schema.

   D. You can grant SELECT and UPDATE object privileges on directories.

8. Which of the following keywords is used with a Data Pump import to copy data from one schema to another?

   A. fromuser and touser

   B. source_schema and target_schema

   C. rename_schema

   D. remap_schema

9. The application development manager asks you to make sure the new Oracle10g database that her team will use has PL/SQL warning enabled and the optimizing compiler set to maximum optimization. What do you have to do to satisfy these requirements?

   A. Nothing. They are the default settings.

   B. The optimizing compiler is set to maximum by default, but you have to set the initialization parameter plsql_warnings to ENABLE:ALL.

   C. plsql_warnings is set to maximum by default, but you need to set plsql_optimize_mode =2 to increase it to maximum.

   D. You need to set both plsql_warnings and plsql_optimize_mode to nondefault settings.

10. Which of the following is not a mode for Data Pump export?

   A. Database

   B. Tablespace

   C. Table

   D. Metadata

11. To perform a Data Pump import from a live database, which parameter needs to be set?

   A. db_link

   B. network_link

   C. dumpfile

   D. directory

12. You perform nightly metadata-only Data Pump exports of your development database. One morning, you get a frantic call from a developer who accidentally dropped a package he had been working on for the past week. Which Data Pump import parameter will you need to extract the package DDL from the dump file?

   A. show

   B. sqlfile

   C. reuse_datafiles

   D. tablespaces

13. What will the following Data Pump import command do?

```
impdp system/password network_link=sys_test
  schemas="GL" remap_schema="GL:GLI" content=both
  nologfile=y include=TABLE:"LIKE 'PROD%'"
```

- **A.** Copy the GL tables whose names start with PROD from the `sys_test` database, placing them into the GLI schema.
- **B.** Copy the GLI tables whose names start with PROD from the `sys_test` database, placing them into the GL schema.
- **C.** Load the data in file `sys_test.dmp` into the table `GLI.products`.
- **D.** Copy the metadata from user GL in `sys_test` into the local database.

14. Your requirements call for loading a lot of data from a flat file dumped from the mainframe into the orders table at night while a few users in Singapore enter orders interactively. You are using SQL*Loader to load the data, but it takes longer than desired. What might you do to speed up the process?

- **A.** Switch to direct path mode.
- **B.** Increase the bind size.
- **C.** Write a Java program to parse and load the data.
- **D.** Write a C program to parse and load the data.

15. Which type of PL/SQL program can be called in the select list of a SQL statement?

- **A.** Trigger
- **B.** Procedure
- **C.** Function
- **D.** None of the above

16. You need to let an application role execute the SLEEP procedure in the DBMS_LOCK package, but do not want to let an application role have access to the other more powerful capabilities of the DBMS_LOCK package. How can you satisfy these requirements best?

- **A.** Grant EXECUTE on `dbms_lock` to user system. Then create a procedure in the system schema that calls DBMS_LOCK.SLEEP. Finally, grant EXECUTE on this procedure to the application role.
- **B.** Grant EXECUTE on DBMS_LOCK to the application role.
- **C.** Grant EXECUTE on DMBS_LOCK.SLEEP to the application role.
- **D.** Write your own procedure to mimic the functionality of the DBMS_LOCK.SLEEP procedure.

17. Which of the following triggering events fire when statistics are gathered on a table?

- **A.** ANALYZE and DDL
- **B.** ASSOCIATE STATISTICS and ANALYZE
- **C.** GATHER STATISTICS and DDL
- **D.** ASSOCIATE STATISTICS and DISASSOCIATE STATISTICS

18. Which Data Pump export mode captures user definitions?

    A. Table mode

    B. Tablespace mode

    C. DBA mode

    D. Schema mode

19. You need to copy the GL schema from production to `qa_test`, changing the tablespace for indexes from `gl_index` to `fin_indx`. What is the best way to satisfy these requirements?

    A. First, use Data Pump to copy the schema without indexes. Then, change the default tablespace for user GL in `qa_test` to `fin_indx`. Next, use Data Pump to copy the indexes. Finally, change the default tablespace for user GL back to `gl_data`.

    B. Use the `dbms_metadata` package to extract table and index DDL. Then, use Notepad (or sed) to edit this DDL, changing the tablespace for the indexes. Finally, run the DDL in the `qa_test` database.

    C. Use Data Pump import, specifying a `remap_datafile` parameter to change the datafile location for indexes.

    D. Use Data Pump import specifying a `remap_tablespace` parameter to change the tablespace location for indexes.

20. Which of the following INSERT statements raises an exception?

    A. `INSERT INTO ORDERS SELECT * FROM STANDING_ORDERS`

    B. `INSERT FIRST WHEN ORDER_TYPE IN (2,5,12) THEN INSERT INTO ORDERS SELECT * FROM STANDING_ORDERS`

    C. `INSERT FIRST WHEN ORDER_TYPE IN (2,5,12) THEN INTO ORDERS SELECT * FROM STANDING_ORDERS`

    D. `INSERT INTO ALL WHEN ORDER_TYPE IN (2,5,12) THEN INTO ORDERS SELECT * FROM STANDING_ORDERS`

Answers to Review Questions

1. B. You cannot insert into a view that contains a CONNECT BY, ORDER BY, or GROUP BY clause.

2. C. A commit makes pending DML changes permanent. When a checkpoint occurs, DBWR flushes dirty buffers to disk, which is independent of transaction boundaries.

3. A. A library can be a database object, but is associated with an operating system shared library. PL/SQL programs include procedures, functions, packages, package bodies, and triggers.

4. D. Using CREATE OR REPLACE PROCEDURE is less typing, but, more importantly, when you drop an object, all privileges granted on that object are dropped as well. When you perform a CREATE OR REPLACE, you do not lose privileges granted on that object.

5. B. You can create a trigger for just about any database event that involves a change to data, but you cannot create a SELECT trigger in Oracle10*g*.

6. B. You can enable triggers with either an ALTER TRIGGER ENABLE statement or with an ALTER TABLE ENABLE ALL TRIGGERS statement.

7. A. The READ and WRITE object privileges are applicable to directory objects; SELECT and UPDATE are not. Directory objects are not owned by any individual schema, so they are like roles and profiles in this regard, not triggers and packages.

8. D. The keywords fromuser and touser are from the older imp import program. Data Pump uses remap_schema (not rename_schema) to map a source to a target schema.

9. B. The default settings are to disable plsql_warnings and enable maximum optimization (level 2).

10. D. Data Pump export modes include database, tablespace, table, and schema. The keyword metadata is used in conjunction with the content parameter. To export only metadata, you specify content=metadata.

11. B. The network_link parameter specifies a database link to the source database.

12. B. To extract the package DDL, you need to specify a sqlfile= and an include parameter.

13. A. The remap_schema parameter defines the source and target schemas, and the include parameter identifies which objects to include in the import job.

14. B. Writing your own Java or C program to do the same thing as SQL*Loader would be a costly decision in terms of development effort. Getting your own program to outperform SQL*Loader would be difficult at best. Direct path loading would certainly speed up the load, but would lock the table exclusively, prohibiting your Singapore users from entering data interactively. Increasing the bind size would allow SQL*Loader to make fewer database calls, resulting in fewer network round-trip communications and potentially improving the performance. The key concept to grasp with this question is that direct path loads lock the table exclusively; therefore they should not be used on active tables.

15. C. Functions can be called in several places, including in the SELECT, WHERE, ORDER BY, and GROUP BY clauses of SQL statements. Triggers are invoked when their trigger event fires. Procedures are invoked as stand-alone statements.

16. A. You cannot grant privileges on only one packaged procedure. You can only grant EXECUTE on the whole package. To be more restrictive in granting privileges, you need to create an intermediate procedure that calls the single procedure you want and grant EXECUTE on that intermediate procedure to the grantee.

17. A. The ASSOCIATE STATISTICS and DISASSOCIATE STATISTICS events fire when an ASSOCIATE STATISTICS or DISASSOCIATE STATISTICS statement is executed, not when statistics are gathered. There is no GATHER STATISTICS triggering event. The triggering events that will fire when statistics are gathered on a table are the ANALYZE and DDL events.

18. D. Table and tablespace modes do not capture user account definitions. Schema mode can, and database mode always captures user definitions. There is no DBA mode.

19. D. Options A and B are a lot of work. The `remap_datafile` parameter applies only to CREATE TABLESPACE and CREATE DIRECTORY statements, not indexes. The `remap_tablespace` parameter tells Data Pump Import to change the tablespace that objects are stored in between the source and the target database.

20. D. Single table inserts must begin with the keywords INSERT INTO and cannot contain the keywords THEN INTO. Multitable INSERT statements cannot begin with the keywords INSERT INTO and may contain the keywords THEN INTO. Option D contains an invalid combination of keywords and will thus raise an exception.

Chapter

8

Managing Consistency and Concurrency

ORACLE DATABASE 10*G*: ADMINISTRATION I EXAM OBJECTIVES COVERED IN THIS CHAPTER:

✓ **Undo Management**

- ▪ Monitor and administer undo.
- ▪ Configure undo retention.
- ▪ Guarantee undo retention.
- ▪ Use the Undo Advisor.
- ▪ Describe the relationship between undo and transactions.
- ▪ Size the undo tablespace.

✓ **Monitoring and Resolving Lock Conflicts**

- ▪ Detect and resolve lock conflicts.
- ▪ Manage deadlocks.
- ▪ Describe the relationship between transactions and locks.
- ▪ Explain lock modes within the Oracle Database 10*g*.

Exam objectives are subject to change at any time without prior notice and at Oracle's sole discretion. Please visit Oracle's Training and Certification website (http://www.oracle.com/education/certification/) for the most current exam objectives listing.

If a database user wants to change their mind after running a *DML (Data Manipulation Language)* statement, Oracle Database10*g* (Oracle 10*g*) retains undo data needed to bring back the data changed by the user since the beginning of a transaction. This same undo data allows the user to view the data in a table as of a point of time in the past. The undo data provides yet another benefit: a query against a table that may be changing after the query started will not see the changes until a new query is issued against the table. Ensuring that the tablespace that holds undo data is sized correctly is an important job for you as a DBA, preventing those late-night phone calls from users who either cannot run their queries to completion or make their nightly updates to the ORDERS table!

Oracle's GUI administration tool, the EM Database Control, makes undo administration and sizing simpler than ever. The Undo Advisor collects statistics on an ongoing basis to help you size the undo tablespace so that DML statements within a transaction can complete successfully while at the same time allowing SELECT statements to complete successfully without receiving the all-too-familiar "Snapshot too old" error; this information is presented in the EM Database Control environment as an easy-to-read graph, making it simple for you to adjust the undo retention and other settings.

Oracle also provides a number of ways to both monitor and resolve locking conflicts in the database. Oracle's locking mechanism keeps locking at the lowest level possible, although users can lock resources at a higher level when necessary. Row-level locking was introduced in Oracle version 6.

The first part of this chapter covers all aspects of undo management: monitoring and administering undo data, ensuring that undo data is available for user transactions, and calculating the size of the undo tablespace. In the last half of this chapter, we'll review the types of locks available and how to manage locking and contention for the same resources by more than one user or transaction. As with undo administration, the EM Database Control environment makes lock management easier than in previous releases of Oracle.

Leveraging Undo Management

Whenever a process or a user session changes data in the database, Oracle saves the old value as it existed before it was modified as undo data. This provides a number of benefits to the database user.

- It lets the user change their mind and roll back, or undo, the change to the database.

- It supports read-consistent queries. Once a query starts, any changes to the query's underlying tables are not reflected in the query's results.

- It supports flashback query, an Oracle feature introduced in Oracle9*i*. Flashback query allows a user to see how a table looked at some point in the past. As long as the undo data still exists for the requested point of time, flashback queries are possible.

In the following sections, we present all aspects of undo management. First, we will show how transactions are related to undo management and how undo records are stored in an undo tablespace along with some of the features supported by undo records. Next, we will show you how to set up the initialization parameters to specify a target for how much undo is retained in the undo tablespace; in addition, we will show you the commands needed to guarantee that undo space is available for SELECT statements at the expense of DML commands.

Monitoring an undo tablespace is not unlike monitoring any other tablespace: you want to make sure that you have enough undo space in the tablespace to satisfy all types of user transactions, but not so much that you're wasting space that can be used for objects in other tablespaces. Therefore, we will present some methods to accurately calculate the optimal amount of undo space you will need. Finally, we will review the notification methods you can use to proactively alert you to problems with the undo tablespace.

Understanding Undo Segments

Undo segments, also known as rollback segments, are similar to other segments in the database, such as table or index segments, in that an undo segment is made up of extents, which in turn are made up of data blocks. Also, an undo segment contains data similar to that stored in a table. However, that is where the similarity ends. Undo segments must be stored in a special type of tablespace called an *undo tablespace*. Although a database can have more than one undo tablespace, only one undo tablespace can be active at any one time. Undo segments contain undo information about one or many tables involved in a transaction. Also, undo segments automatically grow and shrink as needed, acting as a circular buffer—transactions that fill up the extents in an undo segment can wrap around to the beginning of the segment if the first extent is not being used by an active transaction.

At the beginning of a transaction—in other words, when the first DML command is issued after a previous COMMIT or a user first connects to the database—the transaction is assigned to an undo segment in the undo tablespace. Any changes to any table in the transaction are recorded in the assigned undo segment. The names of the current active undo segments can be retrieved from the dynamic performance view *V$ROLLNAME*, as you can see in the following query:

```
SQL> select * from v$rollname;

       USN NAME
---------- ---------------------------
         0 SYSTEM
         1 _SYSSMU1$
         2 _SYSSMU2$
         3 _SYSSMU3$
         4 _SYSSMU4$
         5 _SYSSMU5$
         6 _SYSSMU6$
         7 _SYSSMU7$
```

```
 8 _SYSSMU8$
 9 _SYSSMU9$
10 _SYSSMU10$
```

11 rows selected.

 The data dictionary view DBA_ROLLBACK_SEGS shows both active (online) and inactive (offline) undo segments in both the SYSTEM and undo tablespaces.

The undo segment with an undo segment number (USN) of 0 is an undo segment reserved for exclusive use by system users such as SYS or SYSTEM or if no other undo segments are online and the data being changed resides in the SYSTEM tablespace. In this example, nine other undo segments are available in the undo tablespace for user transactions.

The dynamic performance view *V$TRANSACTION* shows the relationship between a transaction and the undo segments. In the following query, you begin a transaction and then join V$TRANSACTION to V$ROLLNAME to find out the name of the undo segment assigned to the transaction:

```
SQL> set transaction name 'Update clerk salaries';
Transaction set.

SQL> update hr.employees set salary = salary * 1.25
  2      where job_id like '%CLERK';
44 rows updated.

SQL> select xid, status, start_time, xidusn seg_num,
  2         r.name seg_name
  3  from v$transaction t join v$rollname r
  4         on t.xidusn = r.usn
  5  where t.name = 'Update clerk salaries';

XID       STATUS    START_TIME        SEG_NUM SEG_NAME
-------- --------- ----------------- ------- -------------
02002F00 ACTIVE    08/01/04 16:20:10       2 _SYSSMU2$
9A140000

1 row selected.
```

The column XID is the internally assigned, unique transaction number assigned to this transaction, and it is assigned the undo segment _SYSSMU2$. The column XIDUSN (aliased as SEG_NUM in the query) is the undo segment number for _SYSSMU2$. A transaction can reside in only one undo segment; it cannot be moved to another undo segment. However, many different transactions can use the same undo segment.

If an extent in the assigned undo segment fills up and more space is required, the next available extent is used; if all extents in the segment are needed for current transactions, a new extent is allocated for the undo segment.

All undo segments are owned by SYS, regardless of who is making changes in a transaction. Each segment must have a minimum of two extents; the maximum number of extents in an undo segment is high: for an undo tablespace with a block size of 8KB, the default maximum number of extents per undo segment is 32,765.

During a media failure with an undo tablespace, the tablespace can be recovered using archived and online redo log files just as with any other tablespace; however, the instance must be in a MOUNT state to recover an undo tablespace.

> Tablespace recovery is discussed in Chapter 11, "Implementing Database Recovery."

Using Undo Data

Undo data is the old value of data when a process or a user changes data in a table or an index. Undo data serves four purposes in an Oracle database:

- User rollback of a transaction
- Read consistency of DML operations and queries
- Database recovery operations
- Flashback functionality

User Transaction Rollback

In Chapter 1, "Installing Oracle 10*g*," you learned about transactions and how they are managed within the database architecture. At the user level, you might have one or hundreds of *DML* commands (such as DELETE, INSERT, UPDATE, or MERGE) within a particular transaction that need to be undone by a user or a process that is making changes to one or more tables. Undoing the changes within a transaction is called *rolling back* part or all of the transaction. The undo information needed to roll back the changes is called, appropriately, the *rollback information* and is stored in a special type of tablespace called an undo tablespace.

> Configuring and sizing the undo tablespace is covered later in this chapter in the section "Configuring the Undo Tablespace."

When an entire transaction is rolled back, Oracle undoes all the changes since the beginning of the transactions, using the saved undo information in the undo tablespace, releases any locks on rows involved in the transaction, and ends the transaction.

Locks on rows and tables are discussed later in this chapter in the section "Understanding Locks and Transactions."

If a failure occurs on the client or the network, abnormally terminating the user's connection to the database, undo information is used in much the same way as if the user explicitly rolled back the transaction, and Oracle undoes all the changes since the beginning of the transaction, using information saved in the undo tablespace.

Read Consistency

Undo also provides *read consistency* for users who are querying rows involved in a DML transaction by another user or session. When one user starts to make changes to a table after another user has already begun a query against the table, the user issuing the query will not see the changes to the table until after the query has completed and the user issues a new query against the table. Undo segments in an undo tablespace are used to reconstruct the data blocks belonging to the table to provide the previous values of the rows for any user issuing SELECT statements against the table before the DML statements' transaction commits.

For example, the user KELSIEJ begins a transaction at 3:00 P.M. that contains several long-running DML statements against the EMPLOYEES table; the statements aren't expected to finish until 3:15 P.M. As each DML command is issued, the previous values of each row are saved in the transaction's undo segment. At 3:05 P.M., the user SARAHCR issues a SELECT against the EMPLOYEES table; none of the changes made so far by KELSIEJ are visible to SARAHCR. The undo tablespace provides the previous values of the EMPLOYEES table to SARAHCR and any other users querying the EMPLOYEES table between 3:00 P.M. and 3:15 P.M. Even if SARAHCR's query is still running at 3:20 P.M., the query still appears as it did at 3:00 P.M. before KELSIEJ started making changes.

 INSERT statements use little space in an undo segment; only the pointer to the new row is stored in the undo tablespace. To undo an INSERT statement, the pointer locates the new row and deletes it from the table if the transaction is rolled back.

In a few situations, either SARAHCR's query or KELSIEJ's DML statements might fail, either because the undo tablespace is not sized correctly or the undo retention period is too short.

 We will show you how to prevent these failures later in this chapter in the section "Monitoring, Configuring, and Administering Undo."

You can also apply read consistency to an entire transaction instead of just a single SELECT statement by using the SET TRANSACTION statement as follows:

```
SQL> set transaction read only;
Transaction set.
```

Until the transaction is either rolled back or committed, all queries in the transaction see only changes to other tables that were committed before the transaction began. Only the following statements are permitted in a read-only transaction:

- SELECT statements without the FOR UPDATE clause
- LOCK TABLE
- SET ROLE
- ALTER SESSION
- ALTER SYSTEM

In other words, a read-only transaction cannot contain any statement that changes data in a table, regardless of where the table resides. For example, although an ALTER USER command does not change data in the USERS or any other non-SYSTEM tablespace, it does change the data dictionary tables and therefore cannot be used in a read-only transaction.

Database Recovery

The undo tablespace is a key component for database recovery in the case of an instance failure. After the online redo log files bring both committed and uncommitted transactions forward to the point of the instance crash, the undo data in the tablespace is used to roll back the uncommitted transactions.

Flashback Operations

Several flashback options are supported by undo data. Flashback query and the package DBMS_FLASHBACK, introduced in Oracle9i, allow you to query a table as of some point in the past. Flashback table, introduced in Oracle 10g, restores a table as of a point of time in the past using undo data.

Monitoring, Configuring, and Administering Undo

Compared with configuring rollback operations in releases previous to Oracle9i, managing undo in Oracle 10g requires little intervention. However, two particular situations will trigger intervention: either not enough undo space to handle all active transactions, or not enough undo space to satisfy long-running queries that need undo information for read consistency. Running out of undo space for transactions generates messages such as ORA-01650: Unable to extend rollback segment; long-running queries whose undo entries have been reused by current transactions typically receive the ORA-01555: Snapshot too old message.

In this section, we will show you how to configure the undo tablespace using two initialization parameters: UNDO_MANAGEMENT and UNDO_TABLESPACE. We will also present the methods available for monitoring the health of the undo tablespace, as well as using the EM Database Control's Undo Advisor to size or resize the undo tablespace. Using the dynamic performance view V$UNDOSTAT, you can calculate an optimal size for the undo tablespace if the Undo Advisor is not available. Finally, we will show you how to guarantee that long-running queries will have undo entries available, even if it means that a DML transaction fails, by using the RETENTION GUARANTEE option.

Configuring the Undo Tablespace

Manual undo management is not recommended, although it is still the default in Oracle 10g; use manual undo management only for compatibility with Oracle 8i or earlier. To configure automatic undo management, use the initialization parameters UNDO_MANAGEMENT, UNDO_TABLESPACE, and UNDO_RETENTION.

UNDO_MANAGEMENT

The parameter UNDO_MANAGEMENT specifies the way in which undo data is managed in the database: either manually using rollback segments or automatically using a single tablespace to hold undo information.

The allowed values for UNDO_MANAGEMENT are MANUAL and AUTO. To change the undo management mode, you must restart the instance. This parameter is not dynamic, as you can see in the following example:

```
SQL> alter system
  2      set undo_management = manual;

set undo_management = manual
     *
ERROR at line 2:
ORA-02095: specified initialization parameter
            cannot be modified
```

If you are using an SPFILE, you can change the value of this parameter in the SPFILE only and then restart the instance for the parameter to take effect, as follows:

```
SQL> alter system
  2      set undo_management = manual scope=spfile;
System altered.
```

UNDO_TABLESPACE

The parameter UNDO_TABLESPACE specifies the name of the undo tablespace to use for read consistency and transaction rollback.

You can create an undo tablespace when the database is created; you can resize it later or create a new one later. In any case, only one undo tablespace can be active at any given time, unless the value of UNDO_TABLESPACE is changed while the old undo tablespace still contains active transactions. In this case, the old undo tablespace remains active until the last transaction using the old undo tablespace either commits or rolls back; all new transactions use the new undo tablespace.

If UNDO_TABLESPACE is not defined, but at least one undo tablespace exists in the database, the first undo tablespace discovered by the Oracle instance at startup is assigned to UNDO_TABLESPACE. You can find out the name of the current undo tablespace with the SHOW PARAMETER command, as in the following example:

```
SQL> show parameter undo_tablespace
```

```
NAME                      TYPE         VALUE
----------------------    ----------   --------------------
undo_tablespace           string       UNDOTBS1
```

For most platforms, if an undo tablespace is not explicitly created in the CREATE DATABASE command, Oracle automatically creates one with the name SYS_UNDOTBS.

Here is an example of how you can switch the undo tablespace from UNDOTBS1 to UNDO_BATCH:

```
SQL> show parameter undo_tablespace

NAME                      TYPE         VALUE
----------------------    ----------   --------------------
undo_tablespace           string       UNDOTBS1

SQL> alter system set undo_tablespace=undo_batch;
System altered.

SQL> show parameter undo_tablespace

NAME                      TYPE         VALUE
----------------------    ----------   --------------------
undo_tablespace           string       UNDO_BATCH
```

UNDO_RETENTION

The parameter UNDO_RETENTION specifies, in seconds, how long undo information that has already been committed should be retained until it can be overwritten. This is not a guaranteed limit: if the number of seconds specified by UNDO_RETENTION has not been reached, and if a transaction needs undo space, already committed undo information can be overwritten.

To guarantee undo retention, you can use the RETENTION GUARANTEE keywords for the undo tablespace, as you will see later in this chapter in the section "Guaranteeing Undo Retention."

Setting UNDO_RETENTION to zero turns on automatic undo retention tuning. This parameter is continually adjusted to retain just enough undo information to satisfy the longest-running query to date. If the undo tablespace is not big enough for the longest-running query, automatic undo retention retains as much as possible without extending the undo tablespace. In any case, automatic undo retention attempts to maintain at least 900 seconds, or 15 minutes, of undo information.

Regardless of how long undo information is retained, it falls into one of three categories:

Uncommitted undo information Undo information that is still supporting an active transaction and is required in the event of a ROLLBACK or a transaction failure. This undo information is never overwritten.

Committed undo information   Also known as unexpired undo, undo information that is no longer needed to support an active transaction but is still needed to satisfy the undo retention interval, as defined by UNDO_RETENTION. This undo can be overwritten, however, if an active transaction needs undo space.

Expired undo information   Undo information that is no longer needed to support an active transaction and is overwritten when space is required by an active transaction.

Here is an example of how you can change undo retention from its current value to 12 hours:

```
SQL> show parameter undo_retention

NAME                 TYPE         VALUE
-------------------- ----------- -----------------------
undo_retention       integer      600

SQL> alter system set undo_retention = 43200;
System altered.

SQL> show parameter undo_retention

NAME                 TYPE         VALUE
-------------------- ----------- -----------------------
undo_retention       integer      43200
```

Unless you use the SCOPE parameter in the ALTER SYSTEM command, the change to UNDO_RETENTION takes effect immediately and stays in effect the next time the instance is restarted. Note that changing the undo retention from 10 minutes to 12 hours will have a dramatic impact on the amount of space required in your undo tablespace.

Monitoring the Undo Tablespace

Undo tablespaces are monitored just like any other tablespace: if a specific set of space thresholds is not defined, the database default values are used; otherwise, a specific set of thresholds can be assigned. When an undo tablespace's datafiles do not have the AUTOEXTEND attribute set, transactions can fail because too many transactions are vying for too little undo space.

In Figure 8.1, you can see that the undo tablespace UNDOTBS1 is using the default thresholds for the database, issues a warning alert at 85 percent full, and issues a critical alert at 97 percent full. Ideally, you can adjust the undo tablespace when the warning alert is received and solve the space problem before the critical threshold is reached. If the undo tablespace usage tends to spike a lot, you can adjust the thresholds for UNDOTBS1 to send a warning alert at a lower threshold. In this case, the tablespace UNDOTBS1 is only at 50.27 percent capacity.

FIGURE 8.1   The Edit Tablespace UNDOTBS1 screen in EM Database Control

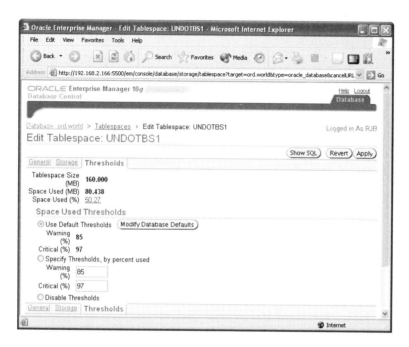

Although you can allow the datafiles in your undo tablespace to autoextend initially, turn off autoextend on its datafiles once you believe that the undo tablespace has been sized correctly. This prevents a single user from accidentally using up large amounts of disk space in the undo tablespace by neglecting to commit transactions as frequently as possible.

Figure 8.2 shows the Undo Management screen in EM Database Control. The current size of the undo tablespace is 160MB, and during the last 7 days the size of this undo tablespace has been sufficient to support the maximum undo generation rate of 977.0 KB/minute.

The EM Database Control uses the data dictionary view V$UNDOSTAT to calculate the undo usage rate and provide recommendations. V$UNDOSTAT collects 10-minute snapshots of the undo space consumption, and in conjunction with UNDO_RETENTION and the database block size, can provide an optimal undo tablespace size. In the following example, you can see the undo usage for the last several 10-minute periods:

```
SQL> select
  2    to_char(begin_time,'yyyy-mm-dd hh24:mi:ss')
  3       starttime,
  4    to_char(end_time,'yyyy-mm-dd hh24:mi:ss')
  5       endtime,
  6    undoblks,
  7    maxquerylen maxqrylen
  8  from v$undostat;
```

STARTTIME	ENDTIME	UNDOBLKS	MAXQRYLEN
2004-08-01 08:46:11	2004-08-01 08:48:47	13	0
2004-08-01 08:36:11	2004-08-01 08:46:11	61	0
2004-08-01 08:26:11	2004-08-01 08:36:11	31	0
. . .			
2004-07-30 09:36:11	2004-07-30 09:46:11	68	0
2004-07-30 09:26:11	2004-07-30 09:36:11	30	0
2004-07-30 09:16:11	2004-07-30 09:26:11	52	0
2004-07-30 09:06:11	2004-07-30 09:16:11	626	190
2004-07-30 08:56:11	2004-07-30 09:06:11	203	0
2004-07-30 08:46:11	2004-07-30 08:56:11	66	0
2004-07-30 08:36:11	2004-07-30 08:46:11	31	0
2004-07-30 08:26:11	2004-07-30 08:36:11	73	0

FIGURE 8.2 The Undo Management screen in EM Database Control

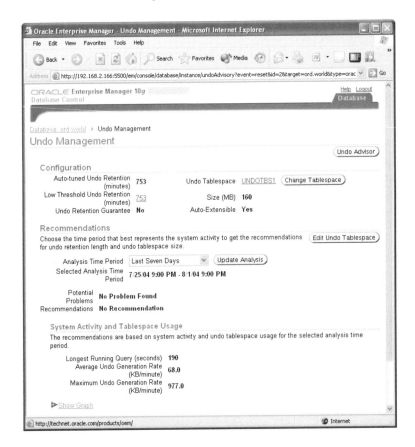

The longest-running query occurred at 9:06 A.M. on July 30, 2004, which is also shown in Figure 8.2.

Running out of space in an undo tablespace can also trigger an ORA-01555: Snapshot too old error. Long-running queries that need a read-consistent view of one or more tables can be at odds with ongoing transactions that need undo space. Unless the undo tablespace is defined with the RETENTION GUARANTEE parameter (described later in this chapter in the section "Guaranteeing Undo Retention"), ongoing DML can use undo space that is needed for long-running queries. As a result, a Snapshot too old error is returned to the user executing the query, and an alert is generated. This alert is also known as a *long query warning alert*.

> This alert can be triggered independently of the space available in the undo tablespace if the UNDO_RETENTION initialization parameter is set too low.

Regardless of how often the Snapshot too old error occurs, the alert is generated at most once during a 24-hour period. Increasing the size of the undo tablespace or changing the value of UNDO_RETENTION does not reset the 24-hour timer. For example, an alert is generated at 10 A.M., and you add undo space at 11 A.M. The undo tablespace is still too small, and users are still receiving Snapshot too old errors at 2 P.M. You will not receive a long query warning alert until 10 A.M. the next day, but chances are you will get a phone call before then!

Sizing the Undo Tablespace Using the Undo Advisor

The EM Database Control *Undo Advisor* helps you determine how large an undo tablespace is necessary given adjustments to the undo retention setting.

In Figure 8.3, the Undo Advisor screen shows the automatically tuned undo retention of 753 minutes and an undo tablespace size of 94MB. If you don't expect your undo usage to increase or you don't expect to need to retain undo information longer than 753 minutes, you can drop the size of the undo tablespace if it is significantly more than 94MB.

On the other hand, if you expect to need undo information for more than 753 minutes, you can see the impact of this increase either by entering a new value for undo retention and refreshing the page or by clicking a point on the graph corresponding to the estimated undo retention. Figure 8.4 shows the results of increasing the undo retention to 103,204 minutes.

To support an undo retention setting of 103,204 minutes given the current undo usage, you must increase the undo tablespace size to 8625MB, or 8.625GB.

Sizing the Undo Tablespace Manually using *V$UNDOSTAT*

In the query you used in the section "Monitoring the Undo Tablespace" earlier in this chapter, you saw a spike in undo usage at 9:06 A.M. with a maximum undo usage of 626 undo blocks per second during that 10-minute interval. To size the undo tablespace using this information, you can use the following calculation:

```
undo_tablespace_size = UR * UPS * DB_BLOCK_SIZE
```

FIGURE 8.3 Auto-tuned undo retention settings

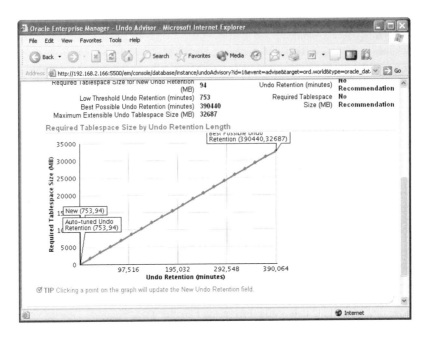

FIGURE 8.4 Specifying new undo retention settings

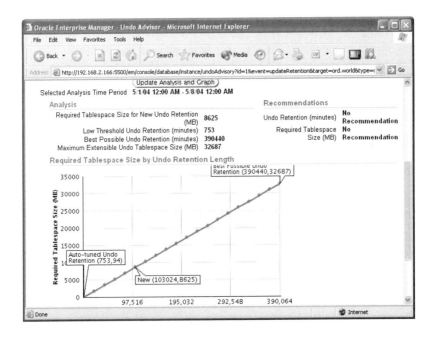

In this calculation, UR is the undo retention from the parameter UNDO_RETENTION, which was set to 43,200 in a previous example. UPS is the maximum undo blocks used per second from the UNDOBLKS column in V$UNDOSTAT. If our database has a block size of 8KB, the size of the undo tablespace should be:

```
undo_tablespace_size = 43200 * 626 * 8192 = 221537894400 = 206GB
```

Add about 10 to 20 percent to this calculation for unexpected spikes in undo usage.

Guaranteeing Undo Retention

By default, undo information from committed transactions (unexpired undo) is overwritten before a transaction fails because of a lack of expired undo. If your database requirements are such that you want long-running queries to succeed at the expense of DML in a transaction, such as in a data warehouse environment where a query can run for hours or even days, you can set the RETENTION GUARANTEE parameter for the undo tablespace.

This parameter is not available as an initialization parameter. Unlike most every other command or procedure in the database, it is not available via the EM Database Control; you must use ALTER TABLESPACE at the command line to set it, as in the following example:

```
SQL> alter tablespace undotbs1 retention guarantee;
Tablespace altered.
```

Turning off the parameter is just as easy, as you can see in the next example:

```
SQL> alter tablespace undotbs1 retention noguarantee;
Tablespace altered.
```

Different undo tablespaces can have different settings for RETENTION. As expected, you cannot set RETENTION for a tablespace that is not an undo tablespace. In the following example, you attempt to change the RETENTION setting for the USERS tablespace, and receive an error message:

```
SQL> select tablespace_name, contents,
  2     retention from dba_tablespaces;

TABLESPACE_NAME                CONTENTS  RETENTION
------------------------------ --------- -----------
SYSTEM                         PERMANENT NOT APPLY
UNDOTBS1                       UNDO      NOGUARANTEE
SYSAUX                         PERMANENT NOT APPLY
TEMP                           TEMPORARY NOT APPLY
USERS                          PERMANENT NOT APPLY
EXAMPLE                        PERMANENT NOT APPLY
OE_TRANS                       PERMANENT NOT APPLY
```

```
SQL> alter tablespace users retention guarantee;

alter tablespace users retention guarantee
*
ERROR at line 1:
ORA-30044: 'Retention' can only be specified
    for undo tablespace
```

Monitoring Locking and Resolving Lock Conflicts

In any database that has more than one user, you will eventually have to deal with locking conflicts when two or more users try to change the same row in the database.

In this section, we present an overview of how locking works in the Oracle database, how users are queued for a particular resource once it is locked, and how Oracle classifies lock types in the database.

At the end of this section, we show you a number of ways to detect and resolve locking issues; we also cover a special type of lock situation: the deadlock.

Understanding Locks and Transactions

Locks prevent multiple users from changing the same data at the same time. Before one or more rows in a table can be changed, the user executing the DML statement must obtain a lock on the row or rows: a lock gives the user exclusive control over the data until the user has committed or rolled back the transaction that is changing the data.

In Oracle 10g, a transaction can lock one row, multiple rows, or an entire table. Although you can manually lock rows, Oracle can automatically lock the rows needed at the lowest possible level to ensure data integrity and minimize conflicts with other transactions that may need to access other rows in the table.

In Table 8.1, both updates to the EMPLOYEES table return to the command prompt immediately after the UPDATE because the locks are on different rows in the EMPLOYEES table and neither session is waiting for the other lock to be released.

TABLE 8.1 Concurrent Transactions on Different Rows of the Same Table

Session 1	Time	Session 2
update employees set salary = salary * 1.2 where employee_id = 102;	11:29	update employees set manager = 100 where employee_id = 109;
commit;	11:30	commit;

Queries never require a lock. Even if another transaction has locked several rows or an entire table, a query always succeeds, using the pre-lock image of the data stored in the undo tablespace.

If multiple users require a lock on a row or rows in a table, the first user to request the lock obtains it, and the remaining users are enqueued using a first-in, first-out (FIFO) method. At a SQL> command prompt, a DML statement (INSERT, UPDATE, DELETE, or MERGE) that is waiting for a lock on a resource appears to hang, unless the NOWAIT keyword is used in a LOCK statement.

The NOWAIT keyword is explained in the next section, "Maximizing Data Concurrency."

At the end of a transaction, when either a COMMIT or a ROLLBACK is issued (either explicitly by the user or implicitly when the session terminates normally or abnormally), all locks are released.

Maximizing Data Concurrency

Rows of a table are locked either explicitly by the user at the beginning of a transaction or implicitly by Oracle, usually at the row level, depending on the operation. If a table must be locked for performance reasons (which is rare), you can use the LOCK TABLE command, specifying the level at which the table should be locked.

In the following example, you lock the EMPLOYEES and DEPARTMENTS tables at the highest possible level, EXCLUSIVE:

```
SQL> lock table hr.employees, hr.departments
  2      in exclusive mode;
Table(s) Locked.
```

Until the transaction with the LOCK statement either commits or rolls back, only queries are allowed on the EMPLOYEES or DEPARTMENTS tables.

In the sections that follow, we will review the lock modes, as well as show you how to avoid the lock enqueue process and terminate the command if the requested resource is already locked.

Lock Modes

Lock modes provide a way for you to specify how much and what kinds of access other users have on tables that you are using in DML commands. In Table 8.2, you can see the types of locks that can be obtained at the table level.

TABLE 8.2 Table Lock Modes

Table Lock Mode	Description
ROW SHARE	Permits concurrent access to the locked table, but prohibits other users from locking the entire table for exclusive access.
ROW EXCLUSIVE	Same as ROW SHARE, but also prohibits locking in SHARE mode. This type of lock is obtained automatically with standard DML commands such as UPDATE, INSERT, or DELETE.
SHARE	Permits concurrent queries but prohibits updates to the table; this mode is required to create an index on a table and is automatically obtained when using the CREATE INDEX statement.
SHARE ROW EXCLUSIVE	Used to query a whole table and to allow other users to query the table, but to prevent other users from locking the table in SHARE mode or updating rows.
EXCLUSIVE	The most restrictive locking mode; permits queries on the locked table but prohibits any DML by any other users. This mode is required to drop the table and is automatically obtained when using the DROP TABLE statement.

Manual lock requests wait in the same queue as implicit locks and are satisfied in a first in, first out (FIFO) manner as each request releases the lock with either an implicit or explicit COMMIT or ROLLBACK.

You can explicitly obtain locks on individual rows by using the SELECT ... FOR UPDATE statement, as you can see in the following example:

```
SQL> select * from hr.employees
  2    where manager_id = 100
  3  for update;
```

This query not only shows the rows that satisfy the query conditions, it also locks the selected rows and prevents other transactions from locking or updating these rows until a COMMIT or a ROLLBACK occurs.

NOWAIT Mode

Using NOWAIT in a LOCK TABLE statement returns control to the user immediately if any locks already exist on the requested resource, as you can see in the following example:

```
SQL> lock table hr.employees
  2  in share row exclusive mode
  3  nowait;
lock table hr.employees
              *
ERROR at line 1:
ORA-00054: resource busy and acquire with NOWAIT specified

SQL>
```

This is especially useful in a PL/SQL application if an alternate execution path can be followed if the requested resource is not yet available. NOWAIT can also be used in the SELECT ... FOR UPDATE statement.

Detecting and Resolving Lock Conflicts

Although locks are a common and sometimes unavoidable occurrence in many databases, they are usually resolved by waiting in the queue. In some cases, you may need to resolve the lock problem manually (for example, if a user makes an update at 4:59 P.M. and does not perform a COMMIT before leaving for the day).

In the next few sections, we will describe in more detail some of the reasons that lock conflicts occur and how to detect lock conflicts and discuss a more specific and serious type of lock conflict: a deadlock.

Understanding Lock Conflicts

In addition to the proverbial user who makes a change at 4:59 P.M. and forgets to perform a COMMIT before leaving for the day, other more typical lock conflicts are caused by long-running transactions that perform hundreds, thousands, or even hundreds of thousands of DML commands in the overnight batch run but are not finished updating the tables when the normal business day starts. The uncommitted transactions from the overnight batch jobs may lock tables that need to be updated by clerical staff during the business day, causing a lock conflict.

Another typical cause of lock conflicts is using unnecessarily high locking levels. In the sidebar "Packaged Applications and Locking" earlier in this chapter, we described a third-party application that routinely locked resources at the table level instead of at the row level to be compatible with every SQL-based database on the market. Developers may unnecessarily code updates to tables with higher locking levels than required by Oracle 10g.

Detecting Lock Conflicts

Detecting locks in Oracle 10g using the EM Database Control makes your job easy; no need to query against V$SESSION, V$TRANSACTION, V$LOCK, and V$LOCKED_OBJECT to see who is locking what resource. In Figure 8.5, you can see the tables locked by the user SCOTT after executing the following statement:

```
SQL> lock table hr.employees, hr.departments
  2      in exclusive mode;
Table(s) Locked.
```

FIGURE 8.5   The Database Locks screen in EM Database Control

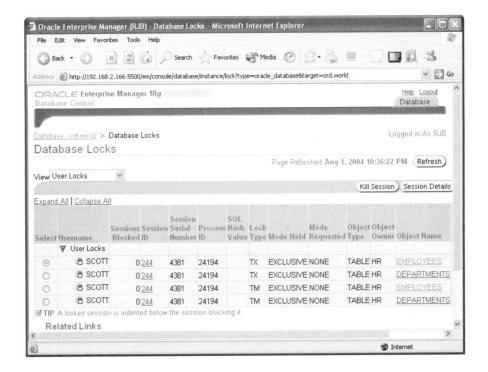

SCOTT has an EXCLUSIVE lock on both the EMPLOYEES and DEPARTMENTS table. You can drill down on the locked object by clicking one of the links in the Object Name column; similarly, you can review other information about SCOTT's session by clicking one of the links in the Session ID column.

Understanding and Resolving Deadlocks

Resolving a lock conflict, the user can either COMMIT or ROLLBACK the current transaction. If you cannot contact the user and it is an emergency, you can select the session holding the lock, and click the Kill Session button in the Database Locks screen of the EM Database Control (refer to Figure 8.5, earlier in this chapter). The next time the user whose session has been killed tries to execute a command, the error message ORA-00028: Your session has been killed is returned. Again, this is an option of last resort: all the statements executed in the session since the last COMMIT are lost.

Real World Scenario

User Education, Locking, and Error Messages

Some of our users who updated their tables using the SQL> command prompt instead of the application would come back from lunch, try to continue their work, and find that they had received an ORA-00028: Your session has been killed error message, which usually initiated a heated discussion with the DBA about lost work due to their session being canceled without notice.

At first, the users thought that the DBA group was either cleaning up unused connections manually or that a new automatic resource management policy was in place, because the details for this error message did not explain why the session was cancelled:

Cause   A privileged user has killed your session and you are no longer logged on to the database.

Action   Log in again if you want to continue working.

As it turns out, the users were not always performing a COMMIT before they left for lunch; the other users who were trying to finish their work could not complete their updates because the rows of the tables were still locked in a transaction that had not yet been committed. They called the DBA, who identified the locking sessions and canceled them, generating the ORA-0002 message for the canceled session.

Oracle error messages are not always clear, and the detailed description of the error message doesn't always help, but at least it provides a starting point for investigating a problem. Make sure that the users can access the Oracle error messages, either via the Internet at www.oracle.com or via an internal shared directory containing all the Oracle documentation for the installation options at your site.

A more serious type of lock conflict is a *deadlock*. A deadlock is a special type of lock conflict in which two or more users are waiting for a resource locked by the other users. As a result, neither transaction can complete without some kind of intervention: the session that first detects a deadlock rolls back the statement waiting on the resource with the error message ORA-00060: Deadlock detected while waiting for resource.

In Table 8.3, two sessions are attempting to update a row locked by the other session.

TABLE 8.3 Deadlock Scenario

Session 1	Time	Session 2
update employees set salary = salary * 1.2 where employee_id = 102;	11:29	update employees set manager = 100 where employee_id = 109;
update employees set salary = salary * 1.2 where employee_id = 109;	11:44	update employees set manager = 100 where employee_id = 102;
ORA-00060: Deadlock detected while waiting for resource	11:45	Control returns to user

After the error message is issued at 11:45, the second UPDATE for Session 1 does not succeed; however, the second UPDATE for Session 2 completes, and the user in Session 2 can now submit another DML statement or issue a COMMIT or ROLLBACK. The user in Session 1 will have to re-issue the second UPDATE.

Summary

In this chapter, we presented the undo tablespace and its importance for the two types of database users: those who want to query a table and receive consistent results, and those who want to make changes to a table and have the option to roll back the data to its state when the transaction started. The undo tablespace provides undo information, or the value of rows in a table before changes were made, for both classes of users. More specifically, undo data facilitates rollback operations, read consistency, certain database recovery operations, and several types of flashback features, some of which were introduced in Oracle9*i* and greatly expanded in Oracle 10*g*.

An undo tablespace can be configured with a handful of initialization parameters: UNDO_MANAGEMENT to define the mode in which undo is managed, with values of either MANUAL or AUTO. The UNDO_TABLESPACE parameter identifies the current undo tablespace, which can be switched while the database is open to users; however, only one undo tablespace can be active at a time.

You can use the EM Database Control to both proactively monitor and resize the undo tablespace, before you get the phone call from the user whose transactions are failing or SELECT statements are not completing. For databases whose long-running queries have priority over successful DML transactions, you can specify that an undo tablespace retain expired undo information at the expense of failed transactions.

In the second part of the chapter, we showed you how to monitor resource locks within a transaction, both at the row level and the table level. Although Oracle usually manages locks at the minimum level to ensure that two sessions do not try to simultaneously update the same row in a table, you can explicitly lock a table at a number of levels. In addition, you can lock a subset of rows in a table to prevent updates or locks from other transactions with the FOR UPDATE clause in the SELECT statement.

Finally, we presented some reasons that lock conflicts occur and how to resolve them; a special kind of lock conflict, called a deadlock, occurs when two users are waiting on a resource locked by the other user. Deadlocks, unlike other types of lock conflicts, are resolved quickly and automatically by Oracle long before any manual lock resolution is attempted.

Exam Essentials

Know the purpose of the Undo Advisor.   Optimize the UNDO_RETENTION parameter as well as the size of the undo tablespace by using Undo Advisor. Use the graph on the Undo Advisor screen to perform what-if analyses given the undo retention requirements.

Be able to monitor locking and resolve lock conflicts.   Identify the reasons for database lock conflicts, and explain how to resolve them. Show an example of a more serious type of lock conflict, a deadlock.

List the features supported by undo data in an undo tablespace.   Enumerate the four primary uses for undo data: rollback, read consistency, database recovery, and flashback operations. Show how the rollback requirements for users that perform long transactions can interfere with read consistency required for query users. Be able to identify and use the method to preserve expired undo at the expense of transactions.

Summarize the steps for monitoring, configuring, and administering the undo tablespace.   Set the initialization parameters required to use an undo tablespace. Be able to review the status of the undo tablespace using EM Database Control, and use the Undo Advisor to resize the undo tablespace when conditions warrant it. Alter the initialization parameter UNDO_RETENTION to configure how long undo information needs to be retained for long-running queries.

List the types of lock modes available when locking a table.   Identify the locks available, from least restrictive to most restrictive. Be able to request a lock with either a LOCK or SELECT statement and return immediately if the lock is not available.

Review Questions

1. What will be the salary of employee number 189 at the completion of the following SQL statements?

```
update emp set salary = 1000 where employee_num = 189;
savepoint save_1;
update emp set salary = salary * 1.1 where employee_num = 189;
savepoint save_2;
update emp set salary = salary * 1.1 where employee_num = 189;
savepoint save_3;
rollback to savepoint save_2;
commit;
update emp set salary = 1500 where employee_num = 189;
savepoint save_4;
rollback to save_4;
commit;
```

   A. 1000

   B. 1100

   C. 1111

   D. 1500

2. Which of the following commands returns an error if the transaction starts with SET TRANSACTION READ ONLY?

   A. ALTER SYSTEM

   B. SELECT

   C. ALTER USER

   D. SET ROLE

3. Which of the following commands is most likely to generate an error message? (Choose two.)

   A. ALTER SYSTEM SET UNDO_MANAGEMENT=AUTO SCOPE=MEMORY;

   B. ALTER SYSTEM SET UNDO_MANAGEMENT=AUTO SCOPE=SPFILE;

   C. ALTER SYSTEM SET UNDO_MANAGEMENT=MANUAL SCOPE=MEMORY;

   D. ALTER SYSTEM SET UNDO_MANAGEMENT=MANUAL SCOPE=SPFILE;

   E. ALTER SYSTEM SET UNDO_TABLESPACE=RBS1 SCOPE=BOTH;

4. Guaranteed undo retention can be specified for which of the following objects?

   A. A tablespace

   B. A table

   C. The database

   D. A transaction

   E. The instance

5. Which dynamic performance view can help you adjust the size of an undo tablespace?

   A. V$UNDOSTAT

   B. V$ROLLSTAT

   C. V$SESSION

   D. V$ROLLNAME

6. Which of the following lock modes permits concurrent queries on a table but prohibits updates to the locked table?

   A. ROW SHARE

   B. ROW EXCLUSIVE

   C. EXCLUSIVE

   D. SHARE ROW EXCLUSIVE

   E. SHARE

7. The highest level at which a user can request a lock is the _____ level.

   A. Schema

   B. Table

   C. Row

   D. Block

8. In the following scenario, two different transactions are updating rows in the same table. What happens at 11:45? (Choose the best answer.)

Session 1	Time	Session 2
update employees set salary = salary * 1.2 where employee_id = 102;	11:29	update employees set manager = 100 where employee_id = 109;
update employees set salary = salary * 1.2 where employee_id = 109;	11:44	update employees set manager = 100 where employee_id = 102;
?	11:45	?

   A. One of the users calls the DBA who immediately kills one of the sessions holding the lock.

   B. The transactions in both Session 1 and Session 2 are both rolled back after both sessions receive an ORA-00060: Deadlock detected while waiting for resource message, and the statements in both transactions must be re-executed, but no other work is lost.

   C. Both Session 1 and Session 2 are killed by Oracle with an ORA-00028: Your session has been killed message and must redo all other statements executed since the last COMMIT.

   D. Session 1 generates an ORA-00060: Deadlock detected while waiting for resource message and rolls back the transaction. The user in Session 2 is then free to roll back or commit their transaction.

9. To retrieve the rollback segment name assigned to a transaction, you can join the dynamic performance view V$TRANSACTION to which other dynamic performance view?

A. V$ROLLSTAT

B. V$ROLLNAME

C. V$UNDOSTAT

D. V$TRANSACTION_ENQUEUE

10. Select the statement that is not true regarding undo tablespaces.

A. Undo tablespaces will not be created if they are not specified in the CREATE DATABASE command.

B. Two undo tablespaces can be active if a new undo tablespace was specified and the old one contains pending transactions.

C. You can switch from one undo tablespace to another while the database is online.

D. UNDO_MANAGEMENT cannot be changed dynamically while the instance is running.

11. To resolve a lock conflict, which of the following methods can you use? (Choose two.)

A. Oracle automatically resolves the lock after a short but predefined time period by killing the session that is holding the lock.

B. The DBA can kill the session holding the lock.

C. The user can either roll back or commit the transaction that is holding the lock.

D. Oracle automatically resolves the lock after a short but predefined period by killing the session that is requesting the lock.

12. If all extents in an undo segment fill up, which of the following occurs next? (Choose all that apply.)

A. A new extent is allocated in the undo segment if all existing extents still contain active transaction data.

B. Other transactions using the segment are moved to another existing segment with enough free space.

C. A new undo segment is created, and the transaction that filled up the undo segment is moved in its entirety to another undo segment.

D. The first extent in the segment is reused if the undo data in the first extent is not needed.

E. The transaction that filled up the undo segment spills over to another undo segment.

13. Which of the following commands returns control to the user immediately if a table is already locked by another user?

A. LOCK TABLE HR.EMPLOYEES IN EXCLUSIVE MODE WAIT DEFERRED;

B. LOCK TABLE HR.EMPLOYEES IN SHARE MODE NOWAIT;

C. LOCK TABLE HR.EMPLOYEES IN SHARE MODE WAIT DISABLED;

D. LOCK TABLE HR.EMPLOYEES IN EXCLUSIVE MODE NOWAIT DEFERRED;

14. Two transactions occur at the wall clock times in the following table. What happens at 10:05?

Session 1	Time	Session 2
`update customer set region = 'H' where state='WI' and county='GRANT';`	9:51	
	9:59	`update customer set mgr=201 where state='IA' and county='JOHNSON';`
`update customer set region='H' where state='IA' and county='JOHNSON';`	10:01	
	10:05	`update customer set mgr=201 where state='WI' and county='GRANT';`

    A. Session 2 will wait for Session 1 to commit or roll back.

    B. Session 1 will wait for Session 2 to commit or roll back.

    C. A deadlock will occur, and both sessions will hang unless one of the users cancels their statement or the DBA kills one of the sessions.

    D. A deadlock will occur, and Oracle will cancel one of the statements.

    E. Neither session is updating the same column, so no waiting or deadlock will occur.

15. Undo information falls into all the following categories except for which of the following?

    A. Uncommitted undo information

    B. Undo information required in case an instance crash requires a roll forward operation when the instance is restarted

    C. Committed undo information required to satisfy the undo retention interval

    D. Expired undo information that is no longer needed to support a running transaction

16. Undo segments are owned by which user?

    A. SYSTEM

    B. The user that initiated the transaction

    C. SYS

    D. The user that owns the object changed by the transaction

17. Undo data in an undo tablespace is not used for which of the following purposes?

   A. Providing users with read-consistent queries

   B. Rolling forward after an instance failure

   C. Flashback queries

   D. Recovering from a failed transaction

   E. Restoring original data when a ROLLBACK is issued

18. Which dynamic performance view shows which transactions are assigned to which undo segment in the undo tablespace?

   A. V$TRANSACTION

   B. V$ROLLSTAT

   C. V$SESSION

   D. V$UNDOSTAT

19. The user SCOTT runs a query at 8:25 A.M. that receives an ORA-01555: Snapshot too old error after running for 15 minutes. An alert is sent to the DBA that the undo tablespace is incorrectly sized. At 10:15 A.M., the DBA checks the initialization parameter UNDO_RETENTION, and its value is 3600; the parameter is sized correctly. The DBA doubles the size of the undo tablespace by adding a second datafile. At 1:15 P.M., the user SCOTT runs the same query and once again receives an ORA-01555: Snapshot too old error. What happens next? (Choose the best answer.)

   A. The DBA receives another alert indicating that the undo tablespace is still undersized.

   B. The user SCOTT calls the DBA to report that the query is still failing.

   C. The second datafile autoextends so that future queries will have enough undo to complete when there is concurrent DML activity.

   D. Resumable Space Allocation suspends the query until the DBA adds another datafile to the undo tablespace, and then the query runs to completion.

20. The EM Database Control Undo Advisor screen uses _____ to recommend the new size of the undo tablespace.

   A. The value of the parameter UNDO_RETENTION

   B. The number of Snapshot too old errors

   C. The current size of the undo tablespace

   D. The desired amount of time to retain undo data

   E. The most recent undo generation rate

Answers to Review Questions

1. D. The last ROLLBACK statement rolls back all DML statements since SAVEPOINT SAVE_4; the last UPDATE was executed before the SAVEPOINT to SAVE_4, therefore the change made by the last UPDATE is unchanged, and the salary remains 1500.

2. C. The ALTER USER command changes data, even though it resides in the data dictionary; no data in a table can be changed in a READ ONLY transaction.

3. A, C. You cannot dynamically change the parameter UNDO_MANAGEMENT after the instance has started. You can, however, change the UNDO_TABLESPACE parameter to switch to another undo tablespace while the instance is up and running.

4. A. Guaranteed undo retention can be set at the tablespace level by using the RETENTION GUARANTEE clause with either the CREATE TABLESPACE or ALTER TABLESPACE command. Only undo tablespaces can have this attribute.

5. A. When database activity is at its peak, the V$UNDOSTAT view, in conjunction with the value for UNDO_RETENTION and DB_BLOCK_SIZE, can be used to calculate an optimal undo tablespace size. Also, the Undo Advisor in the EM Database Control can provide the same optimal tablespace size in a GUI environment.

6. E. SHARE mode permits concurrent queries but prohibits updates to the locked table. SHARE mode is required to create an index on the table.

7. B. The highest level at which a user can request a lock is the table level; the only other lock level available to a user is a row level lock. Users cannot lock at the block or schema level.

8. D. At 11:45, both sessions are waiting for the row locked by the other session. Within a short but predetermined amount of time, Oracle rolls back the statement that detected the deadlock, which could be either session and is not dependent on when each of the transactions started or attempted to update rows locked by other users.

9. B. The column XIDUSN in the view V$TRANSACTION can be joined with the column USN in V$ROLLNAME to retrieve the column NAME in V$ROLLNAME containing the rollback segment name.

10. A. If an undo tablespace is not explicitly created in the CREATE DATABASE command, Oracle automatically creates one with the name SYS_UNDOTBS.

11. B, C. Locks are resolved at the user level by either committing or rolling back the transaction holding the lock. Also, the DBA can kill the session holding the lock as a last resort.

12. A, D. If a transaction fills up an undo segment, either a new extent is allocated for the undo segment or other extents in the segment are reused if the undo data in those extents is no longer needed by other transactions using the same undo segment. Transactions cannot cross segment boundaries in an undo tablespace nor can they move to another segment.

13. B. Regardless of the type of lock requested, NOWAIT is required if you want the command with the lock request to terminate immediately if a lock is already held on the table.

14. D. At 10:01, Session 1 waits for Session 2. At 10:05, a deadlock will occur; Oracle detects the deadlock and cancels one of the statements.

15. B. Undo information is required for instance recovery, but only to roll back uncommitted transactions after the online redo logs roll forward.

16. C. Undo segments are always owned by SYS.

17. B. The online redo log files are used to roll forward after an instance failure; undo data is used to roll back any uncommitted transactions.

18. A. The dynamic performance view V$TRANSACTION contains the column XIDUSN, which is the undo segment number in the current undo tablespace.

19. B. Even if the size of the undo tablespace is adjusted after an undo space problem, only one alert is sent for each 24-hour period. Therefore, the only way that the problem will be resolved promptly is for SCOTT to call the DBA, as the DBA will not receive another alert until the next day when another query fails.

20. D. The Undo Advisor screen uses the desired time period for undo data retention and analyzes the impact of the desired undo retention setting.

Chapter 9

Proactive Database Maintenance and Performance Monitoring

ORACLE DATABASE 10*G*: ADMINISTRATION I EXAM OBJECTIVES COVERED IN THIS CHAPTER:

✓ **Performance Monitoring**

- Troubleshoot invalid and unusable objects.
- Gather optimizer statistics.
- View performance metrics.
- React to performance issues.

✓ **Proactive Maintenance**

- Set warning and critical alert thresholds.
- Collect and use baseline metrics.
- Use tuning and diagnostic advisors.
- Use the Automatic Database Diagnostic Monitor (ADDM).
- Manage the Automatic Workload Repository.
- Describe server generated alerts.

Exam objectives are subject to change at any time without prior notice and at Oracle's sole discretion. Please visit Oracle's Training and Certification website (http://www.oracle.com/education/certification/) for the most current exam objectives listing.

Successful database administrators are always on the lookout for potential database problems that could adversely impact the availability or performance of the systems they manage. Historically, DBAs have resorted to third-party monitoring tools, Oracle's Enterprise Manager suite, or home-grown SQL scripts to gather, store, and analyze database information.

In Oracle Database 10*g* (Oracle 10*g*), however, several new features allow you to easily collect and analyze database performance statistics and proactively respond to problems when they are detected in the database. These new features include the Automatic Workload Repository (AWR), Automated Database Diagnostic Monitoring (ADDM), and the Oracle 10*g* Tuning and Diagnostic Advisors.

In this chapter, we will look at these features in detail.

Proactive Database Maintenance

You can monitor your systems for management and performance problems in essentially two ways: reactively and proactively.

Reactive monitoring involves monitoring a database environment after a performance or management issue has arisen. For example, you start gathering performance statistics using third-party tools, Enterprise Manager, or home-grown scripts after users call to tell you that the system is slow. Obviously, this type of monitoring leaves a lot to be desired, because a problem has already arisen and the users of the system are already impacted. You can use the techniques discussed in this chapter for reactive monitoring, but they are most effective when used to perform proactive monitoring.

Proactive monitoring allows you to identify and respond to common database performance and management issues before, during, or immediately after they occur. Most of the new features in Enterprise Manager (EM) Database Control are geared toward proactive monitoring.

The monitoring tools available in EM Database Control collect their information from a variety of sources (usually the same sources from which your existing third-party tools and home-grown scripts collect their monitoring information): data dictionary views, dynamic performance views, and the operating system. Oracle 10*g* also makes extensive use of the cost-based optimizer statistics for its proactive monitoring. All these sources of information are accessed by the Automatic Workload Repository feature described in the next section.

Automatic Workload Repository

Oracle 10*g* introduces two new background processes—Memory Monitor (MMON) and Memory Monitor Light (MMNL). These processes work together to collect performance statistics directly from the System Global Area (SGA). The MMON process does most of the work by waking up every 60 minutes and gathering statistical information from the data dictionary views, dynamic performance views, and optimizer and then storing this information in the database. The tables that store these statistics are called the *Automatic Workload Repository (AWR)*. These tables are owned by the user SYSMAN and are stored in the SYSAUX tablespace.

To activate the AWR feature, you must set the PFILE/SPFILE parameter STATISTICS_LEVEL to the appropriate value. The values assigned to this parameter determine the depth of the statistics that the MMON process gathers. Table 9.1 shows the values that can be assigned to the STATISTICS_LEVEL parameter.

TABLE 9.1   Specifying Statistics Collection Levels

Collection Level	Description
BASIC	Disables the AWR and most other diagnostic monitoring and advisory activities. Few database statistics are gathered at each collection interval when operating the instance in this mode.
TYPICAL	Activates the standard level of collection activity. This is the default value for AWR and is appropriate for most environments.
ALL	Captures all the statistics gathered by the TYPICAL collection level, plus the execution plans and timing information from the operating system.

Once gathered, the statistics are stored in the AWR for a default duration of 7 days. However, you can modify both the frequency of the snapshots and the duration for which they are saved in the AWR. One way to modify these intervals is by using the Oracle-supplied package DBMS_WORKLOAD_REPOSITORY. The following SQL command shows the DBMS_WORKLOAD_REPOSITORY package being used to change the AWR collection interval to 1 hour and the retention period to 30 days:

```
SQL> execute dbms_workload_repository.modify_snapshot_settings
  (interval=>60,retention=>43200);

PL/SQL procedure successfully completed.
```

The 30-day retention value shown above is expressed in minutes: 60 minutes per hour × 24 hours per day × 30 days = 43,200 minutes.

You can also change the AWR collection interval, retention period, and collection depth using the EM Database Control. Choose Administration ➢ Automatic Workload Repository ➢ Edit on the main screen to open the Edit Settings screen shown in Figure 9.1.

In Figure 9.1, the retention period for statistics gathered by the MMON process is set to 10 days, and statistics are collected every 15 minutes. You can also modify the depth at which statistics are collected by the AWR by clicking the Collection Level link. Clicking this link opens the Initialization Parameters screen in which you can specify any of the three pre-defined collection levels shown in Table 9.1. Figure 9.2 shows the AWR collection level being changed from TYPICAL to ALL.

FIGURE 9.1 Setting AWR statistics collection and retention using EM

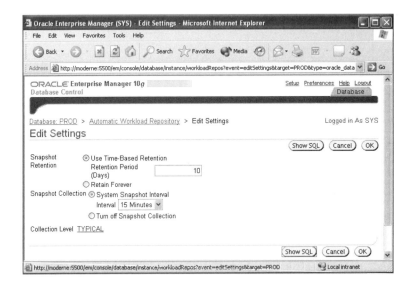

FIGURE 9.2 Changing the AWR statistics collection level

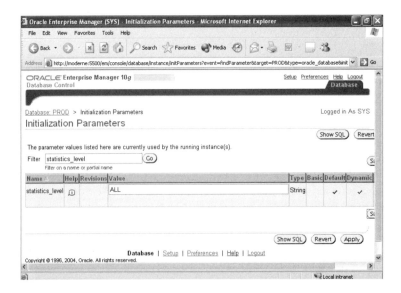

WARNING   Take care when specifying the AWR statistics collection interval. Gathering snapshots too frequently requires additional space in the SYSAUX tablespace and adds additional database overhead each time the statistics are collected.

Once AWR snapshots are taken and stored in the database, the Automatic Database Diagnostic feature uses the statistics as described in the next section.

Automatic Database Diagnostic Monitoring

Following each AWR statistics collection process, the *Automated Database Diagnostic Monitoring (ADDM)* feature automatically analyzes the gathered statistics and compares them to the statistics gathered by the previous two AWR snapshots. By comparing the current statistics to these two previous snapshots, the ADDM can easily identify potential database problems such as CPU and I/O bottlenecks, resource-intensive SQL or PL/SQL, lock contention, and the utilization of Oracle's memory structures within the SGA.

Based on these findings, the ADDM may recommend possible remedies. The goal of these recommendations is to minimize *DB Time*. DB Time is composed of two types of time measures for non-idle database users: CPU time and wait time. This information is stored as the cumulative time that all database users have spent either using CPU resources or waiting for access to resources such as CPU, I/O, or Oracle's memory structures. High or increasing values for DB Time indicate that users are requesting increasingly more server resources and may also be experiencing waits for those resources, which can lead to less than optimal performance. In this way, minimizing DB Time is a much better way to measure overall database performance than Oracle's old ratio-based tuning methodologies.

NOTE   DB Time is calculated by combining all the times from all non-idle user sessions into one number. Therefore, it is possible for the DB Time value to be larger than the total time that the instance has been running.

Once ADDM completes its comparison of the newly collected statistics to the previously collected statistics, the results are stored in the AWR. You can use these statistics to establish baselines against which future performance will be compared, and you can use deviations from these baseline measures to identify areas that need attention. In this manner, ADDM allows you to not only better detect and alert yourself to potential management and performance problems in the database, but also allows you to take corrective actions to rectify those problems quickly and with little or no manual intervention.

The following sections introduce the interfaces, features, and functionality of ADDM and explain how you can use this utility to monitor and manage database storage, security, and performance. We'll begin by examining the EM Database Control tools that you can use to view the results of ADDM analysis.

NOTE   Baselines are discussed later in this chapter in the section "ADDM Alerts."

Using EM Database Control to View ADDM Analysis

EM Database Control graphically displays the results of the ADDM analysis on several screens, including:

- The Performance Findings link under the Diagnostic Summary section of the EM Database Control main screen
- The Performance tab of the EM Database Control main screen
- The ADDM screen located by clicking the Advisor Central link at the bottom of the EM Database Control main screen

Sample output from each of the EM Database Control screens is shown in the following sections.

The EM Database Control Performance Findings Link

The EM Database Control main screen contains a section called Diagnostic Summary. One of the links under this section is called Performance Findings. Figure 9.3 shows this section.

The output in Figure 9.3 shows that ADDM discovered 10 performance-related findings. Clicking the link for these 10 performance findings displays the ADDM summary screen, at the bottom of which is displayed the Performance Analysis section, as shown in Figure 9.4.

FIGURE 9.3 The Diagnostic Summary section of the EM Database main screen

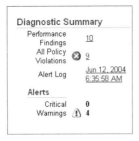

FIGURE 9.4 The Performance Analysis section of the ADDM Summary

		View Snapshots	View Report
Database Time (minutes) **47.22**	Period Start Time	**Jun 13, 2004 9:27:52 AM**	Period Duration (minutes) **12.42**
Task Owner **SYS**	Average Active Sessions **3.8**		

Impact (%) ▽	Finding	Recommendations
59.29	The throughput of the I/O subsystem was significantly lower than expected.	1 Host Configuration
51.55	Individual database segments responsible for significant user I/O wait were found.	4 Segment Tuning
29.41	Individual database segments responsible for significant physical I/O were found.	2 Segment Tuning
28.7	Undo I/O was a significant portion (32%) of the total database I/O.	1 DB Configuration
16.21	SQL statements consuming significant database time were found.	1 SQL Tuning
15.13	The buffer cache was undersized causing significant additional read I/O.	1 DB Configuration
4.1	Waits for redo log buffer space were consuming significant database time.	1 DB Configuration 1 Host Configuration
3.67	Wait event "log file switch completion" in wait class "Configuration" was consuming significant database time.	3 Application Analysis
1.05	The PGA was inadequately sized, causing additional I/O to temporary tablespaces to consume significant database time.	1 DB Configuration

The output in Figure 9.4 shows that the greatest impact to performance is due to bottlenecks related to disk I/O (described by ADDM as "The throughput of the I/O subsystem was significantly lower than expected"). By clicking this link, you can view ADDM's recommendation for correcting this problem, which is shown in Figure 9.5.

ADDM suggests three options for improving the performance of the I/O on this system:

- Stripe and mirror (also known as SAME) all datafiles across multiple disk drives.

- Increase the number of physical disk drives.

- Consider implementing Oracle's Automatic Storage Management feature.

The SAME, or Stripe and Mirror Everything, methodology suggested in Figure 9.5 refers to a database file configuration strategy that is described in this white paper on the Oracle Technology Network: http://otn.oracle.com/deploy/availability/pdf/OOW2000_same_ppt.pdf.

Figure 9.4 also shows that a large portion of our I/O problems are related to specific database tables or indexes: "Individual database segments responsible for significant physical I/O were found." Clicking this link displays the detailed ADDM findings shown in Figure 9.6.

ADDM has essentially identified the SALES_HISTORY table as the source of excessive I/O and recommends that you run the Segment Advisor utility against this table to generate recommendations for improving its performance. The Segment Advisor is described later in this section.

FIGURE 9.5 The ADDM performance finding details for I/O

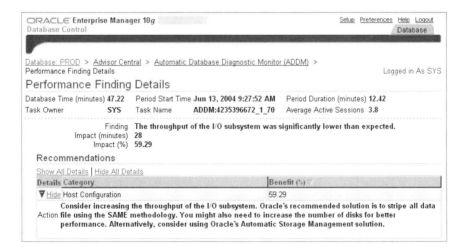

FIGURE 9.6   The ADDM performance details for high I/O segments

Database: PROD > Advisor Central > Automatic Database Diagnostic Monitor (ADDM) >
Performance Finding Details   Logged in As SYS

Performance Finding Details

Database Time (minutes) 47.22	Period Start Time **Jun 13, 2004 9:27:52 AM**	Period Duration (minutes) **12.42**	
Task Owner	**SYS**	Task Name	**ADDM:4235396672_1_70**	Average Active Sessions **3.8**

Finding **Individual database segments responsible for significant physical I/O were found.**
Impact (minutes) **13.89**
Impact (%) **29.41**

Recommendations

Show All Details | Hide All Details

Details	Category	Benefit (%)
▼ Hide	Segment Tuning	21.33

Action **Investigate application logic involving I/O on TABLE "SH.SALES_HISTORY" with object id 50401.**
View Rationale
Message **Run "Segment Advisor" on TABLE "SH.SALES_HISTORY" with object id 50401.**
Action **Run "Segment Advisor" on TABLE "SH.SALES_HISTORY" with object id 50401.**

| ▶ Show | Segment Tuning | 8.08 |

The EM Database Control Performance Tab

You can also click the Performance tab on the EM Database Control main screen to view performance data collected by AWR and analyzed by ADDM. ADDM uses its findings to populate the Sessions: Waiting And Working section of the Performance screen, as shown in Figure 9.7.

Using this section of the Performance screen, you can drill down into detailed information in 11 areas that have been identified as having an impact on performance, from User I/O thorough CPU Used. By clicking the User I/O link, you can drill down into detailed information about user I/O, as shown in Figure 9.8.

The graph in Figure 9.8 shows the times at which the snapshots were taken along its X axis. The lines on the graph show which of the events in the graph's legend experienced the most activity during that snapshot period. The graph output indicates that most of the user I/O activity is experiencing waits for the database event "db file scattered read." This event is caused by the I/O activity that occurs when Oracle experiences a wait while performing a sequential disk read of contiguous blocks from a datafile into the buffer cache—usually when a table is being accessed using a full table scan or fast full index scan.

FIGURE 9.7   Sessions: Waiting And Working section of the Performance screen

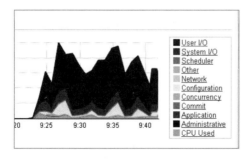

FIGURE 9.8   Detailed user I/O information

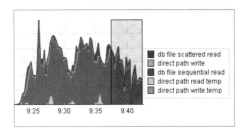

For a complete listing and description of all database wait events, see Appendix C: Oracle Wait Events of *Oracle Database Reference 10*g *Release 1 (10.1)*, Part No. B10755-01.

The Performance screen, shown in Figure 9.9, also contains a Performance Overview section near the bottom that summarizes, in pie graphs, the top SQL and top session wait events identified by ADDM.

Clicking the links in the boxes next to either of these graphs displays details about that item. For example, clicking the link for the SQL statement that experienced the most wait time (35 percent on the graph) shows the output in Figure 9.10.

The output in Figure 9.10 shows that ADDM identified the SQL statement SELECT count(*) FROM SALES_HISTORY as experiencing the most waits during processing. Clicking the link at the bottom of this same screen allows you to view the execution plan for this statement.

FIGURE 9.9   The Performance Overview section of the Performance screen

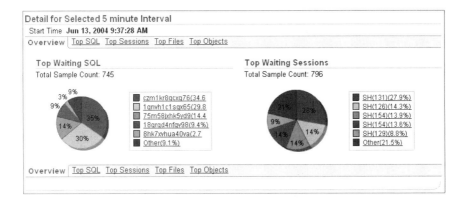

FIGURE 9.10 Drilling down into the Top Waiting SQL

SQL Details: czm1kr8gcxq76

(Run SQL Tuning Advisor)

SQL Text
```
SELECT count(*)
   FROM sales_history
```

Execution Plan | Current Statistics | Execution History | Tuning History

Collected From Target Jun 13, 2004 9:44:04 AM

Data Source	**Cursor Cache**	Plan Hash Value	**1871854880**	Module	**SQL*Plus**
Capture Time	**Jun 13, 2004 9:44:05 AM**	Optimizer Mode	**ALL_ROWS**	Action	**Unavailable**
Parsing Schema	**SH**				

If the execution plan for this query shows that a full table scan of the 900,000+ row SALES_HISTORY table is occurring, then you can see how it might experience I/O waits while retrieving its rows. To view the tuning recommendations that ADDM has generated for this statement, click the Run SQL Tuning Advisor button at the bottom of the screen.

The SQL Tuning Advisor is described later in this chapter.

The Advisor Central Screen

The Advisor Central screen also contains ADDM findings. The link for the Advisor Central screen is at the bottom of the EM Database Control main screen. Click this link to display the Advisor Central screen, the top portion of which is shown in Figure 9.11.

FIGURE 9.11 The Advisor Central screen

Click the ADDM link in the Advisors section of this screen to display a graph, shown in Figure 9.12, that shows all the recent AWR snapshots taken by the MMON process.

As stated earlier, the ADDM automatically compares the most recent AWR snapshot with the last two AWR snapshots when formulating its recommendations. However, you can use this Create ADDM Task screen to manually select any two AWR snapshot times and formulate ADDM recommendations for activity that occurred between those two points in time. To start this process, click the Period Start Time radio button and then select a start date and time by clicking the point in the graph's timeline that corresponds to the beginning period that you want to use. Repeat this process to specify the end process time stamp. Figure 9.13 shows that the start and end time for ADDM analysis have been specified so that they correspond to the two points in time that surround the spike shown in the graph.

FIGURE 9.12   The Create ADDM Task screen

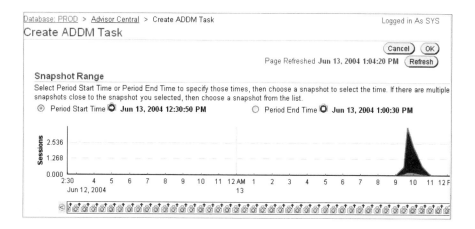

FIGURE 9.13   Manually setting the ADDM analysis period

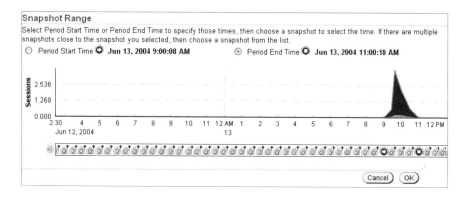

Click OK to analyze the database for possible performance problems between the two specified points in time.

> You can also manually perform an ADDM analysis without the use of EM Database Control by using the addmrpt.sql script located in $ORACLE_HOME/rdbms/admin on Unix systems and %ORACLE_HOME%\rdbms\admin on Windows systems. See Chapter 6 of *Oracle Database Performance Tuning Guide 10g Release 1 (10.1)*, Part Number B10752-01, for details on how to use this script.

The results of this analysis is displayed at the bottom of the ADDM screen that is displayed when the analysis is complete. Figure 9.14 shows an example of the ADDM results for the time interval we chose.

Notice that these findings are similar in nature to the ones displayed by the EM Findings link shown earlier in Figure 9.4. The difference between the two ADDM results is that those in Figure 9.4 are for the last three AWR collection periods as they existed when that page was viewed, whereas the results in Figure 9.14 are for our manually specified time frame. By manually specifying the ADDM analysis period in this way, you can "go back in time" and review previous spikes in performance that may have been missed with real-time monitoring like that shown on the EM Findings link.

Although using EM Database Control to view ADDM results is by far the simplest way to review ADDM recommendations, you can also query the ADDM data dictionary views directly as well. Some of these data dictionary views are discussed in the following section.

Using Data Dictionary Views to View ADDM Analysis

You can use more than 20 data dictionary views to examine the results of ADDM's activities. Four commonly used ADDM views that store the recommendation information we saw in the EM Database Control pages are described in Table 9.2.

FIGURE 9.14   The results of a manually specified ADDM analysis

				View Snapshots	View Report

Database Time (minutes) **134.82** Period Start Time **Jun 13, 2004 9:00:09 AM** Period Duration (minutes) **120.15**
Task Owner **SYS** Average Active Sessions **1.12**

Impact (%) ▽	Finding	Recommendations
45.62	The throughput of the I/O subsystem was significantly lower than expected.	1 Host Configuration
44.68	Individual database segments responsible for significant user I/O wait were found.	5 Segment Tuning
38.97	SQL statements consuming significant database time were found.	5 SQL Tuning
26.92	Individual database segments responsible for significant physical I/O were found.	2 Segment Tuning
26.76	Undo I/O was a significant portion (32%) of the total database I/O.	
11.6	The buffer cache was undersized causing significant additional read I/O.	1 DB Configuration
8.64	Buffer cache writes due to small log files were consuming significant database time.	1 DB Configuration
5.37	Waits for redo log buffer space were consuming significant database time.	1 DB Configuration 1 Host Configuration
4.02	Wait event "log file switch completion" in wait class "Configuration" was consuming significant database time.	3 Application Analysis
3.81	Hard parsing of SQL statements was consuming significant database time.	

TABLE 9.2   ADDM Data Dictionary Views

View Name	Description
DBA_ADVISOR_FINDINGS	Describes the findings identified by the ADDM analysis
DBA_ADVISOR_OBJECTS	Describes the objects that are referenced in the ADDM findings and recommendations
DBA_ADVISOR_RECOMMENDATIONS	Describes the recommendations made based on ADDM findings
DBA_ADVISOR_RATIONALE	Describes the rationale behind each ADDM finding

The following SQL statement shows a sample query on the DBA_ADVISOR_FINDINGS data dictionary view that identifies the type of performance problem that is causing the most impact on the database:

```
SQL> SELECT task_id, type, message
  2  FROm dba_advisor_findings
  3  WHERE impact= (select MAX(impact) FROM dba_advisor_findings);


TASK_ID TYPE       MESSAGE
------- ---------  ---------------------------------------------------
    164 PROBLEM    SQL statements consuming significant database time
                   were found.
```

The output from this query shows that SQL statements being executed in the database are contributing to the poor database performance. By itself, the DBA_ADVISOR_FINDINGS data dictionary view does not identify *which* SQL statements are consuming the database time. Instead, these are shown in the DBA_ADVISOR_OBJECTS data dictionary view and are identified by the TASK_ID value shown in the query on DBA_ADVISOR_FINDINGS. A query on that view, using the TASK_ID of 164 returned by the ADDM session that had the potential for the greatest database impact, returns the SQL statements shown here:

```
SQL> SELECT attr4
  2  FROM dba_advisor_objects
  3  WHERE task_id = 164;


ATTR4
---------------------------------------------------------------------
UPDATE customers SET credit_limit=credit_limit*1.15 WHERE cust_id = :B1
```

```
DELETE FROM sales WHERE time_id BETWEEN '01-JAN-00' and '01-JAN-01';

UPDATE sales_history SET quantity_sold = quantity_sold+10 WHERE
    CHANNEL_ID := B1

SELECT COUNT(*) FROM Sales_history;

SELECT DISTINCT channel_id FROM sales_history;
```

This query shows all the SQL statements that were captured by the AWR during the snapshot period and that were used in the ADDM analysis for that same period.

The DBA_ADVISOR_ACTIONS data dictionary view shows the ADDM recommendations for each finding. The following query shows the recommendations for correcting the performance issues associated with TASK_ID 164, which was identified earlier as being the costliest database activity:

```
SQL> SELECT TRIM(attr1) ATTR1, TRIM(attr2) ATTR2, TRIM(attr3) ATTR3
  2  FROM dba_advisor_actions
  3  WHERE task_id = 164;


ATTR1           ATTR2     ATTR3
----------      ------    ----------
log_buffer      262144    15728640
db_cache_size   25165824  50331648
undo_retention  900       363
```

This output indicates that ADDM recommends that the values for LOG_BUFFER, DB_CACHE_SIZE, and UNDO_RETENTION all be changed from their current values to 15,728,640 bytes, 50,331,648 bytes, and 363 seconds, respectively.

If you want to see the rationale behind each of the actions shown in DBA_ADVISOR_ACTIONS, query the DBA_ADVISOR_RATIONALE data dictionary view. The DBA_ADVISOR_RATIONALE view stores the ADDM recommendations that ADDM has formulated based on the AWR data like those stored in DBA_ADVISOR_FINDINGS and DBA_ADVISOR_OBJECTS. The following example shows a sample query on the DBA_ADVISOR_RATIONALE view using the TASK_ID of 164 identified earlier:

```
SQL> SELECT message
  2  FROM dba_advisor_rationale
  3  WHERE task_id = 164;


MESSAGE
-------------------------------------------------------------------
Buffer cache writes due to small log files were consuming significant
```

```
database time.
```

```
The buffer cache was undersized causing significant read I/O.
```

```
The value of "undo retention" was 900 seconds and the longest running
   query lasted only 330 seconds. This extra retention caused
   unnecessary I/O.
```

 As you can see from the complexity of these examples, examining the ADDM results via the EM Database Control is much easier than accessing the data dictionary views via SQL. From a practical standpoint, you would run SQL queries against these ADDM views only if the EM Database Control were unavailable.

To gain further insight into the recommendations and information gathered by the ADDM, Oracle 10g also provides several advisor utilities in the EM Database Control. These advisors are discussed in the next section.

ADDM Diagnostic Advisors

The ADDM utility also provides several tuning and diagnostic advisors that you can use to examine several common problem areas in your database and then offer suggestions for improving those areas. The diagnostic and tuning advisors include the following:

- SQL Tuning Advisor
- SQL Access Advisor
- Memory Advisor
- Mean Time To Recover Advisor
- Segment Advisor
- Undo Management Advisor

The links to all these advisors are available by clicking the Advisor Central link at the bottom of the EM Database Control main screen. Each of the links listed on the Advisor Central screen is described in the following sections.

The SQL Tuning Advisor

As you saw earlier, the ADDM utility allows you to drill down and view the actual SQL of the statements that are contributing to increasing DB Times. Once the SQL has been identified, you can use the SQL Tuning Advisor to attempt to formulate more efficient SQL execution plans for the offending SQL. Figure 9.15 shows the SQL Tuning Advisor Links screen.

FIGURE 9.15   The SQL Tuning Advisor Links main screen

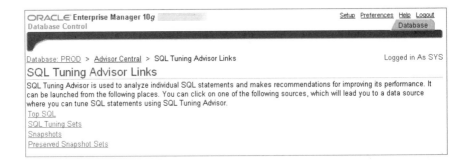

There are four options for the SQL Tuning Advisor: Top SQL, SQL Tuning Sets, Snapshots, and Preserved Snapshot Sets. Table 9.3 compares these options.

TABLE 9.3   Types of Analysis for the SQL Tuning Advisor

Link Name	Description
Top SQL	Allows you to identify and tune the most resource-intensive SQL statements
SQL Tuning Sets	Allows you to group several related SQL statements together for analysis
Snapshots	Allows you to select a specific snapshot to analyze
Preserved Snapshot Sets	Allows you to create and analyze a collection of related snapshots

The following examples use the Top SQL option of the SQL Tuning Advisor. You can view the Top SQL statements in two ways, Spot SQL and Period SQL; each are represented by a tab in the Top SQL screen.

AWR automatically assigns a system-generated name to each SQL statement that is recorded. These names are a combination of 13 numbers and lower-case letters.

Spot SQL graphically displays all the resource wait, I/O, and CPU statistics for SQL statements that have been active in the most recent five-minute interval. By examining the graphical output, you can readily identify which SQL statements caused spikes in these three areas. Figure 9.16 shows a sample Spot SQL screen.

FIGURE 9.16   The Spot SQL tab in the Top SQL screen

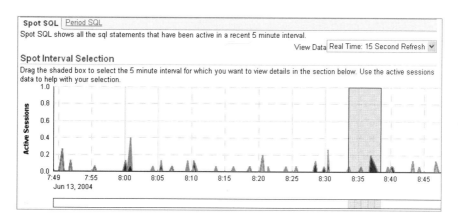

Period SQL allows you to examine the SQL that occurred within the last 24 hours, between two points in time. By examining the graphical output on this screen, you can also easily identify which periods of time experienced spikes in the areas of resource waits, I/O, and CPU. Figure 9.17 shows a sample Period SQL screen.

Regardless of whether you isolate your problem SQL statements using ADDM, Spot SQL, or Period SQL, the process of analyzing that SQL using the SQL Advisor is the same. First, you need to decide which statement you wish to analyze and then click the Run SQL Tuning Advisor button on the SQL Details page shown in Figure 9.18 after selecting that statement from ADDM, Spot SQL, or Period SQL.

FIGURE 9.17   The Period SQL tab in the Top SQL screen

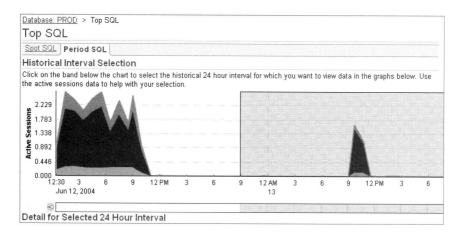

FIGURE 9.18   The SQL Details page

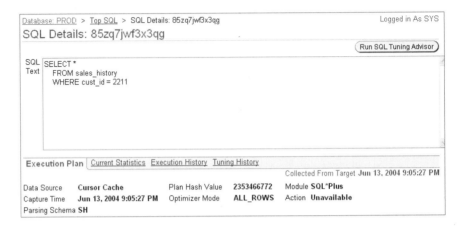

Clicking the Run SQL Tuning Advisor button opens the Schedule Advisor screen. You use this screen to formulate the job that will be submitted to the database when the advisor is actually executed. You specify three elements when running the SQL Tuning Advisor: Description, Scope, and Schedule. Each of these elements is described in Table 9.4.

TABLE 9.4   Elements for Scheduling a SQL Tuning Advisor Job

Job Element	Description
Description	Description of the SQL statement that is being analyzed. Although this is an optional element for submitting a job, it is useful because otherwise Oracle uses a system-generated name for the SQL statement—85zq7jwf3x3qg in Figure 9.18.
Scope	The depth to which the advisor should examine the statement. Possible values are Limited and Comprehensive. The deeper the analysis, the greater the potential for uncovering additional tuning options. You can specify the maximum time that the advisor should spend performing a comprehensive analysis.
Schedule	Specifies when to execute the analysis job. The default value is Immediately, but you can also schedule the job to execute at some time in the future.

Each of these elements is shown in Figure 9.19, which displays a portion of the Schedule Advisor screen.

After you specify the job submission elements, click OK to begin analyzing the specified statement.

Choosing the Comprehensive level of analysis can be time-consuming and resource intensive.

FIGURE 9.19   The SQL Tuning Advisor job scheduling screen

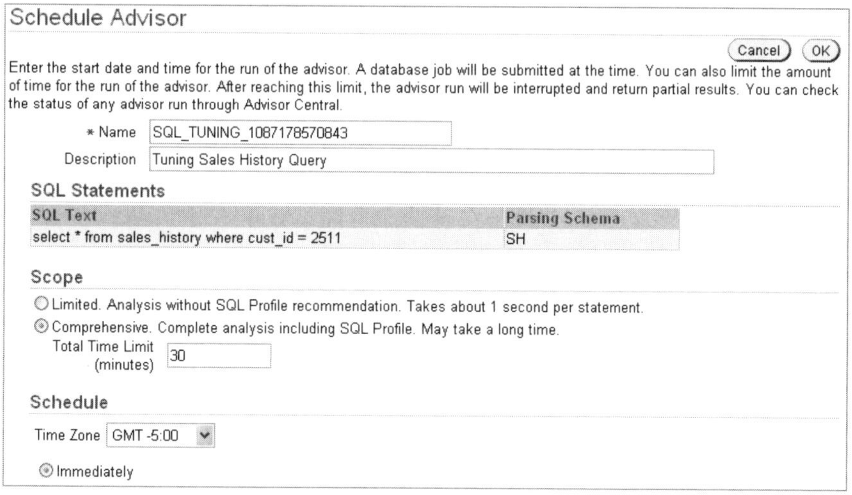

A screen similar to the one shown in Figure 9.20 is displayed once the SQL Tuning Advisor completes its analysis of the specified statement.

In the example in Figure 9.20, the SQL Tuning Advisor is recommending that you add an index to the SALES_HISTORY table. To implement this recommendation, click the Implement button, which will display the Implementation Recommendation screen, as shown in Figure 9.21.

FIGURE 9.20   The completed SQL Tuning Advisor analysis

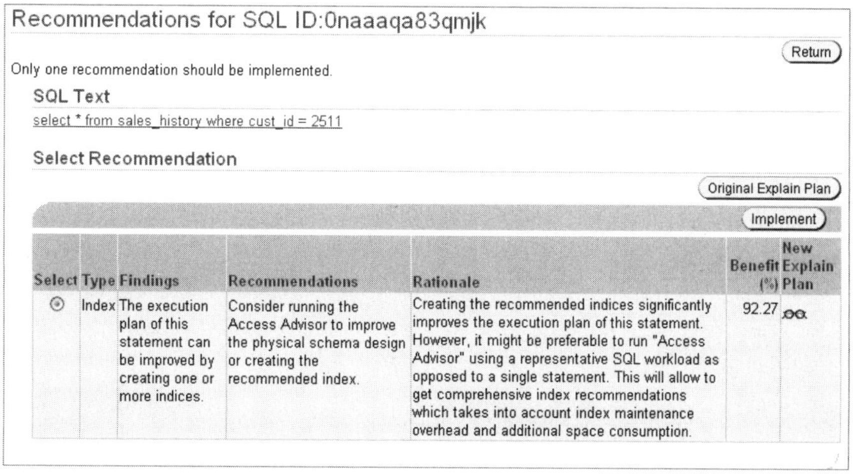

FIGURE 9.21   The SQL Tuning Advisor Implement Recommendation screen

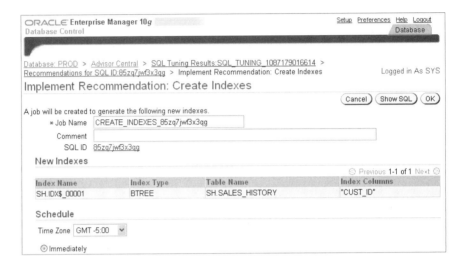

The output in Figure 9.21 shows that the B-Tree index called IDX$_00001 will be created on the CUST_ID column of the SALES_HISTORY table. To review the SQL that will be issued to create this index, click the Show SQL button. If desired, you can modify the generated SQL to rename the index or change its storage parameters. Otherwise, clicking OK submits the job to create the new index. Like the SQL Tuning Advisor, the job can be executed immediately or scheduled to run some time in the future.

Like the SQL identifier, each recommendation is also assigned a system-generated ID made up of a combination of 13 numbers and lowercase letters.

You'll notice that the output in Figure 9.20 also recommends that you use the SQL Access Advisor to further improve the physical design of the schema. This utility is discussed in the next section.

The SQL Access Advisor

You've seen how you can use the SQL Tuning Advisor to identify and create an index to minimize the DB Time for a particular statement. The SQL Access Advisor provides additional support for finding potential schema modifications that you can use to reduce the amount of I/O, CPU, and wait time for a given SQL statement. Figure 9.22 shows the SQL Access Advisor main screen.

FIGURE 9.22 The SQL Access Advisor main screen

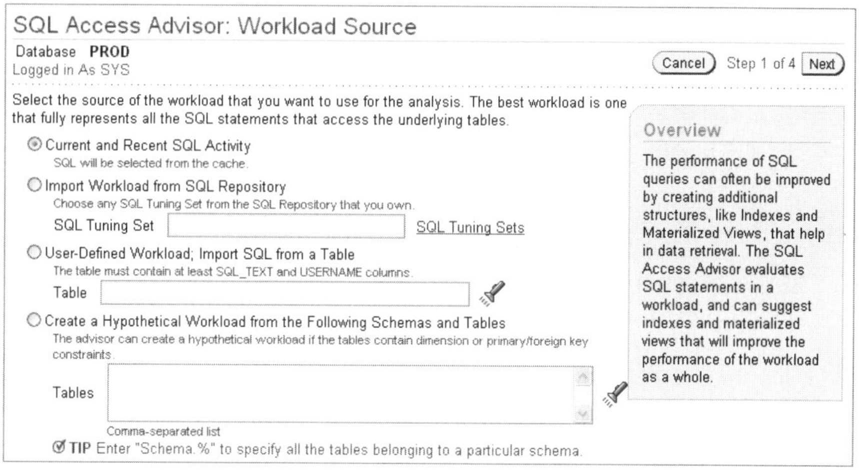

The SQL Access Advisor shows four ways in which you can select the SQL statement to be analyzed. Table 9.5 compares these four techniques.

TABLE 9.5 Comparison of Four Techniques for Selecting SQL to Analyze

Collection Method	Description
Current And Recent SQL Activity	Lets you select the SQL to analyze from what is currently in the SGA
Import Workload From SQL Repository	Lets you analyze a SQL tuning set that was created using the SQL Tuning Advisor
User-Defined Workload; Import SQL From A Table	Lets you perform a tuning analysis on a workload that is not currently running in the database
Create A Hypothetical Workload From The Following Schemas And Tables	Lets you specify a schema against which to generate SQL tuning recommendations

Select the Current And Recent SQL Activity radio button and click Next to display the Recommendation Options screen shown in Figure 9.23.

FIGURE 9.23   The SQL Access Advisor: Recommendation Options screen

SQL Access Advisor: Recommendation Options

Database **PROD**
Logged in As SYS

Cancel Back Step 2 of 4 Next

Recommendation Types

The advisor may recommend indexes or materialized views to reduce the time it takes to read data. However you must balance this benefit against the cost to maintain the additional structures. Select the type of structures to be recommended by the advisor.

⦿ Indexes

◯ Materialized Views

◯ Both Indexes and Materialized Views

☑ TIP Access Advisor jobs generating Materialized View recommendations should be scheduled in maintenance windows.

Advisor Mode

The advisor can run in one of two modes, Limited or Comprehensive. Limited Mode is meant to return quickly after processing the statements with the highest cost, potentially ignoring statements with a cost below a certain threshold. Comprehensive Mode will perform an exhaustive analysis.

⦿ Limited Mode
    Analysis will focus on highest cost statements

◯ Comprehensive Mode

The Advisor can focus its efforts on three options.

- To assess whether the SQL statements will benefit from the addition of an index

- To assess whether the SQL statements will benefit from the addition of a materialized view

- To check for both indexes and materialized views

You can specify the depth level of the analysis as either Limited or Comprehensive.

WARNING   Because Comprehensive tuning analysis can consume a lot of server resources, schedule it when user activity against the database is at its lowest.

Clicking Next after selecting the analysis options displays the scheduling options. Like previous EM Database Control scheduling screens, the time that the analysis will begin, its duration, and its frequency can all be defined on this page.

Finally, clicking Next displays the SQL Access Advisor: Review screen, as shown in Figure 9.24. This screen displays all the options that you specified before clicking Submit to actually begin the analysis.

When the analysis is complete, you return to the Advisor Central screen and a link to the results of the analysis is displayed at the bottom of the screen, as shown in Figure 9.25.

Click the link in the completed analysis table to display the recommendations that the SQL Access Advisor created for SQL statements that were analyzed. Figure 9.26 shows a Recommendations summary screen; the SQL Access Advisor proposed a single recommendation.

FIGURE 9.24   The SQL Access Advisor: Review screen

SQL Access Advisor: Review

Database **PROD**
Logged in As SYS

(Cancel) (Show SQL) (Back) Step 4 of 4 (Submit)

This page allows for review of your chosen input parameters to the SQL Access Advisor.

Task Name   SQLACCESS8929861
Task Description   **SQL Access Advisor**
Scheduled Start Time **Run Immediately**

Options

OPTION △	VALUE
Advisor Mode	Limited Mode
Recommendation Type	Indexes Only
Workload Scope	Partial Workload
Workload Source	SQL Cache
Workload Type	Allow Advisor to Determine Workload Type Based on Workload Content

▶ Show Advanced Options

(Cancel) (Show SQL) (Back) Step 4 of 4 (Submit)

FIGURE 9.25   The completed analysis screen

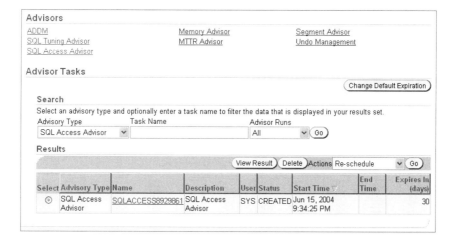

Advisors

ADDM   Memory Advisor   Segment Advisor
SQL Tuning Advisor   MTTR Advisor   Undo Management
SQL Access Advisor

Advisor Tasks

(Change Default Expiration)

Search

Select an advisory type and optionally enter a task name to filter the data that is displayed in your results set.

Advisory Type   Task Name   Advisor Runs
[SQL Access Advisor ▾] [   ]   [All   ▾] (Go)

Results

(View Result) (Delete) Actions [Re-schedule ▾] (Go)

Select	Advisory Type	Name	Description	User	Status	Start Time ▽	End Time	Expires In (days)
⊙	SQL Access Advisor	SQLACCESS8929861	SQL Access Advisor	SYS	CREATED	Jun 15, 2004 9:34:25 PM		30

Clicking Recommendation ID (1) shown in Figure 9.26 displays the details of the SQL Access Advisor recommendation, as displayed in Figure 9.27.

FIGURE 9.26   The SQL Access Advisor Recommendations summary screen

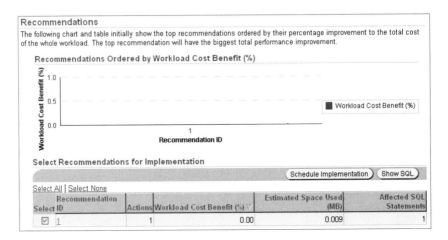

FIGURE 9.27   The SQL Access Advisor recommendation detail screen

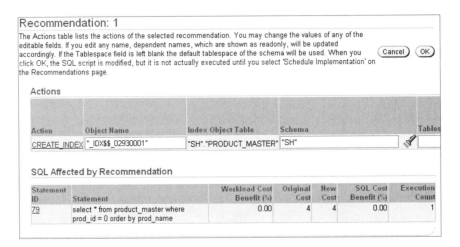

This recommendation indicates that building an index will improve the access path of the SQL statement shown at the bottom of the screen. You can change the default index name of _IDX$$_ 02930001 suggested by the advisor by typing a new name in its place. Additionally, you can also specify the tablespace where the new index should be stored. Clicking OK returns you to the recommendation summary screen shown in Figure 9.26. Click the Schedule Implementation button to schedule the actual creation of the index.

The Memory Advisor

Both the SQL Tuning and Access advisors focus on identifying and tuning the SQL that is having the greatest impact on increasing overall DB Time. Alternatively, you can use the Memory Advisor to gather more global tuning recommendations about all aspects of Oracle's memory structures, including the SGA and user memory structures. You can also access the Memory Advisor from the Advisor Central screen. Figure 9.28 shows the Memory Advisor main screen.

The sizes of four components of the SGA—the Shared Pool, Buffer Cache, Large Pool, and Java Pool—are summarized in tabular and in graphical form. Clicking the Advice buttons next to the Shared Pool and Buffer Cache values tells the Memory Advisor to formulate tuning recommendations for that memory structure. Figure 9.29 shows the Memory Advisor's advice for the Buffer Cache portion of the SGA.

FIGURE 9.28 The Memory Advisor main screen

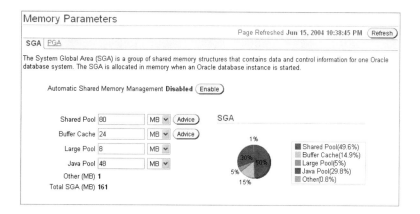

FIGURE 9.29 The Memory Advisor's Buffer Cache recommendation

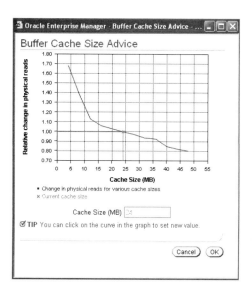

This output shows that as the size of the buffer cache is increased from its current size of 24MB to the recommended size of 48MB, the overall physical reads are reduced by 20 percent (a relative decline from 1.0 to 0.80). This would be beneficial because reads from memory are thousands of times faster than reads from disk.

> If you enable Automatic Shared Memory Management (Figure 9.29 shows that it is disabled for this instance), the ADDM can automatically adjust the size of the Buffer Cache based on its findings.

The main Memory Advisor screen also has a second tab that shows the results of the advisor's analysis of the PGA (Program Global Area) memory that is allocated to each user process. Figure 9.30 shows the PGA tab in the Memory Advisor screen.

Like the SGA screen, the PGA recommendations screen also has an Advice button; click it to view the Memory Advisor's recommendations for improving PGA performance.

The output in Figure 9.31 indicates that the Memory Advisor estimates that if the limit for the aggregate amount of space used for all PGAs were increased from 24MB to 150MB, the resulting cache hit ratios would improve from approximately 75 percent to nearly 100 percent.

> Using cache hit ratios as the primary basis for performance analysis is not recommended. In several situations, high cache hit ratios can exist even when overall performance is poor.

The Mean Time To Recover (MTTR) Advisor

The preceding advisors focused primarily on improving database performance by minimizing user waits for I/O, CPU, and other resources with the goal of minimizing each user's overall DB Time. The Mean Time To Recover (MTTR) Advisor is not concerned with minimizing DB Time, but instead tries to formulate recommendations that minimize the time it takes to perform instance recovery in the case of instance failure. Instance failure can occur when the host server crashes, when any critical SGA background process fails, or if the instance is shut down using the ABORT option. Instance recovery occurs automatically on the first startup following the instance failure. During instance recovery, Oracle uses the undo segments and online redo logs to roll back any uncommitted transactions that were "in flight" when the instance crashed to ensure that all committed transactions are written to disk. As a DBA, you often try to minimize the time it takes to perform this instance recovery so that the database can be brought up quickly.

> In previous Oracle releases, you could use the FAST_START_MTTR_TARGET initialization parameter to specify the maximum allowable instance recovery time (in seconds). This parameter must be set to a non-zero value for the new features described next to work.

FIGURE 9.30 The PGA tab in the Memory Advisor screen

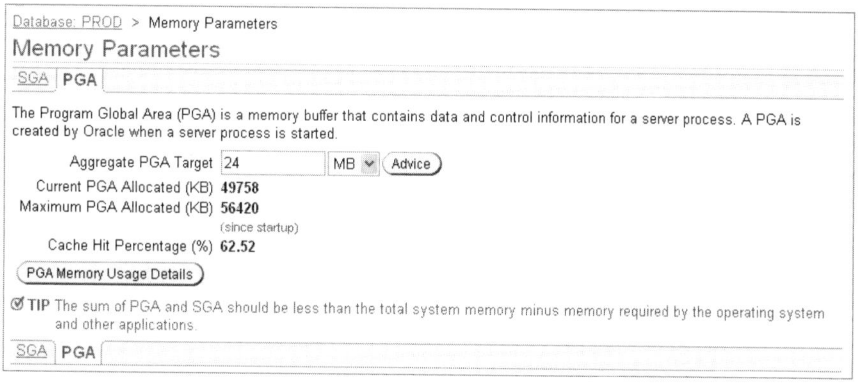

Database: PROD > Memory Parameters
Memory Parameters
SGA PGA
The Program Global Area (PGA) is a memory buffer that contains data and control information for a server process. A PGA is created by Oracle when a server process is started.
Aggregate PGA Target 24 MB Advice
Current PGA Allocated (KB) 49758
Maximum PGA Allocated (KB) 56420
(since startup)
Cache Hit Percentage (%) 62.52
PGA Memory Usage Details
TIP The sum of PGA and SGA should be less than the total system memory minus memory required by the operating system and other applications.
SGA PGA

FIGURE 9.31 The Memory Advisor's PGA recommendations

Oracle Enterprise Manager - PGA Aggregate Target Advi...
PGA Aggregate Target Advice
Cache hit percentage
100%
80%
60%
40%
20%
0%
0
50
100
150
200
250
PGA Target (MB)
Variation of cache hit ratio with PGA target
Current PGA target
Overflow range
Aggregate PGA Target 24 MB
TIP You can click on the curve in the graph to set new value.
Cancel
OK

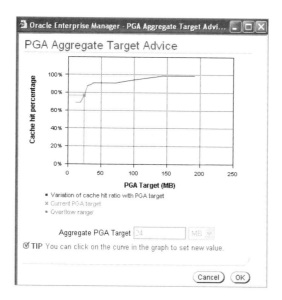

The MTTR Advisor analyzes the database during regular processing and makes recommendations about database and instance parameters that can be modified in order to meet your instance recovery goals. Figure 9.32 shows a portion of the MTTR Advisor recommendation screen.

The output in Figure 9.32 shows that the MTTR Advisor estimates that the current MTTR is 33 seconds. If this MTTR is not acceptable because a Service Level Agreement (SLA) requires a 15-second instance recovery time, then you can specify a new MTTR value of 15 in the Desired Mean Time To Recover box.

FIGURE 9.32 The MTTR Advisor screen

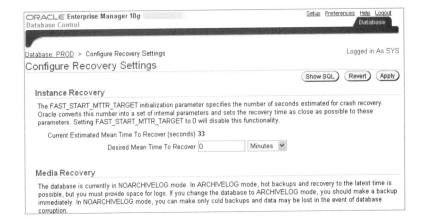

 The MTTR Advisor screen also has Media Recovery and Flash Recovery sections, which are described in more detail in Chapter 10, "Implementing Database Backups" and Chapter 11, "Implementing Database Recovery."

The Segment Advisor

You use the Segment Advisor to identify segments that might benefit from a shrink operation. Segments that can be shrunk are those that the Segment Advisor has found to be needing less space than they are currently allocated. By shrinking or compressing these segments, space is returned to the database for use by other objects, and the total number of I/Os needed to access these objects is reduced, potentially improving the performance of SQL statements that access these objects. Figure 9.33 shows the Segment Advisor main screen.

FIGURE 9.33 The Segment Advisor main screen

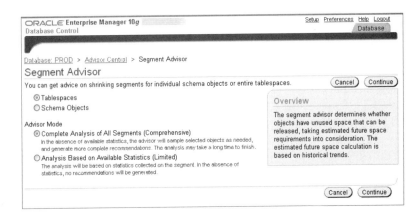

You can analyze potentially compressible segments either at the segment level or at the tablespace level. In addition, you can also specify the degree to which the segments are examined at two levels: Limited and Comprehensive. If you select the Schema Objects and Limited options and then click Continue, the Segment Advisor: Schema Objects screen in Figure 9.34 is displayed.

Initially, no segments are listed for analysis, but click the Add button to specify which segments you want the Segment Advisor to examine. Figure 9.35 shows the screen that is displayed after you select the SUPPLEMENTARY_DEMOGRAPHICS table for segment analysis.

On the screen in Figure 9.35, you can specify how much time the Segment Advisor can take when analyzing the specified segments and how long to store the results of the analysis in the repository. Click Next on this and subsequent screens to display the familiar job scheduling and submissions screens. Once the analysis of the selected segments or tablespaces is complete, the results are displayed at the bottom of the Advisor Central screen, along with all other submitted job results. Click the Segment Advisor Job link to display the Segment Advisor Task screen, which is shown in Figure 9.36.

FIGURE 9.34   The Segment Advisor: Schema Objects screen

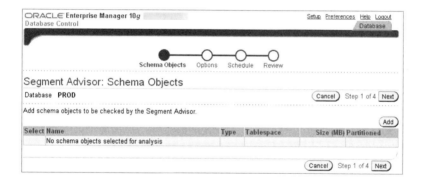

FIGURE 9.35   The Segment Advisor: Options screen

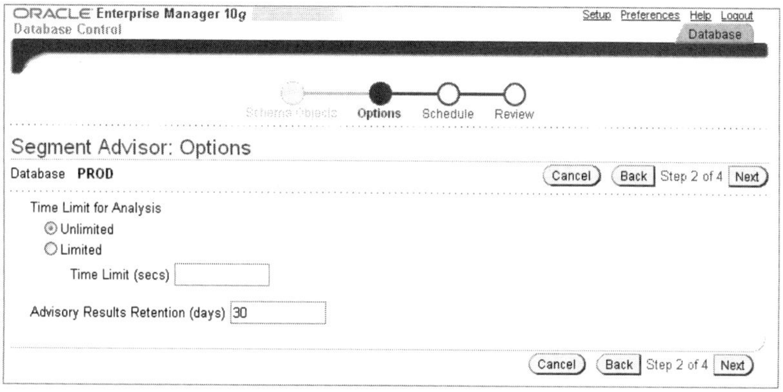

FIGURE 9.36 The Segment Advisor Task screen

The output on this screen shows that the SUPPLEMENTARY_DEMOGRAPHICS table owned by the user SH has been identified as a segment that will benefit from a shrink operation, reducing its allocated space from 4MB to the 1.193MB that the table actually needs to store its data. When shrinking an object identified by the Segment Advisor, there are two shrink options: Compact Segments and Compact Segments And Release Space.

The Compact Segments option compacts the rows in the SUPPLEMENTARY_DEMOGRAPHICS table, but does not release the newly freed space back to the tablespace. This option allows you to put off the more resource-intensive operation of actually releasing the space until later.

The Compact Segments And Release Space option compacts the space in the SUPPLEMENTARY_DEMOGRAPHICS table and also releases the unused space back to the tablespace at the same time. Choosing either of these two compression options displays the familiar job submission screen, which submits the compaction job in the background.

If you have a table that has been compressed using the Compact Segments option and thus does not have its space released, you can later release this space using the SHRINK SPACE option of the ALTER TABLE command, for example: ALTER TABLE supplementary_demographics SHRINK SPACE.

In order for the Segment Advisor to modify segments effectively, you need to enable the ROW MOVEMENT attribute of the affected segments. You can do so using the Options tab in the Edit Table screen or the ALTER TABLE … ENABLE ROW MOVEMENT command.

The Undo Management Advisor

The Undo Management Advisor helps you monitor and proactively respond to potential problems in a common trouble area of any transactional database system: undo segments. When a user starts a DML (Data Manipulation Language) transaction, the before-image of the changed data is buffered in the Database Buffer Cache in the SGA. Copies of these buffers are also written to an *undo segment*, which is stored in the database's undo tablespace. The before-image data stored in the undo segment is used for three important purposes:

- It can be used to restore the original state of the data if the user performing the DML command issues a ROLLBACK command.

- It provides a read-consistent view of the changed data to other users who access the same data prior to the DML user issuing a COMMIT command.

- It is used during instance recovery to undo uncommitted transactions that were in progress just prior to an instance failure.

 In previous releases of Oracle, undo segments were referred to as rollback segments because they are used to roll back a transaction when a ROLLBACK command is issued. However, this term is now generally used to refer to manually managed undo segments, not the system managed undo segments that Oracle recommends be used in Oracle 10*g*.

Once a transaction is assigned to an undo segment, the transaction never switches to a different undo segment, even if the original undo segment was not the most appropriate choice. Because of this, undo segment tuning can be one of the most elusive aspects of database administration. Even when undo activity has reached a steady state and no problems are apparent, the right combination of transactions can cause an undo segment error. This can lead to frustrating undo segment–tuning problems that never completely go away. The goals of undo segment tuning usually ensure the following:

- That database users always find an undo segment to store their transaction before-images without experiencing a wait

- That database users always get the read-consistent view that they need to complete their transactions

- That the database undo segments do not cause unnecessary I/O

 Every database contains at least one undo segment, which is the SYSTEM undo segment. This undo segment is used only for data dictionary read consistency and transaction control.

The most common undo segment–related error message is ORA-01555: Snapshot Too Old. This error can occasionally occur when some users are running long queries and others are simultaneously modifying the data being queried. This scenario can cause the session running the long-running query to be unable to build a read-consistent view of the database, thus causing the ORA-01555 error message.

The Undo Management Advisor helps prevent undo-related problems in the database by monitoring and analyzing undo activity before making recommendations for improving undo performance.

To open the Undo Management Advisor, which is shown in Figure 9.37, click the Undo Management link in the Advisor Central screen in EM Database Control.

The output in Figure 9.37 summarizes the current configuration of the undo management in the database. For example, it shows that the database is currently configured to retain undo information for up to 15 minutes past the time that the transaction that generated the undo was committed or rolled back. It also shows that the current undo tablespace is called UNDOTBS1, is 200MB in size, and does not have the AUTOEXTEND option turned on for its datafiles. It also indicates that the current undo tablespace is too small to support the requested undo retention period of 16 minutes. To meet this undo retention period, the Undo Management Advisor recommends increasing the size of the undo tablespace to 703MB. For details, click the Undo Advisor button to display the screen shown in Figure 9.38.

This output graphically shows how the undo retention time (in minutes along the bottom of the graph) increases to 16 minutes if the size of the undo tablespace increases to 431MB. The graph also shows that the best possible undo retention time that can be obtained with the current undo tablespace size of 200MB is 6 minutes. Implementing these recommendations will minimize database management and performance problems related to undo segments.

FIGURE 9.37   The Undo Management Advisor main screen

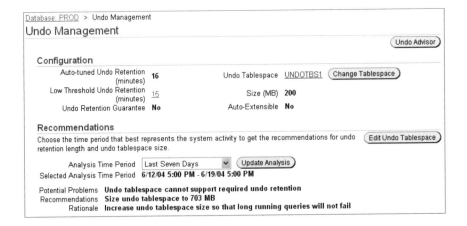

FIGURE 9.38   Details for the Undo Advisor

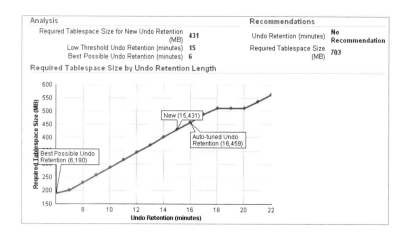

ADDM Alerts

In addition to monitoring and making recommendations on SQL, memory, mean time to recover, segments, and undo activity, ADDM can also be used to proactively monitor the database for other types of problems related to memory, I/O, and CPU utilization, as well as security and space management. To do so, you use ADDM alerts.

ADDM alerts are also an integral part of the ADDM architecture. They notify you when a management or performance issue occurs and begin taking corrective actions—if you configured such actions. By default, the alert notifications are sent to the EM Database Control main screen, as shown in Figure 9.39.

FIGURE 9.39   Sample ADDM alerts

Severity	Category	Name	Message	Alert Triggered	Last Value	Time
⚠	Alert Log	Generic Alert Log Error	ORA-error stack (00600[kcbchg1_6]) logged in C:\ORACLE\RDBMS\ADMIN\PROD\BDUMP\alert_PROD.log.	Jun 11, 2004 11:37:45 PM	0	
⚠	Alert Log	Generic Alert Log Error	ORA-error stack (07445[ACCESS_VIOLATION]) logged in C:\ORACLE\RDBMS\ADMIN\PROD\BDUMP\alert_PROD.log.	Jun 12, 2004 6:37:45 AM	0	
⚠	Alert Log	Generic Alert Log Error	ORA-error stack (00060) logged in C:\ORACLE\RDBMS\ADMIN\PROD\BDUMP\alert_PROD.log.	Jun 19, 2004 3:44:29 PM	0	Jun 19, 2004 3:44:29 PM
⚠	User Audit	Audited User	User SYS logged on from WORKGROUP\MODERNE	Jun 19, 2004 3:45:04 PM	0	Jun 19, 2004 4:59:52 PM
⚠	Response	User Logon Time (msec)	User logon time is 4806 msecs.	Jun 11, 2004 11:25:51 PM	4,756	Jun 20, 2004 9:37:35 AM

You can also configure alerts so that they are sent to you via e-mail. To do so, click the Setup link at the top of the EM Database Control screen to display the Setup screen shown in Figure 9.40.

Click the Notification Methods link on the left to open the Notification Methods screen, which is shown in Figure 9.41.

As shown in Figure 9.41, you'll need to supply three pieces of information:

- The IP address of your network's SMTP mail server

- The name of the user from whom the e-mail address will be sent

- The e-mail address of the user sending the notification e-mails

FIGURE 9.40   The EM Database Control Notification Setup screen

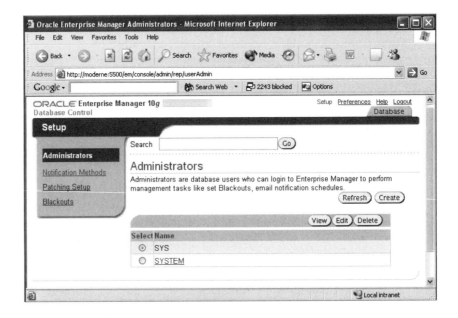

FIGURE 9.41   The EM Database Control Notification Methods screen

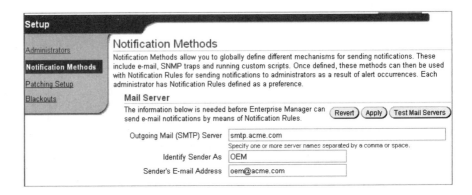

The example in Figure 9.41 uses the server `smtp.acme.com` as the SMTP mail server. This is the server through which EM Database Control will send the ADDM alert e-mails. The name of the user from whom the e-mail address will be sent is shown as OEM. The e-mail address of the user who will be sending the notification e-mails appears in the From box when you receive an alert notification via e-mail. The example in Figure 9.41 shows that the notifications will be using the `oem@acme.com` user account. After you add the e-mail configuration entries, click Apply to save them.

Click the Test Mail Servers button on the Notification Methods screen to confirm that the configuration you've entered is correct.

Once EM Database Control knows how to send notification e-mails when ADDM alert events occur, you need to tell EM Database Control to whom the notification e-mails should be sent. For the user SYS, click the Preferences link at the top of the EM Database Control main screen. To configure e-mail notification information for other users, click the Edit button on the Administrators screen, shown earlier in Figure 9.40.

You can then enter the e-mail address of the DBA who should receive the notification in the box under the E-mail Address column before clicking Apply to save the change. Click the Test button to send a test e-mail message to the address supplied and confirm the e-mail connectivity between EM Database Control and the DBA's e-mail address.

You can also set the message format, long or short, at this time. The short format is useful when you are e-mailing the notifications to a text pager or a cell phone.

After you configure the notification methods, alerts are sent to both the EM Database Control main screen and to the e-mail address specified.

An alert is triggered whenever a monitored event occurs or when a specified database threshold, called a *metric*, is surpassed. Metrics are the statistical performance measurements that are collected and stored in the AWR repository. The ADDM utility then gathers additional database statistics and compares them against the baseline metrics in order to monitor, diagnose, and remedy management problems or poor database performance. There are four default ADDM alerts configured in each database as described in Table 9.6.

TABLE 9.6   Default ADDM Alerts

Alert	Description
Tablespace Space Usage	Alerts you whenever a tablespace's free space falls below 15 percent and again when it falls below 3 percent.
Snapshot Too Old	Alerts you whenever the ORA-01555 error message (described earlier) occurs.

TABLE 9.6 Default ADDM Alerts *(continued)*

Alert	Description
Recovery Area Low On Free Space	Alerts you when the Flash Recovery area is low on free space. See Chapter 10 for details on using the Flash Recovery area.
Resumable Session Suspended	Alerts you whenever an operation that can be resumed goes into a suspended state.

Oracle 10*g* has several additional predefined ADDM alerts, which require a small amount of additional configuration before using. These alerts are defined on the Manage Metrics screen of the EM Database Control. To open this screen, click the Manage Metrics link at the bottom of the EM Database Control main screen. Figure 9.42 shows a portion of the predefined alerts found on the Manage Metrics screen.

Some of the alerts shown in Figure 9.42 include the following:

- The archive destination is more than 80 percent full.

- The archive process is hung and returns an error message.

- The superuser SYS is connecting to the database.

Figure 9.42 also shows that each alert can have two levels of severity: Warning and Critical. These two alert levels allow you to achieve greater granularity. For example, you might want two thresholds set up with regard to the archive destination. One might be a warning threshold that triggers an alert when the archive destination is 80 percent full—causing a message to be displayed on the EM Database Control main screen. In addition, you might want to set up a critical threshold so that you receive an e-mail whenever the archive destination device is 90 percent full. In this manner, you can escalate a potential problem from an EM Database Control console message to an e-mail alert as the problem gets worse.

FIGURE 9.42 A sample of the ADDM Manage Metrics screen

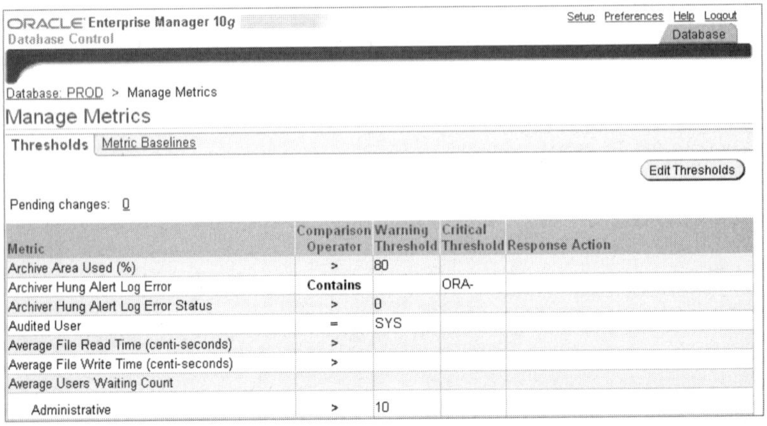

You can also use warning and critical alerts to distinguish between lower severity problems, such as statistics indicating temporary poor performance, and higher severity problems, such as ORA-0600 error messages in the database Alert log. You can achieve this by defining only warning thresholds for lower severity alerts and defining warning and critical alerts for higher severity problems.

Instead of specifying a set value, such as 50 percent and 75 percent for CPU utilization alert levels, you can also raise alerts when CPU utilization exceeds a baseline metric. *Baseline metrics* are gathered during a period of processing that represents normal database activity. Using these baselines, you can raise alerts when relative performance problems occur. For example, rather than raising an alert when the CPU utilization is 50 percent of the available CPU cycles, you can raise an alert when CPU utilization is 50 percent more than the baseline CPU utilization—which itself could be 85 percent of CPU cycles.

To gather baseline metrics, use the Options link on the Metric Baselines tab in the Manage Metrics screen, which is shown in Figure 9.43.

The output in Figure 9.43 shows that no metric baselines have yet been gathered. The AWR can store several baselines, any of which can be used as the basis for the alert system. To gather the first baseline metric, click Create to display the Create Metric Baseline screen, which is shown in Figure 9.44.

Using the Create Metric Baseline screen, you can minimally assign a name and date to the baseline statistics that will be gathered. Optionally, you can also assign a time of day, warning, and alert thresholds. In the example in Figure 9.44, warning alerts have been configured at 85 percent, and critical alerts have been configured at 95 percent.

If no value is supplied for Hour Of Day, baseline statistics are gathered for the entire 24-hour period for the date specified.

FIGURE 9.43 The Metric Baselines tab in the Manage Metrics screen

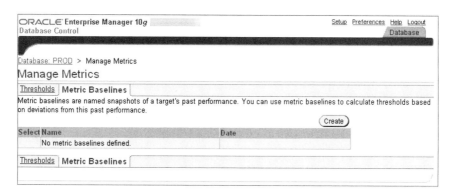

Click Go to capture the current database metrics and then display them at the bottom of the Create Metric Baseline screen, as shown in Figure 9.45.

Using this screen, you can deselect any metrics that you don't want to include in the baseline (all metrics are included by default) or modify the baseline values that were used. Once you tailored these metrics to your needs, you can store them by clicking OK at the top of the page, creating the baseline metric called Initial Server Stats, as shown in Figure 9.46.

FIGURE 9.44   The Create Metric Baseline screen

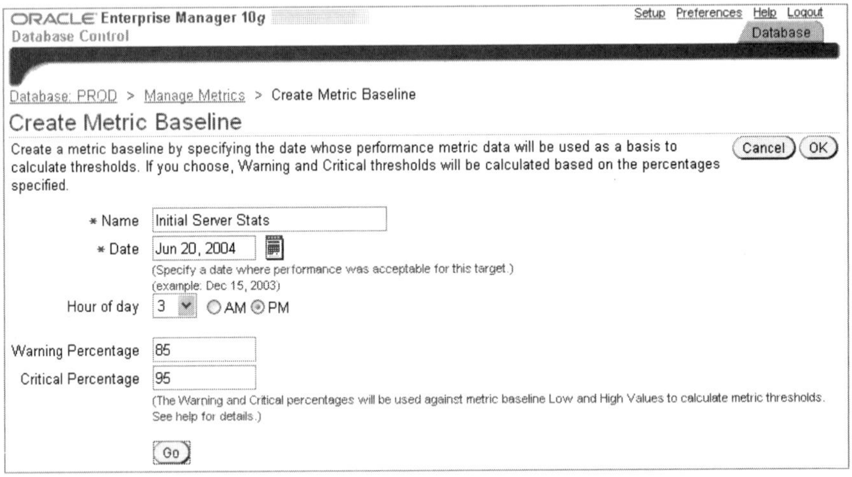

FIGURE 9.45   The summary Metric baseline data

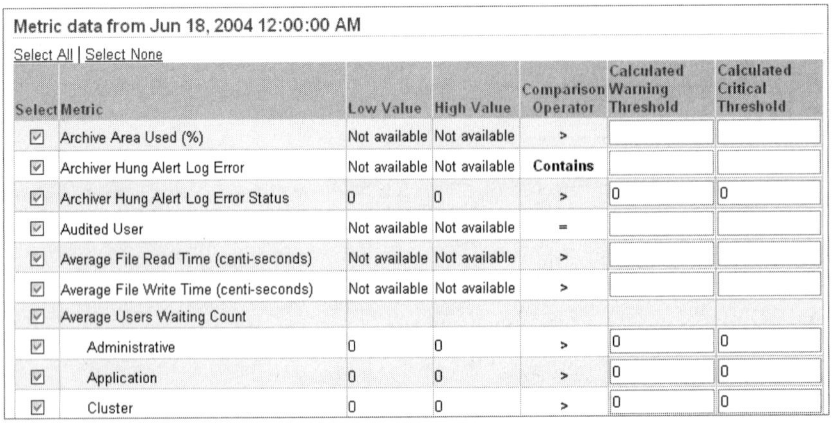

Metric data from Jun 18, 2004 12:00:00 AM

Select All | Select None

Select	Metric	Low Value	High Value	Comparison Operator	Calculated Warning Threshold	Calculated Critical Threshold
☑	Archive Area Used (%)	Not available	Not available	>		
☑	Archiver Hung Alert Log Error	Not available	Not available	**Contains**		
☑	Archiver Hung Alert Log Error Status	0	0	>	0	0
☑	Audited User	Not available	Not available	=		
☑	Average File Read Time (centi-seconds)	Not available	Not available	>		
☑	Average File Write Time (centi-seconds)	Not available	Not available	>		
☑	Average Users Waiting Count					
☑	Administrative	0	0	>	0	0
☑	Application	0	0	>	0	0
☑	Cluster	0	0	>	0	0

The output in Figure 9.46 shows the Initial Server Stats baseline metrics. Clicking this link displays the metrics associated with this baseline. Figure 9.47 shows a sample of the baseline metrics that were established.

The first column shows the name of the metric being monitored, the second column displays the warning values, and the third column displays the critical values that were calculated for that threshold. For example, the baseline warning threshold for the metric Current Open Cursors Count is 784, and the critical threshold is 826.

FIGURE 9.46   The Manage Metrics screen showing new baselines

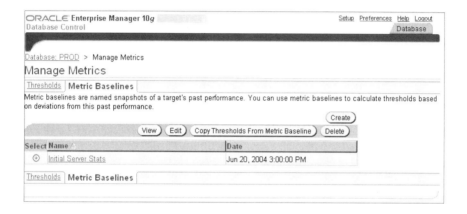

FIGURE 9.47   Sample baseline metric values

CPU Usage (per second)	9	9
CPU Usage (per transaction)	31	33
Consistent Read Blocks Created (per second)	0	0
Consistent Read Blocks Created (per transaction)	0	0
Consistent Read Changes (per second)	0	0
Consistent Read Changes (per transaction)	0	0
Consistent Read Gets (per second)	159	167
Consistent Read Gets (per transaction)	414	436
Consistent Read Undo Records Applied (per second)	0	0
Consistent Read Undo Records Applied (per transaction)	0	0
Cumulative Logons (per second)		
Cumulative Logons (per transaction)	0	0
Current Logons Count	49	52
Current Open Cursors Count	784	826
Cursor Cache Hit (%)	0	0
DBWR Checkpoints (per second)	0	0
Data Block Corruption Alert Log Error		
Data Block Corruption Alert Log Error Status	0	0
Data Dictionary Hit (%)	15	5
Database Block Changes (per second)	140	148
Database Block Changes (per transaction)	447	471

How ADDM Computes Thresholds

When baseline metrics are gathered, the AWR stores the high value and the low value for each metric. The technique that ADDM uses to compute a baseline threshold depends on the comparison operator that is used for specifying the threshold, and on the associated high and low value.

If the metric comparison operator is a greater than (>), the warning threshold for the metric is computed as Metric High Value * (1 + Warning Percentage/100). For example, if the high value for the metric Current Open Cursors Count is 500, the 85 percent warning threshold from Figure 9.44 is 500 * (1 + 85/100) or 925, raising a warning alert whenever the Current Open Cursors Count exceeds 925. Likewise, the critical threshold is 500 * (1 + 95/100) or 975, raising a critical alert whenever the Current Open Cursors Count exceeds 975.

If the metric comparison operator is a less than (<), the warning threshold for the metric is computed as Metric Low Value * (1 – Warning Percentage/100). For example, if the low value for the metric Large Pool Free % is 300MB, the 85 percent warning threshold is 300 * (1 – 85/100) or 45MB, raising a warning alert whenever the percentage of free space in the Large Pool falls below 45MB. Likewise, the critical threshold is 300 * (1 – 95/100) or 15MB, raising a critical alert whenever the free space in the Large Pool falls below 15MB.

Because more than one baseline can be stored in the AWR at one time, EM Database Control gives you a way to choose the baseline that you want to use for alert thresholds. Suppose you have the two baselines shown in Figure 9.48.

To use the metrics associated with the Overnight Processing baseline as the basis for ADDM alerts, simply select that option and click the Copy Thresholds From Metric Baseline button. EM Database Control gives you an opportunity to modify selected metric parameters if needed, before you update the threshold values and see the screen in Figure 9.49.

FIGURE 9.48 Two available baselines

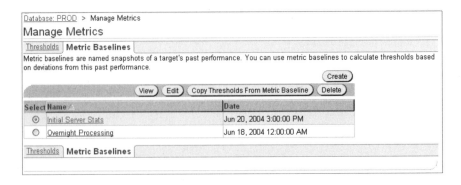

FIGURE 9.49   Baseline metrics update

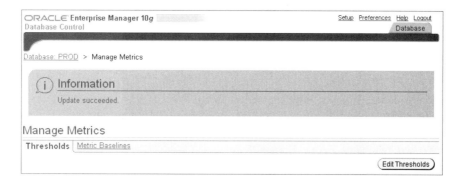

Performance Monitoring

Although AWR, ADDM, and advisors all help you proactively monitor and manage your databases, you can use additional performance-specific features of EM Database Control to further enhance the performance of your database.

However, you should measure exactly how the system is currently performing before beginning any tuning effort. The baseline metrics described in the previous section are a good example of this type of measurement. Using this benchmark, you can then compare the performance of the system after any tuning changes and evaluate their impact.

In addition to these baseline metrics, you can use additional sources of tuning information to monitor and tune database performance. The following section describes these sources.

Sources of Tuning Information

The EM Database Control provides a wealth of information for improving database monitoring and management, but you also need to be aware of several other sources of information about database performance, including:

- The Alert log
- Background and user trace files
- Dynamic performance views
- Data dictionary views

The Alert Log

The Oracle Alert log records informational and error messages for a variety of activities that have occurred against the database during its operation. These activities are recorded in chronological order from the oldest to most recent. The Alert log is found in the `background_dump_dest` directory specified in the PFILE/SPFILE.

The Alert Log frequently indicates whether gross tuning problems exist in the database. Tables that are unable to acquire additional storage, sorts that are failing, and problems with undo segments are all examples of tuning problems that can show up as messages in the Alert log. Most of these messages are accompanied by an Oracle error message.

 ADDM provides a mechanism for sending an alert whenever Oracle errors are detected in the Alert log. Click the Alert Log Content link on the EM Database Control main screen to see the most recent messages.

Background and User Trace Files

Oracle trace files are text files that contain session information for the process that created them. Trace files can be generated by the Oracle background processes, through the use of trace events, or by user server processes. These trace files can contain useful information for performance tuning and system troubleshooting. Background process trace files are found in the directory specified by the BACKGROUND_DUMP_DEST parameter, and the user process trace files are found in the directory specified by the USER_DUMP_DEST parameter. Both of these parameters are defined in the PFILE or SPFILE.

 The 10046 trace event, which can be activated at the instance or session level, is particularly useful for finding performance bottlenecks. See Note 171647.1 at http://metalink.oracle.com for a discussion of using the 10046 trace event as a tuning technique.

Dynamic Performance Views

As described in Chapter 1, "Installing Oracle 10g," Oracle 10g contains approximately 350 dynamic performance views. Table 9.7 contains a partial listing of some of the V$ views that are frequently used in performance tuning.

TABLE 9.7 Sample of Dynamic Performance Views

Name	Description
V$SGASTAT	Shows information about the size of the SGA's components.
V$EVENT_NAME	Shows database events that may require waits when requested by the system or by an individual session. There are approximately 200 possible wait events.
V$SYSTEM_EVENT	Shows events for which waits have occurred for all sessions accessing the system.
V$SESSION_EVENT	Shows events for which waits have occurred, individually identified by session.

TABLE 9.7   Sample of Dynamic Performance Views *(continued)*

Name	Description
V$SESSION_WAIT	Shows events for which waits are currently occurring, individually identified by session.
V$STATNAME	Matches the name to the statistics listed only by number in V$SESSTAT and V$SYSSAT.
V$SYSSTAT	Shows overall system statistics for all sessions, both currently and previously connected.
V$SESSTAT	Shows statistics on a per-session basis for currently connected sessions.
V$SESSION	Shows current connection information on a per-session basis.
V$WAITSTAT	Shows statistics related to block contention.

In general, queries that incorporate V$SYSSTAT show statistics for the entire instance since the time it was started. By joining this view to the other relevant views, you get the overall picture of performance in the database. Alternatively, queries that incorporate V$SESSTAT show statistics for a particular session. These queries are better suited for examining the performance of an individual operation or process. The EM Database Control makes extensive use of these views when creating performance-related graphs such as the one shown in Figure 9.50.

FIGURE 9.50   EM performance graphs based on *V$* views

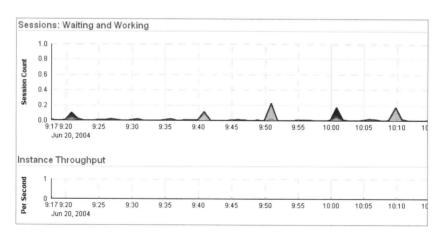

Data Dictionary Views

Depending on the features and options installed, there are approximately 1300 DBA data dictionary views in an Oracle 10g database. Table 9.8 contains a partial listing of some of the DBA views that are used when you tune performance on a database.

TABLE 9.8 A Sampling of Data Dictionary Views

Name	Description
DBA_TABLES	Table storage, row, and block information
DBA_INDEXES	Index storage, row, and block information
INDEX_STATS	Index depth and dispersion information
DBA_DATA_FILES	Datafile location, naming, and size information
DBA_SEGMENTS	General information about any space-consuming segment in the database
DBA_HISTOGRAMS	Table and index histogram definition information
DBA_OBJECTS	General information about all objects in the database, including tables, indexes, triggers, sequences, and partitions

The DBA_OBJECTS data dictionary view contains a STATUS column that indicates, through the use of a VALID or an INVALID value, whether a database object is valid and ready to be used or invalid and in need of some attention before it can be used. Common examples of invalid objects are PL/SQL code that contains errors or references to other invalid objects and indexes that are unusable due to maintenance operations or failed direct-path load processes. Some invalid objects, such as some types of PL/SQL code, dynamically recompile the next time they are accessed, and they then take on a status of VALID again. But you must manually correct other invalid objects, such as unusable indexes. Therefore, proactive database management techniques dictate that you identify and remedy invalid objects before they cause problems for database users.

Identifying Unusable Objects Using Data Dictionary

One way to identify invalid objects is to query the DBA_OBJECTS and DBA_INDEXES data dictionary views to find any invalid objects or unusable indexes and then correct them using the commands shown here:

```
SQL> SELECT owner, object_name, object_type
  2  FROM dba_objects
  3  WHERE status = 'INVALID';
```

```
OWNER            OBJECT_NAME                    OBJECT_TYPE
--------------   ------------------------------ -----------
SH               P_UPDATE_SALES_HISTORY         PROCEDURE
SYS              DBA_HIST_LATCH                 VIEW


SQL> ALTER VIEW sys.dba_hist_filestatxs COMPILE;

View altered.


SQL> ALTER PROCEDURE sh.p_update_sales_history COMPILE;

Procedure altered.


SQL> SELECT owner, index_name, index_type
  2  FROM dba_indexes
  3  WHERE status = 'UNUSABLE';
OWNER            INDEX_NAME                     INDEX_TYPE
--------------   ------------------------------ ----------
HR               JOB_ID_PK                      NORMAL


SQL> ALTER INDEX hr.job_id_pk REBUILD;
```

The ALTER … COMPILE command also works on invalid PL/SQL triggers, packages, package bodies, and functions.

When rebuilding an index using the REBUILD command, the amount of space used by the index is temporarily larger than the actual space needed to store the index. Make sure that adequate space exists in the tablespace before starting the rebuild process; up to 1.5 times the size of the original index is a good rule of thumb.

Identifying Unusable Objects Using EM

EM Database Control also offers a mechanism for fixing invalid database objects. Figure 9.51 shows the Procedures screen. To view it, click the Procedures link on the Administration screen in the EM Database Control.

The Procedures screen shows that the status of the P_UPDATE_SALES_HISTORY procedure is currently INVALID. By selecting the Compile option from the Actions drop-down list, you can begin the recompilation process.

Selecting the Compile option, and then clicking Go causes the procedure to recompile and displays the Edit Procedure screen shown in Figure 9.52.

In the output in Figure 9.52, the procedure returned an error during recompilation. Scrolling to the bottom of this screen shows the messages associated with the error as shown in Figure 9.53.

Once the error condition is corrected (in other words, the missing SALES_HISTORY_VIEW view is re-created), the procedure can again be recompiled using the Compile button, after which the successful completion screen is displayed (see Figure 9.54).

FIGURE 9.51   The Procedures screen in the EM Database Control

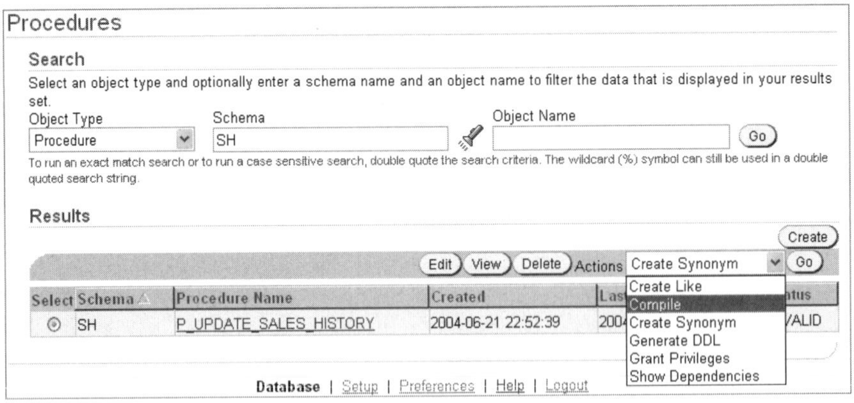

FIGURE 9.52   The Edit Procedure screen

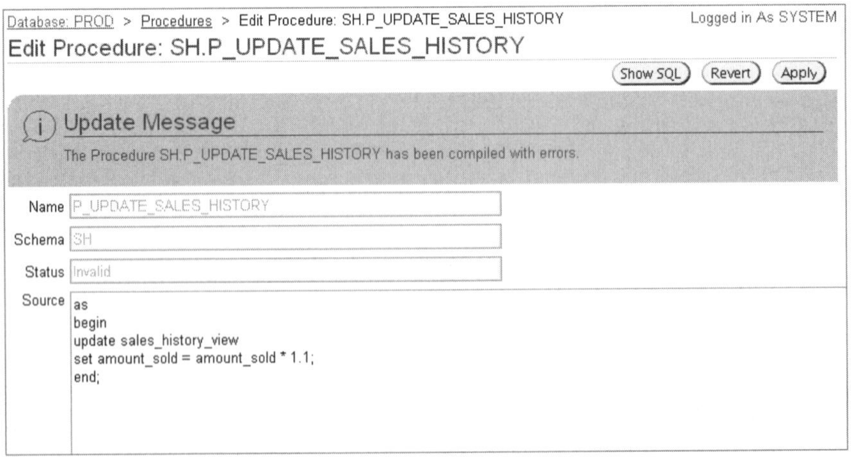

Using the Indexes screen, you can also use EM Database Control to rebuild indexes that are in an unusable state. Click the Indexes link in the Administration screen to open the Indexes screen. The example in Figure 9.55 shows that the JOB_ID_PK index is currently in an unusable state.

FIGURE 9.53   Error messages in the Edit Procedure screen

Errors | Line # = 4 Column # = 8 Error Text = PL/SQL: ORA-00942: table or view does not exist
Line # = 4 Column # = 1 Error Text = PL/SQL: SQL Statement ignored

(Show SQL) (Revert) (Apply)

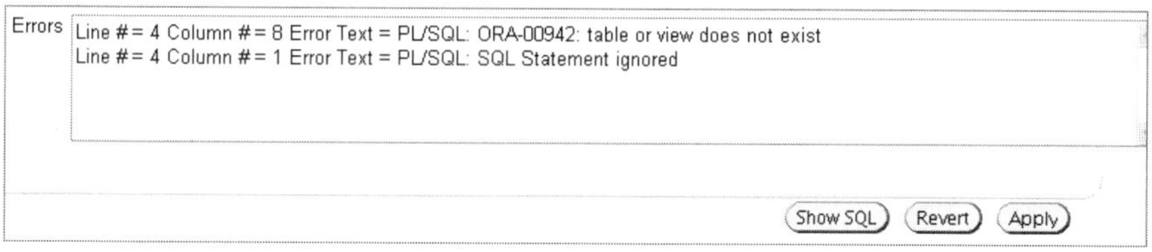

FIGURE 9.54   Successful compilation of the Edit Procedure screen

Database: PROD > Procedures > Edit Procedure: SH.P_UPDATE_SALES_HISTORY   Logged in As SYSTEM
Edit Procedure: SH.P_UPDATE_SALES_HISTORY

(Show SQL) (Revert) (Apply)

(i) Update Message

The Procedure SH.P_UPDATE_SALES_HISTORY has been compiled successfully.

Name   P_UPDATE_SALES_HISTORY
Schema SH
Status Valid
Source as
begin
update sales_history_view
set amount_sold = amount_sold * 1.1;
end;

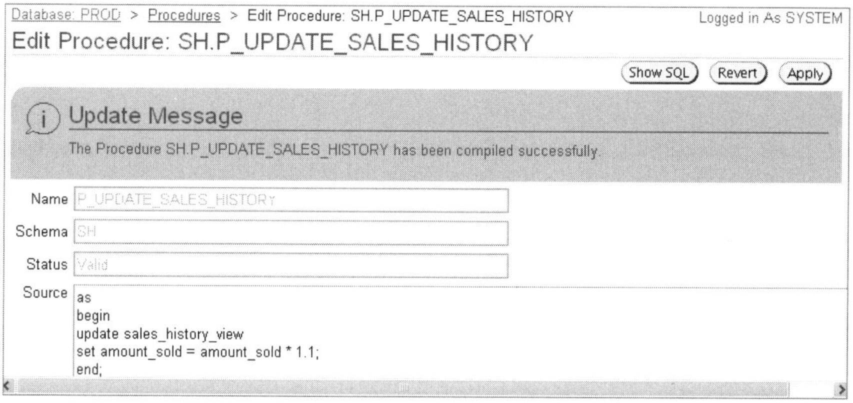

FIGURE 9.55   The Indexes screen showing an unusable index

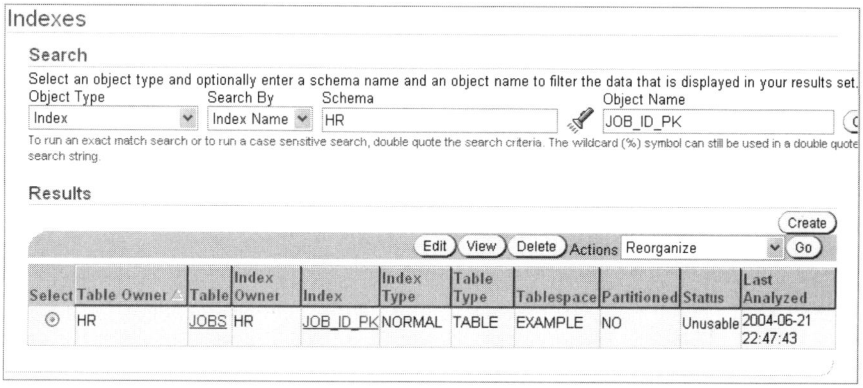

Indexes

Search

Select an object type and optionally enter a schema name and an object name to filter the data that is displayed in your results set.

Object Type	Search By	Schema		Object Name	
Index	Index Name	HR		JOB_ID_PK	

To run an exact match search or to run a case sensitive search, double quote the search criteria. The wildcard (%) symbol can still be used in a double quote search string.

Results

(Create)

(Edit) (View) (Delete) Actions Reorganize ▼ (Go)

Select	Table Owner △	Table	Index Owner	Index	Index Type	Table Type	Tablespace	Partitioned	Status	Last Analyzed
⊙	HR	JOBS	HR	JOB_ID_PK	NORMAL	TABLE	EXAMPLE	NO	Unusable	2004-06-21 22:47:43

To begin the recompilation process, select the Reorganize option from the Actions drop-down list, as shown in Figure 9.56.

Click Go to display the second screen of the Reorganize Objects Wizard, which is shown in Figure 9.57.

Click the Set Attributes or Set Attributes By Type button to modify the index's attributes—such as the tablespace that it will be stored in or its storage parameters—before rebuilding. Click Next to display the third screen of the Reorganize Objects Wizard, partially shown in Figure 9.58.

Using this screen, you can control how the index is rebuilt. For example, you can select the rebuild method, either offline or online, that is best suited for your environment. Offline rebuilds are faster but impact application users who need to access the index. Online rebuilds have minimal impact on users but take longer to complete. You can also specify a "scratch" tablespace where Oracle stores the intermediate results during the rebuild process. Redirecting this activity to another tablespace helps minimize potential space issues in the index's tablespace during the rebuild. You can also specify whether to gather new optimizer statistics when the index build is complete. Click Next on this screen to generate an impact report, as shown in Figure 9.59.

FIGURE 9.56 The Indexes screen showing the Reorganize action

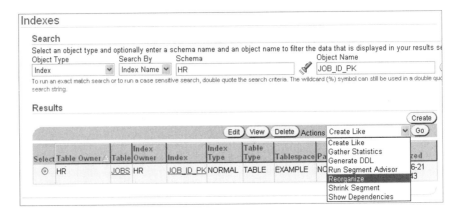

FIGURE 9.57 The second Reorganize Objects screen

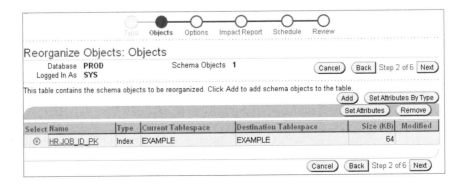

FIGURE 9.58   The third Reorganize Objects screen

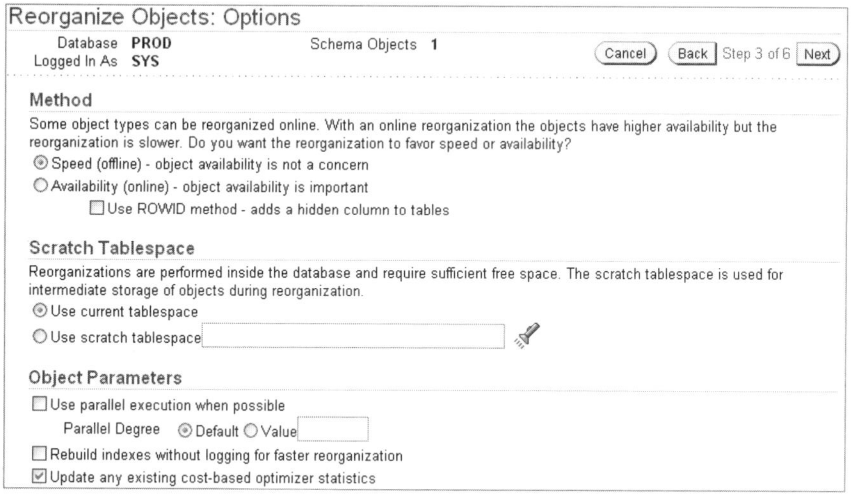

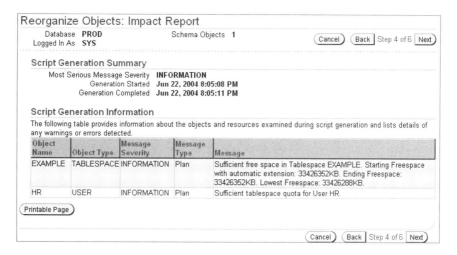

FIGURE 9.59   The Reorganize Objects: Impact Report screen

The output indicates that there is adequate space in the EXAMPLE tablespace for the unusable JOBS_ID_PK index. Clicking Next displays the job scheduling screen shown in Figure 9.60.

Like the earlier job-scheduling example in this chapter, you can use this screen to assign a job description and to specify the start time for the job. Clicking Next submits the job and rebuilds the unusable index according to the parameters you defined.

Storing Database Statistics in the Data Dictionary

Some columns in the DBA views are not populated with data until the table or index referenced by the view is analyzed. For example, the DBA_TABLES data dictionary view does not contain values for NUM_ROWS, AVG_ROW_LEN, BLOCKS, and EMPTY_BLOCKS, among others, until the table is analyzed. Likewise, the DBA_INDEXES view does not contain values for BLEVEL, LEAF_BLOCKS, AVG_LEAF_BLOCKS_PER_KEY, and AVG_DATA_BLOCKS_PER_KEY, among others, until the index is analyzed. These statistics are useful not only to you, but also are critical for proper functioning of the cost-based optimizer.

The *cost-based optimizer (CBO)* uses these statistics to formulate efficient execution plans for each SQL statement that is issued by application users. For example, the CBO may have to decide whether to use an available index when processing a query. The CBO can only make an effective guess at the proper execution plan when it knows the number of rows in the table, the size and type of indexes on that table, and how many the CBO expects to be returned by a query. Because of this, the statistics gathered and stored in the data dictionary views are sometimes called *optimizer statistics*. In Oracle 10g, there are several ways to analyze tables and indexes to gather statistics for the CBO. These techniques are described in the following sections.

Automatic Collection of Statistics

If you created your database using the Database Configuration Assistant GUI tool, your database is automatically configured to gather table and index statistics every day between 10:00 P.M. and 6:00 A.M. However, the frequency and hours of collection can be modified as needed using EM Database Control.

Manual Collection of Statistics

You can also configure automatic statistics collection for manually created databases using manual techniques. Collecting manual statistics is also useful for tables and indexes whose storage characteristics change frequently or that need to be analyzed outside the normal analysis window of 10:00 P.M. and 6:00 A.M. You can collect manual statistics through EM Database Control or using the built-in DBMS_STATS PL/SQL package.

Manually Gathering Statistics Using EM

You can use the EM Gather Statistics Wizard to manually collect statistics for individual segments, schemas, or the database as a whole. To start the wizard, click the Maintenance link on the EM Database Control screen. This wizard walks you through five steps, beginning with the Introduction screen.

Click Next on the Introduction screen to open Step 2 in the wizard, and select the method to use when gathering the statistics shown in Figure 9.61.

As you can see, three primary statistics options are available: Compute, Estimate, and Delete. The Compute option examines the entire table or index when determining the statistics. This option is the most accurate, but also the most costly in terms of time and resources if used on large tables and indexes. The Estimate option takes a representative sample of the rows in the table and then stores those statistics in the data dictionary. The default sample size is 10 percent of the total table or index rows. You can also manually specify your own sample size if desired. You can also specify the sample method, telling EM Database Control to sample based on a percentage of the overall rows, or blocks, in the table or index. The Delete option removes statistics for a table or index from the data dictionary.

If you specify a sample size of 50 percent or more, the table or index is analyzed using the Compute method.

After choosing a collection and sampling method, click Next to display the Object Selection screen, as shown in Figure 9.62.

FIGURE 9.61   The Default Method screen of the Gather Statistics Wizard

Gather Statistics Wizard: Default Method

(Cancel) (Back) | Step 2 of 5 | Next)

The method you've specified here will be used as default method for all selected objects. The statistics will be stored in the data dictionary and used by the cost-based optimizer.

Which one of the following methods would you like to choose?

- ⦿ Compute statistics based on all the rows of the selected objects
- ○ Estimate statistics based on some of the rows of the selected objects. This method is faster but the statistic is less accurate.
    Estimate Percentage
    - ⦿ Default - Oracle determines the best sample size for good statistics
    - ○ Percentage [   ]
    Sample Method
    - ⦿ Row Sample - More accurate but may need to process more data
    - ○ Block Sample - More efficient if the data is randomly distributed on disk
- ○ Delete statistics

(Cancel) (Back) | Step 2 of 5 | Next)

This screen lets you focus your statistics collection by schema, table, index, partition, or the entire database. Figure 9.63 shows the COSTS and PRODUCTS tables being selected at the target for the analysis when the Table option is selected.

Click OK to display the statistics summary screen shown in Figure 9.64.

Click the Options button to specify the analysis method, sample method, and other options related to the gathering the table statistics, and then click Next to move to the fourth EM Gather Statistics Wizard screen, as shown in Figure 9.65.

The output in Figure 9.65 shows the scheduling details of the job that will be used to launch the gathering of the statistics for the specified tables. Accepting the default values generates a system job ID and runs immediately for one time only. If desired, you can change the frequency and time for the statistics-gathering process. Click Next to display the final screen of the EM Gather Statistics Wizard, which is shown in Figure 9.66.

FIGURE 9.62   The Object Selection screen of the Gather Statistics Wizard

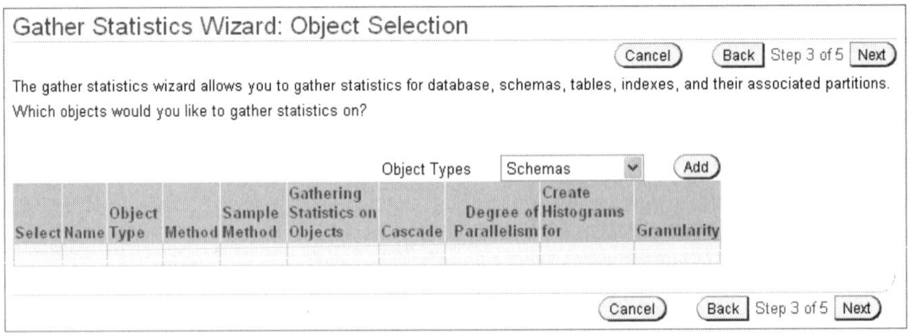

FIGURE 9.63   Selecting tables to be analyzed

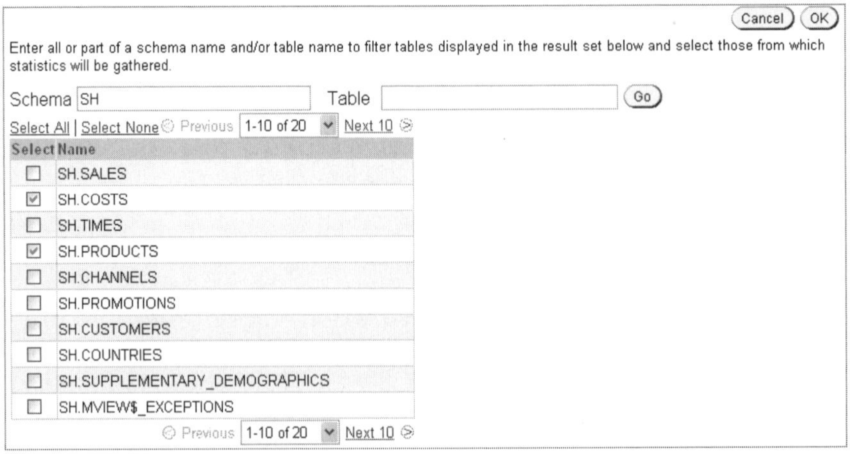

FIGURE 9.64   The statistics summary screen

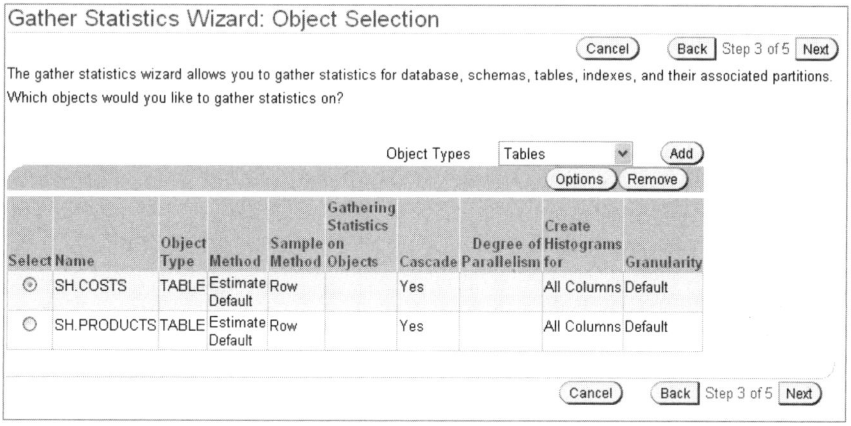

FIGURE 9.65   The Schedule Analysis screen of the Gather Statistics Wizard

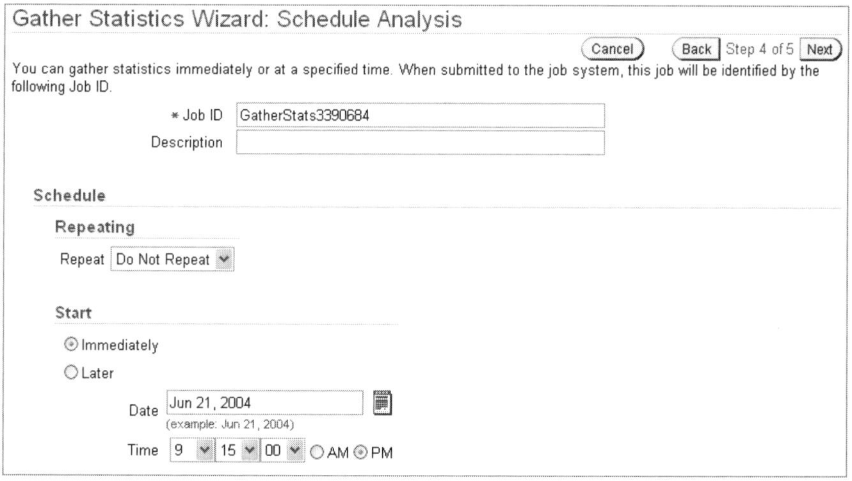

Figure 9.66 summarizes all the specifics of the statistics-gathering job that the wizard built. Click Submit to submit the analysis to Oracle's job-handling system, where it is executed according to the schedule specified previously. Its execution status is displayed on the Scheduler Jobs summary screen shown in Figure 9.67.

Once the job is complete, it is moved to the Run History tab on the Scheduler Jobs screen where its output can be inspected for job success or failure and any associated runtime messages.

FIGURE 9.66 The Review screen of the Gather Statistics Wizard

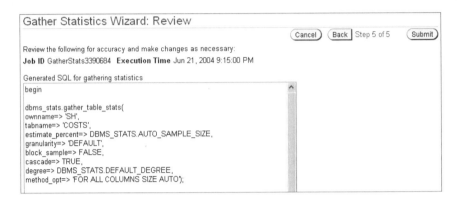

FIGURE 9.67 The Scheduler Jobs summary screen

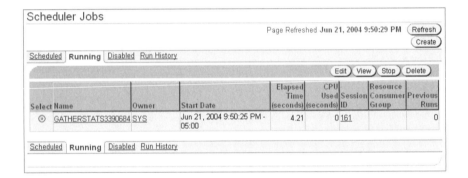

Manually Gathering Statistics Using *DBMS_STATS*

The output in Figure 9.66 shows that the EM Gather Statistics Wizard uses the DBMS_STATS PL/SQL package when it gathers statistics. You can also call the DBMS_STATS PL/SQL package directly from a SQL*Plus session. Some of the options for the DBMS_STATS package include the following:

- Back up old statistics before new statistics are gathered. This feature allows you to restore some or all of the original statistics if the CBO performs poorly after updated statistics are gathered.

- Gather table statistics much faster by performing the analysis in parallel.

- Automatically gather statistics on highly volatile tables and bypass gathering statistics on static tables.

The following example shows how the DBMS_STATS packages can be used to gather statistics on the PRODUCT_HISTORY table in SH's schema:

```
SQL> EXECUTE DBMS_STATS.GATHER_TABLE_STATS ('SH','PRODUCT_HISTORY');
```

You can use the DBMS_STATS package to analyze tables, indexes, an entire schema, or the whole database. A sample of some of the procedures available within the DBMS_STATS package are shown in Table 9.9.

TABLE 9.9   Procedures within the *DBMS_STATS* Package

Procedure Name	Description
GATHER_INDEX_STATS	Gathers statistics on a specified index
GATHER_TABLE_STATS	Gathers statistics on a specified table
GATHER_SCHEMA_STATS	Gathers statistics on a specified schema
GATHER_DATABASE_STATS	Gathers statistics on an entire database

For complete details of the many options available in the DBMS_STATS package, see Chapter 93, "DBMS_STATS," in *PL/SQL Packages and Types Reference 10*g *Release 1 (10.1)*, Part Number B10802-01.

The presence of accurate optimizer statistics has a big impact on two important measures of overall system performance: throughput and response time.

Important Performance Metrics

Throughput is another example of a statistical performance metric. *Throughput* is the amount of processing that a computer or system can perform in a given amount of time, for example, the number of customer deposits that can be posted to the appropriate accounts in four hours under regular workloads. Throughput is an important measure when considering the scalability of the system. *Scalability* refers to the degree to which additional users can be added to the system without system performance declining significantly. New features such as Oracle Database 10*g*'s Grid Computing capabilities make Oracle one of the most scalable database platforms on the market.

Performance considerations for transactional systems usually revolve around throughput maximization.

Another important metric related to performance is response time. *Response time* is the amount of time that it takes for a single user's request to return the desired result when using an application, for example, the time it takes for the system to return a listing of all the customers who purchased products that require service contracts.

🌐 Real World Scenario

Telling ADDM about Your Server I/O Capabilities

Both throughput and response time are impacted by disk I/O activity. In order for ADDM to make meaningful recommendations about the I/O activity on your server, you need to give ADDM a reference point against which to compare the I/O statistics it has gathered. This reference point is defined as the "expected I/O" of the server. By default, ADDM uses an expected I/O rate of 10,000 microseconds (10 milliseconds). This means that ADDM expects that, on average, your server will need 10 milliseconds to read a single database block from disk.

Using operating system utilities, we performed some I/O tests against our large storage area network disk array and found that the average time needed to read a single database block was about 7 milliseconds (7000 microseconds). To give ADDM a more accurate picture of our expected I/O speeds, we used the DBMS_ADVISOR package to tell ADDM that our disk subsystem was faster than the default 10 millisecond value:

```
EXECUTE DBMS_ADVISOR.SET_DEFAULT_TASK_PARAMETER('ADDM', 'DBIO_EXPECTED', 7000);
```

Without this adjustment, the ADDM might have thought that our I/O rates were better than average (7 milliseconds instead of 10 milliseconds) when in fact they were only average for our system. The effect of this inaccurate assumption regarding I/O would impact nearly every recommendation that the ADDM made and would have almost certainly resulted in sub-par system performance.

 Performance tuning considerations for decision-support systems usually revolve around response time minimization.

EM Database Control can be used to both monitor and react to sudden changes in performance metrics like throughput and response time.

Using EM Database Control to View Performance Metrics

EM Database Control provides a graphical view of throughput, response time, I/O, and other important performance metrics. To view these metrics, click the All Metrics link at the bottom of the EM Database Control main screen to display the All Metrics screen, which is partially displayed in Figure 9.68.

Click the metric you want to examine to expand the available information. Figure 9.69 shows a partial listing of the expanded list for the Throughput metric.

Click the Database Block Changes (Per Second) link to display details on the number of database blocks that were modified by application users, per second, for any period between the last 24 hours and the last 31 days. Figure 9.70 shows the Database Blocks Changes detail screen.

FIGURE 9.68 The EM Database Control All Metrics screen

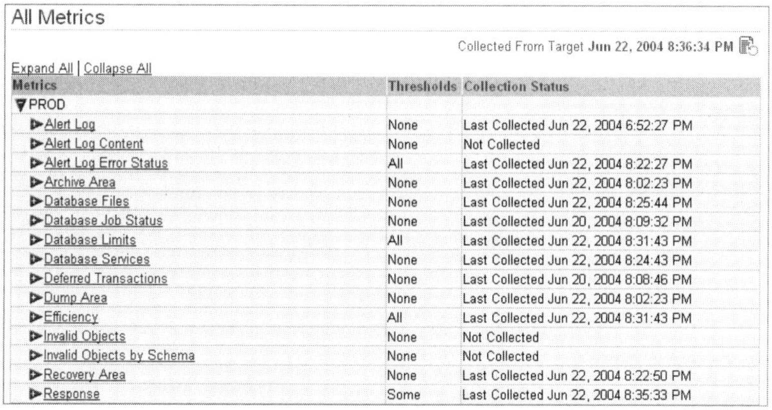

All Metrics

Collected From Target Jun 22, 2004 8:36:34 PM

Expand All | Collapse All

Metrics	Thresholds	Collection Status
▼PROD		
▶Alert Log	None	Last Collected Jun 22, 2004 6:52:27 PM
▶Alert Log Content	None	Not Collected
▶Alert Log Error Status	All	Last Collected Jun 22, 2004 8:22:27 PM
▶Archive Area	None	Last Collected Jun 22, 2004 8:02:23 PM
▶Database Files	None	Last Collected Jun 22, 2004 8:25:44 PM
▶Database Job Status	None	Last Collected Jun 20, 2004 8:09:32 PM
▶Database Limits	All	Last Collected Jun 22, 2004 8:31:43 PM
▶Database Services	None	Last Collected Jun 22, 2004 8:24:43 PM
▶Deferred Transactions	None	Last Collected Jun 20, 2004 8:08:46 PM
▶Dump Area	None	Last Collected Jun 22, 2004 8:02:23 PM
▶Efficiency	All	Last Collected Jun 22, 2004 8:31:43 PM
▶Invalid Objects	None	Not Collected
▶Invalid Objects by Schema	None	Not Collected
▶Recovery Area	None	Last Collected Jun 22, 2004 8:22:50 PM
▶Response	Some	Last Collected Jun 22, 2004 8:35:33 PM

FIGURE 9.69 An expanded list of Throughput metrics

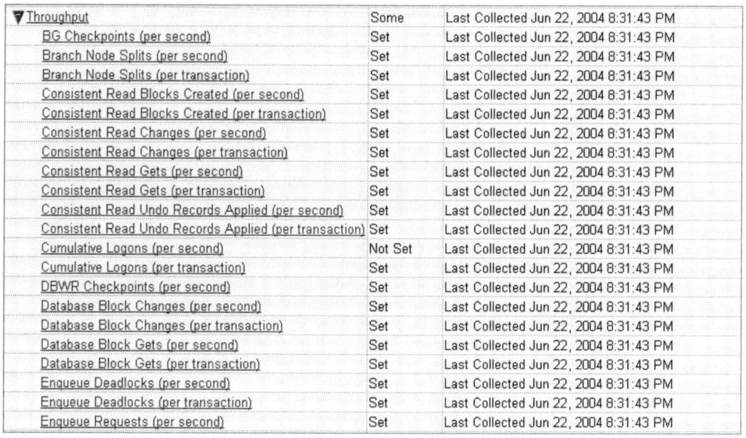

▼Throughput	Some	Last Collected Jun 22, 2004 8:31:43 PM
BG Checkpoints (per second)	Set	Last Collected Jun 22, 2004 8:31:43 PM
Branch Node Splits (per second)	Set	Last Collected Jun 22, 2004 8:31:43 PM
Branch Node Splits (per transaction)	Set	Last Collected Jun 22, 2004 8:31:43 PM
Consistent Read Blocks Created (per second)	Set	Last Collected Jun 22, 2004 8:31:43 PM
Consistent Read Blocks Created (per transaction)	Set	Last Collected Jun 22, 2004 8:31:43 PM
Consistent Read Changes (per second)	Set	Last Collected Jun 22, 2004 8:31:43 PM
Consistent Read Changes (per transaction)	Set	Last Collected Jun 22, 2004 8:31:43 PM
Consistent Read Gets (per second)	Set	Last Collected Jun 22, 2004 8:31:43 PM
Consistent Read Gets (per transaction)	Set	Last Collected Jun 22, 2004 8:31:43 PM
Consistent Read Undo Records Applied (per second)	Set	Last Collected Jun 22, 2004 8:31:43 PM
Consistent Read Undo Records Applied (per transaction)	Set	Last Collected Jun 22, 2004 8:31:43 PM
Cumulative Logons (per second)	Not Set	Last Collected Jun 22, 2004 8:31:43 PM
Cumulative Logons (per transaction)	Set	Last Collected Jun 22, 2004 8:31:43 PM
DBWR Checkpoints (per second)	Set	Last Collected Jun 22, 2004 8:31:43 PM
Database Block Changes (per second)	Set	Last Collected Jun 22, 2004 8:31:43 PM
Database Block Changes (per transaction)	Set	Last Collected Jun 22, 2004 8:31:43 PM
Database Block Gets (per second)	Set	Last Collected Jun 22, 2004 8:31:43 PM
Database Block Gets (per transaction)	Set	Last Collected Jun 22, 2004 8:31:43 PM
Enqueue Deadlocks (per second)	Set	Last Collected Jun 22, 2004 8:31:43 PM
Enqueue Deadlocks (per transaction)	Set	Last Collected Jun 22, 2004 8:31:43 PM
Enqueue Requests (per second)	Set	Last Collected Jun 22, 2004 8:31:43 PM

The output in Figure 9.70 shows that average block changes per second were 3,784, with a high value of 11,616. You can also see that the Warning threshold associated with this metric is 85 and that the Critical threshold is 95 block changes per second and that there were two occurrences of exceeding one or both of those thresholds.

EM Database Control also provides a rich source of performance-tuning information on the Performance tab of the EM Database Control main screen. The Performance tab is divided into three sections of information (as shown in Figures 9.71, 9.72, and 9.73):

- Host
- Sessions
- Instance Throughput

The Host section of the Performance tab shows run queue length and paging information for the host server hardware. The Run Queue Length graph indicates how many processes were waiting to perform processing during the previous one-hour period. The Paging Rate graph shows how many times per second the operating system had to page out memory to disk during the previous one-hour period. Figure 9.71 shows a sample of performance graphs for run queue and paging activity.

In addition to other metrics, the Sessions: Waiting And Working section of the Performance tab always shows CPU and I/O activity per session for the previous one-hour period. Figure 9.72 shows the Sessions: Waiting And Working section of the Performance main screen.

The final section of the Performance main screen, Instance Throughput, is shown in Figure 9.73.

FIGURE 9.70   The database block changes metric detail

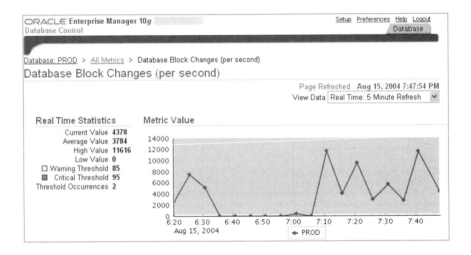

FIGURE 9.71   Host performance metrics

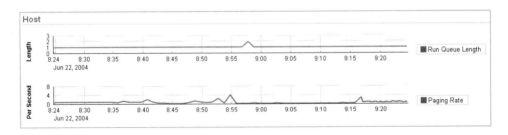

FIGURE 9.72   Session performance metrics

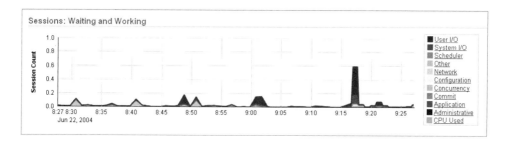

FIGURE 9.73   Instance Throughput performance metrics

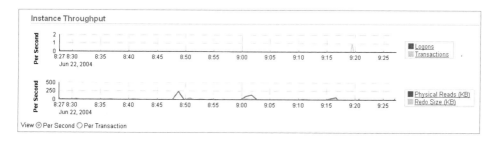

This portion of the Performance tab graphically depicts the logons and transactions per second and the physical reads and redo activity per second. You can also view these metrics on a per transaction basis instead of per section, by clicking the Per Transaction button below the graph.

Using EM Database Control to React to Performance Issues

Suppose you notice a drop in database performance within the last 30 minutes. Using the EM Database Control Performance tab, you can drill down into the detail of any of the performance metrics summarized on the tab and identify the source of the problem using techniques described in the "Using EM Database Control To View ADDM Analysis" section earlier in this chapter.

Summary

Oracle 10*g* provides many tools for proactively identifying and fixing potential performance and management problems in the database. At the core of the monitoring system is the Automatic Workload Repository (AWR), which uses the MMON background process to gather statistics from the SGA and store them in a collection of tables owned by the user SYSMAN.

Following each AWR statistics collection interval, the Automatic Database Diagnostic Monitoring (ADDM) feature examines the newly gathered statistics and compares them with the two previous AWR statistics to establish baselines in an attempt to identify poorly performing components of the database. The ADDM then summarizes these findings on the EM Database Control main and Performance screens. Using these screens, you can identify and examine the SQL statements that are contributing the most to DB Time. You can further explore the opportunities for improving the performance or manageability of your database using the EM Database Control advisors, which include the SQL Tuning Advisor, SQL Access Advisor, Memory Advisor, Mean Time To Recover Advisor, Segment Advisor, and Undo Management Advisor.

Using the SQL Tuning Advisor, you can identify the SQL statements that have had the greatest performance impact on the database. You can then examine these statements using the SQL Access Advisor to determine if adjustments can be made to improve the execution paths for these statements and therefore minimize their impact on total DB Time.

The Memory Advisor suggests changes that can potentially improve Oracle's use of memory within the SGA and PGA.

The Mean Time To Recover Advisor helps you determine if your database is properly configured to meet service-level agreements for instance recovery in the event of a server failure or an instance crash.

The Segment Advisor helps you determine which segments are using excess storage space and which might benefit from a shrink operation. Shrinking these segments not only frees storage space for use by other segments, but also minimizes the number of physical I/Os required to access the segments.

Using the Undo Management Advisor, you can monitor and manage undo segments to minimize the likelihood of ORA-01555, Snapshot Too Old error messages, and improve the application's overall read consistency.

You can also configure ADDM alerts to notify you via the EM Database Control or e-mail whenever the performance of the database varies from established baselines or target levels. Available storage space, excessive wait times, and high I/O activity are all examples of events that you can monitor using alerts.

In addition to EM Database Control, you can find indicators of database performance in the database Alert log, user and background trace files, data dictionary views, and dynamic performance views. Some data dictionary views do not contain accurate information about the segments in the database until after statistics are collected on those objects. Therefore, you can automatically collect segment statistics through the use of EM Database Control jobs.

Invalid and unusable database objects also have a negative impact on performance and manageability. You can monitor and repair invalid and unusable objects using the data dictionary and the EM Database Control Administration screen.

EM Database Control summarizes several important performance metrics on the EM Database Control main screen. These metrics include performance statistics for the host server, user sessions, and instance throughput.

Exam Essentials

Understand the Automatic Workload Repository. Describe the components of the AWR and how they are used to collect and store database performance statistics.

Describe the role of Automatic Database Diagnostic Monitor. Know how ADDM uses the AWR statistics to formulate tuning recommendations using historical and baseline metrics.

Explain how each advisor is used to improve performance. Describe how you can use each of the EM Database Control advisors shown on the Advisor Central screen to improve database performance and manageability.

Describe how alerts are used to monitor performance. Show how you can configure the EM Database Control alert system to alert you via the console or e-mail whenever a monitored event occurs in the database.

Identify and fix invalid or unusable objects. Understand the techniques you can use to identify invalid procedures, functions, triggers, and views and how to validate them. Know how to find unusable indexes and how to fix them.

Understand sources of tuning information. Know in which dynamic performance views, data dictionary views, and log files tuning information can be found.

Review Questions

1. Which of the following components of Oracle architecture stores the statistics gathered by the MMON process?

   A. ADDM

   B. AWR

   C. Data dictionary views

   D. Dynamic performance views

2. Which of the following options for the PFILE/SPFILE parameter STATISTICS_LEVEL turns off AWR statistics gathering and ADDM advisory services?

   A. OFF

   B. TYPICAL

   C. ALL

   D. BASIC

3. The following graphic is from the Sessions: Waiting And Working section of the EM Database Control Performance screen. Using this output, which of the following is the primary source of user wait activity?

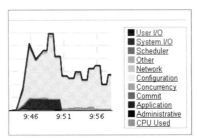

   A. CPU Used

   B. User I/O

   C. System I/O

   D. Configuration

4. The following graphic shows the SQL statements that are having the greatest impact on overall DB Time. Which statement has had the greatest impact?

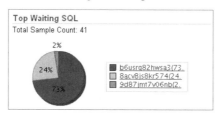

- **A.** 9d87jmt7vo6nb(2.
- **B.** 8acv8js8kr574(24.
- **C.** b6usrq82hwsa3(73.
- **D.** None of the above was highest.

5. Suppose you have used EM Database Control to drill down into ADDM findings and have found that a single SQL statement is causing the majority of I/O on your system. Which of the following advisors is best suited to troubleshoot this SQL statement?

- **A.** SQL Tuning Advisor
- **B.** SQL Access Advisor
- **C.** Both A and B
- **D.** Neither A or B

6. Nearly all the advisors submit their analysis activities to the database in the form of a job. When the analysis job is submitted, which option for job scope adds the least overhead to the system?

- **A.** Limited
- **B.** Restricted
- **C.** Comprehensive
- **D.** Thorough

7. Using the Top SQL link of the EM Database Control Performance screen produces the output shown in the following graphic. Approximately which time interval produced the highest activity for this monitored event?

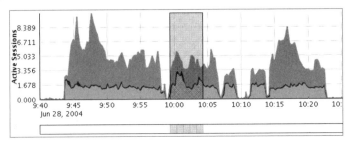

A. 9:45 to 9:50

B. 10:00 to 10:45

C. 9:55 to 10:10

D. 10:00 to 10:05

8. Which data dictionary view contains information explaining why ADDM made its recommendations?

A. DBA_ADVISOR_FINDINGS

B. DBA_ADVISOR_OBJECTS

C. DBA_ADVISOR_RECOMMENDATIONS

D. DBA_ADVISOR_RATIONALE

9. Which of the following advisors determines if the space allocated to the Shared Pool, Large Pool, or Buffer Cache are adequate?

A. SQL Tuning Advisor

B. SGA Tuning Advisor

C. Memory Advisor

D. Pool Advisor

10. Which of the following advisors determines if the estimated instance recovery duration is within the expected service-level agreements?

A. Undo Management Advisor

B. SQL Access Advisor

C. SQL Tuning Advisor

D. MTTR Advisor

11. If no e-mail address is specified, where will alert information be displayed?

A. In the DBA_ALERTS data dictionary view

B. In the V$ALERTS dynamic performance view

C. In the EM Database Control main screen

D. No alert information is sent or displayed.

12. When you configure an alert, which of the following types of alert thresholds can you use to monitor a tablespace for diminishing free space?

A. Warning threshold

B. Critical threshold

C. Both A and B

D. Neither A or B

13. Multiple baseline metrics can be gathered and stored in the AWR. Why might you want more than one metrics baseline?

A. You might want a separate baseline metric for each user.

B. You might want a separate baseline metric for daytime usage versus off-hours usage.

C. You might want a separate baseline metric for each schema.

D. You would never want more than one baseline metric, even though it is possible to gather and store them.

14. Using EM Database Control, you discover that two application PL/SQL functions and a view are currently invalid. Which of the following might you use to fix these objects? (Choose two.)

A. Shut down and restart the database.

B. Use EM Database Control to recompile the object.

C. Export the invalid objects, drop them, and then import them.

D. Use the ALTER FUNCTION … COMPILE and ALTER VIEW … COMPILE commands.

15. You have just created a database using scripts that you wrote. Now you notice that the automatic collection of database statistics by the EMD_MAINTENANCE.EXECUTE_EM_DBMS_JOB_PROCS procedure is not running. What might be the cause?

A. The PFILE/SPFILE parameter GATHER_STATS=FALSE.

B. Only databases created using Database Configuration Assistant have automatic statistics collection enabled.

C. The SYSMAN user who owns the AWR is not logged in.

D. The operating system does not support automatic statistics collection.

16. Which of the following is a performance metric that could be defined as "the amount of work that a system can perform in a given amount of time"?

A. Response time

B. Uptime

C. Throughput

D. Runtime

17. Which of the following is not one of the three primary sources of performance metric information in the EM Database Control Performance screen?

    A. Host

    B. Session

    C. Instance

    D. Network

18. By default, how long will database statistics be retained in the AWR?

    A. 7 days

    B. 30 days

    C. 7 hours

    D. Indefinitely

19. Your users have called to complain that system performance has suddenly decreased markedly. Where would be the most likely place to look for the cause of the problem in the EM Database Control?

    A. Main screen

    B. Performance screen

    C. Administration screen

    D. Maintenance screen

20. Using EM Database Control, you've identified that the following SQL statement is the source of a high amount of disk I/O:

    `SELECT NAME, LOCATION, CREDIT_LIMIT FROM CUSTOMERS`

    What might you do first to try to improve performance?

    A. Run the SQL Tuning Advisor.

    B. Run the SQL Access Advisor.

    C. Check the EM Database Control main screen for alerts.

    D. Click the Alert Log Content link in the EM Database Control main screen.

Answers to Review Questions

1. B. The MMON process gathers statistics from the SGA and stores them in the AWR. The ADDM process then uses these statistics to compare the current state of the database with baseline and historical performance metrics before summarizing the results on the EM Database Control screens.

2. D. Setting STATISTICS_LEVEL = BASIC disables the collection and analysis of AWR statistics. TYPICAL is the default setting, and ALL gathers information for the execution plan and operating system timing. OFF is not a valid value for this parameter.

3. B. The I/O caused by user activity is the primary source of user waits because it is listed first in the graph's legend. Clicking the User I/O link opens a screen in which you can examine which SQL statements are contributing the most to the user waits.

4. C. The pie graph shows that the SQL statement that has been assigned the identifier of b6usrq82hwsa3(73) contributed to 73 percent of the total time spent servicing the top three SQL statements.

5. C. You can use the SQL Tuning Advisor and SQL Access Advisor together to determine if I/O can be minimized and overall DB Time reduced to the targeted SQL statement.

6. A. The Limited scope has the least impact on the system. The Comprehensive scope is the most detailed, but also makes the greatest demands on the system. There are no job scope options called Restricted or Thorough.

7. D. The shaded area shows that the time interval from approximately 10:00 to 10:05 will be analyzed for Top SQL statements.

8. D. DBA_ADVISOR_RATIONALE provides the rationale for each ADDM recommendation. The ADDM findings are stored in DBA_ADVISOR_FINDINGS. The object related to the findings are shown in DBA_ADVISOR_OBJECTS. The actual ADDM recommendations are found in DBA_ADVISOR_RECOMMENDATIONS.

9. C. The Memory Advisor can help determine whether the overall size of the SGA is appropriate and whether memory is properly allocated to the SGA components.

10. D. The Mean Time To Recover (MTTR) Advisor provides recommendations that you can use to configure the database so that the instance recovery time fits within the service levels that you specified.

11. C. By default, alerts are displayed in the Alerts section of the EM Database Control main screen, even when e-mail notifications are not displayed.

12. C. You can specify both warning and critical thresholds for monitoring the available free space in a tablespace. In this situation, the warning threshold is generally a lower number than the critical threshold.

13. B. Because many transactional systems run batch processing during off-hours, having a relevant baseline for each type of usage pattern yields better results in terms of alerts and ADDM recommendations.

14. B, D. After fixing the issue that originally caused the invalid status, you can use both EM Database Control and SQL to compile an invalid object. Starting and stopping the database will not fix invalid objects. Export/import is also not an appropriate technique for recompiling invalid objects.

15. B. Automatic statistics collection can be started on databases created outside the Database Configuration Assistant by using the Automatic Workload Repository link in the EM Database Control Performance screen.

16. C. Throughput is an important performance metric because it is a overall measure of performance that can be compared against similar measures taken before and after tuning changes are implemented.

17. D. Network information may be contained in the Session Information section of the EM Database Control Performance screen, but only if network issues contributed to session wait times.

18. A. By default, database statistics are retained in the AWR for seven days. You can change the default duration using the EM Database Control Automatic Workload Repository link in the Performance screen or using the DBMS_WORKLOAD_REPOSITORY PL/SQL package.

19. B. The Performance screen of the EM Database Control provides a quick overview of how the host system, user sessions, and throughput are impacted by the system slowdown. You can also drill down into any of these three areas to take a look at details about this slowdown.

20. A. Running the SQL Tuning Advisor provides the most information about how the performance of this SQL statement might be improved. The SQL Access Advisor is run only after the output from the SQL Tuning Advisor indicates that it will be useful. EM Database Control does not store detailed information about I/O activity in either its alerts or the Alert log.

Chapter

10

Implementing Database Backups

ORACLE DATABASE 10*G*: ADMINISTRATION I EXAM OBJECTIVES COVERED IN THIS CHAPTER:

✓ **Backup and Recovery Concepts**

  ▪ Describe the basics of database backup, restore and recovery.

  ▪ Configure ARCHIVELOG mode.

  ▪ Configure a database for recoverability.

✓ **Database Backups**

  ▪ Create consistent database backups.

  ▪ Back up your database without shutting it down.

  ▪ Create incremental backups.

  ▪ Automate database backups.

  ▪ Monitor the flash recovery area.

  ▪ Describe the difference between image copies and backup sets.

  ▪ Describe the different types of database backups.

  ▪ Back up a control file to trace.

  ▪ Manage backups.

Exam objectives are subject to change at any time without prior notice and at Oracle's sole discretion. Please visit Oracle's Training and Certification website (http://www.oracle.com/education/certification/) for the most current exam objectives listing.

Oracle Database 10*g* (Oracle 10*g*) makes it easy for you to configure your database to be highly available and reliable. In other words, you want to configure your database to minimize the amount of downtime while at the same time being able to recover quickly and without losing any committed transactions when the database becomes unavailable for reasons that may be beyond your control.

As a database administrator, your primary goal is to keep the database open and available for users, usually 24 hours a day, 7 days a week. Your partnership with the server's system administrator includes the following tasks:

- Proactively solving common causes of failures

- Increasing the mean time between failure (MTBF)

- Ensuring a high level of hardware redundancy

- Increasing availability by using Oracle options such as Real Application Clusters (RAC) and Oracle Streams (an advanced replication technology)

- Decreasing the *mean time to recover (MTTR)* by setting the appropriate Oracle initialization parameters and ensuring that backups are readily available in a recovery scenario

- Minimizing or eliminating loss of committed transactions by using archived redo logs, standby databases, and Oracle Data Guard

RAC, Streams, Data Guard, and standby databases are beyond the scope of this book, but are covered in more detail in advanced Oracle courseware.

In this chapter, we will first describe the components that you will use to minimize or eliminate data loss in your database while at the same time keeping availability high: checkpoints, redo log files, archived redo log files, and the Flash Recovery area. Next, we will show you how to configure your database for recovery, including a discussion of ARCHIVELOG mode and other required initialization parameters. Once your environment is configured, you will need to know how to actually back it up, using both operating system commands and the RMAN utility. Finally, we will show you how to automate and manage your backups as well as how to monitor one of the key components in your backup strategy: the Flash Recovery area. In Chapter 11, "Implementing Database Recovery," we will show you how to use the files created and maintained during your backups to quickly recover the database in the event of a database failure.

Oracle's GUI administration tool, the Enterprise Manager (EM) Database Control, makes backup configuration and performing backups easier than in any previous release of Oracle. Most, if not all, of the functionality available with the command-line interface is available in a GUI interface to save time and make backup operations less error prone.

Understanding and Configuring Recovery Components

A number of structures and events in the database directly support backup and recovery operations. The control files maintain the list of database files in the database, along with a record of the most recent database backups (if you are using RMAN for your backups). The *checkpoint* (CKPT) background process works in concert with the database writer (DBW*n*) process to manage the amount of time required for instance recovery; during instance recovery, the redo log files are used to synchronize the datafiles. For more serious types of failures such as media failures, archived redo log files are applied to a restored backup copy of a datafile to synchronize the datafiles and ensure that no committed transactions are lost. Finally, the Flash Recovery area, new to Oracle 10*g*, is a common area for all recovery-related files that makes your job much easier when backing up or recovering your database.

To maximize your database's availability, it almost goes without saying that you want to perform regularly scheduled backups. Most media failures require some kind of restoration of a datafile from a disk or tape backup before you can initiate media recovery.

In addition to regularly scheduled backups (see the section "Automating Backups" near the end of this chapter), you can configure a number of other features to maximize your database's availability and minimize recovery time: multiplexing control files, multiplexing redo log files, configuring the database in ARCHIVELOG mode, and using a Flash Recovery area.

Control Files

The control file is one of the smallest, yet one of the most critical, files in your database. Recovering from the loss of one copy of a control file is relatively straightforward; recovering from the loss of your only control file or all control files is more of a challenge and requires more advanced recovery techniques.

Recovering from the loss of a control file is covered in Chapter 11.

In the following sections, we will give you an overview of the control file architecture as well as show you how to maximize the recoverability of the control file in the section "Multiplexing Control Files."

Control File Architecture

The *control file* is a relatively small (in the megabyte range) binary file that contains information about the structure of the database. You can think of the control file as a metadata repository for the physical database. It has the structure of the database—the datafiles and redo log files that constitute a database. The control file is created when the database is created and is updated with the physical changes, for example, whenever you add or rename a datafile.

The control file is updated continuously and should be available at all times. Don't edit the contents of the control file; only Oracle processes should update its contents. When you start up the database, Oracle uses the control file to identify the datafiles and redo log files and opens them. Control files play a major role when recovering a database.

The contents of the control file include the following:

- The database name to which the control file belongs. A control file can belong to only one database.

- The database creation time stamp.

- The name, location, and online/offline status information of the datafiles.

- The name and location of the redo log files.

- Redo log archive information.

- Tablespace names.

- The current *log sequence number*, which is a unique identifier that is incremented and recorded when an online redo log file is switched.

- The most recent checkpoint information.

 Checkpoints are discussed in more detail later in this chapter in the section "Understanding Checkpoints."

- The beginning and ending of undo segments.

- Recovery Manager's backup information. Recovery Manager (RMAN) is the Oracle utility you use to back up and recover databases.

The control file size is determined by the MAX clauses you provide when you create the database:

- MAXLOGFILES

- MAXLOGMEMBERS

- MAXLOGHISTORY

- MAXDATAFILES

- MAXINSTANCES

Oracle preallocates space for these maximums in the control file. Therefore, when you add or rename a file in the database, the control file size does not change.

When you add a new file to the database or relocate a file, an Oracle server process immediately updates the information in the control file. Back up the control file after any structural changes. The log writer (LGWR) process updates the control file with the current log sequence number. CKPT updates the control file with the recent checkpoint information. When the database is in ARCHIVELOG mode, the archiver (ARC*n*) processes update the control file with information such as the archive log filename and log sequence number.

The control file contains two types of record sections: reusable and not reusable. RMAN information is kept in the reusable section. Items such as the names of the backup datafiles are kept in this section, and once this section fills up, the entries are reused in a circular fashion after the number of days specified by the initialization parameter CONTROL_FILE_RECORD_KEEP_ TIME is reached. Therefore, the control file can continue to grow due to new RMAN backup information recorded in the control file until it reaches CONTROL_FILE_RECORD_KEEP_TIME.

Multiplexing Control Files

Because the control file is critical for database operation, at a minimum have two copies of the control file; Oracle recommends a minimum of three copies. You duplicate the control file on different disks either by using the multiplexing feature of Oracle or by using the mirroring feature of your operating system. If you have multiple disk controllers on your server, at least one copy of the control file should reside on a disk managed by a different disk controller.

If you use the Database Configuration Assistant (DBCA) to create your database, three copies of the control files are multiplexed by default. In Figure 10.1, on the DBCA Database Storage screen, you can see that DBCA allows you to specify additional copies of the control file or change the location of the control files.

The next two sections discuss the two ways that you can implement the multiplexing feature: using a client or server-side init.ora (available before Oracle 9i) and using the server-side SPFILE (available with Oracle 9i and later).

FIGURE 10.1   DBCA Storage control files

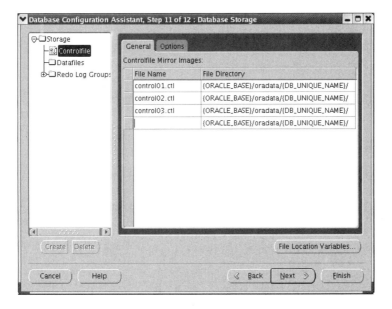

Multiplexing Control Files Using *init.ora*

Multiplexing means keeping a copy of the same control file or other file on different disk drives, ideally on different controllers too. Copying the control file to multiple locations and changing the CONTROL_FILES parameter in the text-based initialization file init.ora to include all control file names specifies the multiplexing of the control file. The following syntax shows three multiplexed control files.

```
CONTROL_FILES = ('/ora01/oradata/MYDB/ctrlMYDB01.ctl',
                 '/ora02/oradata/MYDB/ctrlMYDB02.ctl',
                 '/ora03/oradata/MYDB/ctrlMYDB03.ctl')
```

By storing the control file on multiple disks, you avoid the risk of a single point of failure. When multiplexing control files, updates to the control file can take a little longer, but that is insignificant when compared with the benefits. If you lose one control file, you can restart the database after copying one of the other control files or after changing the CONTROL_FILES parameter in the initialization file.

When multiplexing control files, Oracle updates all the control files at the same time, but uses only the first control file listed in the CONTROL_FILES parameter for reading.

When creating a database, you can list the control file names in the CONTROL_FILES parameter, and Oracle creates as many control files as are listed. You can have a maximum of eight multiplexed control file copies.

If you need to add more control file copies, follow these steps:

1. Shut down the database.

   ```
   SQL> SHUTDOWN NORMAL
   ```

2. Copy the control file to more locations by using an operating system command:

   ```
   $ cp /u02/oradata/ord/control01.ctl /u05/oradata/ord/control04.ctl
   ```

3. Change the initialization parameter file to include the new control file name(s) in the parameter CONTROL_FILES changing this:

   ```
   CONTROL_FILES='/u02/oradata/ord/control01.ctl', \
   '/u03/oradata/ord/control02.ctl', \
   '/u04/oradata/ord/control03.ctl'
   ```

   to this:

   ```
   CONTROL_FILES='/u02/oradata/ord/control01.ctl', \
   '/u03/oradata/ord/control02.ctl', \
   '/u04/oradata/ord/control03.ctl', \
   '/u05/oradata/ord/control04.ctl'
   ```

4. Start up the instance.

   ```
   SQL> STARTUP
   ```

These procedures are somewhat similar to the procedures for recovering from the loss of a control file.

 We will provide examples of control file recovery in Chapter 11.

After creating the database, you can change the location of the control files, rename the control files, or drop certain control files. You must have at least one control file for each database. To add, rename, or delete control files, you need to follow the preceding steps. Basically, you shut down the database, use the operating system copy command (copy, rename, or delete the control files accordingly), modify the init.ora parameter file, and start up the database.

Multiplexing Control Files Using an SPFILE

Multiplexing using a binary SPFILE is similar to multiplexing using init.ora. The major difference is in how the CONTROL_FILES parameter is changed. Follow these steps:

1. Alter the SPFILE while the database is still open:

```
SQL> ALTER SYSTEM SET CONTROL_FILES =
     '/ora01/oradata/MYDB/ctrlMYDB01.ctl',
     '/ora02/oradata/MYDB/ctrlMYDB02.ctl',
     '/ora03/oradata/MYDB/ctrlMYDB03.ctl',
     '/ora04/oradata/MYDB/ctrlMYDB04.ctl' SCOPE=SPFILE;
```

This parameter change takes effect only after the next instance restart by using the SCOPE=SPFILE qualifier. The contents of the binary SPFILE are changed immediately, but the old specification of CONTROL_FILES is used until the instance is restarted.

2. Shut down the database:

```
SQL> SHUTDOWN NORMAL
```

3. Copy an existing control file to the new location:

```
$ cp /ora01/oradata/MYDB/ctrlMYDB01.ctl/ora04/oradata/MYDB/ctrlMYDB04.ctl
```

4. Start the instance:

```
SQL> STARTUP
```

Understanding Checkpoints

The *checkpoint background process* controls the amount of time required for instance recovery. During a checkpoint, CKPT updates the control file and the header of the datafiles to reflect the last successful transaction by recording the last *system change number (SCN)*. The SCN, which is a number sequentially assigned to each transaction in the database, is also recorded in the control file against the datafile name that is taken offline or made read-only.

A checkpoint occurs automatically every time a redo log file switch occurs, either when the current redo log file fills up or when you manually switch redo log files. The DBW*n* processes in conjunction with CKPT routinely write new and changed buffers to advance the checkpoint from where instance recovery can begin, thus reducing the MTTR.

> More information on tuning the MTTR and how often checkpointing occurs can be found in Chapter 11.

Redo Log Files

A *redo log file* records all changes to the database, in most cases before the changes are written to the datafiles.

To recover from an instance or a media failure, redo log information is required to roll datafiles forward to the last committed transaction. Ensuring that you have at least two members for each redo log file group dramatically reduces the likelihood of data loss because the database continues to operate if one member of a redo log file is lost.

> How to recover from the loss of a single redo log group member is covered in Chapter 11; recovery from the loss of an entire log group is covered in *OCP: Oracle 10g Administration II Study Guide* (Sybex, 2005).

In this section, we will give you an architectural overview of redo log files, as well as show you how to add redo log groups, add or remove redo log group members, and clear a redo log group in case one of the redo log group's members becomes corrupted.

Redo Log File Architecture

Online redo log files are filled with redo records. A *redo record*, also called a *redo entry*, is made up of a group of *change vectors*, each of which describes a change made to a single block in the database. Redo entries record data that you can use to reconstruct all changes made to the database, including the undo segments. When you recover the database by using redo log files, Oracle reads the change vectors in the redo records and applies the changes to the relevant blocks.

The LGWR process writes redo information from the redo log buffer to the online redo log files under a variety of circumstances:

- When a user commits a transaction, even if this is the only transaction in the log buffer.

- When the redo log buffer becomes one-third full.

- When the buffer contains approximately 1MB of *changed* records. This total does not include deleted or inserted records.

> LGWR always writes its records to the online redo log file *before* DBW*n* writes new or modified database buffer cache records to the datafiles.

Each database has its own online *redo log groups*. A redo log group can have one or more *redo log members* (each member is a single operating system file). If you have a RAC configuration, in which multiple instances are mounted to one database, each instance has one online redo thread. That is, the LGWR process of each instance writes to the same online redo log files, and hence Oracle has to keep track of the instance from where the database changes are coming. Single instance configurations will have only one thread, and that thread number is 1. The redo log file contains both committed and uncommitted transactions. Whenever a transaction is committed, a system change number is assigned to the redo records to identify the committed transaction.

The redo log group is referenced by an integer; you can specify the group number when you create the redo log files, either when you create the database or when you create a redo log group after you create the database. You can also change the redo log configuration (add/drop/rename files) by using database commands. The following example shows a CREATE DATABASE command.

```
CREATE DATABASE "MYDB01"
. . .
LOGFILE '/ora02/oradata/MYDB01/redo01.log' SIZE 10M,
        '/ora03/oradata/MYDB01/redo02.log' SIZE 10M;
```

Two *log file groups* are created here; the first file is assigned to group 1, and the second file is assigned to group 2. You can have more files in each group; this practice is known as the multiplexing of redo log files, which we'll discuss later in this chapter in the section "Multiplexing Redo Log Files." You can specify any group number—the range will be between 1 and the parameter MAXLOGFILES. Oracle recommends that all redo log groups be the same size. The following is an example of creating the log files by specifying the group number:

```
CREATE DATABASE "MYDB01"
. . .
LOGFILE GROUP 1 '/ora02/oradata/MYDB01/redo01.log' SIZE 10M,
        GROUP 2 '/ora03/oradata/MYDB01/redo02.log' SIZE 10M;
```

Log Switch Operations

The LGWR process writes to only one redo log file group at any time. The file that is actively being written to is known as the *current* log file. The log files that are required for instance recovery are known as the *active* log files. The other log files are known as *inactive*. Oracle automatically recovers an instance when starting up the instance by using the online redo log files. Instance recovery can be needed if you do not shut down the database cleanly or if your database server crashes.

 How instance recovery works is discussed in more detail in Chapter 11.

The log files are written in a circular fashion. A log switch occurs when Oracle finishes writing to one log group and starts writing to the next log group. A log switch always occurs when the current redo log group is completely full and log writing must continue. You can force a log switch by using the ALTER SYSTEM command. A manual log switch can be necessary when performing maintenance on the redo log files by using the ALTER SYSTEM SWITCH LOGFILE command. Figure 10.2 shows how LGWR writes to the redo log groups in a circular fashion.

Whenever a log switch occurs, Oracle assigns a log sequence number to the new redo log group before writing to it. If there are lots of transactions or changes to the database, the log switches can occur too frequently. Size the redo log files appropriately to avoid frequent log switches. Oracle writes to the alert log file whenever a log switch occurs.

> Redo log files are written sequentially on the disk, so the I/O will be fast if there is no other activity on the disk. (The disk head is always properly positioned.) Keep the redo log files on a separate disk for better performance. If you have to store a datafile on the same disk as the redo log file, do not put the SYSTEM, UNDOTBS, SYSAUX, or any very active data or index tablespace file on this disk. A commit cannot complete until a transaction's information has been written to the redo logs, so maximizing the throughput of the redo log files is a top priority.

FIGURE 10.2   Redo log file usage

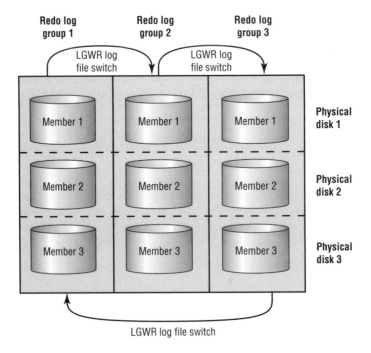

Database checkpoints are closely tied to redo log file switches. We introduced checkpoints earlier in the chapter in the section "Understanding Checkpoints." A checkpoint is an event that flushes the modified data from the buffer cache to the disk and updates the control file and datafiles. The CKPT process updates the headers of datafiles and control files; the actual blocks are written to the file by the DBW*n* process. A checkpoint is initiated when the redo log file is filled and a log switch occurs, when the instance is shut down with NORMAL, TRANSACTIONAL, or IMMEDIATE, when a tablespace status is changed to read-only or put into BACKUP mode, or when other values specified by certain parameters (discussed later in this section) are reached.

You can force a checkpoint if needed, as shown here:

```
ALTER SYSTEM CHECKPOINT;
```

Forcing a checkpoint ensures that all changes to the database buffers are written to the datafiles on disk.

Another way to force a checkpoint is by forcing a log file switch:

```
ALTER SYSTEM SWITCH LOGFILE;
```

The size of the redo log affects the checkpoint performance. If the size of the redo log is smaller compared with the number of transactions, a log switch occurs often, and so does the checkpoint. The DBW*n* process writes the dirty buffer blocks whenever a checkpoint occurs. This situation might reduce the time required for instance recovery, but it might also affect the runtime performance. You can adjust checkpoints primarily by using the initialization parameter FAST_START_MTTR_TARGET. This parameter replaces the deprecated parameters FAST_START_IO_TARGET and LOG_CHECKPOINT_TIMEOUT in previous versions of the Oracle database. It is used to ensure that recovery time at instance startup (if required) will not exceed a certain number of seconds.

Real World Scenario

Redo Log Troubleshooting

In the case of redo log groups, it's best to be generous with the number of groups and the number of members for each group. After estimating the number of groups that would be appropriate for your installation, add one more. I can remember many database installations in which I was trying to be overly cautious about disk space usage, not putting things into perspective and realizing that the slight additional work involved in maintaining either additional or larger redo logs is small in relation to the time needed to fix a problem when the number of users and concurrent active transactions increase.

The space needed for additional log file groups is minimal and is well worth the effort up front to avoid the undesirable situation in which writes to the redo log file are waiting on the completion of writes to the database files or the archived log file destination.

More information on adjusting FAST_START_MTTR_TARGET can be found in Chapter 11.

Multiplexing Redo Log Files

You can keep multiple copies of the online redo log file to safeguard against damage to these files. When multiplexing online redo log files, LGWR concurrently writes the same redo log information to multiple identical online redo log files, thereby eliminating a single point of redo log failure. All copies of the redo file are the same size and are known as a *group,* which is identified by an integer. Each redo log file in the group is known as a *member.* You must have at least two redo log groups for normal database operation.

When multiplexing redo log files, keeping the members of a group on different disks is preferable so that one disk failure will not affect the continuing operation of the database. If LGWR can write to at least one member of the group, database operation proceeds as normal; an entry is written to the alert log file. If all members of the redo log file group are not available for writing, Oracle hangs, crashes, or shuts down. An instance recovery or media recovery can be needed to bring up the database, and you can lose committed transactions.

You can create multiple copies of the online redo log files when you create the database. For example, the following statement creates two redo log file groups with two members in each:

```
CREATE DATABASE "MYDB01"
. . .
LOGFILE
  GROUP 1 ('/ora02/oradata/MYDB01/redo0101.log',
          '/ora03/oradata/MYDB01/redo0102.log') SIZE 10M,
  GROUP 2 ('/ora02/oradata/MYDB01/redo0201.log',
          '/ora03/oradata/MYDB01/redo0202.log') SIZE 10M;
```

The maximum number of log file groups is specified in the clause MAXLOGFILES, and the maximum number of members is specified in the clause MAXLOGMEMBERS. You can separate the filenames (members) by using a space or a comma.

In the following sections, we will show you how to create a new redo log group, add a new member to an existing group, rename a member, and drop a member from an existing group. In addition, we'll show you how to drop a group and clear all members of a group in certain circumstances.

Creating New Groups

You can create and add more redo log groups to the database by using the ALTER DATABASE command. The following statement creates a new log file group with two members:

```
ALTER DATABASE ADD LOGFILE
  GROUP 3 ('/ora02/oradata/MYDB01/redo0301.log',
          '/ora03/oradata/MYDB01/redo0302.log') SIZE 10M;
```

If you omit the GROUP clause, Oracle assigns the next available number. For example, the following statement also creates a multiplexed group:

```
ALTER DATABASE ADD LOGFILE
    ('/ora02/oradata/MYDB01/redo0301.log',
     '/ora03/oradata/MYDB01/redo0302.log') SIZE 10M;
```

To create a new group without multiplexing, use the following statement:

```
ALTER DATABASE ADD LOGFILE
    '/ora02/oradata/MYDB01/redo0301.log' REUSE;
```

You can add more than one redo log group by using the ALTER DATABASE command—just use a comma to separate the groups.

> If the redo log files you create already exist, use the REUSE option, and don't specify the size. The new redo log size will be the same as that of the existing file.

Adding a new redo log group is straightforward using the EM Database Control interface. To do so, click the Administration tab on the database home page, and then click the Redo Log Groups link. You can view and add another redo log group, as you can see in Figure 10.3 on the Redo Log Groups screen.

FIGURE 10.3   The Redo Log Groups maintenance screen

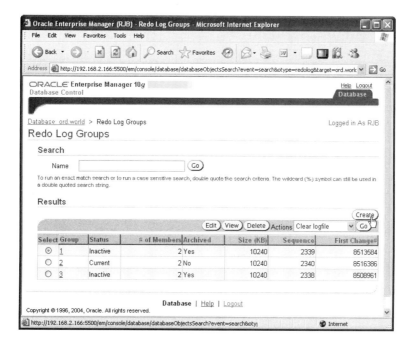

Adding New Members

If you forgot to multiplex the redo log files when creating the database (multiplexing redo log files is the default when you use DBCA) or if you need to add more redo log members, you can do so by using the ALTER DATABASE command. When adding new members, you do not specify the file size, because all group members will have the same size.

If you know the group number, use the following statement to add a member to group 2:

```
ALTER DATABASE ADD LOGFILE MEMBER
'/ora04/oradata/MYDB01/redo0203.log' TO GROUP 2;
```

You can also add group members by specifying the names of other members in the group, instead of specifying the group number. Specify all the existing group members with this syntax:

```
ALTER DATABASE ADD LOGFILE MEMBER
 '/ora04/oradata/MYDB01/redo0203.log' TO
('/ora02/oradata/MYDB01/redo0201.log',
 '/ora03/oradata/MYDB01/redo0202.log');
```

You can add a new member to a group in the EM Database Control by clicking the Edit button in Figure 10.3 and then clicking Add.

Renaming Log Members

If you want to move the log file member from one disk to another or just want a more meaningful name, you can rename a redo log member. Before renaming the online redo log members, the new (target) online redo files should exist. The SQL commands in Oracle change only the internal pointer in the control file to a new log file; they do not change or rename the operating system file. You must use an operating system command to rename or move the file. Follow these steps to rename a log member:

1. Shut down the database.

2. Copy/rename the redo log file member to the new location by using an operating system command.

3. Start up the instance and mount the database (STARTUP MOUNT).

4. Rename the log file member in the control file. Use ALTER DATABASE RENAME FILE 'old_redo_file_name' TO 'new_redo_file_name';.

5. Open the database (ALTER DATABASE OPEN).

6. Back up the control file.

Another way to achieve the same result is to add a new member to the group and then drop the old member from the group, as discussed in the "Adding New Members" section earlier in this chapter and the "Dropping Redo Log Groups" section, which is next.

You can rename a log group member in the EM Database Control by clicking the Edit button in Figure 10.3, clicking Edit again, and then changing the file name in the File Name box.

Dropping Redo Log Groups

You can drop a redo log group and its members by using the ALTER DATABASE command. Remember that you should have at least two redo log groups for the database to function normally. The group that is to be dropped should not be the active group or the current group—that is, you can drop only an inactive log file group. If the log file to be dropped is not inactive, use the ALTER SYSTEM SWITCH LOGFILE command.

To drop the log file group 3, use the following SQL statement:

```
ALTER DATABASE DROP LOGFILE GROUP 3;
```

When an online redo log group is dropped from the database, the operating system files are not deleted from disk. The control files of the associated database are updated to drop the members of the group from the database structure. After dropping an online redo log group, make sure that the drop is completed successfully, and then use the appropriate operating system command to delete the dropped online redo log files.

You can delete an entire redo log group in the EM Database Control by clicking the Edit button (see Figure 10.3, shown earlier) and then clicking the Delete button.

Dropping Redo Log Members

In much the same way that you drop a redo log group, you can drop only the members of an inactive redo log group. Also, if there are only two groups, the log member to be dropped should not be the last member of a group. Each redo log group can have a different number of members, though this is not advised. For example, say you have three log groups, each with two members. If you drop a log member from group 2, and a failure occurs to the sole member of group 2, the instance will hang, crash, and potentially cause loss of committed transactions when attempts are made to write to the missing redo log group, as we discussed earlier in this chapter. Even if you drop a member for maintenance reasons, ensure that all redo log groups have the same number of members.

To drop a redo log member, use the DROP LOGFILE MEMBER clause of the ALTER DATABASE command:

```
ALTER DATABASE DROP LOGFILE MEMBER
'/ora04/oradata/MYDB01/redo0203.log';
```

The operating system file is not removed from the disk; only the control file is updated. Use an operating system command to delete the redo log file member from disk.

> If a database is running in ARCHIVELOG mode, redo log members cannot be deleted unless the redo log group has been archived.

You can drop a member of a redo log group in the EM Database Control by clicking the Edit button (see Figure 10.3, shown earlier), selecting the member to be dropped, and then clicking the Remove button.

Clearing Online Redo Log Files

Under certain circumstances, a redo log group member (or all members of a log group) can become corrupted. To solve this problem, you can drop and re-add the log file group or group member. It is much easier, however, to use the ALTER DATABASE CLEAR LOGFILE command. The following example clears the contents of redo log group 3 in the database:

```
ALTER DATABASE CLEAR LOGFILE GROUP 3;
```

Another distinct advantage of this command is that you can clear a log group even if the database has only two log groups and only one member in each group. You can also clear a log group member even if it has not been archived by using the UNARCHIVED keyword. In this case, it is advisable to do a full database backup at the earliest convenience, because the unarchived redo log file is no longer usable for database recovery.

Archived Redo Log Files

If you only use online redo log files, your database is protected against instance failure but not media failure. Although saving the redo log files before they are overwritten takes additional disk space and management, the increased recoverability of the database outweighs the slight additional overhead and maintenance costs.

In this section, we will present an overview of how archived redo log files work, how to set the location for saving the archived redo log files, and how to enable archiving in the database.

Archived Redo Log File Architecture

An *archived redo log file* is a copy of a redo log file before it is overwritten by new redo information. Because the online redo log files are reused in a circular fashion, you have no way of bringing a backup of a datafile up to the latest committed transaction unless you configure the database in ARCHIVELOG mode.

The process of copying is called *archiving*. ARC*n* does this archiving. By archiving the redo log files, you can use them later to recover a database, update a standby database, or use the LogMiner utility to audit the database activities.

More information on how to use archived redo log files in a recovery scenario can be found in Chapter 11.

When an online redo log file is full, and LGWR starts writing to the next redo log file, ARC*n* copies the completed redo log file to the archive destination. It is possible to specify more than one archive destination. The LGWR process waits for the ARC*n* process to complete the copy operation before overwriting any online redo log file. As with LGWR, the failure of one of the ARC*n* backup processes will cause instance failure, but no committed transactions will be lost because the "Commit complete" message is not returned to the user or calling program until LGWR successfully records the transaction in the online redo log file group.

Real World Scenario

Archive Logging Space Issues

After you configure the database for ARCHIVELOG mode, your job is only half complete. You need to continually make sure that there is enough room for the archived log files, otherwise the database will hang. At least once in every DBA's career, he or she will get a phone call from some users saying that the database has "crashed," while other users are still using the database. It's not until you check the alert log that you discover the archiving process cannot find disk space for a newly filled log file in the archiving destinations.

There should be enough space available for online archived redo log files to recover and roll forward from the last full backup of each datafile that is also online; the remaining archived logs and any previous datafile backups can be moved to another disk or to tape.

Remembering your zero transaction loss strategy (which should be every DBA's strategy), make sure that you do not misplace or delete an archived log file before it is backed up to tape, otherwise you will not be able to perform a complete recovery due to a media failure.

If you use RMAN and the Flash Recovery area for all of your backup files, then you can further automate this process by directing RMAN to maintain enough backups to satisfy a recovery window policy (number of days) or a redundancy policy (multiple copies of each backup). Once an archived log or other backup file is no longer needed for the policy, the files are automatically deleted from the Flash Recovery area.

When the archiver process is copying the redo log files to another destination, the database is said to be in *ARCHIVELOG* mode. If archiving is not enabled, the database is said to be in *NOARCHIVELOG* mode. In production systems, you cannot afford to lose data and should therefore run the database in ARCHIVELOG mode so that in the event of a failure, you can recover the database to the time of failure or to a point in time. You can achieve this ability to recover by restoring the database backup and applying the database changes by using the archived log files.

Setting the Archive Destination

You specify the archive destination in the initialization parameter file. To change the archive destination parameters during normal database operation, you use the ALTER SYSTEM command. Here are some of the parameters associated with archive log destinations and the archiver process:

LOG_ARCHIVE_DEST_n   Using this parameter, you can specify at most 10 archiving destinations. These locations can be on the local machine or on a remote machine where the standby database is located. The syntax for specifying this parameter in the initialization file is as follows:

```
LOG_ARCHIVE_DEST_n =  "null_string" |
((SERVICE = tnsnames_name |
```

```
  LOCATION = 'directory_name')
 [MANDATORY | OPTIONAL]
 [REOPEN [= integer]])
```

For example:

```
 LOG_ARCHIVE_DEST_1 = ((LOCATION='/archive/MYDB01') MANDATORY
   REOPEN = 60)
```

specifies a location for the archive log files on the local machine at /archive/MYDB01. The MANDATORY clause specifies that writing to this location must succeed. The REOPEN clause specifies when the next attempt to write to this location should be made, when the first attempt did not succeed. The default value is 300 seconds.

Here is another example, which applies the archive logs to a standby database on a remote computer.

```
 LOG_ARCHIVE_DEST_2 = (SERVICE=STDBY01) OPTIONAL REOPEN;
```

Here STDBY01 is the Oracle Net connect string used to connect to the remote database. Because writing is optional, the database activity continues even if ARC*n* could not write the archive log file. It tries the writing operation again because the REOPEN clause is specified.

You can also use the EM Database Control web pages to configure the log filenaming and destinations by clicking Configure Recovery Settings in the Maintenance tab. The first destination is on the file system at /u09/oradata/arch01, as you can see in Figure 10.4.

Destination number 10 is the Flash Recovery area using the string USE_DB_RECOVERY_FILE_DEST.

FIGURE 10.4 The log archive destinations

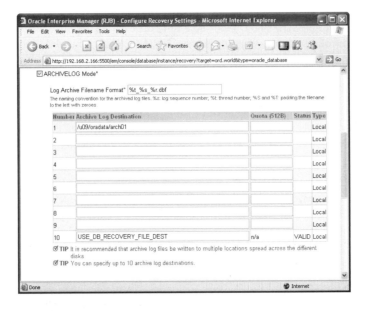

We will tell you about the Flash Recovery area in the section "The Flash Recovery Area."

LOG_ARCHIVE_MIN_SUCCEED_DEST   This parameter specifies the number of destinations that the ARC*n* process should successfully write at a minimum to proceed with overwriting the online redo log files. The default value of this parameter is 1. This parameter cannot exceed the total number of enabled destinations. If this parameter value is less than the number of MANDATORY destinations, the parameter is ignored.

LOG_ARCHIVE_FORMAT   This parameter specifies the format in which to write the filename of the archived redo log files. To ensure that the log files are not overwritten, you use predefined substitution variables to construct the name of each archived redo log file. You can provide a text string and any of the predefined substitution variables. The variables are as follows:

%s	Log sequence number
%t	Thread number
%r	Resetlogs ID: ensures uniqueness even after using advanced recovery techniques that resets the log sequence numbers
%d	Database ID

The format you provide must include at least %s, %t, and %r. If you use the same archived redo log location for multiple databases, you must also use %d. In Figure 10.4 (shown earlier), the log archive filename format is defined as %t_%s_%r.dbf.

Setting *ARCHIVELOG*

Specifying these parameters does not start writing the archive log files. To enable archiving of the redo log files, place the database in ARCHIVELOG mode. You can specify the ARCHIVELOG clause while creating the database. However, you might prefer to create the database first and then enable ARCHIVELOG mode. To enable ARCHIVELOG mode, follow these steps:

1. Shut down the database. Set up the appropriate initialization parameters.

2. Start up and mount the database; ARCHIVELOG mode can be changed only when the database is in the MOUNT state.

Details on instance startup can be found in Chapter 11.

3. Enable ARCHIVELOG mode by using the command ALTER DATABASE ARCHIVELOG.

4. Open the database by using ALTER DATABASE OPEN.

   To disable ARCHIVELOG mode, follow these steps:

1. Shut down the database.

2. Start up and mount the database.

3. Disable ARCHIVELOG mode by using the command ALTER DATABASE NOARCHIVELOG.

4. Open the database by using ALTER DATABASE OPEN.

The dynamic performance view V$DATABASE tells you whether you are in ARCHIVELOG mode, as you can see in this query:

```
SQL> select dbid, name, created, log_mode
  2      from v$database;

     DBID NAME      CREATED   LOG_MODE
---------- --------- --------- ------------
1387044942 ORD       03-MAR-04 ARCHIVELOG

1 row selected.
```

The Flash Recovery Area

As the price of disk space drops, the difference in its price compared with tape is offset by the advantages of using disk as the primary backup medium: Even a slow disk can be accessed randomly a magnitude faster than a tape drive. This rapid access means that any database recovery operation takes only minutes instead of hours.

Using disk space as the primary medium for all database recovery operations is the key component of Oracle 10*g*'s Flash Recovery area. The *Flash Recovery area* is a single, unified storage area for all recovery-related files and recovery activities in an Oracle database.

The Flash Recovery area can be a single directory, an entire file system, or an Automatic Storage Management (ASM) disk group. To further optimize the use of disk space for recovery operations, a Flash Recovery area can be shared by more than one database.

In the following sections, we will cover all major aspects of a Flash Recovery area: what can and should be kept in the Flash Recovery area and how to set up a Flash Recovery using initialization parameters and SQL commands. Also, as with other aspects of Oracle 10*g*, we will show how you can manage most parts of the Flash Recovery area using the Enterprise Manager (EM) Database Control, and we'll introduce some of the more advanced management techniques.

Flash Recovery Area Occupants

All the files needed to recover a database from a media failure or a logical error are contained in the Flash Recovery area. The Flash Recovery area can contain the following:

Control files A copy of the control file is created in the Flash Recovery area when the database is created. This copy of the control file can be used as one of the mirrored copies of the control file to ensure that at least one copy of the control file is available after a media failure.

Archived log files When the Flash Recovery area is configured, the initialization parameter LOG_ARCHIVE_DEST_10 is automatically set to the Flash Recovery area location. The corresponding

ARC*n* processes create archived log files in the Flash Recovery area and any other defined LOG_ARCHIVE_DEST_*n* locations.

Flashback logs If flashback database is enabled, its flashback logs are stored in the Flash Recovery area.

> You can find more information about configuring and using flashback logs with flashback database in *OCP: Oracle 10*g *Administration II Study Guide* (Sybex, 2005).

Control file and SPFILE autobackups The Flash Recovery area holds control file and SPFILE autobackups generated by RMAN if RMAN is configured for control file autobackup. When RMAN backs up datafile #1, which is part of the SYSTEM tablespace, the control file is automatically included in the RMAN backup.

Datafile copies For RMAN BACKUP AS COPY image files, the default destination for the datafile copies is the Flash Recovery area.

> You can find more information on RMAN image copy functions later in this chapter in the section "Using RMAN to Create Backups."

RMAN backup sets By default, RMAN uses the Flash Recovery area for both backup sets and image copies. In addition, RMAN puts restored archived log files from tape into the Flash Recovery area in preparation for a recovery operation.

The Flash Recovery Area and SQL Commands

You must define two initialization parameters to set up the Flash Recovery area: DB_RECOVERY_FILE_DEST_SIZE and DB_RECOVERY_FILE_DEST. Because both of these are dynamic parameters, the instance need not be shut down and restarted for the Flash Recovery area to be usable.

DB_RECOVERY_FILE_DEST_SIZE, which must be defined before DB_RECOVERY_FILE_DEST, defines the size of the Flash Recovery area. To maximize the benefits of the Flash Recovery area, it should be large enough to hold a copy of all datafiles, all incremental backups, online redo logs, archived redo logs not yet backed up to tape, control files, and control file autobackups. At a bare minimum, you need enough space to hold the archived log files not yet copied to tape.

Here is an example of configuring DB_RECOVERY_FILE_DEST_SIZE:

```
SQL> alter system
  2    set db_recovery_file_dest_size = 8g scope=both;
```

The size of the Flash Recovery area will be 8GB, and because we used the SCOPE=BOTH parameter in the ALTER SYSTEM command, the initialization parameter takes effect immediately and stays in effect even after a database restart.

All instances in an RAC database must have the same values for DB_RECOVERY_FILE_DEST_SIZE and DB_RECOVERY_FILE_DEST.

The parameter DB_RECOVERY_FILE_DEST specifies the physical location where all Flash Recovery files are stored. The ASM disk group or file system must have at least as much space as the amount specified with DB_RECOVERY_FILE_DEST_SIZE, and it can have significantly more. DB_RECOVERY_FILE_DEST_SIZE, however, can be increased on the fly if more space is needed and the file system where the Flash Recovery area resides has the space available.

In the following example, we use the directory /OraFlash for the Flash Recovery area, like so:

```
SQL> alter system
  2   set db_recovery_file_dest = '/OraFlash' scope=both;
```

Clearing the value of DB_RECOVERY_FILE_DEST disables the Flash Recovery area; the parameter DB_RECOVERY_FILE_DEST_SIZE cannot be cleared until the DB_RECOVERY_FILE_DEST parameter has been cleared.

The Flash Recovery Area and the EM Database Control

You can create and maintain the Flash Recovery area using the EM Database Control. Click the Maintenance tab, and then click the Configure Recovery Settings link to display the Configure Recovery Settings screen, as shown in Figure 10.5.

FIGURE 10.5 The Configure Recovery Settings screen

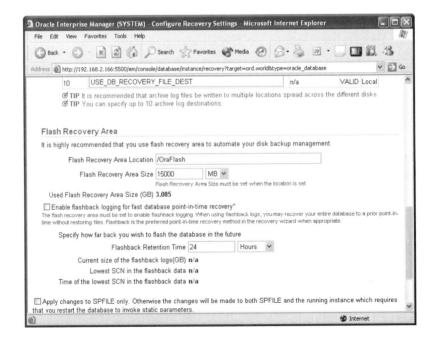

In the Flash Recovery Area section, the Flash Recovery area has been configured for this database in the file system /OraFlash, with a maximum size of 15,000MB (15GB). Just more than 3GB of space is currently used in the Flash Recovery area. Flashback logging has not yet been enabled for this database.

Flash Recovery Area Management

Because the space in the Flash Recovery area is limited by the initialization parameter DB_RECOVERY_FILE_DEST_SIZE, the Oracle database keeps track of which files are no longer needed on disk so that they can be deleted when there is not enough free space for new files. Each time a file is deleted from the Flash Recovery area, a message is written to the alert log.

A message is also written to the alert log in other circumstances. If no files can be deleted, and the recovery area used space is at 85 percent, a warning message is issued. When the space used is at 97 percent, a critical warning is issued. These warnings are recorded in the alert log file, can be viewed in the data dictionary view DBA_OUTSTANDING_ALERTS, and are available in the main screen of the EM Database Control.

When you receive these alerts, you have a number of options. If your retention policy can be adjusted to keep fewer copies of datafiles or reduce the number of days in the recovery window, this can help alleviate the space problems in the Flash Recovery area. Assuming that your retention policy is sound, you should instead add more disk space or back up some of the files in the Flash Recovery area to another destination such as another disk or a tape device.

Performing Backups

Your backup strategy depends on the activity of your database, the level of availability required by your service-level agreements (SLAs), and how much downtime you can tolerate during a recovery effort.

In this section, we'll first review some terminology, and then we will show you a way to back up the control file to a text file that you can edit and use in case of the loss of all control files. Finally, we will introduce Recovery Manager and show you how to make some of the backups we describe in the terminology review.

Understanding Backup Terminology

You can make a whole backup, which backs up the entire database, or you can back up only part of the database, which is called a partial backup. Whole backups and partial backups are known as Oracle backup *strategies*. The backup *type* can be divided into two general categories: full backups and incremental backups. Depending on whether you make your database backups when the database is open or closed, backups can be further categorized into the backup *modes* known as consistent and inconsistent backups.

Your backups can be managed using operating system and SQL commands or entirely by RMAN. Many backup types are only available using RMAN, such as incremental backups; unless you have some specific requirements, it is highly recommended that you use RMAN to implement your backup strategy.

In the following definitions, we'll compare and contrast whole database backups versus partial database backups, full backups versus incremental backups, and consistent backups versus inconsistent backups.

Whole database   A *whole database backup* includes all datafiles and at least one control file. Online redo log files are never backed up; restoring backed up redo log files and replacing the current redo log files will result in loss of data during media recovery. Only one of the control files needs to be backed up; all copies of the control file are identical.

Partial database   A *partial database backup* includes zero or more tablespaces, which in turn includes zero or more datafiles; a control file is optional in a partial database backup. As you may infer, a partial database backup that includes no tablespaces and does not include the control file backs up zero bytes of data to the backup destination.

Full   A *full backup* includes all blocks of every datafile backed up in a whole or partial database backup.

Incremental   An *incremental backup* makes a copy of all data blocks that have changed since a previous backup. Oracle 10*g* supports five levels of incremental backups, from 0 to 4. An incremental backup at level 0 is considered a baseline backup; it is the equivalent of a full backup and contains all data blocks in the datafile(s) that are backed up. Although incremental backups can take less time, the potential downside is that you must first restore the baseline backup and then apply all incremental backups performed since the baseline backup.

Consistent   A *consistent backup*, also known as an *offline backup*, is performed while the database is not open. These backups are consistent because the SCN in the control file matches the SCN in every datafile's header. Although recovering using a consistent backup requires no additional recovery operation after a failure, you reduce your database's availability during a consistent backup as well as risk the loss of committed transactions performed since the consistent backup.

Inconsistent   Although the term *inconsistent backup* may sound like something you might avoid in a database, it is a way to maintain availability of the database while performing backups. An *inconsistent backup*, also known as an *online backup*, is performed while the database is open and available to users. The backup is inconsistent because the SCN in the control file is most likely out of synch with the SCN in the header of the datafiles. Inconsistent backups require recovery when they are used for recovering from a media failure, but keep availability high because the database is open while the backup is performed.

Backing Up the Control File

In addition to multiplexing the control file, you can guard against the loss of all control files by backing up the control file to an editable text file; this backup is called a *backup to trace*. The trace backup is created in the directory specified by the initialization parameter USER_DUMP_ DEST and its format is *sid*_ora_*pid*.trc, where *sid* is the session ID of the user creating the trace backup and *pid* is the process ID of the user creating the trace backup. This special backup of the control file is not a trace file per se; in other words, it is not a dump file or an error report for a failed user or system process. It is rather a proactive rather than reactive report of the contents of the control file, and the report happens to end up in a directory with other trace files.

Back up the control file to trace after any change to the structure of the database, such as adding or dropping a tablespace or creating a new redo log file group. Using the command line to create a backup of the control file is almost as easy as clicking the Backup to Trace button within the EM Database Control:

```
SQL> alter database backup controlfile to trace;
Database altered.
```

Here is an excerpt from the output from the command; note that a lot of editing might be required before using this file to recover your database and control file:

```
--
--      Set #1. NORESETLOGS case
--
-- The following commands will create a new control
-- file and use it to open the database.
-- Data used by Recovery Manager will be lost.
-- Additional logs may be required for media recovery
-- of offline
-- Use this only if the current versions of
-- all online logs are available.
-- After mounting the created controlfile, the following
-- SQL statement will place the database in the
-- appropriate protection mode:
--   ALTER DATABASE SET STANDBY DATABASE TO
--       MAXIMIZE PERFORMANCE
STARTUP NOMOUNT
CREATE CONTROLFILE REUSE DATABASE "ORD"
        NORESETLOGS  ARCHIVELOG
    MAXLOGFILES 16
    MAXLOGMEMBERS 3
    MAXDATAFILES 100
    MAXINSTANCES 8
    MAXLOGHISTORY 454
LOGFILE
  GROUP 1 (
    '/u07/oradata/ord/redo01.log',
    '/u08/oradata/ord/redo01.log'
```

```
  ) SIZE 10M,
  GROUP 2 (
    '/u07/oradata/ord/redo02.log',
    '/u08/oradata/ord/redo02.log'
  ) SIZE 10M,
  GROUP 3 (
    '/u07/oradata/ord/redo03.log',
    '/u08/oradata/ord/redo03.log'
  ) SIZE 10M
-- STANDBY LOGFILE
DATAFILE
'/u05/oradata/ord/system01.dbf',
'/u05/oradata/ord/undotbs01.dbf',
'/u05/oradata/ord/sysaux01.dbf',
'/u05/oradata/ord/users01.dbf',
'/u09/oradata/ord/example01.dbf',
'/u09/oradata/ord/oe_trans01.dbf',
'/u05/oradata/ord/users02.dbf',
'/u06/oradata/ord/logmnr_rep01.dbf',
'/u09/oradata/ord/big_users.dbf',
'/u08/oradata/ord/idx01.dbf',
'/u08/oradata/ord/idx02.dbf',
'/u08/oradata/ord/idx03.dbf',
'/u08/oradata/ord/idx04.dbf',
'/u08/oradata/ord/idx05.dbf',
'/u08/oradata/ord/idx06.dbf',
'/u08/oradata/ord/idx07.dbf',
'/u08/oradata/ord/idx08.dbf',
'/u04/oradata/ord/ORD/datafile/o1_mf_prd01_01059ht2_.dbf',
'/u04/oradata/ord/ORD/datafile/o1_mf_prd02_0105b53n_.dbf',
'/u04/oradata/ord/ORD/datafile/o1_mf_prd03_0105bfp5_.dbf',
'/u04/oradata/ord/ORD/datafile/o1_mf_prd04_0105c2pg_.dbf'
CHARACTER SET WE8ISO8859P1
;
```

Another way to back up your control file is to make a binary copy of it using a similar ALTER DATABASE command, as in the following example:

```
SQL> alter database backup controlfile to
                '/u03/oradata/ctlfile20040911.bkp';
Database altered.
```

Using RMAN to Create Backups

RMAN is the primary component of the Oracle database used to perform backup and recovery operations. You can use RMAN to back up all types: whole or partial databases, full or incremental, and consistent or inconsistent.

RMAN has a command-line interface for advanced configuration and backup operations; the most common backup functions are available via a GUI interface within the EM Database Control. It includes a scripting language to make it easy to automate backups, and it can back up the most critical types of files in your database: datafiles, control files, archived log files, and SPFILEs. It is not used to back up online redo log files (which you should not ever back up anyway), password files, and text-based init.ora files. In other words, RMAN is a "one-stop shopping" solution for your entire backup and recovery needs. In the rare circumstance that you have to back up outside RMAN, you can register the file created during this backup with RMAN for future use in an RMAN recovery scenario.

Due to the relatively static nature of password files and text-based init.ora files, these can be included in the regular operating system backups, or you can back them up manually whenever they are changed.

In the following sections, we will explain the difference between image copies and backup sets and how RMAN handles each of these backup types. After showing you some of the RMAN configuration settings, we will show you some examples of how RMAN performs full and incremental backups, using both the command-line and GUI interface.

Configuring RMAN Backup Settings

Configuring RMAN backup settings is straightforward using the EM Database Control. In the home page, click the Maintenance tab, and then click Configure Backup Settings to open the Device tab screen, as shown in Figure 10.6.

There is a separate section in this screen for your disk device and any tape devices. Under the Disk Settings section, you can control the following parameters:

Parallelism To take advantage of multiple CPUs or disk controllers, increase the value of this parameter to reduce the overall backup time by performing different portions of the backup in parallel.

Disk Backup Location If you are not backing up to the Flash Recovery area, change this value to the location where you want the backups stored.

Disk Backup Type You can choose image copy, backup set, or compressed backup set.

FIGURE 10.6 The Configure Backup Settings: Device screen

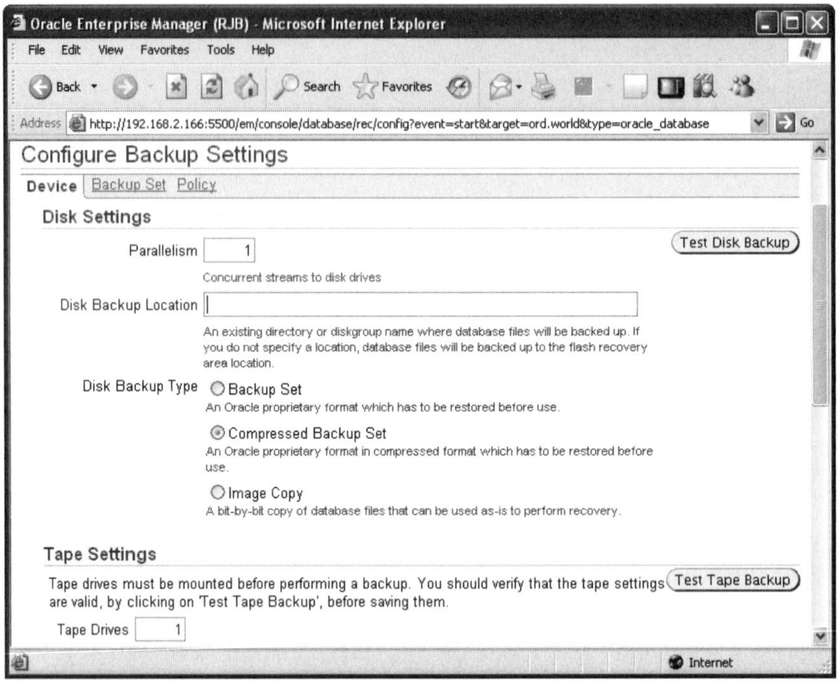

Infrequently used parameters, such as the control file autobackup filename format and the snapshot control file destination filename, are not available from the GUI interface; you must use the RMAN command-line interface to change these values. The following RMAN command-line session uses the RMAN SHOW ALL command to display all default RMAN backup settings:

```
[oracle@oltp oracle]$ rman target /

Recovery Manager: Release 10.1.0.2.0 - Production

Copyright (c) 1995, 2004, Oracle.  All rights reserved.

connected to target database: ORD (DBID=1387044942)

RMAN> show all;

using target database controlfile instead of
      recovery catalog
RMAN configuration parameters are:
CONFIGURE RETENTION POLICY TO REDUNDANCY 1;
CONFIGURE BACKUP OPTIMIZATION ON;
```

```
CONFIGURE DEFAULT DEVICE TYPE TO DISK; # default
CONFIGURE CONTROLFILE AUTOBACKUP ON;
CONFIGURE CONTROLFILE AUTOBACKUP FORMAT FOR
        DEVICE TYPE DISK TO '%F'; # default
CONFIGURE DEVICE TYPE DISK BACKUP TYPE TO COMPRESSED
        BACKUPSET PARALLELISM 1;
CONFIGURE DATAFILE BACKUP COPIES FOR
        DEVICE TYPE DISK TO 1; # default
CONFIGURE ARCHIVELOG BACKUP COPIES FOR
        DEVICE TYPE DISK TO 1; # default
CONFIGURE MAXSETSIZE TO UNLIMITED; # default
CONFIGURE ARCHIVELOG DELETION POLICY TO NONE; # default
CONFIGURE SNAPSHOT CONTROLFILE NAME TO
        '/u01/app/oracle/product/10.1.0/dbs/snapcf_ord.f';
        # default
RMAN>
```

Click the Backup Set tab, and specify the maximum size for a backup set piece (a single file), as you can see in Figure 10.7. In this case, set the maximum backup set piece size to 2GB to make it easier to move files around on file systems whose file size limit is 2GB.

FIGURE 10.7   The Configure Backup Settings: Backup Set screen

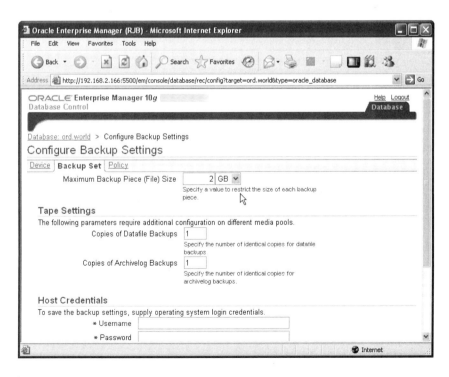

You use the last tab in the Configure Backup Settings screen, the Policy tab, to set a number of other default backup settings, such as automatically backing up the control file with each backup, skipping read-only and offline datafiles, and using a block-change tracking file. A *block-change tracking file* keeps track of changed blocks in each tablespace so that incremental backups need not read every block in every datafile to determine which blocks need to be backed up during an incremental backup. Figure 10.8 shows an example of the Policy tab with a block change tracking file specified.

Understanding Image Copies and Backup Sets

Image copies are duplicates of datafiles or archived redo log files, which means that every block of every file is backed up; you can use RMAN or operating system commands to make image copies. In contrast, *backup sets* are copies of one or more datafiles or archived redo log files that are stored in a proprietary format readable only by RMAN; backup sets consist of one or more physical files and do not include never used blocks in the datafiles being backed up. Backup sets can save even more space by using a compression algorithm designed specifically for the type of data found in an Oracle datafile.

Another difference between image copies and backup sets is that image copies can only be copied to a disk location; backup sets can be written to disk or directly to a tape or other secondary storage device.

FIGURE 10.8 The Configure Backup Settings: Policy screen

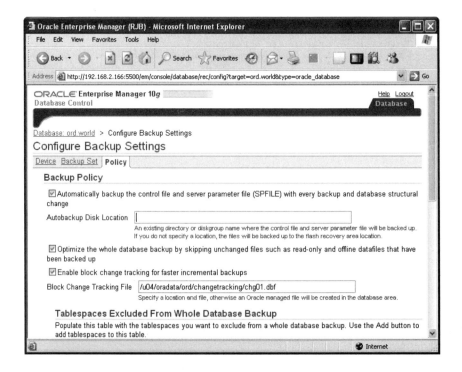

Creating Full and Incremental Backups

The Oracle recommended backup strategy uses RMAN to make a one-time whole-database, baseline incremental level 0 online backup weekly, and then a level 1 incremental backup for the other days of the week. You can easily fine-tune this strategy for your own needs by making, for example, a level 2 incremental backup at noon during the weekdays if heavy DML (Data Manipulation Language) is occurring in the database.

Using RMAN, you can accomplish this backup strategy with just a couple of the RMAN commands that follow. First, here is the baseline level 0 backup at the RMAN command prompt:

```
RMAN> backup incremental level 0
2>      as compressed backupset database;
```

The entire database is backed up using compression to save disk space, in addition to the space savings already gained by using backup sets instead of image copies.

Starting with a baseline level 0 incremental backup, you can make level 1 incremental backups during the rest of the week, as in the following example:

```
RMAN> backup incremental level 1
2>      as compressed backupset database;
```

The options are the same as in our previous example, except that only the blocks that have changed since the last backup are copied to the backup set.

Another variation is to make an incrementally updated backup. An *incrementally updated backup* uses an incremental backup and updates the changed blocks in an existing image copy as if the entire image copy were backed up. In a recovery scenario, you can restore the image copy of the datafile(s) without using an incremental backup; the incremental backup is already applied, saving a significant amount of time during a recovery operation. The following RMAN script shows how an incrementally updated backup works at the command line:

```
run
{
    recover copy of database with tag 'inc_upd_img';
    backup incremental level 1 for
        recover of copy with tag 'inc_upd_img' database;
}
```

This short and cryptic script demonstrates the advantages of using a GUI interface to perform incrementally updated backups. As you can see in Figure 10.9, in the Schedule Backup: Options screen, you can click a check box to perform an incrementally updated backup, in addition to the full backup or incremental backup that we discussed previously in this section.

FIGURE 10.9 Scheduling the backup and specifying the backup type

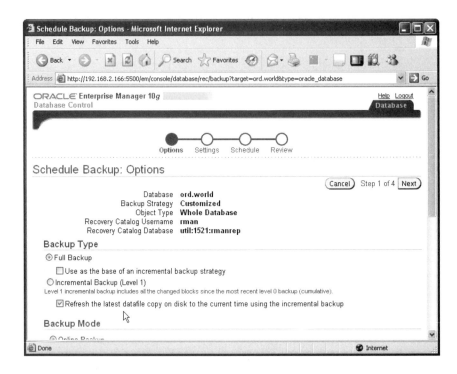

Managing Backups

Managing your database backups is straightforward using the EM Database Control. In this section, we will give you an overview of the RMAN backup and catalog maintenance commands and show you how to monitor the Flash Recovery area and automate backups using the scheduler.

Catalog Maintenance

A number of backup management functions are available in the same screen in the EM Database Control. In the Maintenance tab, click the Manage Current Backups link to open the Manage Current Backups screen, as shown in Figure 10.10.

FIGURE 10.10   The Manage Current Backups screen

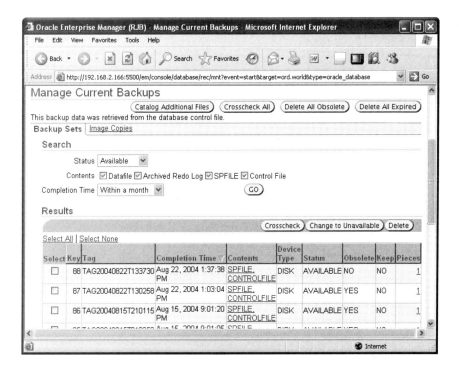

The four buttons at the top perform the following functions:

Catalog Additional Files   Adds any image copy backups made outside RMAN to the RMAN catalog.

Crosscheck All   Double-checks the backup files listed in the catalog against the actual files on disk to make sure that they are all available.

Delete All Obsolete   Deletes all backup files not needed to satisfy the existing retention policy.

Delete All Expired   Deletes the catalog entry for any backups not found when a crosscheck was performed.

Monitoring the Flash Recovery Area

If you are using the Flash Recovery area for all your backups, you want to make sure that you don't run out of space on the disk used for the Flash Recovery area. If your archived redo logs are sent to the Flash Recovery area, and you run out of disk space, redo log archiving halts, and the database is unavailable until you add more disk space or specify an alternate location.

In Figure 10.5, shown earlier in this chapter, we showed you how to create or modify the settings of the Flash Recovery area. In this example, we will use the same screen to monitor the status of the Flash Recovery area. In the Maintenance tab on the database home page, click Configure Recovery Settings to open the screen that displays the current status of the Flash Recovery area (see Figure 10.11) after you scroll to the bottom of the screen.

It appears that the Flash Recovery area is almost full with 14.621GB out of 15GB used. The Flash Recovery area settings screen includes the following information and options:

- The location of the Flash Recovery area

- The size of the Flash Recovery area

- How much of the Flash Recovery area is in use

- An option to configure an advanced recovery feature, flashback database

Click Delete All Obsolete to free up almost 10GB of disk space in the Flash Recovery area. At the RMAN command prompt, the equivalent command is as follows:

```
RMAN> delete noprompt obsolete;
```

Not all information about the Flash Recovery area is available via the EM Database Control interface. For all the details concerning the Flash Recovery area, you can use the dynamic performance view V$RECOVERY_FILE_DEST. After cleaning up obsolete files in the Flash Recovery area, run this query:

```
SQL> select name, space_limit max_size,
  2    space_used used, space_reclaimable obsolete,
  3    number_of_files num_files
  4  from v$recovery_file_dest;
```

NAME	MAX_SIZE	USED	OBSOLETE	NUM_FILES
/OraFlash	1.5729E+10	5367296000	0	526

```
1 row selected.
```

Now, no obsolete files are left in the Flash Recovery area, and we have approximately 5GB used out of 15GB. Currently, 526 files are in the Flash Recovery area; this information is not available via the EM Database Control interface.

Automating Backups

Automating any of the backup operations via the EM Database Control is straightforward. In the database home page, click the Maintenance tab, click Schedule Backup, and select your backup options such as strategy and destination. In step 3, you can specify when the backup will first run, whether it will repeat, and how many times it will repeat. These options are displayed in Figure 10.12.

FIGURE 10.11   Flash Recovery area status

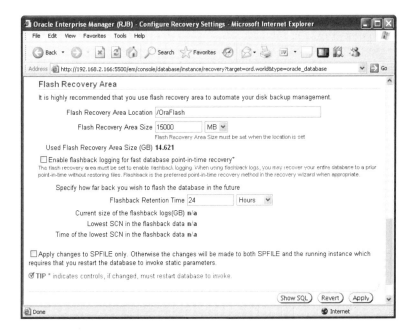

FIGURE 10.12   Scheduling the backup

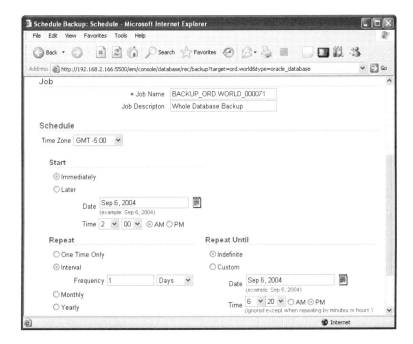

Summary

In this chapter, we presented the database structures that are key elements that need to be multiplexed and backed up to ensure a smooth recovery in the event of a database failure: the control files, online redo log files, and archived redo log files. The control files contain the metadata about every other structure in the database. The online redo log files provide performance benefits to ongoing transactions and ensure that no committed transactions are lost after an instance failure; being able to change the number of redo log groups and the number of members in each group enhances both the availability and performance of the database. Archived redo log files make copies of online redo log files to one or more destinations before they are overwritten by new transactions. The common thread through all three of these structures is multiplexing: creating redundant copies of database components or redundant archival locations to minimize the impact of a media failure.

We also introduced the Flash Recovery area and explained how it is the central location for backups of all database files, control files, initialization parameter files, and archived redo log files in the database. You can manage the Flash Recovery area via the EM Database Control interface or using a SQL command-line interface to set or change database initialization parameters that control its location and size.

Before making database backups, you must understand backup strategies, types, and modes. ARCHIVELOG mode provides many benefits and few downsides, especially in a production environment; NOARCHIVELOG mode, in many ways, restricts the types of backups you can make.

Recovery Manager, or RMAN, provides a number of benefits over manual backup methods using a combination of SQL and operating system commands. You can access most RMAN functionality via the EM Database Control or with a command-line version for advanced backup and recovery techniques. One of RMAN's many benefits is the ability to create compressed backup sets, which not only skips unused blocks in database datafiles, but compresses the blocks before writing to the backup set, saving I/O bandwidth and disk space.

Exam Essentials

Identify the purpose of the redo log files.   Describe the redo log file architecture. Provide details about how to create new redo log file groups and add new members to redo log file groups. Be able to drop redo log group members. Know how to clear online redo log file groups when a log file member becomes corrupted.

Be able to multiplex a control file.   List the steps required to create additional copies of the control file, for both an init.ora file and an SPFILE.

Describe the basic differences between operating a database in *ARCHIVELOG* mode and *NOARCHIVELOG* mode.   Identify the initialization parameters and commands that control the archive process. Briefly describe how archive log information is recorded in the control file.

Identify and discuss backup terminology.   Enumerate the backup strategies, the backup types, and the backup modes. Give examples of how you can combine the strategies, types, and modes in different scenarios.

List the benefits of using RMAN to create backups.   Show how to configure RMAN backup settings via the EM Database Control interface. Differentiate image copies from backup sets. Provide examples of an incremental backup strategy.

Explain the benefits of the Flash Recovery area.   Show how you can access the characteristics and status of the Flash Recovery area using the EM Database Control as well as via dynamic performance views. Describe the database components that can be stored in the Flash Recovery area. Enumerate the initialization parameters that control the location and size of the Flash Recovery area.

Understand backup catalog maintenance.   Show how the EM Database Control interface simplifies cataloging, crosschecking, and cleaning up.

Review Questions

1. Which of the following is the most serious type of redo log file failure?

   A. The loss of an entire redo log file group, but no loss in any other group

   B. The loss of one member of each redo log file group

   C. The failure of the ARC0 background process

   D. The failure of the LGWR background process

2. Which of the following tools or options does not ensure that either no committed transactions are lost or the MTBF is minimized?

   A. Streams

   B. Real Application Clusters

   C. LogMiner

   D. Archived redo logs

   E. Standby databases

3. When the database is in ARCHIVELOG mode, database recovery is possible up to which event or time?

   A. The last redo log file switch

   B. The last checkpoint position

   C. The last commit

   D. The last incremental backup using RMAN

4. From the following, select the true statement regarding image copies and backup sets.

   A. An image copy stores one datafile per image copy, and a backup set can store all datafiles in a single file.

   B. An image copy stores one datafile per image copy, and a backup set consists of one file per datafile backed up.

   C. Both image copies and backup sets use a single file to store all objects to be backed up.

   D. A backup set stores each datafile in its own backup file, but an image copy places all datafiles into a single output file.

5. The option on the EM Database Control backup scheduling options screen that allows you to refresh an image copy on disk with an incremental backup is known as which new RMAN feature?

   A. Incrementally updated backups

   B. Incremental level 0 backups

   C. Compressed image copy refresh

   D. Compressed incremental backups

6. When should the DBA make a trace copy of the control file using ALTER DATABASE BACKUP CONTROLFILE TO TRACE?

    A. After every backup

    B. After multiplexing the control files

    C. Whenever restarting the instance

    D. Whenever the physical structure of the database changes

7. Which of the following is not a step in configuring your database to archive redo log files?

    A. Place the database in ARCHIVELOG mode.

    B. Multiplex the online redo log files.

    C. Specify a destination for archived redo log files.

    D. Specify a naming convention for your archived redo log files.

8. Why are online backups known as inconsistent backups?

    A. Because not all control files are synchronized to the same SCN until the database is shut down

    B. Because both committed and uncommitted transactions are included in a backup when the database is online

    C. Because a database failure while an online backup is in progress can leave the database in an inconsistent state

    D. Because online backups make copies of datafiles while they are not consistent with the control files

9. In the Disk Settings section of the EM Database Control Configure Backup Settings page, which of the following backup settings is not configurable?

    A. Disk Backup Type

    B. Control File Autobackup Format

    C. Disk Backup Location

    D. Parallelism

10. Which of the following initialization parameters specifies the location where the control file trace backup is sent?

    A. USER_DUMP_DEST

    B. BACKGROUND_DUMP_DEST

    C. LOG_ARCHIVE_DEST

    D. CORE_DUMP_DEST

11. Which of the following pieces of information is not available in the control file?

    A. Instance name

    B. Database name

    C. Tablespace names

    D. Log sequence number

12. Which data dictionary view shows that the database is in ARCHIVELOG mode?

   A. V$INSTANCE

   B. V$LOG

   C. V$DATABASE

   D. V$THREAD

13. Which file records all changes made to the database and is used only when recovering an instance?

   A. Archive log file

   B. Redo log file

   C. Control file

   D. Alert log file

14. Which initialization parameter contains the value used as the default for archived log file destination 10?

   A. LOG_ARCHIVE_DEST

   B. STANDBY_ARCHIVE_DEST

   C. LOG_ARCHIVE_DUPLEX_DEST

   D. DB_RECOVERY_FILE_DEST

   E. USE_DB_RECOVERY_FILE_DEST

15. Which of the following commands is a key step in multiplexing control files using an SPFILE?

   A. ALTER SYSTEM SET CONTROL_FILES= '/u01/oradata/PRD/cntrl01.ctl', '/u01/oradata/PRD/cntrl02.ctl' SCOPE=SPFILE;

   B. ALTER SYSTEM SET CONTROL_FILES= '/u01/oradata/PRD/cntrl01.ctl', '/u01/oradata/PRD/cntrl02.ctl' SCOPE=MEMORY;

   C. ALTER SYSTEM SET CONTROL_FILES= '/u01/oradata/PRD/cntrl01.ctl', '/u01/oradata/PRD/cntrl02.ctl' SCOPE=BOTH;

   D. The number of control files is fixed when the database is created.

16. Which statement adds a member /logs/redo22.log to redo log file group 2?

   A. ALTER DATABASE ADD LOGFILE '/logs/redo22.log' TO GROUP 2;

   B. ALTER DATABASE ADD LOGFILE MEMBER '/logs/redo22.log' TO GROUP 2;

   C. ALTER DATABASE ADD MEMBER '/logs/redo22.log' TO GROUP 2;

   D. ALTER DATABASE ADD LOGFILE '/logs/redo22.log';

17. What is the biggest advantage of having the control files on different disks?

   A. Database performance.

   B. Guards against failure.

   C. Faster archiving.

   D. Writes are concurrent, so having control files on different disks speeds up control file writes.

18. To place the database into ARCHIVELOG mode, in which state must you start the database?

　　A. MOUNT

　　B. NOMOUNT

　　C. OPEN

　　D. SHUTDOWN

　　E. Any of the above

19. Which of the following commands places the database in ARCHIVELOG mode?

　　A. ALTER SYSTEM ARCHIVELOG;

　　B. ALTER DATABASE ARCHIVELOG;

　　C. ALTER SYSTEM SET ARCHIVELOG=TRUE;

　　D. ALTER DATABASE ENABLE ARCHIVELOG MODE;

　　E. ALTER DATABASE ARCHIVELOG MODE;

20. Which of the following substitution variables formats are always required for specifying the names of the archived redo log files? (Choose all that apply.)

　　A. %d

　　B. %s

　　C. %r

　　D. %t

Answers to Review Questions

1. **A.** Loss of an entire redo log file group can result in loss of committed transactions that may not yet have been written to the database files. Losing all members of a redo log file group except for one does not affect database operation and does not result in data lost. A message is placed in the alert log file. The failure of LGWR or ARC0 causes an instance failure, but you do not lose any committed transaction data.

2. **C.** The LogMiner tool helps you see which transactions have occurred in the database along with the DML to reverse the changes, but it does not minimize the MTBF or reduce the possibility of committed transaction loss.

3. **C.** In ARCHIVELOG mode, recovery of the database is possible up to the last COMMIT statement; in other words, no uncommitted transactions are lost in ARCHIVELOG mode.

4. **A.** In addition to storing multiple datafiles in a single output file, backup sets do not contain unused blocks and can be compressed.

5. **A.** Incrementally updated backups save time during a recovery operation because fewer incremental backups need to be applied to the restored image copy.

6. **D.** In the rare event that all multiplexed copies of the control file are lost, having a trace copy of the control file reduces the possibility of data loss and reduces downtime during a recovery operation.

7. **B.** Although it is recommended that you multiplex your online redo log files, setting up the archival of your redo log files is not required.

8. **D.** During an online backup, even if all datafiles are backed up at the same time, they are rarely, if ever, in synch with the control file.

9. **B.** Settings such as the control file autobackup filename format and the snapshot control file destination filename must be configured using the RMAN command-line interface.

10. **A.** The trace backup is created in the location specified by USER_DUMP_DEST, and its format is *sid_ora_pid*.trc.

11. **A.** The instance name is not in the control file. The control file has information about the physical database structure.

12. **C.** The V$DATABASE view shows whether the database is in ARCHIVELOG mode or in NOARCHIVELOG mode.

13. **B.** The redo log file records all changes made to the database. The LGWR process writes the redo log buffer entries to the redo log files. These entries are used to roll forward, or to update, the datafiles during an instance recovery. Archive log files are used for media recovery.

14. **D.** DB_RECOVERY_FILE_DEST points to the Flash Recovery area, and this is the default for archived log file destination number 10.

15. A. The location of the new control files is not valid until an operating system copy is made of the current control file to the new location(s) and the instance is restarted. The SCOPE=SPFILE option specifies that the parameter change will not take place until a restart. Specifying either MEMORY or BOTH causes an error, because the new control file does not yet exist.

16. B. When adding log file members, specify the group number, or specify all the existing group members.

17. B. Having the control files on different disks ensures that even if you lose one disk, you lose only one control file. If you lose one of the control files, you can shut down the database, copy a control file, or change the CONTROL_FILES parameter and restart the database.

18. A. To put the database into ARCHIVELOG mode, the database must be in the MOUNT state; the control files and all datafiles that are not offline must be available to change the database to ARCHIVELOG mode.

19. B. You use the ALTER DATABASE ARCHIVELOG command while the database is in the MOUNT state to enable archiving of online redo log files.

20. B, C, D. The substitution variable %d, which represents the database ID, is required only if multiple databases share the same archive log destination.

Chapter

11

Implementing Database Recovery

ORACLE DATABASE 10*G*: ADMINISTRATION I EXAM OBJECTIVES COVERED IN THIS CHAPTER:

✓ **Backup and Recovery Concepts**

- Describe the types of failure that may occur in an Oracle Database.
- Describe ways to tune instance recovery.
- Identify the importance of checkpoints, redo log files, and archived log files.

✓ **Database Recovery**

- Recover from loss of a Control file.
- Recover from loss of a Redo log file.
- Recover from loss of a system-critical data file.
- Recover from loss of a non system-critical data file.

 Exam objectives are subject to change at any time without prior notice and at Oracle's sole discretion. Please visit Oracle's Training and Certification website (http://www.oracle.com/education/certification/) for the most current exam objectives listing.

Oracle Database 10g (Oracle 10g) makes it easy for you to recover from a number of database failures. In Chapter 10, "Implementing Database Backups," we emphasized the importance of checkpoints, redo log files, and archived log files to maintain a high level of availability and recoverability. We also showed you several ways to back up your database. In this chapter, we'll show you how to use those backups effectively when some kind of failure inevitably occurs.

First, we'll review the kinds of failures that can occur in the database; they can occur because of mistakes by users or DBAs or because of hardware or software failures that are out of your direct control. Each of these failures can require little or no action whatsoever, as in the case of an instance failure, but at the other end of the spectrum, a crash of the disk containing the SYSTEM tablespace requires a recovery effort.

We'll then emphasize the importance of checkpoints, online redo log files, and archived redo log files. To balance performance with recoverability, we'll also show you how to tune instance recovery to minimize the amount of time Oracle will require to recover from an instance failure while still providing a reasonable response time for ongoing transactions. In a nutshell, your job is to increase the mean time between failures (MTBF) by providing redundant components where possible and leveraging other Oracle high-availability features such as Real Application Clusters (RAC) and Streams (an advanced replication technology). Going hand in hand with MTBF is decreasing the *mean time to recovery (MTTR)* to ensure compliance with service-level agreements that are in place. Last, but certainly not least, these efforts should help to minimize data loss in such a way that committed transactions are never lost.

Near the end of this chapter, we'll review the steps required to recover from the loss of both system critical and non–system-critical datafiles for databases that are operating in both ARCHIVELOG and NOARCHIVELOG mode. We'll also show you how to recover from the loss of a control file or a redo log file. As with most DBA operations in the database, Oracle's GUI administration tool, the Enterprise Manager (EM) Database Control, makes many of these administration tasks easier and less error prone.

Understanding Database Failure Types

There are six general categories for database-related failures. Understanding what category a failure belongs in will help you to more quickly understand the nature of the recovery effort you need to use to reverse the effects of the failure and maintain a high level of availability and performance in your database. The six general categories of failures are as follows:

Statement A single database operation fails, such as a DML (Data Manipulation Language) statement—INSERT, UPDATE, and so on.

User process   A single database connection fails.

Network   A network component between the client and the database server fails, and the session is disconnected from the database.

User error   An error message is not generated, but the operation's result, such as dropping a table, is not what the user intended.

Instance   The database instance fails unexpectedly.

Media   One or more of the database files is lost, deleted, or corrupted.

In the next six sections, we'll provide details on these failure types and suggest some possible solutions for each failure type. For one particular type of failure, media failure, we'll provide more detailed solutions for recovery later in this chapter.

Statement Failures

Statement failures occur when a single database operation fails, such as a single INSERT statement or the creation of a table. In the list that follows are a few of the most common problems and their solutions when a statement fails.

Attempts to access tables without the appropriate privileges   Provide the appropriate privileges or create views on the tables and grant privileges on the view.

Running out of space   Add space to the tablespace, increase the user's quota on the tablespace, or enable resumable space allocation.

Logic errors in applications   Work with developers to correct program errors or provide additional logic in the application to recover gracefully from unavoidable errors.

Although granting user privileges or additional quotas within a tablespace solves many of these problems, also consider whether there are any gaps in the user education process that might lead to some of these problems in the first place.

User Process Failures

The abnormal termination of a user session is categorized as a *user process failure*; any uncommitted transaction must be cleaned up. The *PMON* (process monitor) background process periodically checks all user processes to ensure that the session is still connected. If the PMON finds a disconnected session, it rolls back the uncommitted transaction and releases all locks held by the disconnected process. Causes for user process failures typically fall into one of these categories:

- A user closes their SQL*Plus window without logging out.

- The workstation reboots suddenly before the application can be closed.

- The application program causes an exception and closes before the application can be terminated normally.

- A user process times out and Oracle disconnects the session.

A small percentage of user process failures is generally no cause for concern unless it becomes chronic; it may be a sign that user education is lacking—for example, training users to terminate the application gracefully before shutting down their workstation.

Network Failures

Depending on the locations of your workstation and your server, getting from your workstation to the server over the network might involve a number of hops: you might traverse several local switches and WAN routers to get to the database. From a network perspective, this configuration provides a number of points where failure can occur. These types of failures are called *network failures*.

In addition to hardware failures between the server and client, a listener process on the Oracle server can fail or the network card on the server itself can fail. To guard against these kinds of failures, you can provide redundant network paths from your clients to the server, as well as additional listener connections on the Oracle server and redundant network cards on the server.

User Error Failures

Even if all your redundant hardware is at peak performance, and your users have been trained to disconnect from their Oracle sessions properly, users can still inadvertently delete or modify data in tables or drop an index. This is known as a *user error failure*. Although these operations succeed from a statement point of view, they might not be logically correct: the DROP TABLE command worked fine, but you really didn't want to drop that table!

If data was inadvertently deleted from a table, and not yet committed, a ROLLBACK statement will undo the damage. If a COMMIT has already been performed, you have a number of options at your disposal, such as using data in the undo tablespace for a Flashback Query or using data in the archived and online redo logs with the LogMiner utility, available as a command-line or GUI interface.

You can recover a dropped table using Oracle's recycle bin functionality: a dropped table is stored in a special structure in the tablespace and is available for retrieval as long as the space occupied by the table in the tablespace is not needed for new objects. Even if the table is no longer in the tablespace's recycle bin, depending on the criticality of the dropped table, you can use either tablespace point in time recovery (TSPITR) or Flashback Database Recovery to recover the table, taking into consideration the potential data loss for other objects stored in the same tablespace for TSPITR or in the database if you use Flashback Database Recovery.

 TSPITR and Flashback Database Recovery are beyond the scope of this book but are covered in more detail in *OCP: Oracle 10g Administration II Study Guide* (Sybex, 2005).

If the inadvertent changes are limited to a small number of tables that have few or no interdependencies with other database objects, Flashback Table functionality is most likely the right tool to bring back the table to a point of time in the past.

Later in this chapter, in the section "Performing Recovery Operations," we'll show you how to recover dropped tables from the recycle bin using Flashback Drop, how to retrieve deleted rows from a table using Flashback Query functionality, use Flashback Table to bring a table back to a point of time in the past along with its dependent objects, and use LogMiner to query online and archived redo logs for the previous state of modified rows.

Instance Failures

An *instance failure* occurs when the instance shuts down without synchronizing all the database files to the same system change number (SCN), requiring a recovery operation the next time the instance is started. Many of the reasons for an instance failure are out of your direct control; in these situations, you can minimize the impact of these failures by tuning instance recovery.

 We will show you how to tune instance recovery later in this chapter in the section "Tuning Instance Recovery."

Here are a few causes for instance failure:

- A power outage
- A server hardware failure
- Failure of an Oracle background process
- Emergency shutdown procedures (intentional power outage or SHUTDOWN ABORT)

In all these scenarios, the solution is easy: run the STARTUP command, and let Oracle automatically perform instance recovery using the online redo logs and undo data in the undo tablespace. If the cause of the instance failure is related to an Oracle background process failure, you can use the alert log and process-specific trace files to debug the problem. The EM Database Control makes it easy to review the contents of the alert log and any other alerts generated right before the point of failure.

Media Failures

Another type of failure that is somewhat out of your control is *media failure*. A media failure is any type of failure that results in the loss of one or more database files: datafiles, control files, or redo log files. Although the loss of other database-related files such as an init.ora file or a server parameter file (SPFILE) is of great concern, Oracle Corporation does not consider it a media failure. The database file can be lost or corrupted for a number of reasons:

- Failure of a disk drive
- Failure of a disk controller
- Inadvertent deletion or corruption of a database file

Following the best practices defined in Chapter 10 by adequately mirroring control files, redo log files, and ensuring that full backups and their subsequent archived redo log files are available will keep you prepared for any type of media failure.

In the next section, we will show you how to recover from the loss of control files, datafiles, and redo log files.

Performing Recovery Operations

Once the inevitable database failure occurs, you can perform a relatively quick and painless recovery operation if you have followed the backup guidelines we presented in Chapter 10 and clearly understand the types of failures presented at the beginning of this chapter.

Before we show you how to perform recovery, however, it is important for you to understand how an Oracle instance starts up and what kinds of failures can occur at each startup phase. Understanding the startup phases is important because some types of recovery operations must occur in a particular phase. Once a database is started, the instance will fail under a number of conditions that we will describe in detail.

Next, we will describe how instance recovery works and how to tune instance recovery, and then show you ways to easily recover from several types of user errors. Finally, we will show you how to recover from media failures due to the loss of both critical and non–system-critical datafiles.

Understanding Instance Startup

Starting up a database involves several phases, from being shut down to being open and available to users. If certain prerequisites are not present, database startup halts, and you must take some kind of remedial action to permit startup to proceed. In the following list are the four basic database states along with their prerequisites after you type the STARTUP command at the SQL*Plus prompt.

SHUTDOWN   No background processes are active. A STARTUP command is used when the database is in this state; the STARTUP command fails if you are in any other state unless you are using STARTUP FORCE to restart an instance.

NOMOUNT   Also known as the STARTED state, the instance must be able to access the initialization parameter file, either as a text-based `init.ora` file or an SPFILE.

MOUNT   In this state, the instance checks that all control files listed in the initialization parameter file are present and identical. Even if one of the multiplexed control files is unavailable or corrupted, the instance does not enter the MOUNT state and stays in the NOMOUNT state.

OPEN   Most of the time spent in instance startup occurs during this phase. All redo log groups must have at least one member available, and all datafiles that are marked as online must be available.

You are notified in a number of ways that a redo log group member is missing or a datafile is missing. If a datafile is missing or corrupted, you will get a message while you are running the STARTUP command, as in this example:

```
SQL> startup

ORACLE instance started.
```

```
Total System Global Area   197132288 bytes
Fixed Size                    778076 bytes
Variable Size              162537636 bytes
Database Buffers            33554432 bytes
Redo Buffers                  262144 bytes
Database mounted.


ORA-01157: cannot identify/lock data file 4 - see DBWR trace file
ORA-01110: data file 4: '/u05/oradata/ord/users01.dbf'

SQL>
```

The message in SQL*Plus shows only the first datafile that needs attention. You will have to use the dynamic performance view V$RECOVER_FILE to display a list of all files that need attention. Here is a query against the view V$RECOVER_FILE and a second query joining V$RECOVER_FILE and V$DATAFILE given the previous STARTUP command:

```
SQL> select file#, error from v$recover_file;

    FILE# ERROR
---------- ---------------------------------------------
        4 FILE NOT FOUND
       11 FILE NOT FOUND

SQL> select file#, name from
  2       v$datafile join v$recover_file using (file#);

    FILE# NAME
---------- -----------------------------------------
        4 /u05/oradata/ord/users01.dbf
       11 /u08/oradata/ord/idx02.dbf
SQL>
```

If a datafile is offline or taken offline, the instance can still start as long as the datafile does not belong to the SYSTEM or UNDO tablespace. Once the instance is started, you can proceed to recover the missing or corrupted datafile and subsequently bring it online. If all files are available, but out of synch, automatic instance recovery is performed as long as the online redo log files can bring all datafiles to the same SCN. Otherwise, media recovery is required using archived redo log files.

If a redo log group member is missing, a message is generated in the alert log, but the database will still open.

Keeping an Instance from Failing

Media failures are not always critical, depending on which type of datafile is lost. If any of the multiplexed copies of the control file are lost, an entire redo log group, or any datafile from the SYSTEM or UNDO tablespace, the instance will fail.

In some cases, the instance becomes unavailable to users but will not shut down; in this case, you can use SHUTDOWN ABORT to force the instance to shut down without resynchronizing the datafiles with the control file. The next time the instance is started, instance recovery will be performed. If you plan on starting up the instance right after using SHUTDOWN ABORT, you can instead use STARTUP FORCE as shorthand for a SHUTDOWN ABORT and a STARTUP.

 Later in this chapter, we will show you how to recover from the loss of a control file, a redo log file member, or one or more datafiles.

Recovering from Instance Failure

As we discussed earlier in this chapter in the section "Instance Failures," an instance failure is any kind of failure that prevents the synchronization of the database's datafiles and control file before the instance is shut down.

Oracle automatically recovers from instance failure during *instance recovery*. Instance recovery is initiated by simply starting up the database with the STARTUP command.

 Instance recovery is also known as crash recovery.

During a STARTUP operation, Oracle first attempts to read the initialization file, and then it mounts the control file and attempts to open the datafiles referenced in the control files. If the data files are not synchronized, instance recovery is initiated.

 We discussed instance startup phases in the section "Understanding Instance Startup" earlier in this chapter.

Instance recovery occurs in two distinct phases: the first phase uses the online redo log files to restore the datafiles to the state before instance failure in a *roll forward* operation; after this step is completed, Oracle uses the undo tablespace to *roll back* any uncommitted transactions. The roll forward operation includes data in the undo tablespace; without a consistent undo tablespace, the roll back operation cannot succeed. Once the roll forward operation completes, the database is open to users while the roll back operation completes. After the roll back phase, the datafiles contain only committed data.

Tuning Instance Recovery

Before a user receives a "Commit complete" message, the new or changed data must first be successfully written to a redo log file. At some point in the future, the same information must be used to update the datafiles; this operation usually lags behind the redo log file write because sequential writes to the redo log file are by nature faster than random writes to one or more datafiles on disk.

As we discussed in Chapter 10, checkpoints keep track of what still needs to be written from the redo log files to the datafiles. Any transactions not yet written to the datafiles are at an SCN after the last checkpoint.

The amount of time required for instance recovery depends on how long it takes to bring the datafiles up-to-date from the last checkpoint position to the latest SCN in the control file. To prevent performance problems, the distance between the checkpoint position and the end of the redo log group cannot be more than 90 percent of the size of the redo log group.

You can tune instance recovery by setting an MTTR target, in seconds, using the initialization parameter *FAST_START_MTTR_TARGET*. The default value for this parameter is zero; the maximum is 3,600 seconds (1 hour).

With a setting of zero, which disables the target, the likelihood that writes to the redo logs wait for writes to the datafiles is reduced. However, if FAST_START_MTTR_TARGET is set to a low nonzero value, writes to the redo logs most likely wait for writes to the datafiles. Although this reduces the amount of time it takes to recover the instance in the case of an instance failure, it affects performance and response time. Setting this value too high can result in an unacceptable amount of time needed to recover the instance after an instance failure.

Two other parameters control instance recovery time:

LOG_CHECKPOINT_TIMEOUT   This is the maximum number of seconds that any new or modified block in the buffer cache waits until it is written to disk.

FAST_START_IO_TARGET   This is similar to FAST_START_MTTR_TARGET, except that the recovery operation is specified as the number of I/Os instead of the number of seconds to finish instance recovery.

Setting either of these parameters overrides FAST_START_MTTR_TARGET. As part of the enhanced manageability features introduced with Oracle9*i*, setting FAST_START_MTTR_TARGET is the easiest and most straightforward way to define your database's recovery time given the time-based constraints included in most typical service-level agreements (SLAs).

The EM Database Control interface makes it easy to adjust FAST_START_MTTR_TARGET. From the Advisor Central screen, accessible at the bottom of the Database Control home page, click MTTR Advisor. In the example in Figure 11.1, you adjust the desired MTTR value to 60 seconds on the Configure Recovery Settings screen.

When you click the Apply button, the new value for FAST_START_MTTR_TARGET goes into effect immediately and stays in effect when the instance is restarted.

FIGURE 11.1   Adjusting MTTR for instance recovery

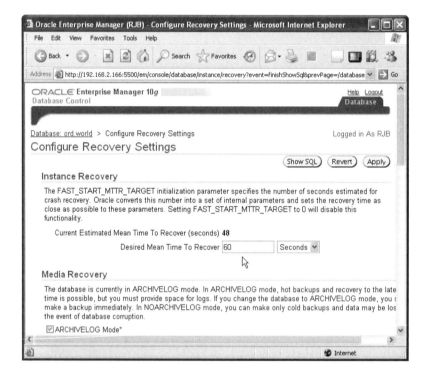

Using the SQL*Plus command line, you can accomplish this task by using the ALTER SYSTEM command, as in this example:

```
SQL> alter system set fast_start_mttr_target=60 scope=both;
System altered.
```

Using SCOPE=BOTH, the new value of the parameter takes effect immediately and stays in effect the next time the instance is restarted.

Recovering from User Errors

Earlier in this chapter, in the section "User Error Failures," we presented a number of scenarios in which a user's data was inadvertently changed or deleted or a table was dropped. In the following sections, we'll show you how to use Flashback Query to retrieve selected rows from a previous state of a table, how to recover a table using Flashback Drop and a tablespace's recycle bin, how to bring back an entire table and its dependent objects (such as indexes) back to a point of time in the past using Flashback Table, and query previous transactions in the online and archived redo logs using the LogMiner utility.

Using Flashback Query

One of the features introduced in Oracle9*i* is called *Flashback Query*. It allows a user to "go back in time" and view the contents of a table as it existed at some point in the recent past. A Flashback Query looks a lot like a standard SQL SELECT statement, with the addition of the AS OF TIMESTAMP clause.

Before users can take advantage of the Flashback Query feature, you, the DBA, must perform two tasks:

- Make sure that there is an undo tablespace in the database that is large enough to retain changes made by all users for a specified period of time. This is the same tablespace that is used to support COMMIT and ROLLBACK functionality (discussed in Chapter 8, "Managing Consistency and Concurrency").

- Specify how long the undo information will be retained for use by flashback queries by using the initialization parameter UNDO_RETENTION. This parameter is specified in seconds; therefore, if you specify UNDO_RETENTION=172800, the undo information for flashback queries can be available for up to two days.

The key to Flashback Query is using the AS OF TIMESTAMP clause in the SELECT statement; you can specify the time stamp as any valid expression that evaluates to a date or time stamp value. In the following example, you want to query the EMPLOYEES table as it existed 15 minutes ago:

```
SQL> select employee_id, last_name, email
  2      from hr.employees
  3  as of timestamp (systimestamp - interval '15' minute)
  4  where employee_id = 101;


EMPLOYEE_ID LAST_NAME              EMAIL
----------- --------------------- --------------------
        101 Kochhar               NKOCHHAR


1 row selected.
```

You can just as easily specify an absolute time of day to retrieve the contents of the row at that time, as in this example:

```
SQL> select employee_id, last_name, email
  2      from hr.employees
  3  as of timestamp
  4      (to_timestamp ('01-Sep-04 16:18:57.845993',
  5                     'DD-Mon-RR HH24:MI:SS.FF'))
  6  where employee_id = 101;


EMPLOYEE_ID LAST_NAME              EMAIL
----------- --------------------- --------------------
        101 Kochhar               NTKOCHHAR
```

If your Flashback Query requires undo data that is no longer available in the undo tablespace, you will receive an error message:

```
SQL> select employee_id, last_name, email
  2     from hr.employees
  3  as of timestamp (systimestamp - interval '10' month)
  4  where employee_id = 101;

select employee_id, last_name, email
       *
ERROR at line 1:
ORA-08180: no snapshot found based on specified time
```

Real World Scenario

Using Flashback Query to Investigate a Customer Complaint

In your custom widget company, an error in the Accounting Department added $2,000 to two orders placed yesterday:

```
SQL> update orders
  2     set order_total = order_total+2000
  3  where order_id in (2367,2361);

2 rows updated.

SQL> select order_id, customer_id, order_total
  2     from orders where order_id in (2367,2361);

  ORDER_ID CUSTOMER_ID ORDER_TOTAL
---------- ----------- -----------
      2361         108    122131.3
      2367         148    146054.8

2 rows selected.
```

Today, the customer with ID 108 called to complain that the bill from his last order (order number 2361) is $2,000 more than expected. Sharon, one of the order-entry clerks, retrieves the row from the ORDERS table with the information for order number 2361:

```
SQL> select order_id, customer_id, order_total
```

```
  2  from orders where order_id = 2361;

 ORDER_ID CUSTOMER_ID ORDER_TOTAL
---------- ----------- -----------
     2361         108     122131.3

1 row selected.
```

Before calling back the customer, Sharon finds out from the Accounting Department that a day ago, two of the orders were incorrectly modified with an additional surcharge. To confirm whether this particular order was affected by the accounting error, she uses a Flashback Query to see if this order had a different order total two days ago:

```
SQL> select order_id, customer_id, order_total from orders
  2      as of timestamp (sysdate - 2)
  3  where order_id = 2361;

 ORDER_ID CUSTOMER_ID ORDER_TOTAL
---------- ----------- -----------
     2361         108     120131.3

1 row selected.
```

This Flashback Query confirms that the order total for this order was $2,000 less two days ago. The AS OF TIMESTAMP clause specifies how far back in the past you want to view the contents of this table. In this case, (sysdate - 2) evaluates to today's date minus two days—in other words, two days ago. Sharon concludes that at some point in the past two days, this was one of the orders that was incorrectly modified. To find all the orders that have the incorrect surcharge, she uses another Flashback Query as a nested query to compare the order totals:

```
SQL> select o.order_id, o.customer_id,
  2    o.order_total "CURR_TOTAL", oo.order_total "ORIG_TOTAL"
  3  from orders o,
  4      (select order_id, order_total from orders
  5       as of timestamp (sysdate - 2)) oo
  6  where o.order_id = oo.order_id and
  7       o.order_total != oo.order_total;

 ORDER_ID CUSTOMER_ID ORDER_TOTAL ORIG_TOTAL
---------- ----------- ----------- ----------
     2361         108     122131.3   120131.3
```

```
        2367         148      146054.8    144054.8

2 rows selected.
```

In this query, Sharon is comparing the entire contents of the current ORDERS table to the entire contents of the ORDERS table as it was two days ago and selecting records in which the order totals don't match. She now knows which records must be updated with the correct order total amount.

Using Flashback Drop and the Recycle Bin

Another user recovery flashback feature, *Flashback Drop*, lets you restore a dropped table without using tablespace point-in-time recovery, as required in previous versions of Oracle. Although tablespace point-in-time recovery could effectively restore a table and its contents to a point in time before it was dropped, it was potentially time-consuming and had the side effect of losing work from other transactions that occurred within the same tablespace after the table was dropped.

In the following two sections, we will talk about the new logical structure available in each tablespace: the recycle bin and how you can query the recycle bin and retrieve dropped objects from it. We will also describe some minor limitations involved in using the recycle bin.

Recycle Bin Concepts

The *recycle bin* is a logical structure within each tablespace that holds dropped tables and objects related to the tables, such as indexes. The space associated with the dropped table is not immediately available but shows up in the data dictionary view DBA_FREE_SPACE. When space pressure occurs in the tablespace, objects in the recycle bin are deleted in a first-in first-out (FIFO) fashion, maximizing the amount of time that the most recently dropped object remains in the recycle bin.

    The recycle bin, new to Oracle 10*g*, is implemented as a data dictionary table.

The dropped object still belongs to the owner and still counts against the quota for the owner in the tablespace; in fact, the table itself is still directly accessible from the recycle bin, as you will see in subsequent examples.

Retrieving Dropped Tables from the Recycle Bin

You retrieve a dropped table from the recycle bin at the SQL command line by using the FLASHBACK TABLE...TO BEFORE DROP command. In the following example, the user GARY retrieves the table ORDER_ITEMS from the recycle bin after discovering that the table was inadvertently dropped:

```
SQL> select order_id, line_item_id, product_id
  2  from order_items
  3  where rownum < 5;
```

```
from order_items
    *
ERROR at line 2:
ORA-00942: table or view does not exist


SQL> flashback table order_items to before drop;

Flashback complete.

SQL> select order_id, line_item_id, product_id
  2  from order_items
  3  where rownum < 5;

  ORDER_ID LINE_ITEM_ID PRODUCT_ID
---------- ------------ ----------
      2355            1       2289
      2356            1       2264
      2357            1       2211
      2358            1       1781

SQL>
```

If the table ORDER_ITEMS was re-created after it was dropped, Gary would add the RENAME TO clause in the FLASHBACK TABLE command to give the restored table a new name, as in the following example:

```
SQL> drop table order_items;

Table dropped.

SQL> flashback table order_items to before drop
  2      rename to order_items_old_version;

Flashback complete.

SQL> select order_id, line_item_id, product_id
  2  from order_items_old_version
  3  where rownum < 5;

  ORDER_ID LINE_ITEM_ID PRODUCT_ID
---------- ------------ ----------
      2355            1       2289
```

2356	1	2264
2357	1	2211
2358	1	1781

SQL>

If the table to be retrieved from the recycle bin was dropped more than once, and you want to retrieve an incarnation of the table before the most recent one, you can use the name of the table in the recycle bin; you can query the view RECYCLEBIN or use the SHOW RECYCLEBIN command.

Using the EM Database Control, you can retrieve a dropped table from the recycle bin on the Perform Recovery: Dropped Objects Selection screen, as shown in Figure 11.2.

The user GARY has one table, ORDER_ITEMS, in the recycle bin that was dropped on June 21, 2004. Subsequent screen in this wizard let you rename the restored tables if a name conflicts with an existing object.

Recycle Bin Considerations and Limitations

A few limitations are associated with the recycle bin:

- Only non-SYSTEM locally managed tablespaces can have a recycle bin. However, dependent objects in a dictionary-managed tablespace are protected if the dropped object is in a locally managed tablespace.

- A table's dependent objects are saved in the recycle bin when the table is dropped, except for bitmap join indexes, referential integrity constraints (foreign key constraints), and materialized view logs.

- Indexes are protected only if the table is dropped first; explicitly dropping an index does not place the index into the recycle bin.

Using Flashback Table

Flashback Table allows you to recover one or more tables to a specific point in time without having to use more time-consuming recovery operations such as tablespace point-in-time recovery or Flashback Database that can also affect the availability of the rest of the database. Flashback Table works in-place by rolling back only the changes made to the table or tables and their dependent objects, such as indexes. Flashback Table is different from Flashback Drop; Flashback Table undoes recent transactions to an existing table, whereas Flashback Drop recovers a dropped table. Flashback Table uses data in the undo tablespace, whereas Flashback Drop uses the recycle bin.

The FLASHBACK TABLE command brings one or more tables back to a point in time before any number of logical corruptions have occurred on the tables. To be able to flashback a table, you must enable row movement for the table. Because DML operations are used to bring the table back to its former state, the ROWIDs in the table change. As a result, Flashback Table is not a viable option for applications that depend on the table's ROWIDs to remain constant.

In the following example, you find out that someone in the HR department has accidentally deleted all the employees in department 60, the IT department, along with the row for IT in the DEPARTMENTS table. Because this happened less than 15 minutes ago, you are sure that there is enough undo information to support a Flashback Table operation.

FIGURE 11.2   The Perform Recovery: Dropped Objects Selection screen

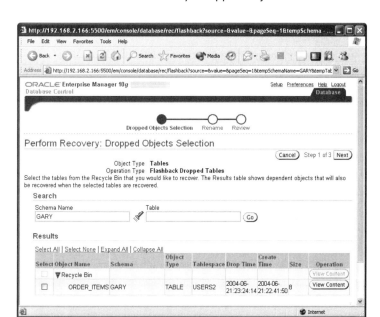

Before performing the Flashback Table operation, you first enable row movement in the two affected tables, as in the following example:

```
SQL> alter table hr.employees enable row movement;
Table altered.
```

```
SQL> alter table hr.departments enable row movement;
Table altered.
```

Before running the FLASHBACK TABLE command, you confirm that the row in DEPARTMENTS for the IT department is still missing using this query:

```
SQL> select * from hr.departments where
  2     department_name = 'IT';
```

```
no rows selected
```

Next, you flash back the table to 15 minutes ago, specifying both tables in the same command, as follows:

```
SQL> flashback table hr.employees, hr.departments
  2     to timestamp systimestamp - interval '15' minute;
```

```
Flashback complete.
```

Finally, you check to see if the IT department is truly back in the table:

```
SQL> select * from hr.departments where
  2     department_name = 'IT';


DEPARTMENT_ID DEPARTMENT_NAME      MANAGER_ID LOCATION_ID
------------- ------------------   ---------- -----------
           60 IT                          103        1400


SQL>
```

If you either flashback too far or not far enough, you can simply rerun the FLASHBACK TABLE command with a different time stamp or SCN, as long as the undo data is still available.

Although the rest of the database is unaffected by a Flashback Table operation, the FLASHBACK TABLE command acquires exclusive DML locks on the tables involved in the flashback. This is usually not an availability issue, because the users who would normally use the table are waiting for the flashback operation to complete anyway!

Integrity constraints are not violated when one or more tables are flashed back; this is why you typically group tables related by integrity constraints or parent-child relationships in the FLASHBACK TABLE command.

Using EM Database Control, you can flashback a table by selecting the Maintenance tab from the EM Database Control home page, and clicking the Perform Recovery link. On the Perform Recovery: Type screen, shown in Figure 11.3, select Tables in the Object Type drop-down box.

FIGURE 11.3 Selecting Tables as the object type for recovery

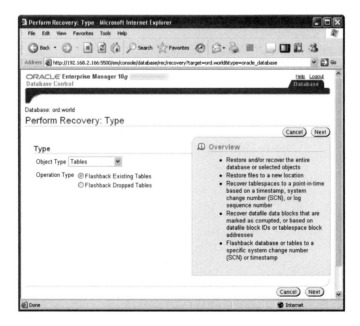

After clicking the Next button, select either Flashback to a Timestamp or Flashback to a Known SCN, and specify the time stamp or SCN as the desired point in time for the recovered table, as you can see in Figure 11.4.

Click Next to skip to step 4 in the recovery dialog, the Perform Recovery: Flashback Tables screen, as shown in Figure 11.5, where you specify the two tables you used in the SQL*Plus command-line example earlier in this section: HR.EMPLOYEES and HR.DEPARTMENTS.

At the end of this sequence of steps, you can view the SQL command that will be executed. In the Perform Recovery: Review screen shown in Figure 11.6, you can see the summary presented before the flashback is initiated, and here is the SQL you see when you click the Show SQL button:

```
FLASHBACK TABLE HR.EMPLOYEES, HR.JOBS,
    HR.DEPARTMENTS, HR.LOCATIONS TO TIMESTAMP
    TO_TIMESTAMP('2004-09-12 01:15:25 PM',
    'YYYY-MM-DD HH:MI:SS AM')
```

The EM Database Control version of the command shows two more tables than in your command-line version of this recovery scenario, HR.JOBS and HR.LOCATIONS, because by default the recovery wizard includes all dependent objects.

FIGURE 11.4   Selecting a time stamp or an SCN for table recovery

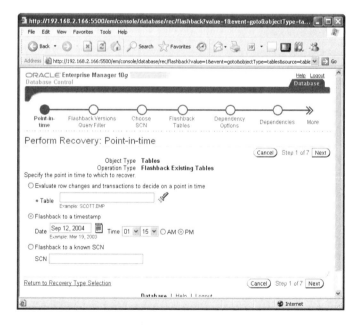

FIGURE 11.5 Selecting tables to flashback

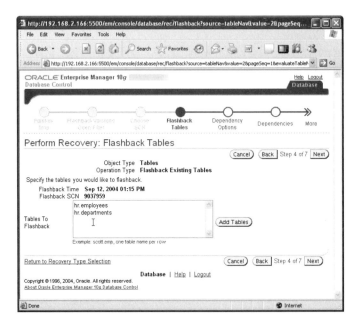

FIGURE 11.6 The Perform Recovery: Review screen

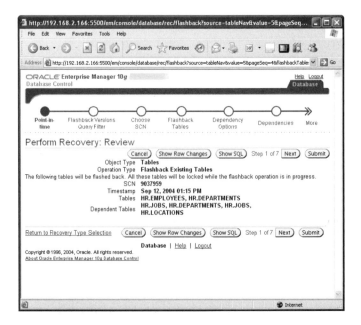

Using LogMiner

Oracle LogMiner is another tool you can use to view past activity in the database. The LogMiner tool can help find changed records in redo log files by using a set of PL/SQL procedures and functions. LogMiner extracts all DDL and DML activity from the redo log files for viewing via the dynamic performance view V$LOGMNR_CONTENTS. In addition to extracting the DDL and DML statements used to change the database, the V$LOGMNR_CONTENTS view also contains the DML statements needed to reverse the change made to the database. This is a good tool for not only pinpointing when changes were made to a table but also for automatically generating the SQL statements needed to reverse those changes.

LogMiner works differently from Oracle's Flashback Query feature. The Flashback Query feature allows a user to see the contents of a table at a specified time in the past; LogMiner can search a time period for all DDL against the table. A Flashback Query uses the undo information stored in the undo tablespace; LogMiner uses redo logs, both online and archived. Both tools can be useful for tracking down how and when changes to database objects took place.

You can configure and use LogMiner either from a SQL command line or via a GUI-based interface within Oracle Enterprise Manager, as shown in Figure 11.7, by choosing Tools ➢ Database Applications ➢ Logminer Viewer.

This LogMiner session initiated through EM shows a sequence of DML statements executed by user GARY against the ORDER_ITEMS table. The SQL Redo column shows the DML statement used to change the ORDER_ITEMS table, and the SQL Undo column shows how to reverse the change made by the DML statement in the SQL Redo column. Double-clicking a row in the report opens a second window that shows the complete text of both the SQL Undo and SQL Redo columns, as shown in Figure 11.8.

FIGURE 11.7   Selecting a DML statement using LogMiner

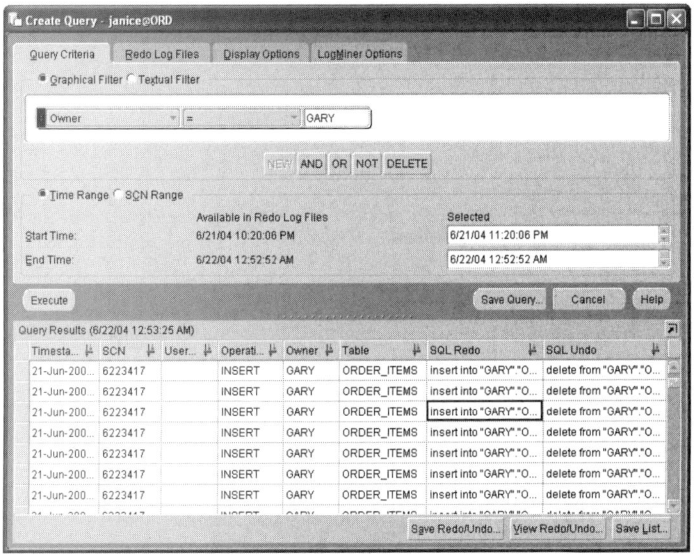

FIGURE 11.8 Using LogMiner to undo a transaction

LogMiner does not actually undo the change; it only provides the statements that you can use to undo the change. You can extract and run any or all DML commands you find in the redo logs, keeping in mind any integrity constraints in place for the tables you are modifying.

Recovering from Loss of a Control File

Losing one of the multiplexed control files immediately aborts the instance. Assuming that you have not lost every control file, recovering from this failure is fairly straightforward.

Recovering from the loss of all control files is covered in *OCP: Oracle 10g Administration II Study Guide* (Sybex, 2005).

Here are the steps to recover from the loss of a control file:

1. If the instance is not shut down, use SHUTDOWN ABORT to force a complete shutdown.

2. Copy one of the good copies of the control file to the location of the corrupted or missing control file. If the corrupted or missing control file resided on a failed disk, copy it to another suitable location instead, and update the initialization parameter file to update the control file reference. Alternatively, you can temporarily remove the reference from the initialization parameter file until you find a suitable location. However, it is highly desirable to maintain at least two, if not more, copies of the control file available in the case of another media failure.

3. Start the instance with STARTUP.

In the following example, you use a server parameter file (SPFILE) for initialization parameters, and you decide to temporarily do without a third multiplexed control file until the disk containing the lost control file is repaired. The initialization parameter file parameter CONTROL_FILES will be changed using the ALTER SYSTEM ... SCOPE=SPFILE command when the instance is started in NOMOUNT mode. You cannot start in MOUNT mode because that mode checks for the existence of all copies of the control file, and as far as the SPFILE is concerned, we are still missing a control file.

The first step is to start the database in NOMOUNT mode, as you can see in this example:

```
SQL> startup nomount

ORACLE instance started.

Total System Global Area  188743680 bytes
Fixed Size                   778036 bytes
Variable Size             162537676 bytes
Database Buffers           25165824 bytes
Redo Buffers                 262144 bytes
SQL>
```

Looking at the dynamic performance view V$SPPARAMETER, you can see that you still have three copies of the control file referenced, but the disk containing the third copy has failed:

```
SQL> select name, value from v$spparameter
  2      where name = 'control_files';

NAME            VALUE
--------------  -------------------------------------------------
control_files   /u02/oradata/ord/control01.ctl
control_files   /u06/oradata/ord/control02.ctl
control_files   /u07/oradata/ord/control03.ctl
```

In the next step, you change the value of CONTROL_FILES in the SPFILE and restart the instance, as you can see here:

```
SQL> alter system set control_files =
  2      '/u02/oradata/ord/control01.ctl',
```

```
   3    '/u06/oradata/ord/control02.ctl'
   4  scope = spfile;

System altered.

SQL> shutdown immediate

ORA-01507: database not mounted

ORACLE instance shut down.

SQL> startup
ORACLE instance started.

Total System Global Area  188743680 bytes
Fixed Size                   778036 bytes
Variable Size             162537676 bytes
Database Buffers           25165824 bytes
Redo Buffers                 262144 bytes
Database mounted.
Database opened.
SQL>
```

Once the instance is restarted successfully, you confirm that the control file is no longer being referenced, as you can see in this query:

```
SQL> select name, value from v$spparameter
  2  where name = 'control_files';

NAME               VALUE
--------------     --------------------------------------
control_files      /u02/oradata/ord/control01.ctl
control_files      /u06/oradata/ord/control02.ctl
```

You still have two multiplexed copies of the control file; therefore, you are covered in case of a media failure of the disk containing one of the remaining control files.

Recovering from Loss of a Redo Log File

A database instance stays up as long as at least one member of a redo log group is available. The alert log records the loss of a redo log group member; as with most database status information, the EM Database Control allows you to easily review the contents of the alert log.

The dynamic performance view V$LOGFILE provides the status of each member of each redo log file member of each redo log group; the STATUS column is defined as follows:

INVALID   The file is corrupted or missing.

STALE   This redo log file member is new and has never been used.

DELETED   The file is no longer being used.

\<blank\>   The redo log file is in use and is not corrupted.

When you are aware of a missing or deleted redo log file group member, follow these three steps to ensure that you maintain a maximum level of redundancy. Losing the remaining member(s) of the redo log group will cause the instance to fail.

1. Verify which redo log file group member is missing.

2. Archive the log file group's contents; if you clear this log file group before archiving it, you must back up the full database to ensure maximum recoverability of the database in the case of the loss of a datafile. Use the command ALTER SYSTEM ARCHIVE LOG GROUP *groupnum*; to force the archive operation. (*groupnum* refers to the redo log group that you want to archive.)

3. Clear the log group to re-create the missing redo log file members using the command ALTER DATABASE CLEAR LOGFILE GROUP *groupnum*;. Alternatively, you can replace the missing member by copying one of the good group members to the location of the missing member; using ALTER DATABASE CLEAR LOGFILE GROUP has the advantage of being platform independent.

In this example, you lose a redo log file group member and check the status of the redo log file groups using V$LOGFILE:

```
SQL> select * from v$logfile
  2  order by group#;


   GROUP# STATUS  TYPE    MEMBER                         IS_
---------- ------- ------ ---------------------------- ---
        1          ONLINE /u07/oradata/ord/redo01.log  NO
        1          ONLINE /u08/oradata/ord/redo01.log  NO
        2          ONLINE /u07/oradata/ord/redo02.log  NO
        2          ONLINE /u08/oradata/ord/redo02.log  NO
        3          ONLINE /u07/oradata/ord/redo03.log  NO
        3          ONLINE /u08/oradata/ord/redo03.log  NO

6 rows selected.

SQL> ! rm /u08/oradata/ord/redo01.log

SQL> select * from v$logfile order by group#;
```

```
GROUP# STATUS  TYPE    MEMBER                        IS_
---------- ------- ------  ----------------------------  ---
     1             ONLINE  /u07/oradata/ord/redo01.log   NO
     1 INVALID ONLINE  /u08/oradata/ord/redo01.log   NO
     2             ONLINE  /u07/oradata/ord/redo02.log   NO
     2             ONLINE  /u08/oradata/ord/redo02.log   NO
     3             ONLINE  /u07/oradata/ord/redo03.log   NO
     3             ONLINE  /u08/oradata/ord/redo03.log   NO
```

```
6 rows selected.
```

It appears that group number 1 has a missing member, so you want to archive group number 1 using the ALTER SYSTEM ARCHIVE command:

```
SQL> alter system archive log group 1;
```

Finally, you can re-create the missing redo log file group member using the ALTER DATABASE command mentioned in step 3:

```
SQL> alter database clear logfile group 1;
```

```
Database altered.
```

Checking the view V$LOGFILE again, you can see that the redo log group member is no longer invalid:

```
SQL> select * from v$logfile order by group#;
```

```
GROUP# STATUS  TYPE    MEMBER                        IS_
---------- ------- ------  ----------------------------  ---
     1             ONLINE  /u07/oradata/ord/redo01.log   NO
     1             ONLINE  /u08/oradata/ord/redo01.log   NO
     2             ONLINE  /u07/oradata/ord/redo02.log   NO
     2             ONLINE  /u08/oradata/ord/redo02.log   NO
     3             ONLINE  /u07/oradata/ord/redo03.log   NO
     3             ONLINE  /u08/oradata/ord/redo03.log   NO
```

```
6 rows selected.
```

By reviewing the contents of the alert log using either the EM Database Control interface by clicking the Alert Log Content link at the bottom of the Database Control home page or by reviewing the file $ORACLE_BASE/admin/ord/bdump/alert_ord.log, you can see the failures associated with the missing redo log group member:

```
Sun Sep 12 17:31:43 2004
ARC1: Evaluating archive   log 1 thread 1 sequence 2500
```

```
Sun Sep 12 17:31:43 2004
Errors in file /u01/app/oracle/admin/ord/bdump/ord_arc1_3717.trc:
ORA-00313: open failed for members of log group 1 of thread 1
ORA-00312: online log 1 thread 1: '/u08/oradata/ord/redo01.log'
ORA-27037: unable to obtain file status
Linux Error: 2: No such file or directory
Additional information: 3
```

Recovering from Loss of a System-Critical Datafile

When you lose a system-critical datafile, in other words, a file from the SYSTEM or UNDO tablespace, the kinds of recovery available depend on whether you are operating in ARCHIVELOG mode or NOARCHIVELOG mode. Oracle strongly recommends operating in ARCHIVELOG mode for any production database that is not read-only.

Loss of a System-Critical Datafile in *NOARCHIVELOG* Mode

The loss of a system-critical datafile in NOARCHIVELOG mode requires complete restoration of the database, including the control files and all datafiles, not just the missing datafiles. As a result, you must reenter any changes made to the database since the last backup.

Loss of a System-Critical Datafile in *ARCHIVELOG* Mode

The recovery of a system-critical datafile in ARCHIVELOG mode cannot proceed while the database is open; recovery must be performed while the database is in the MOUNT state. Because the database is operating in ARCHIVELOG mode, you will not have to reenter any committed transactions in the system-critical datafile.

When a system-critical datafile is lost, such as the datafile for the SYSTEM tablespace, the instance will abort; in the rare circumstance that this does not happen, shut down the database and start it in MOUNT mode, as in this example:

```
SQL> shutdown abort
ORACLE instance shut down.
SQL> startup mount
ORACLE instance started.

Total System Global Area  197132288 bytes
Fixed Size                   778076 bytes
Variable Size             162537636 bytes
Database Buffers           33554432 bytes
Redo Buffers                 262144 bytes
Database mounted.
SQL>
```

From the EM Database Control interface, your only options at this point are to start up the database or perform recovery, as you can see in Figure 11.9.

When you click Perform Recovery, you are prompted for both operating system credentials and database credentials in the Perform Recovery: Credentials screen, as shown in Figure 11.10. Enter these into the appropriate text boxes and click Continue.

FIGURE 11.9 The database status

FIGURE 11.10 The Perform Recovery: Credentials screen

On the Perform Recovery: Type screen, shown in Figure 11.11, select Datafiles as the object type to recover, and click Next. You are going to restore the SYSTEM tablespace's datafile.

On the Perform Recovery: Datafiles screen, shown in Figure 11.12, specify the datafile or datafiles that constitute the SYSTEM tablespace; in this case, it is /u05/oradata/ord/system01.dbf. Click Next.

FIGURE 11.11 The Perform Recovery: Type screen

FIGURE 11.12 The Perform Recovery: Datafiles screen

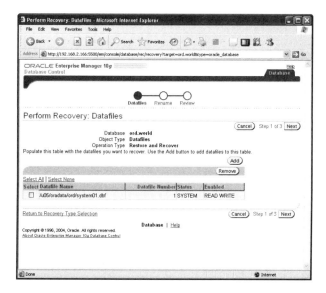

On the Perform Recovery: Rename screen, shown in Figure 11.13, you can restore the datafile to an alternate location. In this case, you want to restore and recover the datafile to the same location, so click Next.

FIGURE 11.13 The Perform Recovery: Rename screen

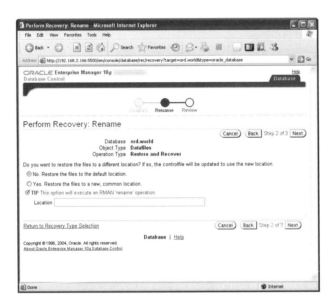

FIGURE 11.14 The Perform Recovery: Review screen

Figure 11.14 shows the final screen before the recovery begins; it includes the RMAN command that is executed when you click Submit.

Clicking Submit runs the RMAN command and initiates the recovery operation. After the recovery operation completes, the EM Database Control provides the output of the RMAN session that recovered the critical datafile, as you can see in Figure 11.15.

Click OK. You can now start up the database by clicking the Startup button in the EM Database Control interface or by issuing the SQL command ALTER DATABASE OPEN, as in this example:

```
SQL> alter database open;
Database altered.
```

Recovering from Loss of a Non–System-Critical Datafile

If you lose a non–system-critical datafile, in other words, not the SYSTEM or UNDO tablespace, your options are similar to those when you lose a system-critical datafile, except that most of your recovery effort in ARCHIVELOG mode can occur while the database is open to users, who can use tablespaces other than the one being recovered.

Loss of a Non–System-Critical Datafile in *NOARCHIVELOG* Mode

As with a system-critical datafile, the loss of a non–system-critical datafile in NOARCHIVELOG mode requires complete restoration of the database, including the control files and all datafiles, not just the missing datafiles. As a result, you must reenter any changes made to the database since the last backup.

FIGURE 11.15   The recovery operation succeeded.

Loss of a Non–System-Critical Datafile in *ARCHIVELOG* Mode

The loss of a non–system-critical datafile in ARCHIVELOG mode affects only objects that are in the missing file, and recovery can proceed while the rest of the database is online. Because you are in ARCHIVELOG mode, no committed transactions in the lost datafile will have to be reentered.

Recovering from the loss of a non–system-critical datafile is not quite as complicated as the recovery from a system-critical datafile that you saw earlier in the chapter; the database is continuously available to all users except for the datafiles being recovered. In the EM Database Control interface, click the Maintenance tab on the EM Database Control home page, and click the Perform Recovery link, as you did in the earlier example. As you can see on the Perform Recovery: Type screen, shown in Figure 11.16, you leave the Object Type as Datafiles and the Operation Type as Recover to Current Time or a Previous Point-in-Time.

Click Next and provide the name of the datafiles to restore; in this case, the USERS tablespace has been corrupted, so you specify the datafiles associated with the USERS tablespace in the Perform Recovery: Datafiles screen, as shown in Figure 11.17. You can use the EM Database Control or the following query to determine the name of the datafile associated with the corrupted datafile, as in this example:

```
SQL> select t.name, d.name
  2     from v$tablespace t join v$datafile d using (ts#)
  3     where t.name = 'USERS';


NAME                     NAME
--------------------     ----------------------------------
USERS                    /u05/oradata/ord/users01.dbf
USERS                    /u05/oradata/ord/users02.dbf
```

FIGURE 11.16   The Perform Recovery: Type screen

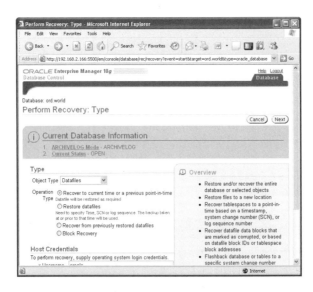

When you click Next, you can recover the datafile and store it in an alternate location in the Perform Recovery: Rename screen, as shown in Figure 11.18. In this example, you restore to the original location.

FIGURE 11.17   The Perform Recovery: Datafiles screen

FIGURE 11.18   The Perform Recovery: Rename screen

Click Next to display step 3 of the recovery operation, the Perform Recovery: Review screen, as shown in Figure 11.19. Not only do you see the RMAN script that will be submitted, but you can edit the script before it is submitted. In addition, you can confirm the datafiles that will be recovered.

When you click Submit, the RMAN script is executed, and the USERS tablespace is recovered. Because the database is in ARCHIVELOG mode, you will not lose any committed transactions in the USERS tablespace.

Alternatively, you can run the RMAN script at the RMAN command prompt, and you will see output similar to the following:

```
[oracle@oltp ord]$ rman target /

Recovery Manager: Release 10.1.0.2.0 - Production

Copyright (c) 1995, 2004, Oracle.  All rights reserved.

connected to target database: ORD (DBID=1387044942)

RMAN>   run { sql 'alter database datafile 4 offline';
             sql 'alter database datafile 7 offline';
             restore datafile 4,7;
             recover datafile 4,7;
             sql 'alter database datafile 4 online';
             sql 'alter database datafile 7 online'; }

using target database controlfile instead of recovery catalog

sql statement: alter database datafile 4 offline

sql statement: alter database datafile 7 offline

Starting restore at 12-SEP-04
allocated channel: ORA_DISK_1
channel ORA_DISK_1: sid=250 devtype=DISK

channel ORA_DISK_1: starting datafile backupset restore
channel ORA_DISK_1: specifying datafile(s) to restore from backup set
restoring datafile 00004 to /u05/oradata/ord/users01.dbf
restoring datafile 00007 to /u05/oradata/ord/users02.dbf
channel ORA_DISK_1: restored backup piece 1
piece handle=/OraFlash/ORD/backupset/
   2004_09_06/o1_mf_nnndf_TAG20040906T233842_0mtgtrod_.bkp
tag=TAG20040906T233842
```

```
channel ORA_DISK_1: restore complete
Finished restore at 12-SEP-04

Starting recover at 12-SEP-04
using channel ORA_DISK_1

starting media recovery

archive log thread 1 sequence 2352 is already on disk as file
    /OraFlash/ORD/archivelog/2004_09_07/
        o1_mf_1_2352_0mtj55w8_.arc
. . .
archive log
filename=/OraFlash/ORD/archivelog/2004_09_12/
        o1_mf_1_2512_0nb127m7_.arc thread=1 sequence=2512
media recovery complete
Finished recover at 12-SEP-04

sql statement: alter database datafile 4 online

sql statement: alter database datafile 7 online

RMAN>
```

FIGURE 11.19   The Perform Recovery: Review screen

Summary

Understanding the types of failures that can occur in the database is critical to deciding the type of action required to recover from the failure. We reviewed the six types of failures in a database: statement, user process, network, user errors, instance, and media.

In addition to knowing how an instance fails, you also need to know what is required to keep a database up and running: all control files, at least one member of each redo log group, and all datafiles for the SYSTEM and UNDO tablespaces. For instance failures, you want to know how long the database will take to recover. Starting with Oracle9*i*, you can use the initialization parameter FAST_START_MTTR_TARGET to specify the target recovery time, making it easier to meet service-level agreements.

Later in the chapter, we presented an overview of how to recover from three of the failure types: instance, user errors, and media. In the discussion on instance failures, we presented the steps required to successfully start up the database, identifying the prerequisites that must be in place for the startup phase to complete.

In many cases, users themselves can solve their errors; Flashback Query can retrieve rows that have been deleted from a table in the past, even after a COMMIT has been performed. Dropped tables are kept in a structure new to Oracle 10*g* called the recycle bin, which lets a user bring back the entire table as long as the space occupied by the table in the tablespace was not required for new objects. Flashback Table brings a table back to a point of time in the past without affecting other objects or users in the database; Flashback Query and Flashback Table are often used as complementary tools when many rows or even a few rows in a table have been lost or inadvertently deleted. Finally, you can access previous transactions against a table from the online and archived redo logs when the self-service recovery tools are not successful in recovering user data.

At the end of the chapter, we visited a couple of media failure scenarios and showed you how to recover from each one of these using the EM Database Control interface while minimizing downtime and preventing any loss of committed transactions.

Exam Essentials

Identify the initialization parameters used to tune instance recovery.   Be able to define the possible values for FAST_START_MTTR_TARGET, FAST_START_IO_TARGET, and LOG_CHECKPOINT_ TIMEOUT. Show the relationship between these parameters and in which situations each is most appropriately used.

List the phases of instance startup.   Show how the database instance moves from SHUTDOWN to NOMOUNT to MOUNT to OPEN, and describe the conditions required in each step before the instance can proceed to the next phase.

Be able to list the types of failures that can occur in a database.   Identify the six types of failures: statement, user process, network, user errors, instance, and media.

List the features supported by Oracle to help users fix their own errors.   Describe each type of user error recovery solution: Flashback Query, Flashback Table, and Flashback Drop.

Be able to use Flashback Query to retrieve previous table data.   Show how Flashback Query can help a user look at the contents of a table at some point of time in the past. Demonstrate the flexibility in specifying the date at which the Flashback Query is executed.

Describe how Flashback Drop is used.   Describe the components of Flashback Drop, such as the recycle bin, and show how it can store a deleted table unless space pressure occurs in the tablespace. Be able to identify the restrictions on the types of objects that can be saved in the recycle bin.

List the steps required to allow Flashback Table to be used on a table.   If a user wants to change the contents of a table to reflect a point of time in the past, show how Flashback Table works and contrast it with Flashback Query. Identify the additional commands needed to allow a table to be flashed back.

Understand how LogMiner works and when it is used.   Identify which database files are used in a LogMiner query. Give an example of when a LogMiner query is the only option for retrieving data changed, deleted, or inserted in a previous transaction.

Identify the three types of database files affected by media failures.   Compare and contrast the loss of control files, redo log file group members, and datafiles, and describe how to recover from the loss of each of these files. Understand how the loss of certain types of datafiles may have a larger impact on availability and recoverability than others.

Review Questions

1. The distance between the checkpoint position in a redo log group and the end of the redo log group can never be what percentage of the smallest redo log group?

   A. 15

   B. 100

   C. 50

   D. 90

   E. None of the above; the distance is relative to the size of the largest redo log group.

2. A database user tries to add a new row to a table, but the tablespace where the table resides is out of space. This type of failure is considered a(n) _____ failure, and the DBA can solve this problem by _____.

   A. User error; providing additional user privileges

   B. User error; increasing the user's quota

   C. Statement failure; enabling resumable space allocation

   D. Statement failure; changing the application logic

3. Which of the following initialization parameters controls the mean time to recover the database, in seconds, after an instance failure?

   A. FAST_START_IO_TARGET

   B. LOG_CHECKPOINT_TIMEOUT

   C. FAST_START_MTTR_TARGET

   D. MTTR_TARGET_ADVICE

   E. FAST_START_TARGET_MTTR

4. What background process frees up locks and rolls back uncommitted changes for an abnormally disconnected session?

   A. ORB0

   B. RBAL

   C. SMON

   D. PMON

5. Which of the following is not a reason for user process failure?

   A. A user's PC suddenly reboots.

   B. The network or an application develops problems.

   C. The DBA kills the user session.

   D. Users terminate SQL*Plus without logging out.

6. Which of the following can help prevent database network failures? (Choose all that apply.)

   A. Configure a backup listener process on the server.

   B. Open more than one session when updating the database.

   C. Configure multiple network cards on the server.

   D. Create a standby database.

7. Identify the statement that is not true regarding the loss of a control file.

   A. A damaged control file can be repaired by using one of the remaining undamaged control files, assuming that there are at least two copies of the control file.

   B. The missing or damaged control file can be replaced while the instance is still active.

   C. You can temporarily run the instance with one less control file, as long as you remove one of the references to the missing control file in the SPFILE or `init.ora` file.

   D. An instance typically fails when one of the multiplexed control files is lost or damaged.

8. Identify the statement that is not true about checkpoints.

   A. Instance recovery is complete when the data from the last checkpoint up to the latest SCN in the control file has been written to the datafiles.

   B. A checkpoint keeps track of what has already been written to the datafiles.

   C. The redo log group writes must occur before a `Commit complete` is returned to the user.

   D. The distance between the checkpoint position in the redo log file and the end of the redo log group can never be more than 90 percent of the size of the largest redo log group.

   E. How much the checkpoint lags behind the SCN is controlled by both the size of the redo log groups and by setting the parameter FAST_START_MTTR_TARGET.

9. The instance can still be started even if some datafiles are missing; this rule does not apply to which tablespaces? (Choose all that apply.)

   A. USERS

   B. SYSTEM

   C. TEMP

   D. SYSAUX

   E. UNDO

10. Select the statement that is not true regarding media failure.

   A. A media failure occurs when the network card on the server fails.

   B. The DBA accidentally deletes one of the datafiles for the SYSTEM tablespace.

   C. There is a head crash on all physical drives in the RAID controller box.

   D. A corrupted track on a CD containing a read-only tablespace causes a query to fail; therefore, a media failure occurs.

11. The loss of a datafile in which two tablespaces requires an instance shutdown to recover the tablespace?

   A. TEMP

   B. SYSTEM

   C. UNDO

   D. SYSAUX

12. To recover a datafile from the SYSTEM or UNDO tablespace, the instance must be in which database state?

   A. NOMOUNT

   B. OPEN

   C. ABORT

   D. MOUNT

13. The STATUS column of the dynamic performance view V$LOGFILE contains what value if one of the redo log file group members has been lost due to a media failure?

   A. INVALID

   B. STALE

   C. DELETED

   D. The column contains a NULL value.

14. Place the following events or actions leading up to and during instance recovery in the correct order.

   1. The database is opened and available.

   2. A non-SYSTEM user attempts to connect to the database, and the connection is refused.

   3. A non-SYSTEM user attempts to connect to the database, and the connection is accepted.

   4. Oracle uses undo segments in the undo tablespace to roll back uncommitted transactions.

   5. Power is lost to the database server.

   6. The DBA issues the STARTUP command at the SQL*Plus prompt.

   7. Oracle applies the information in the online redo log files to the datafiles.

   A. 5, 7, 6, 2, 4, 1, 3

   B. 5, 6, 7, 2, 1, 4, 3

   C. 5, 2, 3, 4, 1, 6, 7

   D. 5, 2, 3, 4, 1, 7, 6

   E. 3, 5, 6, 4, 7, 1, 2

   F. 2, 5, 6, 7, 4, 1, 3

15. The STATUS column of the dynamic performance view V$LOGFILE contains what value if the redo log file group has just been added or the log file group member has just been re-created?

   A. INVALID

   B. STALE

   C. DELETED

   D. The column contains a NULL value.

16. If a datafile is missing when the instance is started, where is the error message recorded?

   A. Only in the alert log.

   B. All missing files are returned directly to the administrator in the SQL*Plus session.

   C. The first missing file is returned directly to the administrator in the SQL*Plus session, and the rest of the missing files are identified in V$RECOVER_FILE.

   D. Only in the alert log and in the DBWR background process trace files.

17. In ARCHIVELOG mode, the loss of a datafile for any tablespace other than the SYSTEM or UNDO tablespace affects which objects in the database?

   A. The loss affects only objects whose extents reside in the lost datafile.

   B. The loss affects only the objects in the affected tablespace, and work can continue in other tablespaces.

   C. The loss will not abort the instance, but will prevent other transactions in any tablespace other than SYSTEM or UNDO until the affected tablespace is recovered.

   D. The loss affects only those users whose default tablespace contains the lost or damaged datafile.

18. Which dynamic performance view shows the datafiles either needing media recovery or missing at instance startup?

   A. V$RECOVER_FILE

   B. V$DATAFILE

   C. V$TABLESPACE

   D. V$RECOVERY_FILE_DEST

   E. V$RECOVERY_FILE_STATUS

19. A fire breaks out in the server room near the routers, and the operations manager cuts off power to all servers, including the database servers. Before the fire is put out, the disk drive containing the SYSTEM tablespace and both network cards on the Oracle database server are destroyed. The user SCOTT was about to create a new table, but the connection was dropped after the power was disconnected from the server. This scenario is primarily an example of what kind of failure?

   A. Network

   B. Instance

   C. Statement

   D. Media

   E. User error

   F. User process

20. Which of the following conditions prevents the instance from progressing through the NOMOUNT, MOUNT, and OPEN states?

A. One of the redo log file groups is missing a member.

B. The instance was previously shut down uncleanly with SHUTDOWN ABORT.

C. Either the SPFILE or init.ora file is missing.

D. One of the five multiplexed control files is damaged.

E. The USERS tablespace is offline with one of its datafiles deleted.

Answers to Review Questions

1. D. The distance (in bytes) between the checkpoint position in a redo log group and the end of the current redo log group can never be more than 90 percent of the size of the smallest redo log group

2. C. The failure of one statement is considered a statement failure, and one way to solve the problem is to enable resumable space allocation.

3. C. The parameter FAST_START_MTTR_TARGET specifies the desired time, in seconds, to recover a single instance from a crash or instance failure. The parameters LOG_CHECKPOINT_TIMEOUT and FAST_START_IO_TARGET can still be used in Oracle 10*g* but should only be used together in an advanced tuning scenario or for compatibility with older versions of Oracle. MTTR_TARGET_ADVICE and FAST_START_TARGET_MTTR are not valid initialization parameters.

4. D. The PMON process periodically polls server processes to make sure that their sessions are still connected.

5. C. A DBA's disconnection of a session is an intentional process termination, not a failure. If a user's PC reboots, the user does not get a chance to log off, and the session is cleaned up by PMON; similarly, disconnecting from the application or SQL*Plus before logging out is considered a user process failure. A network problem can prematurely disconnect a user session, causing a user process failure. In all cases, PMON performs the session cleanup, whether the disconnection was intentional or not.

6. A, C. In addition to configuring a backup listener process and installing multiple network cards, you can also implement connect-time failover and a backup network connection to reduce the possibility of network failures.

7. B. The instance must be shut down, if it is not already down, to repair or replace the missing or damaged control file.

8. D. The distance between the checkpoint position in the redo log file and the end of the redo log group can never be more than 90 percent of the size of the *smallest* redo log group.

9. B, E. If a tablespace is taken offline because a datafile is missing, the instance can still be started as long as the missing datafile does not belong to the SYSTEM or UNDO tablespace.

10. A. If a network card fails, the failure type is network; the actual media containing the database files are not affected.

11. B, C. Only the SYSTEM and UNDO tablespaces require the instance to be shut down when their datafiles need recovery.

12. D. Unlike recovery of non–system-critical tablespaces other than SYSTEM or UNDO that can be recovered with the database in the OPEN state, the database must be in the MOUNT state to recover either the SYSTEM or UNDO tablespace.

13. A. If the redo log file group member has been lost due to a media failure or inadvertent deletion, the STATUS column is set to INVALID when an attempt is made to write redo information to that member.

14. B. Instance recovery, also known as crash recovery, occurs when the DBA attempts to open the database, but the files were not synchronized to the same SCN when the database was shut down. Once the DBA issues the STARTUP command, Oracle uses information in the redo log files to restore the datafiles (including the undo tablespace's datafiles) to the state before the instance failure. Oracle then uses undo data in the undo tablespace to roll back uncommitted transactions.

15. B. If the redo log file group member has never been used, either due to a new redo log file group or a repaired member, the value of STATUS is STALE until the log file member is used to record redo information.

16. C. In addition to reporting the first missing file to the administrator and listing all the missing files in the dynamic performance view V$RECOVER_FILE, the missing datafile(s) are noted in the DBWR background process trace files.

17. B. The loss of one or more of a tablespace's datafiles does not prevent other users from doing their work in other tablespaces. Recovering the affected datafiles can continue while the database is still online and available.

18. A. The dynamic performance view V$RECOVER_FILE contains a list of the datafiles that either need media recovery or are missing when the instance is started.

19. B. The primary failure in this scenario is instance. Subsequently, a network failure will occur when connections are attempted through the burned-out router. However, no connections are possible until the network card in the server is replaced; the instance cannot start because of a media failure on the disk containing the SYSTEM tablespace. It is assumed that the DBA has been configuring this database for fast recovery with both onsite and offsite backups to DVD and tape as well as sending the archived redo logs to a standby database.

20. D. All copies of the control files as defined in the SPFILE or the init.ora file must be identical and available. If one of the redo log file groups is missing a member, a warning is recorded in the alert log, but instance startup still proceeds. If the instance was previously shut down with SHUTDOWN ABORT, instance recovery automatically occurs during startup. Only an SPFILE or an init.ora file is needed to enter the NOMOUNT state, not both. If a tablespace is offline, the status of its datafiles is not checked until an attempt is made to bring it online; therefore, it will not prevent instance startup.

Glossary

A

ADDM   *See* Automated Database Diagnostic Monitoring (ADDM).

anonymous block   An unnamed PL/SQL program.

Application Server Control   *A* web-based component of Enterprise Manager (EM) that monitors Oracle Application Server 10*g* (9.0.4). The Application Server Control lets you monitor and administer a single Oracle Application Server instance, a collection of Oracle Application Server instances, or Oracle Application Server clusters.

archived redo log file   A file that contains the contents of a previously used redo log file. Only created when the database is operating in ARCHIVELOG mode.

ARCHIVELOG mode   A database configuration in which redo log files are copied to the archive log destination, which ensures that they won't be overwritten and lost. These archived logs are used primarily for media recovery.

ARC*n*   An Oracle background process that copies the online redo log files to an archived log destination.

ASM   *See* Automated Storage Management (ASM).

auditing   The monitoring and recording of specific database activities.

Automated Database Diagnostic Monitoring (ADDM)   The process that analyzes the data in the Automatic Workload Repository (AWR) to identify sources of potential performance bottlenecks and recommends solutions for correcting the problem. *See also* Automatic Workload Repository (AWR).

Automated Storage Management (ASM)   A type of storage mechanism that is new in Oracle 10*g*. Oracle manages the storage definitions of the database within a second database used exclusively by ASM to keep track of the disk allocations for your databases.

Automatic Workload Repository (AWR)   The collection of tables, owned by the SYSMAN schema, that stores the performance statistics gathered from the SGA (System Global Area) by the MMON (Memory Monitor) background process.

AWR   *See* Automatic Workload Repository (AWR).

B

BACKGROUND_DUMP_DEST   The Oracle initialization parameter that specifies the directory where the alert log and background process trace files are written.

backup sets   A set of RMAN (Recovery Manager) files that contain the saved data from a backup.

back up to trace   A method of backing up the control file contents to a text file in the location specified by the initialization parameter USER_DUMP_DEST.

baseline metrics   A collection of performance statistics against which current or future database performance is measured to determine if a significant performance deviation has occurred.

bigfile tablespace   A tablespace built on a single data file that can be up to 2^{32} data blocks in size.

block change tracking file   A file created in the same location as the datafiles that tracks the blocks changed since the last incremental backup, saving time during an incremental backup because not all blocks in every datafile need to be checked for changes.

C

cardinality   The number of distinct values in a column or a table.

Cartesian product   The query result produced when a join condition is omitted from a query that references two or more tables in the FROM clause.

change vectors   A description of a change made to a single block in the database.

checkpoint   An event during which the dirty data block buffers are flushed to disk and database files are updated to reflect this action. The database is put into a consistent state.

checkpoint (CKPT) process   The Oracle background process that updates the control file and the datafile headers to reflect the last successful transaction by recording the last System Change Number (SCN).

CKPT   *See* checkpoint (CKPT) process.

column   The vertical space in a table or a view that holds a specific domain of data. In the relational model, an entity has attributes. When this model is implemented in an Oracle database, an entity becomes a table, and an attribute becomes a column.

COMMIT   The SQL command for making permanent the changes effected during a transaction.

connection   The communication channel between the User Process and the Server Process. *See also* Server Process; User Process.

Connection Manager   *See* Oracle Connection Manager.

consistent backup   A backup performed while the database is shut down and unavailable. Also referred to as offline backup.

constraint   An optional schema object that restricts values in the dependent table to a specified condition. Constraints enforce business rules about data.

control file   A small binary file that contains metadata about the physical structure of the database such as the database name, locations of the datafiles and redo logs, and recovery information.

cost-based optimizer   The Oracle optimizer mode that uses statistics about the size, selectivity, and dispersion of the tables and indexes in the database to formulate the most efficient execution plan.

D

database   A collection of control files, datafiles, and redo logs.

database buffer cache   The portion of the SGA (System Global Area) where copies of the data blocks are cached in memory. *See also* System Global Area (SGA).

Database Configuration Assistant (DBCA)   A Java-based tool you can use to create Oracle databases. The DBCA can store and manage definitions of your databases in the form of templates that can be used to make copies of a database.

Database Control   A web-based component of the Enterprise Management Framework for managing Oracle Database 10*g*. The Database Control allows you to monitor and administer a single Oracle database instance or a single Real Application Cluster (RAC) environment.

database templates   XML-based documents that the DBCA creates to store information about database definitions. The documents contain everything the DBCA needs to create a database. *See also* Database Configuration Agent (DBCA).

Database Writer (DBW*n*)   The Oracle background process that is responsible for writing changed data block buffers from the database buffer cache back to the datafiles on disk.

data block   The smallest unit of disk allocation in data or temp files, composed of one or more file system blocks.

Data Control Language (DCL)   The category of SQL commands that control access to database objects, including the GRANT and REVOKE commands.

Data Definition Language (DDL)   The category of SQL commands used to create objects in the database, including CREATE, ALTER, and DROP.

datafiles   The physical database files that store the database's segments, such as tables, indexes, rollback, and partition.

Data Manipulation Language (DML)   The category of SQL commands used to create, modify, or remove data from a table, including INSERT, UPDATE, and DELETE.

DBCA   *See* Database Configuration Assistant (DBCA).

DBMS_DATAPUMP   The PL/SQL (Procedural Language SQL) package that is an API to the Data Pump.

DB Time   A cumulative measure of time spent by the database responding to user requests, including wait times for access to resources such as memory, disk, and CPU for all nonidle user sessions.

DBW*n*   *See* Database Writer (DBW*n*).

DCL   *See* Data Control Language (DCL).

DDL   *See* Data Definition Language (DDL).

deadlock   A special kind of lock conflict that prevents two or more transactions from completing because each transaction has a lock on a resource needed by the other transaction.

dedicated server   A type of connection in which every client connection has an associated dedicated server process on the machine where the Oracle server exists. *See also* Shared Server.

default role   A role initially enabled for every user session.

default tablespace   The tablespace where a user's tables and indexes are stored if not declared explicitly.

directory object   A database object that identifies a file system location. Directory objects are used by data pump jobs.

dispatcher   A process in an Oracle Shared Server environment that manages requests from one or more client connections.

DML   *See* Data Manipulation Language (DML).

dynamic service registration   The ability of an Oracle instance to automatically register its existence with a listener.

E

Emctl   The command-line utility used to stop and start the Oracle Management agent.

Enterprise Manager (EM) Database Control   The web-based GUI tool for managing Oracle environments.

extent management   Defines how free and used extents are managed in a tablespace.

extents   A group of contiguous data blocks allocated to a segment.

Extproc   The default name of the callout process that is used when executing external procedures from Oracle.

F

FAST_START_MTTR_TARGET   An initialization parameter that specifies the desired amount of time, in seconds, to perform instance recovery after an instance failure.

FGA   *See* fine-grained auditing (FGA).

field   The intersection of a column and a row in a table.

fine-grained auditing (FGA)   Special auditing that allows custom rules to be used in monitoring and capturing audit records.

firewall   Generally, a combination of hardware and software that controls network traffic and prevents intruders from compromising corporate network security.

Flashback Database   A flashback feature that lets you recover the entire database to a specific point in time in the past.

Flashback Drop   A flashback feature that retrieves a table after it has been dropped without using other more complicated and disruptive recovery techniques such as point in time recovery or flashback database.

Flashback Query   A feature of the Oracle database that allows a user to view the contents of a table as of a user-specified point in time in the past. How far in the past a flashback query can retrieve rows depends on the size of the undo tablespace and on the setting of the UNDO_ RETENTION system parameter.

Flashback Table   A flashback feature that allows you to recover one or more existing tables to a specific point in time. Flashback table is done in place by rolling back only the changes made to the table or tables and their dependent objects, such as indexes.

Flash Recovery area   A single, unified storage area for all recovery-related files and recovery activities in an Oracle database.

foreign key   A constraint requiring that the value inserted into a column matches the value in a primary or unique key. *See also* self-referencing foreign key.

full backup   A backup that includes all blocks of every datafile backed up in a whole or partial database backup.

function   A PL/SQL (Procedural Language SQL) program that returns a value.

G

Generic Connectivity   One of the Heterogeneous Services offered by Oracle that allows for connectivity solutions based on third-party connection options such as OLEDB (a Microsoft standard) and ODBC (Open Database Connectivity). *See also* Heterogeneous Services.

granule   The unit of contiguous memory used within the SGA (System Global Area) for allocating space to the Shared Pool, database buffer cache, Java Pool, and Large Pool.

grid computing   The concept of spreading Oracle's memory structures across two or more computers on an as-needed basis in order to maximize the performance of the application during peak usage and minimize the use of resources during low usage.

Grid Control   A web-based user interface that communicates with and centrally manages all the components within the Oracle enterprise. From a centralized location, the Grid Control lets you monitor and administer the entire computing environment, including hosts, databases, listeners, application servers, HTTP servers, and web applications.

H

Heterogeneous Services   The facility that lets you communicate with non-Oracle databases and services.

host   The physical machine on which the Oracle server is located. This can be an IP address or a real name that is resolved via some external naming solution, such as DNS.

hostnaming method   A names resolution method for small networks that minimizes the amount of configuration work you must perform.

I

image copies   A bit-for-bit duplicate of datafiles or archived redo log files in a database. You can create image copies using operating system commands or RMAN (Recovery Manager).

inconsistent backup   A backup performed when the database is open and the system change number (SCN) in the datafiles and the control file do not necessarily match. Also referred to as online backup.

incremental backup   A backup that makes a copy of all data blocks that have changed since a previous baseline backup.

incrementally updated backup   A backup that applies an incremental backup to an image copy, reducing the amount of time required in the event of media recovery.

index   An optional schema object to aid data retrieval.

index key   A single occurrence of an index value.

instance   The Oracle SGA (System Global Area) and all the Oracle background processes. *See also* System Global Area (SGA).

instance failure   A circumstance in which the database instance fails unexpectedly, due to a power outage or the failure of an Oracle background process.

instance recovery   The process of synchronizing the contents of each datafile with the control file during instance startup using the online redo log files and data in the undo tablespace.

IP-filtering firewalls   A type of firewall that monitors the network packet traffic on IP networks and filters out packets that either originated or did not originate from specific groups of machines

***i*SQL*Plus**   A web-based version of the SQL*Plus command line and Windows-based products offered by Oracle. You can use this tool to execute queries against a database.

J

Java Pool   The SGA (System Global Area) memory structure where Java code is cached. *See also* System Global Area (SGA).

Java Virtual Machine (JVM)   The software that interprets and executes Java code inside the database.

JVM   *See* Java Virtual Machine (JVM).

L

Large Pool   An optional area in the SGA (System Global Area) used for specific database operations such as backup, recovery, or the UGA (User Global Area), when using the Oracle Shared Server configuration. *See also* System Global Area (SGA); User Global Area (UGA).

least recently used (LRU) algorithm   The mechanism that the Oracle kernel uses to manage the Shared Pool and database buffer caches, whereby the SQL or buffers that have been least recently accessed are those that are overwritten to make room for new SQL or buffers when these requests are made by user Server Processes.

LGWR   *See* log writer.

listener   A server-side process that is responsible for listening and establishing connections to an Oracle server in response to a client connection request.

listener.ora   The configuration file for the Oracle listener located on the Oracle server.

load balancing   The ability of the Oracle listener to balance the number of connections between a group of dispatcher processes in an Oracle Shared Server environment.

localnaming method   A names resolution method that relies on resolving an Oracle Net service name via the tnsnames.ora file.

logging   The recording of the DML (Data Manipulation Language) statements, creation of new objects, and other changes in the redo logs. The process also records significant events, such as starting and stopping the listener, along with certain kinds of network errors. *See also* Data Manipulation Language (DML).

log sequence number   An identifier unique to the database that is incremented and recorded when an online redo log file is switched.

log writer (LGWR)   The background process that writes redo log entries from the Redo Log Buffer to the online redo logs. *See also* Redo Log Buffer.

long query warning alert   An alert generated when a query issues an ORA-01555: snapshot too old error message. This error usually occurs either when there is not enough space in the undo tablespace to hold the previous values of changed data or when the undo retention period for the database is set too low.

`lsnrctl stop`   The command to stop the default Oracle listener.

M

managed targets   Entities that can be monitored and managed within the Oracle Management Framework. These entities include databases, application servers, web servers, applications, and Oracle agents such as the Oracle Net listener and Connection Manager. *See also* Oracle Connection Manager.

mean time to recovery (MTTR)   The average amount of time it takes to recover the database and make it available after an instance failure occurs.

media failure   A failure in which one or more database files is damaged. Media failure applies to control files, redo log files, tempfiles and datafiles.

metadata   Data that describes data. Metadata includes table definitions, stored PL/SQL program code, and privileges, but not the information found in tables.

metric   A measurement that is collected and stored in the AWR (Automatic Workload Recovery) repository. *See also* Automatic Workload Recovery (AWR).

middleware   Software and hardware that sits between a client and the Oracle server. Middleware can provide a variety of functions such as load balancing, security, and application-specific business logic processing.

MTTR   *See* mean time to recovery (MTTR).

multiplexing   Creating multiple copies of a redo log file or control file in different locations so that the loss of one copy does not significantly affect your ability to recover a database.

N

NAMES.DIRECTORY_PATH   An entry found in the `sqlnet.ora` file that defines the net service name search method hierarchy for a client.

Net Service Names   The name of an Oracle service on the network. This is the name the user enters when referring to an Oracle service.

network failure   A failure in the network connection between the client and the database; for example, a router reboot or a failure of a network card in the server.

NOARCHIVELOG mode   A database mode in which redo log files are not written to an archive destination before they are overwritten. A database in NOARCHIVELOG mode can recover only from an instance failure.

n-tier architecture   A network architecture involving at least three computers, typically a client computer, a middle-tier computer, and a database server.

O

OFA   *See* Optimal Flexible Architecture (OFA).

Optimal Flexible Architecture (OFA)   A model for organizing mount points, directory structures, and files so that they will be easier to manage, maintain, and back up.

optimizer statistics   Measures such as number of rows, average row length, number of leaf blocks, and degree of selectivity that are stored as metadata whenever statistics are automatically or manually collected for database tables and indexes.

Oracle Advanced Security   An optional package offered by Oracle that enhances and extends the security capabilities of the standard Oracle server configuration.

Oracle Applications 11*i*   Oracle Corporation's e-business suite of products for businesses, universities, and governments.

Oracle Application Server 10*g*   Oracle Corporation's primary infrastructure product, providing web, portal, forms, reports, and single sign-on capabilities for application developers.

Oracle Collaboration Suite   Oracle Corporation's integrated suite of collaboration products.

Oracle Connection Manager   An optional middleware feature from Oracle that provides multiplexing, network access control, and cross-protocol connectivity.

Oracle Database 10*g*   The latest release of Oracle's flagship database software that provides improved ease of management with grid computing scalability.

Oracle Developer Suite   Oracle Corporation's suite of application design, development, and deployment tools.

Oracle Easy Connect Naming method   A names resolution method for small networks utilizing the TCP/IP protocol, which minimizes the amount of configuration work that you must perform. It is similar to the host naming method but also enables clients to connect to a database server with an optional port and service name as well as the host name of the database.

Oracle Flash Recovery area   A component of the new automated disk-based recovery mechanisms in Oracle 10*g*. Flash Recovery is designed to simplify your life in terms of Oracle backups by providing a centralized location to maintain and manage all the files related to database backups.

Oracle Management Agent   A process that identifies and collects data about entities of interest within the Oracle Management Framework.

Oracle Management Framework   An integrated set of tools that lets you perform traditional tasks more easily and efficiently as well as providing an effective mechanism for monitoring components within the enterprise.

Oracle Management Repository   A database that contains monitoring and configuration information collected about the managed targets in the Oracle Management Framework.

Oracle Management Service   A Java-based web component that is the actual interface you use to monitor and control managed targets within the Oracle Management Framework.

Oracle server   The combination of an Oracle instance and database.

Oracle Services   Oracle Corporation's nonsoftware offerings such as education and consulting services.

Oracle Shared Server   A connection configuration that enhances the scalability of the Oracle Server through the use of dispatcher processes and shared server resources. Shared Server allows the server to support a larger number of lightweight concurrent connections by allowing them to share resources.

Oracle Transparent Gateway   A connectivity product that seamlessly extends the reach of Oracle to non-Oracle data stores and allows you to treat non-Oracle data sources as if they were a part of the Oracle environment.

Oracle Universal Installer (OUI)   The Java-based installation tool for installing Oracle software.

OUI   *See* Oracle Universal Installer.

P

package body   The part of a package that contains the program implementation.

package specification   The part of a package that declares its external interface.

partial database backup   A backup that includes zero or more tablespaces, which in turn include zero or more datafiles; a control file is optional in a partial database backup.

password file   The encrypted file that contains the user names and passwords of users who have been granted SYSDBA and SYSOPER privileges.

PFILE   A plain text file that contains database initialization parameters. Oracle reads this file at startup and uses the information to configure various aspects of the Oracle instance and database.

PGA   *See* Program Global Area.

ping   A TCP/IP utility that checks basic network connectivity between two computers.

PMON   *See* process monitor.

port   Used with TCP/IP to name the ends of logical connections, which carry conversations between two computers.

primary key   A constraint that, when defined on one or more columns in a table, requires that all values in that column be unique and not null.

principle of least privilege   Permits only the minimal set of privileges that are required for the situation.

privileges   The assigned permissions to create, modify, remove, or use a database object or a feature.

proactive monitoring   Monitoring the Oracle server for potential issues before they occur, thus avoiding the impact on the database's performance, availability, or manageability.

procedure   A PL/SQL program that is invoked as a stand-alone statement.

Process Monitor (PMON)   The background process that cleans up failed user connections.

Program Global Area (PGA)   An area of memory in which information for each client session is maintained. This information includes bind variable, cursor information, and the client's sort area.

proxy-based firewall   A firewall that prevents information from outside the firewall from flowing directly into the corporate network. The firewall acts as a gatekeeper, inspecting packets and sending only the appropriate information to the corporate network.

Q

query   A category of SQL statement that retrieves rows from database tables.

R

raw device   A disk that does not contain an operating system managed file system. Instead of a file system managing the reading and writing activities, Oracle does so.

reactive monitoring   Monitoring the Oracle server for issues after they have occurred, too late to avoid impacting the database's performance, availability, or manageability.

read consistency   Oracle's read consistency uses undo data to ensure that a statement (or a transaction) sees a set of data that does not change during its execution.

recycle bin   A logical container in each tablespace holding dropped tables that can be retrieved by a database user as long as the space occupied by the deleted object is not required for new objects in the tablespace.

redo entry   A group of *change vectors*. Redo entries record data that you can use to reconstruct all changes made to the database, including the undo segments. Also referred to as redo record.

redo log   The physical files on disk that store the transaction recovery information written from the Redo Log Buffer by the LGWR (log writer) process. *See also* log writer (LGWR).

Redo Log Buffer   The portion of the SGA (System Global Area) where transaction recovery information is stored until it can be written to the redo log files. *See also* System Global Area (SGA).

redo log file   One of the files that constitutes a redo log group. Also referred to as redo log member.

redo log group   A collection of multiplexed (mirrored) redo log files that contain information about changes in the database.

redo log group member   One of the redo logs within a redo log group.

referential integrity   Enforcing business rules within or between tables using primary key and foreign key constraints.

refuse packet   A packet sent via TCP/IP that acknowledges the refusal of some network request.

request queue   A location in the SGA (System Global Area) in an Oracle Shared Server environment in which the dispatcher process places client requests. The shared server process then processes these requests. *See also* System Global Area (SGA).

response queue   The location in the SGA (System Global Area) in an Oracle Shared Server environment where a shared server process places a completed client request. The dispatcher process then picks up the completed request and sends it back to the client.

response time   The time it takes for a single user's request to return the desired result while using an application. Frequently used as a performance measure in data warehouse systems.

role   A mechanism for grouping privileges for ease in administering them

ROLLBACK   The SQL statement to undo a transaction.

rollback   The second phase of instance recovery during which uncommitted transactions are backed out from the datafiles.

rollback segments   Manually managed segments for storing undo information. This information is used for read consistency and recovery purposes. Rollback segments were replaced by system-managed undo segments when automatic undo management was used.

roll forward   The first phase of instance recovery during which information in the online redo log files is applied to the datafiles (including the undo tablespace) to bring the datafiles up to their state before the instance failed.

rolling back   The process of undoing one or more changes to data within a transaction.

row   A single instance of data in a table. In the relational model, a row is analogous to a tupple.

S

scalability   The ability of a system to continue to provide adequate performance as the amount of data, the number of users, or both increase.

SCN   *See* system change number.

segment   A schema object that stores data outside of the data dictionary. Tables and indexes are segments, while constraints and sequences are not.

segment space management   Defines how free space within a segment is managed.

self-referencing foreign key   A foreign key constraint that refers to the primary key column of the same table.

sequences   Schema objects that generate unique integers.

Server Parameter File (SPFILE)   A binary, dynamically modifiable file that stores a list of instance and database configuration parameters.

server process   The operating system process that executes on the host server on behalf of the user. The server process is responsible for parsing and placing SQL statements into the Shared Pool, copying database blocks into the database buffer cache, and placing transaction recovery information into the Redo Log Buffer.

session   The term used to describe a user's connection to an instance.

SGA   *See* System Global Area (SGA).

shadow process   Another name for a dedicated server process. *See also* shared server process.

Shared Pool   The portion of the SGA (System Global Area) where cached SQL statements and supports metadata are stored.

shared server process   Process in an Oracle Shared Server configuration that executes the client requests.

single-tier architecture   A network architecture in which the client and server processes all run on the same computer.

smallfile tablespace   A traditional tablespace that can have multiple datafiles, each limited to 2^{22} data blocks in size.

SPFILE   *See* Server Parameter File (SPFILE).

SQL   *See* Structured Query Language (SQL).

SQL*Loader   The Oracle10*g* bulk load program.

statement failure   The failure of a single database operation such as a DML (Data Manipulation Language) statement; for example, INSERT, UPDATE, and so on. *See also* Data Manipulation Language (DML).

static service registration   The inputting of service name information directly into the `listener.ora` file.

Streams Pool   The portion of the SGA (System Global Area) that is used to cache Oracle queuing information when the Oracle Streams feature is used. *See also* System Global Area (SGA).

Structured Query Language (SQL)   The English-like language developed to allow users to easily query and manipulate the data stored in relational databases.

SYSDBA   A special all-empowering database authorization assigned to users that allows them to perform any database task.

SYSOPER   A special database authorization assigned to users that allows them to perform a variety of database tasks such as startup and shutdown. Its capabilities are not as encompassing as SYSDBA.

system change number (SCN)   A unique number sequentially assigned to each transaction in the database.

System Global Area (SGA)   The shared memory structure that Oracle uses to cache application users' SQL statements, data, index, and rollback buffers, Java, and redo information.

system monitor (SMON)   The background process that is responsible for instance recovery, temporary tablespace management, and space management.

T

table   A segment that is composed of columns and rows.

tablespace   A logical storage area for database segments.

temporary tablespace   The tablespace in which a user's temporary segments are stored.

throughput   The amount of work that an application or the database can perform in a specified amount of time. Frequently used as a performance measure in systems.

tnsnames.ora   The name of the physical file that is used to resolve an Oracle net service name when you are using the localnaming resolution method.

Tnsping   An Oracle-supplied utility used to test basic connectivity from an Oracle client to an Oracle listener.

tracing   A configuration that records all events that occur on a network, even when an error does not occur. This facility can be established at the client, the middle tier, or the server location.

transaction   A unit of work within a series of SQL statements. A statement begins with the user's first DML (Data Manipulation Language) statement and ends with a `COMMIT` or `ROLLBACK` command. *See also* Data Manipulation Language (DML).

trigger A PL/SQL (Procedural Language/SQL) program that is invoked in response to a database event.

two-tier architecture A network architecture that is characterized by a client computer and a back-end server that communicate using some type of network protocol, such as TCP/IP.

U

UGA *See* User Global Area (UGA).

Undo Advisor A tool within the Oracle advisory framework that uses past undo usage to recommend settings for the UNDO_RETENTION parameter as well as an optimal size for the undo tablespace.

undo data The data blocks changed or updated, along with pointers to rows inserted that are stored in an undo tablespace to support read consistency, rolling back, and recovery from failed transactions or an instance crash. Also referred to as rollback information.

undo segment The segment that stores the before image of modified data; used for rollback or transaction recovery purposes.

undo tablespace A special type of tablespace that holds undo data. Only one undo tablespace can be active in the database at any given time.

user error A user operation that does not generate an error message, but whose result was unintended, such as accidentally dropping a table.

User Global Area (UGA) An area in either the SGA (System Global Area) or PGA (Program Global Area) used to keep track of session-specific information. *See also* Program Global Area (PGA); System Global Area (SGA).

User Process The process that runs on the client computer or application server and connects to the instance using a Server Process.

user process failure The failure of a single connection to the database.

V

V$ROLLNAME A dynamic performance view that has one row for each undo segment in the undo tablespace.

V$TRANSACTION A dynamic performance view that has one row for each active transaction in the database.

view A stored query or virtual table. Views don't usually store data but provide access to data in the base tables.

virtual circuit The shared memory structure used by the dispatcher to manage communications between the client and the Oracle server. The shared server processes use virtual circuits to send and receive information to the appropriate dispatcher process.

W

whole database backup A database backup that includes all datafiles and at least one control file.

Index

Note to reader: **Bolded** page numbers refer to main discussions of a topic. *Italicized* page numbers refer to illustrations and tables.

V

W

Project Management Skills for all Levels

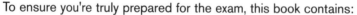

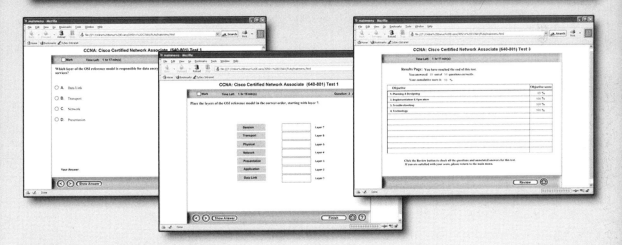

TELL US WHAT YOU THINK!

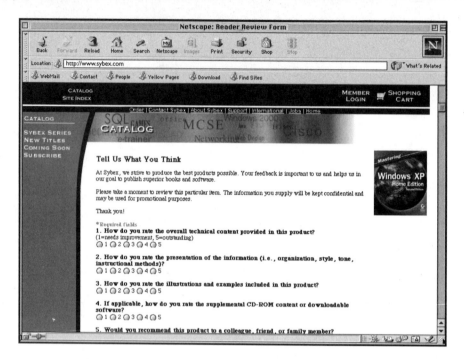

Your feedback is critical to our efforts to provide you with the best books and software on the market. Tell us what you think about the products you've purchased. It's simple:

1. Go to the Sybex website.
2. Find your book by typing the ISBN or title into the Search field.
3. Click on the book title when it appears.
4. Click **Submit a Review.**
5. Fill out the questionnaire and comments.
6. Click **Submit.**

With your feedback, we can continue to publish the highest quality computer books and software products that today's busy IT professionals deserve.

www.sybex.com

SYBEX Inc. • 1151 Marina Village Parkway, Alameda, CA 94501 • 510-523-8233